PRACTICALS IN COST ACCOUNTS

FOR B.COM. PART III; CA INTER; ICWA
AND BANKING EXAMINATIONS

PRACTICALS IN COST ACCOUNTS

FOR B.COM. PART III; CA INTER; ICWA AND BANKING EXAMINATIONS

P.G. ITNAL

ATLANTIC PUBLISHERS AND DISTRIBUTORS

Published by
ATLANTIC PUBLISHERS AND DISTRIBUTORS
B-2, Vishal Enclave, New Delhi-110 027
Phones 5413460, 5429987

Sales Office
4346/4C, Ansari Road, Darya Ganj,
New Delhi-110 002
Phones 3273880, 3285873, 3280451
Fax 91-11-3285873
e-mail gupta.atlantc@axcess.net.in

Typeset at
APD Computer Graphics, Delhi

Printed in India at
Tarun offset Printers

Preface

There are many good books available dealing with theoretical aspects of the subject. The students studying the subject now-a-days attend classes for practical problems and their solutions rather than for theoretical aspects. Therefore, the main objective of this book is to provide solutions to the questions set at the university examinations. The solutions along with the Working Notes, Calculations wherever necessary, help the students to understand the problems easily. In each of the topics covered, maximum possible number of problems of different varieties with satisfactory solutions have been made available. This will create greater confidence among the students in facing the examinations. Only on a few topics the important points and the relevant portion of theoretical aspect has been expressed in minimum words.

It is my sincere and honest efforts to satisfy the students in the subject.

I hope that the students will welcome this book.

I welcome from my friends-colleagues, teaching the subject, the constructive suggestions and the honest expressions about the utility of the said book the purpose for which it is meant. This will help me to accommodate their valuable suggestions.

I am very much thankful to the Publishers, in particulars Dr. K.R. Gupta, Managing Director of Atlantic Publishers and Distributors, New Delhi.

P.G. ITNAL

Contents

Theory Questions

Q. Define "Cost Accounting". Discuss the Superiority of Cost Accounting over Financial Accounting.

OR

Explain any two of the following :

(a) Cost Unit (b) E.O.Q. (c) P/V Ratio.

[K.U.D., April 1998 (O)]

Q 1. What is Material Requisition?

Q 2. What do you mean by Prime Cost?

Q 3. What is Contribution?

Q 4. What is Material Indent?

Q 5. What is Minimum Stock Level?

Q 6. How do you treat Sub-contract Cost in Contract Account?

Q 7. What is Normal Loss in Process Account?

Q 8. What is B.E.P.?

Q 9. What is a Bin-Card?

Q 10. What do you mean by Overhead?

Q 11. What do you mean by Over Recovery of Overhead?

Q 12. Write the Meaning of Machine Hour Rate?

(a) Explain demerits of Marginal Costing Technique.

(b) What is Labour Turnover? What are its causes?

[K.U.D., April 1998 (N)]

Answer any ten questions of the following :

Q 1. What is Cost Unit?

Q 2. What is Variable Cost?

Q 3. What is Re-order Level?

Q 4. What is Material Turn Over Ratio?

Q 5. What is Stories Ledger Cost?

Q 6. What is idle line?

Q 7. What do you mean by over absorption and under absorption of overhead?

Q 8. What is Machine Hour Rate?

Q 9. What do you mean by Passenger k.m. in operating costing.

Q 10. What do mean by work certified?

Q 11. What do mean by abnormal Lon in Process Costing?

Q 12. What is Price Cost?

(II) Explain any four differences between Cost Accounting and Financial Accounting?

(III) Explain briefly the essential characteristics of a Sound Wage system.

[K.U.D., October 1997 (N)]

Answer any ten questions of the following in not more sentences than two.

(a) What is Cost?

(b) State any two objects of Cost Accounting

(c) What is a Joint Product?

(d) What is a By-Product?

(e) What is work uncertified?

(f) What is Economic Order Quantity? (EOQ)

(g) What is Overtime?

(h) What is Abnormal Gain?

(i) What is Overhead?

(j) What is Labour Turn-over Ratio?

(k) State two Examples of Distribution of Overhead?

(l) What is Contribution?

Q 1. What are functions of Stores Department?

Q 2. Distinguish between Halsey and Rowan Plans?

[K.U.D., April 1997 (N)]

Answer any five questions from the following :

(a) Write any two points of distinction between LIFO and FIFO methods of pricing issue.

(b) Write any two points of distinction between line wage and piece wage system of wage payments?

(c) Who prepares material indent and to whom it is sent?

(d) Write any two methods of recovery Factory overhead.

(e) Write the units of measurement of service of the following : Goods, in Transport, and Cinema Theatre.

(f) Write the Formula for Colexlating P/Vratio and Breaks Even Point in Marginal Costing.

[K.U.D., October 1997 (O)]

Q. Distinguish between Cost and Financial Accounting and explain the advantages of Cost Accounting.

OR

Explain any two of the followings :

(a) Break-Even Chart.

(b) Classification of Overheads.

(c) Stock Levels.

(K.U.D., April 1996)

Q. What is Time Keeping ? Explain the different methods of Time Keeping.

OR

What is Break-Even Chart ? What are its advantages and disadvantages ?

(K.U.D., October 1995)

Q. Define Costing and discuss briefly the advantages of costing to the management.

OR

Distinguish between Cost and Financial Accounts.

(K.U.D., April 1995)

Q. What are the essential of a good Costing System?

OR

Define and explain the terms :

(a) Cost units and (b) Cost centre mention the unit of cost in respect of the following industries :

(i) Sugar Mills, (ii) Steel works, (iii) Water supply, (iv) Electricity, (v) Transport.

(K.U.D., October 1994)

Q. Answer the following in at least 2 sentences each :

(1) What do you mean by direct material cost?

(2) Give the formula to calculate Recorder Level.

(3) Give the meaning of Labour Hour Rate.

(4) Mention the mean difference between fixed cost and variable cost.

(5) What do you mean by work-in-progress?

(6) Give the meaning of cost unit.

(7) What is Break-Even Point?

(8) What are Joint Product?

(9) What is "Contribution" in Marginal Costing?

(10) Mention the nature of Industries that adopts "Process Costing".

(K.U.D., April 1994)

Q. Explain the following in one or two sentences :

(i) Economic Order Quantity (E.O.Q.)

(ii) Material Turnover Ratio

(iii) Time Keeping

(iv) Absorption of Overheads

(v) By-Products.

(K.U.D., October 1993)

Q. (a) What method of Costing would you recommend for the following industries?

(i) Chemical, (ii) Ship-Building, (iii) Cycle, (iv) Brick Manufacturing, (v) Cinema Theatre.

(b) Write short notes on any one of the following :

(i) Material Requisition, (ii) Joint product costing.

(K.U.D., April 1993)

Q. Define Cost Accounting and state its advantages.

OR

Write short notes on any two :

(a) Bin Card

(b) Break-Even Chart

(c) Fixed Costs and Variable Cost.

(K.U.D., October 1992)

Q. Mention with reasons the type of costing you will adopt in the following industries :

(a) Cement Factory, (b) Ship-Building, (c) Soap manufacturing, (d) Bicycle manufacturing, (f) Toy making, (g) Garments, (h) Printing Press, (i) Dam Constructions.

(K.U.D., October 1991)

Q. Distinguish between Cost Accounting and Financial Accounting. Briefly explain the advantages of Cost Accounting.

(K.U.D., April 1991)

Q. Distinguish between Cost and Financial Accounting and explain the advantages of a good system of Cost Accounting.

OR

Write short notes on any two :

(i) Economic Order Quantity (E.O.Q.)

(ii) Piece rate system

(iii) Break-Even Chart (B.E.P.)

(iv) What do you mean by Inventory Turnover Ratio?

(K.U.D., October 1990)

Q. (a) What is Cost Accounting? How is it different from Financial Accounting?

(b) What is Time Keeping? Why is it necessary? What are different methods of Time Keeping?

(K.U.D., October 1989)

Q 1. What are the different methods of Remuneration for wage payments? Explain in brief.

Q 2. Explain in brief different methods of Costing?

Q 3. What is Marginal Costing? Explain in brief the following :

(a) Contribution (b) Fixed Cost (c) Variable Cost (d) Profit/Volume Ratio (P/V Ratio).

Q 4. Break-Even Point (B.E.P.)

(Other Questions)

Q. State whether the following statement are True or False.

(1) Sunk costs are irrelevant from the point of view of decision making.

(2) Interior decoration industry use multiple costing.

(3) Bin Card is maintained to record both quantity and values.

(4) Setting up time cost is a Direct Labour Cost.

(5) Overhead cost incurred within the fourwall of the factory are known as factory overheads.

(6) Raw material supply is always the key factor in costing.

(7) A single output or Unit costing is a variant of the process costing.

(8) Benefit derived base is the best base for apportioning the overhead.

(9) Escalation clause is one of the condition of the process costing.

(10) Appropriations shown in Financial Ledger but not taken in Cost Ledger results as showing of more profits in Cost Accounting.

OR

Q. (a) Mention steps which should be taken to install Cost Accounting.

(b) Explain the meaning of Escalation clause.

(K.U.D., April 1985)

1

MATERIAL MANAGEMENT

(a) STORES ROUTINE

(1) Requisition of Materials
(2) Issues of Materials
(3) Stores Control

Requisition of Materials

(a) Fixation of Stock Level.
(b) (1) Minimum Stock Level.
    (2) Recording Level.
    (3) Maximum Stock Level.
    (4) Average Stock Level.
    (5) Danger Level.
    (6) Recording Quantity.

Formula

(a) Minimum Stock Level
= Reorder Level – Average consumption during normal delivery time.

(b) Reordering Level = Maximum consumption × Maximum delivery time.

(c) Maximum Stock Level
= Reordering Level + Reordering quantity – (Minimum consumption × Minimum delivery time.

(d) Danger Level
= Minimum rate of consumption × Emergency delivery time.

Economic Order Quantity (Reordering Quantity)

It is the ideal quantity of material to be purchased at a time. It is determined by considering economics of larger order and cost of carrying cost of stock. The ideal quantity shall be at which both merits and demerits are considered carefully in determining the order quantity.

Economic Order Quantity = E.O.Q.

Formula : $E.O.Q. = \sqrt{\frac{2AO}{C}}$

Where A = Annual consumption in units.
O = Order and receiving cost per order.
C = Cost of carrying inventory per unit per annum.

Problem No. 1

Amit Kumar, a Manufacturer purchased some items of Materials. The invoice gave the following details :

		Rs.
400 Kgs of Material A at Rs. 5 per Kg. (one box)		2,000
200 Kgs of Material B at Rs. 2.50 per Kg. (one box)		500
1000 Kgs of Material C at Rs. 3.50 per Kg. (two boxes)		3,500
Total		Rs. 6,000
Less Trade Discount at 10%		600
		Rs. 5,400
Cash discount at 2½% for payment within 30 days		135
		Rs. 5,265
Add	Rs.	
Carriage	80	
Not returnable boxes @ Rs. 10 each	40	
Insurance	120	
Sales tax @ 4%	216	456
Total		Rs. 5,721

Calculate issue rate for each Material.

Note : Bill could not be paid within 30 days

[K.U.D., April 1998(N)]

Solution :

Calculation of issue Rate of Materials

	Total 1600 Kg	A Kg 400	B Kg 200	C Kg 1000
Invoice value	6,000	2,000	500	3,500
Less Trade discount @ 10%	600	200	50	350
	5,400	1,800	450	3,150
Add Carriage 400 : 200 : 1000	80	20	10	50
Non Returnable cases (1 : 1 : 2)	40	10	10	20
Insurance 2,000 : 500 : 3,500	120	40	10	70
Sales Tax @ 4%	216	72	18	126
Total Cost Rs.	5,856	1,942	498	3,416
Materials in Kg	1,600	400 Kg	200 Kg	100 Kg
Issue Rate per Kg.	Rs. 3.66	Rs. 4.855	Rs. 2.49	Rs. 3. 416

Note : Cash discount was net allowed since the payment was not made within 30 days.

Problem No. 2

The following figures are taken from the records of Pure Chemical Laboratories, Bangalore for the year 1996. The valuation of inventories is Re. 1 Per Litre.

Name of Material	Opening Stocks Litres	Purchases Litres	Closing Stocks Litres
A	20,000	88,000	12,000
B	40,000	130,000	20,000

Calculate the Material turnover ratio of the above materials and express in number of days the average materials in held.

[K.U.D., October 1997(N)]

Solution :

Note : Value of Inventories is Re. 1 per litre

	Material A (Rs.)	Material B (Rs.)
I. Opening Stocks	20,000	40,000
Add Purchases	88,000	130,000
	108,000	170,000
Less Closing Stocks	12000	20,000
Materials Consumed	96,000	150,000

II. Average Stocks = $\frac{\text{Opening Stocks + Closing Stocks}}{2}$; Material A: $\frac{20{,}000+12{,}000}{2} = \frac{32{,}000}{2}$; Material B: $\frac{40{,}000+20{,}000}{2} = \frac{60{,}000}{2}$

Average stocks held: Material A 16,000; Material B 30,000

III. Imventory turnover Ratio = $\frac{\text{Cost of Materials Consumed}}{\text{Cost of Average stock held}}$

$$\text{Material A} = \frac{96{,}000}{16{,}000} = 6$$

$$\text{Material B} = \frac{150{,}000}{30{,}000} = 5$$

The Material A turnover ratio 6 is higher than that of Material B turnover ratio 5.

∴ Material A is fast moving and Material B is slow moving.

IV. Inventory Turnover in days = $\dfrac{\text{Days during the Period}}{\text{Inventory turnover Ratio}}$

Material A = $\dfrac{365}{6}$ = 60.83 or 61 days

Material B = $\dfrac{365}{5}$ = 73 days.

Average stock of Material A is held for 61 days whereas that of Material B is held for 73 days.

Problem No. 3

Bin Card of Bharat Ltd. reveals the following are the details in respects of a Material.

Maximum Consumption in a month of 4 weeks — 800 units

Minimum consumption during the same period — 400 units

Average daily consumption — 24 units (for six days in a week will be 24 × 6 = 144 units)

Normal Delivery Period – 2 weeks.

Economic Order Quantity – 480 units

The factory works for six days in a week

Calculate : (1) Reorder Level

(2) Minimum Stocks Level

(3) Maximum Stocks Level

(4) Average Stocks Level.

[K.U.D., April 1997(N)]

Solution :

Formula :

(1) Reorder Level = Maximum Consumption × Maximum Delivery period

(2) Minimum Stocks Level = Reorder Level – (Average Consumption × Average delivery period)

(3) Maximinimum Stocks Level = Reorder Level + Reorder Quantity – (Minimum Consumption × Minimum delivery period)

(4) Average Stocks Level = 1/2 (Max. Stocks Level + Min. Stocks Level)

Since the information available regarding Normal delivery time 2 weeks only but Max. delivery Period and Min. delivery Period in not given.

∴ On the basis of Average delivery period 2 weeks

Maximum Delivery Period 3 weeks and

Minimum Delivery Period 1 week is taken

Therefore Average Delivery Period = $\dfrac{3+1}{2} = \dfrac{4}{2}$ = 2 weeks

(1) Reorder Level = Max. cons. × Max. delivery period

= 800 × 3 = 2400 units

(2) Maximum Stocks Level = Reorder Level + Reorder Quantity (Economic Order Quantity)

– (Min. cons. × Min. delivery Period.

= 2400 + 480 – (400 × 1)

= 2880 – 400 = 2480 units

(3) Minimum Stocks Level = Reorder Level – Average cons. × Average delivery period

= 2400 – (144 × 2)

= 2400 – 288 = 2112 units

(4) Average Stocks Level = 1/2 (Max. Stock Level + Min. Stocks Level.

= 1/2 (2480 + 2112)

= 1/2 (4592)

= 2296 units

Problem No. 4

The Godavari Pump Co. uses about 75,000 values per year and the usage is fairly constant at 6,250 values per month. The values cost is Rs.1.50 per unit.

When bought in quantities and the cost of carrying is estimated to be 20 per cent of average inventory investment on the annual basis. The cost of placing an order and to process the delivery is Rs. 18. It takes 45 days to receive the delivery from the date of an order and the safely stock of 3250 values desired.

You are required : (a) The most Economic Order Quantity

(b) The order point.

(K.U.D., April 1991)

Solution :

A = Annual consumption is 75,000 units.

O = Cost of placing order Rs. 18.

C = Cost of carrying an inventory Rs. 1.50 @ 20% = 0.30 Ps.

(a) E.O.Q. $= \sqrt{\dfrac{2\ AO}{C}}$

$= \sqrt{\dfrac{2 \times 75{,}000 \times 18}{0.30}}$

$= \sqrt{\dfrac{2 \times 75{,}000 \times 18}{0.30}}$

$$= \sqrt{\frac{27,00,000}{0.30}}$$

$$= \sqrt{90,00,000}$$

$$= \text{3000 Units.}$$

(b) Order Point = Safety stock + Average consumption × Lead time (time to receive order)

$$= 3250 + (6250 \times 45 \text{ days})$$

$$= 3250 + (6250 \times \frac{45}{30})$$

$$= 3250 + 9375$$

$$= \text{12,625 Units.}$$

Problem No. 5

A company uses annually 50,000 units of an item costing Rs. 1.20 each. Order cost is Rs. 45 and inventory carrying cost 15 per cent on the annual average inventory value. Find out E.O.Q.

(K.U.D., October 1990)

Solution :

$$\text{E.O.Q.} = \sqrt{\frac{2\ AO}{C}}$$

A = Annual consumption 50,000 units.

O = Ordering and receiving cost Rs. 45.

C = Cost of carrying inventory 15 per cent of inventory value Rs. 1.20.

= 15% × 1.20 = 0.18 Ps.

Now E.O.Q.

$$= \sqrt{\frac{2\ AO}{C}}$$

$$= \sqrt{\frac{2 \times 50,000 \times 45}{0.18}}$$

$$= \sqrt{2 \times 50,000 \times 45 \times 100}$$

$$= \sqrt{2,50,00,000}$$

$$= \text{5000 Units.}$$

Problem No. 6

Compute an Ideal Order Quantity from the following data :

(1) Consumption of Material A – 6250 units per year.

(2) Expenses of placing and receiving the consignment Re. 0.55 per order and

(3) Cost of storing the Inventory per unit Re. 0.10.

(K.U.D., April 1985)

Solution :

$$\text{E.O.Q.} = \sqrt{\frac{2\ AO}{C}}$$

Where A = Annual Consumption 6250 units.

O = Ordering and receiving cost per order Re. 0.50.

C = Cost of carrying Inventory per annum Re. 0.10.

$$\text{Now E.O.Q.} = \sqrt{\frac{2 \times 6250 \times 50 \times 100}{100 \times 10}}$$

$$= \sqrt{62{,}500}$$

$$\text{E.O.Q.} = 250 \text{ Units.}$$

Problem No. 7

Find out Economic Order Quantity from the following particulars :

Annual consumption – 8000 units.

Cost of Material per unit — Rs. 20.

Cost of placing and receiving one order is Rs. 80.

Annual carrying cost of one unit is 10 per cent of inventory value.

Solution :

$$\text{E.O.Q.} = \sqrt{\frac{2\ AO}{C}}$$

Where A = Annual consumption 8000 units.

O = Ordering and receiving cost per unit.

C = Cost of carrying one unit = 10% of Rs. 20.

= Rs. 2

$$\text{Now E.O.Q.} = \sqrt{\frac{2 \times 8000 \times 80}{2}}$$

$$= \sqrt{6,40,000}$$

$$\text{E.O.Q.} = 800.$$

Problem No. 8

A unit of 'X' cost Rs. 50 and the yearly consumption is 50,625 units.
The cost of placing and receiving one order of material is Rs. 10.
The cost of carrying Inventory is 10 per cent of material cost per annum.
Calculate per cent O.Q.

Solution :

$$\text{E.O.Q.} = \sqrt{\frac{2\text{ AO}}{\text{C}}}$$

Where = A = Annual consumption 50,625 units.

O = Cost of placing an order and receiving Rs. 10.

C = Cost of carrying inventory 10 per cent of Rs. 50 = Rs. 5.

$$\text{Now E.O.Q.} = \sqrt{\frac{2\text{ AO}}{\text{C}}}$$

$$= \sqrt{\frac{2 \times 50,625 \times 10}{5}}$$

$$= \sqrt{2,02,500}$$

$$\text{E.O.Q.} = 450.$$

Problem No. 9

From the following particulars find out Economic Order Quantity and the number of order placed in the year :

Annual consumption 300 units.
Buying cost per order — Rs. 20 + 5
Price per unit — Rs. 250.
Storage and carrying cost as a percentage of Average Inventory is 10 per cent.

Solution :

$$E.O.Q. = \sqrt{\frac{2\ AO}{C}}$$

A = Annual Consumption

O = Ordering and receiving cost – Rs. 20.

C = Cost of carrying inventory is 10 per cent of inventory value – Rs. 250 × $\frac{10}{100}$ = Rs. 25

$$\text{Now E.O.Q.} = \sqrt{\frac{2 \times 300 \times 20}{25}}$$

$$= \sqrt{\frac{12{,}000}{25}}$$

$$= \sqrt{480}$$

$$= 21.9089.$$

Problem No. 10

What is Economic Order Quantity (E.O.Q.) ? Calculate E.O.Q. from the following :

(a) Quantity 600 units annual consumption.

(b) Ordering cost – Rs. 12 per order.

(c) Carrying cost 20 per cent.

(d) Price per unit — Rs. 20.

Solution :

$$E.O.Q. = \sqrt{\frac{2\ AO}{C}}$$

$$= \sqrt{\frac{2 \times 600 \times 12}{20 \times 20\%}}$$

$$= \sqrt{\frac{14,400}{4}}$$

$$= \sqrt{3600}$$

= 60 Units or 10 Order per year.

Problem No. 11

Calculate Economic Order Quantity from the following information :

Consumption of Materials per annum — 10,000 Kgs.

Ordering Cost per order – Rs. 50.

Cost per Kg of raw material – Rs. 2.

Stores Cost = 8% of inventory value.

Solution :

$$\text{E.O.Q.} = \sqrt{\frac{2\ AO}{C}}$$

$$= \sqrt{\frac{2 \times 10,000 \times 50}{2 \times 8\%}}$$

$$= \sqrt{\frac{10,00,000}{0.16}}$$

$$= \sqrt{62,50,000}$$

= 2500 Units or 4 Order per year.

Problem No. 12

A manufacturing company purchases annually 1080 units. The order placing cost is Rs. 300 and the cost of carrying one unit for a year is Rs. 6. Find out Economic Ordering Quantity.

Solution :

$$\text{E.O.Q.} = \sqrt{\frac{2\ AO}{C}}$$

$$= \sqrt{\frac{2 \times 1080 \times 300}{6}}$$

$$= \sqrt{\frac{6,48,000}{6}}$$

$$= \sqrt{1,08,000}$$

= 328.6 or 329 Units.

Problem No. 13

In a factory two materials A and B are used as follows :

Normal usage :	A — 200 Units per week
	B — 100 units per week
Maximum usage :	A — 300 units per week
	B — 150 units per week
Minimum usage :	A — 100 units per week
	B — 50 units per week
Reorder quantity :	A — 1200 Units
	B — 2000 Units
Reorder period :	A — 4 to 6 weeks
	B — 2 to 4 weeks.

Calculate for each material : (a) Reorder level (b) Minimum level (c) Maximum level (d) Average stock level.

(K.U.D., April 1996)

Solution :

(a) Reorder Level = Maximum usage × Maximum Delivery period

Material : A = 300 × 6 = 1800 Units

B = 150 × 4 = 600 Units

(b) Minimum Level = Reorder Level — (Normal usage × Normal Delivery period)

Material : A $= 1800 - (200 \times \frac{4+6}{2})$

$= 1800 - 200 \times 5$

$= 1800 - 1000$

= 800 Units.

B $= 600 - (100 \times \frac{2+4}{2})$

$= 600 - (100 \times 3)$

$= 600 - 300 = 300$ Units.

(c) Maximum Stock Level = Reorder Level + Reorder quantity – (Maximum usage × Minimum Delivery period)

Material : A $= 1800 + 1200 - (100 \times 4)$

$= 3000 - 400 = 2600$ Units.

B $= 600 + 2000 - (50 \times 2)$

$= 2600 - 100 = 2500$ Units.

(d) Average Stock Level = ½ (Maximum stock + Minimum stock)

Material : A = ½ (2600 + 800)

= ½ (3400)

= 1700 Units.

B = ½ (2500 + 300)

= ½ (2800)

= 1400 Units.

Problem No. 14

A manufacturing Company buys certain equipment from outside supplier @ Rs. 30 per unit. Total annual needs are 800 units. The following further details are available : annual return on investment 10 per cent; Rent, Taxes and Insurance per unit per year Re. 1; cost placing an order Rs. 100.

Determine the Economic Order Quantity.

Solution :

E.O.Q. $= \sqrt{\frac{2\ AO}{C}}$

A = Annual Requirement 800 units.

O = Ordering Cost Rs. 100.

Cost of carrying inventory 1 + 3C.

= Rs. 1 + 10% of 30 Return = 1 + 3 = Rs. 4.

E.O.Q. $= \sqrt{\frac{2 \times 800 \times 100}{4}}$

$= \sqrt{40{,}000}$

= 200 Units or 4 Order.

Problem No. 15

Find out Economic Order Quantity and order schedule for Raw materials and Packing materials with the following data given to you :

(1) Cost of Ordering :

Raw Material	Rs. 1000 per order.
Packing Material	Rs. 5000 per order.

(2) Cost of holding Inventory :

Raw Materials	1 Paise per unit per month.
Packing Materials	5 Paise per unit per month.

(3) Production Rate 2,00,000 units per month.

Solution :

E.O.Q. for Raw Materials

$= \sqrt{\frac{2\ AO}{C}}$

$= \sqrt{\frac{2 \times 2{,}00{,}000 \times 1000}{0.01}}$

$= \sqrt{\frac{40{,}00{,}00{,}000}{0.01}}$

= 2,00,000 Raw Materials.

E.O.Q. for Packing Materials

$$= \sqrt{\frac{2 \times 2{,}00{,}000 \times 5{,}000}{0.05}}$$

$$= 2{,}00{,}000 \text{ Units.}$$

Order Schedule one Order per month each.

Problem No. 16

Compute an Ideal Order Quantity from the following data :

Consumption of Material A – 6250 units per month.

Expenses of placing and receiving consignment Re. 0.50 per order and the cost of storing the inventory per unit Re. 0.10.

Solution :

$$\text{E.O.Q.} = \sqrt{\frac{2\text{ AO}}{\text{C}}}$$

$$= \sqrt{\frac{2 \times 6{,}250 \times 0.50}{0.10}}$$

$$= \sqrt{62{,}500}$$

$$= 250 \text{ Units.}$$

Inventory Turnover =
(Expressed in days)

$$\frac{\text{Average Inventory during the period} \times \text{Pays during the period}}{\text{Materials consumed during the period}}$$

$$\text{OR} \quad \frac{\text{Days during the period}}{\text{Material Turnover Ratio}}$$

Materials

Inventory Turnover Ratio expressed in days :

	X	Y	Z
(a)	$\frac{1350 \times 365}{36{,}000}$	$\frac{2100 \times 365}{30{,}000}$	$\frac{3300 \times 365}{4{,}800}$
	13.6875	25.55	250.937
OR :	14 Days	26 Days	251 Days
(b)	$\frac{365}{26.69}$	$\frac{365}{14.29}$	$\frac{365}{1.46}$

Problem No. 17

Find out Economic Order Quantity from the following information : monthly consumption 250 units. Cost of placing and receiving one order Rs. 30. Price per unit Rs. 5. Storage and carrying cost 10 per cent of Inventory value.

Solution :

$$\text{E.O.Q.} = \sqrt{\frac{2\ \text{AO}}{\text{C}}}$$

$$= \sqrt{\frac{2 \times 3000 \times 30}{5 \times 10\%}}$$

$$= \sqrt{\frac{18,00,000}{0.50}}$$

$$= \sqrt{3,60,000}$$

$$= 600 \text{ units or 5 order per year.}$$

Note : 250 Units × 12 = 3000 Units.

Problem No. 18

A manufacturing company uses 200 units of a component every month and buys them entirely from outside suppliers. The order placing and receiving cost Rs. 100 and Annual carrying cost of Rs. 12. Calculate E.O.Q.

(ICWA — Inter)

Solution :

Annual requirements = Monthly 200 units for one year

= 200 × 12 = 2400 Units.

$$\text{E.O.Q.} = \sqrt{\frac{2\ \text{AO}}{\text{C}}}$$

$$= \sqrt{\frac{2 \times 2400 \times 100}{12}}$$

$$= \sqrt{\frac{4,80,000}{12}}$$

$$= \sqrt{40,000}$$

$$= 200 \text{ Units.}$$

Problem No. 19

In a Factory two components X and Y are used as follows :

Normal usage :	X	100 units per week
	Y	50 units per week
Maximum usage :	X	150 units per week
	Y	75 units per week
Minimum usage :	X	50 units per week
	Y	25 units per week

Reordering Quantity X – 600 units; Y – 1000 units.

Reordering period – X 4 to 6 week; Y – 2 to 4 weeks.

Calculate for each components :

(a) Reordering Stock Level (b) Minimum Stock Level

(c) Maximum Stock Level (d) Average Stock Level.

(B'lore, April 1992 & K.U.D., October '86)

Solution :

Stock Levels

(1) Reordering Stock Level : Maximum usage × Maximum Delivery Period

Material : $X = 150 \times 6 = 900$ Units

$Y = 75 \times 4 = 300$ Units

(2) Minimum Stock Level = Reordering Level – (Normal Usage : × Normal Delivery Period)

Material : $X = 900 - (100 \times \frac{4 \text{ to } 6}{2})$

$= 900 - (100 \times 5)$

$= 900 - 500 = 400$ Units.

$Y = 300 - (50 \times \frac{2+4)}{2})$

$= 300 - (50 \times 3)$

$= 300 - 150 = 150$ Units.

(3) Maximum Stock Level = Reorder Level + Reorder Quantity – (Minimum Usage × Minimum Delivery Period)

Material : $X = 900 + 600 - (50 \times 4)$

$= 1500 - 200$

$= 1300$ Units.

$Y = 300 + 1000 - (25 \times 2)$

$= 1300 - 50$

$= 1250$ Units.

(4) Average Stock Level = Minimum Level + ½ Reorder Quantity

X = 400 + ½ × 600 = 400 + 300 = 700 Units.

Y = 150 + ½ × 1000 = 150 × 500 = 650 Units.

OR Average Stock : $\dfrac{\text{Minimum Level + Max Level}}{2}$

$$X = \frac{400 + 1300}{2} = \frac{1700}{2} = 850$$

$$Y = \frac{150 + 1250}{2} = \frac{1400}{2} = 700.$$

Problem No. 20

A manufacturing uses 200 Units of a component every month and buys them extensively from outside supplier.

The order placing cost is Rs. 100 and Annual cost of carrying is Rs. 12. From their set up data calculate E.O.Q.

(ICWA — Inter, 1984)

Solution :

Annual consumption = 200 Units per month for 12 Months.

= 200 × 12

= 2400 Units.

Cost of order placing — Rs. 100

Cost of carrying (annual) — Rs. 12

Now E.O.Q. = $\sqrt{\dfrac{2\,AO}{C}}$

A = Annual consumption = 2400 Units

O = Ordering & Placing cost — Rs. 100

C = Cost Carrying Rs. 12

E.O.Q. $\sqrt{\dfrac{2 \times 2400 \times 100}{12}}$

= $\sqrt{40{,}000}$

= 200 Units.

Problem No. 21

(A) What do you understand by :

(a) Maximum Stock Level

(b) Minimum Stock Level

(c) Reorder Level (Only Theory)

(B) Calculate : (a) Maximum Stock Level (b) Minimum Stock Level
(c) Reorder Level from the following particulars :

Reorder Quantity – 1500 Units.
Reorder Period – 4 to 6 weeks.
Maximum Consumption – 400 units per week
Normal consumption – 300 units per week.
Minimum Consumption – 250 units per week

(K.U.D., October 1990)

Solution :

(1) Reorder Level = Maximum Consumption × Maximum Delivery Period
= 400 × 6 = 2400 Units.

(2) Maximum Stock Level = Reorder + Reorder Quantity – (Minimum Consumption × Minimum Delivery Period)
= 2400 + 1500 – (250 × 4)
= 3900 – 1000 = 2900 Units.

(3) Minimum Stock Level = Reorder Level – (Normal Consumption × Normal Delivery Period)

$$= 2400 - \left(300 \times \frac{4 + 6}{2}\right)$$

= 2400 – (300 × 5)
= 2400 – 1500
= 900 Units.

Problem No. 22

The following information relates to the consumption of a chemical for the month :

Maximum Usage – 2000 Kg., Minimum Usage – 1600 Kg.
Reorder Quantity 2000 Kg.
Delivery Period : Normal – 2 weeks, Minimum – 1 week,
Maximum – 3 weeks.
Annual consumption during 1988 was 24000 Kg.
Calculate : (1) Maximum Stock Level (2) Minimum Stock Level
(3) Material Turnover Ratio

(K.U.D., October 1989)

Solution :

(1) Reorder Level = Maximum consumption × Maximum delivery period

$$= 2000 \times \frac{3}{4} = 1500 \text{ Kgs.}$$

(2) Maximum Stock Level = Reorder + Reorder Quantity – (Minimum Consumption × Min. Delivery time)

$= 1500 + 2000 - (1600 \times \frac{1}{4})$
$= 3500 - 400 = 3100$ Kg.

(3) Minimum Stock Level = Reorder Level – (Normal Usage × Normal Delivery time)

$= 1500 - (1800 \times 2/4)$
$= 1500 - 900 = 600$ Kg.

$$\text{Normal Usage} = \text{Maximum Usage} + \frac{\text{Minimum Usage}}{2}$$

$$= \frac{2000 + 1600}{2} = \frac{3600}{2} = 1800$$

Average Stock Level = Minimum Stock Level + ½ Reorder Quantity

$= 600 + \frac{1}{2} \times 2000$
$= 600 + 1000 = 1600$

$$\text{OR : Average Stock} = \frac{\text{Max Stock Level + Min. Stock Level}}{2}$$

$$= \frac{3100 + 600}{2} = \frac{3700}{2} = 1850$$

$$\text{Material Turnover ratio} = \frac{\text{Material Consumed During the Year}}{\text{Average Stock Level}}$$

$$= \frac{24{,}000}{1600} = 15$$

Note : Particulars of Maximum and Minimum usage for the month need to be converted into weekly.

Problem No. 23

From the following information in respect of Material A and B calculate for each material : (a) Reorder Level (b) Minimum Level (c) Maximum Level and (d) Average Stock Level :

Normal usage	50 units per week each.
Minimum usage	20 units per week each.
Maximum usage	75 units per week each.
Reorder Quantity	A – 300 units
	B – 500 units
Reorder period	A – 4 to 6 weeks
	B – 2 to 4 weeks

(B'lore, April 1988 & K.U.D., April 1977)

Solution :

Stock Levels

(a) Reorder Level = Maximum Usage × Maximum Delivery period

Material : A – 75 × 6 = 450 Units.

B – 75 × 4 = 300 Units.

(b) Minimum Stock Level = Reordering Level – Normal usage × Average delivery period

Material : A $= 450 - (50 \frac{4+6}{2})$

$= 450 - (50 \times 5)$

$= 450 - 250 = 200$ Units.

B $= 300 - (50 \times \frac{2+4}{2})$

$= 300 - 150$

$= 150$ Units.

(c) Maximum Stock Level = Reorder Level + Reorder Quantity – (Minimum Usage × Minimum delivery period)

Material : A $= 450 + 300 - (250 \times 4)$

$= 750 - 100 = 650$ units.

B $= 300 + 500 - (25 \times 2)$

$= 800 - 50$

$= 750$ Units.

Average Stock Level = Minimum Level + ½ (Reorder Quantity)

A $= 200 + (\frac{1}{2} \times 300)$

$= 200 + 150$

$= 350$ Units.

B $= 150 + (\frac{1}{2} \times 500)$

$= 150 + 250$

$= 400$ Units.

Problem No. 24

Two components A and B are used as follows :

Reorder Quantity A – 300 Units

B – 400 Units

Reordering period A – 4 to 6 weeks.

B – 2 to 4 weeks.

Normal usage – 3000 Units per week each

Minimum usage – 1500 Units per week each

Maximum usage – 4500 Units per week each.

You are required to calculate for each of the components :
(1) Maximum Stock Level (2) Minimum Stock Level
(3) Average Stock Level (4) Reorder Level.

(K.U.D., April 1986)

Solution :

(1) Reorder Level = Maximum Level × Maximum Delivery Period

Material : A = 4500 × 6 = 27,000
B = 4500 × 4 = 18,000

(2) Maximum Stock Level = Reordering Level + Reorder Quantity – (Minimum Usage × Minimum Delivery Period)

Material : A = 27,000 + 3000 – (1500 × 4)
= 30,000 – 6,000 = 24,000 Units.
B = 18,000 + 4,000 – (1500 × 2)
= 22,000 – 3000 = 19,000 Units.

(3) Minimum Stock Level = Reordering Level – (Normal Usage × Average Delivery Period)

$$A = 27{,}000 - \left(3{,}000 \times \frac{4+6}{2}\right)$$

= 27,000 – (3,000 × 5)
= 27,000 – 15,000 = 12,000 Units.

$$B = 18{,}000 - \left(3{,}000 \times \frac{2+4}{2}\right)$$

= 18,000 – (3,000 × 3)
= 18,000 – 9,000 = 9,000 Units.

(4) Average Stock Level = Minimum Level + ½ Reorder Quantity

$$\text{or} = \frac{\text{Max. Stock} + \text{Min. Stock}}{2}$$

A = 12,000 + ½ × 3,000
= 12,000 + 1,500 = 13,500 Units. $A = \frac{24000 + 12000}{2} = \frac{36000}{2}$
= 18000

B = 9,000 + ½ × 4,000
= 9,000 + 2,000 = 11,000 Units. $B = \frac{19000 + 9000}{2} = \frac{28000}{2}$
= 14000

Problem No. 25

From the following particulars calculate :

(a) Reorder Level (b) Maximum Stock Level (c) Minimum Stock Level
(d) Average Stock Level (e) Danger Level.

Normal Consumption – 1500 units per week.

Minimum Consumption 750 units per week.

Maximum Consumption 2250 per week.

Reorder quantity — 900 units.

Emergency period — 2 weeks

Reorder period — 3 to 5 weeks.

[B'lore (Modified)]

Solution :

Stock Levels

(a) Reorder Level = Maximum Consumption × Maximum Delivery period
= 2250 × 5 = 11,250 Units.

(b) Maximum Stock Level
= Reorder Level + Reorder Quantity – (Min. Consumption × Min. Delivery period)
= 11,250 + 900 – (750 × 3)
= 12,150 – 2,250 = 9,900 Units.

(c) Minimum Stock Level = Reorder Level – (Normal Consumption × Normal Delivery period)

$$= 11,250 - (1,500 \times \frac{3+5}{2})$$

= 11,250 – 1,500 × 4
= 11,250 – 6000 = 5,250 Units.

(d) Average Stock = Minimum Stock Level + ½ Reorder Quantity
= 5,250 + ½ × 900
= 5,250 + 450 = 5,800 Units.

$$\text{OR : Average Stock} = \frac{\text{Minimum Stock Level + Maximum Stock Level}}{2}$$

$$= \frac{5,250 + 9,900}{2} = \frac{15,150}{2} = 7,575 \text{ Units.}$$

Danger Level = Minimum Consumption × Emergency Delivery Period
= 750 × 2 = 1,500 Units.

Problem No. 26

Following are the particulars of certain item in a manufacturing Company for the month period :

Normal consumption during the month — 900 Units.

Minimum consumption — 800 Units.

Maximum consumption = 1000 Units.

Delivery period : Normal — 2 weeks
Maximum — 3 weeks
Minimum — 1 week
Reorder Quantity = 1,000 Units.

Calculate : (a) Reorder Level (b) Maximum Stock Level
(c) Minimum Stock Level (d) Average Stock.

Solution :

Note : Particulars are given on monthly basis. Whereas delivery period in weekly basis. Therefore consumption be converted into weekly.

(a) Reorder Level = Maximum consumption × Maximum Delivery Period

= 1000 × ¾ = 750 Units.

(b) Maximum Stock Level = Reorder Level + Reorder Quantity – (Minimum Consumption × Minimum Delivery period)

= (750 + 1000) – (800 × ¼)

= 1750 – 200 = 1550 Units.

(c) Minimum Stock Level = Reorder Level – (Normal Consumption × Normal Delivery Period)

= 750 – (900 × 2/4)

= 750 – 450 = 300 Units.

Average Stock Level $= \dfrac{\text{Minimum Stock + Maximum Stock}}{2}$

$= \dfrac{300 + 1550}{2} = 925$ Units.

OR : = Minimum Stock + ½ Reorder Quantity

= 300 + ½ × 1000

= 300 + 500

= 800 Units.

Problem No. 27

Two components of X and Y are used as follows :

Normal Usage	600 Units per week each
Maximum Usage	900 Units per week each
Minimum Usage	300 Units per week each
Reorder Quantity :	X 4800
	Y 7200

Reorder Period : X 4 to 6 weeks
Y 2 to 4 weeks

Calculate each of the components :

(a) Reorder Level (b) Minimum Stock Level

(c) Maximum Stock Level (d) Average Stock Level.

(K.U.D., October 1984)

Solution :

(a) Reorder Level = Maximum Usage × Maximum Delivery Period

X = 900 × 6 = 5400 Units.

Y = 900 × 4 = 3600 Units.

(b) Minimum Stock Level = Reorder Level – (Normal Usage × Average Delivery Period)

$$X = 5400 - (600 \times \frac{4+6}{2})$$

$$= 5400 - (600 \times 5) = 5400 - 3000 = 2400 \text{ Units.}$$

$$Y = 3600 - (600 \times \frac{2+4}{2})$$

$$= 3600 - (600 \times 3) = 3600 - 1800$$

$$= 1800 \text{ Units.}$$

(c) Maximum Stock Level =

Reorder Level + Reorder Quantity – (Min. Usage × Min. Delivery Time)

X = 5400 + 4800 – (300 × 4)

= 5400 + 4800 – 1200 = 10,200 – 1200

= 9000 Units

Y = 3600 + 7200 – (300 × 2)

= 10,800 – 600 = 10,200 Units.

(d) Average Stock Level = Minimum Level + ½ Reorder Quantity

X = 2400 + ½ × 4800

= 2400 + 2400 = 4800 Units.

Y = 1800 + ½ × 7200

= 1800 + 3600 = 5400 Units.

Problem No. 28

From the following particulars regarding a material – calculate :

(a) Reorder Level (b) Maximum Level (c) Minimum Level

(d) Average Stock Level.

Normal usage	100 Units per week
Minimum usage	50 Units per week
Maximum usage	150 Units per week
Reorder Quantity	800 Units
Reorder Period	8 to 12 Weeks.

(K.U.D., M. Com., 1986)

Solution :

Stock Level

(a) Reorder Level = Maximum usage × Maximum delivery period

= 150 × 12 = 1800 Units.

(b) Maximum Level = Reorder Level + Reorder Quantity – (Minimum Usage × Minimum Delivery Period)

= 1800 + 800 – (50 × 8)

= 2600 – 400 = 2200 Units.

(c) Minimum Stock Level = Reorder Level – (Normal Usage × Normal Delivery Period)

$$= 1800 - (100 \times \frac{8 + 12}{2})$$

= 1800 – 1000 = 800 Units.

(d) Average Stock Level = Minimum Stock Level + ½ (Reorder Quantity)

= 800 + ½ × 800

= 800 + 400

= 1200 Units.

$$\text{OR : Average Stock Level} = \frac{\text{Minimum Stock Level + Maximum Stock Level}}{2}$$

$$= \frac{800 + 2200}{2}$$

$$= \frac{3000}{2}$$

= 1500 Units.

Problem No. 29

Shriram Enterprise Manufacturing a special product 'Zed' the following particulars are calculated for the year 1986 :

(a) Monthly demand of 'Zed' 1000 Units.

(b) Cost of placing an order Rs. 100.

(c) Annual carrying cost per unit Rs. 15.

(d) Normal usage 50 units per week.

(e) Minimum usage 25 units per week.

(f) Maximum usage 75 units per week.

(g) Reorder period 4 to 6 weeks.

Compute from the above : (1) Reorder Quantity (2) Reorder Level (3) Minimum Stock Level (4) Maximum Stock Level (5) Average Stock Level.

(C.A., Inter, 1987)

Solution :

Stock Level

(1) Reorder Quantity or Economic Order Quantity :

$$\text{E.O.Q.} = \sqrt{\frac{2\ AO}{C}} = \sqrt{\frac{2 \times 12{,}000 \times 100}{15}} = \sqrt{1{,}60{,}000} = 400 \text{ Units}$$

Monthly demand 1000 for Annual Demand 1000 × 12 = 12000 Units.

(2) Reorder Level = Maximum Usage × Maximum Delivery Period
= 75 × 6 = 450 Units.

(3) Minimum Level = Reorder Level – (Normal usage × Normal Delivery period)

$$= 450 - \left(50 \times \frac{4+6}{2}\right)$$

= 450 – 250 = 200 Units.

(4) Maximum Level = Reorder Level + Reorder Quantity – (Minimum usage × Minimum Delivery Period)
= 450 + 400 – (25 × 4) = 850 – 100
= 750 Units.

(5) Average Stock Level = Minimum Level + ½ Reorder Quantity
= 200 + ½ × 400
= 200 + 200 = 400 Units.

$$\text{OR : Average Stock Level} = \frac{\text{Minimum Stock + Maximum Stock}}{2}$$

$$= \frac{200 + 750}{2} = \frac{950}{2}$$

= 475 Units.

Problem No. 30

From the following particulars for the month; calculate :

(a) Reorder Level (b) Maximum Stock Level
(c) Minimum Stock Level (d) Average Stock Level.

Normal Usage per month 1125 Units.
Maximum usage per month 1500 Units.
Minimum usage per month 1000 Units.
Reorder Quantity 3750 Units.
Reorder Period – Maximum 6 months and Minimum 2 months

(ICWA, Inter)

Solution :

Stock Level

(a) Reorder Level = Maximum Usage × Maximum delivery period

= 1500 × 6 = 9000 Units.

(b) Maximum Stock Level = Reorder Level + Reorder Quantity – (Minimum usage × Minimum delivery period)

= 9000 + 3750 – (1000 × 2)

= 12,750 – 2,000

= 10,750

(c) Minimum Stock Level = Reorder Level – (Normal usage × Normal delivery period)

$$= 9000 - (1125 \times \frac{6+2}{2})$$

= 9000 – 1125 × 4

= 9000 – 4500 = 4500 Units.

(d) Average Stock Level = Minimum Stock Level + ½ × Reorder Quantity

= 4500 + ½ (3750)

= 4500 + 1875 = 6375 Units.

$$\text{OR : Average Stock} = \frac{\text{Minimum Level + Maximum Level}}{2}$$

$$= \frac{4500 + 10750}{2}$$

$$= \frac{15250}{2}$$

= 7625 Units.

Problem No. 31

From the following information calculate :

(a) Reorder Level (b) Reorder Quantity (c) Minimum Stock Level (d) Average Stock Level

Maximum Stock Level = 8000 Units.

Budgeted consumption : Maximum – 1200 Units per month.

Minimum – 800 Units per month.

Estimated delivery time : Maximum – 4 months

Minimum – 3 months.

(a) Reorder Level = Maximum usage × Maximum Delivery period

= 1200 × 4 = 4800 Units.

(b) Reorder Quantity = Maximum Stock Level – Reorder Level + (Minimum usage × Minimum delivery period)

= 8000 – 4800 + (800 × 3)

$= 8000 - 4800 + 2400$

$= 10400 - 4800 = 5600$ Units.

(c) Minimum Stock Level = Reorder Level – (Normal usage × Normal delivery period)

$= 4800 - (1000 \times \frac{4+3}{2})$

$= 4800 - (1000 \times 3.5)$

$= 4800 - 3500$

$= 1300$ Units.

OR : Normal Usage $= \frac{\text{Maximum usage + Minimum usage}}{2}$

$= \frac{1200 + 800}{2} = \frac{2000}{2} = 1000$ Units.

(d) Average Stock = Minimum Level + ½ (Reorder Quantity)

$= 1300 + \frac{1}{2} \times 5600$

$= 1300 + 2800 = 4100$ Units.

OR : Average Stock Level $= \frac{\text{Minimum Stock Level + Maximum Stock Level}}{2}$

$= \frac{1300 + 8000}{2}$

$= \frac{9300}{2}$

$= 4650$ Units.

Problem No. 32

Following are the particulars of manufacturing unit for a certain Material 'A' :

Normal usage – 30 Units per day

Maximum usage during the month of 4 weeks 1000 units.

Minimum usage during the month of 4 weeks 500 units.

Normal usage period 2 weeks (12 days).

Economic Order Quantity (Reorder Quantity 600 units)

Emergency Supply – 5 days.

From the above information calculate :

(a) Reorder Level (b) Maximum Stock Level (c) Minimum Stock Level

(d) Average Stock Level (e) Danger Level.

Solution :

Stock Level

Note : Particulars of Minimum and Maximum usage for the month need to be converted into weeks.

(a) Reorder Level = Maximum usage × Maximum Delivery Period

= 1000 × 2/4 = 500 Units.

(b) Maximum Stock Level = Reorder Level + Reorder Qty. – (Minimum usage × Minimum delivery period)

= 500 + 600 – (500 × 2/4)

= 1100 – 250 = 850 Units.

(c) Minimum Stock Level = Reorder Level – (Normal usage × Normal Delivery period)

= 500 – (30 Units per day × 12 days)

= 500 – 360 = 140 Units.

(d) Average Stock Level = Minimum Level + ½ × Reorder Quantity

= 140 + ½ × 600

= 140 + 300 = 440 Units.

OR : $= \dfrac{\text{Minimum Level} + \text{Maximum Level}}{2}$

$= \dfrac{850 + 140}{2} = \dfrac{990}{2} = 495$ Units.

(e) Danger Level = Normal usage per day × Emergency period

= 30 × 5 = 150 Units.

Problem No. 33

The following details relate the consumption of – Atta (Wheat Floor) in a Bakery :

Consumption Maximum – 400 Kgs per day

Minimum consumption – 250 Kgs per day

Delivery period – 4 to 6 days.

Economic Order Quantity – 25 Quantities consumed during March – 105.75 Qty.

Calculate : (1) Reorder Level (2) Maximum Level (3) Minimum Level (4) Average Stock Level (5) Stock Turnover ratio.

Solution :

Stock Level

(1) Reorder Level = Maximum usage × Maximum delivery period

= 400 × 6 = 2400 Kgs or 2.4 Quintal

(2) Maximum Level = Reorder + Reorder Quantity – (Min. Usage × Min. Delivery time)

= 2400 × 2500 – (250 × 4)

= 4900 – 1000 = 3900 Kgs.

(3) Minimum Level = Reorder Level – (Normal usage × Normal delivery time)

$$= 2400 - \left(\frac{400 + 250}{2} \times \frac{4 + 6}{2}\right)$$

= 2400 – (325 × 5)

= 2400 – 1625 = 775 Kgs.

(4) Average Stock Level = Minimum Level + ½ × Reorder Quantity

= 775 + ½ × 2500

= 775 + 1250 = 2025 Kgs.

$$\text{OR : Average Stock} = \frac{\text{Minimum Level + Maximum Level}}{2}$$

$$= \frac{775 + 3900}{2}$$

$$= \frac{4675}{2}$$

= 2337.5 Kgs.

$$\text{Stock Turnover Ratio} = \frac{\text{Material consumed during period}}{\text{Average Stock}}$$

$$= \frac{10575}{2337.5}$$

= 4.52

Problem No. 34

Two components A and B are used as follows :

Normal Usage 800 Units per week each

Maximum Usage 1200 Units per week each.

Minimum Usage 400 Units per week each.

Reorder Quantity X — 5400

Y — 9800

Reorder Period X — 4 to 6 weeks

Y — 2 to 4 weeks.

Calculate for each components : (a) Reorder Level (b) Maximum Level (c) Minimum Level (d) Average Stock Level.

Solution :

(a) Reorder Level = Maximum Consumption × Max. Delivery time

X = 1200 × 6 = 7200 Units.

Y = 1200 × 4 = 4800 Units.

(b) Maximum Stock Level = Reorder Level + Reorder Quantity – (Min. Consumption × Mini. Delivery Period)

X = 7200 + 5400 – (400 × 4)

= 12600 – 1600 = 11000 Units.

Y = 4800 + 9800 – (400 × 2)

= 14600 – 800 = 6600 Units.

(c) Minimum Stock Level = Reorder Level – (Normal usage × Average Delivery Time)

X $= 7200 - (800 \times \frac{4+6}{2})$

= 7200 – 4000 = 3200 Units.

Y $= 4800 - (800 \times \frac{2+4}{2})$

= 4800 – 2400 = 2400 Units.

(d) Average Stock Level = ½ (Mini. Stock Level + Max. Stock Level)

X = ½ (3200 + 11000)

= ½ × 14200 = 7100

Y = ½ (2400 + 6600)

= ½ × 9000

= 4500 Units.

Problem No. 35

In a manufacturing company uses raw materials for 3 products X, Y and Z following are the particulars :

Raw Materials	Usage per Unit of Product	Reorder Quantity Kg	Delivery Period	Reorder Level Kg	Min. Stock Level Kg	Min. & Max. Usage
X	15 Kg	15000	1 to 3	12000	—	300
Y	6 Kg	7500	3 to 5	1725	—	250
Z	9 Kg	1500	2 to 4	—	3000	350

Weekly production varies from 300 units calculate the Stock Levels of the following :

(a) Maximum Stock of Y (b) Minimum Stock of X

(c) Reorder Level of Z (d) Average Stock Level of X.

Solution :

(a) Maximum Stock Level = Reorder + Reorder Quantity – (Minimum Usage × Minimum Delivery Period)

Y = 7125 + 7500 – (250 × 6 × 3)

= 14625 – 4500 = 10125

(b) Minimum Stock Level = Reorder Level – (Normal Usage × Normal Delivery Period)

X = $15000 - (300 \times 15\text{Kg} \times \frac{1+3}{2})$

= 15000 – (4500 × 2)

= 15000 – 9000 = 6000 Kg.

(c) Reorder Level = Maximum Usage × Max Reorder Period

Z = 350 × 9 Kg × 4 = 12600 Kg.

(d) Average Stock = Minimum Level + ½ Reorder Quantity

X = 9000 + ½ 15000

= 9000 + 7500

= 16500 Kg.

Problem No. 36

Two components of 'X' & 'Y" are used as follows normal usage :

Normal Usage	250 Units per week
Minimum Usage	125 Units per week
Maximum Usage	375 Units per week
Reorder Quantity	X — 1500 Units
	Y — 2500 Units
Reorder Period	X — 4 to 6 weeks
	Y — 2 to 4 weeks.

Calculate : (a) Reorder Level (b) Maximum Level (c) Minimum Level (d) Average Level.

Solution :

Stock Levels

(a) Reorder Level = Maximum Consumption × Maximum Delivery Period

X = 375 × 6 = 2250 Units

Y = 375 × 4 = 1500 Units.

(b) Maximum Level = Reorder Level + Reorder Qty. – (Min. Consumption × Min. Delivery period)

X = 2250 + 1500 – (125 × 4)

= 3750 – 500 = 3259 Units.

Y = 1500 + 2500 – (125 × 2)

= 4000 – 250 = 3750 Units.

(c) Minimum Stock Level = Reorder Level – (Normal consumption × Average delivery period)

X $= 2250 - (250 \times \frac{4+6}{2})$

= 2250 – (250 × 5) = 2250 – 1250 = 1000 Units.

Y $= 1500 - (250 \times (250 \times \frac{2+4}{2})$

= 1500 – (250 × 3)

= 1500 – 750 = 750 Units.

(d) Average Stock Level = Minimum Level + ½ Reorder Quantity

X = 1000 + ½ × 1500 = 1000 + 750 = 1750 Units.

Y = 750 + ½ × 2500 = 750 + 1250

= 2000 Units.

INVENTORY TURNOVER RATIO

Inventory Turnover ratio is also one method of exercising control over the Materials. The Stock Turnover is calculated as follows :

(I) Inventory Turnover Ratio $= \frac{\text{Cost of Materials consumed during Period}}{\text{Cost of Average stock held}}$

Average Stock $= \frac{\text{Opening + Closing Stock}}{2}$

(II) Inventory Turnover in days $= \frac{\text{Days during period}}{\text{Inventory Turnover Ratio}}$ = (M.T.R.)

This helps to compare the turnover of different kinds of materials rate of Turnover ratio.

A Low Turnover Ratio is an indication of slow moving stock. A Low turnover ratio will lead to the disadvantage arising out of over stocking. If the turnover ratio is Zero for a particular item of stock, it means, it is not used during the period. So, it is to be disposed off immediately.

A high turnover ratio is an indication of fast moving stock and less investment in stock.

Problem No. 37

The following are taken from the books of 'X' Co. Ltd. for the year 1989 :

Particulars	Material A	Material B
Opening Stock	25,000	87,500
Closing Stock	15,000	62,500
Purchases	1,90,000	1,25,000

Calculate Inventory Turnover Ratio of the above materials and express the number of days the average inventory held.

(K.U.D., October 1990)

Solution :

Inventory Turnover Ratio

Particulars	Material A	Material B
Opening Stock	25,000	87,500
Add : Purchases	1,90,000	1,25,000
Total Materials	2,15,000	2,12,500
Less : Closing Stock	15,000	62,500
Material consumed during the period	2,00,000	1,50,000
Average Stock		
Opening Stock	25,000	87,500
Add : Closing Stock	15,000	62,500
	40,000	1,50,000
Divided by Two	2	2
Average Stock	20,000	75,000

$$\text{Material Turnover Ratio} = \frac{\text{Cost of Material consumed}}{\text{Average Stock}}$$

	Material A	Material B
	$\frac{2,00,000}{20,000}$	$\frac{1,50,000}{75,000}$
M.T.R. (Ratio)	10 times	2 times

Inventory Turnover Ratio in days :

$$\frac{\text{Days during period}}{\text{Material Turnover ratio}} = \frac{365}{10} \qquad \frac{365}{2}$$

Inventory Turn over in days = 36.5 or 37 days 182.5 or 183 days.

Problem No. 38

The following data are available from the Bin Cards of Joyti Batteries Ltd. for the year 1981 :

Particulars	Material A	Material B	Material C
Opening Stock	7,000	2,000	10,000
Purchases	1,15,000	1,10,000	18,000
Closing Stock	2,000	12,000	12,000

Calculate the material Turnover ratio of A, B & C and express in number of days the average inventory held and comment on the same.

(K.U.D., October 1983)

Solution :

Inventory Turnover Ratio

Particulars	Material A	Material B	Material C
Opening Stock	7,000	2,000	10,000
Add : Purchases	1,15,000	1,10,000	18,000
	1,22,000	1,12,000	28,000
Less : Closing Stock	2,000	12,000	12,000
Materials Consumed	1,20,000	1,00,000	16,000
Average Stock :			
Opening Stock	7,000	2,000	10,000
Add : Closing Stock	2,000	12,000	12,000
	9,000	14,000	22,000
Average Divided by 2 (Two)	2	2	2
Average Stock	4,500	7,000	11,000
Inventory Turnover Ratio : $= \frac{\text{Cost of Materials Consumed}}{\text{Average Stock}}$	$\frac{1,20,000}{4,500}$	$\frac{1,00,000}{7,000}$	$\frac{16,000}{11,000}$
	26.66	14 time	1.5 time
	27 time		Or 2 time
Inventory Turnover Ratio in days $= \frac{\text{Days during period}}{\text{Inventory Turnover ratio}}$	$\frac{365}{27}$	$\frac{365}{14}$	$\frac{365}{2}$
	14 Days	26 Days	183 Days

MATERIAL TURNOVER RATIO

Problem No. 39

The following are taken from the record of M/s Mohan and Co., B'lore fo: the year 1979. The valuation of Inventory is Re.1 per Kg or Litre.

Material	Opening Stock	Purchases	Closing Stock
X	700 Kg	11500 Kg	200 Kg
Y	200 Litre	11000 Litre	1200 Litre
Z	1000 Kg	1800 Kg	1200 Kg

Calculate Inventory Turnover Ratio of the above materials and express i number of days the average Inventory held.

(K.U.D., April 1980

Solution :

(1) Inventory Turnover Ratio = $\frac{\text{Cost of Material Consumed}}{\text{Cost of Average Stock held}}$

(2) Inventory Turnover Ratio (in days) = $\frac{\text{Days During the Period}}{\text{Inventory Turnover Ratio}}$

Particulars	X	Y	Z
Material Consumed :			
Opening Stock	700 Kg	200 Ltr	1000 Kg
Add : Purchases	11500 Kg	11000 Ltr	1800 Kg
	12200	11200	2800
Less : Closing Stock	200	1200	1200
Material Consumed	12000	10000	1600
Average Stock :			
Opening Stock	700	200	1000
Add : Closing Stock	200	1200	1200
	900	1400	2200
Divided by 2 (Two)	2	2	2
	450	700	1100
(1) Inventory Turnover Ratio			
= $\frac{\text{Cost of Material Consumed}}{\text{Cost of Average Stock}}$	$\frac{1200}{450}$	$\frac{10000}{700}$	$\frac{1600}{1100}$
	26.67	14.285	1.45
(2) Inventory Turnover Ratio (in Days) :			
= $\frac{\text{Days During Period}}{\text{Inventory Ratio}}$	$\frac{365}{26.67}$	$\frac{365}{14.29}$	$\frac{365}{1.45}$
	13.68	25.54	251 days
	Or 14 days	Or 26 days	

Problem No. 40

Calculate Inventory Turnover Ratio and express in days from the following particulars :

Normal Usage	1200 Units per day
Reorder Level	12000 Units.
Reorder Quantity	31200
Maximum Stock	36000
Minimum Stock	4800

Solution :

Material Consumed = Maximum Stock – Minimum Stock

= 36000 – 4800 = 31200

$$\text{Average Inventory} = \frac{\text{Maximum Stock} + \text{Minimum Stock}}{2}$$

$$= \frac{36000 + 4800}{2} = 20400 \text{ Units.}$$

Or : Average Inventory = Minimum Stock + ½ × Reorder Quantity

= 4800 + ½ 31200 = 4800 + 15600 = 20400 Units.

$$\text{Inventory Ratio} = \frac{\text{Materials Consumed during the period}}{\text{Average Stock held during the period}}$$

$$= \frac{31200}{20400} = 1.5294.$$

Inventory Turnover Expressed in Days :

(a) $$\frac{\text{Average Inventory} \times \text{Days during the period}}{\text{Material consumed during the period}}$$

$$= \frac{20400 \times 26}{31200} = 17 \text{ days.}$$

Or : $$\frac{\text{Days during the Period}}{\text{Inventory Turnover Ratio}} = \frac{26 \text{ Days}}{1.5294} = 17 \text{ Days.}$$

The Average Stock of 20400 Units is sufficient for 17 days at the Rate of 1200 units per day = 17 × 1200 = 20400 Units.

Problem No. 41

The following are the particulars extracted from the books of X and Co. for the Year 1994 :

Materials	Opening Stock	Purchases	Closing Stock
X	2100 Units	34500 Units	600 Units
Y	600 Units	33000 Units	3600 Units
Z	3000 Units	5400 Units	3600 Units

Calculate Material Turnover Ratio and express in term of Days the Average Inventory held.

Solution :

(I) Material Consumed = Opening Stock + Purchases – Closing Stock.

Materials	X	Y	Z
Opening Stock	2100	600	3000
Add : Purchases	34500	33000	5400
	36600	33600	8400
Less : Closing Stock	600	3600	3600
Material Consumed	36000	30000	4800

(II) Average Stock = $\dfrac{\text{Opening Stock + Closing Stock}}{2}$

	X	Y	Z
Opening Stock	2100	600	3000
Add : Closing Stock	600	3600	3600
	2700	4200	6600
	2	2	2
Average Stock	1350	2100	3300

(III) Inventory Turnover Ratio :

$= \dfrac{\text{Materials Consumed during period}}{\text{Average Stock held during period}}$

X	Y	Z
$\dfrac{36000}{1350}$	$\dfrac{30000}{2100}$	$\dfrac{2100}{4800}$
26.67	14.29	1.46

Expressed in Days :

	X	Y	Z
$= \dfrac{\text{Days during the Period}}{\text{Inventory Turnover Ratio}}$	$\dfrac{365}{26.67}$	$\dfrac{365}{14.29}$	$\dfrac{365}{1.46}$
In days	13.68	25.54	250
	14 Days	26 Days	250 Days

MATERIAL

Material Loss — Wastage, Scrap, Defectives and Spoilage. Material Loss in the nature of wastage, scrap, defective and spoilage.

Treatment

(1) Normal Loss (2) Abnormal Loss.

Normal Loss arises due to the nature of material or Production processes, it is unavoidable.

Treatment : Cost of Normal Loss shall be recovered from the Good units of output.

Abnormal Loss : Abnormal Loss is charged to costing Profit and Loss Account.

Scrap : It possess realisable value and therefore it is credited to costing Profit and Loss Account as income. The Sale value of Scrap may be deducted from the cost of Materials.

Defective Goods : Defective units may be rectified with additional cost and it should be added to the total cost and quantity.

CALCULATION OF COST OF MATERIAL

Problem No. 42

6000 Kg. of wood material costing Rs. 1,08,000 for the manufacturing of 45" size pullover. On the compilation of manufacturing of pullover the following information is furnished :

(a) 2400 pullover of 45" of 2 Kg each manufactured.

(b) 150 Kg wood is scrapped and realised Rs. 1,400.

(c) 300 Kg of offcut were used for the manufactured of another variety of hosing. The market value of this is Rs. 2,700.

(d) 100 pullover were found defective and rectified at an additional material cost of Rs. 1,000.

You are required to find out cost of material of one pullover.

Solution :

Particulars	Qty. Kgs	Amount Rs.
Material issued	6000	1,08,000
Less : Scrap	150	1,400
	5850	1,06,600
Less : Offcuts used for the manufacture of another variety	300	2,700
	5550	1,03,900
Add : Cost of rectification of defective pullover (400)	—	1,000
	5550	1,04,900

	Kgs	Rs.
	5550	1,04,900
Less : Wastage in process Normal Loss Normal Output/Cost.	150	—
Cost of Good Units :	5400	1,04,900

2400 + 300 = 2700 Units (Pullovers of 2 Kg.)

$$\text{Cost per Unit} = \frac{1,04,900}{2700} = \text{Rs. } 38.85$$

Problem No. 43

A Lorry load of Materials of mixed Goods was purchased for Rs. 9,000. These were sorted into the following Grades where market rate was as follows :

Grade	Units	Selling per Unit
A	5000	1.20
B	3000	1.00
C	2000	0.50

Find out the purchases rate per unit of each Grade of the materials assuming that all grades yield the same rate of profit.

(K.U.D., October 1986)

Solution :

Market Value of Materials

Grade	Units	Selling Price per Unit	Total Selling Price
A	5000	1.20	6,000
B	3000	1.00	3,000
C	2000	0.50	1,000
	10000		10,000

Total Sales Price =	10,000
Cost/Purchases Price	9,000
Profit	1,000

$$\text{Profit on Selling Price} = \frac{1,000}{10,000} = 10\%$$

Ascertainment of cost per unit :

Grade	Selling Price Per unit	Profit 10% on selling price	Cost per unit
A	1.20	0.12	1.08
B	1.00	0.10	0.90
C	0.50	0.05	0.45

Verification

Grade	Units	Cost price per unit	Total
A	5000	1.08	5400
B	3000	0.90	2700
C	2000	0.45	900
	10000		9000

Problem No. 44

A consignment consisted of two Chemicals 'A' and 'B'. The invoices gave the following data :

Chemical — A 4000 Kg of Rs. 2.50 per Kg.

Chemical — B 3200 Kg of Rs. 3.25 per Kg.

Sales Tax — Rs. 1836.

Railway freight — Rs. 4.50.

Sales tax is to be apportioned to Chemical — A, Rs. 580.
Chemical — B, Rs. 1256.

Railway Freight is to be charged on the basis of weight.

A shortage of 200 Kg in A and 80 Kg in B was noticed due to breakage.

What stock rate would you adopt for pricing issues assuming a provision of 5% towards further deterioration?

(K.U.D., April 1985)

Solution :

Chemical 'A'

Cost Price 4000 × 2.50	10000
Add : Sales tax	580
Total Cost	10580
Add : Railway Freight	
$\frac{4000}{7200} \times 450 = \frac{5}{9} \times 450$	250
Total Cost	10830
Total Quantity (in Kgs)	4000
Less : Loss of weight	200
	3800
Less : Provision for deterioration 5% of 3800	190
Net Weight	3610

Chemical 'B'

Cost Price 3200 × 3.50	10400
Add : Sales tax	1256
Total Cost	11656
Add : Railway Freight	
$\frac{3200}{7200} \times 450 = \frac{4}{9} \times 450$	200
Total Cost	11856
Total Quantity (in Kgs)	3200
Less : Shortage	80
	3120
Less : Provision for deterioration of 5% of 3120	156
Net Weight	2964

$$\text{Rate per Kg} = \frac{\text{Total Cost}}{\text{Net weight}}$$

$$= \frac{10830}{3610} \qquad = \frac{11856}{2964}$$

= Rs. 3 per Kg = Rs. 4 per Kg.

Problem No. 45

A consignment consisted of two chemicals M & N. The invoice gives the following data :

Chemical 'M' 8000 Kg @ Rs. 5 per Kg	40,000
Chemical 'N' 6400 Kg @ Rs. 6.50 per Kg	41,600
Sales tax	3,264
Railway Freight	1,536
Total Cost	86,400

Shortage of 400 Kg in M and 250 Kg. in N was noticed due to breakage. What is stock rate you would adopt for pricing issues assuming a provision of 5% towards further loss.

(ICWA, Inter)

Solution :

Particulars	Chemicals M	Chemicals N
Cost Price M = 8000 Kg @ Rs. 5 per Kg	40000	—
N = 6400 Kg @ Rs. 6.50 per Kg	—	41600
Add : Sale Tax of Rs. 3,264		
$\frac{40000}{81600} \times 3264 = 1600$ for 'M'	1600	
$\frac{41000}{81600} \times 3264 = 1664$ for 'N'		1664
Add : Railway Freight of Rs. 1536		
$M = \frac{8000}{14400} \times 1536$	853	
$N = \frac{6400}{14400} \times 1536$		683
Total Cost	42453	43947
Total Quantity	8000	6400
Less : Shortage	400	256
	7600	6144
Rate per Unit = $\frac{\text{Total Cost}}{\text{Total Unit}}$	$\frac{42453}{7600}$	$\frac{43947}{6144}$
Cost per Unit	5.59	7.15
Provision 5% Add	0.28	.36
Net Cost per Unit	5.87	7.51
Material Issue Price =	5.87	7.51

Problem No. 46

A consignment consisted of 4 Grades of materials was purchased for Rs. 1,20,000. Storekeeper sorted them and recorded the following :

Grade	A	40000 Units.
Grade	B	8000 Units
Grade	C	10000 Units
Grade	D	12000 Units

The total sales of Grade-A amounted Rs. 16,000 (Rate of Profit being 33-1/3 per cent on cost) and those of Grade-B @ a price of 1.5 time that of A but the rate of profit was 33-1/3 per cent on sales. Similarly Grade-C material was sold for Rs. 50,000 yielding a profit of 20 per cent on sales. Calculate the purchase price of each grade on the basis of above information.

(K.U.D., April 1977 & 1983)

Solution :

Total purchases price of 4 Grade Materials		1,20,000
Grade-A : 4000 Units Sales Price	16,000	

Sales Price per unit = $\dfrac{16000}{4000}$ = Rs. 4

Profit 33-1/3 per cent on cost	
OR : 25% on sales = 25% of 16,000 =	4,000
	12,000

Cost per unit = 12,000/4000 = Rs. 3 per unit.

Grade-B : Sales price is 1.5 time that of A; Sales Price of A — Rs. 4

∴ Sales Price of B – 1.5 times of Rs. 4 = 4 × 1.5 = Rs. 6.

Sales Price of B — Rs. 6 per unit.

Profit 33-1/3 per cent of 6 = 2. Cost Price per Unit = Rs. 4

Total Cost Price = 8000 × 4 = 32,000

Grade-C : 10000 Units, Sales Price	50,000
Profit 20 per cent on Sales price	10,000
Cost price	40,000

Cost price per unit = 40,000/10,000 = Rs. 4 per unit.

The cost price of Grade A, B & C are :

Grades	Units	Cost Price per Unit	Total Cost Price
A	4000	3.00	12,000
B	8000	4.00	32,000
C	10000	4.00	40,000
		Total	84,000
		Total Purchase Price	1,20,000
Balance being the cost price of Grade-D			36,000

Cost per unit = $\dfrac{36,000}{12,000}$ = Rs. 3 per unit.

Verification

Grade	Units	Cost Price per unit Rs.	Total Cost Price Rs.
A	4000	3.00	12,000
B	8000	4.00	32,000
C	10000	4.00	40,000
D	12000	3.00	36,000
		Total Cost Price	1,20,000
		Total Purchase Price	

Problem No. 47

A consignment consisting of 4 Grades of materials was purchased for Rs. 1,80,000. Storekeeper sorted them out and recorded the following Grade-A — 600 Units. Grade-B — 12000 Units. Grade-C — 15000 Uints and Grade-D — 18000 Units.

The total sales of Grade-A amounted to Rs. 24,000 (rate of profit being 33-1/3 per cent of cost) and those of B at a Price 1½ times that of A but the rate of profit was 33-1/3 per cent of sales. Similarly Grade C material was sold for Rs. 75,000, yielding a Profit of 20 per cent on sales.

Calculate the purchases of each grade on the basis of the above information.

Solution :

Grade-A : Total Sales — Rs. 24,000

Number of units — 6000 Units.

Selling price per unit = $\frac{24000}{6000}$ = Rs. 4 per unit.

Rate of profit = 33-1/3 per cent on cost or 25 per cent on sales Price

∴ Total Sales	24,000
Less : Profit 25 per cent on sales	6,000
Cost Price	18,000

Cost price per unit = $\frac{18,000}{6,000}$ = Rs. 3 per unit.

Grade-B : Sales Price 1½ time of A

Sales Price of A — Rs. 4, Sales Price of B 1½ times of Rs. 4

= 4 + 2 = 6 per unit.

Total sales Nos of unit	12000 × 6 =	72,000
Rate of Profit 33-1/3 per cent on sales		24,000
	Cost Price	Rs. 48,000

Cost Price per unit = $\frac{48000}{12000}$ = Rs. 4 per unit.

Grade-C : Total Sales		75,000
Rate of Profit 20 per cent on sales		15,000
Cost Price	Rs.	60,000

Rate per unit = $\frac{60,000}{15,000}$ = Rs. 4 per unit.

			Rs.
Grade-D : Total Purchases Price			1,80,000
Less Cost Price of	A	18,000	
	B	48,000	
	C	60,000	1,26,000
	Cost Price of Grade-D		54,000

Rate per unit = $\frac{54,000}{18,000}$ = Rs. 3 per unit.

Verification

Cost of Price of Materials

Grade	Units	Rate Rs.	Amount Rs.
A	6000	3.00	18,000
B	12000	4.00	48,000
C	15000	4.00	60,000
D	18000	3.00	54,000
	Total Cost of Price		1,80,000

Problem No. 48

The following quotation is received from Mr. Kumar in respect of materials :

500 Kg @ Rs. 10 per Kg.

2000 Kg @ Rs. 8.50 per Kg.

4000 Kg @ Rs. 7.75 per Kg.

Trade discount 20 per cent; cash discount 5 per cent of payment is made within one month. One is required for every 250 Kg. of material and containers are charged at Rs. 25 each but credit with Rs. 20 if returned within one month.

Transport charges for any order Rs. 250.

Storages Rs. 150

Concerns decides to purchases 2000 Kg.

Assuming the payment is made within one month and the containers are also returned. Calculate the material cost per Kg.

Solution :

Purchases of Material in Lot 2000 Kg.

Material Cost 2000 Kg @ Rs. 8.50 per Kg		17,000
Less : Trade discount @ 20% (17,000 × 20/100)		3,400
		13,600
Less : Cash discount @ 5% on 13,600 (13,600 × 5/100)		680
Total Cost		12,920
Add : Transport charges	250	
Add : Storages	150	400
		13,320
Add : Cost container $\frac{2000}{250}$ = 8 × 25		200
Total Cost Price		13,520
Less : Container returned credit @ 20 × 8		160
Net Total Cost Price		13,360

$$\text{Cost Price per Kg.} = \frac{13,360}{2000} = \text{Rs. } 6.68$$

Problem No. 49

A large consignment of materials of variety makes was purchased for Rs. 1,20,000. Later on these were sorted out into following categories whose market rate is given against each :

Category	Units	Selling Price per Unit
M	9000	8.00
N	6000	6.00
P	10500	4.00

Find out the purchase rate per unit of each category of material presuming that all categories yield the same rate of profit.

Solution :

Calculation of Purchase Price

Total Purchase price	1,20,000
Total Sales price	1,50,000
Total Profit	30,000

$$\text{Percentage of Profit on Sales price} = \frac{30,000}{1,50,000} \times 100 = 20 \text{ per cent Profit on Sales.}$$

Category	No. of Units	Sales Price Per unit	Total Sales	Profit % on Sales	Amount of Profit	Purchase price per unit
M	9000	8.00	72,000	20%	1.60	6.40
N	6000	6.00	36,000	20%	1.20	4.80
P	10500	4.00	42,000	20%	0.80	3.20
			1,50,000			

Verification

Grade	No. of Units	Purchase Price	Amount
M	9000	6.40	57,600
N	6000	4.80	28,800
P	10500	3.20	33,600
		Total Purchase Price	1,20,000

MATERIAL INPUT-OUTPUT RATIO

The agricultural products such as oilseeds, paddy, cotton, Jute etc., while put into process of manufacture or conversion into consumable products such as Oil from Oilseeds, Rice from Paddy, Yarn from Cotton, Jute products from raw Jute etc. Yield or output, for example Oilseeds is input and Oil is output for 100 Kg of Oilseeds about 60 Kg of Oil is produced. Here input is 100 Kg output is 60 Kg therefore Input-output Ratio is $\frac{100}{60}$ or $\frac{10}{6}$.

Similarly for other produces such as cotton input is 100 Kg output is 75 Kg of yarn.

Input-output ratio is $\frac{100}{75}$ or $\frac{10}{7.5}$. So also for wheat and wheat products as atta etc.

From the above it is clear that the raw material put into process (to get consumable products) would yield less in quantity in the form of output. Technically it is called as Input-Output Ratio. A standard is fixed to determine the Input ratios and compared with actual performance. It becomes more practical when it is expressed or calculated in terms of cost price of each unit. If the cost price per unit of actual performance is more than the standard cost price, it shows inefficiency in purchasing of raw material.

Many a time particularly in case of agricultural produce — such as cotton grown in different area different variety and thereby quality also differs and hence yield per unit. In all such cases efficiency in buying of material plays an important role which in turn has direct effect on profitability of the organisation. So, material Input-Output ratio is determining factor in framing suitable buying policy.

Problem No. 50

In Spinning Mill yarn is produced from cotton. Following are the particulars extracted from the books of the Mill :

	Standard	Actual.
Input of cotton	10 Kg	10000 Kg
Output Yarn	7 Kg	6000 Kg
Cost per Kg Rs. 42		

Find out Input-Output ratio.

Solution :

Standard Input-Output ratio $\frac{10}{7}$

Actual Input-Output ratio $\frac{10}{6}$ of $\frac{10000}{6000}$

Raw material cost of finished output per Kg. :

Standard = 10/7 × 42 = Rs. 60 per Kg.

Actual = 10/6 × 42 = Rs. 70 per Kg.

The above Input-Output ratio is higher than the standard Input-Output Ratio. The performance is below standard or unfavourable.

Problem No. 51

In a Oil Mill unit uses Oilseeds of certain Grade-A quality costing Rs. 20 per Kg and having Input-Output ratio 125 per cent. Due to low output usual grade of Oilseeds. The mill has to purchase in the market two different Grades of Oilseeds and these were found suitable alternatives to the certain grade A.

Oilseeds	Cost Price per Kg	Input-Output
Grade-B	Rs. 20	110%
Grade-C	Rs. 16	150%

Calculate the cost per Kg of output in each case and recommend which of these Grades preferred in purchasing.

Solution :

The Input-Output ratio varies in both the Grade B and C and also purchase price. It is to be decided on the basis of cost per Kg of Output.

Formula

$$\text{Cost of raw material in finished goods} = \frac{\text{Input}}{\text{Output}} \times \text{Rate per Unit}$$

$$\text{Grade-B} = \frac{110}{100} \times 20 = \text{Rs. 22 per Kg}$$

$$\text{Grade-C} = \frac{150}{100} \times 16 = \text{Rs. 24 per Kg}$$

Grade-B raw material though costly would yield Rs. 22 per Kg in output which is less than the Grade-C. Though the cost price of raw material Grade-C is cheeper than that of the Grade-B. Hence Grade-B is recommended.

Problem No. 52

In a Soap manufacturing company uses Oil-N @ of cost price Rs. 60 per Kg with Input-Output ratio 125 per cent. Due to short supply of particular N Oil the substitutes X, Y and Z is selected as suitable for the product. The following are the particulars :

Oil (Substitute)	Cost Price per Kg	Input-Output Ratio
X	Rs. 60	110%
Y	Rs. 50	120%
Z	Rs. 45	150%

Calculate the cost per Kg of Output in each of these substitutes and give reasons which of these substitutes are preferred and why?

Solution :

The Input-Output ratio varies in all the cases and also the lower cost price may not give the correct answer for our selection.

It is to be decided on the bases of Cost of raw material finished output per Kg. Calculation of cost of raw material in the finished Output = $\frac{\text{Input}}{\text{Output}} \times$ Rate per Unit

Now Substitute :

$$X = \frac{110}{100} \times 60 = \text{Rs. 66 per Kg}$$

$$Y = \frac{120}{100} \times 50 = \text{Rs. 60 per Kg}$$

$$Z = \frac{150}{100} \times 45 = \text{Rs. 67.50 per Kg.}$$

Note : Substitute 'Y' Oil is the lowest cost per Kg. Rs. 60 as compared to other Oils X & Z substitute.

Problem No. 53

In a Spinning Mill two grade of cotton is used to produce yarn. A new variety of raw material named 'X' was introduced as an experiment.

The following are the particulars provided :

Particulars	Grade-A		Grade-B		Grade-X	
	Standard	Actual	Standard	Actual	Standard	Actual
Raw Material :						
Input	10 Kg	10000 Kg	10 Kg	10000 kg	10 Kg	10000 Kg
Output	9 Kg	8000 Kg	8 Kg	9000 Kg	7 Kg	8000 Kg
Cost of Raw material per Kg.	Rs. 36		Rs. 48		Rs. 35	

Find out input-output ratio and state which of these Grades is more advantageous to the Mill.

Solution :

Particulars	Grade-A	Grade-B	Grade-X
Standard Input-Output	$\frac{10}{9} \times 100 = 111\%$	$\frac{10}{8} \times 100 = 125\%$	$\frac{10}{7} \times 100 = 143\%$
Ratio $= \frac{\text{Input}}{\text{Output}} \times 100$			
Actual Input-Output ratio	$\frac{10}{8} = 125\%$	$\frac{10}{9} = 111\%$	$\frac{10}{8} = 125\%$
Raw Material cost	Rs. 36	Rs. 48	Rs. 35
Standard cost of raw material into finished output	$\frac{10}{9} \times 36 = 40$	$\frac{10}{8} \times 48 = 60$	$\frac{10}{7} \times 35 = 50$
Actual cost of raw material into finished output	$\frac{10}{8} \times 36 = 45$	$\frac{10}{9} \times 48 = 53.33$	$\frac{10}{8} \times 35 = 43.7$
Actual cost of raw material into finished output	Rs. 45	Rs. 53.33	Rs. 43.75

In the above three grades A, B & X, Grade 'X' the cost of raw material into finished output is lower than the Grade A & B. Therefore Grade X is more advantageous to the Mill.

MATERIAL PRICING

In a manufacturing Company materials are purchased at different prices on different dates in a month or at different prices in different months of the year since the manufacturing activities are continuous. Materials required for production are issued as and when material requisition Note is received from production departments. Materials issued, pricing policy for issue of materials needs to be adopted accordingly. Following are the possible methods of pricing the issue of materials :

(b) METHODS OF PRICING THE ISSUES

(1) First in First out — FIFO Method (Cover Actual
(2) Last in First out — LIFO Method Cost Price)
(3) Base Stock Method (Under FIFO or LIFO Method)
(4) Average Cost Price :
  (a) Simple Average.
  (b) Periodic Average.
  (c) Weighted Average.
  (d) Periodic-Weighted Average.
(5) Standard Price.
(6) Inflated Price (Under FIFO or LIFO Method)
(7) Market Price.

The following problems dealt herewith would give a perfect knowledge about the various methods of pricing of Issue of materials.

Problem No. 1

Prepare Store Ledger using weighted average price method, from the following particulars.

1996

Jan. 1	Balance 1200 units @ Rs. 3 per unit.
5	Issued to Job No. 1 : 600 units.
8	Purchased 450 units @ Rs. 2.50 per unit.
15	Issued to Job No. 5 : 300 units
20	Issued to Job No. 7 : 400 units
23	Purchased 150 units at Rs. 2.75 per unit.
25	Returned to Stores 50 units from Job No. 7.
27	Purchased 300 units at Rs. 3 per unit.
31	Stores Audit reveals shortage of 20 units due to wrong measurement.

[K.U.D., April 1998 (O)]

Weighted Average Pricing Method

Stores Ledger

Date	Particulars	Receipts			Issues			Balance		
		Units	Rate	Amount	Units	Rate	Amount	Units	Rate	Amount
1996			Rs.	Rs.		Rs.	Rs.		Rs.	Rs.
Jan. 1	Opening Balance	—	—	—	—	—	—	1200	3.00	3600
5	Issued to Job No. 1	—	—	—	600	3.00	1800	600		1800
8	Purchased	450	2.50	1125	—	—	—	600 450 1050	3.00 2.50	1800 1125 2925
15	Issued to Job No. 5	—	—	—	300	2.785	835.5	750		2089.5
20	Issued to Job No. 7	—	—	—	400	2.786	1114	350		915.5
23	Purchased	150	2.75	412.5	—	—	—	500		1328
25	Returned to stores from Job 7	50	2.786	139.3	—	—	—	550		1467.3
27	Purchased	300	3.00	900	—	—	—	850		2367.3
31	Shortage				20	2.785	55.7	830	2.785	2311.6

Note : (1) Returned to stores from Job No. 7. Priced at Issue Price Entry in Receipt column it increases stock balance.

(2) Shortage - Priced as usual
Entry - Issue Column. It reduces balance

Working Note

Issue price under Weighted Average Price Method

$$\text{Weighted Average price} = \frac{\text{Cost of Materials in Stock}}{\text{Quantity in Stock}}$$

Date of issue :

(1) Jan. 5 $= \frac{3600}{1200}$ = Rs. 3 per unit

(2) Jan. 15 = $\frac{2925}{1050}$ = Rs. 2.785

(3) Jan. 20 = $\frac{2089.5}{750}$ = Rs. 2.786

31-1-96 = Shortage :

Price = $\frac{2367.3}{850}$ = Rs. 2.785

Problem No. 2

From the following details write Stores Ledger under Simple Average method.

1977 Jan. 1	—	Opening Balance	150 kgs @ Rs. 5
7		Received	75 kgs @ Rs. 5.20
8		Issued	180 kgs
11		Issued	15 kgs
14		Received	120 kgs @ Rs. 5.40
17		Issued	75 kgs
21		Received	150 kgs at Rs. 5.60
26		Issued	60 kgs
29		Issued	70 kgs
30		Received	100 kgs @ Rs. 5.80

The stocks verification found a shortage of 15 kgs on 16th Jan 1997 and another shortage of 10 kgs. on 31st Jan. 1997.

[K.U.D., October 1977(O)]

Store Ledger-Issue-Price-Simple Average Method

Date	Particulars	Receipts			Issue			Balance		
1997		Units	Rate	Amount	Units	Rate	Amount	Units	Rate	Amount
			Rs.	Rs.		Rs.	Rs.		Rs.	Rs.
Jan. 1	Opening Balance	150	5	750	—	—	—	150	5	750
7	Received	75	5.20	390				150	5	750
								75	5.20	390
8	Issued	—	—	—	180	5.10	918	45	5.20	234
11	Issued	—	—	—	15	5.20	78	30	5.20	156
14	Received	120	5.40	648	—	—	—	30	5.20	156
								120	5.40	648
16	Shortage	—	—	—	15	5.30	79.5	15	5.20	78
								120	5.40	648
17	Issued	—	—	—	75	5.30	397.5	60	5.40	324
21	Received	150	5.60	840	—	—	—	60	5.40	324
								150	5.60	840
26	Issued	—	—	—	60	5.50	330	150	5.60	840
29	Issued	—	—	—	90	5.60	504	60	5.60	336
30	Received	100	5.80	580	—	—	—	60	5.60	336
31	Shortages	—	—	—	10	5.70	57	100	5.80	580
								50	5.60	280
								100	5.80	580

Issue Price : 8-1-97 – $\frac{\text{Total of Prices entering into issue}}{\text{No. of Prices}}$

$\frac{5+5.20}{2} = \frac{10.20}{2} = 5\text{-}10$

16-1-97 Shortage $\frac{5.20+5.40}{2} = \frac{10.60}{2} = 5.30$

17-1-97 = $\frac{5.20+5.40}{2} = \frac{10.60}{2} = 5.30$

26-1-97 = $\frac{5.40+5.60}{2} = \frac{11.00}{2} = 5.50$

31-1-97 = $\frac{5.60+5.80}{2} + \frac{11.40}{2} = 5.70$

Problem No. 3

Prepare Stores Ledger from the following :

Use First in First out (FIFO) Method of Pricing the issue.

1996		
January	1	Opening Stocks 2000 units @ Rs. 2.60 each
	2	Issued 1000 units
	3	Issued 800 units
	4	Purchased 1500 units @ Rs. 2.75 Per unit
	4	Issued 400 units
	5	Issued 320 units
	6	Purchased 1000 units at Rs. 2.90 each
	7	Issued 1400 units
	8	Returned to vendor purchased on 6th January — 30 units
	9	Received back from works order issued on 5th Jan. — 40 units
	10	Issued 500 units
	11	Purchased 500 units @ Rs. 3.20 each
	11	Issued 400 units
	13	Purchased 1500 units at Rs. 3.40 each
	15	Issued 300 units

On 15th January when stock is verified, it found that the actual stock is more by 20 units.

[K.U.D., April 1997(N)]

Solution :

Stores Ledger

First in First out — Issue Price Method

Date Jan. 1996	Particulars	Receipts			Issue			Balance		
		Units	Rate	Amount	Units	Rate	Amount	Units	Rate	Amount
			Rs.	Rs.		Rs.	Rs.		Rs.	Rs.
1	Opening Stocks	2000	2.60	5,200	—	—	—	2000	2.60	5,200
2	Issued	—	—	—	1000	2.60	2,600	1000	2.60	2,600
3	Issued	—	—	—	800	2.60	2,080	200	2.60	520
4	Purchased	1500	2.75	4,125	—	—	—	200	2.60	520
								1500	2.75	4,125
4	Issued	—	—	—	200	2.60	520			
					200	2.75	350	1300	2.75	3,575
5	Issued	—	—	—	320	2.75	880	980	2.75	2,695
6	Purchased	1000	2.90	2,900	—	—	—	980	2.75	2,695
								1000	2.90	2,900
7	Issued	—	—	—	980	2.75	2,695			
8	Returned to vendor Purchased on 6th Jan				420	2.90	1,218	580	2.90	1,682
					30	2.90	87	550	2.90	1,595
9	Received Back from work order Issued on 5th Jan.	40	2.75	110	—	—	—	40	2.75	110
								550	2.90	1,595
10	Issued	—	—	—	40	2.75	110			
					460	2.90	1,334	90	2.90	261
11	Purchased	500	3.20	1,600	—	—	—	90	2.90	261
								500	3.20	1,600
11	Issued	—	—	—	90	2.90	261			
					310	3.20	992	190	3.20	608
13	Purchased	1500	3.40	5,100	—	—	—	190	3.20	608
								1500	3.40	5,100
15	Issued	—	—	—	190	3.20	608			
					110	3.40	374	1390	3.40	4,726
15	Stocks Verification Execess	20	3.40	68	—	—	—	1410	3.40	4,794

Problem No. 4

Prepare Stores Ledger Account using "Last in First Out" method.

01-3-94	Purchased 1,200 units at Rs. 7.50 per unit.
02-3-94	Purchased 2,200 units at Rs. 7.60 per unit.
03-3-94	Issued 500 units.
05-3-94	Issued 700 units.
11-3-94	Issued 800 units.
14-3-94	Returned to stores 200 units which were issued on 3-3-94.
18-3-94	Issued 1,200 units.
23-3-94	Purchases 2,500 units at Rs. 7.40 per unit.
27-3-94	Issued 700 units.
31-3-94	Stock verification showed that material stock was 2,250 units.

(K.U.D., October 1995)

Solution :

Stores Ledger Account (LIFO Method)

Date	Particulars	Receipts			Issue			Balance		
		Qty.	Rate	Amount	Qty.	Rate	Amount	Qty.	Rate	Amount
			Rs.	Rs.		Rs.	Rs.		Rs.	Rs.
1-3-94	Purchases	1200	7.50	9,000	—	—	—	1200	7.50	9,000
2-3-94	Purchases	2200	7.40	16,720	—	—	—	1200	7.50	9,000
								2200	7.60	16,720
3-3-94	Issues	—	—	—	500	7.60	3,800	1200	7.50	9,000
								1700	7.60	12,920
5-3-94	Issued	—	—	—	700	7.60	5,320	1200	7.50	9,000
								1000	7.60	7,600
11-3-94	Issued	—	—	—	800	7.60	1,520	1200	7.50	9,000
								200	7.60	1,520
14-3-94	Return to stores Issued on 3rd	200	7.60	1,520	—	—	—	1200	7.50	9,000
								400	7.60	3,040
18-3-94	Issued	—	—	—	400	7.60	3,040			
					800	7.50	6,000	400	7.50	3,000
23-3-94	Purchased	2500	7.40	18,500	—	—	—	400	7.50	3,000
								2500	7.40	18,500
27-3-94	Issued	—	—	—	700	7.40	5,180	400	7.50	3,000
								1800	7.40	13,320
31-3-94	Excess on Stock	50	7.40	370	—	—	—	400	7.50	3,000
								1850	7.40	13,690

Problem No. 5

Prepare Stores Ledger Accounts from the following particulars using Weighted Average Price Method :

1994

Jan.

1 Balance 500 Units as Re. 1.00 per unit.

3 Issued 100 units to Department 'X'.

8 Received 200 units at Rs. 1.30 per unit.

12 Issued 300 units to Department 'Y'.

14 Received 100 units at Rs. 1.50 per unit.

15 Received 400 units at Rs. 1.40 per unit.

19 It was found that 50 units received on 8th January were defective and returned to the vendors.

22 Issued 250 units to Department 'Z'.

25 Received 500 units at Rs. 1.60 per unit.

29 Issued 400 units to Department 'X'.

31 Department 'Y' returned to the Store Room 100 units issued on 12th January.

(K.U.D., April 1995)

Solution : (Weighted Average Method)

Stores Ledger Account

Date	Particulars	Receipts			Issues			Balance	
Jan. 1994		Qty.	Rate Rs.	Amount Rs.	Qty.	Rate Rs.	Account Rs.	Qty.	Amount Rs.
1	Balance	—	—	—	—	—	—	500	500
3	Issued to Dept-X	—	—	—	100	1.00	100	400	400
8	Received	200	1.30	260	—	—	—	600	660
12	Issued to Dept-Y	—	—	—	300	1.10	330	300	330
14	Received	100	1.50	150	—	—	—	400	480
15	Received	400	1.40	560	—	—	—	800	1,040
19	Returned to Vendor	—	—	—	50	1.30	65	750	975
22	Issued to Dept-Z	—	—	—	250	1.30	325	500	650
25	Received	500	1.60	800	—	—	—	1000	1,450
29	Issued	—	—	—	400	1.45	580	600	870
31	Returned to Stores	100	1.10	110	—	—	—	700	980

Issue Price

(1) 3rd Jan. $\frac{400}{400}$ = 1.00

(2) 12 $\frac{660}{600}$ = 1.10

(3) 22 $\frac{975}{750}$ = 1.30

(4) 29 $\frac{1450}{1000}$ = 1.45

Problem No. 6

An Industry uses a particular raw material which costs Rs. 13.00 per Kg and its Input-Output Ratio is 140 per cent. On account of sudden shortage of this material, the company is compelled to use substitutes. Keeping in view the quality factor, the following two substitutes are considered suitable :

Substitutes	Rate per Kg	Input-Output Ratio
I	Rs. 15.50	120%
II	Rs. 12.00	160%

Recommend which of the above substitutes is beneficial to the Industry.

(K.U.D., October 1994)

Solution :

Since the rate and the Input-Output ratios vary in case of both the substitutes, the decision depends on the cost of each of the substitutes in the finished product per unit.

The cost of raw material in the Finished Product :

$$\text{Cost} = \frac{\text{Input}}{\text{Output}} \times \text{Rate per unit}$$

Or : Input-Output Ratio × Rate per Unit

Substitute Material : I $= \frac{120}{100} \times 15.50$ = Rs. 18.80 per Kg.

II $= \frac{160}{100} \times 12.00$ = Rs. 19.20 per Kg.

Therefore Material substitute I though costly, works out to be economical on account of lower Input-Output Ratio.

Problem No. 7

Prepare a Stores Ledger Account using "Weighted Average Price" method pricing the issue of materials :

1993

January 1 Balance 100 units @ Rs. 50 per unit.
3 Purchased 300 units @ Rs. 60 per unit.
5 Issued 150 units.
10 Issued 50 units.
15 Purchased 200 units @ Rs. 55 per unit.
20 Received back 20 units out of the units issued on 5th Jan.
25 Issued 100 units.

28 Purchased 150 units @ Rs. 65 per unit.
29 Returned to vendor 30 units purchased on 15th January.
31 Stores verification revealed that the actual stock is 430 units.

(K.U.D., April 1994)

Solution : (Under Weighted Average Method)

Stores Ledger Account

Date Jan. 1993	Particulars	Receipts Qty.	Rate Rs.	Amount Rs.	Issues Qty.	Rate Rs.	Amount Rs.	Balance Qty.	Rate Rs.	Amount Rs.
1	Balance	—	—	—	—	—	—	100	50	5,000
3	Purchased	300	60	18,000	—	—	—	400	—	23,000
5	Issued	—	—	—	150	57.5	8,625	250	—	14,375
10	Issued	—	—	—	50	57.5	2,875	200	—	11,500
15	Purchased	200	55	11,000	—	—	—	400	—	22,500
20	Returned to stores Issued on 5th Jan.	20	57.5	1,150	—	—	—	420	—	23,650
25	Issued	—	—	—	100	56.3	5,630	320	—	18,020
28	Purchased	150	65	9,750	—	—	—	470	—	27,770
29	Return to Vendor purchased on 15th	—	—	—	30	55	1,650	440	—	26,120
31	Shortage	—	—	—	10	59.4	594	430	—	25,526

Issue Price : 5th Jan. 93 = $\frac{23,000}{400} = 57.5$ 25th Jan. 93 = $\frac{23,650}{420} = 56.30$

10th Jan. 93 = $\frac{14,375}{250} = 57.5$ 31st Jan. 93 (Shortage) = $\frac{26,120}{440} = 59.40$

Problem No. 8

The following is the record of receipts and issues of materials in a factory during February 1987 :

Feb. 1 Opening Stock 500 Kgs at Rs. 25 per Kg.
3 Issues 200 Kgs.
4 Issues 100 Kgs.
8 Received 200 Kgs at Rs. 24 per Kg.
13 Issues 80 Kgs.
14 Returned from work order to stores 15 Kg at 24 per Kg.
16 Issues 165 Kgs.
20 Received 240 Kgs at Rs. 23 per Kg.
24 Issues 310 Kgs.
25 Received 320 Kgs at Rs. 22 per Kg.
26 Issues 220 Kgs.

Feb. 27 Returned to vendor 50 Kgs. at Rs. 23 per Kg.

28 Issues 50 Kgs.

Issues are to be priced on FIFO Method. Prepare Stores Ledger Account.

(Gulbarga, April 1994 & 1987)

Solution : (Under FIFO Method)

Stores Ledger Account

Date	Particulars	Receipts			Issues			Balance		
Feb. 1987		Qty.	Rate Rs.	Amount Rs.	Qty.	Rate Rs.	Amount Rs.	Qty.	Rate Rs.	Amount Rs.
1	Opening Stock	—	—	—	—			500	25	12,500
3	Issues	—	—	—	200	25	5,000	300	25	7,500
4	Issues	—	—	—	100	25	2,500	200	25	5,000
8	Purchases	200	24	4,800	—	—	—	200	25	5,000
								200	24	4,800
13	Issues	—	—	—	80	25	2,000	120	25	3,000
								200	24	4,800
14	Return to stores	15	24	360	—	—	—	120	25	3,000
								200	24	4,800
								(R) 15	24	360
16	Issues	—	—	—	(R) 15	24	360	170	24	4,800
					120	25	3,000			
					30	24	720			
20	Purchases	240	23	5,520	—	—	—	170	24	4,800
								240	23	5,520
24	Issues	—	—	—	170	24	4,800			
					140	23	3,220	100	23	2,300
25	Purchases	320	22	7,040	—	—	—	100	23	2,300
								320	22	7,040
26	Issues	—	—	—	100	23	2,300			
					120	22	2,640	200	22	4,400
27	Returned to Vendor	—	—	—	50	23	1,150	150	22	3,250
28	Issues	—	—	—	50	22	1,100	100	22	2,200

Note : (1) Returned to stores on 14th 15 Kg at Rs. 24 per Kg. In fact there was no issue at this price earlier. The difference in return to stores Price and the actual Materials issued earlier be accounted to Stores Adjustment Account.

(2) Returned to vendor on 27th 50 Kg at Rs. 23 per Kg is not in stock. The difference in amount be accounted in Stores Adjustment Account.

Problem No. 9

Prepare Stores Ledger accounts for the following transactions using "Last in First out" method :

1-1-89	Opening balance 12,000 Kg at Rs. 7.50 per Kg.
1-1-89	Purchased 22,000 Kg at Rs. 7.60 per Kg.
2-1-89	Issued 5,000 Kg.
5-1-89	Issued 7,000 Kg.
12-1-89	Issued 8,000 Kg.
13-1-89	Surplus from Production Department returned 2,000 Kg (which were issued on 2-1-89).
18-1-89	Issued 12,000 Kg.
22-1-89	Purchased 25,000 Kg at Rs. 7.40 per Kg.
28-1-89	Issued 7,000 Kg.
31-1-89	Stock verified and 500 Kg were found to be in excess.

(K.U.D., October 1993)

Solution : (Under FIFO Method)

Stores Ledger A/c

Date Jan. 1989	Particulars	Receipts Qty.	Receipts Rate Rs.	Receipts Amount Rs.	Issues Qty.	Issues Rate Rs.	Issues Amount Rs.	Balance Qty.	Balance Rate Rs.	Balance Amount Rs.
1	Opening Balance	—	—	—	—	—	—	12000	7.5	90,000
1	Purchases	22000	7.6	1,67,200	—	—	—	12000 22000	7.5 7.6	90,000 1,67,200
2	Issued	—	—	—	5000	7.6	38,000	12000 17000	7.5 7.6	90,000 1,29,200
5	Issued	—	—	—	7000	7.6	53,200	12000 10000	7.5 7.6	90,000 76,000
12	Issued	—	—	—	8000	7.6	60,800	12000 2000	7.5 7.6	90,000 15,200
13	Return from Prod. Dept. issue on 2nd.	2000	7.6	15,200	—	—	—	12000 4000	7.5 7.6	90,000 30,400
18	Issued	—	—	—	4000 8000	7.6 7.5	30,400 60,000	4000	7.5	30,000
22	Purchases	25000	7.4	1,85,000	—	—	—	4000 25000	7.5 7.4	30,000 1,85,000
28	Issues	—	—	—	7000	7.4	51,800	4000 18000	7.5 7.4	30,000 1,33,200
31	Excess in stock verification.	500	7.40	3,700	—	—	—	4000 18500	7.5 7.4	30,000 1,36,900

Problem No. 10

Prepare priced Stores Ledger Account for material 'M' adopting "First in First out" method.

1992

March 1 Opening Stock 500 Kg at Rs. 5 per Kg.

3 Purchases 1,500 Kg at Rs. 4.50 per Kg.

5 Issued 800 Kg.

8 Received 400 Kg at Rs. 4.70 per Kg.

12 Issued 300 Kg.

15 Issued 200 Kg.

18 Returned to stores 200 Kg which were issued on 5th March.

20 Received 800 Kg. at Rs. 5 per Kg.

21 Carriage paid on above consignment Rs. 200.

24 Returned to vendor 100 Kg. from the consignment received on 8th March.

26 Issued 300 Kg.

29 Issued 200 Kg.

31 Stores Audit showed shortage of materials — 50 Kg.

(K.U.D., April 1993)

Solution : (Under FIFO Method)

Stores Ledger Account

Date March 1992	Particulars	Receipts Qty.	Receipts Rate Rs.	Receipts Amount Rs.	Issues Qty.	Issues Rate Rs.	Issues Amount Rs.	Balance Qty.	Balance Rate Rs.	Balance Amount Rs.
1	Opening Stock	—	—	—	—	—	—	500	5.00	2,500
3	Purchases	1500	4.50	6,750	—	—	—	500	5.00	2,500
								1500	4.50	6,750
5	Issues	—	—	—	500	5.00	2,500	1200	4.50	5,400
					300	4.50	1,350			
8	Purchases	400	4.70	1,880	—	—	—	1200	4.50	5,400
								400	4.70	1,880
12	Issues	—	—	—	300	4.50	1,350	900	4.50	4,050
								400	4.70	1,880
15	Issues	—	—	—	200	4.50	900	700	4.50	3,150
								400	4.70	1,880
18	Returned to stores issued on 5th March	200	4.50	900	—	—	—	900	4.50	4,050
								400	4.70	1,880

Date March 1992	Particulars	Receipts Qty.	Receipts Rate Rs.	Receipts Amount Rs.	Issues Qty.	Issues Rate Rs.	Issues Amount Rs.	Balance Qty.	Balance Rate Rs.	Balance Amount Rs.
20	Purchases (Carriage Rs. 200)	800	5.25	4,200	—	—	—	900	4.50	4,050
								400	4.70	1,880
								800	5.25	4,200
24	Returned to Vendor received on 8th	—	—	—	100	4.70	470	900	4.50	4,050
								300	4.70	1,410
								800	5.25	4,200
26	Issued	—	—	—	300	4.50	1,350	600	4.50	2,700
								300	4.70	1,410
								800	5.25	4,200
29	Issues	—	—	—	200	4.50	900	400	4.50	1,800
								300	4.70	1,410
								800	5.25	4,200
31	Shortages of material (Audit report at usual pricing FIFO Method)	—	—	—	50	4.50	225	350	4.50	1,575
								300	4.70	1,410
								800	5.25	4,200

Problem No. 11

From the following particulars prepare Stores Ledger Account using Simple Average Method of Pricing.

1987 Jan.

1	Opening Stock 4000 units @ Rs. 4 per unit.
5	Purchased 500 units at Rs. 5 per unit.
8	Issued 2000 units.
10	Purchased 6000 units @ Rs. 6 per unit.
14	Issued 4000 units.
16	Issued 1000 units.
20	Purchased 3000 units at Rs. 6.50 per unit.
24	Issued 2000 units.
24	Returned to vendor 500 units purchased on 20th Jan.
26	Returned to stores surplus material 200 units on 14th.
28	Purchased 4500 units @ Rs. 5.50 per unit.
30	Issued 7500 units.
31	Stores Audit note shows shortage of 250 units.

[Kuvempu, April 1993 (Modified)]

Solution : (Simple Average Method)

Stores Ledger Account

Date Jan. 1987	Particulars	Receipts Qty.	Receipts Rate Rs.	Receipts Amount Rs.	Issues Qty.	Issues Rate Rs.	Issues Amount Rs.	Balance Qty.	Balance Rate Rs.	Balance Amount Rs.
1	Opening Stock	—	—	—	—	—	—	4000	4.00	16,000
5	Purchases	5000	5.00	25,000	—	—	—	4000 5000	4.00 5.00	16,000 25,000
8	Issues				2000	4.5	9,000	2000 5000	4.00 5.00	8,000 25,000
10	Purchases	6000	6.00	36,000	—	—	—	2000 5000 6000	4.00 5.00 6.00	8,000 25,000 36,000
14	Issued	—	—	—	2000 2000	5.00 5.00	10,000 10,000	3000 6000	5.00 6.00	15,000 36,000
16	Issued	—		—	1000	5.50	5,500	2000 6000	5.00 6.00	10,000 36,000
20	Purchased	3000	6.5	19,500	—	—	—	2000 6000 3000	5.00 6.00 6.50	10,000 36,000 19,500
24	Issued	—	—	—	2000	5.83	11,660	6000 3000	6.00 6.50	36,000 19,500
24	Returned to vendor purchased on 20th	—	—	—	500	6.50	3,250	6000 2500	6.00 6.50	36,000 16,250
26	Returned to stores issued on 14th	200	5.00	1,000	—	—	—	6000 2500 200	6.00 6.50 5.00	36,000 16,250 1,000
28	Purchases	4500	5.50	24,750	—	—	—	6000 2500 200 4500	6.00 6.50 5.00 5.50	36,000 16,250 1,000 24,750
30	Issued	—	—	—	7500	5.75	43,125	1000 200 4500	6.50 5.00 5.50	6,500 1,000 24,750
31	Shortages	—	—	—	250	5.67	1,417.5	750 200 4500	6.50 5.00 5.50	4,875 1,000 24,750
	Closing Stock on 31st January 1987							5450		30,625

Issue Price (Under Simple Average Method)

$$\text{Issue Price} = \frac{\text{No. of Purchase prices included in stock}}{\text{No. of Prices}}$$

Date

(1) 8th Jan. $= \dfrac{4+5}{2} = \dfrac{9}{2} = 4.50$

(2) 14th Jan. $= \dfrac{4+5+6}{2} = \dfrac{15}{3} = 5.00$

(3) 16th Jan. $= \dfrac{5+6}{2} = \dfrac{11}{2} = 5.50$

(4) 24th Jan. $= \dfrac{5+6+6.50}{3} = \dfrac{17.50}{3} = 5.83$

(5) 24th Jan. Return to vendor at purchase price.

(6) 26th Returned to stores at Issue price earlier.

(7) 30th Jan. $= \dfrac{6+6.50+5+5.50}{4} = \dfrac{23}{4} = 5.75$

(8) 31st Jan. shortage $= \dfrac{6.50+5+5.50}{3} = \dfrac{17}{3} = 5.666 = 5.67.$

The same problem answer under Weighted Average method of pricing.

Stores Ledger Account

Date Jan. 1987	Particulars	Receipts Qty.	Rate Rs.	Amount Rs.	Issues Qty.	Rate Rs.	Amount Rs.	Balance Qty.	Rate Rs.	Amount Rs.
1	Opening Stock	—	—	—	—	—	—	4000	4.00	16,000
5	Purchased	5000	5	25,000	—	—	—	9000	—	41,000
8	Issued	—	—	—	2000	4.60	9,200	7000	—	31,800
10	Purchased	6000	6	36,000	—	—	—	13000	—	67,800
14	Issued	—	—	—	4000	5.22	20,880	9000	—	46,920
16	Issued	—	—	—	1000	5.22	5,220	8000	—	41,700
20	Purchased	3000	6.5	1,950	—	—	—	11000	—	61,200
24	Issued	—	—	—	2000	5.56	11,120	9000	—	50,080
24	Returned to vendor purch-ased on 20th.	—	—	—	500	6.50	3,250	8500	—	46,830
26	Returned to stores issued on 14th.	200	5.22	1,044	—	—	—	8700	—	47,874
28	Purchased	4500	5.50	24,750	—	—	—	13200	—	72,624
30	Issued	—	—	—	7500	5.34	40,050	5700	—	39,574
31	Shortage	—	—	—	250	5.34	1,335	5450	—	31,239
	Closing Stock on 31st January 1987							5450		31,239

Issue Price under Weighted Average Method.

$$\text{Issue Price} = \frac{\text{Total amount in Balance}}{\text{Total Quantity in Balance}}$$

(1) Jan. 8 $= \frac{41,000}{9000} = 4.555$ or 4.60

(2) Jan. 14 $= \frac{67,800}{13000} = 5.215$ or 5.22

(3) Jan. 16 $= \frac{46,920}{9000} = 5.215$ or 5.22

(4) Jan. 24 $= \frac{61,200}{11000} = 5.56$

(5) Jan. 24 Return to vendor at Purchase Price.

(6) Jan. 26 Return to stores at issue Price earlier.

(7) Jan. 30 $= \frac{70,536}{13200} = 5.343$ or 5.34

(8) Jan. 31 Shortage $= \frac{30,486}{5700} = 5.343$ or 5.34.

Problem No. 12

From the following particulars prepare Stores Ledger Account using Weighted Average pricing method.

1991 January

1	Opening Balance 50 units @ Rs. 3 per unit.
5	Issued to production 2 units.
7	Purchased 48 units @ Rs. 4 per unit.
9	Issued to production 20 units.
19	Purchase 76 units @ Rs. 3 per unit.
24	Received back into stores issued on 9th, 19 units.
27	Issued to production 10 units.
31	Stores Audit report shows shortage of 10 units.

(K.U.D., 1992)

Solution : (Under Weighted Average Method)

Stores Ledger Account

Date Jan. 1991	Particulars	Receipts Qty.	Rate Rs.	Amount Rs.	Issues Qty.	Rate Rs.	Amount Rs.	Balance Qty.	Rate Rs.	Amount Rs.
1	Opening Stock	—	—	—	—	—	—	50	3.00	150.00
5	Issued	—	—	—	2	3.00	6.00	48	3.00	144.00
7	Purchases	48	4.00	192	—	—	—	96	3.5	336.00
9	Issued	—	—	—	20	3.50	70	76	3.5	266.00
19	Purchases	76	3.00	228	—	—	—	152	3.25	494.00
24	Returns to store (issued on 9th)	19	3.50	66.5	—	—	—	171	3.27	560.50
27	Issued	—	—	—	10	3.27	32.78	161	3.27	527.72
31	Shortages	—	—	—	10	3.27	32.78	151	3.27	494.94

$$\text{Issue Price} = \frac{\text{Total amount in Balance}}{\text{Total units in Balance}}$$

$$\text{5th Jan.} = \frac{150}{50} = \text{Rs. } 3$$

$$\text{9th Jan.} = \frac{336}{96} = \text{Rs. } 3.50$$

$$\text{27th Jan.} = \frac{560.50}{171} = \text{Rs. } 3.278$$

31st Jan. = Shortages priced at latest issue price (i.e. 3.278).

Problem No. 13

Prepare Stores Ledger Account using LIFO pricing method.

January 1991

1 Opening Stock 200 units at Rs. 2 per unit.
2 Issued 150 units.
7 Purchased 100 units @ Rs. 2.20 per unit.
9 Issued 100 units.
15 Purchased 150 units at Rs. 2.40 per unit.
18 Issued 90 units.
20 Issued 10 units.
25 Purchased 180 units @ Rs. 2.50 per unit.
30 Issued 200 units.
31 Stock audit showed excess of 20 units.

(K.U.D., October 1992)

Solution : (Under LIFO Method)

Stores Ledger Account

Date Jan. 1991	Particulars	Receipts			Issues			Balance		
		Qty.	Rate Rs.	Amount Rs.	Qty.	Rate Rs.	Amount Rs.	Qty.	Rate Rs.	Amount Rs.
1	Opening Stock	—	—	—	—	—	—	200	2.00	400
2	Issued	—	—	—	150	2.00	300	50	2.00	100
7	Purchased	100	2.20	220	—	—	—	50	2.00	100
								100	2.20	220
9	Issued	—	—	—	100	2.20	220	50	2.00	100
15	Purchased	150	2.40	360	—	—	—	50	2.00	100
								150	2.40	360
18	Issued	—	—	—	90	2.40	216	50	2.00	100
								60	2.40	144
20	Issued	—	—	—	10	2.40	24	50	2.00	100
								50	2.40	120
25	Purchased	180	2.50	450	—	—	—	50	2.00	100
								50	2.40	120
								180	2.50	450
30	Issued	—	—	—	180	2.50	450	50	2.00	100
					20	2.40	48	30	2.40	72
31	Excess	20	2.40	48	—	—	—	50	2.00	100
								50	2.40	120
		Closing stock on 31-1-1991						100		220

Problem No. 14

Prepare Stores Ledger Account using First in First out (FIFO) method of pricing the issues :

1990

March

1 Balance 500 units @ Rs. 200 per unit.

6 Issued 250 units.

10 Purchased 200 units @ Rs. 190 per unit.

15 Returned to stores 15 units issued on 6th March.

18 Issued 180 units.

22 Purchased 240 units @ Rs. 190 per unit.

23 Issued 300 units.

24 Purchased 320 units @ Rs. 190 per unit.

25 Purchased 200 units @ Rs. 170 per unit.

1990
March

26 Issued 115 units.
27 Returned to vendors 50 units purchased on 24th March.
31 Stores Audit showed a shortage of 10 units.

(K.U.D., April 1992)

Solution : (Under FIFO Issue Price Method)

Stores Ledger Account

Date March 1990	Particulars	Receipts			Issues			Balance		
		Qty.	Rate Rs.	Amount Rs.	Qty.	Rate Rs.	Amount Rs.	Qty.	Rate Rs.	Amount Rs.
1	Balance	—	—	—	—	—	—	500	200	1,00,000
6	Issued	—	—	—	200	200	40,000	300	200	60,000
10	Purchased	200	190	38,000	—	—	—	300	200	60,000
								200	190	38,000
15	Returned to stores issue on 6th March	15	200	3,000	—	—	—	315	200	63,000
								200	190	38,000
18	Issued	—	—	—	180	200	36,000	135	200	27,000
								200	190	38,000
22	Purchased	240	190	45,600	—	—	—	135	200	27,000
								440	190	83,600
23	Issued	—	—	—	135	200	27,000			
					165	190	31,350	275	190	52,250
24	Purchased	320	190	60,800	—	—	—	275	190	52,250
								320	190	60,800
25	Purchased	200	170	34,000	—	—	—	595	190	1,13,050
								200	170	34,000
26	Issued	—	—	—	115	190	21,850	480	190	91,200
								200	170	34,000
27	Returned to Vendor purchased on 24th March	—	—	—	50	190	9,500	430	190	81,700
								200	170	34,000
31	Shortage	—	—	—	10	190	1,900	420	190	79,800
								200	170	34,000

Note : Stores Audit showed on 31st March a shortage of 10 units.

Problem No. 15

The following details are given of a certain material for the month of March 1992 :

March 1992

1 Opening Stock 200 tons @ Rs. 460 per ton.

2 Issued to Job-1, 140 tons.

6 Purchases 350 tons @ Rs. 450 per ton.

8 Condemned due to deterioration in quality and transferred to scrap 30 tons.

9 Issued to Job-2, 80 tons.

14 Issued to Job-3, 210 tons.

17 Purchased 200 tons at Rs. 480 per ton.

20 Issued to Job-4, 120 tons.

25 Purchases 180 tons @ Rs. 470 per ton.

28 Issued to Job-5, 280 tons.

31 Excess found in stock 43 tons reasons traced to the use of wrong measure during the month.

Show the Store Ledger entries under FIFO method of Issue Price.

(Gulbarga, April 1992)

Solution : (Under FIFO Method)

Stores Ledger Account

Date	Particulars	Receipts			Issues			Balance		
March 1992		Qty.	Rate Rs.	Amount Rs.	Qty.	Rate Rs.	Amount Rs.	Qty.	Rate Rs.	Amount Rs.
1	Opening Stock	—	—	—	—	—	—	200	460	92,000
2	Issued to Job-1	—	—	—	140	460	64,400	60	460	27,600
6	Purchases	350	450	1,57,500	—	—	—	60 350	460 450	27,600 1,57,500
8	Condemned due to deterioration and sent to scrap	—	—	—	30	450	13,500	60 320	460 450	27,600 1,44,000
9	Issued to Job-2	—	—	—	60 20	460 450	27,600 9,000	300	450	1,35,000
14	Issued to Job-3	—	—	—	210	450	94,500	90	450	40,500
17	Purchased	200	480	96,000	—	—	—	90 200	450 480	40,500 96,000

Date March 1992	Particulars	Receipts Qty.	Rate Rs.	Amount Rs.	Issues Qty.	Rate Rs.	Amount Rs.	Balance Qty.	Rate Rs.	Amount Rs.
20	Issued to Job-4	—	—	—	90	450	40,500			
					30	480	14,400	170	480	81,600
25	Purchases	180	470	84,600	—	—	—	170	480	81,600
								180	470	84,600
28	Issues to Job-5	—	—	—	170	480	81,600			
					110	470	51,700	70	470	32,900
31	Excess found	43	470	20,210	—	—	—	70	470	32,900
								43	470	20,210
	Closing stock on 31st March 1991							113	470	53,110

Note : (1) Materials condemned due to deterioration in quality and sent to scrap 30 tons priced out of latest purchase price.

(2) Excess found due to wrong measure priced at latest price in stock.

Problem No. 16

(a) What is meant by Minimum Level and Maximum Level ?

(b) Show the following in Stores Ledger Account on FIFO Pricing Method.

Date	Particulars	Units	Rate
1-1-1991	Opening Balance	100	3.80
4-1-1991	Purchases	800	4.00
15-1-1991	Purchases	500	4.20
16-1-1991	Issues	600	—
21-1-1991	Purchases	800	4.60
22-1-1991	Issues	1200	—
24-1-1991	Purchases	1400	4.40
25-1-1991	Return to stores issued 16-1-1991	50	—
27-1-1991	Issues	50	—
31-1-1991	Issues	450	—

On 20th January stock verification revealed a shortage of 20 units.

(Gulbarga, April 1992)

Solution : (Under FIFO Method)

Stores Ledger Account

Date Jan. 1991	Particulars	Receipts Qty.	Rate Rs.	Amount Rs.	Issues Qty.	Rate Rs.	Amount Rs.	Balance Qty.	Rate Rs.	Amount Rs.
1	Opening Balance	—	—	—	—	—	—	100	3.80	380
4	Purchases	800	4.00	3,200	—	—	—	100	3.80	380
								800	4.00	3,200
15	Purchases	500	4.20	2,100	—	—	—	100	3.80	380
								800	4.00	3,200
								500	4.20	2,100
16	Issues	—	—	—	100	3.80	380	300	4.00	1,200
					500	4.00	2,000	500	4.20	2,100
20	Shortage	—	—	—	20	4.00	80	280	4.00	1,120
								500	4.20	2,100
21	Purchases	800	4.60	3,680	—	—	—	280	4.00	1,120
								500	4.20	2,100
								800	4.60	3,680
22	Issues	—	—	—	280	4.00	1,120	—	—	—
					500	4.20	2,100	—	—	—
					420	4.60	1,932	380	4.60	1,748
24	Purchases	1400	4.60	6,160	—	—	—	380	4.60	1,748
								1400	4.40	6,160
25	Returns to stores issued on 16-1-91	50	3.80	190	—	—	—	(R) 50	3.80	190
								380	4.60	1,748
								1400	4.40	6,160
27	Issues	—	—	—	(R) 50	3.80	190	380	4.60	1,748
								1400	4.40	6,160
31	Issues	—	—	—	380	4.60	1,768			
					70	4.40	308	1330	4.40	6,160

Note : (1) Returns to stores are issued first in the next issue immediately.

Problem No. 17

Enter the following in Stores Ledger Account on FIFO bases and show the value of inventory as on 31-3-1991.

1991 March 1. Opening Stock 3000 Kgs @ Rs. 10 Kg.

Purchases		*Issues*	
5th March 91	2000 Kgs @ Rs. 12 per Kg	7th March 91	2500 Kgs
12th March 91	5000 Kgs @ Rs. 15 per Kg	16th March 91	1200 Kgs.
24th March 91	4000 Kgs @ Rs. 16 per Kg	27th March 91	6300 Kgs.

On 18th March 91 Returns to stores 200 Kgs issued on 7th March 91. Stock verification shows shortages of 200 Kgs on 31-3-1991.

(Mysore-Kuvempu, April 1992)

Solution : (Under FIFO Method)

Stores Ledger Account

Date March 1991	Particulars	Receipts Qty.	Receipts Rate Rs.	Receipts Amount Rs.	Issues Qty.	Issues Rate Rs.	Issues Amount Rs.	Balance Qty.	Balance Rate Rs.	Balance Amount Rs.
1	Opening Stock	—	—	—	—	—	—	3000	10	30,000
5	Purchases	2000	12	24,000	—	—	—	3000	10	30,000
								2000	12	24,000
7	Issues	—	—	—	2500	10	25,000	500	10	5,000
								2000	12	24,000
12	Purchases	5000	15	75,000	—	—	—	500	10	5,000
								2000	12	24,000
								5000	15	75,000
16	Issues	—	—	—	500	10	5,000			
					700	12	8,400	1300	12	15,600
								5000	15	75,000
18	Return to stores issued on 7-3-91	200	10	2,000	—	—	—	1300	12	15,600
								5000	15	75,000
								200	10	2,000(R)
24	Purchases	4000	16	64,000	—	—	—	1300	12	15,600
								5000	15	75,000
								200	10	2,000(R)
								4000	16	64,000
27	Issue	—	—	—	200	10	2,000	—	—	—
					1300	12	15,600	—	—	—
					4800	15	72,000	200	15	3,000
								4000	16	64,000
31	Shortage	—	—	—	200	15	3,000	4000	16	64,000
		Value of Closing Stock						4000	16	64,000

(R) = Return to store.

Problem No. 18

Set up Stores Ledger from and enter the following transactions adopting weighted average method.

1991 January

1 Opening Balance 50 units @ Rs. 3 per unit.

3 Issued to production 2 units.

7 Purchased 48 units @ Rs. 4 per unit.

9 Issued 20 units to production.

19 Purchased 76 units @ Rs. 3 per unit.

24 Received back into stores 19 units out of 20 units issued on 9th January.

27 Issued to production 10 units.

31 Stores verification revealed a shortage of 10 units.

(K.U.D., October 1991)

Solution : (Under Weighted Average Method)

Stores Ledger Account

Date Jan. 1991	Particulars	Receipts			Issues			Balance		
		Qty.	Rate Rs.	Amount Rs.	Qty.	Rate Rs.	Amount Rs.	Qty.	Rate Rs.	Amount Rs.
1	Opening Balance	—	—	—	—	—	—	50	3.00	150
3	Issues	—	—	—	2	3.00	6.00	48	—	144
7	Purchases	48	4.00	192	—	—	—	96	—	336
9	Issued	—	—	—	20	3.50	70.00	76	—	266
19	Purchased	76	3.00	228	—	—	—	152	—	494
24	Returns to stores	19	3.50	66.5	—	—	—	171	—	560.50
27	Issued	—	—	—	10	3.278	32.78	161	—	527.72
31	Shortage	—	—	—	10	3.278	32.78	151	—	494.94

$$\text{Issue Price} = \frac{\text{Total Amount in Balance}}{\text{Total Quantity in Balance}}$$

(1) January 3 $= \frac{150}{50} = \text{Rs. } 3$

(2) January 9 $= \frac{336}{96} = 3.50$

(3) January 24 = Returns at Issue Price

(4) January 27 $= \frac{560.50}{171} = 3.278$

(5) January 31 = Shortage priced at latest issue price.

Problem No. 19

Draw Stores Ledger Card recording the following transactions under FIFO Method of pricing material issues.

1987 June

1 Opening Stock 200 units @ Rs. 20 per unit.

5 Received 100 units @ Rs. 22 per unit.

10 Purchased 150 units @ Rs. 24 per unit.
15 Placed order for 200 units with supplier.
20 Purchased 180 units @ Rs. 25 per unit.
24 Purchased 200 units @ Rs. 24 per unit.

Issues were made as follows :

1987 June
2 150 units
12 100 units
28 200 units

1987 June 7th 100 units issued

Stock verification report reveals that there was a shortage of 10 units on 18th June 1987 and an other shortage of 15 units on 26th June.

(Mangalore, April 1991)

Solution : (Under FIFO Method)

Stores Ledger Account

Date June 1987	Particulars	Receipts Qty.	Receipts Rate Rs.	Receipts Amount Rs.	Issues Qty.	Issues Rate Rs.	Issues Amount Rs.	Balance Qty.	Balance Rate Rs.	Balance Amount Rs.
1	Opening Balance	—	—	—	—	—	—	200	20	4,000
2	Issues	—	—	—	150	20	3,000	50	20	1,000
5	Purchases	100	22	2,200	—	—	—	50	20	1,000
								100	22	2,200
7	Issues	—	—	—	50	20	1,000			
					50	22	1,100	50	22	1,100
10	Purchases	150	24	3,600	—	—	—	50	22	1,100
								150	24	3,600
12	Issues	—	—	—	50	22	1,100	100	24	2,400
					50	24	1,200			
18	Shortages	—	—	—	10	24	240	90	24	2,160
20	Purchases	180	25	4,500	—	—	—	90	24	2,160
								180	25	4,500
24	Purchases	200	24	4,800	—	—	—	90	24	2,160
								180	25	4,500
								200	24	4,800
26	Shortages	—	—	—	15	24	360	90	24	2,160
								180	25	4,500
								185	24	4,440
29	Issues	—	—	—	90	24	2,160	70	25	1,750
					110	25	2,750	185	24	4,440

Note : (1) Shortages on 18th and 26th are priced at latest purchases price.
(2) Order placed on 15th is not considered.

Problem No. 20

From the following particulars prepare Stores Ledger pricing issue under FIFO method.

Date	*Purchases Particulars*
3-2-1990	500 Units @ Rs. 12 per unit.
6-2-1990	600 Units @ Rs. 14 per unit.
15-2-1990	700 Units @ Rs. 13 per unit.
20-2-1990	400 Units @ Rs. 15 per unit.
	Issue Particulars
10-2-1990	1000 units.
16-2-1990	800 units.
28-2-1990	40 units.

The stock on February 1st 1990 was 800 units @ Rs. 10 per unit on 18th February stock verification revealed a shortage of 50 units.

(Bangalore, October 1990)

Solution : (Under FIFO Method)

Stores Ledger Account

Date Feb. 1990	Particulars	Receipts Qty.	Receipts Rate Rs.	Receipts Amount Rs.	Issues Qty.	Issues Rate Rs.	Issues Amount Rs.	Balance Qty.	Balance Rate Rs.	Balance Amount Rs.
1	Opening Stock	—	—	—	—	—	—	800	10	8,000
3	Purchases	500	12	6,000	—	—	—	800	10	8,000
								500	12	6,000
6	Purchases	600	14	8,400	—	—	—	800	10	8,000
								500	12	6,000
								600	14	8,400
10	Issues	—	—	—	800	10	8,000	300	12	3,600
					200	12	2,400	600	14	8,400
15	Purchases	700	13	9,100	—	—	—	300	12	3,600
								600	14	8,400
								700	13	9,100
16	Issues	—	—	—	300	12	3,600	100	14	1,400
					500	14	7,000	700	13	9,100
18	Shortages	—	—	—	50	14	700	50	14	700
								700	13	9,100
20	Purchases	400	15	6,000	—	—	—	50	14	700
								700	13	9,100
								400	15	6,000
28	Issues	—	—	—	50	14	700	350	13	4,550
					350	13	4,550	400	15	6,000

Problem No. 21

Prepare a Stores Ledger Account using LIFO method.

1989 January

1 Balance 1200 units @ Rs. 4 per unit.
5 Issued 500 units
10 Purchased 600 units @ Rs. 4.50 per unit
16 Issued 300 units
19 Issued 300 units
22 Purchased 200 units @ 5.75 per unit
25 Issued 300 units
28 Returned to Vendors 150 units out of stock purchased on 10th January 1989.
29 Purchased 500 units @ Rs. 5.50 per unit
31 Issued 120 units
31 Stock verification showed that the materials stock was 650 units.

(K.U.D., April 1990)

Solution : (LIFO Method)

Stores Ledger Account

Date Jan. 1989	Particulars	Receipts Qty.	Receipts Rate Rs.	Receipts Amount Rs.	Issues Qty.	Issues Rate Rs.	Issues Amount Rs.	Balance Qty.	Balance Rate Rs.	Balance Amount Rs.
1	Balance	—	—	—	—	—	—	1200	4.00	4,800
5	Issues	—	—	—	500	4.00	2,000	700	4.00	2,800
10	Purchased	600	4.50	2,700	—	—	—	700 600	4.00 4.50	2,800 2,700
16	Issued	—	—	—	500	4.50	2,250	700 100	4.00 4.50	2,800 450
19	Issued	—	—	—	100 200	4.50 4.00	450 800	500	4.00	2,000
22	Purchased	200	5.75	1,150	—	—	—	500 200	4.00 5.75	2,000 1,150
25	Issued	—	—	—	200 100	5.75 4.00	1,150 400	400	4.00	1,600
28	Returned to Vendors	—	—	—	150	4.50	675	250	4.00	1,050
29	Purchased	500	5.50	2,750	—	—	—	250 500	4.00 5.50	1,050 2,750
31	Issued	—	—	—	120	5.50	660	250 380	4.00 5.50	1,000 2,090
31	Surplus	20	5.50	110	—	—	—	250 400	4.00 5.50	1,000 2,200

Note : Actual = 250 × 4 =1,000

Less : 925

Difference – 75 (On account of Return to vendor of Store Return Price = Rs. 4.50 @ 4.00)

Problem No. 22

From the following particulars prepare Stores Ledger pricing issues under FIFO Method.

Purchases

3rd Feb. 1990 500 units @ Rs. 12 per unit.
6th Feb. 1990 600 units @ Rs. 14 per unit.
15th Feb. 1990 700 units @ Rs. 13 per unit.
20th Feb. 1990 400 units @ Rs. 15 per unit.

Issues

10th Feb. 1990 1000 units.
16th Feb. 1990 800 units.
25th Feb. 1990 400 units.

The stock on February 1, 1990 was 800 units @ Rs. 10 per unit. On 18th February, stock verification revealed a shortage of 50 units.

(Bangalore, October 1990)

Solution : (Under FIFO Method)

Stores Ledger Account

Date Feb. 1990	Particulars	Receipts Qty.	Rate Rs.	Amount Rs.	Issues Qty.	Rate Rs.	Amount Rs.	Balance Qty.	Rate Rs.	Amount Rs.
1	Opening Stock	—	—	—	—	—	—	800	10.00	8,000
3	Purchases	500	12.00	6,000	—	—	—	800	10.00	8,000
								500	12.00	6,000
6	Purchases	600	14.00	8,400	—	—	—	800	10.00	8,000
								500	12.00	6,000
								600	14,00	8,400
10	Issues	—	—	—	800	10.00	8,000	300	12.00	3,600
					200	12.00	2,400	600	14.00	8,400
15	Purchases	700	13.00	9,100	—	—	—	300	12.00	3,600
								600	14.00	8,400
								700	13.00	9,100
16	Issues	—	—	—	300	12.00	3,600	100	14.00	1,400
					500	14.00	7,000	700	13.00	9,100
18	Shortages	—	—	—	50	13.00	650	100	14.00	1,400
								650	13.00	8,450
20	Purchases	400	15.00	6,000	—	—	—	100	14.00	1,400
								650	13.00	8,450
								400	15.00	6,000
25	Issues	—	—	—	100	14.00	1,400	350	13.00	4,550
					300	13.00	3,900	400	15.00	6,000

Problem No. 23

From the following information prepare Stores Ledger under LIFO method.

Date January, 1990	Receipts	Date January, 1990	Issues
1	200 Units @ Rs. 2 per unit	4	125 Units
12	130 Units @ Rs. 3 per unit	14	175 Units.
16	560 Units @ Rs. 2.50 per unit	18	90 Units.

On 20th January 10 units issued on 14th were returned by the department to stores on 31 January stores Audit note shows surplus of 15 units.

(Mangalore, October 1990)

Solution : (LIFO Method)

Stores Ledger Account

Date Jan. 1990	Particulars	Receipts			Issues			Balance		
		Qty.	Rate Rs.	Amount Rs.	Qty.	Rate Rs.	Amount Rs.	Qty.	Rate Rs.	Amount Rs.
1	Purchases	200	2.00	400	—	—	—	200	2.00	400
4	Issues	—	—	—	125	2.00	250	75	2.00	150
12	Purchases	130	3.00	390	—	—	—	75	2.00	150
								130	3.00	390
14	Issues	—	—	—	130	3.00	390	—	—	—
					45	2.00	90	30	2.00	60
16	Purchases	560	2.50	1,400	—	—	—	30	2.00	60
								560	2.50	1,400
18	Issues	—	—	—	90	2.50	225	30	2.00	60
								470	2.50	1,175
20	Return to stores	10	2.00	20	—	—	—	30	2.00	60
								470	2.50	1,175
								10	2.00	20(R)
31	Surplus	15	2.50	37.50	—	—	—	30	2.00	60
								470	2.50	1,175
								10	2.00	20(R)
								15	2.50	37.50(S)

Note : R = Return to stores

S = Surplus.

Problem No. 24

From the following transactions prepare Stock Ledger Account for the month of March 1990, under Base stock method. Base Stock is 200 units; material issue price shall be (a) FIFO (b) LIFO.

1990
March

1	Opening Stock 300 units @ Rs. 2 per unit.
2	Purchased 200 units @ Rs 2 per unit.
10	Purchased 300 units @ Rs. 2.10 per unit.
15	Issued 600 units.
20	Purchased 400 units @ Rs. 2.20 per unit.
25	Issued 300 units.
27	Purchased 500 units @ Rs. 2.10 per unit.
31	Issued 200 units.

(Bangalore, 1990)

Solution : (FIFO Method)

Stores Ledger Account

(Base stock – 200 units)

Date March 1990	Particulars	Receipts Qty.	Rate Rs.	Amount Rs.	Issues Qty.	Rate Rs.	Amount Rs.	Balance Qty.	Rate Rs.	Amount Rs.
1	Opening Stock	—	—	—	—	—	—	300	2.00	600
2	Purchases	300	2.00	400	—	—	—	500	2.00	1,000
10	Purchases	300	2.10	630	—	—	—	500	2.00	1,000
								300	2.10	630
15	Issues	—	—	—	300	2.00	600	200	2.00	400
					300	2.10	630			
20	Purchases	400	2.20	880	—	—	—	200	2.00	400
								400	2.20	880
25	Issues	—	—	—	300	2.20	660	200	2.00	400
								100	2.20	220
27	Purchases	500	2.10	1,050	—	—	—	200	2.00	400
								100	2.20	220
								500	2.10	1,050
31	Issues	—	—	—	100	2.20	220	200	2.00	400
					100	2.10	210	400	2.10	840
		Value of Closing Stock						600	—	1,240

Solution : (Under LIFO Method)

Stores Ledger Account

(Base Stock — 200 units)

Date March 1990	Particulars	Receipts Qty.	Rate Rs.	Amount Rs.	Issues Qty.	Rate Rs.	Amount Rs.	Balance Qty.	Rate Rs.	Amount Rs.
1	Opening Stock	—	—	—	—	—	—	300	2.00	600
2	Purchases	200	2.00	400	—	—	—	500	2.00	1,000
10	Purchases	300	2.10	630	—	—	—	500	2.00	1,000
								300	2.10	630
15	Issues	—	—	—	300	2.10	630			
					300	2.00	600	200	2.00	400
20	Purchase	400	2.20	880	—	—	—	200	2.00	400
								400	2.20	880
25	Issued	—	—	—	300	2.20	660	200	2.00	400
								100	2.20	220
27	Purchased	500	2.10	1,050	—	—	—	200	2.00	400
								100	2.20	220
								500	2.10	1,050
31	Issues	—	—	—	200	2.10	420	200	200	400
								100	2.20	220
								300	2.10	630
	Value of Closing Stock							600	—	1,250

Problem No. 25

With the help of the following information prepare Stores Ledger Account on the basis of Weighted Average Method of pricing of issue of materials.

1988 November	Particulars
1	Opening Stock 240 units @ Rs. 7 per unit.
2	Purchases 400 units @ Rs. 8 per unit.
10	Issues 100 units.
15	Issues 200 units.
18	Issues 240 units.
24	Purchases 400 units @ Rs. 9 per unit.
28	Issues 300 units.
30	150 units Issued.

[Gulbarga, October 1989 (Modified)]

Solution : (Weighted Average Method)

Stores Ledger Account

Date	Particulars	Receipts			Issues			Balance		
Nov. 1988		Qty.	Rate Rs.	Amount Rs.	Qty.	Rate Rs.	Amount Rs.	Qty.	Rate Rs.	Amount Rs.
1	Opening Stock	—	—	—	—	—	—	240	7	1,680
2	Purchases	400	8	3,200	—	—	—	640	—	4,880
10	Issues	—	—	—	100	7.625	762.5	540	—	4,117.5
15	Issues	—	—	—	200	7.625	1,525	340	—	2,592.5
18	Issues	—	—	—	240	7.625	1,830	100	—	762.5
24	Purchases	400	9	3,600	—	—	—	500	—	4,362.5
28	Issues	—	—	—	300	8.725	2,617.5	200	—	1,745
30	Issues	—	—	—	150	8.725	1,308.75	50	—	436.25
				Closing Stock				50		436.25

$$\text{Issue Price} = \text{Weighted Average Method} = \frac{\text{Total Amount in stock}}{\text{Total No. of Units instock}}$$

Date

10. $\dfrac{4{,}880}{640} = 7.625$ 24. $\dfrac{4{,}362.5}{500} = 8.725$

15. $\dfrac{4{,}117.50}{540} = 7.625$ 28. $\dfrac{1{,}745}{200} = 8.725$

18. $\dfrac{2{,}592.5}{340} = 7.525$

Problem No. 26

The following is the record of receipts and issued of a certain material in the factory.

1987

April 1 Opening Stock 50 tons @ Rs. 10 per ton.
Issues 30 tons.
2 Received 60 tons @ Rs. 10.20 per ton.
3 Stock verification loss of 2 tons.
4 Received back from orders 10 tons previously issued at Rs. 9.15 per ton.
5 Issued 40 tons.
6 Received 22 tons @ Rs. 10.30 per ton.
7 Issued 38 tons.

At what price will you issue the materials use to most important method for this purpose and show the comparative results.

(Mangalore, October 1989)

Solution : (Under FIFO Method)

Stores Ledger Account

Date April 1987	Particulars	Receipts Qty.	Receipts Rate Rs.	Receipts Amount Rs.	Issues Qty.	Issues Rate Rs.	Issues Amount Rs.	Balance Qty.	Balance Rate Rs.	Balance Amount Rs.
1	Opening Stock	—	—	—	—	—	—	50	10.00	500
	Issues	—	—	—	30	10	300	20	10.00	200
2	Purchases	60	10.20	612	—	—	—	20	10.00	200
								60	10.20	612
3	Stock Loss	—	—	—	2	10	20	18	10.00	180
								60	10.20	612
4	Returns to stores issued previously	10	9.15	91.50	—	—	—	18	10.00	180
								60	10.20	612
								10	9.15	91.50(R)
5	Issues	—	—	—	10	9.15	91.50			
					18	10.00	180			
					12	10.20	122.40	48	10.20	489.60
6	Received	22	10.30	226.60	—	—	—	48	10.20	489.60
								22	10.30	226.60
7	Issues	—	—	—	38	10.20	489.60	10	10.20	102.00
								22	10.30	226.60

Note : (R) = Returns to stores on 4th are issued immediately in the next issue at the same price.

Solution : (Under LIFO Method)

Stores Ledger Account

Date Jan. 1987	Particulars	Receipts Qty.	Receipts Rate Rs.	Receipts Amount Rs.	Issues Qty.	Issues Rate Rs.	Issues Amount Rs.	Balance Qty.	Balance Rate Rs.	Balance Amount Rs.
1	Opening Stock	—	—	—	—	—	—	50	10.00	500
1	Issues	—	—	—	30	10.00	300	20	10.00	200
2	Received	60	10.20	612	—	—	—	20	10.00	200
								60	10.20	612
3	Stock Loss	—	—	—	2	10.20	20.4	20	10.00	200
								58	10.20	591.60
4	Returns to stores issued previously	10	9.15	91.50	—	—	—	20	10.00	200
								58	10.20	591.60
								10	9.15	91.50

Date Jan. 1987	Particulars	Receipts Qty.	Rate Rs.	Amount Rs.	Issues Qty.	Rate Rs.	Amount Rs.	Balance Qty.	Rate Rs.	Amount Rs.
5	Issues	—	—	—	10	9.15	91.5	20	10.00	200
					30	10.20	306	28	10.20	285
6	Received	22	10.30	226.60	—	—	—	20	10.00	200
								28	10.20	285.60
								22	10.30	226.60
7	Issues	—	—	—	22	10.30	226.60	20	10.00	200
					16	10.20	163.20	12	10.20	122.4

Note : Returns to stores are issued immediately in the next issue.

Problem No. 27

Prepare Stores Ledger Account from the following transactions pricing the issues on LIFO method.

1988

January 1 Received 1000 units @ Rs. 20 per unit.

4 Received 260 @ Rs. 21 per unit.

10 Issued 760 units.

12 Received 400 units @ Rs. 23 per unit.

15 Received 300 units @ Rs. 25 per unit.

20 Issued 600 units.

24 Received 500 units @ Rs. 22 per unit.

31 Issued 400 units.

31 Stores Audit shows shortage of 25 units.

(Gulbarga, April 1989)

Solution : (Under LIFO Method)

Stores Ledger Account

Date Jan. 1988	Particulars	Receipts Qty.	Rate Rs.	Amount Rs.	Issued Qty.	Rate Rs.	Amount Rs.	Balance Qty.	Rate Rs.	Amount Rs.
1	Purchases	1000	20	20,000	—	—	—	1000	20	20,000
4	Purchases	260	21	5,460	—	—	—	1000	20	20,000
								260	21	5,460
10	Issues	—	—	—	260	21	5,460			
					500	20	10,000	500	20	10,000
12	Received	400	23	9,200	—	—	—	500	20	10,000
								400	23	9,200

Date Jan. 1988	Particulars	Receipts Qty.	Rate Rs.	Amount Rs.	Issues Qty.	Rate Rs.	Amount Rs.	Balance Qty.	Rate Rs.	Amount Rs.
15	Received	30	25	7,500	—	—	—	500	20	10,000
								400	23	9,200
								300	25	7,500
20	Issued	—	—	—	300	25	7,500	500	20	10,000
					300	23	6,900	100	23	2,300
24	Received	500	22	11,000	—	—	—	500	20	10,000
								100	23	2,300
								500	22	11,000
31	Issued	—	—	—	400	22	8,800	500	20	10,000
								100	23	2,300
								100	22	2,200
31	Shortage	—	—	—	25	22	550	500	20	10,000
								100	23	2,300
								75	22	1,650

Problem No. 28

The following Transactions took place in respect of Material 'Z' during the month of October 1971.

Date 1971 October	Particulars
1	Opening Stock 200 units @ Rs. 3.50 per unit.
3	Purchased 300 units @ Rs. 4.00 per unit.
5	Issued 400 units.
13	Purchased 900 units @ Rs. 4.30 per unit.
15	Issued 600 units.
23	Purchased 600 units @ Rs. 3.80 per unit.
25	Issued 600 units.

Prepare Stores Ledger Account Pricing materials issued on the basis of :

(a) Simple Average Method and

(b) Weighted Average Method.

(K.U.D., October 1988)

Solution : (Simple Average Method)

Stores Ledger Account

Date Oct. 1971	Particulars	Receipts Qty.	Receipts Rate Rs.	Receipts Amount Rs.	Issues Qty.	Issues Rate Rs.	Issues Amount Rs.	Balance Qty.	Balance Amount Rs.
1	Opening Stock	—	—	—	—	—	—	200	700
3	Purchases	300	4.00	1,200	—	—	—	500	1,900
5	Issued	—	—	—	400	3.75	1,500	100	400
13	Purchases	900	4.30	3,870	—	—	—	1000	4,270
15	Issues	—	—	—	600	4.15	2,490	400	1,780
23	Purchases	600	3.80	2,280	—	—	—	1000	4,060
25	Issued	—	—	—	600	4.05	2,430	400	1,630

Issue Price = (1) 5th Oct. 1971 $= \dfrac{3.50+4}{2} = \dfrac{7.50}{2} = 3.75$

(2) 15th Oct. 1971 $= \dfrac{4+4.30}{2} = \dfrac{8.30}{2} = 4.15$

(3) 25th Oct. 1971 $= \dfrac{4.30+3.80}{2} = \dfrac{8.10}{2} = 4.05$

Solution : (Under Weighted Average Method)

Stores Ledger Account

Date Jan. 1971	Particulars	Receipts Qty.	Receipts Rate Rs.	Receipts Amount Rs.	Issues Qty.	Issues Rate Rs.	Issues Amount Rs.	Balance Qty.	Balance Amount Rs.
1	Opening Stock	—	—	—	—	—	—	200	700
3	Purchases	300	4.00	1,200	—	—	—	500	1,900
5	Issued	—	—	—	400	3.80	1,520	100	380
13	Purchases	900	4.30	3,870	—	—	—	1000	4,250
15	Issues	—	—	—	600	4.25	2,550	400	1,700
23	Purchases	600	3.80	2,280	—	—	—	1000	3,980
25	Issued	—	—	—	600	[illegible]	[illegible]88	400	1,592

Issue Price = (1) 5th October 1971 $= \dfrac{1{,}900}{500} = 3.80$

(2) 15th October 1971 $= \dfrac{4{,}250}{1000} = 4.25$

(3) 25th October 1971 $= \dfrac{3{,}980}{1000} = 3.98.$

Problem No. 29

Prepare Stores Ledger Sheet from the following particulars using Weighted Average Price method.

1987 December

1 Balance 500 Kgs valued at Rs. 10,000
3 Received 1000 Kgs valued at Rs. 21,000
5 Issued 600 Kgs
7 Received 800 Kgs valued @ Rs. 18,000
9 Issued 1000 Kgs
10 Received 200 Kgs valued @ Rs. 4,800
13 Returned to vendor materials purchased on 3rd December 50 Kgs
14 Received 800 Kgs valued at Rs. 18,400
20 Received from Production Department material issued on 5th December Rs. 100
25 Issued 900 Kgs
31 Stock verification showed that the materials stock was 860 Kgs

Note : (1) Material prices are to be rounded of to nearest Paise and material value to nearest rupee.

(2) Write explanatory notes wherever necessary.

(K.U.D., April 1988)

Solution : (Weighted Average Method)

Stores Ledger Account

Date	Particulars	Receipts			Issues			Balance		
Dec. 1987		Qty. Kgs	Rate Rs.	Amount Rs.	Qty. Kgs	Rate Rs.	Amount Rs.	Qty. Kgs	Rate Rs.	Amount Rs.
1	Balance	—	—	—	—	—	—	500	20	10,000
3	Purchase	100	21.00	21,000	—	—	—	1500	20.67	31,000
5	Issued	—	—	—	600	20.67	12,402	900	20.67	18,598
7	Purchase	800	22.50	18,000	—	—	—	1700	21.53	36,598
9	Issued	—	—	—	1000	21.53	21,530	700	21.53	15,068
10	Purchases	200	24.00	4,800	—	—	—	900	22.00	19,868
13	Returned to Vendor purchased on 3rd December	—	—	—	50	21.00	1,050	850	22.14	18,818
14	Purchases	800	23.00	18,400	—	—	—	1650	22.56	37,218
20	Received from Production Issue on 5th	100	20.67	2,067	—	—	—	1750	22.45	39,285
25	Issue	—	—	—	900	22.45	20,205	850	22.45	19,080
31	Surplus	100	22.45	2,245	—	—	—	100	22.45	2,245
31	Closing Stock	—	—	—	—	—	—	860	22.45	21,325

Note : (1) Weighted Average Price is calculated on the basis of

$$\frac{\text{Total amount in Balance}}{\text{Quantity in Balance}} = \text{Issue Price}$$

(2) Returned to Vendor - 50 Kgs are priced @ purchase price Rs. 21 per Kg. Date 3rd December entered in Issue.

(3) Returned from production issued on 5th December entered on receipt column @ issued price Rs. 20.67 increased balance.

(4) Stock as per Stores Ledger A/c is 850 Kgs whereas on verification it was found 860 Kgs the difference is accounted as surplus and entered in receipts column and increased Balance by 10 Kgs Closing stock and Net Balance is 860 Kgs.

Problem No. 30

The Stock of material as on 1-1-1980 was 750 units at Rs. 1.50 per unit. Following is purchases and the issues of this item :

Date	Receipts		Issue
	Qty. (Units)	Rate Rs.	Qty. (Units)
January			
6	—	—	300
9	600	1.65	—
16	450	1.80	—
19	—	—	750
22	—	—	300
25	750	1.95	—
28	—	—	400
31	—	—	300

Prepare Stores Ledger Accounts assuming that the issues are made under Based Stock Method following FIFO Pricing Method. Based Stock is 400 Units.

(Banglore, April 1988)

Solution : (FIFO Method)

Stores Ledger A/c

(Base Stock — 400 units)

Date Jan. 1988	Particulars	Receipts			Issues			Balance		
		Qty.	Rate Rs.	Amount Rs.	Qty.	Rate Rs.	Amount Rs.	Qty.	Rate Rs.	Amount Rs.
1	Opening Stock	—	—	—	—	—	—	750	1.50	1,125
6	Issues	—	—	—	300	1.50	450	450	1.50	675
9	Purchases	600	1.65	990	—	—	—	450	1.50	675
								600	1.65	990
16	Purchases	450	1.80	810	—	—	—	450	1.50	675
								600	1.65	990
								450	1.80	810

Date Jan. 1988	Particulars	Receipts Qty.	Rate Rs.	Amount Rs.	Issues Qty.	Rate Rs.	Amount Rs.	Balance Qty.	Rate Rs.	Amount Rs.
19	Issues	—	—	—	50	1.50	75	400	1.50	600
					600	1.65	990	—	—	—
					100	1.80	180	300	1.80	540
22	Issues	—	—	—	300	1.80	540	400	1.50	600
25	Purchases	750	1.95	1,462.50	—	—	—	400	1.50	600
								750	1.95	1,462.50
28	Issues	—	—	—	400	1.95	780	400	1.50	600
								350	1.95	682.50
31	Issue	—	—	—	300	1.95	585	400	1.50	600
								50	1.95	97.50

Problem No. 31

The following transactions occur in purchase and issue of materials :

Date 1982	Particulars
February	
1	Opening Stock of material 500 tons @ Rs. 200 per ton.
8	Issues 250 tons.
13	Received 200 tons @ Rs. 195 per ton.
14	Returns from department 15 tons to stores issued on 8th.
16	Issue 180 tons.
20	Received 240 tons @ Rs. 190 per ton.
24	Issues 300 tons.
25	Received 320 tons @ Rs. 198 per ton.
26	Issues 115 tons.
27	Returns to vendor purchased on 25th 35 tons.
28	Received 100 tons @ Rs. 200 per ton.

The stock checking on 22nd February 1982 showed a shortage of 10 tons and verifier left a note accordingly. From the above information prepare Stores Ledger Account by adopting the FIFO Method.

[K.U.D., October 1985 (Modified)]

Solution : (Under FIFO Method)

Stores Ledger Account

Date Feb. 1982	Particulars	Receipts Qty.	Rate Rs	Amount Rs.	Issues Qty.	Rate Rs.	Amount Rs.	Balance Qty.	Rate Rs.	Amount Rs.
1	Opening Stock	—	—	—	—	—	—	500	200	1,00,000
8	Issued	—	—	—	200	200	40,000	300	200	60,000
13	Received	200	195	39,000	—	—	—	300	200	60,000
								200	195	39,000
14	Returns to stores	15	200	3,000	—	—	—	315	200	63,000
								200	195	39,000
16	Issued	—	—	—	180	200	36,000	133	200	27,000
								200	195	39,000
20	Received	240	190	45,600	—	—	—	135	200	27,000
								200	195	39,000
								240	190	45,600
22	Shortages	—	—	—	10	190	1,900	135	200	27,000
								200	195	39,000
								230	190	43,700
24	Issued	—	—	—	135	200	27,000	35	195	6,825
					165	195	32,175	230	190	43,700
25	Received	320	198	63,360	—	—	—	35	195	6,825
								230	190	43,700
								320	198	63,360
26	Issued	—	—	—	35	195	6,825	150	190	28,500
					80	190	15,200	320	198	63,360
27	Returns to Vendor purchased on 25th	—	—	—	35	198	6,930	150	190	28,500
								285	198	56,430
28	Received	100	200	20,000	—	—	—	150	190	28,500
								285	198	56,430
								100	200	20,000

Note : Shortage in stock is priced at latest in stock.

Problem No. 32

Following is the summary of the receipts and issues of materials in a factory for the month of February 1984.

1984 February

1 Balance of Stock 5000 Kgs at Rs. 25 per Kg.

3 Issued on Job No. 300 — 700 Kg.

4 Issued on Job No. 301 — 1000 Kgs.

1984 Feb.

10 Received from supplier 2000 Kgs at Rs. 24.50 per Kg.
12 Issued on Job No. 302 — 800 Kgs.
14 Returned surplus materials from Job No. 300 — 150 Kgs.
16 Issued on Job No. 303 — 1800 Kgs.
20 Received from suppliers 2400 Kgs. @ Rs. 24.75 per Kg.
24 Issued on Job No. 304 — 3040 Kgs.
25 Received from supplier 3200 Kgs @ Rs. 24.50 per Kg.
26 Issued on Job No. 305 — 1,120 Kgs.
27 Returned 120 Kgs of defective materials to the vendor from supplies of 20th February.
28 Received from supplier 1000 Kgs at Rs. 25 per Kg.

The stores verifier of the factory noted that on February 15th there was a shortage of 50 Kgs and another 80 Kgs on 27th February. Issues to be priced on the principles of LIFO. Prepare complete account from the above transactions.

(Gulbarga, October 1984)

Solution : (Under LIFO Method)

Stores Ledger Account

Date Feb. 1984	Particulars	Receipts Qty.	Rate Rs.	Amount Rs.	Issues Qty.	Rate Rs.	Amount Rs.	Balance Qty.	Rate Rs.	Amount Rs.
1	Opening Stock	—	—	—	—	—	—	5000	25	1,25,000
3	Issue Job 300	—	—	—	700	25	17,500	4300	25	1,07,500
4	Issue Job 301	—	—	—	1000	25	25,000	3300	25	82,500
10	Received	2000	24.50	49,000	—	—	—	3300	25	82,500
								2000	24.5	49,400
12	Issues Job. 302	—	—	—	800	24.50	19,600	3300	25	82,500
								1200	24.50	29,400
14	Returned to stores from Job. 300	150	25	3,750	—	—	—	3300	25	82,500
								1200	24.50	29,400
								150	25	3,750
15	Shortage	—	—	—	50	25	1,250	3300	25	82,500
								1200	24.50	29,400
								100	25	2,500
16	Issued Job. 303	—	—	—	100	25	2,500			
					1200	24.50	29,400			
					500	25	12,500	2800	25	70,000
20	Received	2400	24.75	59,400	—	—	—	2800	25	70,000
								2400	24.75	59,400

Date Feb. 1984	Particulars	Receipts Qty.	Rate Rs.	Amount Rs.	Issues Qty.	Rate Rs.	Amount Rs.	Balance Qty.	Rate Rs.	Amount Rs.
24	Issued 304				2400	24.75	59,400			
					640	25	16,000	2160	25	54,000
25	Received	3200	24.50	78,400	—	—	—	2160	25	54,000
								3200	24.50	78,000
26	Issued 305	—	—	—	1120	24.50	27,440	2160	25	54,000
								2080	24.50	50,960
27	Returned to Vendors Purchased on 20th.	—	—	—	120	24.75	2,970	2160	25	54,000
								1960	24.50	48,020
27	Shortages	—	—	—	80	24.5	1,960	2160	25	54,000
								1880	24.50	46,060
28	Received	1000	25	25,000	—	—	—	2160	25	54,000
								1880	24.50	46,060
								1000	25	25,000

Note : Returns to vendor on 27th priced at purchased price Rs. 24.75 though on their date the price of Material in stock was 24.50. The difference amount be accounted in "Store Adjustment Account".

Problem No. 33

The stock of Material 'A' as on 1st April 1979 was 250 units @ Rs. 2.50 per unit. Following purchases and issue of material were made subsequently :

Date 1979	Purchases Units	Rate	Issues Date	Units
April			April	
6	50	2.50	12	250
26	350	2.40	27	250
29	200	2.20	30	250
May			May	
18	500	2.30	20	250
26	250	2.10	28	250
June			June	
15	200	2.10	28	250
22	300	2.00	30	250

Prepare a Stores Ledger Account using FIFO Method of pricing and find out stock on 30th June 1979.

(K.U.D., April 1980)

Solution : (Under FIFO Method)

Stores Ledger Account

Date April 1979	Particulars	Receipts Qty.	Receipts Rate Rs.	Receipts Amount Rs.	Issues Qty.	Issues Rate Rs.	Issues Amount Rs.	Balance Qty.	Balance Rate Rs.	Balance Amount Rs.
1	Opening Stock	—	—	—	—	—	—	250	2.50	625
6	Purchases	50	2.50	125	—	—	—	300	2.50	750
12	Issues	—	—	—	250	2.50	625	50	2.50	125
26	Purchases	350	2.40	840	—	—	—	50	2.50	125
								350	2.40	840
27	Issues	—	—	—	50	2.50	125			
					200	2.40	480	150	2.40	360
29	Purchases	200	2.20	440	—	—	—	150	2.40	360
								200	2.20	440
30	Issues	—	—	—	150	2.40	360			
					100	2.20	220	100	2.20	220
May										
18	Purchases	500	2.30	1,150	—	—	—	100	2.20	220
								500	2.30	1,150
20	Issues	—	—	—	100	2.20	220			
					150	2.30	345	350	2.30	805
26	Purchases	250	2.10	525	—	—	—	350	2.30	805
								250	2.10	525
28	Issues	—	—	—	250	2.30	575	100	2.30	230
								250	2.10	525
June										
15	Purchases	200	2.10	420	—	—	—	100	2.30	230
								250	2.10	525
								200	2.10	420
22	Purchases	300	2.00	600	—	—	—	100	2.30	230
								450	2.10	945
								300	2.00	600
28	Issues	—	—	—	100	2.30	230	300	2.10	630
					150	2.10	315	300	2.00	600
30	Issues	—	—	—	250	2.10	525	50	2.10	105
								300	2.00	600
	Closing Stock on 30th June 1979							350		705

Problem No. 34

From the following particulars relating to Material 'A' show how the value of the issues should be arrived at under FIFO Method.

1-1-78	Opening Stock 1000 units @ Rs. 5 per unit.
3-1-78	Purchased 900 units @ Rs. 6 per unit.
7-1-78	Issued to Job No. 137 — 1200 units. MR No. 034.
11-1-78	Purchased 800 units @ Rs. 6.20 per unit.
13-1-78	Purchased 300 units @ Rs. 6.40 per unit.
15-1-78	Issued 400 units to Job No. 141-MR No. 042
17-1-78	Issued 600 units to Job No. 147-MR No. 048.
19-1-78	Purchased 200 units @ Rs. 6.50 per unit.
25-1-78	Issued 600 units to Job No. 150-MR No. 072.
31-1-78	Shortage as per Audit to note — 60 units.

(K.U.D., October 1979)

Solution : (Under FIFO Method)

Stores Ledger Account

Date Jan. 1978	Particulars	Receipts Qty.	Receipts Rate Rs.	Receipts Amount Rs.	Issues Qty.	Issues Rate Rs.	Issues Amount Rs.	Balance Qty.	Balance Rate Rs.	Balance Amount Rs.
1	Opening Stock	—	—	—	—	—	—	1000	5.00	5,000
3	Purchases	900	6.00	5,400	—	—	—	1000 900	5.00 6.00	5,000 5,400
7	Issue-Job. 137 MR No. 034	—	—	—	1000 200	5.00 6.00	5,000 1,200	— 700	— 6.00	— 4,200
11	Purchases	800	6.20	4,960	—	—	—	700 800	6.00 6.20	4,200 4,960
13	Purchases	300	6.40	1,920	—	—	—	700 800 300	6.00 6.20 6.40	4,200 4,960 1,920
15	Issues Job. 141 MR No. 042	—	—	—	400	6.00	2,400	300 800 300	6.00 6.20 6.40	1,800 4,960 1,920
17	Issues Job. 147	—	—	—	300 300	6.00 6.20	1,800 1,860	500 300	6.20 6.40	3,100 1,920
19	Purchased	200	6.50	1,300	—	—	—	500 300 200	6.20 6.40 6.50	3,100 1,920 1,300
25	Issue Job. 105 MR No. 072	—	—	—	500 100	6.20 6.40	3,100 640	200 200	6.40 6.50	1,280 1,300
31	Shortages	—	—	—	60	6.40	384	140 200	6.40 6.50	896 1,300

Problem No. Extra-1/35

From the following particulars concerned to Material 'XY' write up Stores Ledger using :

(a) FIFO Method (b) LIFO Method

(c) Simple average method (d) Weighted average method

for the month of 1991 March.

1991 March

1 Opening Stock on Material 600 units @ Rs. 4 per unit.

2 Issued to Job No. 103, 200 units.

5 Purchased 800 units @ Rs. 4.50 per unit.

8 Issued to Job No. 104 — 650 units.

9 Returned to stores 35 units from Job No. 103.

12 Purchased 700 units @ Rs. 5 per unit.

15 Issued to Job No. 105 — 500 units.

16 Return to vendor 65 units purchased on 12th.

19 Purchased 450 units @ Rs. 5.50 per unit.

22 Purchased 450 units @ Rs. 5.75 per unit.

24 Issued 500 units to job No. 106.

28 Issued to Job No. 107 — 550 units.

29 Transferred 50 units from Job No. 105 to Job No. 106.

31 Stores Audit indicate 75 units shortage due to wrong measure used.

Solution : (Under (FIFO Method)

Stores Ledger Account

Date March 1991	Particulars	Receipts			Issues			Balance		
		Qty.	Rate Rs.	Amount Rs.	Qty.	Rate Rs.	Amount Rs.	Qty.	Rate Rs.	Amount Rs.
1	Opening Stock	—	—	—	—	—	—	600	4.00	2,400
2	Issued Job. 103	—	—	—	200	4.00	800	400	4.00	1,600
5	Purchased	800	4.50	3,600	—	—	—	400	4.00	1,600
								800	4.50	3,600
8	Issues (Job.104)	—	—	—	400	4.00	1,600			
					250	4.50	1,125	550	4.50	2,475
9	Returns from Job No. 103	35	4.00	140	—	—	—	35	4.00	140
								550	4.50	2,475
12	Purchased	700	5.00	3,500	—	—	—	35	4.00	140
								550	4.50	2,475
								700	5.00	3,500

Date	Particulars	Receipts			Issues			Balance		
March		Qty.	Rate	Amount	Qty.	Rate	Amount	Qty.	Rate	Amount
1991			Rs.	Rs.		Rs.	Rs.		Rs.	Rs.
15	Issues Job. 105)	—	—	—	35	4.00	140			
					465	4.50	2,092.50	85	4.50	382.50
								700	5.00	3,500
16	Return to vendor	—	—	—	65	5.00	325	85	4.50	382.50
								635	5.00	3,175
19	Purchased	650	5.50	3,575	—	—	—	85	4.50	382.50
								635	5.00	3,175
								650	5.50	3,575
								450	5.75	2,587.50
22	Purchased	450	5.75	2,587.5	—	—	—	85	4.50	382.50
								635	5.00	3,175
								650	5.50	3,575
								450	5.75	2,587.50
24	Issues	—	—	—	85	4.50	382.50			
	(Job No. 106)				415	5.00	2,075	220	5.00	1,100
								650	5.50	3,575
								450	5.75	2,587.50
28	Issues	—	—	—	220	5.00	1,100	320	5.50	1,760
	(Job No. 107)				330	5.50	1,815	450	5.75	2,587.50
29	Transferred from Job No. 105	50	4.00	200	—	—	—	320	5.50	1,760
	(i.e. return to stores & transfer to Job No. 106)	—	—		50	4.00	200	450	5.75	2,587.50
31	Shortages	—	—	—	75	5.50	412.50	245	5.50	1,347.50
								450	5.75	2,587.50

Note : Transfer from Job No. 105 to stores and transferred to Job No. 106 (Issue to Job No. 106).

Shortages FIFO price method.

Solution : (Under LIFO Method)

Stores Ledger Account

Date	Particulars	Receipts			Issues			Balance		
Feb. 1984		Qty.	Rate Rs.	Amount Rs.	Qty.	Rate Rs.	Amount Rs.	Qty.	Rate Rs.	Amount Rs.
1	Opening Stock	—	—	—	—	—	—	600	4.00	2,400
2	Issued to Job No. 103	—	—	—	200	4.00	800	400	4.00	1,600
5	Purchases	800	4.50	3,600	—	—	—	400 800	4.00 4.50	1,600 3,600
8	Issued to Job No. 104	—	—	—	650	4.50	2,925	400 150	4.00 4.50	1,600 675
9	Return to stores from Job No. 103	35	4.00	140	—	—	—	400 150 (R) 35	4.00 4.50 4.00	1,600 675 140
12	Purchases	700	5.00	3,500	—	—	—	400 150 (R) 35 700	4.00 4.50 4.00 5.00	1,600 675 140 3,500
15	Issued to Job No. 105	—	—	—	35 465	4.00 5.00	140 2,325	400 150 235	4.00 4.50 5.00	1,600 675 1,175
16	Returned to Vendor purchased on 12th	—	—	—	65	5.00	325	400 150 170	4.00 4.50 5.00	1,600 675 850
19	Purchased	650	5.50	3,575	—	—	—	400 150 170 650	4.00 4.50 5.00 5.50	1,600 675 850 3,575
22	Purchased	450	5.75	2,587.50	—	—	—	400 150 170 650 450	4.00 4.50 5.00 5.50 5.75	1,600 675 850 3,575 2,587.50
24	Issued to Job No. 106	—	—	—	450 50	5.75 5.50	2,587.50 275	400 150 170 600	4.00 4.50 5.00 5.50	1,600 675 850 3,300
28	Issued to Job No. 107	—	—	—	550	5.50	3,025	400 150 170 50	4.00 4.50 5.00 5.50	1,600 675 850 275
29	Transferred from Job No. 105 (Return to store)	50	5.00	250	—	—	—	400 150 170	4.00 4.50 5.00	1,600 675 850
	Transferred to Job No. 106	—	—	—	50	5.00	250	50	5.50	275
31	Shortage	—	—	—	50 25	5.50 5.00	275 125	400 150 145	4.00 4.50 5.00	1,600 675 725
	Closing Stock on 31 March 1991							695		3,000

(R) = Returned to Stores.

Solution : (Under Simple Average Method)

Stores Ledger Account

Date March 1991	Particulars	Receipts Qty.	Rate Rs.	Amount Rs.	Issues Qty.	Rate Rs.	Amount Rs.	Balance Qty.	Rate Rs.	Amount Rs.
1	Opening Stock	—	—	—	—	—	—	600	4.00	2,400
2	Issued Job. 103	—	—	—	200	4.00	800	400		1,600
5	Purchased	800	4.50	3,600	—	—	—	400 800		1,600 3,600
8	Issued Job. 104	—	—	—	650	4.25	2,762.50	550		2,537.50
9	Return to Stores	35	4.00	140	—	—	—	585		2,577.50
12	Purchased	700	5.00	3,500	—	—	—	1,285		6,077.50
15	Issued to Job. 105	—	—	—	500	4.25	2,125	785		3,952.50
16	Return to Vendor Purchased on 12th	—	—	—	65	5.00	325	720		3,627.50
19	Purchased	450	5.50	3,575	—	—	—	1370		7,202.50
22	Purchased	450	5.75	2,587.50	—	—	—	1,820		9,790
24	Issued to Job.105	—	—	—	500	5.187	2,593.75	1320		7,194.25
28	Issued to Job. 107	—	—	—	550	5.625	3,093.75	770		4,100.50
29	Transferred from Job. 105 to 106 Return to stores Issued to Job 106	50	4.25	212.50	50	4.25	212.50	770		4,100.50
31	Shortages	—	—	—	75	4.25	318.75	695		3,781.75

$$\text{Simple Average Issue Price} = \frac{\text{No. Purchase Prices}}{\text{No. of Purchases}}$$

$$\text{March - 2} = \frac{4}{1} = 4.00$$

$$\text{March - 8} = \frac{4 + 4.5}{2} = \frac{8.5}{2} = 4.25$$

$$\text{March - 15} = \frac{4.50 + 4 + 5}{3} = \frac{13.5}{4} = 4.50$$

$$\text{March - 24} = \frac{4.50 + 5 + 5.50 + 5.75}{4} = \frac{20.75}{4} = 5.1875$$

$$\text{March - 28} = \frac{5.50 + 5.75}{2} = \frac{11.25}{2} = 5.625$$

March - 29 Transfer from Job 105 to Job 106, Return from Job 105 — at issue price 4.25 and the same is issued to Job 106.

$$\text{March - 31 Shortages} = \frac{5.50 + 5.75}{2} = \frac{11.25}{2} = 5.625$$

Solution : (Under Weighted Average Method)

Stores Ledger Account

Date March 1991	Particulars	Receipts Qty.	Receipts Rate Rs.	Receipts Amount Rs.	Issues Qty.	Issues Rate Rs.	Issues Amount Rs.	Balance Qty.	Balance Rate Rs.	Balance Amount Rs.
1	Opening Stock	—	—	—	—	—	—	600	4.00	2,400
2	Issued to Job. 103	—	—	—	200	4.00	800	400		1,600
5	Purchases	80	4.50	3,600	—	—	—	1200		5,200
8	Issues to Job. 104	—	—	—	650	4.35	2,827.50	550		2,379
9	Return to stores Job. 103	35	4.00	140	—	—	—	585		2,519
12	Purchased	700	5.00	3,500	—	—	—	1285		6,019
15	Issued to Job. 105	—	—	—	500	4.70	2,350	785		3,669
16	Return to Vendor Purchased on 12th	—	—	—	65	5.00	325	720		3,344
19	Purchases	650	5.50	3,575	—	—	—	1370		6,919
22	Purchases	450	5.75	2,587.50	—	—	—	1820		9,506.50
24	Issued to Job. 106	—	—	—	500	5.22	2,610	1320		6,896.50
28	Issued to Job. 107	—	—	—	550	5.22	2,871	770		4,025.50
29	Transferred from Job 105 to Job 106 (i.e. Return to store & Issue to Job 106)	50	4.70	235	50	4.70	235	770		4,025.50
31	Shortage	—	—	—	75	4.70	391.50	695		3,634

Issue Price = Weighted Average Method.

$$\text{Issue Price} = \frac{\text{Total Amount in Balance}}{\text{Total Quantity in Balance}}$$

Issue Price = 2nd March = $\frac{2,400}{600}$ = 4.00. 8th March = $\frac{5,200}{1200}$ = 4.333 or 4.34

15th March = $\frac{6,019}{1285}$ = 4.68 = 4.70. 16th March. Return to vendor at Purchase price.

22th March = $\frac{9,506.50}{1820}$ = 5.223 or 5.22 28th March = $\frac{6,896.50}{1320}$ = 5.22

29th March = Transferred from Job 105 i.e., Issue Price 4.70 Transferred to Job 106 the same issue price.

31st March = Shortages Price = $\frac{4,025.50}{770}$ = 5.22

Problem No. Extra-2/36

- Enter the following transactions in the Stores Ledger of Material 'Y' using LIFO Pricing Method.

July 1984

1 Opening Balance 250 units @ Rs. 2 per unit.

3 Issued 50 units MR No. 21.

6 Received 800 units vide GR No. 6 @ Rs. 2.20 per unit.

7 Issued 300 units MR No. 23.

8 Returned to stores 20 units issued on MR No. 21.

12 Received 300 units GR No. 8 @ Rs. 2.40 per unit.

15 Issued 320 units MR No. 28.

18 Received 100 units GR No. 12 @ Rs. 2.50 per unit.

20 Issue 120 units MR No. 35.

23 Returned to vendor 40 units from GR No. 12 received on 18th.

26 Received 200 units GR No. 18 @ Rs. 2 per unit.

28 Freight charges pair Rs. 100 on purchase GR No. 18.

30 Issued 250 units MR No. 42.

31 Stores audit shows 25 units excess.

Solution : (Under LIFO Method)

Stores Ledger Account

Date July 1984	Particulars	Receipts Qty.	Receipts Rate Rs.	Receipts Amount Rs.	Issues Qty.	Issues Rate Rs.	Issues Amount Rs.	Balance Qty.	Balance Rate Rs.	Balance Amount Rs.
1	Opening Stock	—	—	—	—	—	—	250	2.00	500
3	Issue MR No. 21	—	—	—	50	2.00	100	200	2.00	400
6	Received GR No. 6	800	2.20	1,760	—	—	—	200	2.00	400
								800	2.20	1,760
7	Issue MR No. 23	—	—	—	300	2.20	660	200	2.00	400
								800	2.20	1,100
8	Return to stores MR No. 21	20	2.00	40	—	—	—	200	2.00	400
								500	2.20	1,100
								20	2.00	40
12	Received GR No. 8	300	2.40	720	—	—	—	20	2.00	40
								300	2.40	720
15	Issued MR No. 28	—	—	—	20	2.00	40	200	2.00	400
					300	2.40	720	500	2.20	1,100
18	Received GR No. 12	100	2.50	250	—	—	—	200	2.00	400
								500	2.20	1,100
								100	2.50	250
20	Issues MR No. 35	—	—	—	100	2.50	250	200	2.00	400
					20	2.20	44	480	2.20	1,056
23	Returned to vendor GR No. 12 on 18th	—	—	—	40	2.50	100	200	2.00	400
								440	2.20	968
26	Received GR No.18	200	2.50	500	—	—	—	200	2.00	400
								440	2.20	968
								200	2.50	500
28	Freight charges									
30	Issued MR No. 42	—	—	—	200	2.50	500	200	2.00	400
					50	2.20	110	390	2.20	858
31	Excess (Surplus)	25	2.20	55	—	—	—	200	2.00	400
								415	2.20	913
	Closing Stock on 31st July 84							615		1,313

Note : (1) Returned to stores priced at Issue price such returned material are issued immediate next.

(2) Returned to vendor if materials at purchase is not in stock, the returns to vendor are price purchase price and the difference in price in stock be adjusted to inventory adjustment A/c.

Problem No. Extra-3/37

Prepare a statement showing issue price on the basis of Simple Average and Weighted Average method from the following information :

1986 April

1 Opening Stock 150 units Rs. 10 each.
2 Purchased 250 units at Rs. 11 per unit.
4 Issued 120 units to Job No. 112.
5 Issued 80 units to Job No. 113.
8 Purchased 200 units @ Rs. 12 per unit.
12 Issued 150 units to Job No. 114.
20 Purchased 150 units @ Rs. 14 per unit.
24 Return from Job No. 114 — 30 units.
28 Issued 100 units to Job No. 115.
31 Return to vendor 20 units purchased on 20th.
31 Stores Audit shows shortage of 20 units of materials.

Solution : (Under Simple Average Method)

Store Ledger Account

Date April 1986	Particulars	Receipts Qty.	Receipts Rate Rs.	Receipts Amount Rs.	Issues Qty.	Issues Rate Rs.	Issues Amount Rs.	Balance Qty.	Balance Rate Rs.	Balance Amount Rs.
1	Opening Balance	—	—	—	—	—	—	150		1,500
2	Purchase	250	11	2,750	—	—	—	400		4,250
4	Issue to Job-112	—	—	—	120	10.50	1,326	280		2,924
5	Issue to Job-113	—	—	—	80	10.50	840	200		2,084
8	Purchase	200	12	2,400	—	—	—	400		4,484
12	Issued (Job-114)	—	—	—	150	11.50	1,725	250		2,759
20	Purchases	150	14	2,100	—	—	—	400		4,859
24	Return to stores (Job-114)	30	11.50	345	—	—	—	430		4,514
28	Issued (Job-115)	—	—	—	100	12.33	1,233	330		3,281
31	Return to vendor 20th	—	—	—	20	14	280	310		3,001
31	Shortage	—	—	—	20	12.33	246.60	290		2,754.40

Issue Price : (1) 4th $= \frac{10 + 11}{2} = 10.50$ (2) 5th $= \frac{10 + 11}{2} = 10.50$

(3) 8th $= \frac{11 + 12}{2} = 11.50$ (4) 20th $= \frac{12 + 14 + 11}{3} = 12.33$

Note : Shortage 20 units price at latest Issue price.

Solution : (Under Weighted Average Method)

Stores Ledger Account

Date April 1986	Particulars	Receipts Qty.	Receipts Rate Rs.	Receipts Amount Rs.	Issues Qty.	Issues Rate Rs.	Issues Amount Rs.	Balance Qty.	Balance Rate Rs.	Balance Amount Rs.
1	Opening Balance	—	—	—	—	—	—	150		1,500
2	Purchases	250	11	2,750	—	—	—	400		4,250
4	Issued to Job 112	—	—	—	120	10.625	1,275	280		2,975
5	Issue Job 113	—	—	—	80	10.625	850	200		2,125
8	Purchases	200	12	2,400	—	—	—	400		4,525
12	Issue Job 114	—	—	—	150	11.312	1,697	250		2,828
20	Purchases	150	14	2,100	—	—	—	400		4,928
24	Returns to stores Job 114)	30	11.31	339	—	—	—	430		5,267
28	Issue Job 115	—	—	—	100	12	1,200	330		4,067
31	Return to vendor 20th	—	—	—	20	14	280	310		3,787
31	Shortage	—	—	—	20	12	240	290		3,547

Note : Issue Price

(1) 4th April $= \dfrac{4{,}250}{400} = 10.625$

(2) 5th April $= \dfrac{2{,}975}{280} = 10.625$

(3) 12th April $= \dfrac{4{,}525}{400} = 11.3125$

(4) 28th April $= \dfrac{5{,}267}{430} = 12.24$

Note : 31st April 1986 shortage priced at Rs. 12 per unit latest Issue price.

Problem No. Extra-4/38

Prepare a Statement showing issue price on the basis of (1) Simple Average and (2) Weighted Average method from the following information of material 'X'.

March 1980

1	Purchased 100 units @ Rs. 10 each
2	Purchased 200 units @ 10.20 each
5	Issued 250 units to Job 'A' vide MR No. 12.
7	Purchased 300 units @ Rs. 10.50 each.
10	Purchased 200 units @ Rs. 10.80 each.
13	Issued 200 Units to Job 'B' vide MR No. 17.
18	Issued 200 Units to Job 'C' vide MR No. 17.
20	Purchased 100 units @ Rs. 11 each.
25	Issued 150 units to Job 'D' vide MR No. 25.

Solution : (Simple Average Method)

Stores Ledger Account

Date	Particulars	Receipts			Issues			Balance		
March 1980		Qty.	Rate Rs.	Amount Rs.	Qty.	Rate Rs.	Amount Rs.	Qty.	Rate Rs.	Amount Rs.
1	Purchases	100	10.00	1,000				100		1,000
2	Purchases	200	10.20	2,040				300		3,040
5	Issued MR No. 12				250	10.10	2,525	50		515
7	Purchased	300	10.50	3,150				350		3,665
10	Purchased	200	10.80	2,160				550		5,825
13	Issues MR No. 15				200	10.50	2,100	350		3,725
18	Issues MR No. 17				200	10.65	2,130	150		1,595
20	Purchases	100	11.00	1,100				250		2,695
25	Issues MR No. 25				150	10.90	1,635	100		1,060

Issue Price : (1) 5th March $= \dfrac{10 + 10.20}{2} = 10.10$

(2) 13th March $= \dfrac{10.20 + 10.50 + 10.80}{3} = \dfrac{31.50}{3} = 10.50$

(3) 18th March $= \dfrac{10.50 + 10.80}{2} = \dfrac{21.30}{2} = 10.65$

(4) 25th March $= \dfrac{10.80 + 11.00}{2} = \dfrac{21.80}{2} = 10.90$

STANDARD PRICE METHOD

This method assumes predeterminal price for issue of materials for a specified period. A standard price is fixed after considering fluctuations in material prices based on market condition.

There are two types :

(a) *Basis Standard Price* : Fixed for a long period to facilitate perspective planning.

(b) *Current Standard Price* : Fixed for a short period, flexible to accommodate frequent changes in the material prices.

Standard price is different from actual price difference between stand and price and the actual cost price is known as 'Variance' and it is the indicator of efficiency in purchase of material.

Calculation of Material Price Variance

Variance = Actual Material Receipts (in units) × Standard Price (Units × standard price per unit) – Actual cost price of materials.

If the standard price (as above) is more than the actual price, it is known as positive (+) or profit or favourable variance and it shows efficiency in buying Negative (–) represents (i.e., Actual cost price is more than the standard price charged) unfavourable — or Loss — or debit Balance shows in efficiency in buying.

"Material Variance" Account — is opened to credit-positive variance or profit and Debit-Negative variance or Loss. The final Balance credit/debit or Profit/Loss is transferred to "Costing Profit and Loss Account".

Advantages : (1) It is Simple in operation.

(2) Reasonable comparison between Jobs is made.

(3) Better contract over purchases.

Limitations : (1) It is difficult to fix standard price.

(2) Jobs are not costed at actual cost price.

This results in over charging or under charging of material issues to Jobs.

In a problem where standard price not given it is to be determined by considering :

Closing stock of Material of previous period = Units × Rate = Amount

OR Opening stock of material of current period = Units × Rate = Amount.

+ Debit Balance/Loss i.e., standard price is less than the actual price.

OR – Credit Balance/Profit i.e., Standard Prices is more than the actual cost.

The amount so arrived at is divided by the number units of opening stock — gives the current standard price to be charged to issues.

i.e., Opening stock current period — units × Rate = Amount

(Or Closing stock or previous period)

+ Debit Balance —

Total Amount —

$$\text{Now current standard price} = \frac{\text{Total Amount (as above)}}{\text{No. of units}}$$

= Rate per unit.

OR Opening stock of current period Unix × Rate = Amount

OR Closing stock of previous period —

Actual cost price —

$$\text{Now current standard price} = \frac{\text{Total Amount}}{\text{No. of Units}} = \text{Rate per unit.}$$

Problem No. Extra-5/39 (Standard Price Method)

Stocks are issued at standard price and the following transactions accrued in a specific material.

1985, Jan.

1 Opening stock 10 tons at Rs. 240 per ton.

4 Purchased 5 tons at Rs. 260 per ton.

5 Issued 3 tons.

12 Issued 4 tons.

13 Purchased 3 tons at Rs. 250 per ton.

19 Issued 4 tons.

26 Issued 3 tons.

30 Purchased 4 tons at Rs. 280 per ton.

31 Issued 3 tons.

The debit Balance of price variation on 1st January was Rs. 20. Show the stock account for the material for the month of January indicating how would you deal with difference in material price variance when preparing the Profit & Loss Account for the month.

(ICWA, Inter)

Solution :

Note : In this problem the standard price for issue of materials is not given. Now it is necessary to calculate/ascertain Standard Price.

Calculations of Standard Price :

Value of opening stock 10 Tons × Rs. 120 =	2,400
Add : Debit Balance — Standard Price	20
Was less than the actual cost	
Now value of tons is	2,420

∴ Standard Price for current month would be

$$= \frac{\text{Total Value}}{\text{No. of units}} = \frac{2420}{10} = \text{Rs. 242 per ton.}$$

Solution : (Standard Price — Rs. 242)

Stores Ledger Account

Date Jan. 1985	Particulars	Receipts Qty.	Receipts Rate Rs.	Receipts Amount Rs.	Issues Qty.	Issues Rate Rs.	Issues Amount Rs.	Balance Qty.	Balance Rate Rs.	Balance Amount Rs.
1	Opening Stock	—	—	—	—	—	—	10	240	2,400
4	Purchases	5	260	1,300	—	—	—	15		3,700
5	Issues	—	—	—	3	242	726	12		2,974
12	Issues	—	—	—	4	242	968	8		2,006
13	Purchases	3	250	750	—	—	—	11		2,756
19	Issues	—	—	—	4	242	968	7		1,788
26	Issues	—	—	—	3	242	726	4		1,062
30	Purchases	4	280	1,120	—	—	—	8		2,182
31	Issues	—	—	—	3	242	726	5		1,456
	Closing Stock on 31st January 1985							5		1,456

Material Price Variance Closing Stock :

At Standard Price 5 tons × 242 =	1,210
Actual stock value as above	(–) 1,456
	(–) 246

i.e., Standard Price – buying issue price charged is less than the actual cost price by Rs. 246 i.e., Loss or Debit Balance.

Entry :

(1) Material Price Variance A/c Dr	246	
To Stores Ledger A/c		246
(2) Costing Profit & Loss A/c Dr	246	
To Material Price Variance A/c		246

Problem No. Extra-6/40 (Standard Price Method)

The following are details of purchases and issues of Material 'X' for the month of January 1980.

1980

Jan. 1 Opening Stock 300 units @ Rs. 20 per unit.

2 Purchases 500 units @ Rs. 20 per unit.

8 Purchases 700 units @ Rs. 18 per unit.

9 Issues 600 units.

11 Issues 800 units.

17 Purchases 800 units @ Rs. 20 per unit.

25 Purchases 500 units @ Rs. 25 per unit.

31 Issues 1000 units.

The standard price per unit is Rs. 20 fixed for the year 1980.

Prepare Stores Ledger Account and show the Material Price Variance.

(ICWA, Inter)

Solution :

Stores Ledger Account

Date	Particulars	Receipts			Issues			Balance		
Jan. 1980		Qty.	Rate Rs.	Amount Rs.	Qty.	Rate Rs.	Amount Rs.	Qty.	Rate Rs.	Amount Rs.
1	Opening Stock	—	—	—	—	—	—	300	20	6,000
2	Purchases	500	20	10,000	—	—	—	800		16,000
8	Purchases	700	18	12,600	—	—	—	1500		28,600
9	Issues	—	—	—	600	20	1,200	900		16,600
11	Issues	—	—	—	800	20	16,000	100		600
17	Purchases	800	20	16,000	—	—	—	900		16,600
25	Purchases	500	20	12,500	—	—	—	1400		29,100
31	Issues	—	—	—	1000	20	20,000	400		9,100
		Closing Stock on 31st Jan. 1980						400		9,100

Material Price Variance × Closing stock 400 units at Standard

Price of Rs. 20 per unit = 400 × 20	8,000
Actual closing stock 400 units	9,100
Unfavourable	(–) 1,100

i.e., Standard Price Rs. 20 per unit charged issues is less than the actual cost Price and therefore results in debit balance Rs. 1,100.

Entry :

	Dr	Cr
(1) Material Price Variance A/c Dr	1,100	
To Stores Ledger A/c		1,100
(2) Costing Profit & Loss A/c Dr	1,100	
To Material Price Variance A/c		1,100

Problem No. Extra-7/41 (Under Standard Price Method)

From the following particulars of Material 'X' Purchases and issues for the month of November 1995. Prepare Stores Ledger Account using Standard Price Method. Standard Price @ Rs. 15 per unit for issues of material.

1995

Jan. 1 Opening Stock 600 units @ Rs. 15 per unit.

4 Purchases 525 units @ Rs. 13.50 per unit.

10 Issues 1050 units.

16 Purchases 600 units at Rs. 15 per unit.

25 Purchases 450 units @ Rs. 18 per unit.

29 Issues 750 units.

Determine the price variance giving purchase efficiency and treat of variance in costing.

Solution : (Standard Price Method)

Stores Ledger Account

Date Nov. 1995	Particulars	Receipts Qty.	Receipts Rate Rs.	Receipts Amount Rs.	Issues Qty.	Issues Rate Rs.	Issues Amount Rs.	Balance Qty.	Balance Rate Rs.	Balance Amount Rs.
1	Opening Stock	—	—	—	—	—	—	600	15	9,000
4	Purchases	525	13.50	7,085.50	—	—	—	1125		16,085.50
10	Issues	—	—	—	1050	15	15,750	75		335.50
16	Purchases	600	15	9,000	—	—	—	675		9,335.50
25	Purchases	450	18	8,100	—	—	—	1125		17,435.50
29	Issues	—	—	—	750	15	11,250	375		6,185.50

Material Price Variance :

= (Receipts × Standard Price) – Actual Price

= (1575 × 15) = 23,625 – 24,185.50

= 560.50(–)

= – 560.50 Unfavourable

Entry : (1) Material Variance A/c Dr 560.50
To Stores Ledger A/c 560.50

(2) Costing Profit & Loss A/c Dr 560.50
To Material Variance A/c 560.50

Problem No. Extra-8/42

Ashok Engineering Works values material 'X' issues were charged at standard price fixed on yearly basis. Following are the purchases and issues of material 'X'.

1994

December

1 Opening Stock 5000 units @ Rs. 12 per unit.

4 Issues 2200 units.

8 Purchases 18000 units @ Rs. 11 per unit.

14 Issues 14000 units.

20 Purchases 11000 units @ Rs. 10 per unit.

24 Issues 6000 units.

28 Issues 4500 units.

31 Shortage 1500 units.

Standard Price fixed is Rs. 11 per unit. Prepare Stores Ledger Account and state Material Price Variance.

Solution : (Under Standard Price Method) Standard Price Rs. 11.

Stores Ledger Account

Date Dec. 1994	Particulars	Receipts Qty.	Rate Rs.	Amount Rs.	Issues Qty.	Rate Rs.	Amount Rs.	Balance Qty.	Amount Rs.
1	Opening Stock	—	—	—	—	—	—	5000	60,000
4	Issues	—	—	—	2200	11	24,200	2800	35,800
8	Purchases	18000	11	1,98,000	—	—	—	20800	2,33,800
14	Issues	—	—	—	1400	11	1,54,000	6800	79,800
20	Purchases	11000	10	1,10,000	—	—	—	17800	1,89,800
24	Issues	—	—	—	6000	11	66,000	11800	1,23,800
28	Issues	—	—	—	4500	11	49,500	7300	74,300
31	Shortages	—	—	—	1500	11	16,500	5800	57,800
		29000		3,08,000			3,10,200		

Material Price Variance = (Receipts × Standard Price) – Actual Cost

Opening Stock + Purchase = 5000 + 29000 = 34000 units.

Actual cost of total Purchases + Opening Stock

= 3,08,000 + 60,000 = 3,68,000

Material Price Variance = 34000 × 11 = 3,74,000 – 3,68,000

= 6,000 Favourable (Profit)

Alternatively :

Price Variance = Closing stock at standard – Actual Stock Value

= 5800 × 11 = 63,800 – 57,800

= 6,000 Favourable (Profit).

Problem No. Extra-9/43 (On Standard Price Method)

Following are the particulars of Materials purchases and issues of an engineering works which follows the issue price under standard price method during the month of 1994, December.

1994 December

1 Opening Stock 50 tons @ Rs. 120 per ton.

4 Purchased 25 tons @ Rs. 130 per ton.

6 Issued 15 tons.

10 Issued 20 tons.

18 Purchased 15 tons @ Rs. 125 per ton.

20 Issued 20 tons.

24 Issued 15 tons.

28 Purchased 20 tons @ Rs. 140 per ton.

31 Issued 15 tons.

The debt Balance price variation on 1st December was Rs. 50. Show Stores Ledger Account for the material issue price and how you deal with material price variance.

Solution :

Ascertainment of Standard Price

During the previous month standard price on closing stock was Rs. 120 i.e. Opening Stock during December, remains the same i.e.,

50 tons at Rs. 120 per ton

Now opening stock = 50 × 120 = 6,000

Add : Debit Balance 50

(Being actual cost price is more than the standard Price)

Actual total value 6,050

for 50 units ∴ $\frac{6,050}{50}$ = Rs. 121 per ton

would be the standard price for December 1994.

Solution :

Stores Ledger Account

Date Dec. 1994	Particulars	Receipts Qty.	Rate Rs.	Amount Rs.	Issues Qty.	Rate Rs.	Amount Rs.	Balance Qty.	Rate Rs.	Amount Rs.
1	Opening Stock	—	—	—	—	—	—	50	12	6,000
4	Purchases	25	130	3,250	—	—	—	75		9,250
6	Issued	—	—	—	25	121	3,025	50		6,225
10	Issued	—	—	—	20	121	2,420	30		3,805
18	Purchases	15	125	1,825	—	—	—	45		5,630
20	Issues	—	—	—	20	121	2,420	25		3,210
24	Issues	—	—	—	15	121	1,815	10		1,395
28	Purchases	20	140	2,800	—	—	—	30		4,195
31	Issues	—	—	—	15	121	1,815	15		2,380
		60		7,875			9,680			

Material Price Variance

= (Receipts × Standard Price) – Actual cost

Opening Stock + Purchases (Units)

= 50 + 60 = 110 units.

Opening Stock + Purchases (in amount)

= 6,000 + 7,875 = 13,875 Actual cost.

Material Price Variance

= (110 tons × 121) = 13,310 - 13,875

= 565 Unfavourable

i.e, Actual cost Price is more than standard price.

Entry :		
(1) Material Variance A/c Dr	565	
To Stores Ledger A/c		565
(Debt balance of material variants)		
(2) Costing Profit & Loss A/c Dr	565	
To Material Variance A/c		565

Alternatively :

Material Price Variance = Closing stock at standard price – Closing Stock actual cost.

= 15 tons × 121 = 1,815 – 2,380

= –565 Unfavourable

i.e., Actual closing stock is more than the Standard Price of closing stock in units.

INFLATED PRICE METHOD

Where the material of its natural character losses its weight by evaporation when exposed to nature and/or climate factor. Or breakage of bulk into small units etc. such a loss in weight is termed as unavoidable loss and treated as normal loss.

In calculation of cost price of such material for the purpose of issue to production of the total quantity purchased at certain price,

The Quantity Purchased say	100 units
Less : Normal Loss 10%	10
Good units	90

The total cost — divided by Good units would give the price per unit.

The price so arrived at will be higher than the original cost price per unit.

For example :

Material 'X' was purchased 100 units at a cost of Rs. 180 cost price per unit

$$\frac{180}{100} = 1.80 \text{ per unit.}$$

Now this Material lost its weight by 10%

Quantity purchased 100 units cost = 180

Less : Normal Loss – 10% (100 – 10) = 90

Cost Price for issue is $\frac{180}{90}$ = Rs. 2 per unit.

It is inflated Price.

Original cost price 100 units @ Rs. 180 = Rs. 1.80 per unit. Further at this inflated price material are charged — issued to production by following any of the methods of pricing Issues i.e., FIFO, LIFO and Average Methods etc.

Problem Extra-10/44 (Inflated Price)

The following are the particulars of material 'X' which by its nature it would result is loss of 10% of weight. The issue prices are charged under FIFO method of Pricing.

1994 December

1 Purchased 500 units @ Rs. 9 per unit.
4 Issued 200 units.
8 Purchased 600 units @ Rs. 10 per unit.
12 Issued 300 units.
15 Purchased 600 units @ Rs. 11 per unit.
20 Issued 500 units.
28 Issued 300 units.
30 Surplus found on verification 100 units.

Solution : (Under Inflated Price-FIFO Method)

Stores Ledger Account

Date Dec. 1994	Particulars	Receipts Qty.	Rate Rs.	Amount Rs.	Issues Qty.	Rate Rs.	Amount Rs.	Balance Qty.	Rate Rs.	Amount Rs.
1	Purchased	500	9.00	4,500	—	—	—	500	9.00	4,500
						Less : 10%		50		
								450	10.00	4,500
4	Issues	—	—	—	200	1.00	200	250	10.00	2,500
8	Purchases	600	10	6,000	(*Less* Loss 10%)			250	10.00	2,500
								540	11.11	6,000
12	Issues	—	—	—	260	10.00	2,500	490	11.11	5,444.5
					50	11.11	555.5			
15	Purchased	600	11	6,600	(*Less* Loss 10%)			490	11.11	5,444.5
								540	12.22	6,600
10	Issues	—	—	—	490	11.11	5,444.5			
					10	12.22	122.2	530	12.22	6,477.8
20	Issues	—	—	—	300	12.22	3,666.0	230	12.22	2,811.8
30	Surplus	100	12.22	1,222	—	—	—	330	12.22	4,033.8
		Closing Stock						330	12.22	4,033.8

Note : Calculation shortage of 10% on Purchase quantity and net weight.

Gross	Shortage (10%)	Net Qty.	Rate per unit	Amount Rs.
500	50	450	10.00	4,500
600	60	540	11.11	6,000
600	60	540	12.22	6,600

Problem : Extra-11/45 (Inflated Price)

From the following particulars of Chemicals purchased were subject to Loss of 10% of the quantity purchased. Calculate issue price of materials to production following FIFO Method.

1994 December

1 Opening Stock 200 units at Rs. 6 per unit.
2 Purchases 600 units @ Rs. 5.40 per unit.
6 Purchased 750 units @ Rs. 6.75 per unit.
10 Issues 400 units.
16 Issues 500 units.
18 Returns to vendor 50 units purchased on 6th December.
22 Returned to stores 100 units issued on 16th December.
24 Excess found on verification 50 units.
26 Purchases 600 units @ Rs. 6.50 per unit.
28 Issues 650 units.
31 Shortages 75 units.

Solution :

Working Note

(1) Ascertainment of Net Weight and Inflated Price.

Date	Particulars	Gross Weight	Loss (10%)	Net Weight	Rate Per Unit.	Amount Rs.
1994						
Dec. 2	Purchases	600	60	540	6.00	3,240
6	Purchases	750	75	675	7.50	5,062.50
26	Purchases	600	60	540	7.22	3,900

(2) Returns to vendor purchased on 6th December were priced at purchase price. The price of materials in stock is different — the difference in price should be accounted in Stores Adjustment Account.

(3) Returns to stores are priced at issue price earlier and such returned materials are issued immediately in the next issue.

(4) Excess or surplus and shortage are priced at latest purchase price available in stock.

Solution : (Under Inflated Price FIFO Method)

Stores Ledger Account

Date	Particulars	Receipts			Issues			Balance		
Dec. 1994		Qty.	Rate Rs.	Amount Rs.	Qty.	Rate Rs.	Amount Rs.	Qty.	Rate Rs.	Amount Rs.
1	Opening Stock	—	—	—	—	—	—	200	6.00	1,200
2	Purchases	600	5.40	3,240	(Less Loss 10%)			200	6.00	1,200
								540	6.00	3,240
6	Purchases	750	6.75	5,062.50	(Less Loss 10%)			200	6.00	1,200
								540	6.00	3,240
								675	7.50	5,062.50
10	Issues	—	—	—	200	6.00	1,200	340	6.00	2,040
					200	6.00	1,200	675	7.50	5,062.50
16	Issues	—	—	—	340	6.00	2,040	515	7.50	3,862.50
					160	7.50	1,200			
18	Returns to Vendor Purchased on 6th.	—	—	—	50	6.75	337.50	405	7.50	3,037.50
22	Returns to store issue on 16th.	100	7.50	750	—	—	—	405	7.50	3,037.50
								(R) 100	7.50	750
24	Excess	50	7.50	375	—	—	—	405	7.50	3,037.50
								(R) 100	7.50	750
								(R) 50	7.50	375
26	Purchases	600	6.50	3,900	—	—	—	405	7.50	3,037.50
				(Less Loss 10%)				(R) 100	7.50	750
								(R) 50	7.50	375
								540	7.22	3,900
28	Issues	—	—	—	100	7.50	750			
					50	7.50	375			
					405	7.50	3,037.5			
					95	7.22	685.9	445	7.22	3,214.10
31	Shortages	—	—	—	75	7.22	541.5	370	7.22	2,672.60
	Closing Stock on 31st December 1994							370	7.22	2,672.60

Note : (1) Returns to Vendor purchased on 6th December were priced at purchase price. The price of materials in stock is different — the difference in price should be accounted in Stores Adj. A/c.

(2) Returns to stores are priced at issue price earlier and such returned materials are issued immediately in the next issue.

(3) Excess or Surplus and shortage are priced at a latest Purchase price available in stock.

2

LABOUR

Labour is one of the important factors of production. It deals with human element. It needs careful handling of labour. In Cost Accounting labour is a second important elements of costs. The Labour cost = Wages – Directly affects the cost of production. A satisfied worker produces more output. His work efficiency is identified and is rewarded. A conducive atmosphere is created by providing amenities to keep them satisfied.

Labour classified as :

(a) Direct Labour (b) Indirect Labour

(a) Direct Labour is one which can be identified with output of particular unit. It varies in accordance with output.

(b) Indirect Labour is one which can not be identified with any particular unit of output. Indirectly helps to the production.

Labour Cost Control

It is necessary to exercise control over labour cost since it directly affects the total cost of product.

The following factors are to be considered :

(1) Production planning.

(2) Establishment of standards.

(3) Preparation of labour cost budgets.

(4) Measurement of efficiency of labour.

(5) Labour performance report.

Recruitment and Training of Labour

The Personnel Department looks after the recruitment and training of labour required for organisation.

Personnel department after having collected information from the heads of each department arrange requirements of labour. The personnel department follows the recruitment procedure for labour. Suitable persons are selected for each of the departments.

The recruited labourer is given an understanding the nature of Job to be performed.

Under the Time and Motion study F.W. Taylor the father of the Scientific Management of Labour, states that the existing resources should be utilised to the maximum possible efficiency. So, as to help increase in the production and thereby reducing cost of output. It insist the fixation of standard for each Job in terms of output/time. Increase in the output above the standard and savings in time as compared to standard time fixed for Job, indicates efficiency of Labour in doing the Job. The efficient worker is rewarded.

Labour Turnover

It is always preferable to maintain labour force at stable position. Frequent replacement of Labour force will directly affect the production. Higher Labour turnover ratio increase the cost of production.

Formula calculation of Labour Turnover Ratio :

$$= \frac{\text{No. of persons replaced during the period}}{\text{Average number of workers during the period}} \times 100$$

Time Recording

Control over labourer is exercised by recording the time of entry and exit. Apart from the traditional methods of recording timings of workers, Manual, the most modern and scientific mechanical devices are used to record timing of workers. This will impose discipline among workers and also helps in preparing wage Bill.

Wage Payments

Methods of Remuneration :

(I) Time Wage – Wages paid based on time

Time Wage : (i) Hourly Rate (ii) Day Wages (iii) Monthly Wages.

(II) Payments by Results : Wages linked with production

(a) Piece wage – Wage paid at specific rate based on output.

(b) Incentive plans – It is the combination of time wages + Rewards the worker according to his efficiency.

Earnings – Under Time Wages :

(i) Hours Worked × Rate per Hour

Or (ii) Time taken × Rate per Hour.

High Wages Plan : High day rate or High rate of time wage is paid to efficient worker, so as to encourage such workers who produce more units of output within specified time or increased output above standard output or attains certain percentage of efficiency over standard fixed.

(II) *Piece Wage* : Wages are fixed at specific Rate per unit.

Earnings = No. of units of output × Rate per unit.

(III) *Differential Piece Wage Rate* : Payment of different rates at different levels of efficiency.

Differential Piece Wage (Rate) plans aim at maximum production by giving additional incentives to output at or above standard output. A definite standard of efficiency is set (or fixed) for each Job and for efficiency below standard or above standard different piece rates are paid according to different levels of efficiency.

Differential Piece Rate Schemes

(1) Taylor's system.

(2) Merrick's differential piece rate system.

Taylor's differential piece rate system : F.W. Taylor, father of the scientific management introduced this method on the basis of Time and motion study.

He proposed to improve efficiency of the workers, two rates of payments.

Taylor's Piece Rates

(1) High piece rate for efficiency at or above standards.

(2) Low piece rates for efficiency below standard.

Main Features

(1) There shall be two piece rates : One is lower piece rate for efficiency below standard. Another is higher piece rate at or above standard.

(2) Standard efficiency is determined either in terms of standard time or standard output.

Standard in time and in output are determined based on time and motion study.

(3) If a worker completes the work within standard time, or produces output more than standard output within standard time, he is paid at a higher rate of wages.

If a worker takes more time than the standard time or produces less number of units of output than standard output, he is paid lower rate of wages.

i.e., (a) Higher rate of wages for efficiency at or above standard efficiency.

(b) Lower rate of wages for efficiency below standard efficiency.

TYLOR'S DIFFERENTIAL PIECE RATE SYSTEM

Problem No. 1

From the following particulars find out the amount of cash required for payment of wages in a factory for a particular month.

	Rs.
(a) Wages for Normal hours worked	20,500
(b) Wages for overtime	2,200
(c) Leave wages	1,700
(d) Total ESI Contribution	1,200
(e) Total PF Contribution	3,200

(f) House Rent to be recovered from 30 employees at the rate of Rs. 100 per month per employee.

Ratio of contribution by Employer and Employee is 7 : 5.

Provident Fund Contribution is Equal share of Employer and the Employee.

[K.U.D., April 1998 (N)]

Solution :

Statement of Wage Payment

		Rs.
(a) Wages for Normal Hours worked		20,500
(b) Wages for overtime		2,200
(c) Leave wages		1,700
Total wages		24,400
Less deductions :		
(d) ESI Contribution - 7 : 5 $(1{,}200 \times \frac{5}{12})$	500	
(e) PF Contribution Equal 3,200 × ½	1,600	
House sent recovery PM Rs. 100 for 30 × 100	3,000	
	5,100	5,100
Cash required to pay wages		Rs. 19,300

Problem No. 2

Find out the earnings of Hanumant and Maruti who took 16 Hours and 12 Hours respectively to complete a Job for which Standard time allowed was 18 Hours and the time rate was Rs. 3 per Hour.

Under Halsey Plan

What will be the difference in earnings of these workers if Rowan's Scheme is adopted ?

[K.U.D., April 1998 (O)]

Solution :

Workers :	Hanumant	Maruti
Standard time	18 Hours	18 Hours
Time taken	16 Hours	12 Hours
Time saved	2 Hours	6 Hours
Rate per Hour	Rs. 3	Rs. 3

Earning of workers :

(a) Under Halsey Plan :

$= T \times R + ½ (S–T) \times R$

	Hanumant	Maruti
	$16 \times 3 + ½ (18 - 16) \times 3$	$12 \times 3 + ½ (18 - 12) \times 3$
	$= 48 + ½ (2 \times 3)$	$= 48 + ½ (6 \times 3)$
	$= 48 + ½ \times 6$	$= 48 + 9$
Earnings	= Rs. 51	= 57

(b) Under Rowan Scheme

$= T \times R + R (T \times \frac{S - T}{S})$

	$16 \times 3 + 3 (16 \times \frac{18 - 16}{18})$	$16 \times 3 + 3 (12 \times \frac{18 - 12}{18})$
	$= 48 + 3 (16 \times \frac{2}{18})$	$= 48 + 3 (12 \times \frac{6}{18})$
	$= 48 + 3 (16 \times \frac{1}{9})$	$= 48 + 3 (12 \times \frac{1}{3})$
	$= 48 + 3 \times 1.78$	$= 48 + 3 \times 4$
	$= 48 + 5.34$	$= 48 + 12$
Earning	= Rs. 53.34	= Rs. 60

Difference in earnings —

Halsey plan	Rs. 51	Rs. 57
Rowan plan (Scheme)	Rs. 53.34	Rs. 60
Wages under Rowan Scheme is more	Rs. 2.34	Rs. 3

Problem No. 3

From the following particulars calculate the earnings of workers Manju and Shivappa under Taylor's differential piece Rate system :

Standard time per piece — 90 seconds

Normal rate per hour — Rs. 4

Differential Piece rates :

80% of piece rate below standard

120% of piece rate at or above standard

In a day of 8 hours :

Manju produced – 300 pieces

Shivappa produced – 400 pieces.

[K.U.D., October 1997(N)]

Solution :

Standard time per piece = 90 seconds

Standard output per hour = (90 × 90 = 3600 seconds)

$$= \frac{3600}{90} = 40 \text{ units}$$

Standard output per hour = 40 units

Standard output per day of 8 hours = 40 × 8

Standard output per day of 8 hours = 320 units

Normal rate per hour — Rs. 4.

Normal output per hour = 40 units

$$\text{Normal Rate per unit} = \frac{\text{Rate per hour}}{\text{Units per hour}} = \frac{\text{Rs. 4}}{\text{40 unit}} = 0.10 \text{ Paise}$$

Normal Rate per unit – 10 paise

Workers	Manju (Units)	Shivappa (Units)
Standard output per day of 8 hours	320	320
Actual output per day of 8 hours	300	400
Efficiency – $\frac{300}{320} \times 100 = 93.75\%$ $\frac{400}{320} \times 100 = 125\%$	93.75%	125%
Efficiency	Below standard	Above standard
Taylor's differential piece rate 80% of piece rate – below standard 120% of piece rate at or above standard		
Rate applicabe – Below standard – 80% × 0.10% – Above standard 120% × 0.10%	0.8 paise (300×0.8)	12 paise (400×0.12)
Earning = Rate per unit × No. of units	Rs. 24	Rs. 48
Earnings = Manju – Rs. 24; Shivappa Rs. 48		

Problem No. 4

A worker takes 80 hours to do a job for which the time allowed is 120 hours. His time Rate is Rs. 3 per hour.

Calculate the works cost of the Job under the following methods of payment of wages (i) Time rate (ii) Halsey plan (iii) Rowan plan.

Additional Information :

(1). Material cost Rs. 12

(2) Factory overhead @ 125% of wages.

[K.U.D., October 1997(O)]

Solution :

Standard time allowed – 120 Hours

Actual time taken – 80 Hours

Time saved 40 Hours

Rate Per Hour – Rs. 3.

Earnings of Worker : Time taken – 80 Hours or Actual time worked

Time Rate Rs. 3 Per Hour

Earnings = Time taken × Rate Per Hour

$80 \times 3 = \text{Rs. } 240$

Halsey Plan :

Earnings = Time talgen × Rate + 1/2 (S – T) R

$= 80 \times 3 + 1/2\,(120 - 80)\,R$

$= 240 + 1/2\,(40 \times 3)$

$= 240 + 60 = \text{Rs. } 300$ Ans.

$$\text{Rowan Plan} = T \times R + R\left(T \times \frac{S}{S\ T}\right)$$

$$= 80 \times 3 + 3\left(80 \times \frac{40}{120}\right)$$

$= 240 + 3(80/3)$

$= 240 + 80 = \text{Rs. } 320$ Ans.

Cost Sheet	Time Rate	Halsey Plan	Rowan Plan
Material Cost	120	120	120
Wages	240	300	320
Prime Cost	360	420	440
Factory overhead 125% of wages	300	375	550
Works Cost	660	795	990

Problem No. 5

Anil, Babu and Chandu are the employees of Dev Chand Mills. On a day of 8 hours, they have produced — 15 units, 25 units and 16 units respectively.

Find out their days earnings if,

(i) Standard time per unit – 30 minutes

(ii) Rate Per hour Rs. 10

(iii) Anil is paid according to Taylor's plan.

(iv) Babu is paid according to Halsey plan

(v) Chandu is paid according to straight piece Rate

(vi) Taylor's differential are 75% of piece rate below standard and 125% of piece rate above standard.

[K.U.D., April 1997(N)]

Solution :

Standard time per unit – 30 minutes

Standard output per Hour – 2 units

Rate Per Hour – Rs. 10

Rate Per Unit = 10/2 = Rs. 5 per unit

Normal piece Rate Rs. 5 per unit

Anil : Normal output per day of 8 hours = 8 × 2 = 16 units

Normal output per day of 8 hours = 16 units.

Anil produces – 15 units in a day of 8 hours

Efficiency 100% efficiency – standard output (8 × 2) 16 units.

Anil produces – 15 units in a day of 8 hours.

Efficiency of Anil = $\frac{15}{16} \times 100 = 93.75$ – below standard

Rate applicable under Taylor's Plan

75% of piece below standard

75% × 5 = Rs. 3.75 per unit

Earnings = Units of output × Rate per unit

Earnings of Anil — 15 units × 3.75 = Rs. 56. 25

Halsey Plan :

Earnings = T × R + 1/2 (S-T) R

Where - T = Time taken

S = Standard time

R = Rate per hour

Standard time per unit – 30 minutes

Standard output per hour = 2 units

Standard oupput per day of 8 hours

$$8 \times 2 = 16$$

Standard time for the output of 25 units

Babu : Produced 25 units in a day of 8 hours

H. min.

$$\text{Standard time for output} = \frac{25}{2} = 12.30$$

Time taken – 8 hours

Rate Per Hour — Rs. 10

Earning = J × R + 1/2 (S – T) R

= 8 × 10 + 1/2 (12.30 – 8) 10

= 80 + 1/2 (4.30 × 10)

= 80 + 1/2 (45)

= 80 + 22.50

Babu's Earnings = Rs. 102.50 under Halsey Plan.

Chandu : Produced 16 units

Wages paid under straight piece Rate : E = Units × Rate per unit

Rate Per Hour – Rs. 10

Standard time per unit – 30 minutes

Standard output per hour = 2 units

$$\text{Normal Rate per unit} - \frac{10}{2} = \text{Rs. 5 per unit}$$

Chandu :

Earning = Units of output × Rate per unit.

16 × 5 = Rs. 80

Problem No. 6

M/s Gautam Furnitures received an order for 10 steel tables (Job No. 42) in respect of which of following informations are available.

Complete a Cost sheet for Job No. 42 and calculate Price per table to give a profit of 20% on selling price material :

(1) Steel sheets — 10 sheets @ Rs. 104 per sheet

5 Litres of Paints @ Rs. 200 per litre

Wages :

Cutting — 40 hours @ Rs. 5 per hour

Welding — 60 hours @ Rs. 10 per hour

Finishing — 50 hours @ Rs. 12 per hour

Overhead expenses for these three departments were estimated for the year :

Cutting — Rs. 7,300 for 2920 hours

Welding — Rs. 10,950 for 3650 hours

Finishing — Rs. 8,760 for 3650 hours

Fixed overheads — Rs. 8,176 for 10220 Normal Working hours

[K.U.D., October 1997(O)]

Solution :

Estimated Statement of Cost for Job No. 42

		Rs.
Cost of Materials :		
Steel sheets — 10 sheets × 104	1,040	
Paints — 5 Litre × 200 per litre	1,000	2,040
Direct wages — Hours × Rate per hour		
Cutting — 40 × 5 =	200	
Welding — 60 × 10 =	600	
Finishing 50 × 12 =	600	1,400
Prime Cost		3,440
Factory overhead :		
Cutting — 7,300/2920 = Rs. 2.50 per hour for 40 hours	100	
Welding — 10,930/3650 = Rs. 3.00 per hour for 60 hours	180	
Finishing — 8,760/3650 = Rs. 2.40 per hour for 50 hours	120	400
Fixed overhead — Re. 0.80 paise per hour for 150 hrs. (40 + 60 + 50)		120
Cost of Production		3,960
Add Profit 20% on Sales Price or 25% on Cost Price 25% on Cost 3960 × 25%		990
Selling Price		4,950
Profit 20% Price 4,950 × 20% = 990 Per Table = 4,950/10		495

Problem No. 7

From the following information calculate the earnings of workers A and B as under :

(1) Straight Piece Rate

(2) Differential piece rate system (Taylor's differential piece rate system). Normal Rate per hour Rs. 6.

Standard output per minute — 1 unit. Differential piece rate to be applied 80% of piece rate below standard. 120% of piece rate at or above standard.

In a 8-hour a day : Worker A produces – 450 Units
Worker B produces – 500 Units.

Solution :

Standard production per Minute = 1 Unit

Standard production per hour = 60 × 1 = 60 Units.

Standard output per day of 8 hours = 8 × 60 = 480 Units.

Normal rate per hour = Rs. 6. Normal rate per Unit = $\frac{6}{60}$ = .10 per unit.

Taylor's Differential Piece Rate :

Below Standard Low piece rate = 80% of 0.10 Ps = 0.08 Ps per unit.

Above Standard High piece rate 120% of 0.10 = 0.12 Ps per unit.

Earnings of workers A and B under Straight Piece Rate System :

Earnings = No. of units of output × Rate per unit

Worker A = 450 × 0.10 = Rs. 45

Worker B = 500 × 0.10 = Rs. 50

Taylor's Differential Piece Rate System :

Earnings A = 450 × 0.08 Ps = Rs. 36

Earnings B = 500 × 0.12 Ps = Rs. 60.

Problem No. 8

From the following particulars calculate the earning of wokers A and B as under :

(a) Straight piece rate system.

(b) Differential piece rate system.

Standard time per unit 5 minutes normal rate per hour Rs. 4.80.

In a 9-hour a day : A produces = 90 units.
B produces = 120 units.

Differential piece rate to be applied.

80% of piece rate – below standard

120% of piece rate – at or above standard.

Solution :

Standard output per unit = 5 minutes

Standard output per hour = $\frac{60}{5}$ = 12 units.

Standard output per day of 9 Hours = 12 × 9 = 108 Units.

Normal Piece rate per hour Rs. 4.80

Normal piece rate per unit = Rs. $\frac{4.80}{12}$ = 0.40 Ps.

(a) Differentials Piece Rate

Low piece rate 80% of 0.40 Ps = 0.32 per unit.

High piece rate 120% of 0.40 Ps = 0.48 per unit.

Earnings of Worker Under Straight Piece Rate

Worker A – output = 90 × 0.40 = Rs. 36

Worker B – output = 120 × 0.40 = Rs. 48

(b) Under Differential Piece Rate System

Worker A — output 90 Units below standard

Piece rate to be applied = 0.32 Ps

Earnings = 90 × 0.32 Ps = Rs. 28.80

Worker B — Output 120 Units above standard, rate to be applied 0.48 Ps.

Earnings = 120 × 0.48 Ps = Rs. 57.60.

Problem No. 9

From the following particulars calculate wages earned by worker X and Y under : (a) Straight piece rate and

(b) Taylor's differential piece rate system.

Standard time allowed 10 units per hour.

Normal wages per hour Rs. 6.

Differential rates to be applied.

90% of piece rate when below standard efficiency

125% of piece rate when at or above standard efficiency.

The production on a day of 8 hours.

X – 75 Units

Y – 85 Units.

Solution :

Standard time allowed 10 units per hour.

Standard output per day of 8 hours.

= 10 × 8 = 80 Units.

Normal Wages per hour Rs. 6.

Normal wages per unit = $\frac{6}{10}$ = 0.60 Ps.

Workers		X	Y
Standard output per day	(Units)	80	80
Actual output per day	(Units)	75	85
Efficiency		Below standard	Above standard

Rates to applied under Taylors System	90%	125%
	0.60 × 90% = 0.54 Ps	0.60 × 125% = 0.75 Ps

(a) Earnings of Worker under Straight Piece Rate System :

Worker X = 75 Units × 0.60 Ps = Rs. 45

Y = 85 Units × 0.60 Ps = Rs. 51

(b) Taylor's Differential Piece Rate :

Worker X = 75 × 0.54 Ps = Rs. 40.50

Y = 85 × 0.75 Ps = Rs. 63.75

Problem No. 10

On the basis of the following information calculate the earnings of workers A and B as under :

(a) Straight Piece Rate.

(b) Taylor's differential piece rate system.

Standard production 8 Units per hour.

Normal time rate Rs. 2 per hour.

Differential piece rate to be applied 80% of piece rate below standard 120% of piece rate at or above standard.

In a 9-hour a day A produces – 65 Units and B produces 85 Units.

Solution :

Standard production 8 units per hour

Standard production for a day of 9 hours = 9 × 8 = 72 Units.

Normal time Rate Rs. 2 per hour.

Normal piece rate per unit = $\frac{2}{8}$ = 0.25 Ps per Unit.

Differential piece rate under Taylor's system.

80% of 0.25 Ps = 0.20 Ps below standard.

120% of 0.25 Ps = 0.30 Ps at or above standard.

Workers	A	B
Standard output	72 Units	72 Units
Actual output	65 Units	85 Units
Efficiency of Standard	Below	Above
Rates to be applied per unit	0.20 Ps	0.30 Ps

Earnings of Workers under :

(a) Straight piece rate = 0.25 per Unit :

Worker A = 65 Units × 0.25 Ps = Rs. 16.25

Worker B = 85 Units × 0.25 Ps = Rs. 21.25

(b) Under Taylor's differential piece rates :

Worker A = 65 Units × 0.20 Ps = Rs. 13.00

Worker B = 85 Units × 0.30 Ps = Rs. 25.50.

Problem No. 11

Calculate the earnings of workers X and Y under (a) Straight piece rate (b) Taylor's differential piece rate system from the following information :

Standard production 12 Units per hour.

Normal Time rate Rs. 6 per hour.

In a day of 8-hour : X Produces 90 Units.

Y Produces 110 Units.

Differential rates to be applied as below :

80% of piece wage below standard.

120% of piece wages at or above standard.

Solution :

Standard production per hour — 12 Units.

Standard production per day of 8 hours = 8 × 12 = 96 Units.

Normal time Rate Rs. 6 per hour.

Normal piece Wages $\frac{6}{12}$ = 0.50 Ps per unit.

Workers	X	Y
Standard output	96 Units	96 Units
Actual output	90 Units	110 Units
Efficiency of standard	93.75% Below	113.5% Above
Rates to be applied	80% of 0.50 = 0.40 Ps	120% of 0.50 Ps = 0.60 Ps

Earnings of Workers as under :

(a) Straight Piece Rate = Rs. 0.50 Ps per unit :

Worker X = 90 Units × 0.50 = Rs. 45

Worker Y = 110 Units × 0.50 = Rs. 55

(b) Taylor's differential piece rate :

Worker X = 90 Units × 0.40 = Rs. 36

Worker Y = 110 × 0.60 Ps = Rs. 66

Remarks

The earning of workers under Taylor's differential piece rate system, the worker who produces less than the standard output is paid at lower piece rate i.e., less than the normal piece rate whereas the worker who produces at or above standard output he is paid more than the normal piece rate. Therefore the earnings of workers under this system differ disproportionately.

That is the slow worker or inefficient worker is penalised by paying low rate of wages and fast worker or efficient worker is encouraged by paying higher piece rate.

Problem No. 12

In a company the Standard Time for the Job is 16 hours and the basic wage rate is Rs. 8 per hour. As per the bonus scheme of the company, the worker is to receive his normal rate for hours actually worked and for half the hours saved.

Material cost for the Job is Rs. 79.40 and overhead are charged at Rs. 12 per labour hour.

Calculate :

(a) The earnings of two workers X and Y if they complete the Job in 10 hours and 13 hours respectively.

(b) Effective Labour cost in each case.

(c) The total cost of the Job in each case.

(K.U.D., April 1996)

Solution :

	Workers X	Workers Y
Standard time	16 Hrs	16 Hrs
Time taken	10 Hrs	13 Hrs
Time saved	6 Hrs	3 Hrs

(a) Earnings of Worker X = Time taken × Rate + ½(T.S × R)

= 10 × 8 + ½ (6 × 8)

= 80 + 24 = Rs. 104.00

Worker Y = 13 × 8 + ½ (3 × 8)

= 104 + 12 = Rs. 116.00

(b) Effective Labour Cost = $\frac{\text{Total Cost}}{\text{Hours worked}}$

Worker X = $\frac{104}{10}$

= Rs. 10.40 Rs. 10.40 per hour

Worker Y = $\frac{116}{13}$

= Rs. 8.92 Rs. 8.92 per hour

(c) Total Job Cost

	Worker – X	Worker – Y
Material	79.40	79.40
Labour	104.00	116.00
Overhead Rs. 12 per hour :		
Worker X = 10 Hours × 12	120.00	
Worker Y = Rs. 12 × 13 Hours		156.00
Total Job Cost	Rs. 303.40	351.40

	Worker X	Worker Y
Standard time for the Job	16 Hours	16 Hours
Actual hours worked (Time taken)	10	13
Time saved	6 Hours	3 Hours
Basic rate per hour	Rs. 8	Rs. 8

Problem No. 13

The following particulars apply to a job :

Standard production per hour — 12 units.

Normal rate per hour — Re. 0.60

In a day of 8 hours :

A Produces 64 units.

B Produces 96 units.

C Produces 84 units.

D Produces 100 units.

Calculate the wages of these workers under Merrick's Differential Piece Rate System.

(K.U.D., October 1995)

Solution : (Merrick's Differential Piece Rate Method)

(1) Up to 83% efficiency — Basic Piece rate is paid.

(2) From 83 to 100% efficiency — @ 110% of Basic piece rate.

(3) At or above 100% efficiency — @ 120% of Basic piece rate.

Standard production per hour — 12 units.

Normal Rate per hour — Re. 0.60

Normal Rate per unit — Re. $\frac{0.60}{12} = 0.05$ Paise.

Standard Production per day of 8 hours — $8 \times 12 = 96$ units.

Levels of efficiency — Piece Rate Applicable

$$(\text{Efficiency} = \frac{\text{Actual output}}{\text{Standard output}} \times 100)$$

$$A = \frac{64}{100} \times 100 = 67\% = \text{Basic Rate Price} = 0.05 \text{ paise.}$$

$$B = \frac{96}{100} \times 100 = 100\% = 120\% \text{ of } 0.05 = 0.06 \text{ paise.}$$

$$C = \frac{84}{100} \times 100 = 87.5\% = 110\% \text{ of } 0.05 = 0.055.$$

$$D = \frac{100}{96} \times 100 = 104\% = 0.06.$$

Worker : A — Output — 64 units = Rate 0.05 paise per unit.
$64 \times 0.05 = 3.20 =$ Rs. 3.20

B — 96 units Rate 0.06 paise per unit.
$96 \times 0.06 = 5.76 =$ Rs. 5.76

C — 84 units — rate 0.055
$84 \times 0.055 = 4.62 =$ Rs. 4.62

D — 100 units Rate 0.06
$100 \times 0.06 = 6.00 =$ Rs. 6.00

Workers	Output	% of efficiency	Rate per unit		Amount (Rs.)
A	64	67%	0.05	Basic Rate	3.20
B	96	100%	0.06	120% of Basic	5.76
C	84	87.5%	0.055	110% of Basic	4.62
D	100	104%	0.06	120% of Basic	6.00

Problem No. 14

The following particulars are related to a product :
Standard output per day of 8 hours — 8 units.
Normal wage per day — Rs. 12.
Actual output by Ahmed in a day — 10 units.
Calculate the earnings of Ahmed and also the labour cost per unit under the following methods :

(a) Time Rate (b) Piece Rate
(c) Halsey Plan (d) Rowan Plan.

(K.U.D., April 1995)

Solution :

Standard output per day of 8 hours — 8 units.
Standard output per hour — 1 unit.
Normal wage per day — Rs. 12

$$\text{Normal wage per hour} = \frac{12}{8} = 1.50$$

Standard time per unit — 1 hour
Standard time for 10 units — 10 hours
Time taken — 8 hours.
Time saved (10 – 8) 2 hours.
Earnings of worker Ahmed :

(a) Time wage — per day of 8 hours — Rs. 12
Labour cost per unit — 12/10 = 1.20

(b) Piece wage — per unit 12/8 = 1.50 (Labour cost per unit 1.50)

Actual output = 10 × 1.50 = Rs. 15

(c) Halsey Plan $= T \times R + \frac{1}{2}(TS)R$

$= 8 \times 1.5 + \frac{1}{2}(2 \times 1.50)$

$= 12 + \frac{1}{2} \times 3$

Wage $= 12 + 1.5 = 13.50$

$$\text{Labour cost per unit} = \frac{13.50}{10} = 1.35$$

(d) Rowan Plan $= T \times R + T \times R \dfrac{(S - T)}{S}$

$$= 8 \times 1.50 + 8 \times 1.5 \frac{(10 - 8)}{10} = 14.40$$

Labour cost per unit = 14.40/10 = 1.44

Alternatively :

(a) Standard output per day 8 hours — 8 units
Standard output per hour = 8/8 = 1 unit
Normal wages per day of 8 hours = Rs. 12
Normal wage per hour = 12/8 = Rs. 1.50

(b) Standard time per unit = 10 × 1 = 10 hours
Time taken = 8 hours
Time saved (10 – 8) 2 hours
Rate per hour = Rs. 1.50

Table showing wages of worker Ahmed and the labour cost per unit

Particulars	Time wage	Piece wage	Halsey Plan	Rowan Plan
Wages =	No. of hour worked × Rate P.H.	Units of output × Rate per unit	$= T \times R + \frac{1}{2}(S - T)R$	$= T \times R + \frac{(S - T)}{S} T \times R$
Normal wage				
Rate per hour	Rs. 1.50			
Normal wage				
Rate per unit		Rs. 1.50		
Standard Time			10 hours	10 hours
Time taken			8 hours	8 hours
Rate per hour			Rs. 1.50	Rs. 1.50

Particulars	Time wage	Piece wage	Halsey Plan	Rowan Plan
Wage =	8 × 1.50	10 × 1.50	8 × 1.50 + ½(10 - 8)1.5	$T \times R + \frac{(S-T)}{S} T \times R$
	Rs. 12	Rs. 15	12 + ½ (2 × 1.50)	$8 \times 1.5 + \frac{(10-8)}{10} 8 \times 1.5$
			12 + 1.50	$12 + (\frac{2}{10} \times 12)$
			Rs. 13.50	12 + 2.40
				Rs. 14.40
Labour cost per unit =	12/10	15/10	13.50/10	14.40/10
	Rs. 1.20	Rs. 1.50	Rs. 1.35	Rs. 1.44

Problem No. 15

Calculate the earnings of workers Mohan and Sohan under Straight Piece Rate System and Taylor's Differential Piece Rate System from the following particulars :

Normal rate per hour — Rs. 6.00

Standard time per unit — 30 Seconds.

Differential piece rates :

80% of piece rate below standard.

120% of piece rate at or above standard.

Mohan and Sohan produce 800 Units and 1000 units respectively in a day of 8 hours.

(K.U.D., October 1994)

Solution :

Standard time per unit – 30 Seconds
For 1 Minute – 2 Units
For 60 Minutes – 60 × 2 = 120 Units per hour
For day of 8 hours – 8 × 120 = 960 Units.
Standard output per day (of 8 hours) – 960 Units.
Normal Rate per hour – Rs. 6
Normal output per hour = 120 Units.

$$\text{Normal Rate per unit} = \frac{6}{120} = 0.05 \text{ Ps.}$$

Earning of workers under :

(1) Straight Piece Rate — Mohan — Output = 800 Units × 0.05 = Rs. 40

Straight Piece Rate — Sohan — Output = 1000 Units × .05 = Rs. 50

(2) Time Wage = Rs. 6 per Hour.

Mohan – Worked 8 Hours = 8 × 6 = Rs. 48 per day

Sohan – Worked 8 Hours = 8 × 6 = Rs. 48 per day.

(3) Under Differential Piece rate system : (Taylor's Differential Piece Rate Method)

Standard output per day – 960 Units.

Normal Piece rate per unit – Re. 0.05 Ps.

Differential Piece rate – 80% of Piece rate below standard.

Rate applicable 80% of 0.05 Ps = 0.04 per unit.

120% of Piece rate at or above standard rate applicable – 120%

120% of 0.05 = 0.06 Ps.

Mohan output – 800 Units below standard = 800 × 0.04 = Rs. 32

Sohan output – 1000 Units above standard = 1000 × .06 = Rs. 60

OR : Earnings of workers under Differential Piece rate system :

Particulars	Workers	
	Mohan	Sohan
(1) Standard output in units	960 Units	960 Units
(2) Actual output	800 Units	1000 Units
(3) Percentage of Efficiency	83.33%	104%
(4) Efficiency	Below standard	Above standard
(5) Piece rate applicable	Low piece rate 80% of .05 0.04	High piece rate 120% of .05 0.06
(6) Wage for actual output	800 × .04 Rs. 32	1000 × .06 Rs. 60

OR : Earning of Workers :

Workers	Output	Efficiency	Time wage Rs. 6 per hour	Straight Piece rate – 0.05	Differential Piece rate (i) Low-0.04 (ii) High-0.06
Mohan	800	Below standard	8 × 6 Rs. 48	800 × 0.05 Rs. 40	800 × 0.04 Rs. 32
Sohan	1000	Above standard	8 × 6 Rs. 48	1000 × 0.05 Rs. 50	1000 × 0.06 Rs. 60

Problem No. 16

From the following particulars calculate the earnings of different workers under Taylor's differential piece rate system :

Standard time per unit – 6 minutes.

Normal rate – Rs. 5 per hour.

Differential Piece rates :

80% of piece rate below the standard.

120% of piece rate at or above the standard.

In a day of 8 hours, the production by different workers is as under :

Amar — 70 units; Badekhan — 80 units; Chaplin — 90 units;

Dharmsingh — 100 units.

(K.U.D., April 1994)

Solution : (Taylor's Differential Piece rate system)

Standard time per unit = 6 Minutes.

For one hour (60 minutes) = 60/6 = 10 units.

For one day of 8 hours = 8 × 10 = 80 units.

Standard output per day = 80 units.

Normal rate per hour = Rs. 5; Normal output per hour = 10 units.

Normal rate per unit = Rs. 5/10 = .50 Ps per unit.

Particulars	Amar	Badekhan	Chaplin	Dharmsingh
Standard output units	80	80	80	80
Actual output	70	80	90	100
Efficiency = $\frac{\text{Actual output}}{\text{Standard output}}$	$\frac{70}{80}$	$\frac{80}{80}$	$\frac{90}{80}$	$\frac{80}{100}$
Efficiency Standard	87.5% Below	100% At	112.5% Above	125% Above
Rate Applicable	80% of .50	120% of 0.50 Ps	120% of .50 Ps	120% of .50 Ps
Under Taylor's system (per unit)	0.40 Ps	0.60 Ps	.60Ps	.60 Ps
Wages under Taylor's (Units × Rate)	70 × .40 Rs. 28	80 × .60 Rs. 48	90 × .60 Rs. 54	100 × .60 Rs. 60
Wages under Piece rate (Output × normal)	70 × .50 Rs. 35	80 × .50 Rs. 40	90 × .50 Rs. 45	100 × .50 Rs. 50

Problem No. 17

On a day of 8 hours of work 8 units are to be produced. Hourly wage rate applicable to workers was Rs. 4. Units produced by four workers were : A — 5 Units, B — 10 Units, C — 7 Units, D — 8 Units.

As per Emmerson's Efficiency Plan worker are paid on time basis.

Efficiency	Bonus
From 66-2/3% up to 90% of standard	10% on time wage
At 100% efficiency	20% on time wage

For efficiency over and above 100% bonus will have to be paid at 1 per cent extra for 1 per cent increase in efficiency. Calculate the wages of four workers.

(Gulbarga, April 1994)

Solution :

Earnings of four workers under Emmerson's Efficiency Plan

Particular	Workers			
	A	B	C	D
(1) Standard output (in units)	8	8	8	8
(2) Actual output (in units)	5	10	7	8
(3) Percentage of Efficiency : $= \frac{\text{Actual output}}{\text{Standard output}} \times 100$	62.5%	125%	87.5%	100%
(4) Percentage of Bonus applicable	Nil	20% + 25% (45%)	10%	20%
	Rs.	Rs.	Rs.	Rs.
(5) Wages on time basic per hour Rs. 4 for 8 hours	32.00	32.00	32.00	32.00
(6) Bonus Payable	Nil	14.40	3.20	6.40
Total Wages (5 + 6)	32.00	46.40	35.20	38.40

Problem No. 18

Shri Sai Ltd. has introduced incentive scheme rated on efficiency as under :

Level of Efficiency	Bonus
Upto 70% of standard	Nil
Upto 80% of standard	5% of Basic Wage
Upto 90% of standard	10% of Basic Wage
Upto 100% of standard	15% of Basic Wage.

For an increase of every 1% of efficiency beyond 100%, the bonus also rises by 1%.

Wage Rate per hour Rs. 5.

Standard Time fixed for the job — 10 hours.

Calculate the earnings of workers A, B, C and D who could finished the job taking 8 hours, 9 hours, 10 hours, and 12 hours respectively.

(K.U.D., October 1993)

Statement showing earnings of Workers

Particulars	Workers			
	A	B	C	D
(1) Standard time in hour	10	10	10	10
(2) Actual time taken in hour	8	9	10	12
(3) Percentage of efficiency $= \frac{\text{Standard time}}{\text{Actual time taken}} \times 100$	125%	111%	100%	83.33%
(4) Percentage of Bonus (applicable of basic Wage)	15% + 25%	15 + 11%	15%	10%
(5) Wages – Rate of hour (Time taken × Rate per Hour)	8 × 5 Rs. 40	9 × 5 Rs. 45	10 × 5 Rs. 50	12 × 5 Rs. 60
(6) Bonus payable	40% of 40 Rs. 16	26% of 45 Rs. 11.7	Rs. 7.5	10% of 60 Rs. 6
Total Wages of workers (Wages + Bonus)	40 + 16 56	45 + 11.7 56.7	50 + 7.5 57.5	60 + 6 66

Problem No. 19

In a factory three workers X, Y and Z work in a team and are paid group piece rate. In a particular week they have spent on group piece work as follows :

X – 25 hours; Y – 50 hours; Z – 30 hours.

The balance of time has been spent by them on day work jobs. Their hourly rates are :

X – Re. 0.80; Y – Re. 0.90; Z – Re. 0.50

The group piece rate is 20 paise per unit and the team has produced 400 units in a week. Calculate the earning of workers, if working hours in a week are 50.

(K.U.D., April 1993)

Solution :

Calculation of time wages :	Balance of Hours worked :
X – 25 Hours × 0.80 = 20.00	50 – 25 = 25 × 0.80 = 20.00
Y – 50 Hours × 0.90 = 45.00	50 – 50 = — — —
Z – 30 Hours × 0.50 = 15.00	50 – 30 = 20 × 0.50 = 10.00

Group earnings : (In a week)

In a week = 400 × 0.25 = 100

Less : Time wages = 80

Bonus earned in group 20

Group Bonus shared by workers in proportion to the individual earning on time bases :

Earning	Time base	Ratio	Bonus Rs. 20
X –	20	4	X – 20 × $\frac{4}{16}$ = Rs. 5
Y –	45	9	Y – 20 × $\frac{9}{16}$ = Rs. 11.25
Z –	15	3	Z – 20 × $\frac{3}{16}$ = Rs. 3.75

Total Earnings of Workers :

Workers	Time Wage		Balance of hours		Group Bonus	Total
X	20	+	20	+	5.00	45
Y	45	+	–	+	11.25	56.25
Z	15	+	10	+	3.75	28.75

Problem No. 20

The following particulars apply to an operation of machine :

Standard time per piece — 30 seconds.

Normal rate per hour — Rs. 2.40

Differential rates to be applied : 80% of piece rate below Standard

120% of piece rate at or above Standard.

Worker A — produced 1000 Units per day.

Worker B — produced 900 Units per day of 8 hours.

Calculate the earnings of worker under :

(a) Straight piece rate system.

(b) Taylor's differential piece rate system.

(Gulbarga, April 1993)

Solution :

Standard time per unit — 30 seconds.

Standard output per minute = 60 seconds = 1 minute = 2 Units produced

Standard output per hour = 60 × 2 = 120 Units.

Standard output per day of 8 hours = 120 × 8 = 960 Units.

Normal wage rate per hour = Rs. 2.40

Normal output per hour = 120 Units.

Normal wage rate per unit = $\frac{2.40}{120}$ = 0.02 Ps per unit.

Wages under straight piece rate :

Worker A = Output 1000 units @ Re. 0.02 = Rs. 20

Worker B = Output 900 Units = Re. 0.02 × 900 = Rs. 18

Wages under Taylor's Differential piece rate system :

Worker A — Output $\frac{\text{actual}}{\text{standard}} = \frac{1000}{960} \times 100$ = 104% efficiency above standard

Wages Rate applicable 120% of piece rate i.e., 120% of 0.02 = 0.24

Earnings = Units produced × Rate applicable

= 1000 Units × 0.24 Ps

= Rs. 24.00

Worker B — Output $\frac{\text{actual}}{\text{standard}} = \frac{1000}{960} \times 100$ = 93.75% efficiency of standard.

Wage rate applicable below standard = 80% of 0.02 = 0.016

Wages = Units produced × Rate applicable

= 900 Units × 0.016

= Rs. 14.40

Problem No. 21

Calculate the earnings of a worker under Halsey and Rowan Plan for executing a piece of work in 60 hours as against 75 hours allowed. His hourly rate is .25 Ps per hour. He get a D.A. of Re. 1 per day of 8-hour work.

(K.U.D., October 1992)

Solution :

Halsey Plan

Earning = T × R + ½ (S − T) R

Where T = Time taken

S = Standard time or time allowed

R = Rate per hour

Time taken − 60 hours

Standard time − 75 hours (Time allowed)

Rowan Plan

Earning = $T \times R + T \times R \frac{(S - T)}{S}$

where T = Time taken

S = Standard time or time allowed.

R = Rate per hour.

Time taken − 60 hours

Standard time (Time allowed) = 75 hours

Rate per hour = 0.25 Ps	Rate per hour – 0.25 Ps.
Now Earning $= T \times R + \frac{1}{2} \frac{(S + T)}{S} R$	$E = T \times R + T \times R \frac{(S + T)}{S}$
$= 60 \times 0.25 + \frac{1}{2}(75 - 60) .25$	$= 60 \times 0.25 + 60 \times .25 \frac{(75 - 50)}{75}$
$= 15 + \frac{1}{2}(15 \times 0.25)$	$= 15 + 15 (\frac{15}{75})$
$= 15 + \frac{1}{2}(3.75)$	$= 15 + 3$
$= 15 + 1.875$	= Rs. 18
$= 15 + 1.875$	
= Rs. 16.875	
Total Earning = 16.875	Total Earning = Rs. 18.00
Add : D.A. Re. 1 per day	*Add* : D.A. $\frac{60}{8}$ = 7.50
$\frac{60}{8}$ = 7.50	
24.375	25.50

Alternatively

Earning = 60 × 0.25 =	15.00	Earning = 60 × 0.25 =	15.00
Bonus = ½ (15 × .25)	1.875	Bonus = 15 ($\frac{15}{75}$)	3.00
D.A = 7.50 × 1	7.50	D.A. = 7.50 × 1	7.50
Total Wages	24.375	Total Wages	25.50

Problem No. 22

What will be the earnings of a worker @ Rs. 2.50 per hour. When he takes 120 hours to do the Job for which standard time allowed is 200 hours. Bonus is paid on a sliding scale as follows :

(1) For the first 10% of savings in standard time Bonus is 30% of time saved.

(2) For the second 10% of savings in standard time Bonus is 40% of time saved.

(3) For the third 10% of savings in standard time Bonus is 50% of time saved.

(4) For the fourth 10% of savings in standard time Bonus is 60% of time saved.

(5) For the rest bonus is 70% of time saved.

(K.U.D., April 1992)

Solution :

Standard time	200 Hours
Time taken	120 Hours
Time saved	80 Hours

Percentage of time saved bears to standard time = $\frac{\text{Time Saved}}{\text{Standard time}} \times 100$

$= \frac{80}{200} \times 100 = 40\%$

Bonus Calculation :

			Rs.
(1) First 10% savings	= 200 × 10%	= 20 × 2.50 × 30% =	15.00
(2) Second 10% savings	= 200 × 10%	= 20 × 2.50 × 40% =	20.00
(3) Third 10% savings	= 200 × 10%	= 20 × 2.50 × 50% =	25.00
(4) Fourth 10% savings	= 200 × 10%	= 20 × 2.50 × 60% =	30.00
		Total Bonus	90.00

Bonus : First 10% = 30%

Second 10% = 40%

Third 10% = 50% $= \frac{180\%}{4} = 45\%$

Fourth 10% = 60%

180%

Time saved — 80 Hours : Bonus = 80 Hours × 2.50 × 45% = 90.00

Earnings of worker : E = T × R

= 120 × 2.50 300.00

Total Wages 390.00

Problem No. 23

What will be the earnings of a worker at Rs. 2.25 per hour when he takes 120 hours to do a work for which the standard time allowed is 200 hours. Bonus is paid on sliding scale as follows :

(a) For the First 10% savings in standard time Bonus is 30% of time saved.

(b) For the Second 10% savings in standard time Bonus is 40% of time saved.

(c) For the Third 10% savings in standard time Bonus is 50% of time saved.

(d) For the Fourth 10% savings in standard time Bonus is 60% of time saved.

(e) For the rest Bonus is 70% of time saved.

(K.U.D., April 1992)

Solution :

Standard time	200 Hours
Time taken	120 Hours
Time saved	80 Hours

Standard time 200 Hours. 10% of standard time 200 × 10% = 20 Hours.

Wages on time scale for actual hours worked Rate per hour — Rs. 2.25.

Wages = Actual hours worked × rate per hour

= 120 hours × 2.25 per hour

= Rs. 270

Add : Bonus on sliding scale :

(a)	First 10% savings in standard time 10% of 200 =	20 × 2.25 × 30% =	13.50
(b)	Second 10% savings in standard time 10% of 200 =	20 × 2.25 × 40% =	18.00
(c)	Third 10% savings in standard time 10% of 200 =	20 × 2.25 × 50% =	22.50
(d)	Fourth 10% savings in standard time 10% of 200 =	20 × 2.25 × 60% =	27.00
	Total time saved	80 hours	81.00

Wages for hours worked 120 × 2.25	270.00
Add : Bonus on sliding scale	81.00
Total Wages	351.00

Alternatively : *Bonus on sliding scale :*

1st 10% savings in standard time 10% × 200 =	20 Hours @	30% Bonus
2nd 10% savings in standard time 10% × 200 =	20 Hours @	40% Bonus
3rd 10% savings in standard time 10% × 200 =	20 Hours @	50% Bonus
4th 10% savings in standard time 10% × 200 =	20 Hours @	60% Bonus
Total time saved	80 Hours	180% Bonus

Total percentage of Bonus 180%, average per cent of Bonus $\frac{180}{4} = 45\%$

Bonus = Time saved × Rate per Hour × Average per cent of Bonus

= 80 × 2.25 × 45% = Rs. 81.00

Wages for hour worked 120 × 2.25 = Rs. 270.00

Total Wages Rs. 351.00

Problem No. 24

Shri Veerbhadrappa finished a piece of work in 480 hours as against 600 hours allowed. His hourly rate is Rs. 5. He gets Dearness allowance of Rs. 16 per day of 8 hours worked in addition to his wages.

Calculate his total income under :

(a) Halsey Plan and (b) Rowan Plan

(Mysore, 1992)

Solution :

Standard time (Time allowed)	600 Hours
Time taken	480 Hours
Time saved	120 Hours

Rate per hour Rs. 5

Halsey Plan

Earnings $= T \times R + \frac{1}{2}(S - T) R$

$= 480 \times 5 + \frac{1}{2}(600 - 480)\, 5$

$= 2{,}400 + \frac{1}{2}(120)\, 5$

$= 2{,}400 + \frac{1}{2}(600)$

$= 2{,}400 + 300$

= Rs. 2,700

Add : D.A.

$\frac{16}{8} \times 480 = 960$

Total Wages 3,660

Rowan Plan

Earnings $= T \times R + \frac{(S - T)}{S}\, T \times R$

$= 480 \times 5 + \frac{(600 - 480)}{600}\, 480 \times 5$

$= 2{,}400 + \frac{(120)}{600}\, 2{,}400$

$= 2{,}400 + 1/5 \times 2{,}400$

$= 2{,}400 + 480$

= Rs. 2,880

Add : D.A.

$\frac{16}{8} \times 480 = 960$

3,840

Problem No. 25

Find out remuneration of worker on the basis of (a) Day rate; (b) Piece rate; (c) Halsey plan; and (d) Rowan plan.

1. Name of the worker — Balasangi.
2. Ticket No. 40.
3. Work started 1-1-1991 at 8 a.m.
4. Work completed 5-1-1991 at 12 Noon.
5. Work allotted — Production of 540 units.
6. Work done and approved — 500 units.
7. Time and units allowed — 10 units per hour.
8. Wage rate — Re. 0.80 per hour.
9. Bonus — 40% of the time saved.
10. Worker worked for 9 hours a day.

(K.U.D., October 1991)

Solution :

Approved work = 500 Units.
Standard time for work done = 50 Hours for 500 Units.
Time taken is = 40 Hours (4 days and 4 Hours.)

			Earnings
(a)	Wages under Day Rate System	= 40 Hours × 0.80 =	Rs. 32.00
(b)	Wages under Piece work Rate System	= 50 Hours × 0.80 =	Rs. 40.00
(c)	Wages under Halsey Plan System :		
	40 Hours × 0.80	= Rs. 32.00	
	Bonus 10 Hours × 0.80	= Rs. 3.20	Rs. 35.20
(d)	Wages under Rowan Plan System :		
	40 Hours × 0.80	= Rs. 32.00	
	Bonus Rs. 32 × $\frac{10}{50}$	= Rs. 6.40	Rs. 38.40

Problem No. 26

The daily wage rate guaranteed for a worker is Rs. 1.80 and the standard output fixed for a week is 100 Units representing 100% efficiency. The guaranteed wage rate is paid without bonus to those workers who show efficiency upto 70% of the standard. Beyond this the bonus is payable on a graded scale in the fixed ratio to the increased output as follows :

Efficiency	Bonus payable
90%	10%
100%	20%

Further increase of 1% in bonus is given for every 1% increase in efficiency.

Calculate the total earnings of 4 workers who have worked for a week and their output is as follows :

Worker : A – 50 Units, B – 90 Units, C – 100 Units and D – 120 Units.

(K.U.D., April 1991)

Solution :

Earnings of workers under Emmerson's Efficiency Scheme

	Particulars	Workers			
		A	B	C	D
(1)	Standard output (in units)	100	100	100	100
(2)	Actual output (in units)	50	90	100	120
(3)	Percentage of efficiency $= \frac{\text{Actual output}}{\text{Standard output}} \times 100$	50%	90%	100%	120%
(4)	Bonus percentage payable	Nil	10%	20%	20% + 20%
(5)	Wages for week of 6 days daily wages 1.80 × 6 days	10.80	10.80	10.80	10.80
(6)	Bonus payable	—	1.08	2.16	4.32
	Total Earnings of workers	10.80	11.88	12.96	15:12

Problem No. 27

Anil and Sunil during a week of 49 hours as under :

Anil complete job 'X' in 20 hours against the standard time of 30 hours. He completed job 'Y' during the balance of the time in the week for which standard time was 35 hours.

Sunil completed job 'A' in 34 hours against the standard time of 30 hours. During the balance of the time the completed job 'B' for which standard time was 21 hours.

For jobs 'X' and 'A' Halsey Plan is applicable.

For jobs 'Y' and 'B' Rowan Plan is applicable.

Compute weekly earnings of the two workers. Basic time wage per hour is Rs. 12.

(K.U.D., October 1990)

Solution :

Worker — Anil

Total weekly working hours	48 hours
Completed Job 'X'	20 hours
Job 'Y' balance of figure	28 hours
Job – 'X' = Standard time	30 hours
Time taken	20 hours
Rate per hour	Rs. 12

Halsey Plan Earning $= T \times R + \frac{1}{2}\text{(Time saved)} \times R$

$= 20 \times 12 + \frac{1}{2}(30 - 20)\, 12$

$= 240 + \frac{1}{2}\, 10 \times 12$

$= 240 + \frac{1}{2}\, 120$

$= 240 + 60$

$= 300$

Worker — Sunil

Total weekly working hours	48 hours
Completed Job 'A'	34 hours
Completed Job 'B'	14 hours
Job 'A' Standard time	30 hours
Time taken	34 hours

He has taken more than the standard time. Therefore no premium under Halsey Plan.

Earning $= T \times R = 34 \times 12 = 408$

= Rs. 408

Worker — Anil

Under Rowan Plan :

Job 'Y'

Standard Time	35 hours
Time taken	28 hours

Rate per hour — Rs. 12

Rowan Plan earning $= T \times R + \frac{(S - T)}{S}\, T \times R$

(Worker Anil — Job-'Y') $= 28 \times 12 + \frac{(35 - 28)}{35}\, 28 \times 12$

$= 336 + \frac{1}{5} \times 336$

$= 336 + 67.5$

= Rs. 403.50

Worker — Sunil

Job – 'B' :		
	Standard Time	21 Hours
	Time taken	14 Hours
	Time save	7 Hours

$$\text{Rowan Plan Earning} = T \times R \frac{(S-T)}{S} T \times R$$

$$= 14 \times 12 + \frac{(21-14)}{21} 14 \times 12$$

$$= 168 + \frac{1}{3} \times 168$$

$$= 168 + 56$$

$$= \text{Rs. } 224$$

TAYLOR'S DIFFERENTIAL PIÈCE RATE

Problem No. 28

Calculate the earnings under Taylor's differential piece rate from the given information :

Rate per hour Rs. 6

Standard time per unit 30 minutes.

Differential piece rate to be applied

75% of piece rate below standard

125% of piece rate or above standard

In a 8 hours of a day the actual output of the worker are :

A – 15 Units, B – 25 Units and C – 16 Units.

(K.U.D., October 1990)

Solution :

Standard time per unit 30 minutes.

Standard output per hour 2 units.

Standard output per day of 8 hours = 8 × 2 = 16 Units.

Now standard output per day 16 units.

Normal rate per hour Rs. 6

Normal output per hour 2 units

Normal rate per unit = $\frac{6}{2}$ Rs. 3.

Particulars	Workers		
	A	B	C
Standard output per day in units	16	16	16
Actual output (in units)	15	25	16
Percentage of efficiency	93.75%	156.25%	100%
Differential piece rate to be applied	Below stand.	above stand.	at stand.
75% of piece rate below standard	75% × 3 = 2.25	125% × 3 = 3.75	3.75
Earnings of workers (Output × Rate)	15 × 2.25 Rs. 33.75	25 × 3.75 Rs. 93.75	16 × 3.75 Rs. 60

Problem No. 29

Ramesh runs a small Workshop and employs five workers skilled. The following particulars are extracted from his books for the month of March 1989.

Normal wage rate per worker per hour Rs. 2

Normal output 4 units per day of 8 hours.

Number of working days in a month 25 days.

Actual production during the month 625 Units

You are required to calculate :

(1) Total earnings of each worker.

(2) Effective rate of earnings per hour by each worker.

(3) Labour cost per unit under both incentive system (i.e., Halsey and Rowan).

(K.U.D., April 1990)

Solution :

Time allowed : Standard time :

Normal output 4 units per day of 8 Hours.

Normal time per unit = $\frac{8}{4}$ = 2 Hours.

Actual production during month 625 Units.

For worker time allowed for 625 units × 2 Hours = 1,250 Hours.

Time taken by workers 25 days × 8 Hours = 200 × 5 = 1,000 Hours.

Actual production for 5 workers 625 = $\frac{625}{5}$ = 125 Units Per Worker

Time allowed for 5 workers = 1,250 for 1 worker = 250 Hours.

Time taken by one worker 25 × 8 = 200 Hours.

Time saved by each worker 50 Hours.

Normal Rate per hour Rs. 2

(1) Halsey Plan :

(i) Earning = T × R + ½ (S – T) R

= 200 × 2 + ½ (250 – 200) × 2

= 400 + ½ (50 × 2) = 400 + 50 = 450.00

Effective Rate per hour = $\frac{450}{200}$ = Rs. 2.25

(ii) Labour cost per unit = Total wages paid Rs. 450.00

Total No. of units produced 125.00

Labour cost per Unit

Total Wages paid	450.00
Total No. of units produced	125 Units

Labour cost per unit $= \dfrac{450}{125} =$ Rs. 3.60

(2) Rowan Plan :

$$\text{Earning} = T \times R + \frac{(S - T)}{S} T \times R$$

$$= 200 \times 2 + \frac{(250 - 200)}{250} 200 \times 2$$

$$= 400 + \frac{50}{250} 400$$

$$= 400 + 80 = \text{Rs. } 480.00$$

(ii) Effective Rate per hour $= \dfrac{480}{200} =$ Rs. 2.40

(iii) Labour cost per unit $= \dfrac{480}{125} =$ Rs. 3.84

Earnings of Worker

	Halsey Plan	Rowan Plan
Normal Rate per hour Rs. 2		
Normal output per hour 2 Units.		
Normal cost of Normal output	(2 × 2)	(2 × 2)
	Rs. 4.00	Rs. 4.00
Under Incentive Scheme		
Labour cost	Rs. 3.60	Rs. 3.84
Savings in Labour cost (per Unit)	Re. 0.40 Ps	Re. 0.16 Ps

Problem No. 30

From the following particulars calculate total earnings of the three workers who are paid Merricks Differential piece rate system.

Efficiency	*Piece rate applicable*
Up to 83%	Normal rate applicable
Up to 100%	110% Normal Rate
Above 100%	120% of Normal Rate

Output of three workers for a week : A – 32 Units, B – 37 Units, C – 42 Units. Task output (Standard output) 40 units per week and Normal piece rate Rs. 5 per unit. Also find out their wages if they are paid on straight piece rate basis.

(Gulbarga, October 1990)

Solution :

Statement showing the Earning of workers under Merricks Differential Piece rate

Particulars	Workers		
	A	B	C
(1) Standard output for week	40 Units	40 Units	40 Units
(2) Actual output in units	32 Units	37 Units	42 Units
(3) Percentage of efficiency $\frac{\text{Actual output}}{\text{Standard output}} \times 100$	80%	92.5%	105%
(4) Differential piece rate	Rs. 5	Rs. 5.50	Rs. 6
(a) up to 83% Normal rate Rs. 5			
(b) 83% to 100% = 110% of 5 = Rs. 5.50			
(c) at or above 100% = 120% of 5 = Rs. 6			
Wages = output × Rate	32 × 5	37 × 5.50	42 × 6
	= Rs. 160	= Rs. 203.50	= Rs. 252

Earnings of workers under straight piece rate

Earnings = Actual output × Rate	32 × 5	37 × 5	42 × 5
Rs.	= 160	= 185	= 210

Problem No. 31

Amit and Sunit worked during a week of 48 hours. Amit completed Job–X in 20 hours against standard time of 30 hours.

He completed Job–Y during the balance of time in the week for which standard time was 35 hours.

Sunit : Completed Job–A in 34 hours against standard time of 30 hours during the balance of time he completed Job–B for which standard time was 21 hours.

For Job X and A Halsey plan is applicable, for Job Y and B Rowan plan is applicable. Calculate weekly earning of two workers. Basic time wage per hour is Rs. 12.

(K.U.D., October 1990)

Solution :

Earnings of workers under in a week of 48 Hours :

(a) *Halsey Plan* : Earnings = T × R + ½ (S – T) R

Amit : Job X	=	Standard time	30 Hours
		Time taken	20 Hours
		Time saved	10 Hours
Rate per hour	=	Rs. 12	
Earnings	=	T × R + ½ (S – T) R	
	=	20 × 12 + ½ (30 – 20)12	
	=	240 + ½ (10 × 12)	
	=	240 + 60	
	=	Rs. 300	
Sunit : Job X	=	Standard time	30 Hours
	=	Time taken	34 Hours
	=	Time saved	–4 " (No Bonus payable)
Earnings	=	T × R + ½ (S – T) R	
	=	34 × 12 + No savings in time	
	=	Rs. 408	

(b) *Rowan Plan* : Earnings = $T \times R + \frac{(S - T)}{S} \times T \times R$

Amit : Job Y	=	Standard Time	35 Hours
		Time taken (Balance 48 – 30)	28 Hours
		Time saved	7 Hours
		Rate per Hour Rs. 12.	

Earnings $= T \times R + \frac{(S - T)}{S} T \times R$

$= 28 \times 12 + \frac{(35 - 28)}{35} 28 \times 12$

= 336 + 7/35 × 336

= 336 + 1/5 × 336

= 336 + 67.20

= Rs. 403.20

Sumit :

Standard time	21 Hours
Time taken (48 – 34)	14 Hours
Time saved	7 Hours
Rate per Hour	Rs. 12

$$\text{Earnings} = T \times R + \frac{(S - T)}{S} T \times R$$

$$= 14 \times 12 + \frac{(21 - 14)}{21} 14 \times 12$$

$$= 168 + 7/21 \times 168$$

$$= 168 + 1/3 \times 168$$

$$= 168 + 56$$

$$= \text{Rs. } 224$$

Total Earnings of Workers :

Amit :	Job X – Halsey Plan	Rs.	300.00
	Job Y – Rowan Plan	Rs.	403.20
		Total Rs.	703.20
Sumit :	Job X – Halsey Plan	Rs.	408.00
	Job Y – Rowan Plan	Rs.	224.00
		Total Rs.	632.00

Problem No. 32

During first week of April 1989 a worker Mr. Kalyan manufactured 300 articles. He receives wages for 48 hours a week at the rate of Rs. 4 per hour. The standard time to produce one article is 10 (ten) minutes but under incentive scheme the time allowed is increased by 20%. Calculate his gross wages according to (1) Halsey Plan (2) Rowan Plan.

(Gulbarga, 1990)

Solution :

Ascertainment time taken and time allowed to produce 300 units.

Standard time to produce 1 unit 10 minutes

Standard time to produce 300 units = 300 × 10 = 3000

Standard time for 300 Units = $\frac{3000}{60}$ minutes = 50 Hours.

Time allowed under incentive scheme 20% of 50	= 10 Hours
Time allowed	60 Hours
Time taken	48 Hours
Time saved	12 Hours

Rate per hour — Rs. 4

Statement showing earnings of worker Mr. Kalyan

Particular	Halsey Plan	Rowan Plan
Earnings	$= T \times R + \frac{1}{2}(S - T)R$	$= T \times R + \frac{(S - T)}{S} T \times R$
	$= 48 \times 4 + \frac{1}{2}(60 - 48)\,4$	$= 48 \times 4 + \frac{(60 - 48)}{60} 48 \times 4$
	$= 192 + \frac{1}{2}(12 \times 4)$	$= 192 + \frac{12}{60} \times 192$
	$= 192 + \frac{1}{2}(48)$	$= 192 + \frac{1}{5} \times 192$
	$= 192 + 24$	
	= Rs. 216	$= 192 + 38.40$
		= Rs. 230.40

Problem No. 33

A worker takes 9 hours to complete a Job on daily wages and 6 hours on a scheme of payment by results. His day rate is Re. 0.75 Ps per hour. The material cost of the product is Rs. 4 and the overheads @ 150 per cent of total direct wages.

Calculate the factory cost of the product under : (a) Halsey Plan (b) Rowan Plan (c) Straight piece rate system.

(K.U.D., October 1983 & 85; Gulbarga, April 1991)

Solution :

Standard time 9 hours

Time taken 6 hours

Time saved 3 hours

Rate per hour Re. 0.75 per hour.

Statement showing Earnings of worker

Halsey Plan	Rowan Plan	Straight Plan
$E = T \times R + \frac{1}{2}(S - T)R$	$E = T \times R + (S - T)\,T \times R$	$E = T \times R$
$= 6 \times 0.75 + \frac{1}{2}(9 - 6)\,0.75$	$= 6 \times .75 + \frac{(9-6)}{9} \times .75$	$= 9 \times 0.75$
$= 4.50 + \frac{1}{2}(3 \times 0.75)$	$= 4.50 + 1/3 \times 4.50$	$= 6.75$
$= 4.50 + \frac{1}{2}(2.25)$	$= 4.50 + 1.50$	
$= 4.50 + 1.125$	= Rs. 6	
= Rs. 5.63	= Rs. 6	= Rs. 6.75

Factory cost of product

Particulars	Straight Piece Rate	Halsey Plan	Rowan Plan
Cost of Material	4.00	4.00	4.00
Wages	6.75	5.63	6.00
Prime Cost	10.75	9.63	10.00
Overheads 150% of Direct Wages	10.125	8.45	9.00
	20.88	18.08	19.00

Problem No. 34

Calculate that total wages payable to a worker under Halsey system and Rowan System from the following particulars :

Job No.	Time allowed	Time taken
1	25 Hours	20 Hours
2	30 Hours	28 Hours

The workers are entitled to a fixed D.A. of Rs. 100 per week of 48 hours and basic wage of Rs. 10 per hour.

(B'lore, October 1990)

Solution :

Wages Payable to worker

Particulars	Job No. 1	Job No. 2
Halsey Plan :		
Earnings = $T \times R + \frac{1}{2}(S - T) R$		
Time allowed	25 Hours	30 Hours
Time taken	20 Hours	28 Hours
Time saved	5 Hours	2 Hours
Rate per hour Rs. 10		
	$E = T \times R + \frac{1}{2}(S - T) R$	$E = T \times R + \frac{1}{2}(S - T) R$
	$= 20 \times 10 + \frac{1}{2}(25 - 20)\ 10$	$= 28 \times 10 + \frac{1}{2}(2 \times 10)$
	$= 200 + \frac{1}{2}(5 \times 10)$	
	$= 200 + 25$	$= 280 + 10$
	$= 225$	$= 290$
Add : D.A.	$= 100$	$= 100$
	Rs. 325	Rs. 390

Rowan Plan :

$$E = T \times R + \frac{(S - T)}{S}\ T \times R$$

Time allowed	25 Hours	30 Hours
Time taken	20 Hours	28 Hours
Time saved	5 Hours	2 Hours
	Rate per hour Rs. 10	Rate per hour Rs. 10

$$E = T \times R + \frac{(S - T)}{S} T \times R \qquad E = T \times R + \frac{(S - T)}{S} T \times R$$

$$= 20 \times 10 + \frac{(25-20)}{25} 20 \times 10 \qquad = 28 \times 10 + \frac{(30-28)}{30} 28 \times 10$$

$$= 200 + \frac{5}{25} \times 200 \qquad = 28 \times 10 + \frac{2}{30} 280$$

$$= 200 + \frac{1}{5} \times 200 \qquad = 280 + \frac{1}{15} \times 280$$

$$= 240 \qquad = 280 + 18.67$$

$$= 298.67$$

Add : D.A.	= 100	= 100.00
	Rs. 340	Rs. 398.67

Problem No. 35

Calculate total monthly remuneration of three workers X, Y and Z from the following details :

(a) Standard production per month per worker is 1000 Units.

(b) Actual Production during the month : X — 850 Units, Y — 750 Units, Z — 950 Units.

(c) Piece work rate .10 per unit of actual production.

(d) Additional production bonus is Rs. 10 for each percentage of actual production exceeding 80% actual production over standard

i.e., at 70% bonus

at 80% bonus

at 81 bonus is Rs. 10

at 82% bonus is Rs. 20 and so on.

(e) Dearness allowance Rs. 100 P.M. fixed.

(M'lore, October 1986 & Gulbarga, 1989)

Solution :

Monthly Wages of Workers

Particulars	Workers		
	X	Y	Z
(1) Standard output (in units)	1000	1000	1000
(2) Actual output (in units)	850	750	950
(3) Percentage of Efficiency	85%	75%	95%
(4) Percentage of Bonus applicable Up to 80% Bonus Nil At 81% Rs. 10 and for every 1% increase in efficiency Rs. 10 is payable	5% Rs.	Nil Rs.	15% Rs.
(5) Rate of Bonus Rs. 10	(5 × 10) 50	Nil —	(15 × 10) 150
(6) Wage Piece rate 0.10 Ps per unit	850 × 0.10 85	750 × 0.10 75	750 × 0.10 95
(7) D.A.	100	100	100
	185	175	195
Bonus Payable	50	—	150
Total Wages	235	175	345

Problem No. 36

The standard production in a factory is 10 units per hour for a day of 8 hours. The wage rate is Rs. 6 per hour. Bonus rated efficiency is paid according to a scale as follows :

Levels of Efficiency	Bonus Payable
Up to 60% of Standard	Nil
Above 60% and up to 75%	5%
Above 75% and up to 90%	10%
Above 90% and upto 100%	15%
At 100% of the standard	20%

For an increase of every 1% efficiency beyond 100% the bonus raises by 1%. The output of 6 workers on a day was as follows :

40 Units, 50 Units, 70 Units, 75 Units, 90 Units and 100 Units respectively. Tabulate the earnings of each worker under Emmerson's Efficiency Bonus Plan.

(K.U.D., April 1989)

Solution :

Statement showing Six (6) worker's wages under Emmerson's Efficiency Bonus Plan

Particulars	Workers 1	2	3	4	5	6
(1) Standard output 10 Units per hour for 8 hours (10 × 8)	80	80	80	80	80	80
(2) Actual output	40	50	70	75	80	100
(3) Percentage of efficiency	50%	62.5%	87.5%.	93.75%	112.5%	125%
(4) Bonus percentage applicable	Nil	5%	10%	15%	20%+12.5%	20%+25%
(5) Daily Wages Rs. 6 per hour for 8 hours (6 × 8)	48.00	48.00	48.00	48.00	48.00	48.00
(6) Bonus payable	—	2.40	4.80	7.20	15.60	21.60
Total Wages	48.00	50.40	52.80	55.20	63.60	69.60

Problem No. 37

Daily wage rate guaranteed to workers is Rs. 18 and the standard output fixed for a week of 6 working days is fixed at 100 articles in a factory. Emmerson's efficiency bonus plan is implemented.

The guarantee wage rate is paid without bonus to those workers who show efficiency upto 70% of standard. Beyond 70% efficiency bonus is payable as follows :

Efficiency	Bonus payable
90%	10%
100%	20%

Further increase of 1% in the bonus is given for every 1% increase in the efficiency. Calculate the total earnings of workers A, B, C and D whose output for a week was 50, 90, 100 and 120 Units respectively.

(Gulbarga, October 1988)

Solution :

Statement showing Earnings of workers

	Particulars	Workers			
		A	B	C	D
(1)	Standard output (in units)	100	100	100	100
(2)	Actual output (in units)	50	90	100	120
(3)	Percentage of efficiency	50%	90%	100%	120%
	$= \frac{\text{Actual output}}{\text{Standard output}} \times 100$				
(4)	Bonus payable	Nil	10%	20%	20% + 20%
(5)	Wages for a week (18 × 6)	108	108	108	108
(6)	Bonus Payable	—	10.80	21.60	43.20
	Total Earnings (5 + 6)	108	118.80	129.60	151.20

Problem No. 38

In Anoop Engineering company works standard time for a Job is 16 hours and the basic wage is Rs. 4 per hour. As per bonus scheme instituted by the company, that the worker is to receive his normal wage rate for hours actually worked and for half the hours saved as bonus at hourly rate.

Material for the Job cost Rs. 39.70 and the works on cost is charged on the basis of Rs. 6 per hour.

Calculate : (a) The earnings of the two workers A and B if they complete the Job in 10 hours and 13 hours respectively.

(b) Effect of Labour cost per hour.

(c) Total cost of Job in each case.

(K.U.D., April 1988)

Solution :

Standard time — 16 hours, Basic wage Rs. 4 per hour

Bonus ½ of time saved at hourly rate Job.

		Rs.
Worker-A : Standard time	16 Hours	
Actual hours worked	10 Hours	
Time Saved	6 Hours	
Wages for 10 hours × Rs. 4 (10 × 4)		40.00
Add : Bonus on time saved ½ (6 × 4)		12.00
Time Wages		52.00

Effective Labour cost $\frac{52}{10} = 5.20$

Worker-B :	Hour worked	13 Hours
	Standard time	16 Hours
	Time saved	3 Hours

Wages 13 × 4 =	52.00
Bonus ½ (3 × 4)	6.00
Time Wages	58.00

Labour cost $\frac{58}{13}$ = Rs. 4.46

Statement of Cost in each Case

Particulars	A	B
Material cost	39.70	39.70
Wages	52.00	58.00
Prime Cost	91.70	97.70
Works on cost hours worked @ Rs. 6	60.00	78.00
Total cost of Job	151.70	175.70

Problem No. 39

The standard production in a factory is 10 units per hour for a day of 8 hours. The wage rate is Rs. 16 per day. Bonus rated on efficiency is paid according to scale as follows :

Levels of Efficiency	Bonus % on day wage
Up to 60% of standard	Nil
Above 60% and up to 75%	5%
Above 70% and up to 90%	10%
Above 90% and up to 100%	15%

For an increase of every 1 per cent efficiency beyond 100 per cent efficiency the bonus also rises by 1 per cent. The output of five stokers on a day was as follows :

A — 50 Units, B — 70 Units, C — 75 Units, D — 90 Units, E — 100 Units.

Tabulate the earnings of each worker under Emmerson's Efficiency Plan.

(K.U.D., October 1987)

Solution :

Statement showing Earning of worker under Emmerson's Plan

Particulars	A	B	C	D	E
	Workers				
Standard production					
10 Units per hour for a day of 8 hours × 10	80	80	80	80	80
Actual output	50	70	75	90	100
Percentage of Efficiency	62.5%	87.5%	93.5%	112.5%	125%
Percentage of Bonus	5%	10%	15%	15% + 12.5%	15% + 25%
Day Wages Rs. 16	16.00	16.00	16.00	16.00	16.00
Bonus payable	0.80	1.60	2.40	4.40	6.40
Total Day Wages	16.80	17.60	18.40	20.40	22.40

Problem No. 40

The Standard output of a product has been fixed at 6 units are day of 8 hours in a factory. The normal wages per day is Rs. 12. Determine the total wages of the three workers under :

(a) Halsey Plan and (b) Rowan Plan. When their output has been : Mr. Mallappa — 8 units, Mr. Kallappa — 12 units, Mr. Basappa — 15 units.

(K.U.D., April 1987)

Mr. Mallappa : Output 8 Units

Standard output — 6 units for 8 hours.

For 8 units = $\frac{8}{6} \times 8 = \frac{64}{6} = 10.40$ minutes

Standard time for 8 units 10.40 minutes
Actual time taken 8.00 Hours
Time Saved 2.40 Hours

Normal Rate per day of 8 hours — Rs. 12

Normal rate per hour $\frac{12}{8}$ = Rs. 1.50

Wages Under Halsey Plan : Earnings = T × R + ½ (S – T) R

Earnings = 8 × 1.50 + ½ (10.40 – 8) 1.50

= 12 + ½ (2.40) 1.50

= 12 + 1.20 × 1.50

$$= 12 + \frac{4}{3} \times 1.50$$

$$= 12 + 2 = \qquad \text{Rs. } 14.00$$

Wages Under Rowan Plan : Earnings $= T \times R + \frac{(S - T)}{S} T \times R$

$$\text{Earnings} = 8 \times 1.50 + \frac{(10.40 - 8)}{10.40} 8 \times 1.50$$

$$= 12 + \frac{(2.40)}{10.40} 12$$

$$= 12 + \left(\frac{8}{3} \times \frac{3}{32}\right) 12$$

$$= 12 + 3 = \qquad \text{Rs. } 15.00$$

Mr. Kallappa Output — 12 Units in 8 Hours

Standard time for 6 units — 8 Hours

For 12 units $\frac{8}{6} \times 12 =$ — 16 Hours

Standard time for 12 units — 16 Hours

Time taken — 8 Hours

Time saved — 8 Hours

Normal rate per day of 8 hours Rs. 12

Normal Rate per hour $= \frac{12}{8} = 1.50$

Wages Under Halsey Plan :

$$\text{Earnings} = T \times R + \tfrac{1}{2} (S - T) R$$

$$= 8 \times 1.50 + \tfrac{1}{2} (16 - 8) 1.50$$

$$= 12 + \tfrac{1}{2} (8 \times 1.50)$$

$$= 12 + \tfrac{1}{2} (12)$$

$$= 12 + 6 = \qquad \text{Rs. } 18.00$$

Wages Under Rowan Plan :

$$\text{Earnings} = T \times R + \frac{(S - T)}{S} T \times R$$

$$= 8 \times 1.50 + \frac{(10 - 8)}{16} 8 \times 1.50$$

$$= 8 \times 1.50 + \frac{8}{16} \times 8.00 \times 1.50$$

$$= 12 + ½ \times 12$$

$$= 12 + 6 =$$ Rs. 18.00

Mr. Basappa : Output 15 Units

Standard time 6 units for 8 hours

For 15 units = $\frac{8}{6} \times 15 = 20$ hours

Standard time for 15 units	20 Hours
Time taken	8 Hours
Time saved	12 Hours

Normal Rate per hour $\frac{12}{8}$ = Rs. 1.50

Wages Under Halsey Plan :

Earnings $= T \times R + ½ (S - T) R$

$= 8 \times 1.50 + ½ (20 - 8) 1.50$

$= 12 + ½ (12) 1.50$

$= 12 + 6 \times 1.50$

$= 12 + 9 =$ Rs. 21.00

Wages Under Rowan Plan :

Earnings $= T \times R \ \frac{(S - T)}{S} \ T \times R$

$$= 8 \times 1.50 + \frac{(20 - 8)}{20} \ 8 \times 1.50$$

$$= 12 + (\frac{12}{20}) \ 12$$

$$= 12 + \frac{36}{5}$$

$= 12 + 7.20 =$ Rs. 19.20

	Halsey Plan Rs.	Rowan Plan Rs.
Mr. Mallappa	14.00	15.00
Mr. Kallappa	18.00	18.00
Mr. Basappa	21.00	19.20

Note : From the above it is clear that Mr. Basappa for worker more efficient saves more time and the bonus he get under Rowan Plan is less than the Bonus in Halsey plan and therefore Rowan Plan bonus scheme is disadvantage to a fast worker or more efficient worker.

Problem No. 41

A and B two Workers earn their Wages as under :

Particulars	Worker A	Worker B
(a) Basic Wages	1,000	1,000
(b) Dearness allowance	50%	70%
(c) Provident Fund	8%	8%
(d) Employees State Insurance	2%	2%
(e) Overtime worked	10 Hours	—
(f) Idle time	—	20 Hours

Normal working hours for the month are 200 hours; overtime is paid double the normal rate (Basic Wage) plus D.A. only.

Employer's contribution toward Employees Provident Fund and State Insurance are at equal rates with employees contribution.

This month has 25 working days and one day paid holiday.

Your are required to :

(a) Calculate their total earnings for the month.

(b) Calculate normal wage per hour and overtime wage per hour.

(K.U.D., October 1986)

Solution :

Statement showing Wages of two Workers

Particulars	Workers A	Workers B
(1) Basic wage	1,000	1,000
(2) Dearness allowance 50% and 70%	500	700
(3) Provident Fund 8% and 8%	80	80
(4) E.S.I. 2% and 2%	20	20
(5) Overtime allowance : A = 10 hours at double the rate Basic Wage 1,000; *Add* : D.A. 500; 1,500 / Working hours 200 = 7.50 × 2 × 10 =	150	—
Total Wages	1,750	1,800

Particulars			Workers A	Workers B
Basic Wage			1,000	1,000
D.A.			500	700
Provident Fund			80	80
E.S.I.			20	20
	Normal total wages		1,600	1,800
	Normal working hour		200	
	Normal wages per hour		Rs.	Rs.
Worker-B =	Normal Wages			1,800
	Total working hours	200		180
	Less : Idle time	20		10
	Overtime per hour		15	—
	Normal wages per hour		8	10
	Overtime		15	

Problem No. 42

From the following particulars calculate the earnings of two workers 'A' and 'B' under following methods :

(a) Straight piece rate system (b) Taylor's differential piece rate system.

Standard time per unit — 36 seconds.

Normal rate per hour — Rs. 3

Differential piece rates to be applied.

80% of piece rate when below standard.

120% of piece rate at or above standard.

The output produced by worker in a day of 8 hours.

A — 700 Units, B — 900 Units.

(K.U.D., April 1986)

Solution :

Standard time per unit = 36 Seconds

Standard output per hour i.e., 1 minute = 60 Seconds

60 Minutes = 1 Hour = 60 × 60 = 3600 Seconds

For one unit 36 Seconds $\frac{3600}{36}$ = 100 Units.

Standard output per hour = 100 units.

Normal rate per hour = Rs. 3

Normal rate per unit = Rs. $\frac{3}{100}$ = 0.03 Ps.

Wages under straight piece rate = T × R

Worker A = 700 Units × 0.03 = Rs. 21.00

Worker B = 900 Units × 0.03 = Rs. 27.00

Under Differential piece rate :

Standard output per hour = 100 Units.

Standard output per day 8 hours = 8 × 100 = 800 Units.

Particulars	Worker A	Worker B
(1) Standard output	800 Units	800 Units
(2) Actual output	700 Units	900 Units
(3) Efficiency	Below Standard	Above Standard
(4) Differential piece rate applicable	80% of 0.03 = 0.024	120% of 0.03 = 0.036
(5) Earnings = Units produced × Rate	700 × 0.024 = Rs. 16.80	900 × 0.36 = Rs. 32.40

Problem No. 43

The standard output of product has been fixed at 6 units per day of 8 hours. The normal wage rate per day is Rs. 12. Determine the total wages including bonus payable as under :

(1) Halsey Plan (2) Rowan Plan of wage payment when the output are 5 units, 8 units, 12 units and 15 units per day.

Calculate also the labour cost per unit in each case.

(Gulbarga, April 1986)

Solution :

Standard time 8 hours for 6 units

Standard time for 1 unit $\frac{8}{6}$ = 1.20 Hours

Normal wage rate per day of 8 hours = Rs. 12

Normal wage rate per hour = $\frac{12}{8}$ = Rs. 1.50 Ps

Case No. 1

Output 5 units produced in 8 hours a day

Standard time for 1 unit = 1.20 Hours

Standard time for 5 units = 5 × 1.20 Hour = 6.40 Hours

Time taken to produced 5 units 8.00 Hours

Time saved – negative −1.20 Hours

In this case no bonus is applicable

Now Wages = Time taken × Rate per hour

= 8 × 1.50 = Rs. 12 — No bonus

Labour cost per unit = Rs. $\frac{12}{5}$ = Rs. 2.40

Note : Under Halsey plan and Rowan plan Bonus becomes payable only on the basis of time saved. In this case time taken is more than the Standard time fixed for output. Therefore, the workers will get only wages at hourly rate. In both the Plans the wages payable remain the same.

Case No. 2

Output 8 units in a day of 8 hours

Standard time for 1 unit = 1.20 Hours

Standard time for 8 units = 8 × 1.20 =	10.40 Hours
Time taken to produce 8 units	8.00 Hours
Time saved	2.40 Hours

Rate per hour Rs. 1.50 Ps.

Wages Under Halsey Plan :

$$\text{Wages} = T \times R + \tfrac{1}{2}(S - T)R$$

$$= 8 \times 1.50 + \tfrac{1}{2}\left(\frac{2.40}{60} \times 1.50\right)$$

$$= 12 + \tfrac{1}{2}\left(\frac{8}{3} \times 1.50\right)$$

$$= 12 + \tfrac{1}{2}(4)$$

$$= 12 + 2$$

$$= 14.00$$

Labour cost per unit = $\frac{14}{8}$ = Rs. 1.75

Wages Under Rowan Plan :

$$\text{Wages} = T \times R + \frac{(S - T)}{S} T \times R$$

$$= 8 \times 1.50 + \frac{\frac{(2.40 - 8)}{60}}{10.40} 8 \times 1.50$$

$$= 12 + \left(\frac{\frac{2.40}{60}}{\frac{10.40}{60}} \times 12 \right)$$

$$= 12 + \left(\frac{\frac{8}{3}}{\frac{32}{3}} \times 12 \right)$$

$$= 12 + (8/3 \times 3/32 \times 12)$$

$$= 12 + 3$$

$$= \text{Rs. } 15.00$$

Labour cost per unit = $\frac{15}{8}$ = Rs. 1.875

Case No. 3

Output 12 Units

Standard time for 1 unit = 1.20 Hours

Standard time for 12 units = 1.20 × 12 = 16 Hours

Time taken 8 Hours

Time saved 8 Hours

Rate per hour Rs. 1.50 Ps

Under Halsey Plan :

$$\text{Wages} = T \times R + ½ (S - T) R$$

$$= 8 \times 1.50 + ½ (16 - 8) 1.50$$

$$= 12 + ½ (8 \times 1.50)$$

$$= 12 + 6$$

$$= \text{Rs. } 18$$

Labour cost per unit = $\frac{18}{12}$ = Rs. 1.50

Under Rowan Plan :

$$\text{Wages} = T \times R + \frac{(S - T)}{S} T \times R$$

$$= 8 \times 1.50 + \frac{(16 - 8)}{16} 8 \times 1.50$$

$$= 12 + \frac{8}{16} \times 12$$

$= 12 + 6$

$=$ Rs. 18

Labour cost per unit $= \frac{18}{12} =$ Rs. 1.50

Case No. 4

Output 15 units in a day of 8 hours

Standard time for 1 unit = 1.20

Standard time for 15 units = 15 × 1.20

Standard time = 20 Hours.

Normal wage Rate per hour Rs. 1.50

Under Halsey Plan :

Wages $= T \times R + \frac{1}{2} (S - T) R$

$= 8 \times 1.50 + \frac{1}{2} (20 - 8) 1.50$

$= 12 + \frac{1}{2} (12 \times 1.50)$

$= 12 + \frac{1}{2} (18)$

$= 12 + 9$

$=$ Rs. 21

Labour cost per unit $= \frac{21}{15} =$ Rs. 1.40

Under Rowan Plan :

Earnings $= T \times R + \frac{(S - T)}{S} T \times R$

$= 8 \times 1.50 + \frac{(20 - 8)}{20} 8 \times 1.50$

$= 12 + (\frac{12}{20}) 12$

$= 12 + 7.20$

$=$ Rs. 19.20

Labour cost per unit $= \frac{19.20}{15} =$ Rs. 1.28

Summary statement showing wages in each case under Halsey plan and Rowan plan and Labour cost per unit

Case No.	Output (in units)	Halsey Plan Rs.	Labour Cost per unit Rs.	Rowan Plan Rs.	Labour cost per unit Rs.
Case No. 1	5	12.00	2.40	12.00	2.40
Case No. 2	8	14.00	1.75	15.00	1.875
Case No. 3	12	18.00	1.50	18.00	1.50
Case No. 4	15	21.00	1.40	19.20	1.28

Note : Case No. 3 output 12 units and time saved 8 hours.

(a) Time taken is ½ of standard. The wages in both under Halsey plan and Rowan plan remain the same. Worker gets equal wage in both cases. So, difference between Halsey and Rowan plan is eliminated.

(b) Case No. 4 : Time saved is more that half of the standard time and may be identified as fast worker or more efficient worker.

The bonus amount earned under Rowan Plan is less that the bonus under Halsey Plan. Therefore, the scheme Bonus under Rowan plan is disadvantageous to a fast worker or efficient worker.

Problem No. 44

Two fitters, a labourer and a boy undertake a work on a piece work basis for Rs. 600. Time spent by each worker is 220 ordinary working hours and the rates of pay are :

For two fitters — Re. 0.75 Ps each per hour

For one Labour — Re. 0.50 Ps per hour

Boy — Re. 0.25 Ps per hour

Ascertain the amount of piece work premium and show the amount of it which each worker will receive when it is divided proportionately to the wages paid and show in each case the percentage of the premium bears to the wages payment at ordinary rate to the amount paid for working up :

Add : the cost of material	1,200
Proportion of overhead	450
Of selling expenses	300
For carriage charges	200

Give the total cost?

To return the manufacturer 20% of the total cost at which price must he sell. What will be the profit if reckoned on selling price.

(K.U.D., April 1985)

Solution :

Earnings of workers at ordinary Rate

		Rs.
Fitters	2 × 220 × 0.75 Ps =	330.00
Labour	1 × 220 × 0.50 Ps =	110.00
Boy	1 × 220 × 0.25 Ps =	55.00
	Total Wages	495.00
	Total payment received	600.00
	Premium amount	105.00

Bonus amount paid to worker in proportion to wages

			Ratio			
Fitter 1	Wages	165	3	105 × 3/9	= 35.00	21.20%
Fitter 2	Wages	165	3	105 × 3/9	= 35.00	21.20%
Labour 1	Wages	110	2	105 × 2/9	= 23.33	21.20%
Boy 1	Wages	55	1	105 × 1/9	= 11.67	21.20%
					105.00	

Statement of cost profit and sales Price

		Rs.
Material cost		1,200
Wages (including premium)		600
Prime Cost		1,800
Works overhead		450
Works cost		2,250
Selling and Distribution Expenses :		
Selling Expenses	300	
Carriage charges	200	500
Total cost		2,750
Profit 20 per cent on cost (2,750 × 20%)		550
Selling price		3,300

$$\text{Profit on selling price} = \frac{550}{3,300} \times 100 = 16.67\%$$

Problem No. 45

A batch of four workers consisting of two fitters, a labourers, and a helper undertake a work on piece work basis for Rs. 600. The time spent by each worker is 220 ordinary working hours and the rates of pay are as follows :

For Fitter Rs. 0.75 Ps per hour

For Labourer Rs. 0.25 Ps per hour

For Helper Rs. 0.25 Ps per hour.

Ascertain the amount of piece work premium and show the amount of it which each worker will receive when it is divided proportionately to the time wages paid and show in each case the percentage of premium bears to the wage payment at ordinary rates.

(K.U.D., April 1985)

Solution :

Wages at ordinary rates

	Rs.
Fitter 2 @ Re. 0.75 per hour for 220 hours = 2 × 0.75 × 220 =	330.00
Labour @ Re. 0.25 per hour for 220 hours = 0.25 × 220 =	55.00
Helper @ Re. 0.25 per hour for 220 hours = 0.25 × 220 =	55.00
Total Wages	440.00

Total Payment on piece worth	600.00
Total wages on time basis	440.00
Bonus for worker on piece work of Rs.	160.00

Premium amount is to be distributed among workers on the basis of wages earned :

1st Fitter wages on time bases	Rs. 165	3	3/8
2nd Fitter wages on time bases	Rs. 165	3	3/8
1 Labourer wages on time bases	Rs. 55	1	1/8
1 Helper wages on time bases	Rs. 55	1	1/8

		Rs.
Premium payment to 1st Fitter	= 160 × 3/8 =	60.00
2nd Fitter	= 160 × 3/8 =	60.00
Labour	= 160 × 1/8 =	20.00
Helper	= 160 × 1/8 =	20.00
		160.00

Problem No. 46

Vikas Ltd. has introduced a Bonus system wage payment on a scale rate based on cost reduction and overheads.

The slab rates are as follows :

Up to 10% of savings	5% of the earnings
Up to 20% of savings	15% of the earnings
Up to 40% of savings	30% of the earnings
Up to 70% of savings	40% of the earnings
Above 70% savings	50% of the earnings

The hourly rates of the 3 workers are as under :

A — 0.50 Ps, B — 0.60 Ps, C — 0.55 Ps.

The overhead recovery rate is 500 per cent of the productive wages. The standard cost toward wages and overheads per unit is determined at Rs. 1.20 per unit. If the time taken by A, B and C of finish 100 Units is 26 hours, 30 hours and 20 hours respectively, what is the amount of bonus earned by 3 workers.

(K.U.D., October 1985)

Solution :

Statement showing per cent of savings in cost and Bonus

Worker	Hours taken	Basic Wages P.H.	Total Basic Wage	Overhead 500% on Wage	Total Cost	Standard Cost 100×1.20	Savings cost	Savings in %	Bonus %	Bonus Paid
		(in Ps)	Rs.	Rs.	Rs.	Rs.	Rs.			Rs.
A	26	0.50	13.00	65.00	78.00	120.00	42.00	35%	30%	3.90
B	30	0.60	18.00	90.00	108.00	120.00	12.00	10%	5%	0.90
C	20	0.55	11.00	55.00	66.00	120.00	54.00	45%	45%	4.40

Problem No. 47

Calculate total monthly remuneration of three workers A, B and C from the following data :

(a) Standard production per month per worker 1000 Units. Actual production during the month : A — 850 units, B — 750 Units and C — 950 Units.

(b) Piece work rate 10 Ps per unit (actual production).

(c) Additional production bonus Rs. 10 for each percentage or actual production exceeding 80% — actual production over standard. (eg: 79% Nil, 80% Nil, 81% — Rs. 10, 82% — Rs. 20).

(d) Dearness allowance fixed Rs. 500 per month.

(K.U.D., October 1984)

Solution :

Statement showing total monthly remuneration of workers

Particulars	Workers A	B	C
(1) Standard production (in units)	1000	1000	1000
(2) Actual production (in units)	850	750	950
(3) Bonus payable	85%	75%	95%
Rs. 10 for each percentage	(10 × 5)	—	(10 × 15)
exceeding 80% of standard	50	—	150
(5) Piece Wage Re. 0.10 per unit	85	75	95
(6) Dearness allowances	50	50	50
Total Wages (4 + 5 + 6)			
Monthly remuneration of workers	185	125	295

Problem No. 48

A workman whose basic pay is Rs. 2 per hour is working under Rowan Plan of premium bonus. In addition he receives a cost of living bonus of Rs. 33 per week of 44 hours. During a week he does the following Jobs :

(i) Job X — for which 30 hours are allowed completed in 20 hours.

(ii) Job Y — for which 36 hours allowed completed in 20 hours.

Calculate the workman's earnings and the amount to be charged to each and overhead.

(Gulbarga, October 1984)

Solution :

Statement showing Wages under Rowan Plan

Particulars	Job – X	Job – Y
Standard time	30 Hours	36 Hours
Time taken	20 Hours	20 Hours
Time saved	10 Hours	16 Hours
Rate per hour	Rs. 2	Rs. 2

Wages =

$$T \times R + \frac{(S - T)}{S} T \times R = 20 \times 2 + \frac{(30-20)}{30} 20 \times 2 \qquad = 20{\times}2 + \frac{(36-20)}{36} 20{\times}2$$

$$= 40 + \frac{10}{30} \times 40 \qquad = 40 + \frac{16}{36} 40$$

$$= 40 + 13.33 \qquad = 40 + 17.77$$

$$= \text{Rs. } 53.33 \qquad = \text{Rs. } 57.77$$

Cost of living Bonus is Rs. 33 for 44 hours week. It is proportionately distributed to Job X and Job — Y

$$= \frac{33}{44} \times 20 \qquad = \frac{33}{44} \times 20$$

$$= \text{Rs. } 15 \qquad = \text{Rs. } 15$$

	Job X	Job Y	Total
Wages	Rs. 53.33	Rs. 57.77	Rs. 111.00
Bonus	Rs. 15.00	Rs. 15.00	Rs. 30.00
Overhead	—	—	Rs. 8.00
Total	68.33	72.77	149.00

Problem No. 49

The standard production in a factory is 10 units per hour for a day of 8 hours. Wage rate is Rs. 6 per day. Bonus rated on efficiency is paid according to scale as follows :

Levels of efficiency	Bonus
Upto 60% standard	Nil
Above 60% and up to 75%	5%
Above 75% and up to 90%	10%
Above 90% and up to 100%	15%

For an increase of every 1 per cent efficiency beyond 100 per cent efficiency, the bonus also rises by 1 per cent.

The output of 6 workers on a day was as follows :

A — 40 Units, B — 50 Units, C — 70 Units, D — 75 Units, E — 90 Units and F — 100 Units. Tabulate the earnings of each worker under Emmerson's Efficiency Plan.

(K.U.D., April 1983)

Solution :

Statement showing the earning of 6 workers

Particulars	Workers					
	A	B	C	D	E	F
(1) Standard output for 1 hour - 10 Units (8 × 10 = 80)	80	80	80	80	80	80
(2) Actual output	40	50	70	75	90	100
(3) Percentage of efficiency	50%	62.5%	87.5%	93.5%	112.5%	125%
(4) Bonus percentage applicable	—	5%	10%	15%	15%+12.5% (27.5%)	15%+25% (40%)
(5) Day Wages Rs. 6	6.00	6.00	6.00	6.00	6.00	6.00
(6) Bonus payable	—	0.30	0.60	0.90	1.65	2.40
Total Wages for one day	6.00	6.30	6.60	6.90	7.65	8.40

Problem No. 50

In an Assembly shop P, Q and R work in a team on a Group Job for which they are paid on piece work rate and also on day rate Job. In a 40 hours week they booked the following hours on Group Job which carried a piece wage of Rs. 120, and the balance of hours being spent on individual day rate Job.

Worker	Hours Booked on Group Bonus	Wage rate per hour
P	30 Hours	Rs. 2.00
Q	25 Hours	Rs. 3.00
R	30 Hours	Rs. 1.50

Each worker gets D.A. at Rs. 10 per week.

Tabulate the weekly earning of workers.

(K.U.D., April 1982)

Solution :

Statement showing Group Earnings

Worker	Hours Worked	Rate per Hour	Amount	Ratio	Share in the Group Earnings	
		Rs.				
P	30 Hours	2.00	60.00	4	4/12 × 120 =	40.00
Q	25 Hours	3.00	75.00	5	5/12 × 120 =	50.00
R	30 Hours	1.50	45.00	3	3/12 × 120 =	30.00
		Total Group Wages Rs.				120.00

Statement showing Balance of Hours worked at day Rate

Worker	Balance	Rate per Hour	Amount
P	(40 – 30) 10	Rs. 2.00	20.00
Q	(40 – 25) 15	Rs. 300	45.00
R	(40 – 30) 10	Rs. 1.50	15.00

Statement showing total wages of worker for the week

	P	Q	R
Group Earning	40.00	50.00	30.00
Earnings on Balance of Hours worked	20.00	45.00	15.00
Dearness Allowance	10.00	10.00	10.00
Total Wages	70.00	105.00	55.00

Problem No. 51

What do you understand by Group Incentive Scheme?

In a unit 10 Men work as a Group when the production of the Group exceeds the standard output of 200 units per hour, each man is paid an incentive for the excess production in addition to his wages at hourly rate. The incentive is at half the percentage, the excess production over standard bears to the standard production. Each man (worker) is paid an incentive at the rate of this percentage of wage rate of Rs. 2 per hour. There is no relation between the Individual workman's hourly rate and the Bonus rate. In a week, the hours worked are 500 and the total production is 1,20,000 Units.

(1) Calculate the total amount of Bonus for the week.

(2) Calculate the total earnings of two workers A and B of the group.

Worker A : Worked for 44 hours and the basic rate per hour is Rs. 2.20.

Worker B : Worked for 48 hours and the basic rate per hour is Rs. 1.90.

(K.U.D., April 1981)

Solution :

Actual output per week	1,20,000 Units
Standard output per week for 500 Hours 200 Units per hour	1,00,000 Units
Excess units of output	20,000 Units

Percentage of excess output to standard output = $\frac{20,000}{1,00,000} \times 100 = 20\%$

Bonus rate per hour = Rate per hour × ½ × per cent of excess output

= 2 × ½ × 20%

$= 2 \times \frac{10}{100}$

= Re. 0.20 Ps

Total Bonus = Hours worked × Rate per hour

= 500 × 0.20 = Rs. 100.

Particulars	Worker-A	Worker-B
(1) Hours worked	44 Hours	48 Hours
(2) Rate per Hour	Rs. 2.20	Rs. 1.90
(3) Wages = Hour worked × Rate p.h	= 44 × 2.20	= 48 × 1.90
	= 96.80	= 91.20
Bonus @ Hourly rate 0.20		
Worker A = 44 × 0.20	= 8.80	
Worker B = 48 × 0.20		= 9.60
Total earnings	105.60	100.80

Problem No. 52

Find out the earnings of workers on the basis of Merrick's differential piece rate system from the following particulars :

Piece Rate — 0.10 Ps per unit

Standard production — 120 Units.

Worker : X produces — 90 Units.

Y produces — 100 Units.

Z produces — 130 Units.

Basic piece rate is guaranteed :

Up to 83% of standard production

Workers get premium above 83% as follows :

83% to 100% — 110% of ordinary piece rate

Over 100% — 120% of ordinary piecer rate.

(K.U.D., October 1980)

Solution :

Standard output — 120 Units.

Normal piece rate — 0.10 Ps per unit.

Levels of Efficiency : $\frac{\text{Actual output}}{\text{Standard output}} \times 100$	Rates applicable under Merrick's differential piece rate
Worker : X $\frac{90}{120} \times 100 = 75\%$ Efficiency	Basic Piece Rate — 0.10 Ps
Y $\frac{100}{120} \times 100 = 83.33\%$ Efficiency	110% of 0.10 Ps — 0.11 Ps
Z $\frac{130}{120} \times 100 = 104\%$ Efficiency	120% of .10 Ps — 0.12 Ps

Earnings of Workers

Straight Piece Rate	Merrick's Differential Piece Rate
Worker : X — 90 × 0.10 = Rs. 9.00	90 × 0.10 = Rs. 9.00
Y — 100 × 0.10 = Rs. 10.00	100 × 0.11 = Rs. 11.00
Z — 130 × 0.10 = Rs. 13.00	130 × 0.12 = Rs. 15.60

Problem No. 53

The following particulars apply to a particular Job :

Standard production per hour – 9 Units.

Normal rate per hour – Rs. 1.80

In a 8 hours a day : Ashok produces – 48 Units.

Basavaraj produces – 63 Units.

Chandrashekar produces – 75 Units.

Calculate wages of workers under :

(a) Merrick's differential piece rate

(b) Straight Piece rate.

(K.U.D., October 1978)

Solution :

Standard output per hour – 9 units

Standard output per day of 8 hours = 9 × 8 = 72 units.

Normal Rate per hour – 1.80

Normal Rate per unit = $\frac{1.80}{9}$ = 0.20 Ps

(a) *Merrick's Differential Piece rate :*

(1) Up to 83% efficiency – Basic Piece rate Rs. 0.20 Ps per unit

(2) From 83% to 100% efficiency – 110% of basic piece rate = 0.22 Ps

(3) At or above 100% efficiency = 120% of Basic piece rate = 0.24 Ps.

Levels of efficiency = $\frac{\text{Actual output}}{\text{Standard output}} \times 100$

Rate Applicable under Merricks piece rates :

(1) Ashok = $\frac{48}{72} \times 100 = 67\%$ Basic Piece rate Re. 0.20 Ps

(2) Basavaraj = $\frac{63}{72} \times 100 = 87.5\%$ 110% of 0.20 = Re. 0.22 Ps

(3) Chandrashekar $\frac{75}{72} \times 100 = 104\%$ 120% of 0.20 = Re. 0.24 Ps.

Earnings of Workers

Straight Piece Rate	Merrick's Differential Piece Rate
A — 48 × 0.20 Ps = Rs. 9.60	A — 48 × 0.20 Ps = Rs. 9.60
B — 63 × 0.20 Ps = Rs. 12.60	B — 63 × 0.22 Ps = Rs. 13.86
C — 75 × 0.20 Ps = Rs. 15.00	C — 75 × 0.24 Ps = Rs. 18.00

Problem No. 54

From the following data, prepare a statement showing the cost per day of 8 hours.

(1) Monthly salary (Basic plus D.A.) Rs. 200

(2) Leave salary payable to workman 5% of the above.

(3) Employers contribution to P.F. 8% of salary (including leave salary)

(4) Employers contribution to state insurance 2 per cent salary (-do-)

(5) Amenities to labourers (pro-rata basic) Rs. 17.95 per head per month.

(6) Number of working hours in a month — 200 hours.

(K.U.D., April 1978)

Solution :

Statement showing Labour Cost of Workers per day

Particulars	Rs. Ps.
(1) Monthly salary (Basic + D.A.)	200.00
(2) Leave salary 5% of 200	10.00
(3) P.F. contribution 8% of 210	16.80
(4) E.S.I. contribution 2% of 210	4.20
(5) Amenities	17.95
Total Labour cost per month	248.95

Labour cost per day (per day of 8 Hours) $= \dfrac{\text{Total salary p.m.}}{\text{Total No. of hours}} \times$ No. of Hours a day.

$= \dfrac{248.95}{200} \times 8$ Hours

$=$ Rs. 9.958

MERRICK'S DIFFERENTIAL PIECE RATE SYSTEM

It is an important over Taylor's Differential Piece rate system. It provides basic piece wage rate up to 83% of efficiency. Increase in efficiency is rewarded by increased percentage on basic piece rate.

Three piece rates are applied at different Levels of efficiency or performance. It does not give a guarantee of time wages.

Merrick's Differential Piece rates

(1) Upto 83% efficiency – Ordinary piece rates is paid or Basic piece rate
(2) From 83% to 100 efficiency – @ 110% of Basic piece rate
(3) At or above 100% efficiency – @ 120% of Basic piece rate

Problem No. 55

From the following particulars calculate the earnings of workers A, B and C under :

(a) Straight piece rate system

(b) Merrick's differential piece rate system.

Normal Rate per hour – Rs. 6.00

Standard time per unit – 0.03 Minutes

Output per day of 8 hours is as follows :

Worker : A – 128 Units

B – 150 Units

C – 184 Units.

Solution :

Standard Time per unit – 0.03 Minutes

Standard output per hour = $\frac{60}{3}$ = 20 Units.

Standard output per day = 8 × 20 = 160 Units.
Normal piece rate per hour Rs. 6

Normal rate per unit = $\frac{600}{20}$ Ps = 0.30 Ps per unit

Efficiency = $\frac{\text{Actual output}}{\text{Standard output}} \times 100$

Worker : A – $\frac{128}{160} \times 100$ = 80% Efficiency

B – $\frac{150}{160} \times 100$ = 93.75% Efficiency

C – $\frac{184}{160} \times 100$ = 115% Efficiency

Merrick's Differential Piece Rate

(1) Up to 83% of Efficiency — Basic Piece rate i.e., 0.30 Ps per Unit

(2) From 83% to 100% — 110% of basic Piece rate i.e., 0.30 × 110% = .33 Ps. per Unit

(3) At or above 100% — 120% of basic piece rate i.e., .30 × 120% = 0.36 Ps.

Earnings of Workers Under Merrick's Differential Piece rate

Worker :			
	A	128 × 0.30	= Rs. 38.40
	B	150 × 0.33	= Rs. 49.50
	C	184 × 0.36	= Rs. 66.24

Earnings of Workers Under Straight Piece rate of Re. 0.30

Worker :			
	A	128 × 0.30	= Rs. 38.40
	B	150 × 0.30	= Rs. 45.00
	C	184 × 0.30	= Rs. 55.20

Problem No. 56

The following particulars apply to a particular Job :
Standard production per hour — 18 Units.
Normal Rate per hour — Rs. 7.20

In a day of 8 hours :

A produces — 108 Units.

B produces — 126 Units.

C produces — 162 Units.

Calculate the wages of workers under :

(a) Straight Piece Rate and (b) Merrick's Differential Piece Rate system.

Solution :

Standard production per hour – 18 Units.

Standard production per day = 8 × 18 = 144 Units.

Normal Rate per Hour = Rs. 7.20

Normal Rate per unit = Rs. $\frac{7.20}{18}$ = 0.40 Ps per Unit.

Levels of Efficiency of workers = $\frac{\text{Actual output}}{\text{Standard output}} \times 100$

Worker : A = $\frac{108}{144} \times 100$ = 75% Efficiency

B = $\frac{126}{144} \times 100$ = 87.5% Efficiency

C = $\frac{162}{144} \times 100$ = 112.5% Efficiency

Merrick's Differential Piece Rate

(1) Upto 83% efficiency = Basic piece rate = 0.40 Ps per unit.

(2) From 83% to 100% = 110% of Basic rate = 0.40 × 110% = 0.44 Ps per Unit

(3) At or above 100% = 120% of basic piece rate = 0.40 × 120% = 48 Ps

Straight Piece Rate System	Merrick's Differential Piece Rate
Worker : A — 108 × 0.40 Ps = Rs. 43.20	A — 108 × 0.40 Ps = Rs. 43.20
B — 126 × 0.40 Ps = Rs. 50.40	B — 126 × 0.44 Ps = Rs. 55.44
C — 162 × 0.40 Ps = Rs. 64.80	C — 162 × 0.48 Ps = Rs. 77.76

Problem No. 57

The following are the particulars of a manufacturing company. Standard production per hour – 10 Units.

Normal rate per hour — Rs. 6

In a day of 9 Hours :

A Produces — 68 Units

B Produces — 86 Units

C Produces — 99 Units

Calculate wages of the workers under : (a) Straight piece rate.

(b) Merrick's differential piece rate.

Solution :

Standard output per hour — 10 Units.

Standard output per day of 9 hours = 9 × 10 = 90 Units

Normal rate per hour = Rs. 6

Normal Rate per unit = $\frac{600}{10}$ = 0.60 Ps per unit.

Efficiency of workers : = $\frac{\text{Actual output}}{\text{Standard output}} \times 100$

Workers : A = $\frac{68}{90} \times 100$ = 75.55% (Basic Piece Rate Re. 0.60 Ps)

B = $\frac{86}{90} \times 100$ = 95.55% (110% of 0.60 = Re. 0.66 Ps)

X = $\frac{99}{90} \times 100$ = 110% (120% of 0.60 = 0.72 Ps)

Merrick's Differential Piece Rate

(1) Up to 83% Basic piece rate

(2) From 83% to 100% = 110% piece rate

(3) At or above 100% = 120% of piece rate.

Earning of workers

	Straight Piece Rate	Merrick's Differential Piece Rate
Worker :	A = 68 × 0.60 = Rs. 40.80	A = 68 × 0.60 = Rs. 40.80
	B = 86 × 0.60 = Rs. 51.60	B = 86 × 0.66 = Rs. 57.76
	C = 99 × 0.60 = Rs. 59.40	C = 99 × 0.72 = Rs. 71.28

Problem No. 58

Calculate the earnings of workers A and B under straight piece rate system and Taylor's differential piece rate system from the following particulars :

Normal Rate per hour — Rs. 6.00

Standard time per unit — 30 seconds.

Differential piece rates to be applied 80% of piece rate below standard efficiency

120% of piece rate at or above standard efficiency

Worker : A produces — 850 Units per day of 8 hours.

B produces — 1020 Units per day of 8 hours.

Solution :

Standard production per 30 seconds 1 unit.

Standard production per minute – $\frac{60}{30}$ = 2 Units.

Standard production per hour = 60 × 2 = 120 Units.

Standard production per day of 8 hours = 8 × 120 = 960 Units.

Normal rate per hour = Rs. 6.00

Normal Rate per unit = $\frac{600 \text{ Ps}}{120 \text{ Units}}$ = 0.05 Ps per unit

Taylor's Differential Piece rate :

Low Piece rate — 80% of 0.05 = 0.04 Ps per unit below standard efficiency.

Hight piece rate — 120% of 0.05 = 0.06 Ps per unit at or above standard efficiency.

Earnings of Workers

	Straight Piece Rate System	Taylor's Differential Piece Rate
Worker : A —	850 × 0.05 Ps. = Rs. 42.50	850 × 0.04 Ps = Rs. 34.00
B —	1020 × 0.05 Ps. = Rs. 51.00	1020 × 0.06 Ps = Rs. 61.20

GANT'S TASK AND BONUS PLAN

This plan is based on careful time and motion study. It is the combination of Time wage, Piece wage and Bonus systems.

A standard time is fixed for doing a particular Job or Task. Worker's actual performance is compared with standard time and his efficiency is determined.

(1) If the worker takes more than the standard time (efficiency below 100%) he is paid wages for time taken.

(2) If a worker takes standard time (efficiency 100%) he is paid wages for standard time and a bonus of 20% on the wages earned.

(3) If worker completes the task in less than standard time (efficiency above 100%) he is given wages for standard time plus a bonus of 20% of the wages for standard time.

i.e., if a worker's performance is more than 100% efficiency he is given piece wage plus 20% of piece wage.

With every reduction in time, the plan ensures progressive increase in the total wages. It is also known as progressive rate system.

Advantages

(1) It ensures guaranteed time wage to worker below standard efficiency.

(2) It differentials between efficient and inefficient workers :

(a) i.e., inefficient worker takes more time than the standard time fixed and therefore he is paid time wages.

(b) Efficient worker takes standard time and who completes the task 100% efficiency he is paid time wage + 20% Bonus.

(c) A worker who completes the task in less than the standard time and whose efficiency is more than 100% he is paid piece wages + 20% of piece wage or high piece rate.

GANT'S TASK AND BONUS PLAN

Problem No. 59

From the following data calculate the total monthly remuneration of three workers A, B and C under the Gant's Task Bonus scheme :

(1) Standard production per month — 1500 Units.

(2) Piece work rate 0.75 Ps per unit.

(3) Actual production during the month : A – 1275 Units, B – 1500 Units, C — 1650 Units.

Solution :

Standard production per month — 1500 Units.

Normal piece rate per unit — Re. 0.75 Ps.

Guaranteed month payments — 1500 Units × 0.75 Ps = Rs. 1,125.

Levels of Efficiency	Rate applicable
Worker : A — $\frac{1275}{1500} \times 100 = 85\%$ Efficiency	Below Standard guaranteed time Wage
B — $\frac{1500}{1500} \times 100 = 100\%$ Efficiency	Standard (Standard time Wage + 20% Bonus)
C — $\frac{1650}{1500} \times 100 = 110\%$ Efficiency	Above Standard (Piece Wage + 20% Bonus)

Earnings of Workers	Rs.
A — 1275 units below standard efficiency	1,125.00
B — 1500 Units at standard efficiency + 20% Bonus	1,125.00
Bonus	225.00
	1,350.00
C — 1650 Units above standard (1650 × 0.75 Ps)	1,237.50
Add : 20% Bonus	247.50
	1,485.00

Earnings of Worker : A — Rs. 1,125.00

B — Rs. 1,350.00

C — Rs. 1,485.00

Problem No. 60

The following are the particulars applicable to a work process :

Time Rate Rs. 6 per Hour.

High Task – 60 Units per week (Standard production)

Piece rate above high task — Rs. 7.50 per unit.

In a 40 Hours week the production of workers was as follows :

Worker : A — 51 Units

B — 60 Units

C — 69 Units

D — 75 Units

Calculate the wages of the workers under Gant's Task and Bonus scheme.

Solution :

Time Wages — Rs. 6 per Hour

No. of Hours in a week — 40 Hours.

Time wages per week — 40 × 6 = Rs. 240

High piece rate above standard efficiency — Rs. 7.50 per unit.

GANT'S TASK AND BONUS SCHEME

(1) Efficiency below standard – Guaranteed Time wage.

(2) Efficiency at standard – Time Wage + 20% Bonus

(3) Efficiency above standard – High piece rate on actual output.

Earnings of workers under Gant's Task and Bonus scheme

Worker's % of Efficiency $= \frac{\text{Actual output}}{\text{Standard output}} \times 100$	Rate applicable		Total Wages per week (Rs.)
A $\frac{51}{60} \times 100 = 85\%$ Efficiency	Time Rate (40 × 6)		240.00
B $\frac{60}{60} \times 100 = 100\%$ Efficiency	Time Rate	240.00	
	Add : Bonus 20%	48.00	288.00
C $\frac{69}{60} \times 100 = 115\%$ Efficiency	High Piece Rate (69 × 7.50)		517.50
D $\frac{75}{60} \times 100 = 125\%$ Efficiency	High Piece Rate (75 × 7.50)		562.50

Problem No. 61

Methods of Remuneration :

(1) Straight Piece Rate

(2) Differential Piece Rate : (a) Taylor's Piece Rate

(b) Merrick's Piece Rate

(c) Gant's Task & Bonus system

The following is the output of workers A, B, C and D in a particular 48 hours week.

A — 72 Units, B — 90 Units, C — 96 Units & D — 102 Units.

Guaranteed time rate — Rs. 8 per hour.

Low piece Rate Rs. 3 per unit.

High piece rate Rs. 5 per unit.

High task (standard output) 96 Units.

Show the earnings of workers and the labour cost per unit under :

(a) Straight Piece rate

(b) Differential Piece rate systems :

(1) Taylor's system

(2) Merrick's system

(3) Gant Task and Bonus scheme.

Solution :

Standard output per week — 96 Units.

Normal time rate per hour — Rs. 8

Normal output per hour — $\frac{96}{48}$ = 2 Units per hour.

Normal Rate per unit — $\frac{8}{2}$ = Rs. 4 per unit.

(1) Straight Piece Rate — Rs. 4 per unit.

(2) Differential Piece rate system :

(a) *Taylor's System* : Efficiency :

Below standard — Low piece rate Rs. 3 per unit.

Above standard — High piece rate Rs. 5 per unit.

(b) *Merrick's Differential piece rate* :

(1) Up to 83% efficiency — Ordinary piece rate Rs. 4 per unit.

(2) From 83% to 100% efficiency — 110% of Rs. 4 = Rs. 4.40 per unit.

(3) Above 100% efficiency – 120% of Rs. 4 — Rs. 4.80 per unit.

(3) *Gant's Task and Bonus system* :

(1) Below standard efficiency — Time Wage Rate Rs. 8 per hour.

For week of 48 Hours = 48 × 8 = Rs. 384.00 | Rs.

(2) At Standard Efficiency — Time Wage Rate 384.00

Add : 20% Bonus (384 × 20%) 76.80

460.80

(3) Above standard efficiency — Piece Wage Rs. 4

Add : Bonus 20% of Rs. 4 = 0.80 Ps 4.80

$$\text{Worker's Efficiency} = \frac{\text{Actual output}}{\text{Standard output}} \times 100$$

Worker : A — $\frac{72}{96} \times 100$ = 75% Efficiency below Standard

B — $\frac{90}{96} \times 100$ = 93.5% Efficiency below Standard

C — $\frac{96}{96} \times 100$ = 100% Efficiency at Standard

D — $\frac{102}{96} \times 100$ = 106.25% Efficiency above Standard.

Statement showing the Earning of workers

Standard output = 96 Units

Worker	Actual output	% of efficiency	Straight Piece Rate Rs. 4	DIFFERENTIAL Taylor's	PIECE Merrick's	RATES Gants Task & Bonus System
A	72	75%	72 × 4 = 288	72 × 3 = 216	72 × 4 = 288	384.00
B	90	93.5%	90 × 4 = 360	90 × 3 = 270	90 × 4.4 = 396	384.00
C	96	100%	96 × 4 = 384	96 × 5 = 480	96 × 4.4 = 422.4	460.80
D	102	106%	102 × 5 = 510	102 × 5 = 510	102 × 4.8 = 489.6	489.60
					(102 × 4 =	408.00
					+ 20% Bonus	81.60
						489.60

Problem No. 62

Three workers are working in a factory X, Y and Z. The following particulars apply to them :

Normal Time rate per hour — Rs. 4

Piece rate per unit — Rs. 3

Standard output per hour — 10 Units

In a 40-hour a week the output of workers is as under :

X — 250 Units, Y — 400 Units and Z — 600 Units.

Calculate the earnings of worker under :

(a) Straight Piece rate (b) Taylor's differential piece rate (c) Merrick's differential piece rate (d) Gant's Task & Bonus scheme.

Solution :

Standard output per hour – 10 Units.

Standard output for 40 hours = 40 × 10 = 400 Units.

Normal time rate per hour – Rs. 4

Normal piece rate per unit – Rs. 3

(1) Straightpiece rate Rs. 3 per unit.

(2) Differential Piece rate :

(a) *Taylor's System :*

Below standard low piece rate 90% of 3 = 2.70

At or above standard high piece rate 120% of 3 = 3.60

(b) *Merrick's Differential Piece rate :*

(1) Up to 83% efficiency ordinary piece rate Rs. 3 per unit.

(2) From 83% to 100% efficiency — 110% of 3 = 3.30 per unit.

(3) Above 100% efficiency — 120% of Rs. 3 = 3.60 per unit.

(c) *Gant's Task and Bonus scheme :*

(1) Below standard efficiency – Time Wage rate of Rs. 4 per unit. (40 × 4 = 160)

(2) At standard efficiency — Time Wage + 20% Bonus = 160 + 32 = 192

(3) Above standard efficiency Piece wage + 20% Bonus.

$$\text{Levels of Efficiency} = \frac{\text{Actual output}}{\text{Standard output}} \times 100$$

$$\text{Workers : } X - \frac{250}{400} \times 100 = 62.5\% \text{ Below Standard}$$

$$Y - \frac{400}{400} \times 100 = 100\% \text{ At Standard}$$

$$Z - \frac{600}{400} \times 100 = 150\% \text{ Above Standard}$$

Statement showing the Earnings of workers

Standard output = 400 Units.

Worker	Actual output	% of Efficiency	Straight Piece Rate	Taylor's System	Merrick's Differental Piece Rate	Gant's Task & Bonus scheme
			Rs. 3	Low Rate 2.7 High rate 3.6	Up to 83% Rs. 3 83% to 100% Rs. 3.30 above 100% Rs. 3.60	Below Stand. Time Wage. At Stand. Time Wage + 20% Above Stand. Piece Wage + 20%
X	250	62.75%	250 × 3 = 750	2.50 × 2.7 = 675	250 × 3 = 750	400 × 4 = 1,600
Y	400	100%	400 × 3 = 1,200	400 × 3.6 = 1,440	400 × 3.3 = 1,320	40 × 4 = (1,600 + 320) = 1,920
Z	600	150%	600 × 3 = 1,800	600 × 3.6 = 2,160	600 × 3.6 = 2,160	600 × 3 = 1,800 + 20% 360 2,160

EMMERSON'S EFFICIENCY SCHEME

This scheme guarantees day wage. A standard output is fixed to represent 100% efficiency.

A worker who attains 66-2/3% of efficiency standard gets bonus at given rate. The rate of bonus gradually increases from 66-2/3% to 100%. Bonus will be 20% basic rate.

After 100% efficency bonus will increase @ 1% of basic rate for every 1% rise in efficiency. It is a greater in document to the worker to improve his efficiency. Bonus starts at early stage. It is helpful for beginners.

Formula for calculation of efficiency :

(a) Efficiency on output basis :

$$= \frac{\text{Actual output}}{\text{Standard output}} \times 100$$

(b) Efficiency on Time basis :

$$= \frac{\text{Standard time for actual production}}{\text{Actual time taken}} \times 100$$

Problem No. 63

Daily wage rate guaranteed for a worker is Rs. 45 and the standard output fixed for a week is 150 Units representing 100% efficiency. The guaranteed wage rate is paid without bonus to those workers who show efficiency upto 70% of the standard. Beyond this bonus is payable on graduated scale in the ratio to the increased output as under :

Efficiency	90%	100%
Bonus payable	10%	20%

Further increase of 1% bonus is given for every 1% increase in efficiency. Calculate total earnings of the 4 Workers who have worked for a week and their output was as under :

Worker : A – 75 Units, B – 135 Units, C – 150 Units & D – 180 Units.

Solution :

Earnings of workers under Emmerson's Efficiency scheme

Particulars	Workers			
	A	B	C	D
(1) Standard output in units	150	150	150	150
(2) Actual output (in units)	75	135	150	180
(3) Percentage of Efficiency $= \frac{\text{Actual output}}{\text{Standard output}} \times 100$	50%	90%	100%	120%
(4) Bonus percentage payable	Nil	10%	20%	20% + 20%
(5) Daly wages Rs. 45 for week of 6 days 45 × 6 = 270 (in Rs.)	270	270	270	270
(6) Bonus payable (4 above)	—	27	54	108 (54 + 54)
Total Earnings	270	297	324	378

Problem No. 64

The standard production in a factory is 10 units per hour for a day of 8 hours. The wage rate is Rs. 16 per day. Bonus rated on efficiency is paid according to a scale as follows :

Levels of efficiency	Bonus payable
(1) Up to 60% of standard	Nil
(2) Above 60% of standard up to 75%	5%
(3) Above 75% and up to 90%	10%
(4) Above 90% and up to 100%	15%

For an increase of every 1% efficiency beyond 100% the bonus also rises by 1%. The output of workers on a day was as follows :

A — 50 Units, B — 70 Units, C — 75 Units, D — 90 Units & E — 100 Units.

Tabulate the earnings of each worker under Emmerson's Effciency Bonus plan.

Solution :

Statement showing the earnings of workers under Emmerson's Bonus plan

Particulars	Workers				
	A	B	C	D	E
(1) Standard output (in units)	80	80	80	80	80
(2) Actual output (in units)	50	70	75	90	100
(3) Percentage of efficiency	62.5%	87.5%	93.75%	112.5%	125%
$= \frac{\text{Actual output}}{\text{Standard output}} \times 100$					
(4) Bonus percentage payable	5%	10%	15%	15%+12.5%	15%+25%
(5) Wages for a day	16.00	16.00	16.00	16.00	16.00
(6) Bonus Payable	0.80	1.60	2.40	4.40	6.40
Total Earnings (5 + 6)	16.80	17.60	18.40	20.40	22.40

INCENTIVE WAGE SYSTEM AND BONUS SCHEME

Halsey Plan and Rowan Plan

To encourage higher productivity; a worker may be given additional remuneration for attaining and exceeding 100% efficiency. 100% efficiency may be measured in terms of time or output or cost reduction efficiency more than 100 is reflected in savings of time in doing work or in exceeding output target within a specified time or reduction in cost of production.

Premium Bonus Plan

Premium Bonus plans provide for time wages for actual hours worked plus bonus at a percentage of time saved at hourly rate.

(a) Halsey Plan and (b) Rowan Plan

(a) *Halsey Plan :*

Under this scheme worker is pāid hourly wages for time taken plus a bonus of 50% of time saved at hourly rate a standard time is fixed for every Job.

Earnings under Halsey Plan :

Earnings = Time taken × Rate per hour + ½ (Time saved × Hour Rate)

Or = $T \times R = \frac{1}{2} (Ts \times R)$

Time saved = Standard Time – Time taken

$T \times R + \frac{1}{2} (S - T) R$

Where : T = Time Taken

S = Standard Time

R = Rate per Hour

(b) *Rowan Plan* :

Under this plan bonus is introduced on similar time of Halsey plan proportion to time saved bears to standard time.

$$\text{Earnings} = \text{Time taken} \times \text{Rate per hour} + \text{Rate per hour} \times \text{Time taken} \frac{(\text{Standard time} - \text{Time Taken})}{\text{Standard time}}$$

$$\text{(a)} = T \times R + R \times T \frac{(S - T)}{S}$$

$$\text{(b)} = T \times R + \frac{(S - T)}{S} T \times R$$

Where : T = Time taken; S = Standard time; R = Rate per hour;

Time Saved = Standard time – Time taken

Comparison of Halsey Plan and Rowan Plan

Both the plans are criticised by workers.

Reasons : Full benefit of time saved is not given as the bonus paid in Halsey plan is 50% to worker and 50% to employer, where in case of Rowan plan bonus payable is in proportion to Time saved that bears to standard time.

Rowan plan has another drawback that two workers do the same Job, one is very efficient and another is not so efficient may get the same bonus.

Problem No. 65

Ex : Standard time fixed for a Job — 20 hours.

Worker X takes 12 hours and Y takes 18 hours to complete the Job. Hourly rate is Rs. 2. Calculate wages of workers under Rowan plan.

Rowan Plan

$$\text{Earning} : = T \times R + \frac{(S - T)}{S} T \times R$$

$$X = 12 \times 2 + \frac{(30 - 12)}{30} 12 \times 2$$

$$= 24 + \frac{18}{30} \times 24$$

$$= 24 + 14.40$$

$$= 38.40$$

$$Y = 18 \times 2 + \frac{(30-18)}{30} \times 18 \times 2$$

$$= 36 + \frac{12}{30} \times 36$$

$$= 36 + 14.40$$

$$= 40.40$$

In the above example the bonus payable to workers X and Y is the same.

Worker X : Time taken — 12 Hours.

Time saved is 30 – 12 = 18 Hours efficiency

Y : Time taken — 18 Hours. (Time saved is (30 – 18) 12 Hours not so efficient)

But both get the same amount of bonus.

Alternatively

Earnings of worker X and Y under Rowan Bonus plan :

Worker X

Earning = Time taken × Rate per hour

= 12 × 2 = 24

Bonus on time saved in proportion to standard time — Time taken

= 30 – 12 = 18 Hours.

$$= \frac{(\text{Standard Time} - \text{Time taken})}{\text{Standard Time}} \times \text{Rate per hour} \times \text{Time taken}$$

$$\text{Bonus} = \frac{(S-T)}{S} R \times T$$

$$= \frac{18}{30} \times 2 \times 12$$

$$= \frac{3}{5} \times 24 = 3 \times 4.80 = \text{Rs. } 14.40$$

Worker Y

Earning = T × R

= 18 × 2 = 36

$$\text{Bonus} = \frac{(S-T)}{S} R \times T$$

$$= \frac{(30-18)}{30} 2 \times 18$$

$$= \frac{12}{30} \times 36$$

$= \text{Rs. } 14.40$

In the above case X fact worker — efficient and complete the Job in 12 hours and Time saved in 18 hours — Bonus earned is — Rs. 14.40. Y — show worker not so efficient taken time 18 hours to complete the Job and time saved is 12 hours and the bonus earned in this case also the same amount i.e., Rs. 14.40.

Halsey Plan

Earnings = T × R + ½ (S – T) R

Where T = Time taken

R = Rate per hour

S = Standard Time

S – T = Time Saved.

Problem No. 66

Worker X working a Job completes the work in 20 hours for which standard time fixed is 25 hours. The wage Rate is Rs. 7.50 per hour.

Calculate the Earnings of worker X under Halsey Plan.

Solution :

Earnings = T × R + ½ (S – T) R

= 20 × 7.50 + ½(25 – 20) × 7.50

= 150 + ½ (5 × 7.50)

= 150 + 18.75

= Rs. 168.75

Where T = Time taken

R = Rate per hour

S = Standard time.

Problem No. 67

A worker in a factory who completes the Job in 40 hours. The standard time fixed is 48 hours. The wage rate being Rs. 5 per hour.

Calculate the earnings of worker and Halsey Plan.

Solution :

Halsey Plan :

Earnings = T × R + ½ (S – T) R

= 40 × 5 + ½ (48 – 40) 5

= 200 + ½ (8 × 5)

= 200 + ½ (40)

= 200 + 20

= 220

Alternatively :

Earnings = T × R

= 40 × 5

= 200

Bonus = ½ (S – T) R

= ½ (48 – 40) 5

= ½ (8 × 5)

= ½ × 40

= 20

Earnings = Wages + Bonus

= 200 + 20

= 220.

Problem No. 68

X and Y workers are working in a factory :

X — Completes the Job in 24 Hours and

Y — Completes the Job in 28 Hours.

The standard time fixed for a Job is 36 Hours.

Calculate the earnings of X and Y under Halsey Plan where wage rate being Rs. 6 per hour.

Solution :

Worker X :

Earnings = T × R + ½ (S – T) R

Time taken = 24 Hours.

Standard Time = 36 Hours

Rate per hour = Rs. 6

= 24 × 6 + ½ (36 – 24) 6

= 144 + ½ (12 × 6)

= 144 + ½ (72)

= 144 + 36

= 180

Worker Y : Earnings = T × R + ½ (S – T) R

Time taken = 28 Hours, Standard Time = 36 Hours, Rate per hour = Rs. 6

Earnings = 28 × 6 + ½ (36 – 28) 6

= 168 + ½ (8 × 6)

= 168 + ½ (48)

= 168 + 24

= 190

The above problem under Rowan Plan :

$$\text{Earnings} = T \times R + \frac{(S - T)}{S} T \times R$$

$$\text{Worker X} = 24 \times 6 + \frac{(36 - 24)}{36} 24 \times 6$$

$$= 144 + \frac{12}{36} 144$$

$$= 144 + 48 = 192$$

$$\text{Worker Y} = 28 \times 6 + \frac{(36 - 28)}{36} 28 \times 6$$

$$= 168 + \frac{8}{36} \times 168$$

$$= 168 + 37.32$$

$$= 205.32$$

Problem No. 69

Worker A working in a factory on a Job completes in 16 hours and standard time fixed for a Job is 24 hours. The wage rate being Rs. 5 per hour. Calculate the earning of worker A under Rowan plan.

Solution : (Under Rowan Plan)

$$\text{Earning} = \text{Time taken} \times \text{Rate per hour} + \frac{(\text{Standard Time} - \text{Time taken})}{\text{Standard Time}} \times \text{Time taken} \times \text{Rate per hour.}$$

$$\text{Earnings} = T \times R + \frac{(S - T)}{S} T \times R$$

T = Time taken = 16 Hours.
S = Standard time = 24 Hours.
R = Rate per hour = Rs. 5.

$$= 16 \times 5 + \frac{(24 - 16)}{24} 16 \times 5$$

$$= 80 + \frac{8}{24} \times 80$$

$$= 80 + 26.67 = 106.67.$$

Problem No. 70

A and B two workers working in factory on a particular Job. A completes in 28 hours and B completes in 36 hours. The standard time for Job is fixed 44 hours. The wage rate is Rs. 5 per hour. Calculate the earnings of workers under Rowan plan.

Solution : (Under Rowan Plan)

Earnings $= T \times R + \frac{(S - T)}{S} T \times R$ T = Time taken = 28 Hours.

S = Standard time = 44 Hours.

R = Rate per hour = Rs. 5.

Worker A $= 28 \times 5 + \frac{(44 - 28)}{44} 28 \times 5$

$= 140 + \frac{16}{144} \times 140$

$= 140 + 50.90 = 190.90$

Worker B = Earnings = T × R + (S–T) T × R T = Time taken = 16 Hours.

S = Standard time = 24 Hours.

R = Rate per hour = Rs. 5.

$= 36 \times 5 + \frac{(44 - 36)}{44} 36 \times 5$

$= 180 + \frac{8}{44} \times 180$

$= 180 + 32.72$

$= 212.72$

Problem No. 71

A work man's wage for a guaranteed 44 hours week is Rs. 2 per Hour The estimated time to produce one unit is 30 Minutes.

Time allowed is increased under incentive scheme by 20%.

During one week the worker produced 125 units.

Calculate his gross wages under each of the following methods of remuneration : (1) Time wage, (2) Piece work with guaranteed weekly wages, (3) Halsey premium bonus 50% to the worker, and (4) Rowan plan.

Solution :

Standard time for 1 unit = 30 minutes under incentive scheme.
Time allowed for one unit = 30 minutes

Add : increase by 20% per unit $\frac{6}{36}$ minutes Standard time per unit.

Standard time for 125 units = $125 \times \frac{36}{60} = 75$ Hours.

Rate per hour = Rs. 2, output per hour = 2 units

Rate per unit = $\frac{2}{2}$ = Re. 1 per unit.

(1) *Time wage* : Earnings = Time taken × Rate per hour

= 44 × 2 = Rs. 88.

(2) *Piece Wage method* : Actual output = 125 Units, Rate per unit = Re. 1

Earnings = No. of unit × Rate per unit = 125 × 1 = 125.

(3) Piece wage with guaranteed weekly wages under incentive scheme.

Time allowed – 75 hours, Rate per hour – Rs. 2

Earnings = Time allowed × Rate per hour = 75 × 2 = Rs. 150

(4) *Under Incentive Scheme :* Time allowed = 75 hours.

Under : Halsey premium bonus 50% to worker Time taken = 44 hours

Rate per hour = Rs. 2

$$\text{Earnings} = T \times R + \tfrac{1}{2}(S - T)R$$
$$= 44 \times 2 + \tfrac{1}{2}(75 - 44)2$$
$$= 88 + 31 = \text{Rs. } 119$$

(5) *Rowan Plan* : $\text{Earnings} = T \times R + \frac{(S - T)}{S} T \times R$

$$\text{Earnings} = 44 \times 2 + \frac{(75 - 44)}{75} 44 \times 2$$
$$= 88 + \frac{31}{75} \times 88$$
$$= 88 + 35.37$$
$$= \text{Rs. } 123.37.$$

Problem No. 72

In a manufacturing company worker A takes 18 Hours to complete a Job on daily wages 12 hours on a scheme of payment by results. His day rate is Rs. 3 per hour.

The cost of materials of product is Rs. 30 and the overheads are recovered @ 150% of Direct Wages.

Calculate factory cost of the product under :

(a) Piece Rate system (b) Halsey plan (c) Rowan plan.

Solution :

Standard Time – 18 hours, Time taken — 12 hours, Daily rate — Rs. 3 P.H.

(a) Wages of worker 'A' under Piece rate system :

$$\text{Earnings} = \text{Time taken} \times \text{Rate per hour}$$
$$= 12 \times 3 = 36$$

(b) Halsey Plan : $\text{Earnings} = T \times R + \tfrac{1}{2}(S - T) \times R$

$$\text{Earnings} = 12 \times 3 + \tfrac{1}{2}(18 - 12) \times 3$$
$$= 36 + \tfrac{1}{2}(6 \times 3)$$
$$= 36 + 9 = \text{Rs. } 39$$

(c) Rowan Plan : $\text{Earnings} = T \times R + \frac{(S - T)}{S} T \times R$

$$\text{Earnings} = 12 \times 3 + \frac{(18-12)}{18} 12 \times 3$$

$$= 36 + \frac{6}{18} \times 36$$

$$= 36 + 12 = \text{Rs. } 48$$

Computation of Factory Cost

Particulars	Piece Rate System	Halsey Plan	Rowan Plan
Cost of materials	30.00	30.00	30.00
Wages	36.00	39.00	48.00
Prime Cost	76.00	69.00	78.00
Overheads 150% of Direct Wages	54.00	103.50	117.00
Factory Cost	140.00	172.50	195.00

Problem No. 73

Calculate the Wages of a worker under (a) Halsey Plan (b) Rowan Plan if he executes a piece of work in 72 hours as against 90 hours allowed. His hourly rate is Rs. 4 per hour and he is paid 50% of the time saved under Halsey plan, he gets dearness allowance Rs. 6 per day of 8 hours worked in additions to his wages similarly in case of Rowan plan.

Solution : (Under Rowan Plan)

Standard time — 90 Hours, Time taken — 72 hours, Rate per hour Rs. 4

Under Halsey Plan : Earnings = T × R + ½ (S – T) × R

$$\text{Earnings} = 72 \times 4 + \tfrac{1}{2}(90 - 72) \times 4$$

$$= 288 + \tfrac{1}{2}(18 \times 4)$$

$$= 288 + 36 = 324$$

Under Rowan Plan : $\text{Earnings} = T \times R + \frac{(S - T)}{S} T \times R$

$$\text{Earnings} : = 72 \times 4 + \frac{(90-72)}{90} 72 \times 4$$

$$= 288 + \frac{18}{90} \times 288$$

$$= 288 + 57.60 = 365.60$$

	Rs.
Halsey Plan : Wages	342.00
Add : Dearness allowance Rs. 6 per day of 8 hours	
Standard time – 90 Hours = No. of days = $\frac{90}{8}$ = 11.25	
11.25 × 6 =	67.50
Total Wages	391.50
Rowan Plan : Wages	365.60
Add : Dearness allowance Rs. 6 per day of 8 hours	
Standard time — 90 hours. No. of days $\frac{90}{8}$ = 11.25 × 6 =	67.50
Total Wages	433.10

Problem No. 74

In a manufacturing factory worker X gets basic rate Rs. 5 per hour is working under Rowan System of premium bonus. In addition he gets dearness allowances of Rs. 40 per week of 48 Hours.

During one week he does the following Job :

(1) *Job No. 302* : for which 25 hours are allowed he takes 20 hours to do it.

(2) *Job No. 303* : For which 30 hours are allowed he takes 24 hours to do it.

During the week his waiting time amount to 4 Hours.

Calculate the worker's earnings and the amount to be charged to each Job and to overhead.

Solution :

Earnings of worker X

Job No. 302

Standard Time – 25 Hours

Time taken – 20 Hours

Rate per hour – Rs. 5

$$\text{Rowan Plan : Earnings} = T \times R \; \frac{(S - T)}{S} \; T \times R$$

$$= 20 \times 5 \; \frac{(25 - 20)}{25} \; 20 \times 5$$

$$= 100 + \frac{5}{25} \times 100$$

$$= 100 + 20 = \text{Rs. } 120$$

Job No. 303

Standard time – 30 Hours, Time taken – 24 Hours, Rate per hour — Rs. 5

$$\text{Earnings} = T \times R + \frac{(S-T)}{S} T \times R$$

$$= 24 \times 5 + \frac{(30-24)}{30} 24 \times 5$$

$$= 120 + \frac{6}{30} \times 120$$

$$= 124 + 24 = \text{Rs. } 144$$

Dearness allowance divide between Job No. 302 and Job No. 303 proportionately in ratio of time allowed i.e., 25 + 30 = 55 (Ratio = 25 : 30 or 5 : 6).

For Job No. 302 $= 40 \times \frac{5}{11} =$ Rs. 18.18

For Job No. 303 $= 40 \times \frac{6}{11} =$ Rs. 21.82

Total D.A. Rs. 40.00

Earnings on Job No. 302	Rs.
Wages	120.00
Add : D.A.	18.18
Total Wages	138.18
Earnings on Job No. 303	
Wages	144.00
Add : D.A.	21.82
Total Earnings	165.82

Note : Waiting time of 4 hours to be charged to factory overhead
4 × 5 = Rs. 20.

(Worker is to get wages for idle time and idle time is assumed normal idle time.)

Total Earnings of Worker X :	Job No. 302		138.18
	Job No. 303		165.82
Dearness allowances :	For Job No. 302 =	18.18	
	For Job No. 303 =	21.82	
	Total	40.00	
	Total Earnings		304.00

Problem No. 75 (Rowan Plan problem on as ascertainment of time taken)

In a manufacturing company a worker X completes the Job in a certain number of hours.

The standard time fixed for a Job is 20 Hours and the worker get Rs. 3 per hour. The worker earns bonus at 50%. Rs. 12 under Halsey Plan. Ascertain his total earnings under :

(a) Halsey Plan and (b) Rowan plan.

Solution : (Acertainment of time taken)

The worker X earns bonus @ 50% — Rs. 12

Bonus at 100% will be Rs. 24

The hourly rate of wages Rs. 3

Therefore time saved should be $\frac{24}{3}$ = 8 Hours

Now standard time —	20 Hours
Less : Time saved	8 Hours
Time taken	12 Hours

Rate per hour — Rs. 3

Earnings of worker X under :

Halsey Plan : Earnings T × R + ½ (S – T) × R

Standard time = 20 Hours, Time saved — 8 Hours, Time taken — 12 Hours.

Rate per Hour — Rs. 3

$$\begin{aligned} \text{Earnings} &= 12 \times 3 + \tfrac{1}{2}(20 - 12) \times 3 \\ &= 36 + \tfrac{1}{2}(8 \times 3) \\ &= 36 + \tfrac{1}{2} \times 24 \\ &= 36 + 12 = \text{Rs. } 48 \end{aligned}$$

$$\text{Rowan Plan} = \text{Earnings} = T \times R + \frac{(S - T)}{S} T \times R$$

Standard time — 20 Hours, Time saved — 8 Hours, Time taken — 12 Hours.

Rate per Hour — Rs. 3.

$$\begin{aligned} \text{Earnings} &= 12 \times 3 + \frac{(20 - 12)}{20} 12 \times 3 \\ &= 36 + \frac{8}{20} \times 36 \\ &= 36 + 14.40 = \text{Rs. } 50.40. \end{aligned}$$

Problem No. 76

In a manufacturing company Ashok works on a particular Job for which standard time allowed is 40 hours and the wage Rate Rs. 5 P.H.

The Job is completed by the worker in 26 hours.

The factory overhead charged are @ 75% of standard time.

Calculate the wages of worker Mr. Ashok under :

(a) Halsey Plan (b) Rowan Plan and also prepare comparative statement showing savings in labour cost under both the plans.

Solution :

Halsey Plan : Earnings $= T \times R + \frac{1}{2}(S - T)R$

Standard Time – 40 hours, Time taken – 26 hours, Rate per hour — Rs. 5.

$$\begin{aligned} \text{Earnings} &= 26 \times 5 + \tfrac{1}{2}(40 - 26)\,5 \\ &= 130 + \tfrac{1}{2}(14 \times 5) \\ &= 130 + \tfrac{1}{2}(70) \\ &= 130 + 35 \\ &= \text{Rs. } 165 \end{aligned}$$

Rowan Plan : Earnings $= T \times R + \frac{1}{2}\frac{(S - T)}{S}\,T \times R$

Standard time 40 hours, Time taken — 26 hours, Rate per hour — Rs. 5

$$\begin{aligned} \text{Earnings} &= 26 \times 5 + \frac{(40 - 26)}{40}\,26 \times 5 \\ &= 130 + \frac{14}{40} \times 130 \\ &= 130 + \frac{91}{2} \\ &= 130 + 45.50 \\ &= \text{Rs. } 175.50 \end{aligned}$$

Employer's savings in Labour cost :

		Rs.
(a)	Wages at Standard time (40 × 5)	200.00
	Wages under Halsey plan	165.00
	Savings in Wages	35.00
(b)	Wages at Standard time (40 × 5)	200.00
	Less : Wages under Rowan plan	175.50
	Savings in wages	24.50

Halsey Plan :

			Rs.
	Overhead 75% on standard time		
	Wages @ Standard time 40 × 5 = 200		
	(200 × 75% = 150)		150.00
Less :	Under Halsey Plan Wages 165		
	Overhead 75% of 165		123.75
	Savings overhead		26.25
	Total savings :	In wages	35.00
		In overhead	26.25
		Total Savings	61.25

Rowan Plan :

	Overhead 75% of standard time		
	Wages (45 × 5 = 200)		
	Overhead @ 75% of 200 =		150.00
Less :	Overhead under Rowan plan Wages Rs. 175.50		
	Overhead 75% of 175.50		131.63
		Saving overhead	18.37
	Total savings	(in wages)	24.50
		in overhead	18.37
		Total Savings	42.87
	Total savings in Labour cost :		
	Under Halsey Plan		61.25
	Under Rowan Plan		42.87

Comparative statement showing effect of paying under Halsey & Rowan Plans

Incentive Systems	Normal Wages	Bonus	Total Wages	Employers Savings	Effective rate of earning per hour
(1) Halsey Plan	26 × 5 = 130	35.00	165.00	61.25	$= \frac{\text{Total Wages}}{\text{Actual time taken}}$ $= \frac{165}{26} = 6.35$
(2) Rowan Plan	26 × 5 = 130	45.50	175.50	42.87	$= \frac{\text{Total Wages}}{\text{Actual time taken}}$ $= \frac{175.50}{26} = 6.75$

Problem No. 77

An employee A working under Bonus scheme saves 8 hours in a Job for which the standard time fixed is 40 hours. Calculate the wages payable for time taken under the following alternatives. Rate per hour is Rs. 4.

(1) Employee A receives an increase in hour rate based on percentage that the time saved bears to the time set (i.e. standard time) (Rowan Plan).

(2) A bonus of 10 per cent on award rate is payable when standard time (namely : 100 per cent efficiency) achieved plus a further bonus of 1 per cent on award rate for each 1 per cent increase in excess of 100 per cent efficiency (i.e., Emmerson's Efficiency Plan).

Solution :

Standard time —	40 Hours	Rate per hour Rs. 4
Less : Time saved	8 Hours	
Time taken	32 Hours	

(i) *Earnings Under (Rowan Plan)* : Earnings $= T \times R + \frac{(S - T)}{S} T \times R$

$$\text{Earnings} = 32 \times 4 + \frac{(40 - 32)}{40} 32 \times 4$$

$$= 128 + \frac{8}{40} \times 128$$

$$= 128 + 25.60$$

$$= 153.60$$

(ii) *Premium Bonus – Emmerson's Bonus Plan* :

Standard time – 40 hours, Time taken – 32 hours, Rate per hour — Rs. 4.

$$\therefore \text{Efficiency of worker A} = \frac{\text{Standard time}}{\text{Actual time taken}} \times 100$$

$$= \frac{40}{32} \times 100 = 125\% \text{ of efficiency.}$$

Wages on time basis : Actual time of worker 32 hours, Rate per hour — Rs. 4.

Wages $= T \times R = 32 \times 4 =$ 128.00

Bonus 10 per cent on achieving 100 per cent efficiency $= \frac{10}{100} \times 128 = 12.80$

Add : Bonus of 1 per cent for each per cent :

In excess of 100 per cent efficiency — 125 per cent efficiency

Excess of 100 per cent = 25 per cent

Increase in Bonus $\frac{10}{100} \times 128 =$ 32.00

Total Earnings of Worker A 172.80

Problem No. 78

X worker in manufacturing company works under Rowan system of premium bonus on a basic rate of pay of Rs. 5 per hour. In addition, he receives a cost of living bonus of Rs. 6 per week of 44 hours. During the week he worked on the following Jobs :

Job No. 401 for which 36 hours are allowed, he completes the Job in 20 hours.

Job No. 403 for which time allowed is 30 hours and he completes the Job in 20 hours.

During the week his waiting time amounts to 4 hours. Calculate the earning of worker X and the amount to be charged to each Job and to overheads.

Solution :

	Job No. 401	Job No. 403
Standard time	36 Hours	30 Hours
Time taken	20 Hours	20 Hours
Time saved	16 Hours	10 Hours

Idle time (44 – 20 – 20) = 4 hours

Rate per hour – Rs. 5

Earnings of worker X (Rowan Plan) = Earning $= T \times R + \frac{(S - T)}{S} T \times R$

Job No. 401

$$E = T \times R + \frac{(S - T)}{S} T \times R$$

$$= 20 \times 5 + \frac{(36 - 20)}{36} 20 \times 5$$

$$= 100 + \frac{16}{36} \times 100$$

$$= 100 + 44.40$$

$$= 144.40$$

Job No. 403

$$E = T \times R + \frac{(S - T)}{S} T \times R$$

$$= 20 \times 5 + \frac{(30 - 20)}{30} 20 \times 5$$

$$= 100 + \frac{10}{30} \times 100$$

$$= 100 + 33.33$$

$$= 133.33$$

Cost of living Rs. 66 for 44 hours of week.

Total standard time :

Job No. 401 = 36 Job No. 403 = 30

Cost of living is proportionately divided among Job No. 401 & 403

Standard time 36		Standard time 30, Total cost of living	
$\therefore \frac{36}{66} \times 66 = 36$ cost of living		$\therefore \frac{30}{66} \times 66 = 30$ cost of living	
Total Wages (Under Rowan Plan)		Total Wages (Under Rowan Plan)	
Wages	144.40	Wages	133.33
Add : Cost of living	36.00	Cost of living	30.00
	180.40		166.33

Total earning of worker X = Job No. 401 + Job No. 403 + Waiting time
= 180.40 + 166.33 + 20.00 (4 × 5)
= Rs. 366.73.

Problem No. 79

In a manufacturing company the worker is paid in the existing incentive system of wage payment.

Normal working hours – 5 days of 9 hours Plus 3 shifts of 3 hours each.

Rate of payment – days work Rs. 5 per hour late shift Rs. 7.50 per hour.

Addition at Bonus payable — Rs. 10 per day shifts, Rs. 7.50 late shifts.

The average output per operative for 54 hours week – 160 Articles.

i.e., 5 days of 9 hours =	45 Hours
3 late shifts of 3 hours	9 Hours
	54 Hours

In order to increase output and eliminate overtime, it was dicided to switch over to a system of payment by results. The following information is obtained :

Time rate Rs. 5 per hour. Basic time allowed for 20 Articles – 5 hours piece work Rate — *Add* : 20 per cent to piece Premium Bonus — *Add* : 50 per cent to time.

You are required to show :

(a) Hours worked (b) Weekly earnings (c) No. of articles produced (d) Labour cost per article for one operative under the following systems :

(1) Existing time Rate (2) Straight piece rate system

(3) Halsey Plan (4) Rowan Plan.

Assume that the articles 180 are produced in 45 hours per week under above 2, 3 and 4 system and that the worker earns half the time saved under Halsey plan. The additional Bonus under :

Existing system will be discontinued in the proposed incentive schemes.

Solution :

(a) *Under Existing scheme* : Time Rate =
Normal working hours in a week of 5 days of 9 hours = 5 × 9 = 45 Hours.

	Rs.
Normal Rate per hour — Rs. 5	
Earning = T × R = 45 × 5 =	225.00
Overtime — 3 shifts of 3 hours each = 3 × 3 = 9 Hours	
Overtime wages = T × R = 9 × 7.50 =	67.50
Day shift Bonus for 5 days shift — Rs. 10 = 5 × 10	50.00
Late shifts for 3 days — Rs. 7.50 (3 × 7.50) =	22.50
Total Wages	365.00

(b) *Straight piece rate System* for piece work output 180 articles 45 hours.

Output per hour $\frac{180}{45}$ = 4 units per hour

Normal Rate per hour — Rs. 5 for 45 hours = 45 × 5 =	225.00
Add : 20 per cent to piece 20 per cent of Rs. 225 =	45.00
Total week wages	270.00

Alternatively

Piece rate wages : Normal output per hour — 4 units.
Normal rate per hour — Rs. 5

Normal Rate per unit = $\frac{5}{4}$ = Rs. 1.25

Earnings = Output × Rate per hour = 180 × 1.25 =	225.00
Add : 20 per cent of 225	45.00
	270.00

(c) *Under Halsey Plan* :

Basic time allowed 5 hours for 20 Articles

Premium Bonus *Add* : 50 per cent to time (50 per cent of 5 hours 2½ hours) i.e., 7½ hours for 20 Articles

Time allowed for 180 units × $\frac{7\frac{1}{2}}{20}$ hours

Standard time for 180 units	67½ Hours
Actual time taken	45 Hours
Time saved	22½ Hours

Earnings = T × R + ½ (S – T) R

= 45 × 5 + ½ (67½ – 45) 5

= 225 + ½ (22½ × 5)

= 225 + ½ (112.50)

= 225 + 56.25 = 281.25

(d) *Under Rowan Plan* : Earnings $= T \times R + \frac{(S - T)}{S} T \times R$

Standard time — 67½ hours, Time taken — 45 hours, Rate per hour — Rs. 5.

$$\text{Earnings} = 45 \times 5 \frac{(67\tfrac{1}{2} - 45)}{67\tfrac{1}{2}} 45 \times 5$$

$$= 225 + \left(\frac{22\tfrac{1}{2}}{67\tfrac{1}{2}}\right) 225$$

$$= 225 + 75 = \text{Rs. } 300$$

Statement showing Labour cost under each of method of payment

Methods of Payment or Systems	Hours Worked	Weekly Earnings Rs.	No. of unit of output (in Units)	Cost per unit Rs.	Round up Rs.
(1) Existing Time Rate	54	365.00	180	2.00	2.00
(2) Piece Rate	45	270.00	180	1.50	1.50
(3) Halsey Plan	45	281.25	180	1.562	1.57
(4) Rowan Plan	45	300.00	180	1.66	1.67

Problem No. 80 (Problem on Merit Rating)

Following are the data relating to the workers X, Y and Z, working in a factory on a particular Job :

Normal Rate per hour — Rs. 5. Hours worked by the workers :

X – 60 hours, Y – 48 hours, Z – 72 hours.

The merit rating analysis shows the following efficiency of the workers : X — 80%, Y — 120%, Z — 75%

In addition to the wages paid at the adjusted normal rate (i.e., according to the efficiency rate of the workers) a worker is entitled to dearness allowance as a percentage of his wages at adjusted rate based on cost of living Index number for every 3 point in Index number above 100 points 1% dearness allowance is to be allowed. Now the cost of Index number is 130 points.

Calculate the total earnings of the workers.

Solution :

Earnings of the workers :

Worker X (Earnings) : Normal rate per hour — Rs. 5

Adjusted Normal rate to percentage of efficiency

Adjusted Rate — 5 × 80% = Rs. 4 per hour.

	Rs.
Actual hours worked 60 hours.	
Earnings = No. of hours worked × Rate per hour = 60 × 4 =	240.00
Add : Dearness allowance above 100 Index number = 130	
D.A. for $\frac{30}{3}$ = 10 point per cent of Rs. 240	24.00
	264.00

Worker Y (No. of hours worked — 48 hours)

Normal rate per hour — Rs. 5

Adjusted rate on per cent of efficiency

5 × 120 per cent = Rs. 6 per hour

Earning = No. of hours worked × Rate per Hour = 48 × 6 =	288.00
Add : Dearness allowance above 100 points index Number 130	
D.A. for 30 for every 3 point 1 per cent of D.A.	
$\frac{30}{3}$ = 10 per cent of Rs. 288 =	28.80
Total earnings	316.80

Worker Z : No. of hours worked 72 hours.

Normal rate per hour — Rs. 5

Adjusted rate on per cent of efficiency 5 × 75% = Rs. 3.75 per hour

Earnings = No. of hours worked × Rate per hour = 72 × 3.75 =	270.00
Add : Dearness allowances above 100 point in Index No. 130 for	
every 3 point 1 per cent of D.A. $\frac{30}{3}$ = 10 per cent Rs. 270	27.00
Total Earnings	297.00

GROUP BONUS SCHEME

When a work is carried on in a group, to encourage group workers' efficiency the bonus may be paid to the whole group. The group bonus may be shared by the members (workers) of the group in an agreed ratio. In the absence of any agreed ratio it may be distributed among the workers in the ratio of basic time earnings for time spent by them on a group work.

Group bonus enhances productivity of the group. Under this scheme the efficiency or otherwise of the individual is not considered but group efficiency is determined as a whole and bonus is paid on that basis.

Problem No. 81

In an assembly shop A, B and C work in a team on a group Job (for which they are paid on a piece work rate) and also work on day rate Job. In a 44-hour week they have worked the following hours on group Job which carried a piece wage of Rs. 300, the balance of hours being spent on individual day rate Job.

Workers	Hours worked on Group Job	Wage Rate per Hour
A	36 Hours	Rs. 5.50
B	24 Hours	Rs. 5.00
C	30 Hours	Rs. 4.50

Each worker gets D.A. at Rs. 10 per week. Tabulate weekly Earnings of workers.

Solution :

Group Piece wage earning of Rs. 300 is distributed to workers in the proportion of contribution.

Workers	Hours worked	Rate per hour	Amount	Ratio
A	36	5.00	180.00	$\frac{180}{480}$ = 3/8
B	24	7.50	180.00	$\frac{180}{480}$ = 3/8
C	30	4.00	120.00	$\frac{120}{480}$ = 2/8
			480.00	

Share in the Group earnings :

A	3/8 × 300	=	112.50
B	3/8 × 300	=	112.50
C	2/8 × 300	=	75.00
		Total	300.00

Statement showing Balance of Hours worked at Day wage rate on Job :

A = 44 – 36 = 8 × 5 =	40.00
B = 44 – 24 = 20 × 7.50 =	150.00
C = 44 – 30 = 14 × 4 =	56.00

Weekly Earnings of Group Workers

Workers	Group Earnings	Earnings on balance of hours worked	D.A. per week	Total Amount
A	112.50	40.00	10.00	162.50
B	112.50	150.00	10.00	272.50
C	75.00	56.00	10.00	135.00

Problem No. 82

In a factory 4 workers — two skilled, one semi skilled and one skilled worker undertook the particular Job on piece work basis for Rs. 3,600.

The time spent by each of them is 400 hours and the rates of pay are for Skilled workers 2 — Rs. 2.25 per hour.

Semi skilled worker 1 — Rs. 1.50 per hour

Unskilled worker 1 — Re. 0.75 per hour.

Ascertain the amount of piece work premium and show how the amount of it which each worker will receive when it is divided proportionately to the wages paid and show in each case the percentage of bonus nears to the wage payment at basis rate.

Further from the following particulars calculate total cost :

	Rs.
Cost of material	4,000
Wages (as above)	—
Overhead	1,500
Selling Expenses	1,000
Carriage outward Expenses	600

The manufactures expects return @ 20 per cent on sales price.

Ascertain profit to be made.

Total piece work of Rs. 3,000.

Solution :

Skilled workers 2 — @ Rs. 2.25 × 400 =	1,800
Semi skilled worker 1 — @ Rs. 1.50 × 400 =	600
Unskilled worker 1 — 0.75 Ps × 400 =	300
Total Wages	2,700
Total payment to group workers	3,600
Total wages at ordinary rate	2,700
Bonus premium on working piece work	900

The bonus premium is to be distributed among all workers in proportion to wages paid to them wages at ordinary rate.

Skilled workers — 2 — 1st worker Rs.	900	3/9
2nd worker Rs.	900	3/9
Semi skilled worker — 1	600	2/9
Unskilled worker — 1	300	1/9

Proportionate bonus and percentage of Bonus on Wages.

Skilled workers — 1st — $900 \times 3/9 = 300 = \frac{300}{900} \times 100 = 1/3$

2nd — $900 \times 3/9 = 300 = \frac{300}{900} \times 100 = 1/3$

Semi skilled 1 — $900 \times 2/9 = 200 = \frac{200}{600} \times 100 = 1/3$

Unskilled 1 — $900 \times 1/9 = 100 = \frac{100}{300} \times 100 = 1/3$

Total premium of Rs. 900 distributed among the workers.

Skilled —	1st — 300	33.33% Or 1/3
	2nd — 300	33.33% Or 1/3
Semi skilled	1 — 200	33.33% Or 1/3
Unskilled	1 — 100	33.33% Or 1/3

Statement of Total Cost Profit Selling Price

Cost of Material		4,000
Wage (including premium)		3,600
	Prime Cost	7,600
Works overhead		1,500
	Works Cost	9,100
Selling Expenses		1,000
Carriage outward		600
	Total Cost of sales	10,700
Add : Profit 20 per cent on sales price Or 25% on cost price		2,675
	Selling Price	13,375

(Profit 20 per cent on 13,375 = Rs. 2,675)

Problem No. 83

In an engineering company a particular Job standard time fixed is 36 hours and the basic time wage is Rs. 6 per hour. As per the bonus scheme instituted by the company, that the worker is to get his normal rate for hours actually worked, and for half of the hours saved. Worker A completes the Job in 26 hours and worker B completes the Job in 28 hours. The cost of material for Job is Rs. 165 and the worker on cost be charged on the basis of 150 per cent of Direct wages what would be selling price if profit margin is 25 per cent on cost.

Calculate :

(a) Total wages earned by A and B and the effective Labour cost per hour.
(2) Total cost of Job in each case.

Solution :

Standard Time — 36 hours, Normal rate per hour — Rs. 6

Earnings of Workers	A	B
(1) Standard time	36 hours	36 hours
(2) Rate per hour	Rs. 6.00	Rs. 6.00
(3) Actual time taken	26 Hours	28 Hours
(4) Time saved (1 – 3)	10 Hours	8 Hours
(5) Basic wage (26 × 6)	Rs. 156.00	
(28 × 6)		Rs. 168.00
(6) Bonus ½ of time saved × @ hour ½ (10 × 6)	Rs. 30.00	
½ (8 × 6)		Rs. 24.00
Total Wages	186.00	192.00
(7) Labour cost per hour = $\frac{\text{Total wages}}{\text{No. of hours}}$	$\frac{186}{26} = 7.15$	$\frac{192}{28} = 6.85$
Labour cost per hour Rs.	7.15	6.86

Statement of cost of Job in each Case

Particular	A	B
(1) Material	165.00	165.00
(2) Direct Wages	186.00	192.00
Prime Cost	351.00	367.00
Works on cost 150% of Direct Wages A — 186 × 150%	279.00	
B — 192 × 150%		288.00
	630.00	655.00
Add : Profit 25% on cost	157.50	163.75
Selling Price	787.50	818.75

Problem No. 84

In a manufacturing Co. in the production unit under bonus system, bonus hours are credited to the employees in proportion of time taken which time saved bears to standard time Jobs are carried forward from week to another. No overtime is worked and the payment is made on including those subsequently rejected.

Following are the details provided :

Particulars	Employees		
	X	Y	Z
(1) Basic wages rate per unit	Rs. 6.00	Rs. 7.50	Rs. 7.00
(2) Units issued	3000.00	2800.00	3600.00
	H.M.	H.M.	H.M.
(3) Time allowed for 100 units (in hours)	2.30	3.00	2.45
(4) Time taken	60 hours	89 hours	88 hours
(5) Rejects	200.00	150.00	400.00

H = Hours M = Minutes

From the above information calculate :

(a) The bonus hours and the bonus amount earned

(b) Total Wage cost

(c) The wage cost of each good unit produced.

Solution :

Calculation of standard time = $\frac{\text{Units}}{100} \times$ Time allowed

Units H.M.	Units H.	Units H.M.
$\frac{3000}{100} \times 2.30$	$\frac{2800}{100} \times 3$	$\frac{3600}{100} \times 2.45$
= 75 Hrs	84 Hrs	99 Hrs.

Statement showing Earnings of Workers

Particulars	Employees		
	X	Y	Z
Time allowed (Standard time)	75 hours	84 hours	99 hours
Time taken	60 hours	89 hours	88 hours
Time saved	15 hours	—	11 hours
Calculation of Bonus :			
Bonus = Time Save × $\frac{\text{Time taken}}{\text{Standard time}}$ × Rate	$15 \times \frac{60}{75} \times 6$		$11 \times \frac{88}{99} \times 7$
Bonus	= 72	—	= 68.44

Statement of Earnings Workers

Particulars	Employees		
	X	Y	Z
Earnings = T × R	60 × 6	89 × 7.50	88 × 7
Wages	360.00	667.50	616.00
Add : Bonus	72.00	—	68.44
Total Wages	432.00	667.50	684.44

Particulars	Employees		
	X	Y	Z
Units issued	3000	2800	3600
Units rejected	200	150	400
Good Units	2800	2650	3200
Wage cost of good units / No. of good units	432 / 2800	667.50 / 2650	684.44 / 3200
Cost per unit	0.15 Ps	0.25 Ps	0.21 Ps

Problem No. 85

In a manufacturing factory fifteen workers are working in a group on particular Job, when weekly production of group exceeds a standard output per hour, each worker in the group is paid a bonus for the excess production in addition to his hourly wages.

The amount of bonus is calculated by first determining the percentage by which the group output exceeds the standard output, one half of this percentage is applied to a wage rate of Rs. 10 per hour to determine an hourly Bonus rate irrespective of variations in individual hourly rate. Each worker in a group is paid a bonus. This bonus rate applied to his total hours worked during the week.

The standard output before a bonus can be earned is 200 units per man hour on the basis of production record stated below :

Compute :

(1) The rate of amount of bonus for the week.

(2) The total wages of worker A who worked for 42 hours at a basic Wage Rs. 8 per hour.

Worker B — who worked for 40 hours at basic wage of Rs. 12 per hour

Days	Man hours worked	Production (in units)
Monday	75	19,300
Tuseday	75	19,400
Wednesday	75	20,000
Thursday	75	21,750
Friday	70	18,250
Saturday	45	5,050
Total	415	1,03,750

Solution :

Actual production per week — 1,03,750 Units.

Man hours work in the week — 415 hours.

Rate of production for the group

$$\text{Per man hour} = \frac{\text{Total units}}{\text{Total man hours}} = \frac{1,03,750}{415} = 250 \text{ Units.}$$

Standard output per worker — 200 units

Actual output exceed standard output 50 units.

Per cent of excess output over standard output

$$= \frac{\text{Excess output}}{\text{Standard output}} \times 100 = \frac{50}{200} \times 100 = 25\%$$

Bonus rate per hour = Rate per hour × ½ × per cent of excess output

= 10 × ½ × 25% = Rs. 1.25

Total Bonus for the week = Total man hours × Bonus rate per hour

= 415 × 1.25

= Rs. 518.75

Earnings of workers :

Worker A :

			Rs.
Wages	=	Hours worked × rate per hour	
	=	42 × 8 =	336.00
Bonus	=	Hours worked × Bonus rate per hour	
	=	42 × 1.25	52.50
		Total Earnings	388.50

Worker B :

Wages	=	Hours worked × Rate per hour	
	=	40 × 12	480.00
Bonus	=	Hours worked × Bonus rate per hour	
	=	40 × 1.25	50.00
		Total Earnings	530.00

Labour bonus cost attach to each unit :

$$\frac{\text{Total Bonus for the week}}{\text{Total output for the week}} \text{ of Rs. } \frac{518.75}{1,03,750} = \text{Re. } 0.005 \text{ Ps}$$

Bonus cost per unit = Re. 0.005 Ps.

Problem No. 86

The following particulars relate to the year ending 31st March 1992 for 30 Workers in a factory :

	Rs.
(1) Basic Pay	3,60,000
(2) Dearness allowances	1,80,000
(3) Bonus 20% on wages (Basic)	—
(4) Night shift allowances	64,000
(5) Overtime allowances	48,000
(6) P.F. Deposit for the period	75,000
(7) E.S.I. Contribution	20,200
Recovery towards house Rent	75,000
Supply of provision	1,50,000
Expenses incurred for amentites to Employees	30,000

P.F. is paid in equal shares by employers and employee E.S.I. contribution ratio 7:5. The workers are entitled to 5 per cent of the total days worked as leave with full pay. No. of days worked in a year 300 days of 8 hours a day. Normal idle time is 5 per cent. Calculate Labour cost per hour.

Solution :

Amount Payable to Workers

(1) Basic Pay		3,60,000
(2) D.A.		1,80,000
(3) Bonus 20 per cent of 3,60,000		72,000
(4) Night shift allowances		64,000
(5) Overtime allowances		48,000
(6) P.F. Deposits employer's contribution ½ × 75,000		37,500
(7) E.S.I. contribution employer at 7/12 × 20,200		11,783
(8) Expenses for amenities		30,000
Total wages		8,03,283
		8,03,283
Less : Recovery : House Rent	75,000	
Supply of provision	1,50,000	2,25,000
Net payment to workers		5,78,283

Hours worked : 300 days × 8 Hours × 30 Workers		72,000 Hours
Less : Leave with pay 5 per cent of 72,000 Hours	3,600	
Idle time (Normal 5% of 68,400)	3,420	7,020 Hours
Actual working hours		64,980 Hours

$$\text{Labour cost per hour} = \frac{\text{Total wages}}{\text{No. of working Hrs.}} = \frac{8,03,283}{64,980} = \text{Rs. } 12.36$$

(PROBLEMS ON TIME WAGES AND MONTHLY PAYMENT)

Problem No. 87

Mr. Mohan working in a factory is paid monthly Wages. The following are the details :

(1) Basic Wages Rs. 1,125
(2) Dearness allowance Rs. 875
(3) Bonus 10 per cent of Basic Payment.
(4) Employers contribution towards provident fund 8-1/3 per cent
(5) 1 per cent towards E.S.I.
(6) Leave on full pay 1/20 days worked.
(7) Employers maintains a canteen for subsidised tea and Lunch provided to workers and monthly subsidiary is Rs. 9,000.
Total numbers of workers 300. Normal idle time 20 per cent of the total working hours. The average working days in a month 25 days of 8-hour a day.

Calculate total wages of Mohan and the labour cost per hour.

Solution :

Total Monthly Wages

(1) Basic Pay	1,125.00
(2) Dearness allowance	875.00
(3) Bonus 10% on Rs. 1,125	112.50
(4) Employer's contribution to P.F. 8-1/3% of Rs. 1,125	93.75
(5) E.S.I. Contribution 1 per cent of 1,125	11.25
(6) Proportionate canteen subsidiary $\frac{9000}{300}$	30.00
Total Wages	2,247.50

No. of working hours 25 days of 8 hours (25 × 8)	200 Hours
Less : 1/20 day leave with full pay $\frac{200}{20}$ =	10 Hours
	190 Hours
Less : Normal idle time 20 per cent of working hours (190 × 20%)	38 Hours
Effective working hours in a month	152 Hours

$$\text{Labour Cost per hour} = \frac{\text{Total monthly wages}}{\text{Effective working hours}}$$

$$= \frac{2,247.50}{152}$$

= Rs. 14.786.

Problem No. 88

Mr. Raju is working in a factory draws the monthly salary. Details of salary drawn is as follows :

(1) Basic Pay Rs. 1,500

(2) D.A. Rs. 950

(3) P.F. contribution of employee's 10 per cent of basic.

(4) Bonus @ 10 per cent of basic.

(5) E.S.I. — Employer's contribution 1 per cent of Employee's contribution ½ per cent.

(6) Employer maintains a canteen for workers where subsidised tea and lunch are provided subsidies to the canteen is Rs. 12,000; total No. of workers are 400.

(7) Normal idle time 20 per cent. The worker is entitled to 15 days earned leave during the year.

(8) No. of working days in a year — 300 days of 8 hours a day.

Calculate total pay of worker and the Labour cost per hour.

Solution :

Total Wages for the Month

(1) Basic pay	1,500
(2) D.A.	950
(3) Bonus 10 per cent of basic	150
(4) Employee's contribution to P.F. 20 per cent of Basic pay	150
(5) Employer's contribution to E.S.I. 1 per cent of basic	15
(6) Canteen subsidies proportionate $\frac{12,000}{400}$	30
Total Monthly Wages	2,795

No. of working hours per month

Working days in year 300 × 8 hours	2,400 Hours
Less : 15 days leave with pay (15 × 8)	120 Hours
	2,280 Hours
Less : Normal idle time 20% of 2,280	456 Hours
Effective working hours in year	1,824 Hours

$$\text{Working hours per month} = \frac{1,824}{12} = 152 \text{ Hours.}$$

$$\text{Labour cost per hour} = \frac{\text{Total Wages}}{\text{Effective working hours}}$$

$$= \frac{2,795}{152}$$

$$= \text{Rs. } 18.38.$$

Problem No. 89

The following particulars relate to the year ending 31st March 1993 for 40 workers :

(1) Basic Wages	1,50,000
(2) D.A.	75,000
(3) Night shift allowances	28,800
(4) Overtime allowances	21,000
(5) P.F. deposit for the year	36,000
(6) E.S.I. contribution	8,424
(7) Recovery towards House Rent	30,600
(8) Recovery towards supply of provision	50,000
(9) Expenses for provide amenities	12,000

Other Informations :

(1) P.F. is paid in equal share by Employer and Employee.

(2) Contribution to E.S.I. in the ratio of 7 : 5 by the Employer and Employees respectively.

(3) The workers are entitled to 5% of the total days worked as leave on full pay.

(4) The numbers of days worked 300 in the year normal idle time is 5 per cent of working in hours.

(5) Daily working hours — 8 hours.

Solution :

Total Labour cost per Year for the year ending 31-3-1993

(1) Basic Pay		1,50,000
(2) D.A.		75,000
(3) Night shift allowances		28,800
(4) Overtime allowances		21,000
(5) P.F. Deposit	36,000	
Less : Employee's contribution 50%	18,000	18,000
(6) E.S.I. contribution	8,424	
Less : Employees contribution (8,424 × 5/12)	3,510	4,914
(7) Employees Amenities		12,000
Total Labour Cost		3,09,714
Less : Recovery of Hours Rent	30,600	
Supply of provision	50,000	80,600
Net Labour cost		2,29,114

Calculation of working hours

300 Days × 8 hours × 40 Workers	96,000
Less : 5% on 96,000	4,800
	91,200
Less : 5% Normal idle time	4,560
Total Working hours	86,640

$$\text{Labour Cost per hour} = \frac{\text{Total Labour cost}}{\text{Total working hours}}$$

$$= \frac{3{,}09{,}714}{86{,}640}$$

$$= \text{Rs. } 3.57.$$

Problem No. 90

In a manufacturing factory X and Y working on a particular Job to produce 260 Units and 220 Units respectively for which time allowed is 15 minutes per unit and 10 units per minute respectively credited to workers for every hour time saved a basis is paid 50% of basic rate which is Rs. 12 per hour for both employees. The basic working week is 44 hours. Hours worked in excess of 44 hours are paid at a time plus 1/3.

X completes his units in 47 hours.

Y completes his units in 40 hours. (But worked for full week)

Due to defective material, 10 units of X and 5 units of Y are subsequently scraped although all units produced are paid.

You are required to calculate the worker X and Y the following :

(a) Total wages payable (b) Amount of bonus payable

(c) The labour cost per good unit.

Solution :

Statement of Earning of Workers

Particulars	Worker - X Units	Worker - Y Units
Units produced	260	210
Time allowed 15 minutes per unit		
For One hour = 4 Units ($\frac{60}{15}$)		
Time for producing	260 Units 65 Hours	220 Units 55 Hours.
Standard time	65 Hours	55 Hours
Time taken	47 Hours	40 Hours
Time saved	18 Hours	15 Hours
Rate per hour	Rs. 10	Rs. 10

Particulars	Worker - X Units	Worker - Y Units
Bonus 50 per cent of Basic Rs. 10	Rs. 5	Rs. 5
Bonus = Time saved × Rate per hour	18 Hours × 5	15 Hours × .5
	= Rs. 90	= Rs. 75
Time Wages for week	44 Hours × Rs. 10	40 Hours × Rs. 10
	= Rs. 440	= Rs. 400
Add : Bonus	= Rs. 90	= Rs. 75
Overtime (47 – 44) 3 hours		
Time wage = 3 × 10 = 30		
Add : 1/3 of 30 10	= Rs. 40	= —
Total Wages	Rs. 570	Rs. 475
Units Produced	260 Units	220 Units
Less : Units scraped	10 Units	5 Units
Good Units	250 Units	215 Units
Labour cost per Unit = $\frac{\text{Total Wage}}{\text{No. of good Units}}$	$\frac{570}{250}$	$\frac{475}{215}$
	= Rs. 2.28	= Rs. 2.28

Note : Worker Y is paid on actual time worked on Job since he is provided another Job for work for remaining period (44 – 40) 4 Hours work and paid separately.

Problem No. 91

In a manufacturing company the working hours for the month is 200 hours, Overtime allowances is paid at double the normal rate plus D.A. only. Employers contribution to Provident Fund and Employees State Insurance (E.S.I.) are at equal rates with employee contribution. The following are the particulars of workers X and Y who are paid monthly wages.

Particulars	Workers X	Workers Y
(a) Basic Wages	1,750	2,050
(b) Deaness allowance 80% of Basic	1,400	1,640
(c) Provident Fund on basic	10%	10%
(d) Employees State Insurance (E.S.I.)	2%	2%
(e) Overtime worked	15 Hours	—
(f) Idle time paid	—	20 Hours

Calculate the total earning of workers X and Y and also ascertain normal wage rate per hour and overtime wage per hour.

Solution :

Statement of Wages of Workers

Particulars	Worker X	Worker Y
(a) Basic Wage	1,750.00	2,050.00
(b) Dearnes allowances 80 per cent of basic wage	1,400.00	1,640.00
(c) Provident Fund 10 per cent of basic wage	175.00	205.00
(d) E.S.I. 2 per cent of basic wage	35.00	41.00
(e) Overtime 15 Hours (Double the rate on basic) 1,750; *Add* : D.A. 1,400; = 3,150		
Normal working = $\frac{3,150}{200}$ 15.75		
Overtime hour rate (15.75 × 2) = 31.50		
for 15 × 31.50 = 472.50	472.50	
Total Wages	3,832.50	3,936.00

Calculation of Normal Wages of Workers

Particulars	Worker A	Worker B
(1) Basic Wages	1,750	2,050
(2) D.A.	1,400	1,640
(3) P.F.	175	205
(4) E.S.I.	35	41
	3,360	3,936
Worker Normal Rate	$\frac{3,360}{200}$	$\frac{3,936}{180}$
Workers Normal Rate	16.80	21.37
Overtime Wages	31.50	—

Problem No. 92

From the following particulars you are required to prepare a statement of labour cost of 8 hours per day :

(1) Monthly salary (Basic) 1,050 (in Rs.)

(2) Leave salary 5% of Basic pay

(3) Employer's contribution to P.F. 10% (1 & 2)

(4) Employer's contribution to State Insurance 3% of (1 & 2)

(5) Pro-rata expenditure on amenities to labourers — Rs. 56.125

(6) No. of working hours in a month — 200 hours.

Solution :

Statement showing Labour Cost per day of 8 hours

Particulars	Rs.
(1) Monthly Salary (Basic)	1,050.00
(2) Leave salary 5% of basic (5% × 1,050)	52.50
(3) Employer's contribution to P.F. 10% of 1 & 2 (1,050 + 52.50 = 1,112.50 × 10%)	111.25
(4) E.S.I. Contribution 3% of 112.50	33.37
(5) Amenities to Labourers	56.13
Total Monthly salary	1,303.25

$$\text{Labour cost per Day (8 Hours)} = \frac{\text{Total Salary}}{\text{No. of hours in a month}} \times \text{No. of hours in day}$$

$$= \frac{1{,}303.25}{200} \times 8$$

$$= \text{Rs. } 52.13$$

Problem No. 93

In a manufacturing concern Emmerson's Bonus Scheme was introduced with a guarantee of day wages of Rs. 35 per day.

The standard output is fixed at 300 units per week representing 100% efficiency. The guaranteed wage rate is paid without bonus to those workers who show efficiency up to 70% of standard. Beyond this bonus is payable on a graded scale in the fixed ratio to the increased output as under :

Efficiency	Bonus Payable
90%	10%
100%	20%

Further increase of 1% in bonus is given for every 1% increase in efficiency.

Calculate the total earning of 5 workers, worked for a week and their output was as under :

A – 150 Units, B – 255 Units, C – 270 Units, D – 300 Units & E – 375 Units.

Solution :

Statement showing the earnings of workers under Emmerson's Plan

Particulars	Workers				
	A	B	C	D	E
(1) Standard output	300	300	300	300	300
(2) Actual output	150	255	270	300	375
(3) Percentage of Efficiency	50%	85%	90%	100%	125%
(4) Bonus Percentage	—	—	10%	20%	20% + 25%
(5) Day wage for week (35 × 6)	210	210	210	210	210
(6) Bonus Payable	—	—	21	42	94.50
Total Wages	210	210	231	252	304.50

Problem No. 94

In a manufacturing Co. the Emmerson's efficiency Bonus system was introduced with day. Wages guaranteed up to 70% of standard efficiency no bonus is payable above 70% and upto 100% efficiency, a bonus is payable on a graded scale.

@ 100% efficiency and above bonus is payable as per the Emmerson's efficiency bonus scheme.

In a factory standard output per hour 5 units of 8 hours a day is fixed. Rate per hour is Rs. 4.50. The output of workers A, B, C and D for the week (6 Days) is 240 Units, 252 Units, 264 Units and 300 Units respectively.

Calculate that total earnings of workers.

Solution :

Standard output per hour 5 Units

For 8 hours day = (8 × 5) = 40 Units

For 6 Days of week (6 × 40) = 240 Units.

Rate per Hour = 4.50

Emmerson's Efficiency Bonus Scheme :

Up to 70% efficiency no bonus guaranteed.

At 100% efficiency — 20% Bonus

Above 100% efficiency 1 per cent Bonus for every 1 per cent increase in efficiency.

Statement showing Wages of Worker for the Week
Under Emmerson's Efficiency Bonus Scheme

Particulars	Workers A	B	C	D
(1) Standard output (in units)	240	240	240	240
(2) Actual output	240	252	264	300
(3) Percentage of Efficiency	100%	105%	110%	125%
(4) Percentage of Bonus applicable	20%	20%+5%	20%+10%	20%+25%
	Rs.	Rs.	Rs.	Rs.
(5) Day wages for week (4.5 × 8 × 6)	216.00	216.00	216.00	216.00
(6) Bonus Payable	43.20	54.00	64.80	97.20
Total Wages for week	259.20	270.00	280.80	313.20

Problem No. 95

A manufacturing company has introduced a bonus system of wage payment at sales rates based on cost reduction towards labour and overheads the slab rate beings :

Up to 10% of savings — 5% Bonus of the Earnings
Up to 20% of savings — 15% Bonus of the Earnings
Up to 40% of savings — 30% Bonus of the Earnings
Up to 70% of savings — 40% Bonus of the Earnings
Above 70% of savings — 50% Bonus of the Earnings

The rate per hour for 3 workers A, B and C are Rs. 2.00, Rs. 2.50 and Rs. 2.25 respectively. The overhead recovery rate is 500% on productive wages. The standard cost toward wages and overhead per unit is determined at Rs. 5 per unit.

If time taken by A, B and C to produce 400 units is 50 hours, 70 hours and 40 hours respectively what is the amount of bonus earned by each of the worker.

Solution :

Statement showing per cent of savings in cost and the rate of Bonus applicable

Worker	Hours taken	Basic Wages per Hour	Total Basic Wage	Overhead @ 500% of Wage	Total Cost	Standard Cost	Savings in time	Savings in %	Bonus % applicable	Bonus Amount
						(200×5)				
A	50	2.00	100	500	600	1,000	400	40%	30%	180
B	70	2.50	150	750	900	1,000	100	10%	5%	45
C	40	2.25	90	450	540	1,000	460	46%	40%	216

Problem No. 96

In an engineering shop a worker is paid Rs. 2 per hour. The standard time fixed for the Job is 250 hours and actual time taken to complete the Job is 175 hours.

The plan of payment of bonus on sliding scale is as under :

Sliding scale of Bonus :

(a) Within first 10% of savings in standard time Bonus 40% of time saved.

(b) Within second 10% of savings in standard time 50% of time saved.

(c) Within third 10% of savings in standard time 60% of time saved.

(d) Within fourth 10% of savings in standard time 70% of time saved.

(e) For the rest of Bonus is 75% of time saved.

Calculate the earning of the work wages and Bonus.

Solution :

Standard time	250 Hours
Time taken	175 Hours
Time saved	75 Hours

Rate per hour Rs. 2

Total time saved on standard time :

First 10% of standard time 250 × 10%	=	25 Hours
Second 10% of standard time 250 × 10%	=	25 Hours
Third 10% of standard time 250 × 10%	=	25 Hours
Time Saved Total		75 Hours

Earnings of worker = Time taken × Rate per hour

= 175 × 2

= 350 Rs. 350.00

Bonus :

(a) First 10 per cent savings in standard time (25 × 2 × 40 per cent)	20.00	
(b) Second 10 per cent savings in standard time 50 per cent (25 × 2 × 50%)	25.00	
(c) Third 10 per cent savins in standard time 60 per cent (25 × 2 × 60%)	30.00	75.00
Total Earnings of Worker		425.00

Problem No. 97

In a Vijay Engineering Works the four workers produced : X — 1800 Units, Y — 4200 Units, M — 3000 Units, Z — 1200 Units.

The wages rate paid to the workers under :

(a) Straight Piece rate 0.60 Ps per unit.

(b) Differential piece works under which first 1200 units are paid at 0.20 Ps per unit the rate increase by 0.10 Ps per unit for each subsequent 600 units produced.

Calculate the wages of workers under :

(a) Straight piece rate method.

(b) Under differential piece system.

(c) The total cost per unit.

(d) The average cost per unit.

Solution :

(a) Earnings Under Straight Piece Rate System

Workers	Units Produced	Rate per unit	Total Wages
X	1800	0.60 Ps	1,080
Y	4200	0.60 Ps	2,520
M	3000	0.60 Ps	1,800
N	1200	0.60 Ps	720
	10200		6,120

$$\text{Average Cost} = \frac{\text{Total Cost}}{\text{No. of Units}} = \frac{6,120}{10200} = \text{Re. } 0.60 \text{ Ps}$$

(b) Differential Piece Rate : (1) First up to 1200 Units 0.20 Ps per unit
(2) For subsequent 600 Units increase 0.10 Ps. per unit

Particulars	Workers			
	X	Y	M	N
Units proudced	1800	4200	3000	1200
(1) Wages for first 1200 × 0.20 Ps	240	240	240	240
(2) Wages for subsequently 600 × .30 Ps	180	180	180	
(3) Wages for next 600 × 0.40	—	240	240	—
(4) Wages for next 600 × 0.50	—	300	300	—
(5) Wages for next 600 × 0.60	—	360	—	—
(6) Wages for next 600 × .70	—	420	—	—
Total Wages	420	1740	960	240

$$\text{Average Cost per Unit} = \frac{\text{Total Wages}}{\text{Total Units produced}} = \frac{3,560}{10200} = 0.349 \text{ or } 0.35 \text{ Ps}$$

Problem No. 98

What will be the earnings of a worker who is paid Rs. 2.50 per hour when he takes 180 hours to complete a Job work for which time allowed is 300 hours. The plan of payment of Bonus is on a sliding scale as under :

Percentage of Savings in Standard time	Bonus paybale % on time saved
(1) Within first 10% savings	40% of time saved
(2) Within second 10% savings	50% of time saved
(3) Within third 10% savings	60% of time saved
(4) Within fourth 10% of savings	70% of time saved
(5) For the rest of the bonus is at	75% of time saved.

Solution :

Standard time	300 Hours
Time taken	180 Hours
Time saved	120 Hours

10% of savings in standard

Calculation of Bonus for 120 Hours time saved : Rs.

			Rs.
(i)	First 10% savings	= 300 × 10% = 30 Hours × 2.50 × 40% =	30.00
(ii)	Second 10% savings	= 300 × 10% = 30 Hours × 2.50 × 50% =	37.50
(iii)	Third 10% savings	= 300 × 10% = 30 Hours × 2.50 × 60% =	45.00
(iv)	Fourth 10% savings	= 300 × 10% = 30 Hours × 2.50 × 70% =	52.50
		Total Bonus	165.00

Earnings = Time worked × Rate per hour

= 180 × 2.50

= 450

Add : Bonus as above 165

Total Wages 615

Alternatively :

Average per cent of Bonus 55 per cent of time saved.

Time saved = 120 × 2.50 = 300 × 55% = Rs. 165

Alternatively calculation of Average per cent = Total Bonus payable per cent on time saved

$$= \frac{220\%}{4}$$

= 55%.

3

Costing Overheads

Definition

The indirect portion of the total cost constitutes the overhead cost which is the aggregate of :

(a) Indirect Material Cost.

(b) Indirect wages and

(c) Indirect expenses and indirect costs are those which are incurred for the benefit of number of cost centres or cost units. Indirect costs, therefore, can not be conveniently identified with a particular cost centres or cost units.

Cost Centres or Cost Units

(a) Functional classification.

(b) Classification with regard to behaviour of the expenditure.

(c) Element-wise classification.

(A) *Functional-wise classification*

When the overheads are classified with major activity division of an organisation.

(a) Manufacturing overhead.

(b) Administrative overhead.

(c) Selling & Distribution overheads.

(d) Research and Development Expenses.

(B) *Classification with regard to behaviour of expenditure*

Some expenses do not change with volume of production/output and others change after a certain stage and still others with changes in volume of output. They are :

(a) Fixed overhead Expenses like — Rent of the Building, Depreciation on Building, office, staff salary, Interest on Capital etc.

(b) Semi variable overhead — It is an overhead partly fixed and partly variable.

Semi variable overheads may be :

(1) Fixed Expenses remain at the same position within certain stage of output :

Plant capacity, Factory building, staff etc., increase in plant capacity beyond its optimum capacity (maximum capacity) and also factory building needs expanded to accommodate more number of plants and staff supervisory and administrative needs to be expanded to carry out increased productive activities.

E.g. : If the productive capacity installed is 100 units or less than that a certain fixed expenditure is incured, beyond 100 units say capacity doubled, then increase, in plant, factory building and staff etc. increase and this stage become variable and up to 100 units capacity remains fixed. Therefore the overhead on such situation be treated as fixed + (plus) variable and is called same variable or semi fixed overhead, e.g. Telephone charges, postage up to certain weight etc.

(c) *Variable Overheads* — Variable overheads vary/change in proportion to output. Increase in the output increases overheads and decrease in output decreases overheads, Indirect expenses on material and wages etc.

(C) *Element-wise classification*

This classification was done according to the nature and source of expenditure.

(1) *Indirect Material* : e.g. Lubricants, Cotton waste, cost of materials of small value etc.

(2) *Indirect Wages* : e.g. Leave with pay, overtime duty, Nights shift Bonus, Holding pay etc. — factory supervisor salary etc.

(3) *Indirect Expenses :* e.g. Repairs and maintenance, depreciation, taxes, expenses on amenities to workers, entertainment, sports facility, canteen, Hospital for worker, Education facility for workers' children etc.

Steps — While apportioning the overheads to the Production Department :

(1) Collection of overheads.

(2) Classification of overheads.

(3) Allocation and apportionment of overheads.

(4) Absorption of overheads.

Collection of Overheads

(1) Stores Requisition. (2) Wage analysis sheet for Indirect Labour for Indirect Materials. (3) Expenses vouchers for Indirect Expenses.

Departmentalisation of Overheads

After the collection of overheads, the next stage is the allocation and apportionment of overheads to various departments. It is known as Departmentalisation of overheads. Department in factory may be broadly divided into :

(a) Service Departments.

(b) Production Departments.

Basis for apportionment of overheads : Suitable basis for apportionment of overheads to Production Departments and Service Department is to be adopted.

Basis

(1) Service or use or benefits derived to Departments

(2) Survey of existing conditions.

(3) Ability to pay or ability to bear by the Department.

Table : Overhead Cost and Basis for Distribution

(1) Amenities to workers, canteen Expenses. General Welfare Expenses. Others benefits — ESI, P.F. Contribution by the Employer.	No. of Employees. Or wages for each Department.
(2) Depreciation on Plant & Machinery, Equipment, Fire Insurance	Capital Value
(3) Lighting	No. of Light point or floor area houses used etc.
(4) Power	Horse power of machine (H.P.)
(5) Steam	On consumption basis.
(6) Delivery Expenses	Weight, volume or ton K.M.
(7) Audit Fee	Sales
(8) Stores Expenses	Materials consumed in value
(9) Other Overhead Expenses	Direct Material Direct Labour hour rate Or Machine hour rate.

Absorption of Overheads

Overhead absorption is "the allotment of overhead to cost unit". The term 'recovery' or 'Application' are also used in the same sense.

The following are the common basis used :

(1) Percentage on Direct Material Cost $= \frac{\text{Overhead}}{\text{Direct Material}} \times 100$

(2) Percentage of Direct Labour Cost $= \frac{\text{Overhead}}{\text{Direct Labour Cost}} \times 100$

(3) Percentage on Prime Cost $= \frac{\text{Overhead}}{\text{Prime Cost}} \times 100$

(4) Labour Hour Rate $= \dfrac{\text{Overhead}}{\text{Labour Hours Rate}}$

(5) Machine Hour Rate $= \dfrac{\text{Overhead}}{\text{Machine Hours Rate}}$

(a) Computation of Labour Hour Rate : $\dfrac{\text{Total Wages}}{\text{No. of labour hours worked}}$

(b) Computation of Machine Hour Rate :

Basis of apportionment of Machine Expenses

Expenses	Basis
(I) *Standing Charges :*	
(1) Rent, Rates, Taxes, etc.	(1) Area used or space occupied by Machine
(2) Lighting & Healing	(2) Floor area or No. of light points.
(3) Supervision charged	(3) Time devoted to each machine
(4) Insurance (Fixed)	(4) Capital Value.
(II) *Machine Expenses*	
(1) Power and steam	Horse power (H.P.) of machine
(2) Depreciation on machine	$\dfrac{\textit{Cost} + \text{Installation charges} - \text{Scrap}}{\text{Life in term of Machine hours}}$
(3) Repairs & Maintenance	Cost of Repairs actual
(4) Consumable items : Lubricants, Oil etc.	Cost/Machine hours.
(5) Oil consumption per hour, cost per Litre.	Actual.

Re-apportionment of Service Departments — Cost to Production Departments

Service Departments costs are to be re-apportioned to production department is known as the secondary Distribution. The basis for the apportionment of Service Department to Production Departments.

Service Department Costs (1)	Basis of Apportionment (2)
(1) Maintenance Department Repairs, Planning, Time keeping.	Hours worked for each Department or Direct Labour Rate, or Machine hour Rate.
(2) Personnel Department	Rate of labour Turnover.
(3) Store-Keeping Dept.	No. of requisition or value of Material.
(4) Welfare service — Canteen, Recreation, Hospital etc.	No. of Employees.
(5) Purchases Department	Value of materials purchases.

(1)	(2)
(6) Building Service Department	Floor area.
(7) Fire Protection	Capital value.
(8) Power	Horse power or H.P. or machine hour rate.

METHODS OF RE-APPORTIONMENT

(Service Department costs — reapportionment under these methods)

(1) *Direct Distribution.* Service Department costs are distribution to Production Department whereas the services rendered by one service department to other service departments are neglected.

(2) *Step Ladder.* Under this method the costs of most serviceable department is first apportioned to the other Service Departments and Production Departments. The next service department is taken up and its cost apportioned and this process is continued till the cost of the last Service Departments cost is apportioned. The cost of last Service Departments cost is apportioned only to Production Departments.

Limitation. It does not consider the services enjoyed by the other Service Departments.

(3) *Simultaneous Equation Method.* The Limitation in the above that is the benefit received from one service department to another service department is not fully accounted. The simultaneous method, does take into account and ascertain the true cost of service department rendering service to each other. It involves calculation in a most scientific way.

(4) *Repeated Redistribution Method.* Under this method costs of Service Department are distributed again and again among other departments until the figure become nil.

Problem No. 1

The following particulars relate to Shankaling Paints (Pvt.) Ltd.

(a) Departmental Overheads

Production Departments	Rs.	Service Departments	Rs.
A	600	X	234
B	700	Y	300
C	800		

(b) Absorption of Service Department Costs

	Production Department			Service Department	
	A	B	C	X	Y
Service Depts.					
X	20%	30%	40%	—	10%
Y	40%	10%	30%	20%	—

(c) Absorption Method to be followed — Simultaneous Equation Method

(d) Final out Machine Hour rate, if Machine Hours worked are :

A — 3960 B — 3292 C — 2038

[K.U.D., April 1998 (N)]

Solution :

The Service Department Expenses are apportioned to production departments under Simultaneous Equation Method.

Now Let X : be the total of X Service Department.

Y : be the total of Y Service Department.

X = 234 + 20% of Y — I

Y = 300 + 10% of X — II

Now Equation-I X = 234 + 1/5 (300 + 1/10^{X})

= 234 + 1/5 × 300 + 1/50^{X}

= 234 + 60 + 1/50^{X}

X – 1/50 ^{x} = 294

49/5 ^{x} = 294

X = 294 × 50/49 = 300

X = 300 Total Cost of X Service Department

Now Equation-II Y = 300 + 1/10^{x}

Substitute value of X =

Y = 300 + 1/10 × 300

= 300 + 30

Y = 330 Total Cost of Y Service Department

Note : It should be noted that the Service Department n — total cost includes inter Service Department of Y — 10%.

Therefore net amount of X Service Department will be (300 – 10% of 300) Rs. 270 only should be apportioned.

Similarly Service Department Y include inter Service Department of X — 20%. The net amount will be (330 – 20% of 330) Rs. 264.

Apportion of Service Departments Cost to Production Departments

		Production Departments		
		A	B	C
		Rs.	Rs.	Rs.
As per Primary Distribution Summary		600	700	800
Apportionment of Service Departments				
Costs X — 2 : 3 : 4 $\frac{270}{9}$	30	60	90	120
Y — 4 : 1 : 3 $\frac{264}{8}$	33	132	33	99
Verify A - 600 + X - 234 Total 2,634	Rs.	792	823	1,019

B - 700 Y - 300

C - 800

2,100 + 534

Machine Hour Rate =	$\frac{\text{Total Cost}}{\text{No. of Machine Hour}}$	$\frac{792}{3,960}$	$\frac{823}{3,292}$	$\frac{1019}{2,038}$
Machine Hour Rate		Re. 0.20	0.25	0.50

Problem No. 2

Find out Machine Hour Rate adopting Simultaneous Equation Method from the following details :

Particulars	Production Departments			Service Departments	
	A Rs.	B Rs.	C Rs.	X Rs.	Y Rs.
(1) Indirect Labour	1,200	2,000	1,000	500	1,000
(2) Depreciation	2,500	1,600	200	300	200
(3) Sundries	900	2,100	900	200	300
(4) Rent	2,400	4,800	2,000	2,000	800
(5) Electricity	800	2,000	500	400	300
Total	7,800	12,500	4,600	3,400	2,600
Estimated Machine Hours	1000	2450	1380	—	—
Apportionment of Service Department Cost					
X	30%	40%	20%	—	10%
Y	10%	20%	50%	20%	—

[K.U.D., April 1998 (O)]

Solution :

Let X — be the total of X Service Department

and Y — be the total of Y Service Department

Now X = 3,400 + 20% of Y - I

Y = 2,600 + 10% of X - II

X = 3,400 + 20% × 2,600 + 1/10^x

= 3,400 + 1/5 × 2,600 + 1/10^x

= 3,400 + 520 + 1/50^x

x – 1/50^x = 3,920

Now 49/50^x = 3,920

X = 3,920 × $\frac{50}{49}$

X = 4,000 X = Service Department = X = 4,000

Now Equation No. II

Y = 2,600 + 10% X

Substitute Value of X

Y = 2,600 + 1/10 × 4,000

Y = 2,600 + 400

Y = 3,000 Total Cost of Service Department - Y

Note : It should be noted that the Service Department X Total Cost includes 10% to Y Service Department.

X = 4,000 – 10%

X = 4,000 – 400

X = 3,600. Total Cost of X Service Department apportioned

Similarly Y = 3,000 includes 20% to X Service Department

Y = 3,000 – 20%

= 3,000 – 600

Y = 2,400

Apportionment of Service Departments Costs of Production Departments

	Production Department		
	A	B	C
	Rs.	Rs.	Rs.
As per Primary Distribution Summary	7,800	12,500	4,600
Apportionment Service Department Costs			
X — 36,00 4	1,200	1,600	800
Ratio 3 : 4 : 2 3,600 × 1/9 = 400			
Y — 2,400 3			
Ratio 1 : 2 : 5 = 2,400 × 1/8 = 300	300	600	1,500
Total A + B + C = 30,900	9,300	14,700	6,900

Verification

Total of A	7,800	Estimated			
		Machine Hours	1000	2450	1380
B	12,500				
C	4,600				
Total Production Dept.	24,900	Machine Hour			
+ Service Department X	3,400	Rate	9,300 / 1000	14,700 / 2450	6,900 / 1380
Y	2,600				
Total	30,900	Machine Hour Rate	Rs. 9.30	6.00	5.00

Problem No. 3

From the data given below calculate the Machine Hour Rate per annum :

	Rs.
(1) Rent of the Department (space occupied by Machine 1/5 of the Department)	780
(2) Lighting (No. of Men in the Department 12) 2 men engaged on this Machine	288
(3) Insurance	36
(4) Waste Cotton, oil etc.	60
(5) Salary of foreman (he devoles 1/4 of his time on this Machine)	6,000

Cost of Machine in Rs. 9,200 and it has an estimated scrap value of Rs. 200

It is ascertained from the past experience :

(i) that the Machine will work for 1800 hours per annum

(ii) that it will incur expenditure of Rs. 1125 p.a. in respect of repairs and maintenance

(iii) that it consumes 5 units of power per hour at cost of 60 paise per unit.

(iv) that working life of the Machine will be 10 years.

[K.U.D., October 1997(N)]

Solution :

Computation of Machine Hour Rate

	Per Annum	Per Hour
I. Standing Charges (Fixed Expenses)	Rs.	Rs.
(i) Rent – (1/5 × 780) 156	156	
(ii) Lighting – (1/12 × 288)	48	
(iii) Insurance	36	
(iv) Salary of Foreman (1/4 × 6,000)	1,500	
Total Standing Charges	1,740	

$$\text{Hourly Rate} = \frac{\text{Total Cost}}{\text{Total No. of Working Hours}} = \frac{1{,}740}{1800} \quad 0.97$$

0.9666

II. Machine Expenses

(i) Cotton waste, oil etc. Hourly Rate = $\frac{\text{Rs. 60 p.a.}}{1800} = 0.033$ 0.03

(ii) Depreciation - Hourly rate = $\frac{\text{Cost} - \text{Scrap}}{\text{Life}} = \frac{9{,}200 - 200}{18000} = \frac{9000}{18000}$ 0.50

	Per Annum	Per Hour
Working Hours – 1800 p.a. for 10 years = (1800 × 10)		
(iii) Repairs & Maintenance - Hourly rate = $\frac{1125}{1800}$ = 0.625		0.63
(iv) Power Per hour 5 units cost per unit 60 paise 5 × 0.60 =		3.00
Machine Hour Rate Rs.		5.13

Machine Hour Rate – Rs. 5.13

Problem No. 4

A Manufacturing Company has three Production Departments namely, A, B & C and two Service Departments namely,

(a) Transport and (b) Power Supply.

The departmental overheads are obtained in a summarised form as under :

Production Departments	Rs.	Service Departments	Rs.
A	10,000	Transport	4,000
B	6,000	Power Supply	6,000
C	5,000		

Overheads of Service Departments are as under :

Departments	A	B	C	Transport	Power Supply
Transport	40%	30%	10%	—	20%
Power Supply	20%	40%	30%	10%	—

Prepare a statement showing a distribution of Service Departments expenses to Production Departments by repeated distribution method.

[K.U.D., October 1997(O)]

Solution :

Repeated Distribution Summary

Particulars	Production Departments A	B	C	Service Dept. Transport	Power Supply
	Rs.	Rs.	Rs.	Rs.	Rs.
As per Primary Distribution Summary	10,000	6,000	5,000	4,000	6,000
Transport 40% 30% 10% — 20%	1,600	1,200	400	-4,000	800
	11,600	7,200	5,400	—	6,800
Power Supply 20% 40% 30% — 10%	1,360	2,720	2,040	680	6,800
	12,960	9,920	7,440	680	—

Particulars	Production Departments A Rs.	B Rs.	C Rs.	Service Dept. Transport Rs.	Power Supply Rs.
Transport 40% 30% 10% — 20%	272	204	68	–680	136
	13,232	10,124	7,505	—	136
Power Suppy 20% 40% 30% — 10%	27.20	54.4	40.80	13.6	–13.6
	13,259.20	10,178.40	7,548.80	13.6	—
Transport 40% 30% 10% — 20%	5.44	4.08	1.36	–13.6	2.72
	13,264.64	10,182.48	7,550.16	—	2.72
Power Suppy 20% 40% 30% — 10%	.55	1.10	.82	0.25	-2.75
	13,265.19	10,183.58	7,550.98	0.25	—
Transport	.11	.12	.12	–0.25	—
Total	13,265.30	10,183.70	7,551.10	0	—

Or

The same problem may be answered under Simultaneous Equation Method.

Solution :

Let 'T' be the Total of Transport

Let P be the Total of Power Supply

(i) Transport — T = 4,000

(ii) Power Suppy = 6,000

I ∴ T = 4,000 + 10% P

II P = 6,000 + 20% T

Substituting the value of P in Equation - I

$$T = 4{,}000 + 10\% (6{,}000 + 20\% T)$$
$$= 4{,}000 + 10\% (6{,}000 + 1/5\ T)$$
$$= 4{,}000 + 600 + 1/50\ T$$
$$= 4600 + 1/50\ T$$
$$T - 1/50\ T = 4{,}600$$
$$\frac{49}{50} T = 4{,}600$$
$$T = 4{,}600 \times \frac{50}{49} = 4{,}694$$
$$T = 4{,}694$$

Now value of P

$$P = 6{,}000 + 20\% T$$

Substitute value of T

$$P = 6{,}000 + 1/5 \times 4694$$
$$= 6{,}000 + 938.8 \text{ or } 939$$
$$P = 6{,}939$$

Note — The total cost of two Service Departments namely, Transport 4,694 and Power Supply 6,939 are inclusive of services rendered by one Service Department to another Service Department.

∴ The Total Cost of Transport — (Rs. 4,694 – 20%) (4,694 – 939) Rs. 3,755 only be apportioned.

Similarly Power Supply — 6,939 – 10% T = (6,939 – 690) = 6,245 only be apportioned.

Overhead Distribution of Service Dept. — Transport & Power Supply to Production Departments

Particulars	Total	Production Departments		
		A	B	C
	Rs.	Rs.	Rs.	Rs.
As per Primary Distribution summary	21,000	10,000	6,000	5,000
Service Dept. Cost				
Transport ratio 4 : 3 : 1	3,755	1,878	1,408	469
3,755 × 1/8 = 469.375				
Power Supply ratio 2 : 4 : 3	6,245	1,388	2,775	2,082
6,245 × 1/9 = 693.88 = 694				
	31,000	13,266	10,183	7,551

The Anwers :

Under Repeated Distribution of Service Departments — Transport and Power Supply and under Simultaneous Equation Methods are the same.

Problem No. 5

M/s. Vijay Engineering Ltd., provides the following information for the period 1990. It has three Production Departments — A, B & C and Two Service Departments X & Y.

Particulars	Production Departments			Service Departments	
	A	B	C	X	Y
	Rs.	Rs.	Rs.	Rs.	Rs.
(1) Direct Materials	45,000	90,000	90,000	67,500	67,500
(2) Direct Wages	90,000	1,35,000	1,80,000	45,000	90,000
(3) Assets values (Plant)	2,70,000	1,80,000	1,35,000	45,000	45,000
(a) Area occupied (Sq Mtr)	375	625	125	125	125
(b) Staff (No. of Employee)	250	375	375	125	125
(c) Electricity (H. watts)	10000	7500	5000	2500	2500
(d) Light Points (Nos)	15	24	6	9	6

Expenses for the period

(1)	General Overheads	2,70,000
(2)	Rent, Rate, etc.	1,23,750
(3)	Motive Power	24,750
(4)	Lighting	4,500
(5)	Stores Expenses	18,000
(6)	Amenities to staff	67,500
(7)	Depreciation	67,500
(8)	Repairs & Maintenance	13,500

Apportion the Expenses of Service Departments :

X — Proportionate to Direct Wages.

Y — In the ratio of 5:2:2:1 to Departments A, B, C and X respectively.

Solution :

Production Overhead Distribution Summary

Particulars	Total	Production Departments			Service Departments	
		A	B	C	X	Y
	Rs.	Rs.	Rs.	Rs.	Rs.	Rs.
(1) Direct Material	3,60,000	45,000	90,000	90,000	67,500	67,500
(2) Direct Wages	5,40,000	90,000	1,35,000	1,80,000	45,000	90,000
(3) General Overhead (2,70,000 × 1/12) 22,500 (Basis: D. Wages) (2:3:4:1:2)	2,70,000	45,000	67,500	90,000	22,500	45,000
(4) Rent, Rate etc. 1/11 × 1,23,750 = 11,250 (Basis : Area) (3:5:1:1:1)	1,23,750	33,750	56,250	11,250	11,250	11,250
(5) Motive Power 1/11 × 24,750 (Basis : K.W.H.) (4:3:2:1:1)	24,750	9,000	6,750	4,500	2,250	2,250
(6) Lighting (1/20 × 4,500 = 225) (Basis : Lightpoint) (5:8:2:3:2)	4,500	1,125	1,800	450	675	450
(7) Stores Exp. 1/16 × 18,000 = 1,125 (D. Material 2:4:4:3:3)	18,000	2,250	4,500	4,500	3,375	3,375

Particulars	Total	Production Departments			Service Departments	
		A	B	C	X	Y
	Rs.	Rs.	Rs.	Rs.	Rs.	Rs.
(8) Amenities to staff 1/10 × 67,500 = 6,750 (Basis : No. of Employees) (2:3:3:1:1)	67,500	13,500	20,250	20,250	6,750	6,750
(9) Dept. on Plant 1/15 × 67,500 = 4,500 (B : Plant Value) (6:4:3:1:1)	67,500	27,000	18,000	13,500	4,500	4,500
(10) Repairs & Maintenance 1/15 × 13,500 = 900 (B : Plant Value) (6:4:3:1:1)	13,500	5,400	3,600	2,700	900	900
Total	5,89,500	1,37,025	1,78,650	1,47,150	1,64,700	2,31,975
	5,89,500	1,37,025	1,78,650	1,47,150	52,200	74,475
				Materials	67,500	67,500
				Wages	45,000	90,000
					1,12,500	1,57,500

Apportionment of Overheads of Service Departments X and Y to Production Departments under repeated distribution methods.

Particulars	Total	Production Departments			Service Depts.	
		A	B	C	X	Y
	Rs.	Rs.	Rs.	Rs.	Rs.	Rs.
(1) As per Primary distribution summary	5,89,500	1,37,025	1,78,650	1,47,150	52,200	74,475
(2) Service Depts. (X – Basis Proportion to Direct wage 2:3:4:2) (1/11 × 52,200 = 4,745)		9,490	14,235	18,985	–52,200	9,490
		1,46,515	1,92,885	1,66,135	—	83,965
(3) Y – Basis-given 5:2:2:1 = 1/10 × 83,965 = 8,396.5		41,983	16,793	16,793	8,396	–83,965
		1,88,498	2,09,678	1,82,928	8,396	—

Particulars	Total	Production Departments			Service Dept.	
		A	B	C	X	Y
	Rs.	Rs.	Rs.	Rs.	Rs.	Rs.
(4) X – Basis (2:3:4:2 = 1/11 × 8396 = 763)		1,526	2,289	3,055	–8,396	1,526
		1,90,024	2,11,967	1,85,983	—	1,526
(5) Y – Basis (5:2:2:1) 1/10 × 1526 = 152.6		761	306	306	153	–1,526
		1,90,785	2,12,273	1,86,289	153	—
(6) X – Basis (2:3:4:2) 1/11 × 153 = 14		28	42	55	–153	28
		1,90,813	2,12,315	1,86,344	—	28
(7) Y – Basis (5:2:2:1) 1/10 × 28 = 2.80		16	6	6	—	–28
	5,89,500	1,90,829	2,12,321	1,86,350	—	—
Actual = 14:5.60:5.60 Rounded up = 16:6:6						

Problem No. 6

A company has 3 production departments X, Y and Z and one service department P. The following figures are available for one month of 25 working days of 8 hours each day :

Particulars	Service Dept.	Production Departments			Total
	P	X	Y	Z	
(1) Power and Lighting	480	400	600	720	2,200
(2) Supervision	—	—	—	—	4,000
(3) Rent	—	—	—	—	2,000
(4) Labour	—	—	—	—	6,000
(5) Other Expenses	800	800	1,600	1,600	4,800
Other Information :					
(1) Ratio of time devoted by supervisor	2	3	3	2	
(2) Number of workers	5	15	20	10	
(3) Area (Square feet)	500	600	800	600	
(4) Service by P to other Departments	—	30%	50%	20%	

Calculate Labour hour rate for each production departments.

(K.U.D., April 1996)

Solution :

Overhead Distribution Summary

Particulars	Basis	Total	Service Dept. — P	Production Departments X	Y	Z
(1) Power & Light	Actual given	2,200	480	400	600	720
(2) Supervision	Time devoted 2:3:3:2	4,000	800	1,200	1,200	800
(3) Rent (area)	Square feet 5:6:8:6	2,000	400	480	640	480
(4) Labour welfare	No. of workers 1:3:4:2	6,000	600	1,800	2,400	1,200
(5) Other Expenses	Actual given	4,800	800	800	1,600	1,600
Total		19,000	3,080	4,680	6,440	4,800
Apportionment of Service Department Expenses to Production Department (30%, 50%, 20%)			–3,080	+924	+1,540	+616
Total Overhead Expenses			—	5,604	7,980	5,416

$$\text{Labour Hour Rate} = \frac{\text{Overhead}}{\text{No. of Labour hours}}$$

	X	Y	Z
	15 × 25 × 8	20 × 25 × 8	10 × 25 × 10
Labour Hours	3000	4000	2000

$$\text{Labour Hour Rate} = \frac{\text{Overhead}}{\text{No. of Labour hours}}$$

$$= \frac{5{,}604}{3000} \quad \frac{7{,}980}{4000} \quad \frac{5{,}416}{2000}$$

Labour Hour Rate	=	1.868	1.995	2.708

Problem No. 7

In a factory there are three Production Departments A, B, C and two service departments "Workshop" and "Power supply". The expenses of these departments for the month of March 1995 are as follows :

Production Depts.	Service Depts.	Rs.
A — 8,000	Workshop	2,340
B — 7,000	Power supply	3,000
C — 5,000		

The expenses of Service Departments are charged on a percentage basis as shown below :

Depts.	A	B	C	Workshop	Power Supply
(1) Workshop	10%	30%	50%	—	10%
(2) Power Supply	30%	10%	40%	20%	—

Reapportion the Service Department expenses to Production Departments under simultaneous equation method.

(K.U.D., October 1995)

Solution :

The Service Department expenses are apportioned to Production Departments under simultaneous equation method.

Let X be the Workshop Department.

Y be the Power supply Department.

X = 2,340 + 20% of Y

Y = 3,000 + 10% of X

Now X = 2,340 + 1/5 (3,000 + 1/10X)

X = 2,340 + 600 + 1/50X

X = 1/50 X = 2,940

49/50X = 2,940

X = 2,940 × 50/49

X = 3,000

Now Y = 3,000 + 1/10 × 3,000

= 3,000 + 300

= 3,300

Now the workshop expenses of Rs. 3,000 includes the inter service Department Power supply 10%. The net amount to be apportioned (3,000 – 10%) Rs. 2,700 only.

Similarly power supply expenses Rs. 3,300 includes the inter service Department = workshop – 20%.

The net amount – to be apportioned (3,300 – 20%=2,640 only)

Apportionment of the Service Department expenses to Production Departments under simultaneous equation method :

Expenses	Production Departments		
	A	B	C
(1) As per Primary Distribution summary	8,000	7,000	5,000
(2) Service Department Expenses (Workshop (3000 – 10% = 2,700) Ratio = 1:3:5 = 2,700 × 1/9	300	900	1,500
(3) Power supply (3,300 – 20%) 2,640 Ratio = 3:1:4 = 2,640 × 1/8	990	330	1,320
	9,290	8,230	7,820

Alternatively

The same problem may be answered under repeated distribution of service department expenses to production department. The answer will remain the same under both the methods.

Repeated Distribution Method

Particulars	Production Depts.			Service Depts.	
	A	B	C	Workshop	Power Supply
	Rs.	Rs.	Rs.	Rs.	Rs.
(1) Primary Distribution summary	8,000	7,000	5,000	2,340	3,000
(2) Workshop Expenses Ratio = 1:3:5:1	234	702	1,170	–2,340	234
	8,234	7,720	6,170	—	3,234
(3) Power Supply (3:1:4:2)	970	323	1,293	648	–3,234
	9,204	8,025	7,463	648	—
(4) Workshop (1:3:5:1)	65	194	324	–648	65
	9,269	8,219	7,787	—	65
(5) Power Supply (3:1:4:2)	20	6	26	13	–65
	9,289	8,225	7,813	13	—
(6) Workshop (1:3:5:1)	1	5	7	–13	—
Total	9,290	8,230	7,820	—	—

Total — Production Department	A	8,000	9,290
	B	7,000	8,230
	C	5,000	7,820
			25,340
Service Department			
Workshop		2,340	
Power Supply		3,000	
		25,340	

Problem No. 8

In a factory there are 4 Production Departments A, B, C & D and Service Departments X and Y. The departmental overheads are obtained in a summarised form as under :

Production Departments	Service Departments
A – Rs. 1,270	X – Rs. 750
B – Rs. 1,460	Y – Rs. 340
C – Rs. 990	
D – Rs. 830	

The expenses (overheads) of services departments are charged out on percentage basis as given below :

	Production Departments				Service Departments	
	A	B	C	D	X	Y
X Service Department	10%	30%	20%	20%	—	20%
Y Service Department	30%	20%	30%	10%	10%	—

Reapportion the service departments overheads to production departments under simultaneous equation method.

Further ascertain overhead recovery rate in each production department, A, B, C and D in which estimated working hours are 2,000, 3,000, 2,600 and 1,600 respectively.

(K.U.D., April 1995)

Solution :

Ascertainment of Total overheads of each of the Service department :

I $X = 750 + 1/10Y$

II $Y = 340 + 1/5X$

Equation I :

$X = 750 + 1/10\ (340 + 1/5X)$

$\therefore\ X = 750 + 34 + 1/50X$

Now $Y - 1/50X = 784$

$\therefore\ 49/50X = 784$

$X = 784 \times 50/49$

$= 800$

Equation – II :

$Y = 340 + 1/5X$

$\therefore\ Y = 340 + 1/5 \times 800$

$Y = 340 + 160$

$Y = 500$

Total cost of Service Departments :

X – Rs. 800 and Y – Rs. 500

include the cost of service rendered by one service department to another service department. Therefore out of Total cost of Service Department :

$X = 800 - 20\% = (800 - 160)$ Rs. 640

Similarly Total cost of Service Department of

Y = 500 – 10% = (500 – 50) Rs. 450

will be apportioned to Production Departments.

Statement showing the apportionment of Service Department Overheads to Production Departments

Particulars	Total	Production Departments			
		A	B	C	D
	Rs.	Rs.	Rs.	Rs.	
As per Primary Distribution Summary	4,550	1,270	1,460	990	830
Service Department – X (1:3:2:2) 1/8 of 640 = 80	640	80	240	160	160
Service Department – Y (3:2:3:1)	450	150	100	150	50
Total Overheads	5,640	1,500	1,800	1,300	1,040
Overhead Recovery rate		1,500	1,800	1,300	1,040
Working Hours		2000	3000	2600	1600
Recovery rate		0.75	0.60	0.50	0.65

The same problem may be answered under repeated distribution method also.

Repeated Distribution of Overheads of Service Department to Production

Particulars	Total	Production Departments				Service Depts.	
	Rs.	A	B	C	D	X	Y
As per Primary Distribution Summary	5,640	1,240	1,460	990	830	750	340
Service Department :							
X		75	225	150	150	–750	150
		1,345	1,685	1,140	980	—	490
Y		147	98	147	49	49	–490
		1,492	1,783	1,287	1,029	49	—
X		5	15	10	9	–49	10
		1,497	1,798	1,297	1,038	—	10
Y		3	2	3	2	—	–10
Total Overheads		1,500	1,800	1,300	1,040	—	—
Working Hour		2000	3000	2600	1600		
		0.75	0.60	0.50	0.65		

Problem No. 9

Divya Ltd. has three production departments, namely A, B & C and two service departments namely "Transport" and "Power Supply". The departmental overheads are obtained in a summarised form as under :

Production Departments	Service Departments
A – Rs. 3,393	Transport – Rs. 1,000
B – Rs. 4,657	Power Supply – Rs. 500
C – Rs. 3,530	

Overheads of Service Departments are apportioned as under :

	A	B	C	Transport Department	Power Supply Department
Transport Department	30%	40%	10%	—	20%
Power Supply Department	40%	30%	20%	10%	—

Estimated working hours of Production Departments A, B & C are 2000, 2500 and 1800 respectively.

Prepare a statement showing the distributions of Service Departments expenses to Production Department by Repeated Distribution method and find out overhead recovery rate in Production Departments A, B and C.

(K.U.D., October 1994)

Solution :

Distribution of overheads of Service Departments to Production Departments under Repeated Distribution method

Particulars	Production Departments			Service Deptartments	
	A	B	C	Transport	Power Supply
	Rs.	Rs.	Rs.	Rs.	Rs.
As per Primary summary	3,393	4,657	3,530	1000	500
Transport Department	300	400	100	−1000	+ 200
	3,693	5,057	3,630	—	700
Power Supply Department	280	210	140	70	−700
	3,973	5,267	3,770	70	—
Transport Department	21	28	7	−70	14
	3,994	5,295	3,777	—	14
Power Supply Department	5.6	4.2	2.8	1.4	−14
	3,999.6	5,299.2	3,779.8	1.4	—
Transport Department	0.42	0.56	0.14	−1.4	0.28
	4,000.02	5,299.76	3,779.94	—	0.28
Power Supply Department	0.10	0.14	0.04	—	−0.28
	4,000.12	5,299.90	3,779.98	—	—
Roundup	4,000	5,300	3,780	—	—

Overheads Recovery Rate :	A	B	C
Working hours	$\frac{4,000}{2000}$	$\frac{5,300}{2500}$	$\frac{3,780}{1800}$
Recovery Rate =	Rs. 2	Rs. 2.12	Rs. 2.10

Solution :

The same problem : Distribution of overheads of Service Department to Production Department under Simultaneous Equation Method.

Let T — be the Total of Transport.

P — be the Total of Power supply.

∴ T = Rs. 1000 + 10% of P and

P = Rs. 500 + 20% of T

Now T = 1000 + 10% of P

P = 500 + 20% T

Substituting the value of P.

$$T = 1000 + \frac{10}{100} \times (500 + 1/5T)$$

$$T = 1000 + 1/10 \times 500 + 1/5T$$

$$T = 1000 + 50 + 1/50T$$

$$T = 1/50T = 1050$$

$$49/50T = \frac{1,050 \times 50}{49} = \frac{52,500}{49}$$

$$T = 1,070.50 \text{ Or} = 1,071.$$

Now $P = 500 + 1/5 \times 1,070.50$

$P = 500 + 214$

$P = 714$

Please remember that the above total cost of two Service Departments is inclusive of the cost of service rendered by each to other.

Therefore Total cost Transport Department

of Rs. 1,071 – 20% = 857 and of

Power supply = Rs. 714 – 10% = Rs. 643.

Or

Solution :

Apportionment of Service Department expenses to Production Department under Simultaneous Equation Method

Particulars	Total	Production Departments		
		A	B	C
	Rs.	Rs.	Rs.	Rs.
As per Primary Distribution summary	11,580	3,393	4,657	3,530
Transport (1,071 – 214)	857	321	429	107
Power supply (714 – 71) (Base 4:3:2)	643	286	214	143
Total	13,080	4,000	5,300	3,780
Overheads Recovery :				
Overhead / Working hour	4,000 / 2000	5,300 / 2500		
Recovery Hourly Rate	Rs. 2	Rs. 2.12		Rs. 2.10

Problem No. 10

In a factory, there are three production departments A, B and C and two service departments X and Y. The departmental expenses for the month of January 1993 were given below :

Production Departments			Service Departments	
A	B	C	X	Y
1,65,000	3,60,000	2,50,000	12,000	10,000

The service department expenses are allocated on a percentage basis as follows :

Service Departments	Production Departments			Service Departments	
	A	B	C	X	Y
X	30%	20%	30%	—	20%
Y	40%	30%	20%	10%	—

Prepare a statement showing the distribution of service departments expenses to the three production departments under "The Repetitive Distribution Method".

(K.U.D., April 1994)

Solution : (Repetitive Distribution of overheads of Service Department Expenses to the Production Department)

Particulars	Total	Production Departments			Service Depts.	
		A	B	C	X	Y
	Rs.	Rs.	Rs.	Rs.	Rs.	Rs.
As per Primary distribution summary	7,75,000	1,65,000	3,60,000	2,50,000	12,000	10,000
X – Service Dept.	12,000	3,600	2,400	3,600	-12,000	2,400
Y – Service Dept.	10,000					
	7,97,000	1,68,600	3,62,400	2,53,600	—	12,400
Service Depts.						
Y – 4:3:2:1		4,960	3,720	2,480	1,240	-12,400
		1,73,560	3,66,120	2,56,080	1,240	—
X – 3:2:3:2		372	248	372	-1,240	248
		1,73,932	3,66,348	2,56,452	—	248
Y – 4:3:2:1		99	74	50	25	-248
		1,74,031	3,66,442	2,56,502	25	—
X – 3:2:3:2		7.5	5	7.5	-25	5
		1,74,038.5	3,66,447	2,56,509.5	—	5
Y – 4:3:2:1		2	2	1		-5
	7,97,000	1,74,040.5	3,66,449	2,56,510.50	—	—

Alternatively

The same problem may be answered under Simultaneous Equation method. The result remains the same.

Solution : (Simultaneous Equation method)

Service Department X – Rs. 12,000

Service Department Y – Rs. 10,000

Let us have equation : X – 12,000 + 10/100 of Y

Y – 10,000 + 20/100 of X

i.e., X = 12,000 + 1/10Y

Y = 10,000 + 1/5X

Now Equation X = 12,000 + 1/10 (10,000 + 1/5 X)

= 12,000 + 1000 + 1/5 X

= 13,000 + 1/5 X

X – 1/50 X = 13,000

$$\frac{49\,X}{50} = 13{,}000$$

X = 13,000 × 50/49

X = 13,265 (rounded up)

Now Y = 10,000 + 1/5 Y

Y = 10,000 + 1/5 X 13265

= 10,000 + 2,653

= 12,653

Now Service Department : X = 13,265

Y = 12,653

The apportionment of Service Department X would be (Rs. 13,265 Less 20% = 13,265 – 2,653 = Rs. 10,612) and the Service Department = Y would be (Rs. 12,653 *Less* 10% i.e., 12,653 – 1,265 = Rs. 11,388).

Distribution of the overheads (Expenses) of service departments X and Y to production departments A, B and C under Simultaneous Equation method

Particulars – Expenses	Total	Production Departments		
		A	B	C
	Rs.	Rs.	Rs.	Rs.
(1) As per Primary distribution summary	7,75,000	1,65,000	3,60,000	2,50,000
(2) Service Department – X (13,265 – 20%) Ratio : 3:2:3	10,612	3,979.5	2,653	3,979
(3) Service Department – Y (12,653 – 10%) Ratio – 4:3:2 (Fractions roundup)	11,388	5,061	3,796	2,531
Total	7,97,000	1,74,040.5	3,66,449	2,56,510.50

Problem No. 11

Following are the annual charges incurred in a machine shop where manual Labour in almost nil and where work is done by means of exactly :

(1) Rent and rate for the shop 9,600

(2) Depreciation on each machine 1,000

(3) Repairs and maintenance for all machines 2,000

(4) Power consumed @ 0.05 Ps per unit for shop 6,000

(5) Electric charges is for lighting in the shop 1,080

(6) Attendants : There are two attenders in shop each being paid Rs. 120 pm.

(7) Supervision : For the supervision of all five machines there is a supervisor whose salary is Rs. 500 pm.

(8) Sundry supplies such as lubricants, grease etc. for the shop — Rs. 900

(9) The machine uses 10 units of power per hour.

(Kuvempu, April 1994)

Solution :

Computation of Machine Hour Rate

Particulars	Per Annual	Per Hour Rate
(I) *Standing Charges :*		
(1) Rent and Rate = $\frac{9,600}{5}$ = 1,920	1,920	
(2) Depreciation	1,000	
(3) Attenders = 2 × 120 = 240 × 12 = $\frac{2,880}{5}$	576	
(4) Supervisor salary 500 × 12 = 6000 × 1/5	1,200	
Total Cost	4,696	
No. of working hour = on power consumption 0.05 per unit × 10 = 0.50 = 6000 × 1/5 = 1200	2400	
1200 × 100/50 = 2400 Hours		1.956
(II) *Machine Expenses :*		
(1) Repairs & Maintenance 2000 × 1/5 = $\frac{400}{2400}$		0.166
(2) Electric Charges = 1,080 × 1/5 = $\frac{216}{2400}$		0.09
(3) Power 0.05 per unit for 10 units = 10 × 0.05		0.50
(4) Sundry Expenses = 900 × 1/5 = $\frac{180}{2400}$		0.075
Machine Hour Rate		2.787

Problem No. 12

From the expenses given below, calculate machine hour rate for the month of January 1992 :

(a) Rent (space occupied by the machine is 1/5 of the Department) Rs. 600.

(b) Insurance Rs. 48.

(c) Cotton waste Oil etc. Rs. 120.

(d) Salary of supervisor (1/5 of his time is spent on this machine) Rs. 6,000.

The above expenses are annual expenses.

The cost of the machine was Rs. 66,000 with a scrap value of Rs. 6,000. From the past experience it is assumed that the life of the machine is 20,000 hours. Repairs and maintenance cost is estimated to be Rs. 5,000 throughout the life of the machine. The power consumption of the machine is 10 units per hour at 5 paise per unit. The machine is expected to run 200 hours in the month.

(K.U.D., October 1993)

Solution :

Calculation of Machine Hour Rate for Jan. 1992

Particulars	Cost for month	Machine Hour Rate
(I) Standing Charges		
(1) Rent Rs. 600 $\times \frac{1}{5} \times \frac{1}{12} = 10$	10	
(2) Insurance 48 $\times \frac{1}{12}$	4	
(3) Cotton Waste Oil etc. = $\frac{120}{12} \times 1$	10	
(4) Salary of supervisor = 6,000 × 1/5 × 1/12	100	
	124	
Machine hour rate = $\frac{124}{200} = 0.62$ (200 hours in a Month)		0.62
(II) Repairs & Maintenance = $\frac{5000}{20000}$		0.25
Depreciation = $\frac{\text{Cost} - \text{Scrap}}{\text{Life}} = \frac{66,000 - 6,000}{20000}$		3.00
Power 10 units per hour 0.05 Ps per unit 10 × .05		0.50
Machine Hour Rate	Rs.	4.27

Problem No. 13

The following details have been extracted from cost records of Chandrahas Metals Ltd. :

Materials — Rs. 72,000

Direct Wages — Rs. 60,000

Hours of machine operation — 20,000

Labour hours worked — 24,000

Total overheads of the department — Rs. 48,000

On an order executed in the department during this period, the relevant data were :

Materials used — Rs. 4,000
Labours hours — 1,650
Direct wages — Rs. 3,600
Machine hours — 1,200

Prepare a comparative statement of cost of this job order under :

(i) Direct Labour cost method.
(ii) Direct labour hour rate method.
(iii) Machine hour rate method.

(K.U.D., April 1993)

Solution :

Calculation :

(1) Percentage of Labour Cost = $\frac{\text{Overhead}}{\text{Labour Cost}} \times 100 = \frac{48000}{6000} \times 100 = 80\%$

(2) Direct Labour hour rate = $\frac{\text{Overhead}}{\text{Labour hours}} = \frac{48000}{24000}$ = Rs. 2 per hour

(3) Machine hour rate = $\frac{\text{Overhead}}{\text{Machine hour}} = \frac{48000}{20000}$ = Rs. 2.40 per hour

Comparative Statement of Cost

Particulars	Direct Labour cost	Labour Hour Rate	Machine Hour Rate
Materials Cost	4,000	4,000	4,000
Direct Wages	3,600	3,600	3,600
Prime Cost	7,600	7,600	7,600
Factory Overhead :			
(1) Labour cost = 80% of 3,600	2,880	—	—
(2) Labour hour rate = Rs. 2	—	3,300	—
(3) Machine hour rate = 2.40 × 1200	—	—	2,880
Total	10,480	10,900	10,480

Problem No. 14

From the budgeted figures of Mysore Metal Works :

(a) Prepare normal overhead application Rate using :

(1) Direct Labour Rate method.
(2) Direct Labour Cost method.
(3) Machine hour rate method.

Budgeted figures :

Estimated factory overhead for the year	58,000
Estimated direct labour hours	134600 Hours
Estimated Labour cost	97,500
Estimated Machine hours	50500 Hours.

(b) Prepare a comparative statement of cost showing the result of application of each of the above to Job No. 84 from the data given below :

Cost of Direct Materials consumed	(Rs.)	420
Direct Wages	(Rs.)	450
Direct Labour hours (in Hours)		300
Machine Hours (in Hours)		200

(Gulbarga, April 1993)

Solution :

(1) Labour Hour Rate $= \dfrac{\text{Overhead}}{\text{Labour hours}} = \dfrac{58,000}{134600} = 0.43$

(2) Labour Cost (%) $= \dfrac{\text{Overhead}}{\text{Labour Cost}} \times 100 \; \dfrac{58,000}{97,500} = 59.5\%$

(3) Machine Hour Rate $= \dfrac{\text{Overhead}}{\text{No. of Machine hours}} = \dfrac{58,000}{50500} = 1.15$

Comparative Statement of Cost

Particulars	Direct Labour Cost	Labour Hour Rate	Machine Hour Rate
(1) Direct Material consumed	420	420	420
(2) Direct Wages	450	450	450
Prime Cost	870	870	870
Factory Overheads :			
(1) Labour cost 59.5% on Direct Wages	267.75	—	—
(2) Labour hour rate 300 × 0.43	—	129	—
(3) Machine Hour Rate 200 × 1.15	—	—	230
Cost of Production (Works Cost)	1,137.75	999	1,100

Problem No. 15

From the following particulars compute Machine Hour Rate :

Cost of Machine	11,000
Scrap value	1,000
Repairs for the effective working life	1,500
Standing charges for 4 weekly period	1,600

Power used 6 units per hour @ 0.05 Ps per unit.

Effective working Life 10000 Hours.

Hours worked in 4 weekly period 120 Hours.

(Kuvempu University, April 1993)

Solution :

Computation of Machine Hour Rate

Particulars	4 Weekly period Total	Rate per Hour
(I) *Standing Charges*		
4 Weekly Hours worked $\frac{1,600}{120}$	1,600	13.33
(II) *Machine Expenses*		
Depreciation $= \frac{\text{Cost} - \text{Scrap}}{\text{Effective working life}}$		
$= \frac{11,000 - 1,000}{10000}$ = Re. 1		1.00
Rapirs for effective working life = $\frac{1,500}{10000}$		0.15
Power used = 6 units per hour @ 0.05 Ps per unit (6 × 0.05 = 0.30)		0.30
Machine Hour Rate	Rs.	14.78

Note : Power consumption 6 units per hour 0.05 Ps per unit per hour for 120 hours (120 × 6 = 720 units).

Total units =	720	Per hour 6 Units
Rate per unit	× .05	
		@ Re. 0.05 Ps
Total amount Rs.	36.00	(6 × 0.05 = 0.30)

Problem No. 16

The following details are extracted from the books of Mohan Machine Tools Ltd., which has a separate Machine shop. The details given below are in respect of four of the (identical) machines cost of machine is Rs. 1,80,000. Estimated scrap value is 5% at the end of effective life.

Effective life in 15 Years.

Expected to run for 4800 hours in a year.

It is estimated loss due to Normal repairs is 300 hours.

Further Loss due to stagger 1500 hours.

Other details of machine shop :

(1) Wages and Bonus of two operators each operator is incharge of two machines of Rs. 12,000 p.a. each.

(2) Rent and rates of the shop of Rs. 6,000 p.a.

(3) General lighting of the shop Rs. 500 pm.

(4) Insurance premium per quarter per machine Rs. 400.

(5) Cost of repairs and maintenance per machine Rs. 625 pm.

(6) Shop supervisor's salary per month Rs. 1,000.

(7) Power consumption of the machine per hour 60 units @ Rs. 10 per 100 units.

(8) Other factory overheads chargeable to shop Rs. 8,000 p.a.

The supervisor is expected to devote 1/5 of his time for supervising a machine.

You are required to compute machine hour rate from the above particulars.

(Kuvempu, October 1993)

Solution :

Computation of Machine Hour Rate (Machine Total — 4)

	Per Annum Total	Per Hour Rs.
(I) *Standing Charges*		
(1) Rent and Rates of the shop 6,000 × 1/4	1,500	
(2) Wages and Bonus	6,000	
Two operators each in charge of two machines		
one operator paid Rs. $\frac{12,000}{2} = 6,000$		
(3) General Lighting of the shop 500 × 12 = 6,000 × ¼ =	1,500	
(4) Insurance Premium per Quarter per machine 400 × 4	1,600	
(5) Factory overhead chargeable p.a for the shop 8,000 × ¼ = 2,000	2,000	

	Per Annum Total	Per Hour Rs.
(6) Shop supervisor salary Rs. 1,000 × 12 = 12,000 × 1/5 = 2,400	2,400	
(7) Depreciation $= \frac{\text{Cost} - \text{Scrap}}{\text{Life}} = \frac{1,80,000 - 9,000}{19} = \frac{1,71,000}{19} = 9,000$	9,000	
Total Standing charges	24,000	8.00

Machine Working Hours 4800
Less : Loss due to Rep. 300
4500
Less : Loss due to shortage 1500
Effective Hours 3000

Total Cost $= \frac{24,000}{3000} =$ Rs. 8 per Hour.

(II) *Machine Expenses*

(1) Repairs and Maintenance per Machine 625 × 12

$= \frac{7,500}{3000} =$ Rs. 2.50 — 2.50

(2) Power consumption
per hour 60 units for 3000 = 60 × 3000 = 18,000
per 100 units Rs. 10 Cost Rs. 10
per unit 0.10 per 100 units = 180 × .10

$\frac{1800}{3000}$ p.a. for 1 unit × .10 Ps for 60 × .10 = 6.00 — 6.00

Machine Hour Rate of Rs. 16.50

Problem No. 17

Calculate Machine Hour Rate for Machine No. 101 from the particulars given below :

The department has three machine of equal value.

(a) Cost of Machine Rs. 10,000

(b) Estimated life of Machine 15000 hours.

(c) Estimated scrap value of machine Rs. 1,000
(d) Hour worked during the year — 1500 hours.
(e) Machine occupies 1/5 of the floor space in Department for which Rent and lighting charges amounted to Rs. 3,500 per annum.
(f) Machine consumes 10 units of power per hour @ .10 Ps per unit.
(g) Repairs and Maintenance throughout the working life of the machine is estimated @ Rs. 3,600.
(i) Cost of supervision and other expenses for 3 Machines amounted to Rs. 4,500 per annum.

(K.U.D., October 1992)

Solution :

Computation of Machine Hour Rate — 1500 Hours p.a.

Particulars		per annum Rs.	per hour Rs.
(I) *Standing Charges*			
(1) Rent & Lighting	$3{,}500 \times \frac{1}{5}$	700	
(2) Insurance	$1{,}275 \times \frac{1}{3}$	425	
(3) Supervision and Other charges	$4{,}500 \times \frac{1}{3}$	1,500	
Total Fixed Expenses		2,625	
Working hours p.a. 1500 Hours for Rs. 2,625 $= \frac{2{,}625}{1500}$			1.75
(II) *Machine Expenses*			
(1) Depreciation $= \frac{\text{Cost} - \text{Scrap}}{\text{Life in hours}} = \frac{10{,}000 - 1000}{15000}$			0.60
(2) Power = .10 Ps per unit for 10 units (10 × .10)			1.00
(3) Repairs and Maintenance $= \frac{3{,}600}{15000} =$			0.24
Machine Hour Rate	= Rs. 3.59 or 3.60		3.59

Problem No. 18

Calculate Machine hour rate for Machine No. 101 from the particulars given below. The department have five Machines of similar types and value.

(a) Rent of the Department Rs. 4,805 per annum.
(b) Depreciation on each Machine Rs. 500 p.a.
(c) Repairs and Maintenance of the Department Rs. 1,000 p.a.
(d) Light charges of the department Rs. 540 p.a.
(e) Attendants — two attendants in the department and each is paid Rs. 60 per month.
(f) Supervision — One supervisor in the department who is paid @ Rs. 250 per month.
(g) Cotton waste and lubricants for the department Rs. 945 p.a.
(h) Higher purchase instalment payable for machine Rs. 1,200 p.a.
(i) Each Machine consumes 10 units of power at Re. 1.00 for 15 units.
(j) Each Machine will work 1200 hours per annum.

(K.U.D., April 1992)

Solution :

Computation of Machine Hour Rate

Sundry Charges :		
(a) Rent – 4,805 × 1/5 =	961	
(b) Cotton waste & Lubricants 495 × 1/5 =	99	
(c) Light charges 540 × 1/5 =	108	
(e) Attender 2 × 60 × 12 = 1,440 × 1/5	288	
(f) Supervisor 1 × 250 × 12 = 3,000 × 1/5	600	
(h) Higher purchase instalment on Interest 300 × 1/5	60	
	2,116	
Total Standing charges / Total No. of Hours p.a. $\frac{2,116}{1200}$		1.7633
Machine Expenses :		
(b) Depreciation – $\frac{500}{1200}$		0.416
(c) Repairs & Machine $\frac{1000}{1200} \times 1/5$		0.166
(i) Power – 10 units $\frac{1200}{10} = \frac{1.20}{15}$		0.125
Machine Hour Rate		2.436

Problem No. 19

From the particulars furnished below compute a machine Hour Rate (Including shop expenses) :

Name of the equipment	—	BAML Mobile Crane No. 333054
Date of Purchase	—	01-04-1985
Make	—	BAML Load Lift Corporation Ltd.
Cost	—	Rs. 50,000
Power	—	Diesel 10 H.P. Engine
Estimated Life	—	10 years
Depreciation	—	12½ p.a. on original cost.
Insurance	—	Rs. 300 p.a.
Repairs	—	Rs. 800 p.m.
Consumable stores	—	300 p.m.
Rent	—	Rs. 800 p.m.

Supervision 01/5 for the machine Rs. 1,300 p.a. Assume that the crane can work for 200 Hours in a month and has actually worked for 80% of the Normal working hours. Cost of diesel Oil etc. per hour — Rs. 1.50.

(Mysore, April 1992)

Solution :

Computation of Crane Mobile per Hour

	Total Cost (p.a.) Rs.	Per Hour Rs.
(I) *Standing Charges :*		
(1) Rent (800 × 12 = 9,600)	9,600	
(2) Insurance	300	
(3) Supervision salary (1,300 × 1/5)	260	
(4) Depreciation cost of Rs. 50,000 @ 12½%	6,250	
Total Standing charges	16,410	
Working Hours per month 200 Hours actual		
Working hours 80% of 200 = 160 × 12 = 1920 Hours		
Annual Working Hours 1920 and Total cost 16,410	$\frac{16,410}{1920}$	8.55
(II) *Machine Expenses :*		
(1) Repairs (700 × 12 = $\frac{8,400}{1920}$) =		4.37
(2) Consumable stores (300 × 12 = $\frac{3,600}{1920}$)		1.87
(3) Cost of Diesel Oil		1.50
Mobile Crane Rate per Hour		Rs. 16.30

Problem No. 20

A Machine Cost — Rs. 90,000

Scrap value at the end of effective life of 19 years 5%.

The machine is expected to run per annum 2400 Hours.

Estimated loss due to normal repairs 150 Hours.

Further loss for setting up 750 Hours.

The other details in respect of machine shop are :

(a) Wages of two operators (each in charge of two machine) 6,000 p.a.

(b) Rent, rate of the shop Rs. 3,000 p.a.

(c) General lighting of the shop of Rs. 250 p.m.

(d) Insurance of this machine Rs. 200 per Quarter.

(e) Cost of repairs & maintenance per machine Rs. 250 p.m.

(f) Shop supervisor salary Rs. 500 p.m.

(g) Power consumption of machine 20 units per hour cost per 100 units of Rs. 10.

(h) Other factory overhead for the shop Rs. 4,000 p.a.

There are four identical machines in the shop. The supervisor is expected to devote 1/5 of his time on this machine.

Compute Machine Hour Rate.

[Mysore, April 1992, (Mod. October)
Gulbarga, April 1990, C.A. Inter]

Solution :

Computation of Machine Hour Rate

	Total Cost (p.a.) Rs.	Per Hour Rs.
(I) *Standing Charges :*		
(a) Wages of operator = Rs. $\frac{6,000}{2}$ p.a. = 3,000	3,000	
(b) Rent and Rate for shop = $\frac{3,000}{4} \times ¼$	750	
(c) Insurance per Quarter 200 × 4 = 800	800	
(d) General Lighting for shop 250 × 12 = 3,000 × ¼	750	
(e) Shop supervisor salary 500 × 12 = 6,000 × 1/5	1,200	
(f) Depreciation = $\frac{\text{Cost} - \text{Scrap}}{\text{Life}} = \frac{90,000 - 4,500}{19}$ $= \frac{85,500}{19}$	4,500	
Total Standing charge	11,000	

			Total Cost (p.a) Rs.	Per Hour Rs.
Hours Worked	2400			
Less : Normal repairs	150	Machine Hour Rate	$\frac{11,000}{1500}$	7.33
	2250			
Less : Loss due to setting up	750			
	1500	Effective Working Hours		

(II) *Machine Expenses* :

(f) Repairs & Maintenance $250 \times 2 = \frac{3,000}{1500}$ 2.00

(g) Power 20 units per hour 1500 Hours Cost 100 units Rs. 10

$20 \times 1500 = 3,000$ Units = for $\frac{30,000}{100} \times 10$

$= \frac{3,000}{1500} = 2.00$ 2.00

Machine Hour Rate 11.33

Problem No. 21

In a factory there are 4 production departments A, B, C and D and two service departments X and Y. The expenses are as follows :

Production Departments Rs.		Service Departments Rs.	
A —	12,000	X—	2,750
B —	8,000	Y—	1,900
C —	6,000		
D —	5,000		

The expenses of service departments are charged on percentage basis as given below :

Departments	Production Departments				Service Departments	
	A	B	C	D	X	Y
X Service Department	20%	30%	15%	15%	—	20%
Y Service Department	30%	20%	20%	20%	10%	—

Reapportion the service departments, expenses to production departments under simultaneous equation method.

(K.U.D., October 1991)

Solution :

Simultaneous Equation Method :

$$X = 2{,}750 + 10\% \text{ of } Y = 2{,}750 + \frac{1}{10} Y$$

$$Y = 1{,}900 + 20\% \text{ of } X = 1{,}900 + \frac{1}{5} X$$

$$X = 2{,}750 + 190 + \frac{1}{50} X$$

$$X = \frac{1}{50} X = 2{,}940$$

$$\frac{49}{50} X = 2{,}940$$

$$\therefore X = 2{,}940 \times \frac{50}{49} = \text{Rs. } 3{,}000$$

$$Y = 1{,}900 + \frac{1}{5} (3000)$$

$$= 1{,}900 + 600 = \text{Rs. } 2{,}500$$

$$= \text{Rs. } 2{,}500$$

Secondary Distribution Summary

Particulars	Production Departments			
	A Rs.	B Rs.	C Rs.	D Rs.
As per Primary Summary	12,000	8,000	6,000	5,000
Add : Service Department X-expenses reapportioned (3,000)	600	900	450	450
Add : Service Department Y-expenses reapportioned (2,500)	750	500	500	500
Total	13,350	9,400	6,950	5,950

Problem No. 22

The total factory overhead of department A for the month of July 1990 amounted Rs. 20,000. The following additional information is also obtained in respect of the department.

(i) Number of articles produced 5000 units.

(ii) Total direct material cost of Rs. 50,000.

(iii) Number of labour hours worked 10000 Hours.

(iv) Number of machine hours worked 2000 Hours.

From the above you are required to establish the factory overhead absorption rates on the following basis :

(a) Rate per unit (b) As percentage direct material cost

(c) Rate per labour hour worked (d) Rate per machine hour worked.

(K.U.D., October 1991)

Solution :

$$\text{(a) Rate per unit} = \frac{\text{Factory overhead}}{\text{No. of units produced}} = \frac{20{,}000}{5000} = \text{Rs. 4 per unit}$$

$$\text{(b) As a percentage of Direct Material cost} = \frac{\text{Factory overhead}}{\text{Material Cost}} \times 100$$

$$= \frac{20{,}000}{80{,}000} \times 100 = 25\%$$

$$\text{(c) Labour Hour Rate} = \frac{\text{Factory overhead}}{\text{Labour Hours}} = \frac{20{,}000}{10{,}000} = \text{Rs. 2 per Hour}$$

$$\text{(d) Machine Hour Rate} = \frac{\text{Factory overhead}}{\text{Machine Hours}} = \frac{20{,}000}{2{,}000} = \text{Rs. 10 per Hour}$$

(a) Rate per Unit = Rs. 4

(b) Percentage of Factory Overhead on Direct Material cost = 25%

(c) Labour Hour Rate = Rs. 2 per Hour.

(d) Machine Hour Rate Rs. 10 per Hour.

Problem No. 23

Calculate the Machine Hour Rate from the following particulars :

(1)	Life of the machine	10 Years
(2)	Cost of the machine	Rs. 80,000
(3)	Cost of freight and installation of the machine	Rs. 20,000
(4)	Scrap value after 10 years of life	Rs. 10,000
(5)	Rent, Rate and Taxes for the shop (per Quarter)	Rs. 3,000
(6)	Shop supervisors salary (per Quarter)	Rs. 6,000
(7)	Insurance premium for the machine (per annum)	Rs. 600
(8)	Estimated repairs and maintenance charge during the life	Rs. 10,000
(9)	Factory lighting per month	Rs. 2,400
(10)	Power 5 units per hours @ 20 Ps per unit	
(11)	Estimated working hours — per annum 2000 Hours.	

The machine occupies ¼ of the Factory shop and lighting should be apportioned on this basis. The supervisor is expected to devote 1/6th of his time for supervising machine.

(Mangalore, April 1991)

Solution :

Computation of Machine Hour Rate

	Total Cost (p.a.) Rs.	Per Hour Rs.
(I) *Standing Charges :*		
(1) Rent, Rate & Taxes per Quarter 3,000 × 4 = 12,000 × ¼ = 3,000	3,000	
(2) Insurance	600	
(3) Factory Lighting (P.M. 2400 × 12 = 28,800 × ¼ = 7,200	7,200	
(4) Shop supervision salary per quarter (6000 × 4 = 24,000 × 1/6 = 4,000)	4,000	
(5) Depreciation = $\frac{\text{Cost + Instalment – Scrap}}{\text{Life}}$ $= \frac{80,000 + 20,000 - 10,000}{10 \text{ Years}} = \frac{90,000}{10}$	9,000	
	23,800	
$\frac{\text{Total Cost}}{\text{Machine Hours}} = \frac{23,800}{2000}$ = 11.90 Machine Hour Rate		11.90
(II) *Machine Expenses :*		
(1) Repairs & Maintenance $\frac{10,000}{10} = \frac{1,000}{2000}$		0.50
(2) Power (5 Units per Hour @ 0.20 Ps per Unit) 5 × 0.20 = 1.00		1.00
Machine Hour Rate		13.40

Problem No. 24

A Limited Company has three Production Departments 'A', 'B', 'C' and one Service department 'S'. The following figures are available for one month of 25 days of 8 hours each. All these departments work for all the days and with full attendance.

	Total	S	A	B	C
		Departments			
	Rs.	Rs.	Rs.	Rs.	Rs.
(I) *Expenses*					
(i) Power and Lighting	1,100	240	200	300	360
(ii) Supervision	2,000	—	—	—	—
(iii) Rent	500	—	—	—	—
(iv) Welfare	600	—	—	—	—
(v) Other	1,200	—	—	—	—
	5,400				
(II) *Other Information :*					
(i) Supervisors' Salary	30%	30%	20%	20%	
(ii) Number of workers	10	30	40	20	
(iii) Floor area (Sq. ft.)	500	600	800	600	
(iv) Service to Production Departments	—	50%	30%	20%	

Calculate Labour Hour Rate per each department.

(K.U.D., October 1990)

Solution :

Overhead Distribution Summary

Particulars	Basis for allocation	Total	Service Dept.	Production Departments A	B	C
		Rs.	Rs.	Rs.	Rs.	Rs.
(1) Power and Lighting	Actual	1,100	240	200	300	360
(2) Supervision	3:3:2:2	2,000	600	600	400	400
(3) For Rent	For area 5:6:8:6	500	100	120	160	120
(4) Welfare	No. of workers 1:3:4:2	600	60	180	240	120
(5) Others	Actual	1,200	200	200	400	400
Total		5,400	1,200	1,300	1,500	1,400
(5) Service Department re-distribution to Production Departments 5:3:2			–1,200	600	360	240
Total Amount			—	1,900	1,836	1,640

Computation of Labour Hours Rate

Total No. of hours worked	A	B	C
25 days of 8 Hours (25 × 8 = 200)	200 × 30	200 × 40	200 × 20
	6000	8000	4000
Labour Hour Rate = $\frac{\text{Total Overhead}}{\text{No. of hours worked}}$ =	$\frac{1,900}{6000}$	$\frac{1,836}{8000}$	$\frac{1,640}{4000}$
Labour Hour Rate	= Re. 0.316	Re. 0.229	Re. 0.41

Problem No. 25

X Co. Ltd. has three production departments and two service departments. The following figures are extracted from the books of the company :

Expenses :

Rent	20,000
Indirect Wages	6,000
Depreciation	40,000
Lighting	2,400
Power	6,000
Others	40,000

Other Particulars :

	Production Departments			Service Departments	
	A	B	C	D	E
(1) Floor space (Sq. ft.)	4,000	5,000	6,000	4,000	1,000
(2) Light points	20	30	40	20	10
(3) Direct Wages	9,000	6,000	9,000	9,000	7,000
(4) H.P. of Machine	75	30	35	10	—
(5) Value of Machine	1,20,000	1,60,000	2,00,000	10,000	10,000
(6) Working Hours	3113	2014	2033	—	—

The expenses of service departments D and E are to be apportioned as follows :

	Production Departments			Service Departments	
	A	B	C	D	E
Department D Cost	20%	30%	40%	—	10%
Department E Cost	40%	20%	20%	20%	—

You are required to distribute the Service Departments expenses to the Production Departments A, B & C under Simultaneous Equation method.

(B'lore University, 1990)

Solution :

Working Note :

Let X be the total of Service Department D

Y be the total of Service Department E

Equation (i) $X = 15{,}950 + 20\% \text{ of } Y$

(ii) $Y = 10{,}050 + 10\% \text{ of } X$

Now (i) $X = 15{,}950 + 1/5\,(10{,}050 + 1/10\,X)$

$= 15{,}950 + 2{,}010 + 1/50\,X$

$X - 1/50 = 17{,}960$

$$\frac{49}{50} X = 17{,}960 \times \frac{50}{49}$$

$= 18{,}326.53$

$= 18{,}327$

(ii) $Y = 10{,}050 + 1/10\,(18{,}327)$

$= 10{,}050 + 1{,}832.7$

$= 11{,}882.70$

$= 11{,}883$

Primary Distribution Summary Apportionment of Indirect Expenses/ Overheads to Production Departments to Service Departments

Expenses	Basis for apportion-ment	Total	Production Departments			Service Depts.	
			A	B	C	D	E
		Rs.	Rs.	Rs.	Rs.	Rs.	Rs.
(1) Rent 1/20 × 20000	Space 4:5:6:4:1	20,000	4,000	5,000	6,000	4,000	1,000
(2) Indirect Wages	D. Wages 9:6:9:9:7	6,000	1,350	900	1,350	1,350	1,050
(3) Depreciation 1/50 × 40,000	Value 12:16:20:1:1	40,000	9,600	12,800	16,000	800	800
(4) Lighting 1/12 × 2,400	Light points 2:3:4:2:1	2,400	400	600	800	400	200
(5) Power 1/30 × 6,000	H.P. 15:6:7:2	6,000	3,000	1,200	1,400	400	—
(6) Other 1/40 × 40,000	D. Wages 9:6:9:9:7	40,000	9,000	6,000	9,000	9,000	7,000
Total		1,14,400	27,350	26,500	34,550	15,950	10,050

Simultaneous Equation Method :

The total cost of Service Department

D = Rs. 18,327 includes 10% of E

E = Rs. 11,883 includes 20% of D as the service rendered by one Servic Department to another service departments.

Therefore the net amount of Service Departments :

D = would be (Rs. 18,327 - 10%) = Rs. 16,494

E = would be (Rs. 11,883 - 20%) = Rs. 9,506

Secondary Distribution Apportionment of Service Department Cost to Production Departments

Particulars	Basis	Total	Production Departments		
			A	B	C
		Rs.	Rs.	Rs.	Rs.
(1) As per Primary Distribution summary		88,400	27,350	26,500	34,550
(2) Service Dept. Cost D – 1/9 × 16,494 = 1,832.66	2:3:4	16,494	3,665	5,498	7,331
E = 1/8 × 9,506 = 1,188.25	4:2:2	9,506	4,753	2,376	2,377
		1,14,400	35,768	34,374	44,258

	A	B	C
Total Cost	35,786	34,374	44,258
No. of working hours	3,113	2,014	2,033
Machine Hour Rate = Total cost / No. of working hours	35,768 / 3113	34,374 / 2014	44,258 / 2033
Machine Hour Rate (in Rs.)	11.489	17.067	21.769

Under the same problem the service department cost may be apportioned under repeated distribution method.

Particulars	Basis	Total	Production Departments			Service Depts.	
			A	B	C	D	E
		Rs.	Rs.	Rs.	Rs.	Rs.	Rs.
(1) As per primary distribution		1,14,400	27,350	26,500	34,550	15,950	10,050
Apportionment of % Service Dept. (1) Dept. - D 1/10 × 15,950 = 1,595	2:3:4:1		·3,190	4,785	6,380	–15,950	1,595
			30,540	31,285	40,930	—	11,645

Particulars	Basis	Total	Production Departments			Service Depts.	
			A	B	C	D	E
		Rs.	Rs.	Rs.	Rs.	Rs.	Rs.
(2) Dept. -E 1/10 × 11,645 = 1,164.5	4:2:2:2		4,658	2,329	2,329	2,329	–11,645
			35,198	33,614	42,259	2,329	—
(3) Dept. - D 1/10 × 2,329 = 233	2:3:4:1		465	699	932	–2,329	233
			35,663	34,313	44,191	—	233
(4) Dept. - E 1/10 × 233 = 23.30	4:2:2:2		93	47	47	46	–233
			35,756	34,360	44,238	46	—
(5) Dept. - E 1/10 × 46 = 4.60	2:3:4:1		9	14	18	–46	5
			35,765	34,374	44,256	—	5
(6) Dept. - E 1/10 × 5 = 0.50	4:2:2:2		3	—	2	—	–5
Total Amount			35,768	34,374	44,258	—	—

$$\text{Machine Hour Rate} = \frac{\text{Total Cost}}{\text{No. of Hours}}$$

$$= \frac{35{,}768}{3113} = \frac{34{,}374}{2014} = \frac{44{,}258}{2033}$$

Machine Hour Rate = 11.489 17.067 21.769

Problem No. 26

In a factory the following expenses are incurred :

(a) Power consumption of this machine Rs. 9,000 p.a.

(b) Repairs and Maintenance for the entire working life of the machine — Rs. 16,000.

(c) Oil waste etc. and for this machine Rs. 1,800 p.a.

Other Expenses of the entire factory for the year :

(1) Rent and rates	27,000
(2) Lighting	1,200
(3) Supervision	3,750
(4) Sundry Expenses	15,000

Other Information :

Area of the factory 10,000 sq. feet. Area occupied by this machine is 2000 sq. feet. Cost of Machine 60,000. Estimated life of the machine 10 Years. There are 16 workers in the factory out of them 4 attend to this machine. The degree of supervision is 2/5 to this machine.

The factory will work for 2000 hours per annum.

(Bangalore, B.Com., October 1990)

Solution :

Computation of Machine Hour Rate

	Total Cost (p.a.) Rs.	Per Hour Rs.
(I) *Standing Charges :*		
(1) Rent and Rate 27,000 × 1/5	5,400	
(2) Lighting 1,200 × 1/5	240	
(3) Supervision 3,750 × 2/5	1,500	
(4) Sundry Expenses 15,000 (apportioned on the basis of area 15,000 × 1/5 = 3,000)	3,000	
Total Standing Charges	16,140	
Machine Working Hours 2000 = $\frac{\text{Total Cost}}{\text{No. of Hours}}$ =	$\frac{16,140}{2000}$	
Machine Hour Rate		8.07
(II) *Machine Expenses :*		
(1) Power $\frac{9,000}{2000}$		4.50
(2) Repairs & Maintenance $\frac{16,000}{10 \text{ Years}} = \frac{1,600}{2000}$		0.80
(3) Oil wastage etc. = $\frac{1,800}{2000}$		0.90
Total		14.27
Machine Hour Rate		14.27

Problem No. 27

Reghavendra Co. Ltd. has three production departments namely X, Y and Z and one service department namely P. The factory works for 25 days in a month for 8 hours a day. Following are the particulars for a month :

Overheads	Total	Service Dept. P	Production Departments X	Y	Z
	Rs.	Rs.	Rs.	Rs.	Rs.
(1) Power & Lighting	2,200	480	400	600	720
(2) Supervision Salary	4,000	—	—	—	—
(3) Rent	2,000	—	—	—	—
(4) Labour welfare	6,000	—	—	—	—
(5) Other Expenses	4,800	800	800	1,600	1,600
Additional Information :					
Ratio time devoted by supervisor		2	3	3	2
No. of workers		5	15	20	10
Area occupied (sq ft)		500	600	800	600
Service by Department 'P' to other Departments			30%	50%	20%

Required :

(1) Labour hour rate for each Department.

(2) Overheads to be charged for a Job if it passes through department X and Z requiring 10 and 20 man hours of work respectively.

(K.U.D., October 1989)

Solution :

Overhead Distribution Summary

Particulars	Basis for apportion-ment	Total	Service Dept. P	Production Departments X	Y	Z
		Rs.	Rs.	Rs.	Rs.	Rs.
(1) Power & Lighting	Actuals	2,200	480	400	600	720
(2) Supervision salary	Ratio 2:3:3:2	4,000	800	1,200	1,200	800
(3) Rent	Area 5:6:8:6	2,000	400	480	640	480
(4) Labour welfare	No. of Worker 1:3:4:2	6,000	600	1,800	2,400	1,200
(5) Other Expenses	Actual	4,800	800	800	1,600	1,600
		19,000	3,080	4,689	6,440	4,800
Absorption of Cost of Service Department	Ratio given 30%, 50%, 20%		–3,080	924	1,540	616
Total Cost			—	5,604	7,980	5,416

Computation of Labour Hour Rate

Particulars	Production Departments X Rs.	Y Rs.	Z Rs.
Total Cost as above	5,604	7,980	5,416
Total Labour Hours in a Month (25 days × 8 Hours per day = 200)	(25 × 200) = 3000 Hrs	(20 × 200) 4000 Hrs	(10 × 200) 2000 Hrs
Labour Hour Rate = $\frac{\text{Total Cost}}{\text{No. of Labour Hrs.}}$	$\frac{5,604}{3000}$	$\frac{7,980}{4000}$	$\frac{5,416}{2000}$
Labour Hours Rate	1.868	1.995	2.708
Overhead to be charged for Job			
Department X = 10 Mens × 1.868	18.68	—	—
Department Z = 20 Mens × 2.708	—	—	54.16

Problem No. 28

A machine costs Rs. 50,000 and is deemed to have a scrap value of Rs. 5,000 at the end of effective life of 10 years.

The machine is expected to run for 1,500 Hours p.a.

The details in respect of machine Shop are :

(1)	Wages of two operators per annum each (Each operators operate two Machines)	6,000
(2)	Rent and rates of the shop (per annum)	3,000
(3)	General Lighting of the shop (per month)	250
(4)	Insurance Premium for the Machine (per quarter)	200
(5)	Cost of Repairs & Maintenance (per month)	250
(6)	Shop supervisor's Salary (per month)	500
(7)	Power consumption of Machine per hour 200 units @ Rs. 10 per 100 units.	
(8)	Factory overhead charges to the shop (per annum)	4,000

There are four identical Machines in the shop.

The supervisor is expected to devote 1/5 of his time on each machine. Compute Machine Hour Rate from the above details.

(K.U.D., April 1989)

Solution :

Computation of Machine Hour Rate

	Total Cost (p.a.) Rs.	Per Hour Rs.
(I) *Standing Charges :*		
(a) Rent and Rate Rs. $\frac{3,000}{4}$ p.a. for 4 months	750	
(b) General Lighting for the shop 250 × 12 = 3,000 (3,000 × ¼ = 750)	750	
(c) Insurance premium (200 × 4)	800	
(d) Supervisor's salary = 500 × 12 = 6,000 × 1/5	1,200	
(e) Factory Overhead charge 4,000 × ¼	1,000	
Total Standing Charges	4,500	
$\frac{\text{Total Standing Charges}}{\text{No. Machine Hour}}$	$\frac{4,500}{1,500}$	3.00
(II) *Machine Expenses :*		
(f) Wages of operators $\frac{6,000}{2} = \frac{3,000}{1500} =$		2.00
(g) Repairs & Maintenance 250 × 12 = $\frac{3,000}{1500}$ =		2.00
(h) Depreciation = $\frac{\text{Cost} - \text{Scrap}}{\text{Life}} = \frac{50,000 - 5,000}{10}$ $= \frac{45,000}{1500}$		3.00
(i) Power = 20 units per hour for 1500 Hours (20 × 1500 = 30,000 units for 100 units Rs. 10 = $\frac{3,000}{100} \times 10 = \frac{3,000}{1500}$		2.00
Machine Hour Rate		12.00

Problem No. 29

Calculate Machine Hour Rate for the machine No.7 which is one of the seven machines in operation in a department of a factory.

You are furnished with the following information :

(1)	Cost of Machine No. 7	10,000
(2)	Estimated Scrap value at the end of life of 10 years	1,000
(3)	No. of working hours per annum	1800 Hours

(4) Machine No. 7 occupies one-fifth of the area
(5) Rent, rate and lighting per annum Rs. 3,500
(6) Charges for this machine per annum Rs. 2,000
(7) Oil, Cotton waste etc. for this machine per annum Rs. 300
(8) Repairs & Maintenance throughout the working life of the machine Rs. 3,600
(9) Cost of supervision application to this machine No. 7 p.a. Rs. 1,500.

(Gulbarga, October 1989)

Solution :

Computation of Machine Hour Rate

	Total Cost (p.a.) Rs.	Per Hour Rs.
(I) *Standing Charges :*		
(1) Rent, Rates and Lighting 3,500 × 1/5 p.a.	700	
(2) Supervision 1,500 p.a.	1,500	
(3) Depreciation $= \frac{\text{Cost} - \text{Scrap}}{\text{Life}} = \frac{10{,}000 - 1{,}000}{10}$	900	
Total Standing Charges	2,100	
Machine Hour Rate $= \frac{\text{Total Cost}}{\text{No. hours}} = \frac{2{,}100}{1800}$		1.17
(II) *Machine Expenses :*		
(1) Oil, Cotton waste etc. $\frac{300}{1800} = 0.17$		0.17
(2) Repairs & Maintenance $\frac{3{,}600}{10} = \frac{360}{1800}$		0.20
(3) Power $\frac{2{,}000}{1800} = 1.11$		1.11
Machine Hour Rate		2.65

Problem No. 30

Deepa Ltd. has three production departments, namely A, B & C and four Service Departments, namely, Canteen, Personnel, Maintenance and Stores departments. The Departmental overhead are obtained in a summarised form as under :

Production Departments		Service Departments	
A —	8,000	Canteen —	2,000
B —	12,000	Personnel —	2,500
C —	6,000	Maintenance	6,000
		Stores	4,000

Following information are also obtained :

No. of employees in different departments are as follows :

A — 25, B — 30, C — 20, Canteen — 5, Personnel — 2, Maintenance — 10 and Stores — 10

You are asked to distribute stores Expenses as under :

Maintenance — 10%, Dept. A — 20%, Dept. B — 40% and Dept. C — 30%.

The maintenance department renders service to Departments :

A — 30%, B — 50% and C — 20%.

Distribute the service departments expenses to production departments under Step Ladder Method. Write your assumptions whenever necessary.

(K.U.D., April 1988)

Solution :

Assumptions :

Canteen Department and Personnel Department serve the maximum other departments. Since the expenses of personnel department are more than the canteen department. The Personnel Department expenses are first distributed to other departments and then canteen. Expenses order of distributed as under :

(1) Personnel Department (2) Canteen Department
(3) Stores Department (4) Maintenance Department

(Step Ladder Method)

Secondary Distribution Summary

Distribution of Service Department expenses to other Service Departments & Production Departments

Particulars	Service Departments				Production Depts.		
	P	C	S	M	A	B	C
	Rs.	Rs.	Rs.	Rs.	Rs.	Rs.	Rs.
(a) As per Primary Distribution	2,500	2,000	4,000	6,000	8,000	12,000	6,000
Service Department Expenses							
(1) Personnel Department Basis — No. of Employees (Canteen - 5, Stores - 10, Maintenance - 10, A - 25, B - 30, C - 20. 1:2:2:5:6:4)	-2,500	125	250	250	625	750	500
	—	2,125	4,250	6,250	8,625	12,750	6,500
(2) Canteen Department (Basis – 2:2:5:6:4)		−2,125	224	224	559	671	447
	—	—	4,474	6,474	9,184	13,421	6,947

Particulars	Service Departments				Production Depts.		
	P	C	S	M	A	B	C
	Rs.	Rs.	Rs.	Rs.	Rs.	Rs.	Rs.
(3) Stores Department (Basis — 1:2:4:2)	—	—	-4,474	497	994	1,989	994
	—	—	—	6,791	10,178	15,410	7,941
(4) Maintenance Department (Basis — given 3:5:2)	—	—	—	-6,791	2,091	3,486	1,394
Total (40,500)	—	—	—	—	12,269	18,896	9,335

Department	Basis	Canteen	Stores	Mainten.	A	B	C
(1) Personnel Department	No. of Employees	5	10	10	25	30	20
		1	2	2	5	6	4
(2) Canteen Department	No. of Employees		Stores	Maintenance	A	B	C
			10	10	25	30	20
			2	2	5	6	4
(3) Stores Department	Given			Maintenance	A	B	C
				10%	20%	40%	30%
(4) Maintenance Depart.	Given				A	B	C
					30%	50%	20%

Problem No. 31

From the following details compute the hourly rate of a machine installed in a shop :

		Rs.
(1)	Capital cost of the machine	9,000
(2)	Installation charges	1,000
(3)	Scrap value after the expiry of its life of 10 years	2,000
(4)	Rent of the shop per quarter	300
(5)	General lighting of the shop per month	20
(6)	Supervision salary per month	200
(7)	Insurance per month of machine	5
(8)	Cost of repairs & maintenance per annum	100
(9)	Power consumption — 2 units per hour @ Rs. 5 per 100 units	
(10)	Estimated working hours of the machine 2000 hours per annum.	

The supervision in the shop is expected to devote 1/5 of his time for this machine. The machine occupies ¼ of the area of shop.

(Gulbarga, October 1988)

Solution :

Computation of Machine Hour Rate

	Per Annum Total Cost Rs.	Per hour Rs.
(I) *Standing Charges :*		
(1) Rent — per Quarter 300 × 4 = 1,200 × ¼	300	
(2) General Lighting p.m. 20 × 12 = 240 × ¼	60	
(3) Supervisor's Salary 200 × 12 = 2,400 × 1/5	480	
(4) Insurance 5 × 12 = 60	60	
Depreciation = $\frac{\text{Cost + Installation charges} - \text{Scrap}}{\text{Life}}$		
$= \frac{9{,}000 + 1{,}000 - 2{,}000}{10 \text{ Years}} = \frac{8{,}000}{10}$	800	
Total Standing Charges	1,700	
Machine Hours p.a. 2,000	$\frac{1{,}700}{2000}$	0.85
(II) *Machine Expenses :*		
(1) Repairs & Maintenance $\frac{100}{2000}$		0.05
(2) Power Consumption = 2 units per hour cost Rs. 5 per 100 units = 2 × 0.05 = 0.10		0.10
Machine Hour Rate		1.00

Problem No. 32

From the following particulars compute machine hour rate :

(1) Rent, Rate (for the Dept.)	12,000
(2) Lighting & Heating (for the Dept.)	3,000
(3) Supervisions salary (in the Dept.)	6,000
(4) Insurance (for the Dept.)	3,000
(5) Lubricants and cotton waste (for the machine)	300

Additional Information

(a) The cost of Machine is Rs. 16,000 and Scrap value at the end of its life Rs. 1,000 (of 10 years).

(b) The machine will work for 2000 hours during the year.

(c) The machine occupies 1/4 of the space in the Department.

(d) 3 out of 18 light and heating points are for the machine.

(e) Supervisor devotes 20% of his time over this machine.

(f) There are five machines of the same cost in the Department.

(g) Estimated cost of repairs & maintenance over the life of machine is Rs. 1,000.

(h) That the machine consumes 4 units per hour @ Rs. 0.50 per unit.

(K.U.D., October 1987)

Solution :

Computation of Machine Hour Rate

	Per Annum	Per Hour
(I) *Standing Charges :*	Rs.	Rs.
(1) Rent & Rates (for the Dept - 12,000 × ¼)	3,000	
(2) Lighting & Heating (3,000 × 3/18)	500	
(3) Supervision salary (6,000 × 20/100)	1,200	
(4) Insurance (3,000 × 1/5)	600	
Total Standing Charges	5,300	
Standing charges per hour = $\frac{5,300}{2000}$ = 2.65		2.65
(II) *Operation Expenses :*		
(5) Lubricant oil & cotton waste $\frac{300}{2000}$		0.15
(6) Depreciation = $\frac{\text{Cost} - \text{Scrap}}{\text{Life}} = \frac{16,000 - 1,000}{10}$ $\frac{1500}{2000}$		0.75
(7) Repairs & Maintenance $\frac{1,000}{10} = \frac{100}{2000}$		0.05
(8) Oil – 4 Ltr. per hour cost 0.50		2.00
Machine Hour Rate (per Hour)		5.60

Problem No. 33

Production Department has five different groups of machines :

Machine Groups	Lubrication	Repairs & Maintenance	Depreciation
	Rs.	Rs.	Rs.
1	7,000	12,000	24,000
2	6,000	18,000	32,000
3	3,500	10,000	16,000
4	9,000	12,500	48,000
5	4,500	7,500	64,000

(1) Insurance on Building 20,000
(2) Power consumption 1,62,000
(3) Rent, Rates & Taxes etc. 60,000
(4) Consumable stores 1,01,640
(5) Insurance on Machinery 36,800
(6) Supervisions salary 46,200
(7) General Expenses 1,84,800

The necessary data for apportionment of expenses are as follows :

Group	Effective	Area occupied (Sq Mtr)	Book value of Machine (in Lakhs)	Machine Hours
1	25	90	24,000	24,000
2	30	120	3,20,000	14,400
3	10	40	1,60,000	24,000
4	50	150	4,80,000	18,000
5	20	100	6,40,000	12,000

Calculate Machine Hour Rate for each of the five groups of machine showing clearly the basis of apportionment used.

(B'lore University, October 1987)

Solution :

Primary Distribution of Overheads of Machine Groups

Particulars	Basis apportionment	Total	Machine Groups 1 Rs.	2 Rs.	3 Rs.	4 Rs.	5 Rs.
Standing Charge :							
(1) Rent 1/50 × 60,000	Space 9:12:4:15:10	60,000	10,800	14,400	4,800	18,000	12,000
(2) Insurance on Building 1/2 × 20,000	-do-	20,000	3,600	4,800	1,600	6,000	4,000
(3) Supervision salary 1/77 × 46,200	20:12:20:15:10	46,200	12,000	7,200	12,000	9,000	6,000
(4) General Expenses 1/77 × 1,84,800	-do-	1,84,800	48,000	28,800	48,000	36,000	24,000
(5) Depreciation	Actual given	1,84,800	24,000	32,000	16,000	48,000	64,000
(6) Insurance 1/23 × 36,800 = 1600	3:4:2:6:8	36,800	4,800	6,400	3,200	9,600	12,800
Total Standing Charges		5,31,800	1,03,200	93,600	85,600	1,26,600	1,22,800

Particulars	Basis apportionment	Total	Machine Groups				
			1	2	3	4	5
			Rs.	Rs.	Rs.	Rs.	Rs.
(1) Power consumption (5:6:2:10:4)	H.P.	1,62,000	30,000	36,000	12,000	60,000	24,000
(2) Consumable Store 1/77 × 1,01,640 20:12:20:15:10	Machine Hours	1,01,640	26,400	15,840	26,400	19,800	13,200
(3) Lubricants	Actual given	30,000	7,000	6,000	3,500	9,000	4,500
(4) Repairs & Maintenance	Actual given	60,000	12,000	18,000	10,000	12,500	7,500
Total Cost		8,85,440	1,78,600	1,69,440	1,37,500	2,27,900	1,72,000

Machine Hour Rate

= Total Cost / No. of Hour worked	1,78,600 / 24000	1,69,440 / 14400	1,37,500 / 24000	2,27,900 / 18000	1,72,000 / 12000
Machine Hour Rate (in Rs.)	7.44	11.77	5.729	12.66	14.33

Problem No. 34

Alfa Ltd. has three Manufacturing Departments A, B and C and One Service Department 'S'. The following figures are available for one month of 25 working Days of 8 Hours day. All the departments worked all days with full attendance.

	Total	Service Dept. S	Manufacturing Departments A	B	C
	Rs.	Rs.	Rs.	Rs.	Rs.
(I) *Expenses*					
(1) Power & Lighting	2,200	480	400	600	720
(2) Supervision	2,000	—	—	—	—
(3) Rent	1,000	—	—	—	—
(4) Welfare	1,200	—	—	—	—
(5) Other Expenses	2,400	400	400	800	800
(II) *Other Information :*					
(1) Supervision salary		30%	30%	20%	20%
(2) No. of Workers		10	30	40	20
(3) Floor Area (sq ft)		500	600	800	600
(4) Service to Production Dept.		—	50%	30%	20%

Calculate Labour Hour rate for each Production Department.

(K.U.D., April 1987)

Solution :

Overheads Distribution Summary

Particulars	Basis for apportionment	Total	Service Dept. S	Production Depts. A	B	C
		Rs.	Rs.	Rs.	Rs.	Rs.
(I) Standing Charges						
(1) Power & Lighting	Actual given	2,200	480	400	600	720
(2) Supervision	Ratio given (3:3:2:2)	2,000	600	600	400	400
(3) Rent	Floor area (5:6:8:6)	1,000	200	240	320	240
(4) Welfare	No. of workers (1,3,4,2)	1,200	120	360	480	240
(5) Other	Ratio given	2,400	400	400	800	800
Total Standing Charges		8,800	1,800	2,000	2,600	2,400
(II) Allocation of Service Department Expenses to Production Department	Given		1,800	2,000	2,600	2,400
			–1,800	900	540	360
Total			—	2,900	3,140	2,760

Computation of Labour Hours

$$= \frac{\text{Overhead}}{\text{Labour Hour}} \qquad = \qquad \frac{200\times30}{6{,}000} \qquad \frac{200\times40}{8{,}000} \qquad \frac{200\times20}{4{,}000}$$

Labour Hour Rate

$$= \frac{\text{Total Amount}}{\text{Total No. of hours}} \qquad \frac{2{,}900}{6{,}000} \qquad \frac{3{,}140}{8{,}000} \qquad \frac{2{,}760}{4{,}000}$$

$$= \quad 0.48 \text{ Ps} \qquad 0.39\text{Ps} \qquad 0.69\text{Ps}$$

Problem No. 35

From the Budgeted figures of Bharat Metal Works calculate overhead recovery rate using (1) Direct Labour Hour Rate method, (2) Machine Hour Rate method and (3) Labour Cost Rate method.

Budgeted figures for the year :

(a) Estimated Factory overheads	1,72,125	
(b) Estimated Labour hours worked	24,590	Hours
(c) Estimated Labour cost	2,29,500	
(d) Estimated Machine Hours worked	45,900	Hours

Prepare a comparative statement of cost showing the result of each of the above rates to Job No. 105, from the data given below. Cost of Direct Materials Rs. 1,040. Cost of Direct Labour Rs. 1,575. Direct Labour hours worked — 324 Hours. Machine Hours worked 710 Hrs.

(K.U.D., October 1986)

Solution :

Working Note

(1) Direct Labour Hour Rate $= \dfrac{\text{Estimated Factory Overhead}}{\text{Estimated Labour Hours}}$

$= \dfrac{1{,}72{,}125}{24590} = 6.99 = \text{Rs. } 7 \text{ per Hour}$

(2) % of Labour Cost Rate Method $= \dfrac{\text{Estimated Factory Overhead}}{\text{Estimated labour cost}}$

$= \dfrac{1{,}72{,}125}{2{,}29{,}500} \times 100$

$= 75\%$

(3) Machine Hour Rate $= \dfrac{\text{Estimated Factory Overhead}}{\text{Estimated Machine Hours worked}}$

$= \dfrac{1{,}72{,}125}{45900}$

= Rs. 3.75 per hour.

Comparative Statement of Cost

Particulars	Labour Hour Rate	Labour Cost	Machine Hour Rate
Direct Material	1,040	1,040	1,040
Direct Wages	1,575	1,575	1,575
Prime Cost	2,615	2,615	2,615
Factory Overhead			
(a) Direct Labour Hour Rate Rs. 7 per hour rate = 324 × 7 = 2,268	2,268	—	—
(b) Labour cost method 75% of Direct wages $1{,}575 \times \frac{75}{100} = 1{,}181.25$	—	1,181.25	—

Particulars	Labour Hour Rate	Labour Cost	Machine Hour Rate
(c) Machine Hour Rate Rs. 3.75 per hour Machine Hour worked = 710 × 3.75 = 2,662.5	—	—	2,662.5
Total Cost	4,883	3,796.25	5,277.5

Problem No. 36

Calculate the Machine Hour Rate for the year 1985 to cover the following overhead expenses relating to Machine No. 105 :

(1)	Capital cost of Machine	20,000
(2)	Estimated Scrap value	4,000
(3)	Rent of the Shop per quarter	600
(4)	General Lighting of the shop per month	40
(5)	Shop supervision's salary per month	400
(6)	Insurance premium per annum	120
(7)	Repairs and Maintenance per annum	200

(8) Power consumption of the machine 20 units per hour @ 20 Ps per unit.

(9) The Machine occupies ¼ of total shop area.

(10) The supervisor in the shop is expected to devote 1/5 of the time on this Machine.

(11) General Lighting expenses are to be apportioned on the basis of shop area.

(12) The Estimate Life of the Machine is 20000 Hours.
Machine Hours worked 2000 Hours for the year.

(K.U.D., April 1986)

Solution :

Computation of Machine Hour Rate for the year 1985

	Per Annum Total Cost Rs.	Per Hour Rs.
(I) *Standing Charges :*		
(1) Rent per quarter Rs. 600 × 4 = 2,400 × ¼	600	
(2) General Lighting per month 40 × 12 = 480 × ¼	120	
(3) Shop supervisor's salary 400 × 12 = 4,800 × 1/5	960	
(4) Insurance premium per annum	120	
Total Standing Charges	1,800	

	Per Annum Total Cost Rs.	Per Hour Rs.
Machine Hour per Year = 2000 = $\frac{1,800}{2000}$ = 0.90		0.90
(II) *Machine Expenses :*		
(1) Power consumption = 20 × 0.20 =		4.00
(2) Repairs and Maintenance $\frac{200}{2000}$ = 0.10		0.10
(3) Depreciation = $\frac{\text{Cost} - \text{Scrap}}{\text{Life in Hours}} = \frac{20,000 - 4,000}{20,000} = \frac{16000}{20000}$		0.80
Machine Hour Rate		5.80

Problem No. 37

Harsha Ltd. has three Production Departments and two Service Departments. Particulars of Expenses of the respective departments are as follows :

Production : Departments A — 800, B — 700, C — 500

Service Departments D — 234 E — 300

The expenses of service departments are charged out on a percentage basis as follows :

Production Departments			Service Departments	
A — 20%,	B — 40%,	C — 30%	D —	E — 10%
E — 40%	20%	20%	20%	—

Using the above particulars, apportion the Service Departments expenses to various Production Departments by adopting Simultaneous Equation Method.

(K.U.D., October 1985)

Solution :

Let X be the Total of Service Department — D

Let Y be the Total of Service Department — E

(1) Now

$$
\begin{aligned}
X &= 234 + 20\% \text{ of } Y \\
Y &= 300 + 10\% \text{ of } X \\
X &= 234 + 20\% (300 + 1/10X) \\
&= 234 + (1/5 \times 300 + 1/5 \times 1/10X) \\
&= 234 + 60 + 1/50X \\
&= 234 + 1/50X \\
X - 1/50\ X &= 294 \\
49/50\ X &= 294 \\
X &= 294 \times \frac{50}{49} \\
X &= 300 \text{ Service Department} - D
\end{aligned}
$$

(2) Y = 300 + 1/10 of X
Y = 300 + 10% of 300
= 300 + 30
= 330

The total cost Service Department

D — Rs. 300 includes 10% of E

E — Rs. 330 included of 20% of D as the service rendered by one Service Department to another Service Dept.

Therefore the Net amount of Service Department :

D — would be (300 — 10%) = 270

E — Would be (330 — 20%) = 264

Apportion to Production Departments.

Apportionment of Service Department Overhead to Production Dept.

Particulars	Basis	Total	Production Depts. A	B	C
As per Primary Distribution Summary		2,000	800	700	500
Apportionment of Overhead of Service Department					
D — (300 - 10% = 270) Or 1/9 × 270 = 30)	2:4:3:9	270	60	120	90
		2,270	860	820	590
E — (330 - 20%) = 264	4:2:2	264	132	66	66
		2,534	992	886	656

Problem No. 38

The following expenses have been incurred in respect of a shop having 4 identical machines :

(1)	Rent and Rates	6,000	per annum
(2)	Power consumed by the shop	.10	Ps per unit (4,800 p.a.)
(3)	Repairs	1,000	per annum
(4)	Light for the shop	800	p.a.
(5)	Shop Supervisor's salary	600	per month.
(6)	Lubricants etc.	100	per month.
(7)	Depreciation per machine	600	per annum
(8)	Hire purchase instalment for the machine (including interest Rs. 300)	800	

(9) There are two attenders in a shop each getting Rs. 60 per month.

(10) Each machine consumes 10 units of power per hour.

Calculate the Machine Hour Rate.

(K.U.D., April 1985)

Solution :

Calculation of Machine Hour Rate

	Per Annum Rs.	Per Hour Rs.
(1) Rent & Rates (6,000 × ¼)	1,500	
(2) Lighting (800 × ¼)	200	
(3) Supervision (600 × 12 × ¼)	1,800	
(4) Attenders (2 × 60 × 12 × ¼)	360	
(5) Hire-Purchases interest (300 × ¼)	75	
(6) Lubricants (100 × 12 × ¼)	300	
Total	4,295	
Hourly Rate = $\frac{4,295}{1200}$ = 3.529 or 3.53		3.53
Machine Expenses :		
(1) Power consumed 10 units @ .10 Ps per unit		1.00
(2) Repairs 1,000 × 1/4 = $\frac{2.50}{1200}$ = 0.208		
(3) Depreciation $\frac{600}{1200}$ 0.50 0.708		0.70
Machine Hour Rate		5.23

Note : Units consumed $\frac{4,800}{10}$ × 100 = 48,000 Total for 4 Machines

Per Machine = $\frac{48,000}{4}$ = 12000 Units.

Hours in a year 10 units per hour for 12000 Hours = $\frac{12000}{10}$ = 1200 Hrs.

Problem No. 39

The following information relates to the activities of a Production Department for a certain period in a factory :

Materials used	72,000
Direct Wages	60,000
Machine Hours	20000 Hours.
Labour Hour worked	24000 Hours.
Overhead chargeable to the Department	48,000

On one order carrying out in the Department during the period, the relevant data are available :

Material used	4,000
Labour Hours	1650 Hours.
Direct Wages	3,300
Machine Hours	1200 Hours.

Prepare comparative Statement of cost of this order by using the following three methods of recovery of overhead :

(1) Direct Labour Hour Rate method.
(2) Direct Labour Cost Rate method.
(3) Machine Hour Rate method.

(Gulbarga, October 1985)

Solution :

Calculation Overhead Recovery under the methods of :

(1) Direct Labour Hour Rate Method = $\frac{\text{Overhead}}{\text{Labour Hours}} = \frac{48{,}000}{24{,}000} =$ Rs. 2 per Hour.

(2) Direct Labour Cost Method = % of Recovery of overhead on the basis of labour cost = $\frac{\text{Overhead}}{\text{Direct Wages}} \times 100 = \frac{48{,}000}{60{,}000} \times 100$ = 80% of Wages.

(3) Machine Hour Rate Method = $\frac{\text{Overhead}}{\text{Machine Hours}} = \frac{48{,}000}{20000} =$ Rs. 2.40

Comparative Cost Statement of an Order

	Labour Hour Rate Method Rs.	Labour Cost Rate Method Rs.	Machine Hour Rate Method Rs.
(1) Materials uses	4,000	4,000	4,000
(2) Direct Wages	3,300	3,300	3,300
Prime Cost	7,300	7,300	7,300
Factory Overhead :			
(1) Labour Hour Rate Rs. 2 per Hour Hours 1650 × 2	3,300	—	—
(2) Percentage of Direct Wages 80% of Direct Wages (80% of 3,300 = 2,640)	—	2,640	—
(3) Machine Hour Rate Rs. 2.40 per Hour Machine Hour 1200 × 2.40	—	—	2,880
Works Cost Or Cost of Production	10,600	9,940	10,180

Problem No. 40

A Machine shop contains four newly purchased machines each occupying practically equal space and the value of each of machine respectively : A - Rs. 20,000, B - Rs. 25,000, C - Rs. 3,000 and D - Rs. 40,000.

The following are expenses per Machine shop :

(1) Rent	10,000
(2) Rates & Water	4,250
(3) Light & Heat	3,150
(4) Power - A	5,100
B	5,000
C	12,000
D	14,500
(5) Administrative Expenses	9,500
(6) Running Expenses and Works sundries	20,000

Prepare a machine hour rate for each machine presuming 45 hours a week and 50 weeks in a year's 80% of the yearly hours utilisation. The life of the Machine is 10 years without any scrap value.

(K.U.D., October 1984)

Solution :

Computation of Machine Hour Rate

Particulars	Basis for allocation	Total Cost	A	B	C	D
(I) *Standing Charges :*						
(1) Rent	Equally	10,000	2,500	2,500	2,500	2,500
(2) Rates & Water	Equally	4,250	1,062	1,062	1,062	1,063
(3) Light & Heating	—	3,150	787	787	788	788
(4) Administration	Equally	9,500	2,375	2,375	2,375	2,375
(5) Depreciation = $\frac{\text{Cost}}{\text{Period}} = \frac{20,000}{10}$	10% on cost	11,500	2,000	2,500	3,000	4,000
		38,400	8,724	9,224	9,726	10,726
(II) *Machine Expenses :*						
Power	Actual	36,600	5,100	5,000	12,000	14,500
Running Expenses	On power used 51:50:120:145	20,000	2,787	2,732	6,557	7,923
Total Cost			16,611	16,856	28,284	33,149
No. of Hours Worked in a year (No. of Hours = $45 \times 50 \times \frac{80}{100}$ = 1800)			1800	1800	1800	1800
Machine Hour Rate = $\frac{\text{Cost}}{\text{No. of hours}}$			$\frac{16,611}{1800}$	$\frac{16,956}{1800}$	$\frac{28,284}{1800}$	$\frac{33,149}{1800}$
		=	9.228	9.42	15.71	18.416

Problem No. 41

Calculate Machine Hour Rate for the month of January 1987 to cover the overhead expenses given below relating to a machine.

(1)	Rent of the department (1/5 are occupied)	780 p.a.
(2)	Lighting (out of 12 points 2 are for Machine)	288 p.a.
(3)	Insurance	36 p.a.
(4)	Cotton wastage	60 p.a.
(5)	Formen's salary (¼ for the machine)	6,000 p.a.
(6)	Cost of the Machine	9,200
(7)	Scrap value	200
(8)	It is assumed that the machine will work for 1800 Hours per annum and it will incurred Rs. 1,125 for repairs and maintenance.	
(9)	Throughout the life of the machine is 10 years.	
(10)	Power consumption 5 units per hour @ cost of 6 Ps per unit.	

(K.U.D., October 1976, Gulbarga, April 1987)

Solution :

Computation of Machine Hour Rate

	Total Cost (p.a.) Rs.	Per Hour Rs.
(I) *Standing Charges :*		
(1) Rent — 780 × 1/5 = 156	156	
(2) Lighting 288 for 12 Points = $\frac{288}{12} \times 2$	48	
(3) Insurance	36	
(4) Forman's salary 6,000 × ¼	1,500	
(5) Depreciation = $\frac{\text{Cost} - \text{Scrap}}{\text{Life}} = \frac{9{,}200 - 200}{10}$	900	
Total Standing Charges	2,640	
Machine Hour Rate = $\frac{\text{Total Cost}}{\text{No. of Hours}}$	$\frac{2{,}640}{1800}$	1.47
(II) *Machine Expenses :*		
(1) Repairs & Maintenance for life period 10 years $\frac{1{,}125}{10} = \frac{112.5}{1800} = 0.0625$		0.0625
(2) Cotton waste etc. $\frac{60}{1800}$		0.03
(3) Power consumption 5 units per hour cost 0.06 Ps (5 × 0.06 = 0.30)		0.30
Machine Hour Rate		1.8625

Problem No. 42 (Simultaneous Equation Method)

AB Co. Ltd. a manufacturing unit has four Production Departments — I, II, III & IV and Two Service Departments — Transport and Power Supply.

Production Departments				Service Departments	
I	II	III	IV	Transport	Power Supply
4,500	4,050	3,600	3,150	2,475	1,710

The service departments expenses are charged to production departments on a percentage basis given below :

	Production Departments				Service Departments	
	I	II	III	IV	Transport	Power Supply
Transport	10%	30%	20%	20%	—	20%
Power Supply	30%	20%	30%	10%	10%	—

Using the above particulars apportion the service departments expenses to various production departments on the basis of Simultaneous Equation method.

Solution :

Let 'T' be the total of Transport Department 'P' be the total of Power Supply Department

$$\therefore \quad T = 2,475 + 10\% \text{ of } P$$
$$P = 1,710 + 20\% \text{ of } T$$
$$\text{Now } T = 2,475 + 1/10\ (1,710 + 1/5\ T)$$
$$= 2,475 + 171 + 1/50\ T$$
$$= 2,646 + 1/50\ T$$
$$\text{Now } T - 1/50 = 2,646$$
$$49/50\ T = 2,646$$
$$T = 2,646 \times \frac{50}{49}$$
$$T = 2,700 \text{ (Transport)}$$
$$\text{Power } P = 1,710 + 1/5$$
$$= 1,710 + 1/5 \times 2,700$$
$$= 1,710 + 540$$
$$= 2,250 \text{ (Power supply)}$$

Now the Total cost of Transport of Rs. 2,700

Total cost of Power supply of Rs. 2,250

The above Total cost of Service Departments include the cost of Service Departments to another rendered by one service department to another service department. Therefore Transport cost — apportion to Production Department will be only (2,700 — 20%) of Rs. 2,160.

Similarly power supply costs — Rs. 2,250 — 10% Transport Rs. 2,025.

Apportionment of Overheads of Service Departments to Production Departments

Particulars	Total Cost	Production Departments I	II	III	IV
As per Primary Distribution summary	15,300	4,500	4,050	3,600	3,150
Service Department					
Transport Basis (1:3:2:2 = 8) 1/8 × 2,160 = 270	2,160	270	810	540	540
	19,485	5,445	5,310	4,815	3,915

The same problem may be apportioned under repeated distribution method

Particulars	Basis	Production Departments I	II	III	IV	Service Depts. Trans-port	Power supply
As per Primary Distribution summary		4,500	4,050	3,600	3,150	2,475	1,710
Service Depts.							
(1) Transport Dept.	1:3:2:2:2	247.5	742.5	495	495	-2,475	495
		4,747.5	4,792.5	4,095	3,645	—	2,205
(2) Power supply	3:2:3:1:1	661.5	441	661.5	221.5	220	-2,205
		5,409	5,233.5	4,756.5	3,866	220	—
(3) Transport	1:3:2:2:2	22	66	44	44	—	44
		5,431	5,299.5	4,800.5	3,910	—	44
(4) Power supply	3:2:3:1:1	14	11	14	5	—	—
		5,445	5,310	4,815	3,915	—	—

Problem No. Extra-1/43

The following information relates to the activities of a manufacturing concern for the month of October 1990 :

Materials	1,80,000
Direct Wages	1,50,000
Machine operation during the month	24000 Hours.
Labour hours worked	30000 Hours.
Overhead chargeable to the Departments	Rs. 1,20,000

On one order carrying out in the department during the period the following particulars are provided :

Material issued	10,000
Direct Wages	8,250

Labour hour worked	1,800 Hours
Machine hours	1,400 Hours.

Prepare comparative statement of cost of the order by using the following methods of recovery of overheads :

(a) Direct Labour hour rate method.

(b) Direct Labour cost method.

(c) Machine hours rate method.

Solution :

Working Note

Ascertainment of (a) Labour Hour Rate (b) Labour Cost (c) Machine Hour Rate.

(a) Direct Labour Hour Rate $= \dfrac{\text{Overhead}}{\text{Labour Hour worked}}$

$= \dfrac{1{,}20{,}000}{30000} = \text{Rs. } 4 \text{ per Hour.}$

(b) Direct Labour cost method $= \dfrac{\text{Overhead}}{\text{Labour cost}} \times 100$

$= \dfrac{1{,}20{,}000}{1{,}50{,}000} \times 100 = 80\% \text{ of Direct wage}$

(c) Machine Hour Rate $= \dfrac{\text{Overheads}}{\text{Machine Hours}} = \dfrac{1{,}20{,}000}{24000} = \text{Rs. 5 per hour.}$

Comparative Statement of Cost of an Order

Particulars	Direct Labour cost	Labour Hour Rate	Machine Hour Rate
Materials Issued	10,000	10,000	10,000
Direct Wages	8,250	8,250	8,250
Prime Cost	18,250	18,250	18,250
Factory Overhead (Recovery)			
(a) Direct Labour cost method 80% of Direct Wages $= \frac{80}{100} \times 8250$	6,600		
(b) Labour Hour Rate Rs. 4 per Hour Hours worked 1800 × 4		7,200	
(c) Machine Hour Rate Rs. 5 per hour Hours worked 1400 × 5			7,000
Works Cost	34,850	25,450	25,250

Problem No. Extra-2/44

Vijay Engineering Co. Ltd. provides the following budgeted figures :

Budgeted Figures :

Estimated Factory Overheads	1,45,000
Estimated Direct Labour	1,81,250
Estimated Labour Hours	36250 Hours.
Estimated Machine Hours	29000 Hours.

Prepare :

Normal Overhead Recovery rate using :

(1) Direct Labour cost method.

(2) Labour hours rate method.

(3) Machine Hour rate method.

The company has received an order for the product what would be the cost of such product if :

Cost of materials used	3,780
Direct Wages	4,050
Direct Labour Hours	900 Hours
Machine Hours	600 Hours

Prepare a comparative statement using the above information for the executing the order and also show the overhead recovery rate on budgeted figures.

Solution :

Working Note

Ascertainment of overhead recovery rate on budgeted figures.

(1) Direct Labour Cost Method $= \dfrac{\text{Overhead}}{\text{Direct Labour cost}} \times 100$

$= \dfrac{1,45,000}{1,81,250} \times 100 = 80\%$ of Direct Wages.

(2) Labour Hour Rate Method $= \dfrac{\text{Overhead}}{\text{Labour Hours}} = \dfrac{1,45,000}{36250} =$ Rs. 4 per Hour.

(3) Machine Hour Rate Method $= \dfrac{\text{Overhead}}{\text{Machine Hours}} = \dfrac{1,45,000}{29000} =$ Rs. 5 per Hour.

Comparative Statement of Cost of an Order

Particulars	Direct Labour Cost Rs.	Labour Hour Rate Rs.	Machine Hour Rate Rs.
Materials Issued	3,780	3,780	3,780
Direct Wages	4,050	4,050	4,050
Prime Cost	7,830	7,830	7,830
Factory Overhead Recovery under :			
(1) Direct Labour cost 80% of Direct Wages (4,505 × 80%)	3,240	—	—
(2) Labour Hour Rate Rs. 4 per Hour (900 × 4 = 3,600)	—	3,600	—
(3) Machine Hour Rate Rs. 5 per Hour (600 × 5 = 3,000)	—	--	3,000
Works Cost or Cost of Production	11,070	11,430	10,830

Problem No. Extra-3/45

From the following data compute an hourly Machine rate assuming that the machine room will work 90% capacity throughout the year and that a break down of 10% is normal. There are seven festival holidays exclusively Sundays. The working hours are 8 on weekly days and on 4 Hours on Saturdays. There are 40 Machines of the same type.

Expenses per annum	3,120
Power and lighting	1,280
Foreman's salary	2,400
Grace cost etc.	660
Machine repairs	1,446
Depreciation	2,031.60
	10,937.60

(C.A. Final)

Solution :

Computation of Machine Hour Rate

Particulars	Per Annum Total Cost Rs.	Per Hour Ps.
(I) *Standing Charges*		
(1) Lighting	1,280	
(2) Foreman's Salary	2,400	
(3) Depreciation	2,031.6	
Total Standing Charges	5,711.6	
		Machine Hour Rate
		$= \frac{\text{Expenses}}{\text{No. of Hours}}$
		$= \frac{273.44}{2016}$
		= 0.1356 Or .14
(II) *Machine Expenses*		
(1) Power	3,120	
(2) Grease, Oil etc.	660	
(3) Machine repairs	1,446	
Total Expenses	10,937.6	

$$\text{Exp. per Machine} = \frac{\text{Total Exp.}}{\text{No. of Machine}} = \frac{10,937.6}{40}$$

$$= 273.44$$

Calculation of Machine Hours

Days in a year	365
Less : Holidays	7
	385
Less : Sundays in a year	52
	306
Less : Saturdays in a year	52
	254
Full Working days	254
Full Working Days (254 × 8)	2,032
Add : Saturdays (52 × 4)	208
Total Working Hours	2,240
Less : Normal Loss 10%	224
Effective Working Hours	2,016

Problem No. Fxtra-4/46

A manufacturing company installed a machine costing Rs. 4,95,000. Expected scrap value of Rs. 30,000 and Estimated life 15 years. The normal working hours p.a. 6000 Hours with including of 10% preventive maintenance. The following information is provided for the machine :

	Rs.	
(1) Rent	10,700	p.a.
(2) Lighting	225	p.m.
(3) Power — .50 Ps per unit	2,150	p.m.
(4) Supplies	8,100	p.a.
(5) Repairs	16,200	p.a.
(6) Wages for the operator Rs. 15 per hour		
(7) Supervisor's salary	3,500	p.m.

Ascertain machine hour rate.

If the machine is idle for want of material 60 hours in a year. How much is the loss?

Solution :

Computation of Machines Hour Rate

Particulars		Per Annum Rs.	Per Hour Rs.
(I) *Standing Charges :*		10,700	
(1) Rent		2,700	
(3) Supervisor's salary 3,500 × 12		42,000	
(4) Depreciation $= \dfrac{\text{Cost} - \text{Scrap value}}{\text{Life}}$			
$= \dfrac{4,95,000 - 30,000}{15}$		31,000	
		86,400	
Total Cost		$\dfrac{86,400}{5400}$	16.00
No. of working hour	60,000		
Less : preventive maintenance 10%	6,000		
(II) *Machine Expenses :*			
(1) Power = 3,150 × 12 $= \dfrac{2,37,800}{5400}$			7.00
(2) Suppliers $= \dfrac{8,100}{5400} =$			1.50
(3) Repairs $= \dfrac{16,200}{5400}$			3.00
(4) Wages for operators			15.00
Machine Hour Rate			42.50

Problem No. Extra-5/47

A manufacturing company installed two Big Machines and four small machines identical each others in both the cases. Following are the particulars :

(1) Big machines 2 — Area occupied ¼. Employees engaged 6 on each Machine.

(2) Small machines 4 — Area occupied ½ of the big machine. Employees 4 on each machine.

(3) Each of the 6 machines — Estimated working hours per year 4200 hours — effective working life — for Big machine 60000 Hours; for Small machines — 4500 hours.

(4) Cost of machines — Big Rs. 1,60,000 — Scrap value of Rs. 25,000.
Small — Rs. 1,14,000 — Scrap value of Rs. 15,000.

(5) Power consumption cost — 0.60 Ps per unit.
Big machines — 40 units per hour
Small machines — 12 units per hour.

(6) Repairs and maintenance — Estimated cost for each Big machine — Rs. 30,000 and Small machine Rs. 11,250 during effective life.

(7) The supervisor is paid Rs. 42,000 per year and he attends ½ of his time for machines — all the six machines.

(8) Rent, rates of factory of Rs. 30,000 per annum.

(9) Lighting per annum Rs. 2,856 on the basis workers engaged.

(10) Calculate machine hour rate for Big machines and small machines.

Solution :

Computation of Machine Hour Rate

Particulars			Big Machines-2	Small Machines-4
(I) *Standing Charges :*				
(1) Rent rate etc.	Big	Small		
Rs. 30,000 × ½ = 15,000 × ½	7,500		7,500	
30,000 × ½ = 15,000 × ¼ =		3,750		3,750
(2) Lighting Rs. 8,564				
Basis — No. of workers	12	16		
2,856 × 3/7 = 1,224/2	1,224		612	
2,856 × 4/7 = 1,632/4		1,632		408
(3) Supervisor's salary Rs. 42,000 × ½ = 2,100				
No. of machines 2 + 4 = 6 equally				
21,000/6 =			3,500	3,500
Total Standing Charges			11,612	7,658

Particulars			Big Machines-2	Small Machines-4
Hourly Rate :				
Effective working hour 4200 Hours				
$= \frac{\text{Standing Charges}}{\text{Effective Working Hours}}$	$\frac{11,612}{4200}$	$\frac{7,658}{4200}$	= 2.76	= 1.82
(II) *Machine Expenses :*				
Repairs & Maintenance :				
$= \frac{\text{Total Amount}}{\text{Effective life in hours}}$	$\frac{30,000}{60000}$	$\frac{11,250}{4500}$	0.50	0.25
Depreciation $= \frac{\text{Cost} - \text{Scrap}}{\text{Life in hour}} =$				
Big $= \frac{1,60,000 - 25,000}{60000}$	$= \frac{1,35,000}{60000} =$		2.25	
Small $= \frac{1,14,000 - 15,000}{45000}$	$= \frac{99,000}{45000} =$			2.20
Power – Big Machine = 0.60 per unit @ 40 hours =			24.00	
Small Machine = 0.60 × 12				7.20
Machine Hour Rate			29.51	11.47

Problem No. Extra-6/48

X Co. Ltd. a manufacturing company is divided into four departments A, B, and C are Production Departments and D is the Service Department. The actual costs for the year 1990 were as follows :

Expenses

(1)	Employers Liability for Insurance	3,750
(2)	Depreciation on Plant	11,250
(3)	Repairs to Plant	15,000
(4)	Rent	25,000
(5)	Supervision	37,500
(6)	Fire Insurance in respect of stock	12,500
(7)	Power	22,500
(8)	Light	3,000

The following information is available in respect of the four Departments :

Particulars	Departments			
	A	B	C	D
(1) Area in sq metre	3,750	2,750	2,250	1,250
(2) No. of Employees	60	45	30	15
(3) Total wages	1,50,000	1,00,000	75,000	50,000
(4) Value of plant	6,00,000	4,50,000	3,00,000	1,50,000
(5) Value of stock	3,75,000	2,25,000	15,000	—
(6) H.P. of plant	32	24	16	8

Apportion the costs to the various departments on the most equitable basis.

Solution :

Overheads (Primary) Distribution Summary

Particulars	Basis	Total	Production Departments			Service Dept.
			A	B	C	D
		Rs.	Rs.	Rs.	Rs.	Rs.
(1) Employer's Liability for Insurance	No. of Employees 4:3:2:1	3,750	1,500	1,125	750	375
(2) Depreciation on Plant	Value of Plant 4:3:2:1	11,250	4,500	3,375	2,250	1,125
(3) Repairs to Plant	Value of Plant 4:3:2:1	15,000	6,000	4,500	3,000	1,500
(4) Rent	Area 15:11:9:5	25,000	9,375	6,875	5,625	3,125
(5) Supervision	No. of Employees 4:3:2:1	37,500	15,000	11,250	7,500	3,750
(6) Fire Insurance in respect of stock	Stock Value 5:3:2	12,500	6,250	3,750	2,500	—
(7) Power	H.P. 4:3:2:1	22,500	9,000	6,750	4,500	2,250
(8) Light	Floor area 15:11:9:5	3,000	1,125	825	675	375
Total		1,30,500	52,750	38,450	26,800	12,500

4

Methods of Costing

(A) UNITS OR OUTPUT COSTING

Problem No. 1

Martin Ltd. Belgaum is Manufacturing Mono-bloc Motors. From the details relating to manufacturing operations for the year ended 31-12-1997, prepare a costs sheet.

	Rs.
Work-in-progress on 1-1-97	66,000
Work-in-progress on 31-12-97	54,000
Stock of Raw Materials	
on 1-1-1997	2,25,000
on 31-12-1997	2,04,000
Purchases during the year 1997 (Raw Materials)	4,77,000
Direct Labour	1,71,000
Manufacturing Expenses	84,000

Administration overhead 6% on works cost seelling overhead 2% of sales. Production and Sales 300 motors @ Rs. 3,000 each.

[K.U.D., April 1998 (N)]

Solution :

Statement of Cost for the year 1997

	Rs.	Rs.
Raw material on 1-1-97	2,25,000	
Add : Purchases during the year	4,77,000	
	7,02,000	
Less : Closing stock on 31-12-97	2,04,000	
Materials consumed		4,98,000
Direct Labour		1,71,000
Prime Cost		6,69,000

	Rs.	Rs.
		6,69,000
Factory overhead		84,000
Manufacturing Expenses		7,53,000
Add : Work-in-Progress on 1-1-97		66,000
		8,19,000
Less : Work-in-Progress on 31-12-97		54,000
Works cost		7,65,000
Administrative overhead 6% on works cost		
6% × 7,65,000		45,900
Cost of Production		8,10,900
Selling overhead 2% of sales		
Sales 300 × 3,000 = 9,00,000		18,000
		8,28,900
Sales — 300 × 3,000		9,00,000
Profit		71,100

Problem No. 2

The following particulars relate to the manufacture of 200 tons of superfine paper manufactured by Bemser Paper Mills Ltd. for the month ended 31st December 1996.

Direct Materials :

Paper Pulp — 250 tons at Rs. 100 per ton

Other Materials — 200 tons at Rs. 15 per ton

Direct Labour :

40 Skilled men at Rs. 6 per day for 25 days

40 Unskilled men at Rs. 2 per day for 25 days

Direct Expenses :

Special Equipment Rs. 3,000

Special Services Rs. 1,000

Works Overhead :

Fixed 70% of Direct Labour

Variable 100% of Direct Wages

Administrative overhead 10% of works cost selling and distribution overhead 15% of works cost sales of scrap material Rs. 800

Scrap value of special equipment after use in manufacture is nil.

Find out cost per ton of manufactured paper.

[K.U.D., April 1998 (O)]

Solution :

Statement of Cost of Superfine Paper 200 tons

	Rs.	Rs.
(I) Direct Materials :		
Paper Pulp - 250 tons × Rs. 100 per ton	25,000	
Other Material 200 tons × Rs. 15 per ton	3,000	28,000
(II) Direct Labour :		
Skilled - 40 × 6 per day × 25 days	6,000	
Unskilled - 40 × 2 per day × 25 days	2,000	8,000
(III) Direct Expenses :		
Special Equipment	3,000	
Special Services	1,000	4,000
Prime Cost		40,000
(IV) Works Overhead		
Fixed - 70% Direct Labour 70% × 8000		5,600
Variable 100% of Direct Labour 100% × 8,000		8,000
Works Cost		53,600
Less Scrap Sold (Material)		4,800
Works Cost		52,800
(V) Administrative Overhead		
10% of works cost - 10% × 52,800		5,280
Total Cost of Production		58,080
(VI) Selling and Distribution Overhead		
15% of Works Cost - 15% × 52,800		7,920
Total Cost of Sales		66,000

$$\text{Cost per ton} = \frac{\text{Total Cost}}{\text{Output in tons}} = \frac{66{,}000}{200} = \text{Rs. } 330 \text{ per ton}$$

Problem No. 3

The records of Genius Pen Co. show the following figures of expenses for the year ending 31-12-1996 when the production was 10,000 Pens :

	Rs.
Materials consumed	15,000
Direct wages	10,000
Variable production overhead	20,000
Variable selling overhead	40,000
Administrative overhead	15,000
Selling price per pen	15

It is expected that in 1997 :

(a) Production will be 20,000 pens

(b) Prices of material will go up by 33-1/3%

(c) Variable selling and Administrative overhead will rise by 50% and Rs. 5,000 respectively.

What would be cost and selling price per pen in 1997 if it is desired to maintain the same rate of Profit on sales as in 1996 ?

[K.U.D., October 1997(N)]

Solution :

Production of Pens — 10000

Statement of Cost of Pen for 1996

	Total Cost	Cost per pen
Materials consumed	15,000	1.50
Direct wages	10,000	1.00
Prime Cost	25,000	2.50
Factory overhead :		
Variable production overhead	20,000	2.00
Factory Cost	45,000	4.50
Administrative overhead	15,000	1.50
Cost of Production	60,000	6.00
Variable selling overhead	40,000	4.00
Cost of sales	100,000	10.00
Selling Price Per Pen — Rs. 15 for 10000 Pens	150,000	15.00
Profit	Rs. 50,000	5.00

$$\text{Percentage of Profit on cost of sales} = \frac{50,000}{100,000} \times 100 = 50\%$$

Estimated Statement of Cost of Pens for 1997

Production in 1997 — estimated 20000

		Cost per Pen Rs. Ps.	Total Cost (20000) Rs.
Materials consumed Rs. 1.30 =	1.50		
Add Increases by 33-1/3% of 1.50	+ 0.50	2.00	40,000
Direct Wages		1.00	20,000
Prime Cost		3.00	60,000
Factory overhead :			
Variable Production Overhead		2.00	40,000
Factory Cost		5.00	100,000
Administrative overhead 1996	Rs. 15,000		
Increase Add for 1997	5,000	1.00	20,000
Cost of Production		6.00	120,000
Variable selling overhead — Per Pen — Rs.	4.00		
Add Rise by 50% of Rs. 4 =	2.00	6.00	120,000
Cost of Sales		12.00	240,000
Percentage of Profit on cost 50%		6.00	120,000
Cost per Pen	12.00		
Adv. Profit 50%	6.00		
	18.00	18.00	360,000

Estimated Selling Price Rs. 18 Per pen for 1997

Percentage of Profit in 1996 50% is retained in 1997

Problem No. 4

The Sahadri Paper Co. supplies you the following details from the Cost records on materials :

	Rs.
Stocks on 1-1-1997	1,12,500
Stocks on 31-1-1997	1,37,250
Direct Wages	78,750
Indirect Wages	4,125
Works-in-Progress on 1-1-97	42,000
on 31-1-97	52,000
Sales	3,00,000
Purchases of Materials	99,000
Factory Rent, Rates and Power	22,500

Depreciation of Plant Machinery	5,250
Expenses on purchases	2,250
Carriage outward	3,750
Advertising	5,250
Office Rent or Taxes	3,750
Travellers Salary and Commission	9,750
Stocks of Finished Goods on 1-1-97	81,000
on 31-1-97	46,000
Sale of scrap	1,125

[K.U.D., October 1997(O)]

Solution :

Statement of Cost for the month of January 1997

		Rs.	Rs.
I.	Raw material — Opening Stocks 1-1-97	1,12,500	
	Add Purchases	99,000	
		2,11,500	
	Less Closing Stocks 31-12-97	1,37,250	
	Material consumed	74,250	
	Expenses on Purchases	2,250	76,500
	Direct wages		78,750
	Prime Cost		1,55,250
II.	Factory overhead :		
	Indirect wages	4,125	
	Factory Rent, Rates & Power	22,500	
	Depreciation on Machinery	5,250	27,150
	Factory Cost		1,82,400
III.	Work-in-Progress on 1-1-97		42,000
			2,24,400
	Less Closing W.I.P. on 31-1-97		52,000
			1,72,400
	Less Scrap sold		1,125
	Cost of Production		1,71,275
IV.	Office Overhead		
	Office Rent, taxes etc.		3,750
	Total Cost		1,75,025
	Finished Goods :		
	Opening Stocks on 1-1-97		81,000
			2,56,025
	Less Closing Stocks on 31-1-97		46,000

V.	Selling of Distribution overhead		2,10,025
	Carriage outward	3,750	
	Advertising	5,250	
	Travellers Salary and Commission	9,750	
		18,750	18,750
	Cost of sales		2,28,775
VI.	Sales Price		3,00,000
	Profit	Rs.	71,225

Problem No. 5

A P Scooters Ltd. find that in 1996 total cost of producing 100 scooters was Rs. 20,00,000, which were sold at Rs. 22,000 each. The cost consists of —

Material Rs. 8,00,000
Direct wages Rs. 9,00,000
Factory overhead Rs. 1,80,000
Office overhead Rs. 94,000
Distribution overhead Rs. 260 per Scooter

For 1997 the Cost estimate is :

(a) that each Scooter will require
Material — Rs. 9,000
Labour — Rs. 9,000

(b) that factory overhead will bear the same relation to wages in the previous period

(c) that the percentage of office overhead on Factory cost will be the same as in the past and

(d) that there will be an increase of Rs. 60 per scooter in Selling and Distribution overhead.

Prepare a statement showing the profit that the company would make per scooter if it increases the sales price of scooter by Rs. 2,000.

[K.U.D., April 1997(N)]

Solution :

Statement of Cost for the year 1996

	Rs.
Material	8,00,000
Direct Wages	9,00,000
Prime Cost	17,00,000
Factory overhead	1,80,000
Factory Cost	18,80,000
Office overhead	1,94,000
Total Cost	19,74,000
Distribution overhead Rs. 260 per scooter for 100 = 100 × 260	26,000
Total Cost of sales	20,00,000
Sales Price per scooter Rs. 22,000 for 100 =	22,00,000
Profit	2,00,000

For 1997 Cost Estimate

(a) A scooter require Material Rs. 9,000 per unit
Labour Rs. 9,000 per unit

(b) Percentage of factory overhead on wages :

$$\frac{\text{Factory overhead}}{\text{Wages}} \times 100 = \frac{1,80,000}{9,00,000} \times 100 = 20\% \text{ of wages}$$

(c) Percentage of office overhead to factory cost :

$$\frac{\text{Office overhead}}{\text{Factory Cost}} \times 100 = \frac{94,000}{1,88,000} \times 100 = 5\% \text{ of F.}$$

(d) Selling and Distribution overhead :

Increase of Rs. 60 per scooter i.e. Rs. 260 + 60 = Rs. 320

Sales Price will increase by Rs. 2,000

Rs. 22,000 + 2,000 = Rs. 24,000 per Scooter

Estimated Cost Statement for 1997

	Per Scooter Rs.
Direct Material	9,000
Direct Labour	9,000
Prime cost	18,000
Factory overhead : 20% of wages — 20% of 9,000 =	1,800
Factory Cost	19,800
Office overhead : 5% of Factory Cost = 5% of 19,800	990
Total Cost	20,790
Selling and Distribution overhead Rs. 260 + 60 = Rs. 320 per scooter	320
Cost of Sales	21,110
Sales Price Rs. 22,000 + 2,000 = Rs. 24,000	24,000
Profit per scooter	2,890

	in 1996	in 1997
Profit per Scooter	Rs. 2,000	Rs. 2,890
Percentage on Sales	$\frac{2,000}{24,000} \times 100 = 9.09$	$\frac{2,890}{24,000} \times 100 = 12.04\%$

Percentage of Profit on sales in 1997 is higher than 1996.

Problem No. 6

Samarath Company has received an enquiry for the supply of 2000 steel folding chairs. The cost are estimated as under :

Raw materials — 100000 Kg at Re. 1 per Kg.

Direct Wages — 10000 Hours at Rs. 4 per hour.

Variable Overhead :

(a) Factory Rs. 2.40 per Labour hour

(b) Selling and Distribution — Rs. 16,000

Fixed Overhead

(a) Factory Rs. 6,000

(b) Selling and Distribution — Rs. 14,000

Prepare a statement showing the price to be fixed per chair which will yield a profit 20% on selling price.

(K.U.D., April 1996)

Solution :

Statement of Estimated Cost and Price (No. of Chairs produced 2000)

	Rs.	Rs.
Raw materials 100000 Kg. @ Rs. 1 per Kg.		1,00,000
Direct Wages 10000 hours @ Rs. 4 per hour		40,000
Prime Cost		1,40,000
Factory Overheads :		
(a) Variable Rs. 2.40 per chair (2000 × 2.40)	4,800	
(b) Fixed	6,000	10,800
Works cost		1,50,800
Administrative Overhead :		
Selling and Distribution :		
Variable	16,000	
Fixed	14,000	30,000
Total cost or Cost of sales		1,80,800
Profit — 20% on selling price or 25% on cost		45,200
Selling price		2,26,000

Selling price Rs. 2,26,000 for 2000 = $\frac{2,26,000}{2000}$ = 113 Rs. per Chair.

Problem No. 7

The Beena Ltd., is producing two types of pens "Deluxe" and "Popular". The manufacturing costs for the year ended 31st March 1992 were :

Direct Materials	1,60,000
Direct Wages	2,20,000
Production overheads	60,000
Total	4,40,000

It is ascertained that :

(a) Direct materials in "Deluxe" type pen cost twice as much as that of "Popular" type.

(b) Direct wages in "Popular" type pen were 60% of those for "Deluxe" type.

(c) Production overhead was 40 paise per pen for both types.

(d) Administration overhead for each type was 150% of direct wages.

(e) Selling cost as 50 paise per pen for both the types.

(f) Production during the year was :
"Deluxe" type — 50,000 pens of which 45,000 were sold.
"Popular" type — 1,00,000 pens of which 90,000 were sold.

(g) Selling prices were Rs. 10 per pen of "Deluxe" type and the profit made on each type of pen.

Prepare a statement showing the total cost per pen of each type and the profit made on each type of pen.

(K.U.D., April 1995)

Solution :

Calculation :

(a) Allotment of Material Cost :

Let X be the material cost of popular type

Material Cost in Deluxe pen will be 2X.

Now : Deluxe pen = 2X, Popular Pen = X

$\therefore$ = 50,000 × 2 X + 1,00,000 X = 1,60,000

= 1,00,000 X + 1,00,000 X = 1,60,000

Now = 2,00,000X = 1,60,000

$\therefore$ X $= \dfrac{1,60,000}{2,00,000}$

X = 0.80 Paise

Now substitute X-value i.e. X is the cost of material of Popular Pen = 0.80 Paise.

Deluxe pen cost of Material — 1.60

Popular pen cost of Material — 0.80

Material cost — Deluxe 50,000 × 1.60 = 80,000

Popular 1,00,000 × 0.80 = 80,000

1,60,000

(b) *Direct Wages :*

Let Deluxe type — wages are X

and popular type will be X 60/100

Deluxe — 50,000X Popular 1,00,000 X 60/100 = 2,20,000

50,000X + 60,000X = 2,20,000

1,10,000X = 2,20,000

Now X = 2,20,000 / 1,10,000

Now X Rs. 2 per pen

Wages per Pen

Deluxe = Rs. 2 × 50,000 = 1,00,000

Popular = 60% of 2 = 1.20 × 1,00,000 = 1,20,000

(1,00,000 + 1,20,000 = 2,20,000)

(c) Production overhead .40 paise per pen

Deluxe — 50,000 × 0.40 = 20,000

Popular — 1,00,000 × 0.40 = 40,000

60,000

(d) Administration overheads 150% of Direct wages

Deluxe — Rs.1,50,000 (1,00,000 × 150%)

Popular — Rs. 1,80,000 (1,20,000 × 150%)

(e) Selling Cost = 0.50 Paise per pen

Deluxe — 45,000 × 0.50 = 22,500

Popular — 90,000 × 0.50 = 45,000

Statement of Cost and Profit

Production— No. of Pens	Total Cost	Deluxe Pen Total (50000)	Deluxe Pen Cost per Pen	Popular Type Total (100000)	Popular Type Cost per Pen
(1) Materials	1,60,000	80,000	1.60	80,000	0.80
(2) Wages	2,20,000	1,00,000	2.00	1,20,000	1.20
Prime Cost	3,80,000	1,80,000	3.60	2,00,000	2.00
Production Overhead	60,000	20,000	0.40	40,000	0.40
Works Cost	4,40,000	2,00,000	4.00	2,40,000	2.40

Production— No. of Pens	Total Cost	Deluxe Pen Total (50000)	Deluxe Pen Cost per Pen	Popular Type Total (100000)	Popular Type Cost per Pen
Administrative Overhead 15% of Direct Wage	3,30,000	1,50,000	3.00	1,80,000	1.80
Cost of Production	7,70,000	3,50,000	7.00	4,20,000	4.20
Less : Closing Stock Deluxe 5000 × 7 } Popular 10000 × 4.20	77,000	35,000	—	42,000	—
Cost of Pens sold	6,93,000	3,15,000	7.00	3,78,000	4.20
Deluxe 45,000 Selling Exp. } Popular 90,000	67,500	22,500	.50	45,000	0.50
Cost of Sales	7,60,000	3,37,500	7.50	4,23,000	4.70
Selling Price	10,80,000	4,50,000	10.00	6,30,000	7.00
Deluxe — 10 } Profit : Popular — 7	3,19,500	1,12,500	2.50	2,07,000	2.30

Problem No. 8

The company's records show the following particulars for the 1992 :

Production and sales	100 Fans
	Rs.
Direct materials	25,000
Direct labour	10,000
Direct charges	1,000
Works overheads	9,000
Office overhead	5,000
Selling overhead	5,000
Profit	11,000

You ascertain that 80% of the works overhead fluctuates directly with production and 70% of selling overheads fluctuate with sales. It is anticipated that the company would produce 500 fans per annum for the year 1993 and that direct labour charges per unit will be reduced by 10%. While fixed works overhead charges will increase by Rs. 2,400. Office overhead and fixed selling overhead charges are expected to show an increase of 10% and 20% respectively but otherwise no changes are anticipated.

Prepare a statement of Cost and Profit for the year 1993.

(K.U.D., October 1994)

Solution :

Statement of Cost and Profit for the year 1992

Particulars	Total Rs.	Cost per unit Rs.
Production and sales 100 Fans		
Direct Materials	25,000	250
Direct Labour	10,000	100
Direct Expenses (Charges)	1,000	10
Prime Cost	36,000	360
Works Overhead :		
Variable — 8% of 9,000	7,200	72
Fixed — 20% of 9,000	1,800	18
Works Cost	45,000	450
Office Overhead : Fixed	5,000	50
Cost of Production	50,000	500
Selling Overhead :		
Variable — 70% of 5,000	3,500	35
Fixed — 30% of 5,000	1,500	15
Cost of sales	55,000	550
Add : Profit 20%	11,000	110
Sales Pirce	66,000	660

Estimated Cost and Profit Statement for the year 1993

Particulars	Cost per Unit	Total
Direct Material	250	1,25,000
Direct Labour — 100 – 10% (100 – 10)	90	45,000
Direct Charges	10	5,000
Prime Cost	350	1,75,000
Works Overhead : Variable	72	36,000
Fixed — 1800 + 2400	8.40	4,200
Works Cost	430.40	2,15,200
Office Overhead : Fixed + Increase (5000 + 500)	11	5,500
Cost of Production	441.40	2,20,700
Selling Overhead : Variable	35	17,500
Fixed + Increase (1500 + 300)	3.60	1,800
Cost of Sales	480	2,40,000
Profit 20% on Cost	96	48,000
Sales Price	576	2,88,000

Problem No. 9

A company manufactures two types of pens namely "Hero" and "Raja". Following are the details of costs for the year ended 31st March 1993 :

Direct Materials	:	1,30,000
Direct Labour	:	1,10,000
Production Overhead	:	72,500

Following further information is available :

(i) The direct materials in "Raja" pen was 40% of that in "Hero".

(ii) The direct labour cost in "Hero" pen was twice as much as that in "Raja" pen.

(iii) Production overhead per pen was in the ratio of 5:3 (Hero and Raja).

(iv) Administration overhead for each type of pen was 100% of direct labour cost.

(v) Selling and distribution expenses was Rs. 1.50 per pen for both types.

(vi) Following was the production and sales during the year :

"Hero" pens — 20,000 of which 18,000 were sold @ Rs. 22 each.

"Raja" pens — 15,000 of which 14,000 were sold @ Rs. 14 each.

Prepare a Statement showing the Cost and Profit per pen of each type.

(K.U.D., April 1994)

Solution :

Calculations :

(I) Allocation of Material Cost :

Let X be the Material cost of "Hero" pen

Now 40/100 X will be material cost of "Raja" a pen

$\therefore$ 20,000 X + 15,000 × 40/100X :

= 20,000X + 6000X = 1,30,000

= 26,000X = 1,30,000

Now X = $\frac{1,30,000}{26,000}$ = Rs. 5 per pen = X = Rs. 5 Cost of Material per Pen

Substitute X value = i.e. Hero Pen

Material Cost of Hero Pen = Rs. 5

Raja pen = 40% of 5 = Rs. 2 per pen.

Now = Hero pen — 20,000 × 5	=	1,00,000
Raja pen 15,000 × 2	=	30,000
		1,30,000

(II) Labour Cost : Let labour cost in Raja pen is X

Now Labour cost in Hero pen will be 2X

$\therefore$ 20000 × 2X + 15000X	=	1,10,000
40000X + 15000X	=	1,10,000
55000X	=	1,10,000

$$X = \frac{1,10,000}{55000}$$

= Rs. 2

Substitute value of X in Raja a pen = Rs. 2

Hero pen = Rs. 2 × 2 = Rs. 4

Labour charges — Hero pen = 20000 × 4 = 80,000

Raja pen = 15000 × 2 = 30,000 1,10,000

(III) *Production Overhead ratio 5:3* :

Hero Pen = 5 × 20000 = 1,00,000

Raja pen = 3 × 15000 = 45,000

1,45,000

$$1,45,000 = 72,500 = \frac{72,500}{1,45,000} = \text{Re. } 0.50 \text{ Ps per pen.}$$

Hero Pen = 5 × 0.50 = 2.50 per pen

= 20000 × 2.50 = 50,000 50,000

Raja Pen = 3 × 0.50 = 1.50 per pen

= 15000 × 1.50 = 22,500 22,500

72,500

Statement of Cost and Profit for the year ending 31-3-1993

Particulars	Total Cost	Hero Pen Total	Hero Pen per pen	Raja Pen Total	Raja Pen per pen
Output		20,000		15,000	
Direct Materials Cost	1,30,000	1,00,000	5.00	30,000	2.00
Direct Labour	1,10,000	80,000	4.00	30,000	2.00
Prime Cost	2,40,000	1,80,000	9.00	60,000	4.00
Production Overheads	72,500	50,000	2.50	22,500	1.50
Works Cost	3,12,500	2,30,000	11.50	82,500	5.50
Administrative Overhead 100% Direct Wages	1,10,000	80,000	4.00	30,000	2.00
Cost of Production	4,22,500	3,10,000	15.50	1,12,500	7.50
Less : Closing stock (i) Hero Pen 2000 × 15.5 (ii) Raja pen 1000 × 7.5	38,500	31,000	—	7,500	—
Cost of production of goods sold	3,84,000	2,79,000	15.50	1,05,000	7.50
Selling and Distribution Expenses per pen	48,000	27,000	1.50	21,000	1.50
Cost of Sales	4,32,000	3,06,000	17.00	1,26,000	9.00
Sales 18000	5,92,000	3,96,000	22.00	1,96,000	14.00
Profit	16,000	90,000	5.00	70,000	5.00

Problem No. 10

Shri Ram Enterprises make two types of articles M and N. The firm has produced 1,000 units of M and 500 units of N. The following expenses are incurred on two articles :

	Rs.
Materials	3,00,000
Direct Wages	1,80,000
Machine expenses	42,000
Consumable stores	20,000
Depreciation	28,000
Workshop expenses	1,50,000
Administrative and selling Exp. (to be apportioned on the basis of sale of units produced)	80,000

Additional Information :

	M : N
Material Cost ratio per unit	1 : 2
Labour Cost ratio per unit	3 : 2
Machine utilisation ratio per unit	2 : 3

Selling price per unit — M Rs. 750; N Rs. 900

Calculate the Cost and Profit per unit of M and N.

(K.U.D., October 1993)

Solution :

For the purpose of apportioning expenditure between two articles, the ratio are to be calculated as under :

(1) Material ratio	= M :	1000 × 1 = 1000
(Ratio Equal)	N :	500 × 2 = 1000
(2) Labour ratio	= M :	1000 × 3 = 3000
(Ratio = 3 : 1)	N :	500 × 2 = 1000
(3) Machine utilisation	= M :	1000 × 2 = 2000
(Ratio = 4 : 3)	N :	500 × 3 = 1500

Statement of Cost and Profit

Particulars	Basis for Apportionment	Ratio	Total Rs.	M Rs.	N Rs.
No. of Units Produced				1000 units	500 units
(1) Material	Material	Equal	3,00,000	1,50,000	1,50,000
(2) Direct Wages	Labour	3 : 1	1,80,000	1,35,000	45,000
Prime Cost			4,80,000	2,85,000	1,95,000
(3) Factory Overhead :	Machine				
(a) Machine Expenses	Utilisation	4 : 3	42,000	24,000	18,000
(b) Consumable Stores	Material	1 : 1	20,000	10,000	10,000
(c) Depreciation	Machine Utilisation	4 : 3	28,000	16,000	12,000

Particulars	Basic for Apportionment	Ratio	Total Rs.	M Rs.	N Rs.
(d) Workshop Expenses	Labour	3 : 1	1,50,000	1,12,500	37,500
Works Cost			7,20,000	4,47,500	2,72,500
(4) Administration and Selling expenses Sales of Units 7,50,000 : 4,50,000	Sales Value	75 : 45 or 5 : 3	80,000	50,000	30,000
Cost of Sales			8,00,000	4,97,500	3,02,500
Selling Price M - 1000 × 750 N - 500 × 900			12,00,000	7,50,000	4,50,000
Profit			4,00,000	2,52,500	1,47,500

		M	N
Cost per unit	$= \frac{\text{Total Cost}}{\text{No. of Units}}$	$\frac{4,97,500}{1000}$	$\frac{3,02,500}{500}$
Cost per unit	=	Rs. 497.50	Rs. 605
Sales Price per unit	=	Rs. 750	Rs. 900
Profit per unit		Rs. 252.5	Rs. 295

Problem No. 11

The following information relates to the manufacture of a standard product during April 1991 :

Raw Material — Rs. 15,000

Direct Labour — Rs. 9,000

Machine hour rate — Rs. 5

Machine hours worked — 900 hours

Administrative Overheads — 20% of works cost

Selling overheads — Re. 0.50 per unit.

Units produced — 17100 units.

Units sold — 16000 units at Rs. 4 per unit.

Prepare the Statement of Cost showing Cost and Profit per unit sold.

(K.U.D., April 1993)

Solution :

Statement of Cost and Profit

	Rs.	Rs.
Raw materials	15,000	
Direct Labour	9,000	
Prime Cost		24,000
Factory Overheads : Machine hour rate = 900 × 5		4,500
Works Cost		28,500
Administrative Overhead (20% of works cost) 28,500 × 20%		5,700
Cost of production		34,200

$$\text{Cost of production per unit} = \frac{\text{Total Cost}}{\text{Units produced}}$$

$$= \frac{34,200}{17100} = \text{Rs. 2 per unit.}$$

Less : Closing stock = 17100 units produced

Closing stock $\frac{16000}{1100}$ " sold × 2 — 2,200

Cost of production of units sold (16000 × 2)	32,000
Selling Overhead = 16000 × .50	8,000
Cost of sales — of units sold (16000)	40,000
Sales 16000 × 4 =	64,000
Profit	24,000

Cost of production = Rs. 2

Cost of sales per unit = 2.50

Selling Price per unit = Rs. 4.00

$$\text{Profit per Unit} = \frac{24,000}{16000} = \text{Rs. } 1.50$$

Problem No. 12

The Managing Director of a manufacturing company insists you as to the minimum price at which he can sell his output of one of the departments of the organisation which is included to mass production in future. The company's records show the following particulars for this department for the past year :

Production and sales : 100 Units

Direct materials	3,900
Direct Labour	2,100
Direct charges	300

Works on cost		2,100
Office on cost		840
Selling on cost		960
	Total Cost	10,200
	Profit	2,550
	Sales	12,750

(1) It is ascertained from the records that 40% of works on cost fluctuates directly with production and 70% of selling cost fluctuates with sales.

(2) It is anticipated that the department would produce 1000 units per annum and that the direct labour charges per unit will be reduced by 20% which fixed works on cost charges will increase by Rs. 900.

(3) Office on cost and fixed selling on cost charges are expected to show an increase of 25% besides the above no other charges are anticipated.

Prepare cost sheet for submission to your client so as to earn the same rate of profit in future production.

(B'lore University, April 1993)

Solution :

Statement of Cost and Profit

Particulars		100 Units Total cost	100 Units Cost per Unit	1000 Units Total cost	1000 Units Cost per Unit
(1) Direct material		3,900	39.00	39,000	39.00
(2) Direct Labour (per unit)	21.00	2,100	21.00	16,800	16.80
Less : Reduction by 20%	4.20				
	16.80				
(3) Direct Expenses		300	3.00	3,000	3.00
Prime Cost		6,300	63.00	58,800	58.00
(4) Works on cost 2,100					
Variable 40% of 2,100	840	840	8.40	8,400	8.40
Fixed 60% of 2,100	1,260	1,260	12.60	2,160	2.16
Works cost		8,400	84.00	69,360	69.36
(5) Office on cost	840				
Add : Increase 25% of 840	210				
For 100 units per unit 10.50	10,500	840	8.40	10,500	10.50
Cost of production		9,240	92.40	79,860	79.86
(6) Selling on cost Rs. 960					
Variable 70% of 960 = 672		672	6.72	6,720	6.72
Fixed 30% 960 = 288		288	2.88	—	—

Particulars		100 Units		1000 Units	
		Total cost	Cost per Unit	Total cost	Cost per unit
For 1000 Units Fixed =	288				
Add : Increase by 25% of 288	72	—	—	360	0.36
	360				
Cost of sales		10,200	102.00	86,940	86.94
Profit :					
Cost Rs. 102 profit 25.50					
per cent of profit on cost 25%		2,550	25.50	—	21.735
Sales Price		12,750	127.50	86,940	108.675

Advise to Client : It is advised to produced 1000 Units the cost price per unit will be Rs. 86.94 is cheaper than when 100 Units are produced. Even the sales price is Rs. 108.675 is cheaper than the earlier price when 100 Units are produced @ sales price Rs. 127.50 though the percentage of profit remains the same.

Problem No. 13

The following figures are extracted from the books of factory after close of the year :

(1)	*Raw Materials* :	
	Opening stock	14,000
	Purchases during the year	1,00,000
	Closing stock	10,000
(2)	Direct wages	20,000

(3) Works overhead 50% on Direct Wages.

(4) Stores overhead on materials is 10 per cent of cost of material.

(5) 10 per cent of the castings were rejected being not upto the specification and a sum of Rs. 800 was realised in sale of scrap.

(6) 10 per cent of the finished casting were found to be defective in manufacture and were rectified by expenditure of a additional works overhead charges to the extent of 20 per cent on proportionate direct wages.

(7) The total Gross output of casting during the year 2000 tons. Find the manufacturing cost of saleable casting per ton.

(Gulbarga, April 1993)

Solution :

Statement of Cost

		Out put in tons (2000 units)	Total Cost
(1) *Raw material* : Raw material consumed :			
Opening stock	14,000		
Add : Purchases during the year	1,00,000		
	1,14,000		
Less : Closing stock	10,000		1,04,000
(2) Direct Wages			20,000
Prime Cost			1,24,000
(3) Works overhead 50% on direct wages (20,000 × 50%)			10,000
			1,34,000
(4) Stores overhead on material 10 per cent on cost of material (1,04,000 × 10% = 10,400)			10,400
Total Cost of Gross output		2000	1,44,400
Less : Sale of scrap costing 10 per cent of casting		20	800
Cost of good units of finished casting		1800	1,43,600
Add : Additional works overhead on 10 per cent finished casting found defective rectification expenses 20 per cent of direct wages :			
Proportionate :			
10 per cent of finished casting 1800 × 10% = 180			
for 2000 tons 20,000 Wages			
for 180 = 20,000/2000 × 180 = 1800 × 20% = 360			360
Total cost of manufacture (of saleable casting)		1800	1,43,960

$$\text{Cast per ton} = \frac{\text{Total cost}}{\text{Output in tons}}$$

$$= \frac{1,43,960}{1800}$$

$$= 79.97$$

Cost per ton = Rs. 80 (rounded up)

Problem No. 14

A Company manufactured and sold 2000 calculators in the year 1989. The following are the particulars :

Materials	1,60,000
Wages	2,40,000
Factory overheads	1,00,000
Office overheads	1,80,000
Selling & Distribution overheads	60,000
Sales	8,00,000

For the year 1990 it is estimated that :

(a) Production and sales will be 2,400 calculators.

(b) Materials cost will increase by 20%.

(c) Wages will increase by 5%.

(d) Factory overheads will increase in proportion to the combined cost of materials and wages.

(e) Selling and Distribution cost per unit will remain the same.

(f) Office expenses will not be effected by increase in production.

Prepare a Statement of Cost showing the Price at which 2400 calculators are to be manufactured in 1990 so as to give a Profit of 10 per cent on Sales.

(K.U.D., October 1992)

Solution :

State of Cost for 1990 Budgeted Production 2400 Units

Particulars	Total Cost Rs.	Cost per unit Rs.
Materials — $\frac{1,60,000}{2000} \times 2400 \times \frac{120}{100}$ = Rs. 80		
Add : 20% $\frac{16}{96}$	2,30,400	96.00
Wages $\frac{2,40,000}{2000}$ = 120 + 5% = 126 × 2400 =	3,02,400	126.00
Prime Cost	5,32,800	222.00
Factory overheads $\frac{1,00,000}{2000}$ = 50 + 25% =		
222 × $\frac{25}{100}$ = 55.50		55.50
(5,32,800 × 25%)	1,33,200	
Works Cost	6,66,000	277.50

Particulars	Total Cost Rs.	Cost per unit Rs.
Office overheads = (not affected increase)	1,80,000	75.00
Cost of Production or Total cost	8,46,000	352.50
Selling and Distribution Overheads		
$\frac{60,000}{2000}$ = Rs. 30 per unit (2400 × 30)	72,000	30.00
Cost of Sales	9,18,000	382.50
Add : Profit 10 per cent on Sales Price		
Or : Cost is 90 for 9,18,000 × 10 profit		
$= 9,18,000 \times \frac{10}{90} =$	1,02,000	42.50
Sales Price	10,20,000	425.00

Problem No. 15

From the following figure prcpare a cost sheet for 3 months ending 31-12-1975 and also a tender for the supply of 750 fans to retain the same percentage of profit as was previous period.

Completed stock on 1-10-1975	Nil
Completed stock on 31-12-1975	20,250
Stock of raw material on 1-10-75	5,000
Stock on raw material on 31-12-75	3,500
Factory wages	75,000
Indirect charges	12,500
Materials purchased	32,500
Sales	1,12,500
Number of fans manufactured	3000

(Gulbarga, April 1992; Mysore, April 1979)

Solution :

Statement of Cost for 3 months ending 31-12-1975

(1) *Raw materials* :		
Opening stock on 1-10-1975	5,000	
Add : Purchases	32,500	
	37,500	
Less : Closing stock on 31-12-75	3,500	34,000

(2) Factory wages		75,000
Prime Cost		1,09,000
(3) Factory overhead (indirect charges)		12,500
Works cost		1,21,500

Cost of production for 3000 fans cost per fan

$= \frac{1,21,500}{3000} = 40.50$ per fan produced 3000 fans

Less : Closing stock	500	20,250
Fans sold	2500	1,01,250

(Value of closing stock per fan 40.50 × 2500 = 20,250)

(Cost of Fans sold = 2,500 Fans of Rs. 1,01,250)

Sales Price per Fan = $\frac{1,12,500}{2500}$ = Rs. 45 per Fan 1,12,500

Profit 11,250

Percentage of profit = $\frac{11,250}{1,12,500} \times 100 = 10\%$

Quotation Price for 750 Fans = 750 × 45 = 33,750

Additional Problem No. 16

M/s M.T. Shoe Co. manufacture two types of shoes — A and B. Production cost for the year ended 31st March 1990 were :

Direct Material	:	15,00,000
Direct Wages	:	8,40,000
Production overhead	:	3,60,000

There was no work-in-progress in the beginning or at the end of the year. It is ascertained that :

(a) Direct material in type A shoes consist twice as much as that in 'B' type shoes.

(b) Direct wages for type 'B' shoes were 60% of those for type A shoes.

(c) Administrative overhead for each type was 150% of Direct wage.

(d) Production overhead was same per pair of A & B type.

(e) Selling cost was Rs. 1.50 per pair.

(f) Production during the year were :

Type A — 40000 pairs of which 36000 were sold

Type B — 120000 pairs of which 100000 were sold.

(g) Selling price was Rs. 44 per pair for type A

Rs. 28 per pair for type B.

Prepare statement showing Cost and Profit.

Solution :

Calculations :

(1) Material Cost — Allocation

Let type B — Material cost be — X

Type A's material cost be 2X.

$$\therefore 1{,}20{,}000X + 2X\ 40{,}000 = 15{,}00{,}000$$
$$1{,}20{,}000X + 80{,}000X = 15{,}00{,}000$$
$$2{,}00{,}000X = 15{,}00{,}000$$
$$X = \frac{15{,}00{,}000}{2{,}00{,}000}$$
$$= \text{Rs. } 7.50$$

Material Cost X = Rs. 7.50 per pair.

Substitute Material cost type B = Rs. 7.50

Material cost type A = Rs. 15.00

Material cost type A = 40,000 × 15 = Rs. 6,00,000

Material cost type B = 1,20,000 × 7.50 = 9,00,000

(2) *Wages :*

Let X be the labour charges for A for B will be $\frac{60X}{100}$

$$40{,}000X + 1{,}20{,}000 \times \frac{60X}{100} = 8{,}40{,}000$$
$$40{,}000X + 72{,}000\ X = 8{,}40{,}000$$
$$1{,}12{,}000\ X = 8{,}40{,}000$$
$$X = \frac{8{,}40{,}000}{1{,}12{,}000}$$
$$X = \text{Rs. } 7.50 \text{ per pair.}$$

Substitute X type A = Rs. 7.50

Substitute X type B = Rs. 7.50 × 60/100

= Rs. 4.50 per pair.

Wages type A = 40,000 × 7.50 = 3,00,000

B = 1,12,000 × 4.50 = 5,40,000   8,40,000

(3) Production Overhead = Rs. $\frac{3{,}60{,}000}{1{,}60{,}000}$ = 2.25 per pair.

Type A = 40,000

Type B = $\frac{1{,}20{,}000}{1{,}60{,}000}$

Type A = 40000 × 2.25 = 90,000

Type B = 1,20,000 × 2.25 = 2,70,000

OR

Solution :

Allocation of Material cost :

(1) Let type B Material be — X

Type — A material cost would be — 2X

$\therefore$ Material for Type — B = 1,20,000X

Type — A = 40,000 2X

Now 1,20,000X + 80,000X = 15,00,000

2,00,000X = 15,00,000

$$X = \frac{15,00,000}{2,00,000}$$

= Rs. 7.50 per pair.

Type B Material cost = 7.50 per pair

Type A Material cost = 7.50 × 2 = 15 per pair.

(2) *Wages :*

Let X be labour charges for type A

$$\text{For type B} = \frac{60X}{100}$$

$$\therefore 40,000X + 1,20,000 \times \frac{60X}{100}$$

= 40,000X + 72,000X = 8,40,000

1,12,000X = 8,40,000

$$X = \frac{8,40,000}{1,12,000}$$

= Rs. 7.50 per pair.

X Type A — 7.50 per pair

$$B — \frac{60}{100} \times 7.50 \text{ Rs.} = 4.50 \text{ per pair.}$$

(3) Production overhead — on the basis of output

			Ratio	A		B
Type A	40,000	1				
Type B	1,20,000	3		1	:	3

Production overhead Rs. 3,60,000

Type A	3,60,000 × ¼	=	90,000
Type B	3,60,000 × ¾	=	2,70,000
	Total		3,60,000

Statement of Cost and Profit for the year ending 31st March 1990

Particulars	Total	Type 'A' shoe Total		Type 'B' shoe Total	
Direct Material	15,00,000	6,00,000	15.00	9,00,000	7.50
Wages	8,40,000	3,00,000	7.50	5,40,000	4.50
Prime Cost	23,40,000	9,00,000	22.50	14,40,000	12.00
Production overhead	3,60,000	90,000	2.25	2,70,000	2.25
Works Cost	27,00,000	9,90,000	24.75	17,10,000	14.25
Administrative Expenses 15% of Direct wages	12,60,000	4,50,000	11.25	8,10,000	6.75
Cost of production	39,60,000	14,40,000	36.00	25,20,000	21.00
Less : Closing stock A — 40,000 × 36 = B — 20,000 × 21 =	5,64,000	1,44,000	—	4,20,000	—
Cost of Goods sold	33,96,000	12,96,000	36.00	21,00,000	21.00
Selling Expenses	2,04,000	54,000	1.50	1,50,000	1.50
Cost of Sales	36,00,000	13,50,000	37.50	22,50,000	22.50
Sales : Type A = 36,000 × 44 = Type B = 1,00,000 × 28 =	43,84,000	15,84,000	44.00	28,00,000	28.00
Profit	7,84,000	2,34,000	6.50	5,50,000	5.50

Additional Problem No. 17

M/s Software Co. Ltd. manufactures and sells Refrigerators two types namely Deluxe Frize and Standard Frize.

The following are the particulars of production during the year 1994 :

Direct Material Cost	Rs.	1,36,00,000
Direct Wages	Rs.	85,80,000
Production overhead	Rs.	7,50,000

There are no work-in-progress in the beginning and at the end of the year.

It was ascertained that :

(1) Direct Material cost in Deluxe Frize consists of twice as much as that of Standard Frize.
(2) Direct wages for Standard Frize were 40% of those for Deluxe Frize.
(3) Product overhead per unit remain the same in both the cases.
(4) Administrative overheads for each was 150% of Direct wages.
(5) Selling cost per unit was Rs. 675.
(6) Production during the year were :
Deluxe Frize — 2500 units of which sold 2400 units.
Standard Frize — 3500 units of which sold 3200 units.

(7) Selling Price per Unit :
Deluxe Frize — Rs. 12,500
Standard Frize — Rs. 6,500

Prepare statement showing Cost and Profit for type and the Total Profit.

Solution :

(1) Material cost — Rs. 1,36,00,000

Let Standard Frize — Material cost be X

and Deluxe Frize — material cost twice of Standard Frize-*i.e.*, 2X.

$$\text{Now}\quad 3500X + 2500 \times 2X = 1{,}36{,}00{,}000$$

$$\therefore\quad 3500X + 5000X = 1{,}36{,}00{,}000$$

$$8500X = 1{,}36{,}00{,}000$$

$$X = \frac{1{,}36{,}00{,}000}{8{,}500}$$

$$= 1{,}600$$

X = Standard Frize = 1600

2X = Deluxe Frize = 2 × 1600 = 3200

Now Deluxe Frize 2500 × 3200	=	80,00,000
Standard Frize 3500 × 1600	=	56,00,000
Total		1,36,00,000

(2) Direct Wages — Rs. 85,80,000

Let X be the Direct wages for Deluxe Frize and

$$\text{Standard Frize} = \frac{40X}{100}$$

$$\text{Now}\quad 2500X + 3500 \times \frac{40X}{100} = 85{,}80{,}000$$

$$2500X + 1400X = 85{,}80{,}000$$

$$3900X = 85{,}80{,}000$$

$$X = \frac{85{,}80{,}000}{3900}$$

$$= 2{,}200$$

Now Deluxe Frize X — 2,200

$$\text{Standard Frize}\ \frac{40X}{100} = 2{,}200 \times \frac{40}{100} = 880$$

Now Deluxe Frize 2500 × 2,200	=	55,00,000	
Standard Frize 3500 × 880	=	30,80,000	85,80,000

(3) Production Overhead = Rs. 7,50,000

Deluxe Frize = 2500, Standard Frize = 3500 Total = 6000

$$\frac{\text{Total Cost}}{\text{No. of units}} = \frac{7,50,000}{6000} = 125 \text{ per unit.}$$

Deluxe Frize 2500 × 125	=	3,12,500
Standard Frize 3500 × 125	=	4,37,500
Total		Rs. 7,50,000

Statement of Cost and Profit for the year ended 1994

Production : Deluxe Frize = 2500 units.
Standard Frize = 3500 units

Particulars	Total	Deluxe Frize		Standard Frize	
		Cost per unit	Total	Cost per unit	Total
	Rs.	Rs.	Rs.	Rs.	Rs.
Direct Material	1,36,00,000	3200	80,00,000	1600	56,00,000
Direct Wages Deluxe 2200 Standard 40% of 2200	85,80,000	2200	55,00,000	880	30,80.000
Prime Cost	2,21,80,000	5400	1,35,00,000	2480	86,80,000
Factory Overhead					
Production Cost	7,50,000	125	3,12,000	125	4,37,500
Works Cost	2,29,30,000	5525	1,38,12,500	2605	91,17,500
Administrative Overhead 150% of Direct Wage	1,28,70,000	330	82,50,000	1320	46,20,000
Cost of Production of Deluxe — 2500 Standard — 3500	3,58,00,000	8825	2,20,62,500	3925	1,37,37,500
Less : Closing stock Deluxe — 100 Standard — 300	-20,60,00	—	-8,82,500	—	-11,77,500
Cost of Goods sold	3,37,40,000	8825	2,11,80,000	3925	1,25,60,000
Add : Selling cost	37,80,000	675	16,20,000	675	21,60.000
	3,75,20,000	9500	2,28,00,000	4600	1,47,20,000
Selling Price	5,08,00,000	12500	3,00,00,000	6500	2,08,00,000
Profit	1,32,80,000	3000	72,00,000	1900	60,80,000

Productions	Total Profit	Cost per unit	Unit sold	Profit per unit
Deluxe	72,00,000	9,500	2400	3,000
Standard	60,80,000	4,600	3200	1,900

Problem No. 18

From the following data find out an appropriate Cost Sheet from the generating Costs of Electricity per unit in an Iron Foundry during March 1991 :

(1) Fuel : Cost at the beginning of the month — 500 tons.
Supply during the month — 1100 tons.
Balance at the end of the month — 400 tons.
Annual contract for the supply of coal.
For colliery Rs. 10 per ton. Add 10% to cover freight and handling charges.

(2) Oil 10 tons @ Rs. 250 per ton.

(3) Water — 50000 gallons. Pumping charges 0.25 Ps per 100 gallons.

(4) Depreciation of steam boiler :
Capital Value — Rs. 24,000 @ 12% p.a.

(5) Salaries and Wages of Boiler House :
10 men @ Rs. 100 per month each.
40 coolies @ Rs. 20 per month each.

(6) Recovery on account of sales of Ashes 100 tons @ Re. 1 per tons.

(7) Salaries and Wages of Generating station :
50 men @ Rs. 100 per month each.
20 coolies @ Rs. 20 per month each.

(8) Repairs and maintenance of the generating equipment Rs. 2,600.

(9) Depreciation on Generating Equipment :
Capital value Rs. 1,20,000 @ 12½% p.a.

(10) Share of Administration charges — Rs. 1,750.

(11) No. of units generated 1,46,000.

(12) Loss in process — 2000 units.

(K.U.D., October 1991)

Solution : (Electricity Generating or Power House)

Statement of Cost of Electricity Generation

		Rs.	Rs.
(A) *Steam Production* : (Cost + Freight) (10 + 1 = 11)			
(1) Fuel — Opening stock	500 × 11	5,500	
Add : Purchases	1100 × 11	12,100	
		17,600	
Less : Closing Stock		4,400	13,200
(2) Oil — 10 tons @ Rs. 250 per ton =			2,500
(3) Water 50000 gallons @ Re. 0.25 per 100 gallons			
$50000 \times \frac{25}{100} \times \frac{1}{100} =$			125

(4) Depreciation steam boilder : on 24,000 @ 12% p.a. for 1 month		240
(5) Salary & Wages : Men 10 × 100 =	1,000	
Coolies 40 × 20 =	800	1,800
Total Cost		17,865
Less : Recovery by sale of Ashes		100
Cost of steam production		17,765
(B) *Electricity Generation Cost* :		
(7) Salary and Wages : Men 50 × 100 =	5,000	
Coolies 20 × 20 =	400	5,400
(8) Repairs & Maintenance		2,600
(9) Depreciation of Equipments : $1{,}20{,}000 \times \frac{25}{2} \times \frac{1}{100} \times \frac{1}{12} =$		1,250
Cost of Generating Electricity		27,015
(10) Administrative charges		1,750
Total Cost		28,765

$$\text{Cost per Unit} = \frac{28{,}765}{144000} = 0.20 \text{ per unit (Approx. 0.20 Ps.)}$$

Note : Total Units Produce = 1,46,000 Units.
Loss in Process = 2,000 Units
Net Units Produce = 1,44,000 Units

Problem No. 19

The following information relates to the production of T.V. sets for the year 1985 :

1. Materials — Rs. 14,00,000.
2. Direct wages — Rs. 10,80,000.
3. Factory Overheads — Rs. 3,24,000.
4. Administrative Overheads — Rs. 2,24,320.
5. 350 T.V. sets were manufactured and sold at Rs. 12,000 each during the year 1985.

For the year 1986 it is estimated that :

(a) Each T.V. set will require materials of Rs. 3,200 and Direct Wages Rs. 3,800.

(b) Factory overheads are charged as a percentage of Direct Wages.

(c) Administrative Overheads are charged as a percentage or works cost.

Prepare a statement and show the profit to be made per unit, if the selling price of the set is going to be reduced by Rs. 200.

(K.U.D., October 1991)

Solution :

Statement showing Cost of Production for 1985

Particulars	Amount (Rs.)
Materials	14,00,000
Labour	10,80,000
Prime Cost	24,80,000
Add : Factory Overhead	3,24,000
Works Cost	28,04,000
Add : Administration Overhead	2,24,320
Total Cost	30,28,320
Sales Price 350 × 12000	42,00,000
Profit	11,71,680

$$\text{Cost per unit} = \frac{30,28,320}{350} = 8,652$$

Sales	12,000
Profit per Unit	3,348

(1) *Percentage of Factory Overhead to Wages*

$$= \frac{3,24,000}{1,08,000} \times 100 = 30\%$$

(2) *Percentage of Administration Overhead to Works Cost*

$$= \frac{2,24,320}{28,04,000} \times 100 = 8\%.$$

Cost and Profit Statement for 1986

Particulars	Amount (Rs.)
Materials	3,200
Add : Labour	3,800
Prime Cost	7,000
Add : Factory Overhead 30% of wages	1,140
Works Cost	8,140
Add : Administration Overhead 8% Works Cost	651
Total Cost	8,791
Add : Profit	3,009
Sales Price	11,800

Problem No. 20

The following particulars relate to slate manufacturing company for the month of March 1990 :

(1) Slates quarried 10,000 tons on which Royalty of Rs. 2 per ton paid.
(2) Wages Rs. 40,000, Coal Rs. 10,000, Internal Transport Rs. 20,000.
(3) Works overhead 20% on Direct charges.
(4) Office overhead 10% on works cost.
(5) Cost of removal of overburden, .01 Ps per slate manufactured.
(6) Opening stock 10,000 slates.
(7) Manufactured slates purchased at Re. 1 per slate.
(8) Slate sold 1,00,000 @ Rs. 2 per slate
(9) Closing stock 30,000 slates.
(10) Selling expenses .10 Ps per slate sold.

You are required to prepare the statement of Cost and Profit for month of March 1990.

(K.U.D., April 1991)

Solution :

Statement of Cost and Profit for the Month March 1990

Particulars		
(1) Direct Materials :		
Royalty 10000 tons @ Rs. 2 each	20,000	
Direct Wages	40,000	
Coal	10,000	
Internal Transport	20,000	90,000
(2) Works overhead 20% on Direct Expenses (90,000 × 20% = 18,000)		18,000
		1,08,000
Add : Cost of removal of overburden on slate .01 Ps per slate manufactured 1,00,000 × 0.01		1,000
Works cost		1,09,000
(3) Office overhead 10% on 1,09,000		10,900
Total Cost of production		1,19,900
(4) Selling and Distribution Expenses		10,000
		1,29,900
Add : Purchased manufactured slates @ Re. 1 per slate		20,000
		1,49,900
Less : Closing stock (Slates 30000 × 1.199)		35,970
		1,13,930
Add : Selling overhead .10 paise per slate		10,000
		1,23,930
Sales		2,00,000
Profit		76,070

Ascertainment of slates manufactured :		Nos.
Sales		1,00,000
Add : Closing stock		30,000
		1,30,000
Less : Opening stock	10,000	
Purchased from outside	20,000	30,000
Slates (Sales and Manufactured during the month)		1,00,000

$$\text{Cost of Production per unit} = \frac{\text{Total Cost}}{\text{No. of Units}} = \frac{1,19,900}{1,00,000} = 1.199.$$

Closing stock valued at Cost of Production = Rs. 1.199

Closing Stock — Slates = 30000 × 1.199 = 35,970.

Problem No. 21

A manufacturer makes two kinds of Toys X and Y. The following particulars relate to these toys for the year 1988 :

Particulars	Toy-X	Toy-Y
(1) Number of toys manufactured	4000 Units	1000 Units
(2) Materials	3,140	2,650
(3) Wages	9,400	5,700
(4) Power (Direct Cost)	2,100	1,410
(5) Factory supervision Rs. 3,600 for both		
(6) Packing charges Rs. 400 for both		
(7) Management and selling expenses Rs. 6,200 for both.		

You are required to prepare a statement showing cost of each kind of toy when ready for despatch taking into account the following :

(A) Factory supervision to be charged in proportion in Direct cost.

(B) Packing Expenses to be apportioned in the ratio that the Direct cost plus factory supervision cost of X bears to similar cost of Y.

(C) Management and selling expenses to be charged in proportion to the toys manufactured.

(K.U.D., October 1990)

Solution :

Statement of Cost of manufactured Toy

Particulars	Toy-X	Toy-Y
Number of toys manufactured	4000 Units	1000 Units
(1) Direct materials	3,140	2,650
(2) Direct Wages	2,400	5,700
(3) Power (Direct cost)	2,100	1,410
Prime Cost	14,640	9,760

Particulars	Toy-X	Toy-Y
Factory Overhead :		
Factory supervision Rs. 3,600 Basis in proportion to Direct cost	2,160	1,440
Works Cost	16,800	11,200
Selling and Distribution Expenses :		
Packing charges Rs. 400 (Basis Works cost)	240	160
Management and Selling Expenses Rs. 6,200 (Basis in proportion of production) Toy = X 4,000 : Toy = Y 1,000 (4 : 1) Toy = X — 4/5 × 6,200 = 4,960 Toy = Y ¼ × 6,200 = 1,240	4,960	1,240
Cost of sales	22,000	12,600
Cost per Unit Toy-X $\frac{22,000}{4,000}$ Toy-Y $\frac{12,600}{1,000}$	Rs. 5.50	Rs. 12.60

Working Note

(1) Factory supervision Rs. 3,600 apportioned in proportion to Direct cost.

Direct Cost	Toy-X	Toy-Y	Total
	14,640	9,760	24,400
	$\frac{14,640}{24,400} \times 3,600$	$\frac{9,760}{24,400} \times 3,600$	
	= 2,160	= 1,440	

(2) Packing charges Rs. 400 apportioned on works cost.

Works Cost	Toy = X	Toy = Y	Total
	16,800	11,200	28,000
	$\frac{16,800}{28,000} \times 400$	$\frac{11,200}{28,000} \times 400$	
	= 240	160	

(3) Management and selling Expenses Rs. 6,200 basis in proportion to production.

Toy = X	Toy = Y		Total
4,000	1,000	(4:1)	5,000
4/5 × 6,200	1/5 × 6,200		
4,960	1,240		

Problem No. 22

M/s Ashok Company Limited manufactured and sold 2000 cameras in the year ending 31-12-1985. The summarised Trading and Profit and Loss Account is as under :

Trading and Profit and Loss A/c for the year 1985

Particulars	Rs.	Particulars	Rs.
To Cost of materials	1,60,000	By Sales	8,00,000
To Direct Wages	2,40,000		
To Manufacturing Cost	1,00,000		
To Gross Profit c/d	3,00,000		
	8,00,000		8,00,000
To Management and staff salaries	1,20,000	By Gross Profit b/d	3,00,000
To Rent, Rates and Insurance	20,000		
To Selling Expenses	60,000		
To General Expenses	40,000		
To Net Profit	60,000		
	3,00,000		3,00,000

For the year ending 31-12-1986 it is estimated that :

(1) Output and sales will be 2,400 cameras.

(2) Prices of Raw materials will rise by 20% on previous levels.

(3) Wages rate will rise by 5%.

(4) Manufacturing costs will rise in proportion to combined cost of materials and wages.

(5) Selling cost per unit remain unchanged.

(6) Other Expenses will remain unaffected by the rise in output.

You are required to submit a statement for the Board of Directors showing the price at which cameras should be marketed so as to show a profit of 10% on the selling Price.

(K.U.D., April 1990)

Solution :

Statement of Cost for 1986 — Estimated Output 2,400 Units

		Total Cost Rs.	Cost per Unit Rs.
Cost of materials $\frac{1,60,000}{2,000}$	80		
Add: Increase 20% of 80 = 16	16		
	96	2,30,400	96.00
Direct Wages $\frac{2,40,000}{2,000} \times 2,400 \times \frac{105}{100}$		3,02,400	126.00
Prime Cost		5,32,800	222.00
Manufacturing $\frac{1,00,000}{2,000} \times 2,400 \times \frac{222}{200}$		1,33,200	55.50
Works Cost		6,66,000	277.50
Administrative Overheads :			
Manager and Staff salaries	1,20,000		
Rent, Rates and Insurance	20,000		
General Expenses	40,000	1,80,000	75.00
Cost of Production		8,46,000	352.50
Selling Expenses $\frac{60,000}{2,000}$ = Rs. 30		72,000	30.00
Cost of Sales		9,18,000	382.50
Add : Profit 10% on Selling Price			
i.e., $\frac{10}{90} \times 9,18,000 = 1,02,000$		1,02,000	42.50
Sales Price		10,20,000	425.00

Sales Price Rs. 10,20,000 for 2,400 Cameras and Rs. 425 per Unit.

Problem No. 23

Arun Manufactures Products X and Y. From the following particulars prepare statement of cost showing cost of each product for the year ending 1989 and Selling Price :

	X	Y
No. of units produced	10,000	5,000
Direct Expenses	Rs.	Rs.
Materials	6,500	3,500
Labour	20,000	7,250
Power	3,500	1,250

Other Expenses :

(a) Packing Expenses 7,500

(b) Selling and Management Expenses 10,500

(c) Factory supervision 8,750

Selling price is to be fixed at a profit of 10% on Selling Price.

(B'lore, October 1990)

Statement of Cost, Profit and Selling Price

Particulars	Product X	Product Y
(I) No. of units Production	10000	5000
(II) *Direct Expenses :*		
Materials	6,500	3,500
Labour	20,000	7,250
Power	3,500	1,250
Prime Cost	30,000	12,000
(III) Factory Overhead 8,750		
Basis Prime cost 30,000 : 12,000 5 : 2 = 42,000		
$X = \frac{30,000}{42,000} \times 8,750 = 6,250$	6,250	2,500
$Y = \frac{12,000}{42,000} \times 8,750 = 2,500$		
Works Cost	36,250	14,500
(IV) Office Overhead and Selling and Distribution Expenses :		
(a) Packing Expenses 7,500	5,357	2,143
On basis of works cost 36,250 : 14,500		
$\frac{36,250}{50,750} \times 7,500 = 5,357$		
$\frac{14,500}{50,750} \times 7,500 = 2,143$		

Particulars	Product X	Product Y
(b) Selling and management expenses on the basis of units produced 10,000 : 5,000 (2 : 1) X — 2/3 × 10,500 = 7,000 Y — 1/3 × 10,500 = 3,500	7,000	3,500
Cost of Sales	48,607	20,143
Profit 10% on selling price If selling price is 100 Profit is 10 Cost 90 For cost of 90 48,607 10 $X = 48{,}607 \times \frac{10}{90} = 5{,}400$ $Y = 20{,}143 \times \frac{10}{90} = 2{,}238$	5,400	2,238
Selling Price	54,007	22,381
Selling Price per Unit =	$\frac{54{,}007}{10000}$	$\frac{22{,}381}{5000}$
=	Rs. 5.40	Rs. 4.476

Problem No. 24

A Television manufacturing company finds that in 1989 it costs Rs. 6,16,000 to manufacture 200 B & W television which were sold at Rs. 4,000 each cost was made up of :

Materials	2,00,000
Direct Wages	3,00,000
Factory overhead	60,000
Office overhead	56,000
Total	6,16,000

For the year 1990 the company estimates to sell 300 T.V. and

(a) That the television will require the same cost of materials and wages.

(b) That the factory overhead will bear the same relation to direct wages as was in previous year.

(c) That the percentage of office overhead on factory cost will be the same as in previous year.

Prepare a statement of cost for 1990 and find out the estimated total profit and per unit if the selling price is enhanced by Rs. 80 per television.

(Gulbarga, April 1990)

Solution :

Statement of Cost for 1989 — No. of T.V. 200 produced

		Total Cost	Cost per Unit
Materials		2,00,000	1,000
Direct Wages		3,00,000	1,500
	Prime Cost	5,00,000	2,500
Factory Overhead		60,000	300
	Works Cost	5,60,000	2,800
Office Overhead		56,000	280
	Cost of production	6,16,000	3,080
Sales price Rs. 4,000 per unit		8,00,000	4,000
	Profit	1,84,000	920

Statement of Estimated Cost for 1990 — No. of T.V. 300

		Total Cost	Cost per Unit
(I) Materials per unit (1,000 × 300)		3,00,000	1,000
(II) Direct Wages per unit (1,500 × 300)		4,50,000	1,500
	Prime Cost	7,50,000	2,500
(III) *Factory Overhead :* Percentage of Factory overhead on direct wages $\frac{\text{Factory overhead}}{\text{Direct Wages}} \times 100 = \frac{60{,}000}{3{,}00{,}000} \times 100 = 20\%$; $4{,}50{,}000 \times 20\% = 90{,}000$		90,000	300
	Works Cost	8,40,000	2,800
(IV) *Office Overhead* : Percentage of office overhead on factory cost $\frac{\text{Office overhead}}{\text{Works cost}} \times 100 = \frac{56{,}000}{5{,}60{,}000} \times 100 = 10\%$; $= 8{,}40{,}000 \times 10\% = 84{,}000$		84,000	280
	Total Cost	9,24,000	3,080
(V) Sales Price per Unit Rs. 4,000; *Add* : Increase 80; 4,080		12,24,000	4,080
	Profit	3,00,000	1,000

	Rs.		
Total Cost for 300 T.V.	9,24,000	Sales price per unit	Rs. 4,080
Per T.V. Cost	3,080	Cost price per unit	Rs. 3,080
Total Profit for 1990	3,00,000	Profit per unit	Rs. 1,000
Cost per T.V.	3,080		
Profit per T.V.	1,000		

Problem No. 25

The records of Roopa Enterprises show the following figures of expenses for the year ending 31-12-1988 when the output was 1000 Units :

Direct Materials :	
Stock on 1-1-1988	15,000
Stock on 31-12-1988	30,000
Purchases	1,45,000
Direct Wages	75,000
Direct Expenses	5,000
Factory Overhead (60% Variable)	35,000
Administrative Overhead (Fixed)	15,000
Selling Overhead (30% Variable)	24,000

Prepare a statement of Estimated cost 1989 and find cost per unit using the following information :

(1) The output is expected to be 3000 Units.
(2) Direct Wages are expected to decline by 10%.
(3) Fixed Factory overhead would go up Rs. 4900.
(4) Administration overhead will rise by 20%.
(5) Fixed selling overhead will rise by 25%.

(K.U.D., October 1989)

Solution :

Statement of Cost for the year 1988

		Total Cost	Output (1000 Units)
Direct Materials : Stock on 1-1-1988	15,000		
Add : Purchases	1,45,000		
	1,60,000		
Less : Closing stock	30,000	1,30,000	130.00
Direct Wages		75,000	75.00
Direct Expenses		5,000	5.00
Prime Cost		2,10,000	210.00
Factory Overhead : 35,000 (Variable 60%)	= 21,000	21,000	21.00
Fixed 40%	= 14,000	14,000	14.00
Works Cost		2,45,000	245.00
Administrative Overhead 15,000 (Fixed)		15,000	15.00
Total Cost		2,60,000	260.00
Selling Overhead (24,000)			
Variable 30% of 24,000		7,200	7.20
Fixed 70% of 24,000		16,800	16.80
Cost of selling		2,84,000	284.00

Estimated Cost of 1989

Output 3000 Units

		Cost per Unit	Total Cost
Direct materials		130.00	3,90,000
Direct wages	75.00		
Less : Decline 10% of 75	7.50	67.50	2,02,500
Direct Expenses		5.00	15,000
Prime Cost		202.50	6,07,500
Factory overhead variable		21.00	63,000
Factory overhead Fixed	14,000		
Add : Increase	4,900	6.30	18,900
Works Cost		229.80	6,89,400
Administration overhead			
Fixed	15,000		
Add : Increase 20%	3,000	6.00	18,000
Total Cost		235.80	7,07,400
Selling overhead variable		7.20	21,600
Fixed	16,800		
Add : Increase 25%	4,200	7.00	21,000
Cost of Sales		250.00	7,50,000
Cost per Unit		250.00	
Total Cost			7,50,000

Problem No. 26

M/s Carona shoes company manufactures two types of shoes A and B. The production cost for the year ended 31st March 1989 were :

Direct Materials	15,00,000
Direct Wages	8,40,000
Production Overhead	3,60,000
Total	27,00,000

There was no work-in-progress.

At the beginning or at the end of the year it is ascertained that :

(1) The Direct materials in type A shoes consists twice as much as that of Type B shoes.

(2) The Direct wages for type B shoes were 60% of those for type A.

(3) Production overhead was the same per pair of A and B type shoes.

(4) Administrative overhead for each was 150% of direct wages.

(5) Selling cost was Rs.1.50 per pair.

(6) Production during the year were :
Type A 40,000 pairs of which 36,000 were sold.
Type B 1,20,000 pairs of which 1,00,000 were sold.

(7) Selling price was Rs. 44 pair for type A and Type B Rs. 28 per pair shoes.

Prepare a statement showing cost and profit.

(K.U.D., April 1989)

Solution :

Working Note

(1) Apportionment of cost of production i.e., materials, wages and production overhead to Type A shoes and Type B shoes.

Total cost of material — Rs. 15,00,000

Let be the Type B shoes consume material X and that of Type A shoes be 2X.

Therefore $X + 2X = 15,00,000$

Now $= X \times 1,20,000 + 2X \times 40,000 = 15,00,000$

$1,20,000X + 80,000X = 15,00,000$

$2,00,000X = 15,00,000$

$$X = \frac{15,00,000}{2,00,000}$$

X = Rs. 7.50 cost of materials

2X = Rs. 15 twice that of X.

Substitution X = Type B shoes — 1,20,000 pairs

Cost of Type B shoes = 1,20,000 × 7.50 = 9,00,000

Type A shoes = 40,000 pairs. Cost of A Type shoes = 40,000 × 15 = 60,00,000

Total Material Cost Rs. 15,00,000

Apportioned to	Type A shoes	6,00,000
	Type B shoes	9,00,000
	Total	15,00,000

(2) Direct Wages Rs. 8,40,000. Let Wages for type A shoes be X and for Type B shoes be 60% of X

Therefore $40,000X + 1,20,000 \times 60\% X$

$= 40,000X + 72,000X = 8,40,000$

$= 1,12,000X = 8,40,000$

$$X = \frac{8,40,000}{1,12,000} = 7.50 \text{ per pair.}$$

Substitute X for Type A shoes Rs. 7.50 per pair.

Type B shoes Rs. 7.50 × 60% = 4.50 per pair.

Total Wages = Rs. 8,40,000 Type A shoes 40,000 × 7.50 = 3,00,000
Type B shoes 1,20,000 × 4.50 = 5,40,000
8,40,000

(3) Production overhead per pair of shoes for both Type A and Type B is same.

Production overhead Rs. 3,60,000

Apportioned in ratio of output Type A 40,000 and Type B 1,20,000

Ratio = 1 : 3 = Type A = 3,60,000 × ¼ = 90,000

Type B = 3,60,000 × 3/4 = 2,70,000.

Statement of Cost and Profit

Particulars	Total Cost	Type A Shoes 40,000 Pairs		Type B shoes 1,20,000 Pairs	
		Cost per pair	Total Cost	Cost per pair	Total Cost
(1) Direct Material	15,00,000	15.00	6,00,000	7.50	9,00,000
(2) Wages	8,40,000	7.50	3,00,000	4.50	5,40,000
Prime Cost	23,40,000	22.50	9,00,000	12.00	14,40,000
(3) Production overhead apportioned in the ratio 1:3	3,60,000	2.50	90,000	2.25	2,70,000
Work Cost	27,00,000	24.75	9,90,000	14.25	17,10,000
(4) Administrative overhead 150% of Direct Wages	12,60,000	11.25	4,50,000	6.75	8,10,000
Cost of production	39,60,000	36.00	14,40,000	21.00	25,20,000
of Type A 40,000 pair shoes Type B 1,20,000 pair shoes					
The production sales closing A — 40,000 36,000 4,000 B — 1,20,000 1,00,000 20,000					
Less : Closing Stock	5,64,000		1,44,000		4,20,000
Cost of production of Sold shoes	33,96,000		12,96,000		21,00,000
Selling overhead Type A 36,000 × 1.50 Type B 1,00,000 × 1.50	2,04,000	1.50	54,000	1.50	1,50,000
Cost of Sales	36,00,000	37.50	13,50,000	22.50	22,50,000
Sales Price Type A Rs. 44 Type B Rs. 28	43,84,000	44.00	15,84,000	28.00	28,00,000
Profit	7,84,000	6.50	2,34,000	5.50	5,50,000

Problem No. 27

Prepare cost sheet from the following information relating to article X :

Stock on 1st January 1988 :	
Raw materials	4,000
Finished goods (400 Units)	3,200
Purchases of Raw materials	24,000
Direct wages	20,000
Works on cost	8,400
Work-in-progress :	
On 1st January 1988	960
On 31st January 1988	3,200
Office administrative overhead	1,600
Stock on 31st December 1988 :	
Raw materials	4,400
Finished Goods (800 Units)	?
Sale of Finished products	60,000

Selling expenses were calculated to be 0.20 Ps per unit

Total production during 1988 was 6400 Units.

Calculate cost and profit per unit also.

(K.U.D., April 1989)

Solution :

Working Note

Calculation of No. of units sold :

Finished goods in Units	
Opening Stock	400
Add : Produced during the year	6,400
Total production	6,800
Less : Closing stock unit	800
Total No. of units sold	6,000

Statement of Cost and Profit (Output 6400 Units)

Raw materials :	
Opening stock on 1-1-1988	4,000
Add : Purchases	24,000
	28,000
Less : Closing stock 31-12-1988	4,400

Raw material consumed	23,600
Direct Wages	20,000
Prime Cost	43,600
Works on Cost	8,400
	52,000
Works-in-progress :	
Opening stock 1-1-1988	960
	52,960
Less : Closing stock 31-12-1988	3,200
Works Cost	49,760
Office and Administrative overhead	1,600
Total cost of production	51,360

Units of output — 6400

Cost of Finished goods :

$$\text{per Unit} = \frac{\text{Total Cost}}{\text{Units Production}} = \frac{51{,}360}{6400} = 8.025$$

Add : Opening stock of finished goods (400 Units)	3,200
	54,560
Less : Closing stock of finished goods (800 Units @ Rs. 8.025 = 6,420)	6,420
Cost of Finished Goods Sold	48,140
Add : Selling Expenses for 6,000 × 0.20 = 1,200	1,200
Total cost of goods sold	49,340
Sales Price	60,000
Profit	10,660

Cost of Production of 6400 Units	51,360
Cost of Finished Goods (800 Units @ Rs. 8.025)	6,420
Profit	10,660

Problem No. 28

M/s A B C Ltd. furnished the following data relating to the manufacture of a product during the year 1986 :

Production	1000 units
Materials	20,000
Labour	12,000
Office overhead	4,000
Factory overhead	8,000
Selling Expenses	1,000

Profit 25% on selling Price.

The company decides to produce 1500 Units in 1987.

It is estimated that :

(1) The cost of materials will increase by 20%.

(2) The labour cost will increase by 10%.

(3) 50% Factory overhead and office overhead are fixed and other 50% are variable.

(4) Selling Expenses per unit will be reduced by 20%.

(5) The rate of profit will remain the same.

Prepare a statement for 1987 showing (a) Total profit (b) Selling price per Unit.

(K.U.D., October 1988 and B'lore, April 1985)

Solution :

Statement of Cost for 1986 — Output 1000 Units

Particulars	Total Cost	Cost per Unit
Materials	20,000	20.00
Labour	12,000	12.00
Prime Cost	32,000	32.00
Factory overhead	8,000	8.00
Works Cost	40,000	40.00
Office overhead	4,000	4.00
Total Cost	44,000	44.00
Selling Expenses	1,000	1.00
Cost of Sales	45,000	45.00
Profit 25% on selling price Or 1/3 on cost 1/3 × 45,000	15,000	15.00
Selling Price	60,000	60.00

Estimated Statement of Cost for 1987 — Output 1500

Particulars			Total Cost	Cost per Unit
Material	20.00			
Add : Increase by 20%	4.00	24.00	36,000	24.00
Labour Cost	12.00			
Add : Increase by 10%	1.20	13.20	19,800	13.20
Prime Cost			55,800	37.20
Factory overhead	8.00			
50% Variable Rs. 4 per unit (4 × 1500)			6,000	4.00
Fixed 8,000 × 50% = 4,000			4,000	2.67
Works Cost			65,800	43.87

Particualars	Total Cost	cost per Unit
Office Overhead per unit 4		
Variable 50% of Rs. 4 (Rs. 2 × 1500)	3,000	2.00
Fixed Cost 4,000 × 50% = Rs. 2,000	2,000	1.33
Total Cost	70,800	47.20
Selling Expenses per unit Re. 1	1,200	0.80
Cost of Sales	72,000	48.00
Less : Reduced by 20% (1 – 0.20 = 0.80)		
Sales price	96,000	64.00
Estimated Profit for the Year 1987	24,000	16.00

Rate of Profit 1/3 or Cost = 72,000 × 1/3 = Rs. 24,000
or 25% on Selling price = 96,000 × 25% = Rs. 24,000

Problem No. 29

The records of Archana enterprises show the following figures of expenses for the year ending 31-12-1987 :

Materials Opening stock (1-1-1987)	6,000
Purchases during the year	58,000
Stock on 31-12-1987	12,000
Labour	14,000
Chargeable Expenses	2,000
Office Expenses	6,000
Factory overheads	14,000
Marketing charges	6,000

The annual output was 1000 Units. The Budgeted output for the year 1988 2500 Units.

Prepare a statement of estimated cost for 1988.

The following information may be useful in this regard :

(1) Labour cost may decline by 20%.

(2) 40% of works overheads are variable (fluctuate with change in volume).

(3) Fixed works overheads are expected to go up by Rs. 6,000.

(4) 40% of marketing expenses are fixed.

(5) Office expenses and fixed marketing expenses may increase by 25%.

(K.U.D., April 1988)

Solution :

Statement of Cost for the year 1987 (Output 1000 Units)

		Total Cost	Cost per Unit
Materials : Opening stock	6,000		
Add : Purchases	58,000		
	64,000		
Less : Closing stock	12,000		
Material consumed		52,000	52.00
Labour : Wages		14,000	14.00
Chargeable Expenses		2,000	2.00
Prime Cost		68,000	68.00
Factory Overheads		14,000	14.00
Works cost		82,000	82.00
Office Expenses		6,000	6.00
Total Cost		88,000	88.00
Marketing Charges		6,000	6.00
Sales Price		94,000	94.00

Budgeted Cost for the year 1988 (Output 2500 Units)

			Cost per Unit	Total Cost
Materials (52 × 2500 = 1,30,000)			52.00	1,30,000
Labour Wages	14.00			
Less : decline 20%	2.80	11.20 × 2500	11.20	28,000
Chargeable Expenses (2 × 2500 = 5,000)			2.00	5,000
Prime Cost			65.20	1,63,000
Works Overhead	14,000			
Variable 40% × 14,000 = $\frac{5,600}{1000}$ = 5.60 × 2500			5.60	14,000
Fixed 60% × 14,000 = 8,400 + 6,000 = 14,400			5.76	14,400
Works Cost			76.56	1,91,400
Office Expenses	6,000			
Add : Increase 25% (1,500)	1,500		3.00	7,500
			79.56	1,98,900
Marketing Expenses :	6,000			
Fixed 40% × 6,000 = 2,400				
Add : Increase 25% 600			1.20	3,000
Variable cost 60% × 6,000 = $\frac{3,600}{1000}$			3.60	9,000
Total Cost (Sales)			84.36	2,10,900

Problem No. 30

Mr. Ashok furnishes the following data relating to the manufacture of a standard product during December 1986 :

Raw materials consumed		Rs. 15,000
Direct Labour cost		Rs. 9,000
Machine hour rate		Rs. 5
Machine hour worked	(in Hours)	900
Administrative overheads 20% on works cost.		
Selling overhead	(per unit)	Re. 0.50
Units produced	(in units)	17100
Units sold	(in units)	16000

Selling Price per unit @ Rs. 4 per unit.

Your are required to prepare a statement of cost showing of cost and profit per unit sold.

(K.U.D., October 1987)

Solution :

Statement of Cost

Raw material consumed	15,000
Direct Labour charges	9,000
Prime Cost	24,000
Factory Expenses : Machine hour rate Rs. 5 per hour (900 × 5 = 4,500)	4,500
Works Cost	28,500
Administrative overhead 20% on works cost (28,500 × 20%)	5,700
Total Cost	34,200

Cost per Unit = $\frac{34,200}{17,100}$ = Rs. 2 per Unit.

Statement of Profit

Cost of production of 16000 Units Rs. 2 per Unit (16000 × 2)	32,000
Add : Selling overhead Re. 0.50 per unit (16000 × 0.50)	8,000
Total Cost of sales	40,000
Sales price @ Rs. 4 per unit (16000 × 4)	64,000
Profit on sales	24,000

Per unit Profit = $\frac{24,000}{16000}$ = Rs. 1.50

Cost per Unit = Rs. 2.50 per unit. ($\frac{40000}{16000}$ = Rs. 2.50)

Problem No. 31

The following figures are obtained from records of Factory :

Materials issued	64,000
Wages	56,000

Factory overhead @ 60% of wages.

Out of the materials issued Rs. 800 worth of goods have been returned to the stores and Rs. 400 transferred to other Jobs. 10% of the production has been scrapped as bad and a further 20% has been brought up to specification by increasing the factory overheads to 80% of the wages. If the scrapped production fetches only Rs. 470, find the production cost per unit of the finished product if the product (including the quantity scrapped) to be 100 Unit.

(K.U.D., April 1987)

Solution :

Statement of Cost

Particulars			Units	Total Cost	Cost per Unit
			100		
(1) Materials issued		64,000			
Less : Returned to stores	800				
Less : Transferred	400	1,200		62,800	628
(2) Wages				56,000	560
Prime Cost				1,18,800	1,188
(3) Factory overhead 60% of wages (56,000 × 60%)				33,600	336
Works Cost				1,52,400	1,524
Less : Scrap sold 10% of production (100 × 10%)			10	470	
			90	1,51,930	
Additional factory overhead 20% of 100 units					
Increasing factory overhead 80%					
Existing 60% — increased to 80%					
Net increase 20% on wages					
Rs. 560 per unit when 60% of wages for 20 Units					
= 560 × 20 = 11,200					
Add : Increase 20% of 11,200 × 20%				2,240	
Total cost of production				1,54,170	

$$\text{Cost per unit} = \frac{\text{Total cost}}{\text{No. of units}} = \frac{1,54,170}{90} = \text{Rs. } 1,713.$$

Problem No. 32

Following particulars are taken from the record of Vijay Metal Works :

Materials Issued	72,000
Wages paid	60,000

Factory expenses are 50% of Wages.

Out of the materials issued Rs. 1,500 worth of materials have been returned to the stores and Rs. 500 worth of materials are transferred to other Jobs.

5% of the production has been scrapped as bad and a further 15% of total production has been brought up to the specification by increasing the factory overhead to 60% of wages proportionately. If the scrapped production fetches Rs. 1000 find the production cost per unit of the finished goods. The total gross output during the period was 200 Units.

(K.U.D., October 1986)

Solution :

Statement of Cost Output — 200 Units

Materials issued		72,000	
Less : Returned to stores	1,500		
Less : Transferred to the other Jobs	500	2,000	
Material consumed		70,000	
Wages paid		60,000	
Prime Cost			1,30,000
Factory overhead 50% of wages 50% of 60,000			30,000
Factory Cost			1,60,000
Less : Scrap 5% of 200 Units = 10 Units			1,000
			1,59,000
Additional Factory overhead 15% of 200 = 30 Units @ 10% of Wages (60% — 50% = 10%) 10% of 60,000			
10% of 60,000 = $\frac{6,000}{200}$ = 30 × 30 = 900			900
Total Cost			1,59,900

Total production 200 — 5% = 10 = 190 Units.

$$\text{Cost per Unit} = \frac{1,59,900}{190} = \text{Rs. } 832 \text{ per Unit Cost.}$$

Problem No. 33

The following figures have been taken from the records of the Rico Calculators Ltd. for the year ending 31-12-1984 :

(1)	Stock of materials 1-1-1984	30,000
(2)	Stock of materials 31-12-1984	10,000
(3)	Purchases of materials	60,000
(4)	Wages paid	90,000
(5)	Factory Expenses	20,000
(6)	Administrative Expenses	9,000
(7)	Stock of Finished goods 1-1-84	10,000
(8)	Stock of Finished goods 31-12-1984	50,000
(9)	Sales	2,12,000

(10) Total number of machine hours worked during the year — 5000 Hours.

(11) Total number labour hours worked during the year — 4500 Hours.

(12) Total number of calculators produced during the year 1984 — 5000 Units.

The company was required to quote for the supply of 1000 calculators during the year 1985.

The calculators to be quoted are of uniform quality and makes and similar to those manufactured during the year 1984.

However, as from 1st Jan. 1985 the cost of materials has increased by 10% and Factory Labour by 5%.

The Estimated machine hour for the quotation order are 1000 hours and estimated labour hour required are 900 Hours.

The factory expenses are recovered on the basis of labour hour worked.

Prepare a Statement showing the Price to be quoted to give the same percentage of Net Profit on sales as was returned during 1984.

(K.U.D., April 1986)

Solution :

Statement of Cost for the year 1984

Total Units Produced — 5000 Units			
(1) Raw materials : Opening stock	30,000		
Add : Purchases	60,000		
	90,000		
Less : Closing stock	10,000	16.00	80,000
(2) Direct Wages Paid		18.00	90,000
Prime Cost		34.00	1,70,000

	Per unit	Total
(3) Factory Expenses	4.00	20,000
Works Cost	38.00	1,90,000
(4) Administrative Overhead	1.80	9,000
Cost of production	39.80	1,99,000
Add : Opening stock of Finished Goods 1-1-1984		10,000
		2,09,000
Less : Stock of Finished stock 31-12-84		50,000
Cos. of Goods sold	31.80	1,59,000
Sales Price	42.40	2,12,000
Profit	10.60	53,000

Percentage of Profit on sales = $\frac{53,000}{2,12,000} \times 100 = 25\%$ on Sales

II. Statement Cost of Quotation Order for 1000 Units for 1985

		Cost per unit	Total Cost
(1) Materials Cost per unit	= 16.00		
Add : Increase by 10%	1.60	17.60	17,600
(2) Wages Basis Labour hour — Rate Wages for 1984 – 90,000 Hours Worked 4500 = .20 Ps per Hour for 900 Hours Increase by 5% = 900 + 18,000 = 18,900		18.90	18,900
Prime Cost		36.50	36,500
(3) Factory Overhead recovered on the basis of machine Hour $\frac{\text{Factory Overhead}}{\text{Machine Hour}} = \frac{20,000}{5000}$ = Rs. 4 per hour		4.00	4,000
Works Cost		40.50	40,500
(4) Administrative Overhead Recovery Basis Labour Hours $\frac{\text{Administrative Overhead}}{\text{Labour Hours}} = \frac{9,000}{4,500}$ = Rs. 2		1.80	1,800
Cost of Production		42.30	42,300
Profit 25% on Sales Or 1/3 on Cost (42,300 × 1/3)		14.10	14,100
Sales Price		56.40	56,400

Problem No. 34

From the following data prepare a cost and profit statement of popular stores manufacturing company for the year 1985 :

(1)	Stock of material 1-1-1985	35,000
(2)	Stock of material 31-12-1985	4,900
(3)	Purchases of materials	52,500
(4)	Direct Wages	95,000
(5)	Factory Expenses	17,500
(6)	Establishment Expenses	10,000
(7)	Completed stock on 1-1-1985	Nil
(8)	Completed stock on 31-12-1985	35,000
(9)	Sales	1,89,000

No. of stoves manufactured during the year 1985 — 4000.

The company wants to quote for a contract for supply of 1000 stoves during the year 1986.

The stove to be quoted are uniform in the previous year. It is estimated that during 1986 :

Cost of material increase by 15% and Factory labour by 10%.

Prepare a statement showing the price to be quoted to give the same percentage of profit on turnover as was realised during the year 1985 assuming that the cost per unit of overhead charged will be same as in the previous year.

(Mangalore, April 1991 & Gulbarga, 1986)

Solution :

Statement of Cost and Profit for the year 1985

(1) Raw materials : Opening stock 1-1-85	35,000		
Add : Purchases	52,500		
	87,500		
Less : Closing stock 31-12-85	4,900	82,600	20.65
(2) Direct Wages		95,000	23.75
Prime Cost		1,77,600	44.40
(3) Factory overhead : Factory Expenses		17,500	4.375
Works Cost		1,95,100	48.775
(4) Office overhead : Establishment Expenses		10,000	2.50
Cost of production		2,05,100	51.275
Cost of production of 4000 stoves	2,05,100		
Add : Opening stock of completed stores	Nil		
	2,05,100		

Less : Closing stock of completed stoves	35,000	
	1,70,100	1,70,100
Cost of completed stoves sold		1,70,100
Sales Price		1,89,000
		18,900

Percentage of profit on sales = $\frac{\text{Profit}}{\text{Sales}} \times 100$

$= \frac{18,900}{1,89,000} \times 100 = 10\%$

Quotation Price Statement of Cost for 1986

Quotation for 1000 Stoves			
(1) Raw materials per unit	20.65		
Add : Increase by 15%	3.0975	23,747.50	23.7475
(2) Wages per Unit	23.75		
Add : Increase by 10%	2.375	26,125.00	26.1250
Prime Cost		49,872.50	49.8725
(3) Factory overhead per unit no charges		4,375.00	4.3750
Works Cost		54,247.50	54.2475
(4) Office overhead per unit no charges		2,500.00	2.5000
Cost of sales		56,747.50	56.74775
Add : Profit 10% on sales Or			
$\frac{10}{90} \times$ on Cost = $\frac{10}{90} \times 56,747.50$ =		6,305.277	6.305
Quotation Price		63,053.777	63.0537

Problem No. 35

The following Trading and Profit and Loss Account of Water Ltd. for the year ending 31-12-1982 in which 800 Units were sold by the company.

Trading and Profit and Loss Account

To Cost of materials	32,000	By Sales	1,60,000
To Direct wages	48,000		
To Manufacturing wages	20,000		
To Gross Profit	60,000		
	1,60,000		1,60,000
To Salaries	24,000	By Gross Profit b/d	60,000
To Rent	4,000		
To Selling Expenses	8,000		
To General Expenses	12,000		
To Net Profit	12,000		
	60,000		60,000

Following Estimates were made by the Costing Department for the year 1983 :

(1) The output and the sales will be 1000 Units.

(2) The cost of materials will rise by 25% over the previous year level.

(3) Wages during the year will rise 12½%.

(4) Manufacturing wages will rise in proportion to the combined cost of materials and wages.

(5) Selling cost per unit will remain unchanged.

(6) Other expenses will remain unaffected by the rise in output.

From the above prepare a cost sheet (Cost statement) showing the price at which the product would be marketed so as to show a profit of 10% on the Selling Price.

(K.U.D., April 1985)

Statement of Cost for 1983 (Estimated Output 1000 Units)

Cost of materials = $\frac{32,000}{800} \times 1000 =$	40,000		
Add : Increase by 25% of 40,000 =	10,000	50,000	50.00
Direct Wages = $\frac{48,000}{800} = 60,000 =$	60	67,500	67.50
Add : Increase 12 ½% of 60 = 7,500 =	7.50		
Prime Cost		1,17,500	117.50
Factory Overhead :			
Manufacturing Expenses			
$\frac{20,000}{8,000} = 25 \times \frac{117.50}{100} = 29.375 \times 1000 =$		29,375	29.375
(Or $\frac{20,000}{800} \times 1000 \times \frac{117.50}{100} = 29,375$)			
Works Cost		1,46,875	146.875
Office Oveheads :			
Salaries	24,000		
Rent	4,000		
General Expenses	12,000	40,000	40.000
Cost of production		1,86,875	186.875
Selling cost per unit = $\frac{8,000}{800} = 10 \times 1000$		10,000	10.000
Total Cost		1,96,875	196.875
Add : Profit 10% on Selling Price			
i.e., $\frac{10}{90} \times 1,96,875 =$		21,875	21.875
Total Selling Price		2,18,750	218.750

Profit 10% on Selling Price 2,18,750 = 21,875
(2,18,750 × 10% = 21,875)

Problem No. 36

The following extract of costing information relates to a commodity for the six months ending 30th June 1981 :

(1)	Purchases (Raw materials)	30,000
(2)	Direct Wages	25,000
(3)	Rent and Insurance of works	10,000
(4)	Carriage inwards	390
(5)	Stock on 1st Jan. 1981 : Raw materials	5,000
	Finished Product (1000 Kgs)	4,000
(6)	Stock on 30th June 1981 : Raw materials	5,500
	Finished Product (2000 Kgs)	8,000
(7)	Work-in-progress 1st Jan. 1981	1,200
	Work-in-progress 30th June 1981	4,000
(8)	Cost of Factory supervision	2,000
(9)	Sales of finished product	75,000

(10) Advertising discount allowed and selling Expenses amount to 0.25 Paise per Kg. sold. 16000 Kg of the commodity were produced during the year.

Prepare a Statement showing :

(a) The value of raw materials used.

(b) The cost of output for the period.

(c) The cost of Turnover for the period.

(d) The Net profit for the period.

(e) The net profit per Kg. of commodity.

(K.U.D., October 1984)

Solution :

Working Note

	Kgs.
Output during the Period	16,000
Add : Opening Stock	1,000
	17,000
Less : Closing stock	2,000
Finished Stock Sold	15,000
Selling Expenses 0.25 Ps per Kg = 15,000 × 0.25 Ps)	Rs. 3,750

Statement of Cost

	Rs.	Rs.
Raw materials : Opening stock	5,000	
Add : Purchases	30,000	
	35,000	
Less : Closing stock	5,560	
	29,440	
Add : Carriage Inward	390	
Total cost of materials consumed	29,830	29,830
Direct Wages		25,000
Prime Cost		54,830
Factory Overheads :		
Rent, Insurance of works	10,000	
Cost of factory supervision	2,000	12,000
Works Cost		66,830
Work-in-progress on 1-1-1981		1,200
		68,030
Less : Work-in-progress on 30-6-1981		4,000
Cost of production		64,030
Add : Finished stock : Opening 1000 Kg × 4		4,000
		68,030
Less : Closing stock 2000 × 4 =		8,000
Cost of Goods sold		60,030
Selling Expenses 0.25 Ps per Kg for 15000 × 0.25 =		3,750
Cost of Sales		63,780
Selling Price		75,000
Profit		11,220

$$\text{Net Profit per Kg.} = \frac{11,220}{15000} = \text{Re. } 0.748$$

Problem No. 37

The following figures have been extracted from the record of the company for the year 1981 :

Direct Material	70,000
Direct Wages	60,000
Factory overhead	30,000
Administrative overhead	48,000
Selling overhead	32,000
Distribution overhead	16,000
Profit	64,000

A work order has been executed in 1982 and the following expenses have been incurred :

Material	10,000
Wages	6,000

Assuming that the rate of factory overhead has gone up by 20%

The administrative overhead has gone up by 10%

Selling overheads are Rs. 3,000

Distribution overhead are Rs. 134

Prepare a cost sheet and find out at what price would be the product be sold so as to earn the same rate of profit on the selling Price.

(K.U.D., April 1984)

Solution :

Statement of Cost for the year 1981

(1) Direct materials		70,000
(2) Direct Wages		60,000
Prime Cost		1,30,000
(3) Factory overhead		30,000
Works Cost		1,60,000
(4) Administrative overhead		48,000
Cost of production		2,08,000
(5) Selling and Distribution overhead :	Selling overhead	32,000
	Distribution overhead	16,000
Total Cost		2,56,000
Profit 20% on sales or 25% on cost		64,000
Sales		3,20,000

Statement of Estimated Cost for the year 1982

(1) Direct Material		10,000.00
(2) Direct Wages		6,000.00
Prime Cost		16,000.00
(3) Factory overhead 50% on Direct wages = 6,000 × 60% =		3,000.00
Works Cost		19,000.00
(4) Administrative overhead 30% on works cost (19,000 × 30%)		5,700.00
		24,700.00
(5) Selling and Distribution overhead :	Selling overhead	3,000.00
	Distribution overhead	134.00
Total Cost or Cost of Sales		27,834.00
Profit 20% on sales or 25% on cost 25% × 27,834 = 6,958.50		6,958.50
Sales Price		34,792.50

Working Note

Calculating of percentages of :

(1) Factory overhead as a percentage on Direct Wages

$$\frac{\text{Factory Overhead}}{\text{Direct Wages}} \times 100 = \frac{30{,}000}{60{,}000} \times 100\% = 50\% \text{ Direct Wages}$$

(2) Administrative overhead as a percentage on works cost

$$\frac{\text{Administrative Overhead}}{\text{Works Cost}} \times 100 = \frac{48{,}000}{1{,}60{,}000} \times 100 = 30\% \text{ on works cost}$$

(3) Percentage Profit on Selling price $= \frac{\text{Profit}}{\text{Selling Price}} \times 100 = \frac{64{,}000}{3{,}20{,}000} \times 100$

X = 20% Selling Price. = 20%

Problem No. 38

The following data relates to the manufacture of standard product during the four weeks ending 28th October 1975 :

Raw materials	20,000
Direct Wages	12,000
Machine hours worked 950 Hours	
Machines Hour rate Rs. 2 per Hour	
Office overhead 15% on works cost	
Selling overhead Re. 0.37 Ps per unit	
Units Produced 20,000 Units.	
Units sold @ Rs. 2.50 each — 18,000 Units.	

Prepare a state of cost from the above showing :

(a) Cost of production per unit.

(b) Profit for the period.

(K.U.D., October 1982)

Solution :

Statement of Cost 4 Weeks ending 28th October 1975

(1) Raw materials consumed	20,000
(2) Direct Wages	12,000
Prime Cost	32,000
(3) Factory overhead machine hour worked 950 × 2	1,900
Works Cost	33,900
(4) Office overhead 15% on works cost 15% of 33,900	5,085
Cost of production	38,985

Note : Cost of production of 20000 Units Rs. 38,985

$$\text{Cost per unit} = \frac{38{,}985}{20000} = 1.9492 = 1.95$$

No. of units produced	20,000	38,985.00	
No. of units sold	18,000	35,086.50	
Closing stock of Finished units	2,000	3,898.50	3,898.50
Cost of No. of units 18,000 sold			35,086.50
(6) Selling overhead Re. 0.37 Ps per unit (.37 × 18000)			6,660.00
Cost of units 18,000 sold			41,746.50
Sales Price Rs. 2.50 per unit = 2.50 × 18000			45,000.00
Profit			3,253.50

Problem No. 39

Modern manufacturing submits the following information on 31st March 1981 :

(1) Sales for the year	2,75,000
(2) Inventory at the beginning of the year :	
Finished Goods	7,000
Work-in-progress	4,000
(3) Purchase of Raw materials for the year	1,10,000
Raw material at stock at the beginning of the year	3,000
Raw material at the end of the year	4,000
(4) Direct Labour	65,000
(5) Factory overhead 60% of the Direct Labour	
(6) Inventory at the end of the year :	
Work-in-progress	6,000
Finished Goods	8,000
(7) Other Expenses for the year	

Selling Expenses 10% of sales and Administrative Expenses 5% of sales.

Prepare a Statement of Cost.

(K.U.D., 1983 & C.A. Inter, 1977)

Solution :

Statement of Cost for the year ending 31-3-1981

(1) Raw materials : Stock at the beginning	3,000	
Add : Purchases during the year	1,10,000	
	1,13,000	
Less : Closing stock at the end of year	4,000	1,09,000
(2) Direct Labour		65,000
Prime Cost		1,74,000

(3) Factory overhead 60% of Direct Wages (60% of 65,000)	39,000
	2,13,000
Add : Work-in-progress in the beginning	4,000
	2,17,000
Work-in-progress at the end	6,000
Total work cost	2,11,000
(4) Administrative overhead 5% on sales value of Rs. 2,75,000	13,750
	2,24,750
Add : Finished stock in the beginning	7,000
	2,31,750
Less : Finished Stock at the end	8,000
Total cost of production	2,23,750
(5) Selling Expenses 10% on sales value (10% of 2,75,000)	27,500
Cost of sales	2,51,250
Sales Price	2,75,000
Profit	23,750

Problem No. 40

Patil Brother, Hubli manufactures two types of articles in their S.S.I. unit branded as P and Q. The output during February 1982 was :

P — 1,000 Units

Q — 1,500 Units.

The expenses incurred during the month were :

Materials	8,00,000
Wages	1,60,000
Stores Expenses	40,000
General works overhead	1,44,000
Labour welfare expenses	11,200
Depreciation on plant @ 10% on Rs. 8,00,000	
Administrative and selling overheads	3,38,000
Machine hours worked during the month — 3000 Hours	
machine Hour Rate @ Rs. 4	

Other Particulars :	P		Q
Material cost ratio per unit	3	:	2
Labour cost ratio per unit	1	:	2
Machine utilisation ratio	1	:	1

Administrative and selling overheads were to be allocated in the ratio of works cost.

Prepare total cost of production and cost per article P and Q.

(K.U.D., 1982)

Solution :

Working Note

Calculation of Ratio for Apportionment of Expenses

Particulars	Cost Ratio P	Cost Ratio Q	Apportionment Ratio P	Apportionment Ratio Q
	Units	Units		
(1) Material Cost Ratio	1,000	1,500		
	× 3	× 2		
	3,000	3,000	1	: 1
(2) Labour Cost Ratio	1,000	1,500		
	× 1	× 2		
	1,000	3,000	1	: 3
(3) Machine Utilisation Ratio	1,000	1,500		
	× 1	× 1		
	1,000	1,500	2	: 3

(4) Stores Expenses apportioned as a percentage on material cost.

$$\frac{\text{Stores Expenses}}{\text{Material cost}} \times 100 = \frac{40{,}000}{8{,}00{,}000} \times 100 = 5\% \text{ on material cost}$$

Material cost

P = 4,00,000 × 5% = 20,000

Q = 4,00,000 × 5% = 20,000

(5) General work overhead and labour welfare expenses apportioned as a percentage on Direct wages :

(a) $\frac{\text{General Works Overhead}}{\text{Direct Wages}} \times 100 = \frac{1{,}44{,}000}{1{,}60{,}000} \times 100 = 90\%$ of wages.

(b) $\frac{\text{Labour Welfare}}{\text{Direct Wages}} \times 100 = \frac{11{,}200}{1{,}60{,}000} \times 100 = 7\%$ of wages.

(6) Administrative and selling overheads as percentage on works cost

(a) $\frac{\text{Administrative Overhead}}{\text{Works Cost}} \times 100$

(b) $\frac{\text{Selling Overhead}}{\text{Works Cost}} \times 100$

(7) Depreciation apportioned on the basis of machine utilisation Ratio = 2 : 3 (as above)

Statement of Cost Production — P and Q

Particulars	Basis for Apportionment Ratio	Total Cost Rs.	Products P — 1000 Rs.	Q — 1500 Rs.
(1) Materials Cost	1 : 1	8,00,000	4,00,000	4,00,000
(2) Wages	1 : 3	1,60,000	40,000	1,20,000
Prime Cost		9,60,000	4,40,000	5,20,000
(3) Factory Overhead				
(a) Stores Expenses	as a percentage on Material cost 5%	40,000	20,000	20,000
(b) General works overhead	Direct Wages	1,44,000	36,000	1,08,000
$\frac{\text{General works overhead}}{\text{Direct Wages}} \times 100 =$ i.e. $\frac{1,44,000}{160000} \times 100 = 90\%$				
(c) Labour Welfare Exp.	Direct Wages			
$\frac{\text{Labour Welfare Exp.}}{\text{Direct Wages}} \times 100$				
$\frac{11,200}{1,60,000} \times 100 =$	7%	11,200	2,800	8,400
(d) Depreciation Plant cost 8,00,000 Depreciation = 10%	Machine utilisation 2 : 3	80,000	32,000	48,000
Works Cost		12,35,200	5,30,800	7,04,400
(4) Administrative and selling overhead	on works cost %			
$\frac{\text{Admin. and selling overhead}}{\text{Works Cost}} \times 100$				
$\frac{3,38,000}{12,35,200} \times 100 = 27.364\%$		3,38,000	1,45,248	1,92,752
Total Cost		15,73,200	6,76,048	8,97,152

Problem No. 41

A manufacturing Co. produces 500 Units of an article by incurring the following Expenses :

Raw materials	8,900
Direct Wages	5,600
Production overhead	20% on prime cost
Administrative overhead	10% on Factory cost

Selling and Distribution Expenses	860
Total Sales	25,000

The company wants to supply 100 Units of the article on special order.

Ascertain the price to be quoted, expecting the same percentage of profit as above from the following particulars :

Material cost expected	2,000
Direct Wages	1,000
Selling and Distribution Expenses	40

(K.U.D., October 1980)

Solution :

Statement of Cost and Profit

(Output — 500 Units)

Raw materials	8,900
Direct Wages	5,600
Prime Cost	14,500
Product overhead 20% on 14,500	2,900
Factory Cost	17,400
Administration Exp. 10% of 17,400	1,740
Total Cost	19,140
Selling and Distribution Exp.	860
Total Cost of Sales	20,000
Selling Price	25,000
Profit	5,000

$$\text{Per cent of Profit on Sales} = \frac{5{,}000}{25{,}000} \times 100 = 20\%$$

$$\text{Or per cent Profit on Cost} = \frac{5{,}000}{20{,}000} \times 100 = 25\%$$

Estimate of Cost and Profit

(Output 100 Units)

Raw materials	2,000
Direct Wages	1,000
Prime Cost	3,000
Production Overhead 20% on 3,000	600
Works Cost	3,600
Administrative Exp. 10% on 3,600	360
Total cost of production	3,960
Selling and Distribution Exp.	40
Total Cost of Sales	4,000
Add : Profit 25% on cost $\frac{25}{100} \times 4{,}000$	1,000
Selling Price	5,000

Problem No. 42

X Co. Ltd. manufacture two types of M and N kitchen (home) appliances. The total expenses during the year 1990 as shown by the books of the company Product M — 900 Units and Product N — 1200 Units are as under :

	Total Cost Rs.
(1) Materials	2,97,000
(2) Direct Wages	18,000
(3) Stores overhead	29,700
(4) Operating expenses of machine	6,600
(5) Depreciation	3,300
(6) Administrative and selling expenses	60,277
(7) Works general overhead	45,000
(8) Labour amenities	2,250

Other data available to you are :

	Products M	N
Direct material cost ratio	1 :	2
Driect labour cost ratio	2 :	3
Machine utilisation ratio	1 :	2

Calculate the cost of each type of products per unit giving reasons for the basis of apportionment adopted by you.

(Extra — 1)

Solution :

Calculation of Ratio for Apportionment Expenses

	Cost Ratio M	Cost Ratio N	Apportionment Ratio M	N	
(1) Material Cost Ratio	900 × 1 = 900	1200 × 2 = 2,400	900	2,400	= 3 : 8
(2) Direct Labour Cost Ratio	900 × 2 = 1,800	1200 × 3 = 3,600	1,800	3,600	= 1 : 2
(3) Stores overhead apportioned as a % on material cost	$\frac{\text{Stores overhead}}{\text{Material cost}} \times 100$	$= \frac{29,700}{2,97,000} \times 100$	= 10% on Material cost.		
(4) Machine operating Expenses : Basis Machine utilisation ratio	900 × 1 = 900	1200 × 2 = 2,400	900	2,400	= 3 : 8
(5) Depreciation machine	Machine utilisation ratio				3 : 8

	Cost Ratio M	Cost Ratio N	Apportionment Ratio M	N
(6) and (7) (a) Works General Expenses				
(b) Labour amenities Expenses : basis direct labour cost ratio			1	: 2
(8) Administrative and selling : Basis as percentage on works cost				
$= \frac{\text{Administrative and Selling Exp.}}{\text{Works overhead}} \times 100 = \frac{60,277}{4,01,850} \times 100 = 15\%$ on works cost.				

Statement of Cost of Products M and N

Particulars	Basis for Apportionment	Total Cost	Products M	N
	Ratio			
(1) Direct Material Cost	3 : 8	2,97,000	81,000	2,16,000
(2) Direct Labour	1 : 2	18,000	6,000	12,000
Prime Cost		3,15,000	87,000	2,28,000
(3) *Factory overhead :*				
(a) Stores overhead	Material cost 10%	29,700	8,100	21,600
(b) Operating of machine Exp.	Machine utilisation 3 : 8	6,600	1,800	4,800
(c) Works general overhead	Labour cost ratio 1 : 2	45,000	15,000	30,000
(d) Labour amenities	as above	2,250	750	1,500
(e) Depreciation	Machine utilisation 3 : 8	3,300	900	2,400
Works Cost		4,01,850	1,13,550	2,88,300
(4) Administrative and selling Expenses : basis as a percentage on works cost	as a percentage on works cost 15%	60,277	17,032	43,245
Cost of Sales		4,62,127	1,30,582	3,31,545
Total No. of units produced			900 Units	1200 Units
Cost per Unit			145.09	276.2875
			Rs. 145	Rs. 276

Problem No. 43

The following figures relate to an Iron Foundry for the year 1994 :

(1)	Raw materials : Opening Stock	52,500
	Purchases during the year	3,75,000
	Closing stock	37,500
(2)	Direct wages	75,000

(3) Works overhead 60% of Direct Wages.

(4) Stores overhead on materials 10% on cost of material.

(5) 10% of the castings were rejected being not up to the specification and a sum of Rs. 3,000 was realised on sale of scrap.

(6) 15% of finished casting were found to be defective in manufacturing and were rectified by the expenditure of additional works overhead charged to the extent of 20% on the proportionate to Direct wages.

The total gross output of casting during the year was 3000 tons. Find out the manufacturing cost of the saleable casting per ton.

(Extra — 2)

Solution :

Statement of Cost for the year 1994

		Output (in tons)	Total Cost (in Rs.)
Output during the Year		3000	
(1) Raw Materials : Opening stock	52,500		
Add : Purchases during the year	3,75,000		
	4,27,500		
Less : Closing stock	37,500		3,90,000
(2) Direct Wages			75,000
Prime Cost			4,65,000
(3) Works overhead 60% of Direct Wages (75,000 × 60%)			45,000
(4) Stores overhead on material cost 10% (3,90,000 × 10%)			39,000
Works Cost			5,49,000
Cost of production output in tons		3000	
Less : 10% of casting rejected : 10% of 3000 and scrap sold		300	3,000
Cost of good Units		2700	5,46,000
Additional works overhead charged on defective units 15% of 2700 = 405 rectified @ 20% of Direct Wages			2,025
Proportionate $\frac{75,000}{3000} \times 405 = 10,125 \times 20\% = 2,025$			
Manufacturing cost of saleable casting		2700	5,48,025

$$\text{Cost per ton of casting} = \frac{\text{Total cost}}{\text{Output in tons}} = \frac{5,48,025}{2700} = 202.97 \text{ or Rs. } 203$$

Problem No. 44

A B Co. Ltd. manufactures a certain product 10000 units per month. The following are the particulars of cost structure of the product :

(1)	Direct material cost per Unit	75
(2)	Direct Labour	50
(3)	Works overhead Fixed (Rs. 6,50,000)	65
	Variable	100
		290
(4)	Selling and distribution overhead	
	Fixed (2,50,000)	25
	Variable	35
		350
(5)	General Administration Fixed (5,00,000)	50
(6)	Margin of profit	100
	Selling Price	500

Due to increase in demand and consequent extension of delivery dates and dissatisfaction of customers, the management decided to provide for an output of 15000 units per month in the next year (against anticipated demand of 18000 units) which would involve a capital outlay of Rs. 8,00,000 on which interest and finance charges would amount to 12% per annum. Prepare a comparative consolidated cost statement showing anticipated margin of profit for the present output of 10000 units and the proposed output of 15000 units. Assume that the coming year there will be an alround increase of 5% in different items of expenses except fixed expenses due to proposed increase in output (if the proposal is adopted) there will be increase of 25% in fixed overheads and 20% in Fixed selling and distribution Expenses and 10% in general administration apart from the interest and financial charges. It is decided to maintain the present level of sales an increase of 2% in sales price is possible and figures should be taken for the level of production at 10000 units per month.

(Extra — 3)

Solution :

Comparative Statement of Cost and Profit

Particulars			10,000 Units Cost per unit Rs.	10,000 Units Total Cost Rs.	15,000 Units Cost per Unit Rs.	15,000 Units Total Cost Rs.
(1) Direct material cost per unit			75.00			
Add : Increase 5%			3.75			
			78.75	7,87,500	78.75	11,81,250
(2) Direct Labour		50.00				
Add : Increase 5%		2.50	52.50	5,25,000	52.50	7,87,500
Prime Cost			131.25	13,12,500	131.25	19,68,750
(3) Works overhead :						
Variable		100				
Add : Increase		5	105.00	10,50,000	105.00	15,75,000
Fixed	6,50,000		65.00	6,50,000	54.16	8,12,500
Add : Increase 25% for 15000 Units	1,62,500					
	8,12,500					
Works Cost			301.25	30,12,500	290.41	43,56,250
(4) Office overhead :			50.00	5,00,000	36.67	5,50,000
(a) General and adiministration overhead — Fixed	5,00,000					
Add : Increase of 10% only for 15000 units	50,000					
	5,50,000					
(b) Interest on capital invested Rs. 8,00,000 @ 12% p.a. 96,000 for one month 96,000 × 1/12 = 8,000 only for 15000 Units			—	—	00.59	8,000
			351.25	35,12,500	327.67	49,14,250
(5) Selling and Distribution overhead						
Variable		35.00				
Add : Increase 5%		1.75	36.75	3,67,500	36.75	5,51,250
Fixed Expenses :	2,50,000					
Add : Increase for 15000 units @ 20%	50,000		25.00	2,50,000	20.00	3,00,000
Cost of Sales			413.00	41,30,000	384.42	57,65,500
Selling Price for 10,000 Units	500					
Add : Increase 2%	10		510	51,00,000	500.00	75,00,000
for 15000 – 500	510					
Profit			97.00	9,70,000	115.58	17,34,500

Problem No. 45

XY Co. Ltd. having normal manufacturing capacity 100% is 2,00,000 units per year. The estimated cost of production is as under :

Direct Materials cost	Rs. 10 per unit
Direct Labour	Rs. 8 per unit
Subject to a minimum of Rs. 70,000 p.m.	Indirect Expenses
Fixed	4,50,000 per year.
Variable	Rs. 6 per unit.

Semi variable Rs. 1,80,000 @ 60% capacity and an additional of Rs. 60,000 for every 20% increase in capacity on any part thereof each unit of Raw material yields scrap which is sold at 20% of the cost price of material.

In 1994 the factory worked @ 60% capacity for the first 4 months an at 90% capacity for the remaining period of 8 months. During the first 4 months the selling price per unit was Rs. 40. What would be the price in the remaining period of 8 months to yield a total profit of Rs. 10,50,000 for the year.

(Extra — 4)

Solution :

Working Note

(a) (1) Capacity @ 100% per year — 2,00,000 Units.

(2) Capacity @ 60% for 4 months = 2,00,000 × 60% × 4/12 = 40,000 Units.

(3) Capacity @ 90% for 8 months = 2,00,000 × 90% × 8/12 = 1,20,000 Units.

(b) *Indirect Expenses* :

Semi variable —	Upto 60% capacity	1,80,000 p.a.
	Next 20% capacity	60,000 p.a.
	Next 20% or part thereof	60,000 p.a.
		3,00,000

Rs. 1,80,000 p.a. @ 60% capacity, @ 60% up to 4 months.
= 1,80,000 × 4/12 =60,000 for 4 months.

Per annum Rs. 3,00,000 for 8 months = 3,00,000 × 8/12 = 2,00,000 for 8 months

Statement of Cost Output @ 100% Capacity : 2,00,000 Units

Units Produced	@ 60% capacity 4 months 4000 units		@ 90% capacity 8 months 120000 units	
	Cost per Unit	Total Cost	Cost per Unit	Total Cost
(1) Direct Material Cost	10.00	4,00,000	10.00	12,00,000
Less : Scrap sold 20% of cost	2.00	80,000	2.00	2,40,000
	8.00	3,20,000	8.00	9,60,000

Units Produced	@ 60% capacity 4 months 4000 units		@ 90% capacity 8 months 120000 units	
	Cost per Unit	Total Cost	Cost per Unit	Total Cost
(2) Direct Wages Rs. 8 per unit Subject to a minimum of Rs. 70,000 p.m. (a) Units 40,000 × 8 = 3,20,000 Or 70,000 p.m for 4 months 2,80,000 (b) Units 1,20,000 × 8 = 9,60,000 Or Rs. 70,000 × 8 months 5,60,000	8.00	3,20,000	8.00	9,60,000
Prime Cost	16.00	6,40,000	16.00	19,20,000
(3) Works Overhead Indirect Expenses (i) Fixed 4,50,000 per year for 4/12 (ii) 4,50,000 × 8/12 = 3,00,000	3.75	1,50,000	2.50	3,00,000
Variable : Per Unit	6.00	2,40,000	6.00	7,20,000
(3) Semi variable Rs. 1,80,000 @ 60% (a) @ 60% — 1,80,000 × 4/12 (b) @ 90% 1,80,000 @ 60% Rs. 3,00,000 p.a. for 8 months 3,00,000 × 8/12	1.50	60,000	1.67	2,00,000
Total Cost	27.25	20,90,000	26.17	31,40,000
(a) Sales price for first 4 months sales price for the remaining 8 months would be Rs. 34.50	40.00	16,00,000	34.50	41,40,000
Profit	12.75	5,10,000	8.33	10,00,000

Note : Total profit for the year Expected in Rs.	15,10,000
Less : Profit for first 4 months	5,10,000
Desired profit for the remaining 8 months period	10,00,000
Therefore add desired profit to total cost you get .	31,40,000
Sales Price total amount *Add* : Profit	10,00,000
Sales Price	41,40,000

$$\text{Sales Price per Unit} = \frac{41,40,000}{120000} = \text{Rs. } 34.50$$

Problem No. 46

X Co. intends to submit a tender you are given the following particulars :

(1)	Stock of Finished Goods on 31-12-1970	72,800
(2)	Stock of Raw materials on 30-6-1971	35,360
(3)	Stock of Raw materials on 31-12-1970	33,280
(4)	Stock of Finished Goods on 30-6-1971	78,000
(5)	Purchases of raw materials	7,59,200
(6)	Office Overhead	70,161
(7)	Production Wages	5,16,880
(8)	Works Overhead	1,29,220
(9)	Sales of finished goods	15,39,200

From the above details find out :

(1) Percentage of works cost on cost of productive Wages.

(2) Percentage of office on cost to works cost.

(3) On the basis of the above percentage prepare a tender sheet after taking into consideration of the following particulars :

(a) Cost of Raw materials 75,000

(b) Wages 40,000

(c) Net Profit to be provided @ 15% on Selling Price.

(K.U.D., October 1979)

Solution :

Statement of Cost for Period of 6 Months from 1st Jan. 71 to 30-6-71

(1)	Raw materials : Opening stock on 31-12-70	33,280	
	Add : Purchases	7,59,200	
		7,92,480	
	Less : Closing Stock	35,360	7,57,120
(2)	Wages		5,16,880
	Prime Cost		12,74,000
(3)	Works Overhead		1,29,220
	Works Cost		14,03,220
(4)	Office Overhead		70,161
	Cost of production		14,73,381
	Add : Opening stock of Finished Goods on 31-12-1970		72,800
			15,46,181
	Less : Closing stock of Finished Goods on 30-6-71		78,000
	Cost of production of Finished Goods sold		14,68,181
	Sales of Finished Goods		15,39,200
	Profit		71,019

Working Note

Calculation of percentage :

(a) Percentage of works cost on cost of production Wages

$$\frac{\text{Works cost}}{\text{Productive Wages}} \times 100$$

$$= \frac{1,29,220}{5,16,880} \times 100 = 25\% \text{ on Wages.}$$

(b) Percentage of Office on cost to works cost

$$= \frac{\text{Office on Cost}}{\text{Works Cost}} \times 100$$

$$= \frac{70,161}{14,03,220} \times 100 = 5\% \text{ on Works cost.}$$

Statement of Cost and Profit and Tender

(1) Raw materials	75,000
(2) Wages	40,000
Prime Cost	1,15,000
(3) Works on Cost 25% on Direct Wages (40,000 × 25%)	10,000
Works Cost	1,25,000
(4) Office on Cost 5% on works cost (1,25,000 × 5%)	6,250
Cost of production	1,31,250
Add : Profit 15% on Selling Price	
If Sales Price 100 for cost Price	
Profit 15 85 1,31,250 15	
Cost Price 85	
$= 1,31,250 \times \frac{15}{85} = 23,162$	23,162
Tender Price	1,54,412

Verification :

Sales Price 1,54,412 × 15% = Rs. 23,162

(B) OPERATING COSTING

Problem No. 1

From the following information, calculate total Kms. and total passenger Kms. :

No. of Buses — 5

Days operated in the month — 25 days

Round trips made by each bus — 4

Distance between two places — 20 Kms.

Capacity of the Bus — 50 passengers.

Normal passengers travelling — 90% capacity

[K.U.D., April 1998(N)]

Solution :

(a) Total Kms. Run —

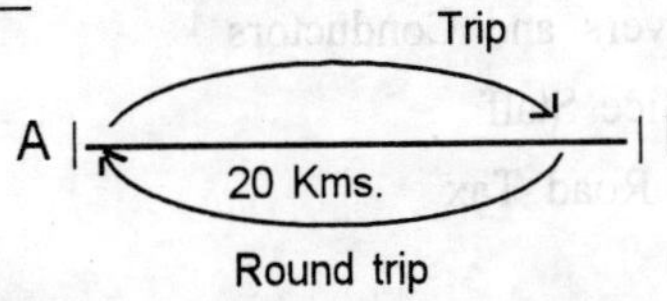

(a) No. of Buses × distance × Round Trip × No. of days

$5 \times 20 \times (2 \times 4) \times 25 = 20000$ Kms.

(b) Passenger Kms. Capacity

$5 \times 2 \times (2 \times 4) \times 25 \times (50 \times 90\%)$

$20,000 \times 45 = 9,00,000$

Passenger Kms. = 9,00,000

Ans — (a) Total Kms. — 20,000

(b) Total Passenger Kms. = 9,00,000

Problem No. 2

Gajanan Transport Company operates 4 buses between Sirsi and Mundagod. the distance between Sirsi and Mundagod is about 50 Kms. Capacity of each bus is 50 passengers, but on an average the bus runs 25% empty. All the buses run all the days of a month. Each making two round trips each day. Following particulars of expenditure are obtained from the books of the company for the month of November 1997 :

	Rs.
Wages of drivers and Conductors	24,000
Salaries of office staff	10,000
Diesel oil etc.	88,000
Repairs	10,800
Insurance and Road Tax	22,000

Depreciation	13,200
Other fixed expenses	12,000

Find out —

(a) The cost per passenger Kms.

(b) The bus fare to be charged from Sirsi to Mundagod adding a $33\frac{1}{3}$ % on bus fare.

[K.U.D., April 1998(N)]

Solution :

Statement of Operating Cost

	Rs.	Rs.
I. Fixed Expenses or Standing Charges		
Wages of Drivers and Conductors	24,000	
Salaries of Office Staff	10,000	
Insurance and Road Tax	22,000	
Depreciation	13,200	
Other fixed expenses	12,000	81,200
II. Maintenance Charges		
Repairs		10,800
III. Operating Charges		
Diesel Oil etc.		88,000
Cost per Passenger per Km Re. 0.11 paise for Total Cost		1,00,000

50 Kms. 50 × 0.11 Rs. 5.55

Add Profit $^1/_3$ or ½ Cost 2.77

Rs. 7.32

Bus fare = 7.32

Cost per Passenger Km. = $\frac{100000}{900000}$ = 0.11

Cost per Passenger Km. = 0.11.

Passenger Kms. =

No. of Buses × distance × Round Trips × Capacity × No. of days.

4 × 50 Kms × (2 × 2) × 50 × 75% × 30 = 900000 Passenger Kms.

Problem No. 3

Chaiga Power Corporation Ltd., provides the following details relating to the year ended 31st December 1996 :

	Rs.
Direct Labour	33,000
Supervisory Salaries	10,500
Lubricants and Stationery	21,000
Repairs and Maintenance	42,000
General Administration	18,000

Coal consumed ½ Kg per Kwh and the cost of Coal Rs. 7,000 per ton.

Total Units generated during the year — 58600 Kwh.

Corporation Charges depreciation @ 5% p.a. on its Assets

Consider interest @ 6% p.a. on Capital Cost of Rs. 2,00,000.

Prepare a Cost Sheet showing the Cost per Kwh. of Electricity generated.

[K.U.D., April 1998(O)]

Solution :

Statement of Operating Cost Power Generated 58600 Kwh

	Total Cost Rs.	Cost per Kwh. Rs.
I. Fixed Expenses or Standing Charges :		
(1) Supervisory Salaries	10,500	
(2) General Administration	18,000	
(3) Depreciation on Capital Cost @ 5% p.a. on its assets - Rs. 2,00,000	10,000	
(4) Interest on Capital - Rs. 2,00,000 @ 6% on Rs. 2,00,000	12,000	
	50,500	
Cost per Kwh. $\frac{50500}{58600}$		0.867
II. Operating Costs :		
Coal consumed ½ Kg. per Kwh $\frac{58600}{2}$ 29300 Kgs.		
29300 Kgs. per ton 1000 Kgs. = 29.30 Ton cost Rs. 7000 per ton		
29.30 × 7000 =	2,05,100	
Direct Labour	33,000	
Lubricant and Stationary	21,000	
Repairs & Maintenance $\frac{3,01,100}{58600}$ Cost per Kwh	42,000	5.138
	3,01,100	6.005

Cost per Kwh Rs. 6.00

Problem No. 4

Jagadamba Transport Company runs four buses between Hubli and Sirsi. The distance between Hubli and Sirsi is about 100 Km. The seating capacity of each bus is 40 passengers.

The following particulars are obtained from the Books of the Company for the month of November 1996 :

		Rs.
(1)	Salary of 4 drivers — each per month	3,000
(2)	Salary of 4 conductors — each per month	2,000
(3)	Diesel cost at Re. 1 per Km.	
(4)	Repairs and Maintenance Re. 0.20 per Km.	
(5)	Cost each bus - Rs. 4,50,000	
(6)	Life of each bus — 5 years	
(7)	Interest and other charges	22,500
(8)	Commission to agents who bring Passengers — Re. 1 per passenger per trip	
(9)	Miscellaneous expenses	6,700

Actual passengers carried were 75% of the total seating capacity. All the buses run for 30 days. Each bus makes one round trip per day.

Find out cost per passenger Km.

How much he should charge to a passenger for a trip, from Sirsi to Hubli, when he wants to earn a profit of 20% on the bus fare.

[K.U.D., October 1997(N)]

Solution :

Working Note

Calculation of passenger Km.

No. of Buses × Distance × No. of Trips × No. of Days × Capacity × % capacity used

4 × 100 × 2 × 30 × 40 × 75% = 7,20,000 Passenger Km.

Kilometres Run — in a month of 30 days

No. of Buses × Distance × Trips × No. of days

4 × 100 × 2 × 30 = 24000 Km. run in a month.

Statement of operating cost for the month.

No. of Buses — 4. Distance – 100 Km. No. of Trips 2. No. of days 30.

Total No. of Km. run — 4 × 100 × 2 × 30 = 24000 Km.

	Total Cost
I. Standing Charges :	Rs.
Salary — Drivers — 4 × 3,000 each per month	12,000
Salary — Conductors — 4 × 2,000 each per month	8,000
Interest and other charges	22,500
II. Miscellaneous Expenses	6,700
Depreciation : $\frac{\text{Cost}}{\text{Life}}$ $\frac{4,50,000}{5}$ each Bus 90,000 $\frac{1}{12}$ × PM No. of buses = 7,500 × 4	30,000
Total Standing Charges	79,200
III. Operating expenses :	
Diesel oil cost at Re. 1 P.M. for 24000 Km.	24,000
Repairs and Maintenances Rs. 0.20 P. Km. × 24000 Km.	4,800
Total Cost	1,08,000

Total cost for the month — Rs. 1,08,000

Total Passenger Km. 7,20,000

Cost per passenger Km. = $\frac{1,08,000}{7,20,000}$ = 0.15 Paise

Re. 0.15 paise per passenger Km.

Cost per Passenger Km. Re. 0.15 paise

Distance from Hubli to Sirsi — 100 Km.

Cost Price per Passenger — 0.15 paise × 100 =	Rs. 15
Add Commission to agent per Passenger	1
Cost per Passenger	Rs. 16
Add Profit 20% on bus fare or 25% on Cost - 25% of 16 =	4
From Hubli to Sirsi — Bus fare per passenger	Rs. 20

Problem No. 5

Shyamalal Transport Company supplies the following details in respect of a Vehicle :

	Rs.
Cost of Vehicle	1,50,000
Road Licence fee per year	600
Insurance Charges per year	300

Garage Rent per year	1,200
Drivers wages per month	1,500
Cost of Diesel oil per litre	8
Kilometre per litre	16 Km.
Proportionate Charges for tyre and maintenance	0.20 paise
Estimated Life	300000 Km.
Estimated annual Km.	30000

Ignore interest on capital

Calculate Cost per Km.

[K.U.D., October 1997(O)]

Solution :

Statement of Operating Cost of Vehicle

	Total Cost per year	Per Km.
	Rs.	Rs. Ps.
I. Standing Charges		
Road Licence fee per year	600	
Insurance Charges per year	300	
Garage Rent per year	1,200	
Drivers wages Rs. 1,500 pm × 12	18,000	
Total Cost	20,100	
Estimated annual Km. 30000		
Cost per Km. = $\frac{20,100}{30000}$ =		0.67
II. Maintenances Charges		
Proportionate Charges for tyre and Maintenance		0.20
III. Operating Charges :		
Diesel oil - Cost - Rs. 8 per litre		
Per Litre - 16 Km. - cost per Km $\frac{8}{16}$ =		0.50
Depreciation = $\frac{\text{Cost}}{\text{Life}} = \frac{1,50,000}{300,000}$ = 0.50 × 30000 = 15,000		0.50
Cost per Km.		1.87

Problem No. 6

Sai Plaza is star class Hotel.

Find out the total Room Days for the year 1996 from the details given below :

(i) Single Bed Suits — 50; Double Bed Suits — 20

(ii) Normal occupancy in Summer :

Single Bed Suit — 80%; Double Bed Suits 50%

(iii) November, December, January and February are winter months

(iv) Occupancy in winter :

Single Bed Suit — 40%, Double Bed Suits — 20%

[K.U.D., April 1997(N)]

Solution :

No. of Suits in Hotel :

(i) Single Bed Suit - 50 (ii) Double Bed Suits - 20

Summer Period : March, April, May & June = 4 months.

Winter Period : November, December, January & February - 4 months

Rainy Seasons-period : Remaining of 4 months

(Remaining 4 months rainy season period occupancy is not given. It is presumed that summer period occupancy rate is continued.)

Occupancy - Room days :

(a)	In Summer Period — 4 months — 30 days in a month		
	Single Bed Suit — 50 × 80% = 40 × 120 days =	4,800	Roomdays
	Double Bed Suits — 20 × 50% = 10 × 120 days =	1,200	6,000
(b)	Winter Period — 4 months - 30 days in a month = 120 days		
	Single bed Suit - 50 × 40% = 20 × 120 = days = 2400 days		
	Double Bed Suits - 20 × 20% = 4 × 120	480	2,880
(c)	Rainy Season Period — 4 months = 4 × 30 = 120 days		
	(It is pressumed that summer period occupancy rate is continued)		
	Single Bed Suit — 50 × 80% = 40 × 120 days =	4,800	
	Double Bed Suits — 20 × 50% = 10 × 120 days =	1,200	6,000
	Total Room days		14,880

Problem No. 7

Gadag City Bus Service Company runs the following fleet of buses within the limits of Gadag city :

10 Buses of 50 passenger carrying capacity.

15 Buses of 40 passenger carrying capacity.

On an average each bus makes 10 trips per day covering a distance of 8 Km. in each trip and 75% of the seats are occupied. The annual records show that 5 buses are generally required to be kept away from roads each day for repairs.

The following expenses were incurred by the company during August 1994 :

(1) Garage Rent, Rates and Insurance	3,000	
(2) Road and Vehicle Tax	1,800	
(3) Salary : (i) Chief Operating Manager	1,500	
(ii) 3 Assistant Managers	800	each
(iii) 4 Supervisors	400	each
(iv) 25 Drivers	240	each
(v) 30 Cleaners	100	each
(vi) Office Staff	4,000	
(4) Consumable Stores	4,500	
(5) Petrol and Diesel	24,500	
(6) Lubricants	5,000	
(7) Replacement of Tyres and tubes	1,750	
(8) Gas and Electricity	350	
(9) Miscellaneous Expenses	500	
(10) Repairs	3,000	
(11) Depreciation	6,500	

Prepare operating cost and show the cost per passenger Km.

(K.U.D., April 1996)

Solution :

Statement of Operating Cost for the month of August 1994

Particulars	Rs.	Rs.
(I) *Standing Charges*		
Garage Rent, Rates and Insurance		3,000
Road and Vehicle Tax		1,800
Salary : (1) Chief operating manager	1,500	
(2) Asst. Managers 3 × 800	2,400	
(3) Supervisors 4 × 400	1,600	

Particulars	Rs.	Rs.
(4) Drivers 25 × 240	6,000	
(5) Cleaners 30 × 100	3,000	
(6) Office staff	4,000	18,500
Depreciation		6,500
Total Standing Charges		29,800
(II) *Repairs and Maintenance*		
Replacement of tyres and tubes	1,750	
Gas and Electricity	350	
Miscellaneous Expenses	500	
Repairs	3,000	5,600
(III) *Operating Charges*		
Consumable stores	4,500	
Petrol and Diesel	24,500	
Lubricants	5,000	34,000
Total Expenses		69,400

Working Note

Calculations of Passenger Km.

No. of Bus × C. Distance × No. of trips × No. of days × Capacity

(a) 10 × 8 × 10 × 31 × (50 × 75%) = 9,30,000

(b) 15 × 8 × 10 × 31 × (40 × 75%) = 11,16,000

Total Passenger Km. 20,46,000

Less : $\frac{5 \times 20,46,000}{25}$ = 20% of total passenger Km. laid off for repairs 4,09,200

Total passenger Km. 16,36,800

$$\text{Cost per Passenger Km.} = \frac{\text{Total Cost}}{\text{Passenger Km.}} = \frac{69,400}{16,36,800} = 0.0423998 \text{ Or } 0.0424$$

Problem No. 8

The following information relates to Vasavi Talkies for the year ending 31-12-93 :

(a) Salaries :

(i) One Manager Rs. 1,600 p.m.

(ii) 10 Gate Keepers Rs. 400 p.m. each

(iii) 2 Operators Rs. 800 p.m. each

(iv) 4 Clerks Rs. 500 p.m. each

(b) Electricity Bill — Rs. 23,310
(c) Carbon — Rs. 14,470
(d) Sundry Expenses Rs. 10,850
(e) Advertisement Rs. 69,420
(f) Office Expenses Rs. 36,000
(g) Hire Print Rs. 2,81,400

The premises are valued at Rs. 12,00,000 and its estimated life is 15 years. Projector and Equipment cost Rs. 6,40,000 on which 10% depreciation is to be charged. Daily 3 shows are run throughout the year. The total capacity is 625 seats which are divided into 3 classes as follows :

Janata Circle — 250 seats.
Deluxe Circle — 250 seats.
Lords Circle — 125 seats.

(i) 20% of total seats remain vacant.
(ii) Weightage to be given to 3 classes in the ratio 1:2:3.

Determine the rates for each class if the management expects 30% return on gross proceeds. Ignore entertainment tax.

(K.U.D., October 1995)

Solution :

Statement of Operating Cost of Vasavi Talkies for the year ended 31-12-1993

Particulars		Rs.	Rs.
Fixed Cost :			
(a) Salary :			
(i) Manager	1,600 × 12	19,200	
(ii) Gate Keepers	10 × 400 × 12	48,000	
(iii) Operators	2 × 800 × 12	19,200	
(iv) Clerks	4 × 500 × 12	24,000	
Office Expenses		36,000	
Depreciation on Machinery	6,40,000 × 10%	64,000	
Building (Life)	$\frac{12,00,000}{15}$	80,000	2,90,000
(b) Variable Cost (Operating Cost) :			
Electricity Bill		23,310	
Carbon		14,470	
Sundry Expenses		10,850	
Hire Print		2,81,400	
Advertisement		69,420	
			3,99,450
Total			6,89,850

Calculation of Man shows :

(1) Capacity used — 80% only 20% vacant

Janata Circle —	250 × 80%	= 200 seats.
Deluxe Circle —	250 × 80%	= 200 seats.
Lords Circle —	125 × 80%	= 100 seats.

(2) Total No. of shows during the year = 365 × 3 = 1095 no. of shows.

(3) Man shows during the Year :

Class	No. of seats × No. of shows × weightage	
Janata Circle	= 200 × 1095 × 1	= 2,19,000
Deluxe Circle	= 200 × 1095 × 2	= 4,38,000
Lords Circle	= 100 × 1095 × 3	= 3,28,500
Total Man shows		9,85,500

$$\text{Cost per man show} = \frac{\text{Total Cost}}{\text{Total Man show}}$$

$$= \frac{6,89,850}{9,85,500}$$

$$= 0.70 \text{ Paise}$$

Add 30% on Gross Proceed

$$\frac{30}{70} \times .70 = .30 \text{ Ps} \qquad \frac{0.30 \text{ Ps.}}{1.00 \text{ Re.}}$$

Rate to be charged with due weightage :

Jana Circle	Re. 1 × 1 = Re. 1
Deluxe Circle	Re. 1 × 2 = Rs. 2
Lords Circle	Re. 1 × 3 = Rs. 3

Problem No. 9

Madhuri Transport Co. runs a mini bus with a capacity of 25 seats. It holds licence to operate between two cities which are 25 Kms. apart. It runs mini bus for 30 days in a month and on an average 80% of seating capacity is utilised. The bus makes two round trips each day.

The bus costs Rs. 2,40,000 with 10-year life.

Other expenses per month are as under :

Driver's Salary per month	800
Conductor's Salary per month	600
Manager's Salary per month	900
Cleaner's Salary per month	500
Garage rent per month	300
Rent, Lighting etc. per month	500

Repairs and maintenance per month	400
Annual Tax	3,600
Diesel and oil (Re. 0.70 per Km.)	

The driver and conductor are given 10% of fare as commission to be divided equally between the two. The margin of profit expected was 20% of fare. Fix fare per passenger Km.

(K.U.D., April 1995)

Solution :

(Operating Cost of Transport Passenger)

Calculation of Total Passenger Kms.

Distance × No. of Trips × Capacity × No. of days.

25 Kms × 2 × 2 × 25 (80/100) × 30

= 100 × 20 × 30 = 60,000 Passenger Kms.

Total Kms = 25 × 2 × 2 × 30 = 100 × 30 = 3,000 Kms run.

Total Passenger Kms 60,000 — Total Kms run 3000

I. *Standing Charges :*		
Manager's Salary per month	900	
Garage Rent per month	300	
Rent Lighting a/c per month	500	
Annual Tax (3,600 × 1/12)	300	
Depreciation $\left[\frac{\text{Cost}}{\text{Life}} \quad \frac{2,40,000}{10} = \frac{24,000}{12}\right]$	2,000	4,000
II. *Operating Cost :*		
Driver's salary p.m.	800	
Conductor's salary p.m.	600	
Cleaner's salary p.m.	500	
Diesel and Oil (0.70 × 3000)	2,100	
Repairs and maintenance	400	4,400
Total Cost		8,400
Add : 10% Commission		1,200
20% Profit		2,400
Total takings		12,000

Fare to be charged per passenger Km. = $\frac{12,000}{60,000}$ = 0.20 Paise.

(2) *Calculation of Commission* : If Total takings 100

Driver's & Conductor commission 10% of 100	10	
Margin of Profit 20%	20	30
		70

Cost before Commission & Profit :

Commission & Profit for 8,400 = 8,400 × 30/70 = 3,600

Commission 10% 1,200 = Driver — 600 and Conductor — 600

20% Profit = Rs. 2,400.

Problem No. 10

Channagiri Transport Company supplies the following details in respect of a truck of 5 ton capacity :

Cost of Truck	6,20,000	
Scrap value at the end of the life	20,000	
Diesel, Oil, grease	50	per trip each way
Repairs and maintenance	2,500	per month
Driver's wage	5,000	per month
Cleaner's wage	2,000	per month
Insurance	6,000	per year
Tax	3,000	per year
General supervision charges	15,000	per year

Estimated life of truck is 10 years. The truck carries goods to and from Bijapur city covering a distance of 50 miles each way.

On outward trip freight is available to the extent of full capacity and on return 60% of capacity.

Assuming that the truck runs on an averages 25 days a month work out :

(a) Operating cost per ton-mile.

(b) Rate per ton per trip that the company should charge if a profit of 50% on freightage is to be earned.

(K.U.D., October 1994)

Solution :

Statement of Operating Cost of a Truck

(I) *Standing Charges* :

(1) Insurance $6000 \times \frac{1}{12} =$	500
(2) Taxes $3,000 \times \frac{1}{12} =$	250
(3) General supervision charges $15,000 \times \frac{1}{12}$	1,250

(4) Depreciation	$= \dfrac{\text{Cost} - \text{Scrap}}{\text{Life}}$	
	$= \dfrac{6,20,000 - 20,000}{10}$	
	$= 60,000 \times \dfrac{1}{12}$	5,000
(5) Driver's wage		5,000
(6) Cleaner's wage		2,000
		14,000

Ton Mile : Onward Trip — 5 × 50 × 25 = 6,250
Return Trip 5 × 60/100 × 50 × 25 = 3,950
Ton Mile = 10,000

Cost per ton Mile = $\dfrac{14,000}{10,000}$		1.40
(II) *Maintenances Charges* :		
Repairs & Maintenance	$\dfrac{2,500}{10,000}$ =	0.25
(III) *Operating Charges* :		
Diesel, Oil, grease etc. — 50 × 2 × 25 = 2,500		0.25
	Cost per ton Mile	1.90

Working Note

(1) Total ton Mileage
Onward Trip — 5 × 50 × 25 = 6,250
Return — 5 × 60/100 × 50 × 25 = 3,750
Ton Mile 10,000

(2) Freightage to be charged :
Operating cost — per ton Mile — Rs. 1.90
Operating cost per ton per trip — 1.90 × 50 = Rs. 95
Add : Profit 50% on freightage (100% on cost) Rs. 95
Freightage per ton per trip Rs. 190

Problem No. 11

Good Luck Transporters charge Rs. 300 per tonne for a 5 tonne lorry load from Gadag to Belgaum. The charge for return trip is Rs. 280 per tonne. In the month of December 1992, K.A. 26-7722 has made 10 outward journeys with full load (from Gadag to Belgaum) out of which 3 tonnes were unloaded at Hubli twice in the month. It returned without any load once only from Hubli. The expenses are as follows :

(i) Annual standing charges — Rs. 96,000
(ii) Annual maintenance charges — Rs. 48,000
(iii) Monthly running charges — Rs. 9,250.

You are asked to find out the cost per tonne-Kilometre and also the profit in the month of December 1992 assuming that no concession is made delivery at the intermediate stages.

Following is the additional data :

Distance between Hubli and Gadag — 60 Kms.

Distance between Belgaum and Gadag — 160 Kms.

The vehicle carried a load of 8 tons 5 times in the month while returning from Belgaum but was once caught by the police and fined Rs. 5,000.

(K.U.D., April 1994)

Solution : (Calculation of Ton-Km.)

From Gadag 60 Kms to Hubli 100 Kms Belgaum

Total 160 Kms.

Lorry capacity — 5 tons

Onward trips — 10 full load from Gadag to Belgaum = 160 Kms.

of Which 3 tons — Unloaded at Hubli — 60 Kms 2 times.

On return without any load once in a month from Hubli.

Gross — Ton-Km	= 5 ton × 160 Kms × 10 times × 2	
	= 16000 Kms	
Less : Actual load not carried		
(i) Load Hubli to Belgaum = 10 Kms × 3 ton × 2 times = 600		
(ii) *Less* : Returned without load (Once in a month) from Hubli to Gadag = 5 tons × 6 Kms		300
		900
(16000 – 900 = 15100)		15100
Add : Extra Load : While return from Belgaum to Gadag.		
Extra Load = (8 – 5) 3 tons		
160 Kms × 3 tons × 5 times =		2400
Total ton Kms		17500

Alternatively : Calculation of Ton Km.

Onward Trip — from Gadag to Belgaum :		
5 Trip × 8 tons × 160 Kms	=	6,400 Kms
2 Trip × 5 tons × 60 Kms	=	600 Kms
2 Trip × 2 tons × 100	=	400
3 tons unloaded at Hubli		7,400 Kms
Return Trip from Belgaum to Gadag :		
5 Trip × 8 tons × 160 Kms	=	6,400
4 Trip × 5 tons × 160	=	3,200
1 Trip × 5 ton × 100	=	500
		10,100 Kms
Total onward Trip	=	7400 Kms
Return Trip	=	10100 Kms
		17500 Kms.

Statement of Cost (Operating Cost Per Month)

		Rs.
Standing charges $\frac{96,000}{12}$	=	8,000
Maintenance charges = $\frac{48,000}{12}$	=	4,000
Monthly running charges		9,250
Total Cost		21,250

Total ton Kms = 17500

Cost per ton = $\frac{21,250}{17500}$ = Rs. 1.214

Profit for the month

	Rs.
Freight Collected :	
(i) From Gadag to Belgaum Rs. 300 per ton — for 5 tons × 10 times = 300 × 5 × 10 =	15,000
(ii) Return trip Belgaum to Gadag Rs. 280 × per ton for 5 ton × 10 times 280 × 5 × 10	14,000
(iii) Additional freight from Belgaum to Gadag for Extra Load 3 ton × 5 times × Rs. 280 per ton 3 × 5 × 280	4,200
Total	33,200
Less : Cost as above	21,250
	11,950
Less : Abnormal Loss Fine	5,000
Net Profit	6,950

Note : Fine of Rs. 5,000 is not a regular expenses. Therefore it is not included in total cost.

Problem No. 12

A Transport company owns 4 buses having 40 passenger seats each. It has the licence to play between two towns which have 50 Kms. distance each bus makes one to and from trip day on all 30 days in a month. On an average 75% seats are filled :

The estimated expenses for a month are as follows :

	Rs.
Salary of Drivers, Conductors etc	12,000
Office salary	5,000
Diesel	20,000
Depreciation	13,000
Repairs and maintenance	5,000
Insurance, Tax and Garage Rent	8,000
Interest and other expenses	10,000
Resale value of tyres	1,000

Calculate the cost per passenger Kilometre.

(K.U.D., October 1993)

Solution :

Operating Cost of 4 Buses — Cost per Passenger Km.

	Rs.	Total Cost
(I) *Standing Charges*		
(1) Salary of Drivers, Conductors etc.	12,000	
(2) Office Salary	5,000	
(3) Insurance, Taxes and Garage Rent	8,000	
(4) Depreciation	13,000	
(5) Interest and other Expenses	10,000	
Total	48,000	
Less : Resale of Tyres	1,000	47,000
(II) Repairs and maintenance		5,000
(III) Operating Charges (Diesel)		20,000
Total Cost		72,000

Total Cost 72,000

Total Passenger Km $\frac{72,000}{3,60,000}$

Cost per Passenger Km = 0.20 Ps per passenger.

Passenger Km = No. of buses × No. of Trip × Distance × No. of days × Capacity
= 4 × 1 × (50 × 2) × 30 × (40 × 75/100)
= 4 × 100 × 30 × 30 = 3,60,000 Passenger Km.

Problem No. 13

Karnataka State Employees Association has constructed a building at Bijapur with 20 rooms having two beds in each room for providing lodging facilities to the Government employees visiting the city.

The following expenses have been incurred during the year 1991 :

(a) Manager's Salary — Rs. 500 per month.

(b) Salary of 4 attenders — Rs. 300 per month each.
(c) Light Bill — Rs. 6,000
(d) Fuel (For supply of hot water) — Rs. 4,400
(e) Washing charges of bedsheets etc. Rs. 3,800
(f) Depreciation on : Building Rs. 3,00,000 at 5% p.a.
Furniture Rs. 1,00,000 at 10% p.a.
Bedsheets Rs. 25,000 at 20% p.a.
(g) White washing and maintenance → Rs. 16,000
(h) Printing and Stationery — Rs. 3,000
(i) Administrative charges — Rs. 8,000.

A canteen is run on contract basis and the sum received from the contractor is Rs. 4,000. The visitors are classified in to two categories viz. (i) Government servants; (ii) Others. The visitors other than Government employees are charged at double rate. The occupancy ratio is about 80% for the year. Calculate the rent per bed per day assuming that the visitors of both the classes are in equal ratio.

(K.U.D., April 1993)

Solution : (Lodging)

Operating Costing

		Rs.	
(I) *Fixed Expenses :*			
(a) Manager's Salary = 500 × 12		6,000	
(b) Salary of attenders — 4 × 300 × 12		14,400	
(c) Light Bill		6,000	
(d) Printing & Stationery		3,000	
(e) Administrative charges		8,000	
(f) Depreciation :			
Building = 3,00,000 × 5% =	15,000		
Furniture = 1,00,000 × 10%	10,000		
Badsheet = 25,000 × 20%	5,000	30,000	
Total Fixed Cost			67,400
(II) *Maintenance Expenses :*			
(d) Fuel (for hot-water supply)		4,400	
(e) Washing charges		3,800	
(g) White washing		16,000	24,200
Total Cost			91,600
Less : Cash received from canteen contractor			4,000
(Net) Total Cost of operating			87,600

$$\text{Cost per day per visitor} = \frac{87{,}600}{17520} = \text{Rs. } 5$$

Cost per bed per day = Rs. 5 of Govt. Employee.

Others double Rs. 5 × 2 = Rs. 10

Calculation of Guest day :

No. of rooms × No. of beds = 20 × 2 = 40

Occupancy = 80% = 40 × 80% × 365 = 11680 Guest days.

$$\text{Ratio} = \text{visitors} = \text{Equal} : \frac{11680}{2} = 5840 \text{ Govt. Employees}$$

= 2 × 5840 Others.

= 11680 Others.

Total = 5840 + 11680 = 17520.

$$\text{Charges} = 1 : 2 = \text{Cost per day} = \frac{\text{Total Cost}}{\text{No. of Guest}}$$

$$= \frac{87{,}600}{17520}$$

= Rs. 5.

Problem No. 14

From the following information of a Transport Company calculate the cost per Km :

Cost of Bus	Rs.	50,000
Kms run (annual)	Kms	30000
Licence fee (annual)	Rs.	1,500
Insurance (annual)	Rs.	1,400
Garage Rent (annual)	Rs.	1,000
Supervision (annual)	Rs.	2,000
Drivers wage per hour	Rs.	5
Diesel cost per Litre	Rs.	6
Kms per Litre	Kms	10
Repairs and Maintenance per Km	Rs.	2
Tyre Cost per Km	Re.	1
Estimated life of Bus	Kms	100000

Charges 10% interest p.a. the cost of Bus.

The bus runs 50 Kms per hour on an average.

(K.U.D., October 1992)

Solution :

Operating Cost of Transport of Bus

Particulars	per annum Rs.	per Km Rs.
Fixed Charges (Annual) :		
Road Licence fee	1,500	
Insurance	1,400	
Garage Rent	1,000	
Supervision	2,000	
Drivers wages Rs. 5 per hour 50 Kms for 30000 Kms i.e., $5 \times \frac{30,000}{50} =$	3,000	
Interest @ 10% on cost of Bus Rs. 50,000	5,000	
Depreciation $\frac{\text{Cost}}{\text{Life}} = \frac{50,000}{1,00,000} \times 30000$	15,000	
Total	28,900	
$\frac{\text{Total fixed charges}}{\text{No. of Kms run}} = \frac{28,900}{30000} =$		0.96
Variable Charges : or Operating Cost		
Repairs & Maintenance		2.00
Tyre cost		1.00
Diesel per litre Rs. 6 for 1 litre = 10 Kms		0.60
Operating Cost Rs. 4.56 or 4.60		4.56

Problem No. 15

A Transport Company owns two buses of X and Y. From the following information calculate cost per kilometre :

Particulars		Bus-X	Bus-Y
(1) Cost of Bus	Rs.	50,000	30,000
(2) Kms run (annual)	Kms	30000	12000
(3) Licence fees (annual)	Rs.	1,500	1,500
(4) Insurance fee (annual)	Rs.	1,400	1,000
(5) Garage Rent (annual)	Rs.	1,000	500
(6) Supervision (annual)	Rs.	2,000	2,000
(7) Driver's Wages per hour	Rs.	5	5
(8) Diesel Cost per Litre	Rs.	6	6
(9) Kms per Litre	Kms	10	10
(10) Repairs and Maintenance per Km	Kms	2	2

Particulars		Bus-X	Bus-Y
(11) Tyre cost per Km	Re.	1	0.60
(12) Estimated life of Bus	Kms	100000	75000

Charges 10% interest per annum on cost of Bus. The buses run 50 Kms per hour on an average.

(K.U.D., April 1992)

Solution :

Operating Cost of Buses

Particulars	Bus-X	Bus-Y
(I) *Standing Charges*	Rs.	Rs.
(1) Licence fees	1,500	1,500
(2) Insurance	1,400	1,000
(3) Garage Rent	1,000	500
(4) Supervisior	2,000	2,000
(5) Interest on Capital @ 10% on cost		
Bus-X 50,000 × 10%	5,000	
Bus-Y 30,000 × 10%		3,000
	10,900	8,000
Cost per Km :		
Bus-X = $\frac{10,900}{30,000}$ =	0.363	
Bus-Y = $\frac{8,000}{12,000}$ =		0.667
(II) *Repairs & Maintenance* (per Km)	2.00	3.00
(III) *Operating Cost*		
Drivers Wages per hour Rs. 5 running 50 Kms		
$\therefore$ 1 Km = $\frac{5}{50}$ = 1/10	0.10	0.10
Diesel Cost per litre Rs. 6		
Bus-X = $\frac{6}{10}$ = 0.60	0.60	
Bus-Y = $\frac{6}{15}$ = 0.40		0.40
Tyre Cost per Km	1.00	0.40
Depreciation = $\frac{\text{Cost}}{\text{Life}}$		
Bus-X = $\frac{50,000}{100000}$ =	0.50	
Bus-Y = $\frac{30,000}{75000}$ =		0.40
	4.563	5.167
Cost per Km	4.56	5.17

Problem No. 16

The data given related to "Metro talkies" for the year ending 31st March 1988 :

(1) Salaries :

(i) One Manager	Rs.	800	per month
(ii) 10 Gate Keepers	Rs.	200	per month
(iii) 2 Operators	Rs.	400	per month
(iv) 4 Clerks	Rs.	250	per month

(2) Electricity and Oil	Rs.	11,655
(3) Carbon	Rs.	7,235
(4) Miscellaneous Expenditure	Rs.	5,425
(5) Advertisement	Rs.	34,710
(6) Administrative expenses	Rs.	18,000
(7) Hire for print	Rs.	1,40,700

The premises are valued Rs. 6,00,000 and its estimated life is 15 years. Projects and equipment cost is Rs. 3,20,000 on which 10% depreciation is to be charged.

Daily 3 shows are run throughout the year. Total capacity is 625 seats which are divided into three classes as follows :

Janata Circle	250 seats
Sunman Circle	250 seats
Lords Circle	125 seats

Ascertain cost per man-show assuming that :

(i) 20% of the total seats remain vacant and

(ii) Weightage to be given to the three classes in the ratio 1:2:3.

Determine the rates for each class if the management expects 30% return on gross proceeds. Ignore entertainment tax.

(K.U.D., October 1990)

Solution : Operating Costing on Cinema House

Statement of Cost for the year 1988

	Amount Rs.	Total Amount Rs.
(I) *Standing Charges/Fixed Expenses*		
(a) Salaries — Manager 1 × Rs. 800 PM × 12 months	9600	
Gate Keepers 10 × Rs. 200 PM × 12 months	24000	
Operators — 2 × Rs. 400 PM × 12 months	9600	
Clerks — 4 × Rs. 250 PM × 12 months	12000	
	55200	
(b) Administrative overhead		

		Amount Rs.	Total Amount Rs.
(c) Depreciation :		18,000	
On premises Rs. $\frac{6,00,000}{15 \text{ years}}$ =	40,000		
Projector & Equipments — 320000 @ 10%	32,000	72,000	1,45,200
(II) *Maintenance Costs or Variable Costs*			
(1) Electricity and oil		11,655	
(2) Carbon		7,235	
(3) Miscellaneous Expenditure		5,425	
(4) Advertisement		34,710	
(5) Hire for Print		1,40,700	1,99,725
Total Costs			3,44,925

Total Costs for the year Rs. 3,44,925

Working Note

Total Capacity — 100%
Less : vacancy — 20%
Capacity utilised 80% only

Total No. of Shows during period
365 days × 3 = 1095 Shows

Total No. of Seats

(1) Janata Circle — 250 × 80% = 200
(2) Sanman Circle — 250 × 80% = 200
(3) Lords Circle — 125 × 80% = 100
500 seats

Calculation of Man-Shows

Class	No. of seats	No. of shows during year	Weightage	Man-shows
(1) Janata Circle	200	1095	1	2,19,000
(2) Sanman Circle	200	1095	2	4,38,000
(3) Lords Circle	100	1095	3	3,28,500
			Total	9,85,500

Cost per man-show :

Total Cost — Rs. 3,44,925 Re.

Total No. of Man-Shows 985500

$$\text{Cost per Man-show} = \frac{3,44,925}{985500} = 0.35$$

Add : Profit 30% on Gross

$$\frac{30}{70} \times 0.35 = 0.15$$

Re. 0.50

Rate to be charged per man-show is Re. 0.50

Rate with due weightage to different classes :

(1) Janata Circle —	Re. 0.50 × 1 = Re. 0.50
(2) Sanman Circle	Re. 0.50 × 2 = Re. 1.00
(3) Lords Circle	Re. 0.50 × 3 = Rs. 1.50

Problem No. 17

The city municipality arranges for the removal of garbage by means motor vehicle. The following vehicles are maintained :

No. of Vehicles	Specifications
20	5 tons Lorries
30	4 tons Lorries
50	3 tons Lorries
40	2 tons Lorries

On an average each Lorry makes six trips a day and in each trip lorries cover an average distance of 5 Km. Each Lorry carried garbage weighting only 60% of the capacity taking an annual average. 20% of the Lorries are laid for repairs every day.

The conservancy work is carried daily. Following are the month charges incurred on conservancy transport.

Items of Expenses	Monthly charges
(1) Salary of the superintendent (Motor vehicle Dept.)	2,000
(2) Salaries of the three transport foremen Rs. 500 each	
(3) Wages of drivers Rs. 150 each for 140 drivers.	
(4) Wages of mazdoor (Labour) Rs. 75 for 280 mazdoors.	
(5) Consumable stores	16,000
(6) Petrol	60,000
(7) Lubricants	15,000
(8) Replacement of Tyres, tubes and other part & accessories	5,000
(9) Garage Rent and Rates (Adjust the books of muncipality)	3,000
(10) Gas and Electric charges	1,000
(11) Miscellaneous charges	12,000

There is a repair workshop attached to the motor vehicles department which also carries out repairs for the office cars and other vans and vehicles. 50% of the superintendent stipulated salary is debited to workshop and the remaining stipulated charges to be borne by conveyance transport department and the services of the workshops are Rs. 10,000 a month assuming that the month consists of 30 days. Calculate cost per ton for removal of garbage.

(Mysore, April 1994 & C.A. Final)

Solution : (Calculation of Ton Kms for the month)

(1) Ton Km	= No. of Lorries × capacity in ton × No. of Trips × distance × days.		
	= 20 × (5 × 60%) 6 × 5 × 30 =		
	= 20 × 3 × 6 × 5 × 30	54,000	
	Less : Lay off for repairs 20%	10,800	43,200
(2) Ton Km	= 30 × (4 × 60%) 6 × 5 × 30		
	= 30 × 2.40 × 6 × 5 × 30	64,800	
	Less : Lay off for repairs 20%	12,960	51,840
(3) Ton Km	= 50 × (3 × 60%) 6 × 5 × 30		
	= 50 × 1.80 × 6 × 5 × 30	81,000	
	Less : Lay off 20%	16,200	64,800
(4) Ton Km	= 40 × (2 × 60%) 6 × 5 × 30		
	= 40 × 1.20 × 6 × 5 × 30	43,200	
	Less : Lay off for Repairs 20%	8,640	34,560
	Total Ton Kms		1,94,400

Statement of Operating Cost of Lorries
(Total Cost per month)

	Rs.	
(I) *Standing Charges :*		
(1) Salaries of superintendent 2000 × 50% only	1,000	
(2) Salaries of three transport foremen (3 × 500)	1,500	
(3) Wages of Drivers (150 × 140)	21,000	
(4) Wages of mazdoors (75 × 280)	21,000	
(5) Garage Rent	3,000	
Total Standing Charges		47,500
(II) *Repairs & Maintenance Charges :*		
(1) Workshop repairs and servicing charges	10,000	
(2) Replacement of tyres and tubes and other Exp.	5,000	
(3) Gas and Electric charges	1,000	16,000
(III) *Operating Charges :*		
(1) Consumable stores	16,000	

	Rs.	Rs.
(2) Petrol	60,000	
(3) Lubricants	15,000	
(4) Misc. Expenses	12,000	1,03,000
Total Expenses		1,66,500

$$\frac{\text{Total Expenses for the month}}{\text{Total ton Kms for the month}} = \frac{1,66,500}{194400}$$

Cost per ton Km = 0.85648

Or Approximately = 0.86 Ps per lorry Km.

Problem No. 18

Work out appropriate cost sheet from the unit cost per passenger mile for the year 1980-81 for Passenger buses run by a Transport company. Following are the figures extracted from the books of the company.

(1) 5 Passenger buses costing Rs. 5,00,000, Rs. 1,20,000, Rs. 45,000, Rs. 55,000 and Rs. 80,000 respectively.
Yearly Depreciation of vehicles 20% of the cost.
(2) Annual repairs and Maintenance and spare parts are 80% of Depreciation.
(3) Wages of 10 Drivers @ Rs. 100 each per month.
(4) Wages of 20 cleaners @ Rs. 50 each per month.
(5) Yearly rate of Interest @ 4% on capital.
(6) Rent of six garages Rs. 50 each per month.
(7) Directors fees @ Rs. 400 p.m.
(8) Office and E.S.I. Rs. 1,000 p.m.
(9) Licence and Taxes @ Rs. 1000 for every six months.
(10) Realisation by sale of old Tyres and Tubes @ Rs. 3,200 for six months.
(11) 900 Passengers were carried over 1600 Mile during the year.

[K.U.D., October 1990 (Modified), I.C.W.A. Final]

Solution :

Working Note No. 1

(1) Depreciation 20% of cost per annum.

Buses	Cost of Buses
1	50,000
2	1,20,000
3	45,000
4	55,000
5	80,000
Total Cost of Buses	3,50,000

Depreciation 20% on 3,50,000 = 70,000

(2) Repairing and Maintenance 80% of Depreciation

70,000 × 80% = 56,000

Statement of Operating Cost of 5 Buses

(I) *Standing Charges* :		
(1) Wages of Drivers 10 × 100 = 1,000 × 12	12,000	
(2) Wages of cleaners 20 × 50 = 1,000 × 12	12,000	
(3) Interest on capital @ 4% p.a on 3,50,000	14,000	
(4) Rent of six garages 6 × 50 p.m. = 300 × 12	3,600	
(5) Directors fees Rs. 400 p.m. × 12	4,800	
(6) Office and E.S.I. Rs. 1,000 p.m. × 12	12,000	
(7) Licence fee Taxes Rs. 1,000 for six months (1,000 × 2)	2,000	
(8) Depreciation p.a.	70,000	
Total Standing Charges		1,30,400
(II) *Repairs and Maintenance* : 80% of Depreciation		56,000
Total Cost		1,86,400
Less : Sale of Tyre and Tubes 3,200 × 2 =		6,400
Total cost for the year		1,80,000

Total cost = Rs. 1,80,000

Total No. of Passenger Mile 1440000

$\therefore$ Cost per Passenger Mile = $\frac{180000}{1440000}$ = Re. 0.125

Working Note No. 2

Calculation of total Passenger mile per year 900 × 1600 = 1440000

Problem No. 19

A bus runs between Mysore and Bangalore for 30 days in a month covering a distance of 150 Kms. each way making a round trip daily. The normal capacity of the bus is 60 Passengers. It is generally full. Calculate the total Passenger Kms.

(Mysore, B.B.M., 1992)

Solution :

Calculations of Passenger Kms

Mysore to Bangalore

Passenger Kms. = No. of buses × Distance × Trip × Capacity × No. of days.

= 1 × 150 × 2 × 60 × 30

= 540000 Passenger Kms.

Problem No. 20

A transport company is running 5 Buses between two cities which are 40 Kms. apart, seating capacity of each bus is 50 passengers. Actual passengers carried were 80% of the seating capacity. Each bus made one trip per day. All the buses run all the days of the month. Find out the total passenger Kms. covered during the month of November 1991.

(Mysore, April 1992)

Solution :

Calculation of total passenger Kms.

Passenger Kms. = No. of Buses × Distance × Trips × Capacity × No. of days.
= 5 × 40 Kms. × 2 × (50 × 80% C.C. × 30 days)
= 400 × 40 × 30
= 480000 Passenger Kms.

Problem No. 21

Calculate the cost per Km. of a vehicle from the following data :

(1)	Value of vehicle	15,000
(2)	Road licence fee per year	500
(3)	Insurance charges per year	100
(4)	Garage Rent per year	600
(5)	Drivers wages per month	200
(6)	Cost of petrol per litre	0.80 Ps.
(7)	Kilometre per litre — 8 Kms.	
(8)	Proportionate charges for tyre and maintenance per Km.	0.20 Ps.
(9)	Estimated life (in Kms.) 150000	
(10)	Estimated annual Kms. 6000	
(11)	Ignore interest on capital.	

(I.C.W.A., Inter)

Solution :

Statement of Operating Cost (Annual Kms. 6000) .

(I) *Standing Charges* :		
(1) Road Licence Fees	500	
(2) Insurance	100	
(3) Garage Rent	600	
(4) Drivers wages — 200 × 12	2,400	
Total Standing Charges	3,600	
Cost per Km. = $\frac{3,600}{6000}$		0.60

(II) *Repairs and Maintenance :*

(i) Charges for tyres 0.20

(ii) Depreciation = $\frac{\text{Cost}}{\text{Life in Km.}} = \frac{15,000}{150000}$ 0.10

(III) *Operating Charges :*

Cost of petrol per Litre 0.80 Ps. $\frac{0.80}{8}$ = 0.10

Km. per Litre 8 Kms.

Total operating cost per Km. 1.00

Problem No. 22

Shri Gundu Rao own a bus which runs between Mysore and Bangalore 10 days in a month covering a distance of 300 Kms. in a round trip. It halts at Mysore every day. The bus goes another 10 days in a month towards Hassan covering a distance of 240 Kms. in a round trip.

For the rest of 4 days in a month it runs in the local city covering a distance of 40 Kms. daily.

The normal capacity of the bus is 50 Passengers. It generally 10% vacant during its Bangalore trip. 80% full during Hassan trip and always full during the city. Calculate the total passenger Kms. per month.

(Mysore, April 1992)

Solution :

Calculations of Total Passenger Kms.

(1) From Mysore (Distance 300 Kms. Round trip) to Bangalore		
= No. of buses × Distance × No. of days × Capacity		
= 1 × 300 × 10 × 50		
= 1,50,000 Kms.		
Less : 15,000 Vacant 10%		1,35,000
(2) Mysore to Hassan		
80% capacity 1 × 240 × 10 × 50 =	1,20,000	
Less : 20% Vacant	24,000	96,000
(3) Local city 1 × 40 × 4 × 50 =		8,000
Total passenger Kms.		2,39,000

Problem No. 23

Hotel Fidalgo, Goa provides economy Lodging facilities. From the following information, ascertain the Rent to be charged in a suitable statement from :

(1) Single Rooms — 20
Double Rooms — 30

(2) Annual Expenses Summary :

(a) Salary : (i) Manager @ Rs. 1,200 p.m.
(ii) Accountant Rs. 1,000 p.m.
(iii) Two Receptionists Rs. 800 p.m. each.
(iv) Two clerks @ Rs. 500 p.m. each
(v) Ten attenders @ Rs. 300 p.m. each.

(b) Lighting and Heating Rs. 30,000.

(c) Interior decoration and garden upkeep Rs. 22,500.

(d) Licence fees Rs. 14,070.

(e) Repairs and Maintenance Rs. 18,000.

(f) Depreciation on Building @ Rs. 5% on 10,00,000.

(g) Depreciation on Furnishing @ 10% on Rs. 2,50,000.

(h) Miscellaneous Expenses Rs. 20,000.

(i) Insurance and water Rs. 22,000.

(3) Occupancy ratio :

(a) During summer (30 Weeks) :
Single Rooms 100% Double Rooms 90%

(b) During winter (22 Weeks) :
Single Rooms and Double Rooms 50%

(4) Profit Margin 20% on cost.

(5) For the purpose of fixing rentals having regard to the space and facilities the Double room shall be considered 1½ of Single room.

(K.U.D., April 1990)

Solution :

Statement of Cost — Hotel & Lodging

Fixed Expenses :		
(1) Salary :		
(a) Manager Rs. 1,200 p.m. × 12	14,400	
(b) Accountant 1,000 × 12	12,000	
(c) Receptionist 2 × 800 × 12	19,200	
(d) Clerks 2 × 500 × 12	12,000	
(e) Attenders 10 × 300 × 12	36,000	93,600
(2) Lighting and Heating		30,000
(3) Interior decoration and garden upkeep		22,500
(4) Licence Fee		14,070
(5) Repairs and maintenance		18,000

(6) Depreciation on Building @ 5% on 10,00,000	50,000
(7) Depreciation on Furnishing @ 10% on 2,50,000	25,000
(8) Miscellaneous Expenses	20,000
(9) Insurance & Water	22,000
	2,95,170
Add : Expected Profit 20% on cost	59,034
Total	3,54,204

Calculation :

Computation of Guest days :	Single Room	Double Room 90%
Summer (30 Weeks)	30 × 7 × 20 = 4,200	30 × 7 × 27 = 5,670
Winter (22 Weeks)	22 × 7 × 10 = 1,540	22 × 7 × 15 = 2,310
Guest Days	5,740	7,980

Double Rooms considered 1½ time of Single Rooms.

Guest days for Double Room in terms of their equivalent Single Room.

Guest days will be : Double Room Guest days 7,980 × 1½ = 7,980 × 3/2

= 11970 Guest days.

Total Guest days = 5,740 + 11,970 = 17,710 Guest days.

Rental to be charged per guest for Single Room.

$$= \frac{\text{Total Amount}}{\text{Guest days}} = \frac{3{,}54{,}204}{17710} = \text{Rs. } 20$$

Rent for Single Room — Rs. 20

Double Room 20 × 3/2 = 20 + 10 = 30

(one and halftimes) 1½ = 3/2.

Problem No. 24

A person owns a bus which runs between Bangalore and Mysore and back for 10 days in a month. The distance between Bangalore and Mysore is 130 Kms. The bus completes the trip from Bangalore and Mysore and will be back on the same day. The bus goes Nandi Hills for another 10 days. The distance between Bangalore and Nandi Hills is 60 Kms. This trip is also completed on the same day.

For the rest 4 days of its operation it runs in the Local city daily distance covered is 30 Kms. Calculate the charge to be made by the person when he went to earn a profit of 25% on his taking.

Other informations are as follows :

(1) Cost of the bus	3,00,000
(2) Depreciation 20% p.a.	20% p.a.
(3) Salary of clerk	250 p.m.
(4) Insurance	7,500 p.a.

(5) Diesel consumption 10 Kms. per litre costing of Rs. 4 per litre.
(6) Token Tax 6,000 p.a.
(7) Repairs & Maintenance 2,500 p.m.
Lubricant Rs. 10 per 100 Kms.
(8) Permit fees 1,500 p.m.
(9) Normal passengers 50 persons

The bus generally occupies 90% of the capacity.

(Bangalore, October 1990)

Solution :

Statement of Operating Cost of Bus Per Month

Particulars	Total Cost per Month Rs.	Cost per Km. Re.
(I) *Standing Charges*		
(1) Depreciation 20% p.a. on 3,00,000 = 60,000 × 1/12	5,000	
(2) Salary of clerk	250	
(3) Insurance 7,500 × 1/12	625	
(4) Token 6,000 × 1/12	500	
(5) Permit Fee	1,500	
Total Standing Charges	7,875	
Km. run':		
(1) Bangalore to Mysore = 2 × 130 × 10 = 2,600		
(2) Bangalore to Nandi = 2 × 60 × 10 = 1,200		
(3) Bangalore local city = 30 × 4 120		Cost per Km.
3,920		= 0.699
(II) *Repairs and Maintenance*	2,500	*Add*
Lubricant Rs. 10 per 100 Kms.	392	Profit 25%
(III) *Operating Cost*		on taking or
Diesel consumption 10 Kms. per litre	1,568	1/3 on cost
cost per Litre Rs. 4		1/3 × 0.699
Cost per Km. = $\frac{4}{10}$ = 0.40 (3,920)		= 0.233
		Charge to
	12,335	be made 0.932
Cost per Km. = $\frac{\text{Cost}}{\text{Kms.}} = \frac{12,335}{176400} =$	0.0699263	0.0699 or 0.07

Calculation of Kms. run =No. of buses × Trip × Distance × No. of days × Capacity

(1) Bangalore to Mysore	= 1 × 2 × 130 × 10 × (50 × 90%)	1,17,000
(2) Bangalore to Nandi	= 1 × 2 × 60 × 10 × (50 × 90%)	54,000
(3) Bangalore Local City	= 1 × 1 × 30 × 4 × (50 × 90%)	5,400
Total passenger Kms.		1,76,400

Problem No. 25

A transport company having a fleet of trunks to carry waste materials. The company has the following capacity Vehicles :

No. of Vehicles	Capacity
40	5 Tons
20	4 Tons
50	3 Tons

On an average each Lorry makes five trips a day and in each trip covers an average distance of five Km. The Lorry carries only 75% of its capacity. 20% of the Lorries are laid off for repair every day.

Following charges incurred during the month :

	Rs.
Salary of the supervisor	2,000 per month
Salary of foremen — 3	600 per month each
Wages of drivers	200 each for 110 drivers
Wages of cleaners	100 each for 220 cleaners
Consumable stores	16,000
Diesel	60,000
Lubricants	14,000
Replacement of tyre	6,000
Garage Rent	3,000
Electricity charges	1,000
Other Expenses	12,000

During the month old tubes and tyres were auctioned for Rs. 3,000 assuming that a month consist of 30 days.

Calculate cost per ton Km.

(M'lore, April 1990)

Solution :

Statement of Operating Cost of Lorries for the month

(I) *Standing Charges*		
(1) Salary of supervisor	2,000	
(2) Salary of foremen (3 × 600)	1,800	
(3) Wages of Drivers (200 × 110)	22,000	
(4) Wages of cleaners (100 × 220)	22,000	
(5) Garage Rent	3,000	
(6) Electricity Charges	1,000	
(7) Other Expenses	12,000	
Total Standing Charges	63,800	63,800

(II) *Repairs and Maintenance*		
Replacement of Tyres	6,000	
Less : Sale of old Tubes and Tyres	–3,000	3,000
(III) *Operating Expenses*		
Consumable stores	16,000	
Diesel	60,000	
Lubricant	14,000	90,000
Total Cost		1,56,800

$$\text{Cost per ton Km.} = \frac{\text{Total cost}}{\text{Ton Km.}}$$

$$= \frac{1,56;800}{193500} = 0.81 \text{ Ps.}$$ 0.81 paise

Working Note

Calculation of ton Km.

= No. of Lorries × Trips × Distance × days × Lodging capacity × per cent Loading

(1) 40 × 5 × 5 × 30 × 5 × 75%	=	1,12,500
(2) 20 × 5 × 5 × 30 × 4 × 75%	=	45,000
(3) 50 × 5 × 5 × 30 × 3 × 75%	=	84,375
Total ton Km.		2,41,875
Less : Laid off for repairs		48,375
Ton per Km.		1,93,500

Problem No. 26

A person owns a mini Bus which runs between Bangalore and Mysore and back for 10 days in a month. The distance between Bangalore and Mysore is 150 Kms. The bus completes the trip from Bangalore to Mysore and will be back; goes to Nandi Hills for another 10 days in a month. The distance between Bangalore and Nandi Hills is 60 Kms. This trip is also completed on the same day.

For the rest of 5 days in a month it operates in Local City daily covering a distance of 30 Kms. The mini Bus capacity is 25 seats, generally it is running in full capacity in local city area and Bangalore-Mysore and Bangalore-Nandi Hills also.

Calculate the charges to be made by the owners of mini Bus when he wants to earn a profit of 25% on his taking.

Other information are as follows :

	Rs.
(1) Cost of Bus	3,00,000
(2) Depreciation 20% p.a.	
(3) Salary of a clerk	1,250 p.m.
(4) Driver's salary	1,750 p.m.
(5) Conductor's salary	1,250 p.m.

(6) Insurance per Quarter 4,000

(7) Lubricants Rs. 10 per 100 Kms.

(8) Diesel consumption 10 Kms. per litre cost Rs. 6 per litre.

(9) Token tax per annum 9,000

(10) Repairs and Maintenance 3,000 p.m.

(11) Permit fees 2,500 p.m.

[Bangalore, October 1990 (Modified)]

Solution :

Statement of Operating Cost of Mini Bus for the Month

		Total Cost per month
(I) *Standing Charges*		
(1) Depreciation 20% p.a. on 3,00,000 = 60,000 × 1/12 =	5,000	
(2) Salary of clerk	1,250	
(3) Driver's salary	1,750	
(4) Conductor's Salary	1,250	
(5) Insurance per Quarter Rs. 4,000 × 1/3	1,250	
(6) Token tax Rs. 9,000 p.a. for 1 month	750	
(7) Permit tax	2,500	
Total Standing Charges		13,750
(II) *Repairs and Maintenance* :		3,000
(III) *Operating Charges* :		
Lubricants Rs. 10 for 10 Kms. 4,350		435
Diesel consumption 10 Kms. per Litre cost per litre Rs. 6 for 4,350 Kms.		2,610
Total Cost		19,795

$$\text{Cost per passenger Km} = \frac{\text{Total cost}}{\text{Total passenger Kms}} = \frac{19{,}795}{108750} = 0.18\text{ Ps.}$$

Cost per passenger Km. = 0.18 Ps.

Profit 25% on taking on

Or 1/3 on cost $\frac{0.06\text{ Ps.}}{0.24\text{ Ps.}}$ Charge to per passenger = 0.25 Ps. Km.

Working Note

(I) *Calculations of Passenger Kms.* :

(1)	Bangalore to Mysore = 1 × 2 × 150 × 10 × 25	75,000 Kms.
(2)	Bangalore to Nandi Hills and Back = 1 × 2 × 60 × 10 × 25	30,000 Kms.
(3)	Bangalore Local City = 1 × 1 × 30 × 5 × 25	3,750 Kms.
	Total Passenger Kms.	1,08,750

(II) *Calculation Total running Kms.*

(1)	From Bangalore to Mysore = 1 × 2 × 150 × 10	3,000
(2)	From Bangalore to Nandi Hills = 1 × 2 × 60 × 10	1,200
(3)	Bangalore City (Local) = 1 × 30 × 5	150
		4,350

(III) *Calculation of Profit and takings*

Cost per passenger Km.	0.18
Profit 25% on takings Or 1/3 on cost	0.06
Passenger 24 Paise Km.	0.24 Or 0.25 Ps.

If 100 is taking

25 Profit

75 Cost. Therefore 1/3 on cost.

Problem No. 27

Mr. Sohan Singh has started transport business with a fleet of 10 taxies. The varies expenses incurred by him are as follows :

(1)	Cost of each taxi	75,000
(2)	Salary of office staff	1,500 p.m.
(3)	Salary of garage staff	2,000 p.m.
(4)	Rent of garage	1,000 p.m.
(5)	Drivers salary per taxi	400 p.m.
(6)	Road taxes and repairs per taxi	2,160 p.a.
(7)	Insurance premium @ 4% p.a. on cost	
(8)	The life of taxi estimated 3,00,000 Kms and at the end of which is estimated to be sold at Rs. 15,000 the taxi runs on an average 4000 Kms. per month.	
(9)	Petrol consumption is 9 Kms per litre costing of Rs. 9 per litre.	
(10)	Oil and other sundry expenses amounted to cost Rs. 10 for 100 Kms.	

Calculate the cost of running a taxi per Km. If the Line charges is Rs. 2 per Km find out the profit Mr. Sohan Singh may expect the first year of operation.

(Gulbarga, October 1990)

Solution :

Statement of Operating Cost Monthly running 4000 Kms

	Total cost per Month	Cost per Km.
(I) *Standing Charges*		
(1) Salary of office staff 1,500 × 1/10	150	
(2) Salary of garage staff 2,000 × 1/10	200	
(3) Rent of garage 1,000 × 1/10	100	
(4) Driver's salary per taxi per month	400	
(5) Road taxes and repairs per taxi 2,160 × 1/12	180	
(6) Insurance premium 4% of 75,000 = 3,000 × 1/12	250	
(7) Depreciation : $\frac{\text{Cost} - \text{Scrap}}{\text{Life}}$		
$\frac{75{,}000 - 15{,}000}{3{,}00{,}000} = \frac{60{,}000}{3{,}00{,}000} \times 4{,}000$	800	
Total Standing Charges	2,080	
Running Kms per month = 4,000 Kms		
Cost per Km = $\frac{2{,}080}{4{,}000} = 0.52$		0.52
(II) *Operating Cost*		
Petrol consumption 9 Km per litre		
Cost per litre Rs. 9		
Cost of petrol per Km. = $\frac{9}{9} = 1.00$		1.00
Oil and other sundry expenses cost Rs. 10 per 100 Kms		
Cost per Km. $\frac{10}{100} = 0.10$		0.10
Operating cost per Km		1.62

Profit earned :

Hire charges	2.00
Cost per Km	1.62
Profit per Km	Re. 0.38

Problem No. 28

Dharwad Transport Company runs fleet of Buses as follows :

No. of Buses	Carrying Capacity
10	60 Passengers each
·5	40 Passengers each

Each Bus makes four trips in a day covering a distance of 5 Kms per Trip. On an average 75% of seats are occupied in each Trip. Assuming that the company operates fleet 25 days in a month, ascertain operating cost per passenger Kilometre taking in to account following further information :

(1)	Wages of 15 Drivers @	250 p.m each
(2)	Diesel	4,375 p.m.
(3)	Repairs	2,500 p.m
(4)	Tyres and Tubes	1,375 p.m.
(5)	Depreciation	90,000 p.a.
(6)	Garage Rent	9,000 p.a.
(7)	Interest on capital	12,000 p.a.
(8)	General supervision	750 p.m.
(9)	Oil, Grease, cotton waste etc.	500 p.m.

(K.U.D., October 1989)

Solution :

Statement of Operating Cost of Transport

	Cost per Month	Total	Cost per Passenger Km.
(I) *Fixed Expenses*			
(1) Drivers wages 15 × 250	3,750		
(2) Garrage Rent 9,000 × 1/12	750		
(3) Interest on capital 12,000 × 1/12	1,000		
(4) General Supervision	750	6,250	0.0104
(II) *Maintenances*			
(1) Repairs	2,500		
(2) Tyres & Tubes	1,375	3,875	0.00645
(III) *Running Charges*			
(1) Diesel	4,375		
(2) Depreciation 90,000 × 1/12	7,500		
(3) Oil, Grease, cotton waste etc.	500	12,375	0.0206
Total cost		22,500	0.0375

Calculation of passengers Km. : = No. of bus × No. of trip × No. of day × C. distance × Km. Trip

(I) = (10 × 4 × 25) (60 × 75%) × 5 × 2 = 1000 × 45 × 10 = 4,50,000

(II) = (5 × 4 × 25) (40 × 75%) × 5 × 2 = 500 × 30 × 10 = 1,50,000

Passenger Km. 6,00,000

$$= \text{Cost per Passenger Km.} = \frac{22{,}500}{6{,}00{,}000} = 0.0375.$$

Problem No. 29

Murali Travels is a Transporting company is running a fleet of six Buses between two towns 75 Kms. apart. Seating capacity of each bus is 40 passengers. The following particulars are available for the month of November 1988 :

(1)	Wages of Drivers and Conductors and cleaners	14,400
(2)	Salaries of office and supervisory staff	6,000
(3)	Diesel and other Oil	41,280
(4)	Repairs and maintenance	4,800
(5)	Taxes and Insurance	9,600
(6)	Depreciation	15,600
(7)	Interest and other charges	12,000

Actual passenger carried on an average 80% of the seating capacity. All the buses ran on all the days of the month. Each bus made one trip per day covering a distance of 150 Kms.

Find out the cost per Passenger Km.

(Gulbarga, April 1989)

Solution :

Working Note

Calculation of Passenger Kilometre

Passenger Km. = No. of Bus × Distance × No. of trips × days × Capacity
= 6 × 150 × 1 × 30 × (40 × 80%)
= 864000 (8,64,000 Passenger Km.)

Statement of Operating Cost of 6 Buses for the month

	Total Cost per Month	Total Cost Rs.
(I) *Standing Charges*		
(1) Wages of Drivers, conductors and cleaners	14,400	
(2) Salaries of office and supervisory staff	6,000	
(3) Taxes and Insurance	9,600	
(4) Depreciation	15,600	
(5) Interest and other charges	12,000	
Total Standing Charges	57,600	57,600

	Total Cost per Month	Total Cost Rs.
(II) *Repairs and Maintenance*	4,800	4,800
(III) *Operating Cost*		
Diesel and other Oil	41,280	41,280
Total Cost		1,03,680

Total Cost of operating Buses 1,03,680

Total Passenger Km. 8,64,000

$$\text{Per Passenger Km.} = \frac{1,03,680}{8,64,000} = \text{Re. } 0.12$$

Problem No. 30

A Bus with a capacity of 50 passengers makes a return trip from Belgaum to Hubli Via Dharwar per day. This distance between Belgaum to Dharwar is 75 Kms. (approx.) and between Dharwar to Hubli 25 Kms. (approx.) during onward journey the bus is full of capacity upto Dharwar but only 60% full between Dharwar-Hubli on the other hand on return trip it is full to capacity from Hubli to Dharwar but carries 80% of capacity between Dharwar-Belgaum.

The following information is provided to you :

(1)	The bus runs on an average 25 effective days in a month	
(2)	Cost of the Bus	2,50,000
(3)	Estimated Scrap value after 10 years of effective Life	70,000
(4)	Road Licence tax etc. per year	5,000
(5)	Insurance charges per year	1,000
(6)	Garage Rent per year	6,000
(7)	Drivers and conductors wages per month	2,000
(8)	Cost of Diesel per Litre	4
(9)	Kilometre per Litre	8 Kms.
(10)	Proportionate charges of tyres and maintenance Re. 0.20 Km.	

(K.U.D., October 1988)

Solution :

Working Note 1

Calculation of passenger Km. = From Belgaum to Dharwar — 75 Kms.
From Dharwar to Hubli — 25 Kms.
= No. of trip × Distance × Capacity × days.

(a) Onward Journey :		
Belaum to Dharwar	= 1 × 75 × 50 × 100% × 25 =	93,750
Dharwar to Hubli	= 1 × 25 × 50 × 60% × 25 =	18,750
(b) On Return Journey :		
Hubli to Dharwar	= 1 × 25 × 50 × 100% × 25 =	31,250
Dharwar to Belgaum	= 1 × 75 × 50 × 80% × 25 =	75,000
	Passenger Km.	2,18,750

Statement of Operating Cost for the month

(I) *Standing Charges* :		
(1) Road Licence, taxes per year 5,000 × 1/12	417	
(2) Insurance charges per year 1,000 × 1/12	83	
(3) Garage Rent per year 6,000 × 1/12	500	
(4) Drivers and conductors wages per month	2,000	
(5) Depreciation $= \frac{\text{Cost} - \text{Scrap}}{\text{Life in Year}} = \frac{2,50,000 - 70,000}{10}$		
$= \frac{1,80,000}{10} = 18,000 \times 1/12$	1,500	
Total Standing Charges	4,500	4,500
(II) *Repairs and Maintenance* : Re. 0.20 Ps per Km.		1,000
Total No. of Kms = 5,000 × 0.20 = 1,000		
(III) *Operating Cost* :		
Diesel = cost per Litre Rs. 4		
per Litre 8 Kms.		
Cost per Km. 4/8 = 0.50 Ps.		
Total Kms 5,000 × 0.50 = 2,500		2,500
Total cost per month		8,000

$$\frac{\text{Total cost per month}}{\text{No. of passenger Kms.}} = \frac{8,000}{2,18,750} = 0.3657 \quad \text{Or } 0.366$$

Working Note 2

Total Kms. running = 100 × 2 × 25 = 5,000 Kms.

Problem No. 31

The Karnataka Roadways has a fleet of 20 Trucks. Each Truck covers a distance of 300 Kms per day and the carrying capacity of the truck is 10 tons. On an average loading is available for the trucks at 90% capacity effective working days in a month are excluding the days of lay off on account of repairs which are estimated to be 5%. Following are the particulars :

(1) Cost of a Truck	1,60,000
(2) Estimated useful Life — 5 years.	
(3) Salary to Driver and Cleaner per truck per month	1,000
(4) Re-sale value after 5 years	60,000
(5) Taxes and Insurance per truck per year	2,500
(6) Maintenance, Repairs etc. for all trucks per year	24,000

(7) Tyres & Tubes etc. per truck per year 7,200

(8) Diesel Oil etc. per 10 Kms. Rs. 40.

Calculate cost of operating Truck per ton Km.

(K.U.D., October 1987)

Solution :

Statement of Operating Cost of Truck

(I) *Fixed Expenses :*		
Salary to Drivers and Cleaners Rs. 1,000 × 12	12,000	
Taxes and Insurance	2,500	
Depreciation = $\frac{\text{Cost} - \text{Scrap}}{\text{Life}} = \frac{1,60,000 - 60,000}{5}$	20,000	34,500
(II) *Maintenance :*		
Repairs & Maintenance $\frac{24,000}{20}$	1,200	
Tyres & Tubes per truck	7,200	8,400
(III) *Operating Expenses :*		
Direct Oil etc. per 100 Kms. Rs. 40		
Per day 300 Kms. per 100 Kms. Rs. 40		
For 300 Kms. Rs. 120		
Total Kms. run 300 for 25 days = 7,500 × 12		
90,000 – 5% (90,000 – 4,500 = 85,500 × 40%)	34,200	34,200
Total Cost		77,100

Total Ton Km. = (300 Kms. × 1) × (25 days × 12) × (10 × 90%)

= 300 × 300 × 9 = 8,10,000

Less : Lay off 5% 40,500

Effective total ton Km. 7,69,500

$$\text{Cost per ton Km.} = \frac{\text{Total Cost}}{\text{Ton Km}} = \frac{77,100}{7,69,500} = 10 \text{ cost per ton Km.}$$

Problem No. 32

Speed Transport Company supplies the following details in respect of a 10 ton capacity Vehicle :

(1) Cost of Truck 1,80,000

(2) Estimated Life 10 Years

(3) Diesel Oil, Grease etc. 15 each way

(4) Repairs and maintenance 500 p.m.

(5)	Driver's wage	800 p.m.
(6)	Cleaner's wage	400 p.m.
(7)	Insurance	2,500 p.a.
(8)	Tax	2,400 p.a.
(9)	General supervising charges	9,600 p.a.

The truck carries goods to and from a city covering a distance of 50 Miles each way in one day. On outward trip freight is available to the extract of full capacity and on return 20% capacity.

Assuming the truck run on an average of 25 days in month work out :

(a) Operating cost per ton Mile.

(b) Rate per ton that the company should charge if a profit of 50% on freightage is to be earned.

(Gulbarga, October 1987)

Solution :

Working Note

Calculation of ton Mile :

On Outward trip	= No. of Bus × Trip × distance × capacity × days	
	= 1 × 1 × 50 × 10 × 25	12,500
On Return trip	= 1 × 1 × 50 × (10 × 20%) × 25	2,500
	Total Ton Mile	15,000

Statement of Opening Cost of Truck for the month

(I) *Standing Charges :*		
(1) Drivers Wages	800	
(2) Cleaners Wages	400	
(3) Insurance per year 2,500 × 1/12	208	
(4) Taxes per year 2,400 × 1/12	200	
(5) General supervising charges per year 9,600 × 1/12	800	
(6) Depreciation $\frac{\text{Cost}}{\text{Life}} = \frac{1,80,000}{10 \text{ Year}}$ = 18,000 × 1/12	1,500	
Total Standing Charges		3,908
(II) *Repairs and Maintenance*		500
(III) *Operating Charges*		
Diesel Oil, Grease etc. Rs. 15 each		
Onward return No. of days		
2 × 25 × 15		750
Total Cost per month		5,158

Total Cost = Rs. 5,158

Total Ton Mile 15000

$$\text{Cost per ton Mile} = \frac{\text{Cost}}{\text{Ton Mile}} = \frac{5,158}{15000} = 0.343866 \text{ or } 0.344$$

Freightage to be charged operating cost per ton mile Re.	0.344
Profit 50% on freightage or 100% on cost	0.344
Freightage per ton per Mile	0.688

Freight for 50 Mile = 50 × 0.688 = Rs. 34.40 per ton for 50 Mile.

Problem No. 33

Find out the cost per unit of Electricity generated for the month of April 1985 :

(1) Fuel coal 1200 tons @ Rs. 11 per ton
Coke 500 tons @ Rs. 15 per ton
Handling charges of fuel at 50 Ps per ton
Ash removal charges 160 tons @ 0.25 Ps per ton

(2) Cost of water pumped from the river was 1,60,000 Gallons at 37½ Ps per 1000 Gallons.

(3) Oil 50 gallons @ Rs. 4 per gallon

(4) Credit on account of :
(a) Sale of Ash 280 tons @ Re. 0.25 Ps per ton
(b) Cost of steam supplied to the manufacturing shops 3000 units @ Rs. 10 per 1000 Units.

(5) Salaries and wages of staff per month Rs. 1,025.

(6) Depreciation : Boiler @ 6% per annum on cost of Rs. 20,000
Generator @ 4% p.a. on the cost of Rs. 1,20,000.
Building @ 1% p.a. on the cost of Rs. 12,000.

(7) The monthly technical supervision charges amounted to Rs. 985.
Total units generated 97,000 Units.
Loss due to leakage 1,000 Units.

(K.U.D., April 1986)

Solution :

Statement of Operating Cost of Power House

Electricity Generated	97,000 Units
Less : Loss due to leakage	1,000 Units
	96,000 Units

(I) *Steam Production :*

(1)	Coal 1200 Tons @ Rs. 11 per ton	13,200	
	Coke 500 × 15	7,500	
	Handling charges of the fuel 1200 + 500 = 1700 × .50	850	
	Ash removal charges 160 × 0.25	40	21,590
(2)	Water Pumping charges $\frac{1,60,000}{1,000} \times 0.375 = 60$		60
(3)	Oil 50 gallons @ Rs. 4 @ 50 × 4 =		200
(4)	Depreciation :		
	Boiler cost 1,20,000 @ 6% p.a. 1,200 × 1/12	100	
	Building cost 12,000 × 1% = 120 × 1/12	10	110
	Steam Production Total cost		21,590
Less : credits :	(1) Sale of Ash 280 × 0.25 Ps	70	
	(2) Cost of steam $\frac{30,000}{1,000} \times 10$	300	– 370
			21,590

(II) *Electricity Generate*

(1)	Salaries and Wages of staff per month	1,025	
(2)	Technical supervision charges	985	
(3)	Depreciation generator @ 4% on 1,20,000 4,800 × 1/12	400	2,410
	Total Cost		24,000

Total cost Rs. 24,000

Total units generated 96,000

Per unit $= \frac{24,000}{96,000} =$ Re. 0.25

Cost per unit Re. 0.25 Ps.

Problem No. 34

Shri Ram Transport runs Lorries to carry sulphate from Gokak to Savalatti. The distance between Gokak and Savalatti is 25 Miles. Lorries do not get return load. The Lorries employed in the month of June 1983 were :

	5 ton Lorries	21
	4 ton Lorries	15
	3 ton Lorries	20
Total Tons	12 Total Lorries	56

The work is carried on daily but 20% of Lorries are laid down for repairs every day. The following are the expenses in the month of June 1983 :

(1)	Petrol	60,000
(2)	Oil	8,100
(3)	Driver salary — 80 Driver (per Month each Driver)	300
(4)	Coolies 150 (per month each Coolie)	200
(5)	Manager's Salary	1,500 p.m.
(6)	Machines remuneration (3 Machines — each per month)	300 p.m.
(7)	Garage Rent	2,000
(8)	Maintenance	2,000
(9)	Replacement of Tyres	12,000
(10)	Workshop overhead (applicable to Vehicle Dept.)	7,050
(11)	Other Expenses	5,200
(12)	Depreciation	10,000

One-half of the Manager salary is to be debited to this Dept (Motor vehicle Dept.). Calculate cost per ton mile. Above stated employees are permanent employees except Coolies.

(K.U.D., October 1985)

Solution :

Working Note

Capacity		Lorries				
5	Ton	21	=	5 × 21	=	105
4	Ton	15	=	4 × 15	=	60
3	Ton	20	=	3 × 20	=	60
		Total Tons				225

Total monthly ton Miles :

= Days in a month × Trip per day × Miles per trip × Capacity

= 30 × 1 × 25 × 225 = 1,68,750 Ton Miles 1,68,750

Less : 20% Lay off	33,750
Net Ton Mileage	1,35,000

Statement of Operating Cost of Vehicles

(I) *Standing Charges :*		
(1) General Manager Salary (1500 × ½)	750	
(2) Salaries of 3 Machines (300 × 3)	900	
(3) Drivers Salaries (300 × 80)	24,000	
(4) Garage Rent	2,000	
(5) Depreciation	10,000	37,650

(II) *Maintenance Expenses :*		
Workshop overhead	7,050	
Replacement of Tyres etc.	12,000	
Maintenance	2,000	21,050
(III) *Operating Expenses :*		
Petrol	60,000	
Oil	8,100	
Wages of Coolies (150 × 200)	30,000	
Other Expenses	5,200	1,03,300
Total Cost		1,62,000

$$\text{Cost per Ton Mile} = \frac{1{,}62{,}000}{1{,}35{,}000} = \text{Rs. } 1.20$$

Problem No. 35

A person owns a bus which runs between Mumbai to Pune and back for 10 days in a month. The distance from Mumbai to Pune is 150 Miles. The bus completes the trip from Mumbai to Pune and back in the same day. The bus goes another 10 days in a month towards Virar. The distance from Mumbai to Virar is 120 Miles. The trip is also completed in the same day. For the rest 4 days of its operation in a month it runs in the local city. Daily distance covered in local city is 40 miles.

Calculate the rate the person should charge from passenger, when he wants to earn the Profit of 33-1/3% on his taking. The other information are given below :

Cost of the Bus	60,000
Depreciation (20% per Annum)	20% p.a.
Salary of Driver	35 p.m.
Salary of conductor	350 p.m.
Salary of part-time accountant	160 p.m.
Insurance	1,680 p.a.
Diesel consumption 4 Miles per Litre.	
Cost of Diesel Re. 1 per Litre.	
Bus Tax	600 p.a.
Oil, Grease etc.	Rs. 10 per 100 Miles
Repairs and maintenance	500 p.m.
Permit fees	284 p.m.
Normal capacity 50 persons.	

The Bus is generally occupied 90% of the capacity when it goes to Pune and 80% when it goes to Virar. It is also full when it run within the city. Passenger tax is 20% of the fare charged.

(K.U.D., April 1985)

Solution :

Statement of Operating Cost of Bus

	Cost per Month	Total	Cost per Mile
(I) *Fixed Cost :*			
Salary of Driver	350		
Salary of Conductor	350		
Salary of part-time accountant	160		
Insurance 1,680 p.a. (1,680 × 1/12)	140		
Bus Tax 600 p.a. (600 × 1/12)	50		
Permit fees 284 p.m.	284	1,334	0.239
(Cost per Mile = $\frac{1,334}{5,560}$)			
(II) *Maintenance* : Repairs & Maintenance $\left(\frac{500}{5560}\right)$		500	0.089
(III) *Running Charges :*			
Diesel consumption 4 miles per litre			
Cost Re. 1 per Litre Total Mile $\frac{5,560}{4}$ =	1,390		
Oil, Grease etc. Rs. 10 per 100 Mile			
for $\frac{5,560}{100}$ = 55.60 × 10	556		
Depreciation cost 60,000 @ 20%			
12,000 p.a. (12,000 × 1/12 = 1,000)	1,000	2,946	0.529
Total Cost per Month		4,780	0.857
			Or 0.86

Calculation : Passenger Miles

(a) Mumbai to Pune 150 Miles × 10 days = 150 × 2 × 10 =	3,000
(b) Mumbai to Viral = 120 Miles × 10 days = 120 × 2 × 10 =	2,400
(c) Mumbai Local — 40 Miles × 4 days = 40 × 4 =	160
Total Miles Run	5,560

Miles Run × Passenger Capacity

(a) Mumbai to Pune = 3,000 × (50 × 90%) = 3,000 × 45 =	1,35,000	
(b) Mumbai to Virar = 2,400 × (50 × 80%) = 2,400 × 40 =	96,000	
(c) Mumbai Local = 160 × (50 × 100%) = 160 × 500 =	8,000	2,39,000

(II) Cost per Passenger Mile = $\dfrac{\text{Total Cost}}{\text{Passenger Mile}} = \dfrac{4,780}{239,000}$ = 0.02 Ps

Add : Profit 33-1/3% $\dfrac{0.02 \times 100/3}{200/3} = 0.02 \times \dfrac{100}{3} \times \dfrac{3}{200}$ 0.01 Ps

0.03 Ps

Add : Passenger tax 20% of 0.03 = 0.006 0.006 Ps

Total 0.036 Ps

Cost per Passenger Mile = Re. 0.036

Problem No. 36

Union Transport company supplies the following details in respect of 5 ton capacity :

Cost of Truck	90,000
Estimated Life	10 Years
Diesel, Oil, Grease (per trip each way)	15
Repairs and Maintenance	500 p.m.
Driver's wage	500 p.m.
Clerk's wage	500 p.m.
Cleaner's wage	250 p.m.
Insurance	4,800 p.a.
Tax	2,400 p.a.
General supervision charges	4,800 p.a.

The truck carries goods to and from the city covering a distance of 50 miles each way. Onward trip freight is available to the extent of full capacity and on return 20% of capacity. Assuming that the Truck runs on an average 25 days a month work out :

(a) Operating cost per truck mile.

(b) Rate per ton per trip that the company should charge if a profit of 50% on freightage is to be earned.

(K.U.D., October 1984)

Solution :

Calculations :

(a) Total miles & ton Mile : Onward Trip =

= No. of trips × distance × capacity × No. of days in month

= 1 × 50 × (5 × 100%) × 25

= 50 × 5 × 25 6,250

Return Trip = 1 × 50 (5 × 20%) × 25

= 50 × 1 × 25 1,250

Total ton mile 7,500

Statement of Operating Cost Ton Miles — 7500

Particulars	Total cost per Month	Cost per ton Mile
(I) *Fixed Cost :*		
(1) Driver's wage	500	
(2) Cleaner's wage	250	
(3) Insurance (Rs. 4,800 × 1/12)	400	
(4) Tax (Rs. 2,400 × 1/12)	200	
(5) General supervision charges 4,800 × 1/12	400	
Total Cost	1,750	
Cost per to Mile = $\frac{1,750}{7,500}$ = 0.233		0.233
(II) *Repairs & Maintenance*	500	0.066
(III) *Operating Expenses :*		
Depreciation = $\frac{\text{Cost}}{\text{Life}} = \frac{90,000}{10}$ 9,000 × $\frac{1}{12}$	750	0.10
Diesel, Oil, Grease Rs. 15 per trip per day (15 × 2 × 25 = 750)	750	0.10
Total Cost	3,750	0.50

Cost per ton mile = $\frac{3,750}{7,500}$ = 0.50

Freight Charges :	Rs.
Cost per trip = 50 × 0.50	25
Add : Profit 50% on freightage i.e., 100% on cost	25
Freight per trip	50

Problem No. 37

From the following Data relating to two different vehicles, A and B compute the cost per running Mile :

	Vehicle A	Vehicle B
Mileage run (Annual) (in Miles)	15000	6000
Cost of Vehicle	25,000	15,000
Road Licence fees (Annual)	750	750
Insurance (Annual)	700	400
Garage Rent (Annual)	600	500
Supervision and salary	1,200	1,200

	Vehicle A	Vehicle B
Driver wage per hour	3	3
Cost of fuel per litre	3.00	3.00
Miles run per litre	20 Miles	15 Miles
Repairs & Maintenance per mile	1.65	2
Tyres Expenses per Mile	0.80	0.60
Estimated Life of vehicle (Miles)	1,00,000	75,000

Charge interest @ 5% per annum on cost of vehicle. The vehicles run 20 Miles per hour on an average.

(K.U.D., April 1984)

Solution :

Statement of Operating Cost of Vehicles

Particulars	Vehicle-A Total Cost	Vehicle-A Cost per Mile	Vehicle-B Total Cost	Vehicle-B Cost per Mile
	Rs.		Rs.	
Mileage Run (Annual) (in Miles)	15,000		6,000	
(I) *Fixed Expenses :*				
(1) Road Licence Fee (per annum)	750		750	
(2) Insurance (per annum)	700		400	
(3) Garage Rent (per annum)	600		500	
(4) Supervision salary (per annum)	1,200		1,200	
(5) Interest @ 5% on cost :				
Vehicle-A = 25,000 × 5%	1,250			
Vehicle-B = 15,000 × 5%			750	
Total Cost	4,500		3,600	
Cost per Mile = $\frac{\text{Total Cost}}{\text{Total Miles}}$				
A = $\frac{4,500}{15,000}$ = 0.30 B $\frac{3,600}{6,000}$ = 0.60		0.30		0.60
(II) *Maintenance :*				
Repairs & Maintenance :				
A = 1.65 × 15,000	24,750	1.65		
B = 2.00 × 6,000			12,000	2.00
Tyre Expenses :				
A = 15000 × .80 B = 6000 × 0.60	12,000	0.80	3,600	0.60

Particulars	Vehicle-A Total Cost	Vehicle-A Cost per Mile	Vehicle-B Total Cost	Vehicle-B Cost per Mile
	Rs.		Rs.	
(III) *Operating Expenses :*				
Cost of fuel per Litre Rs. $\frac{3}{20}$ Rs. $\frac{3}{15}$	2,250	0.15	1,200	0.20
Mile run per litre (A = 15000 × .15 = 2,250) (B = 6000 × .20 = 1,200)				
Drivers Wages per Hour (A = 0.15 × 15,000 = 2,250 = 3/20 = .15) (B = .15 × 6000 = 3/20 = .15)	2,250	0.15	900	0.20
Depreciation :				
(A = $\frac{25,000}{1,00,000}$ = 0.25 × 15,000) (B = $\frac{15,000}{75,000}$ = 0.20 × 6,000)	3,750	0.25	1,200	0.20
	49,500	3.30	22,500	3.75
Cost per Mile =	$\frac{49,500}{15,000}$	3.30	$\frac{22,500}{6,000}$	3.75

Problem No. 38

From the following data you are required to ascertain the cost of running the lorry per ton mile :

Total tonnage carried in a week 30 tons.

Total mileage in a week 600 miles details of the above are as follows :

Days	Miles	Tons
Monday	120	6
Tuesday	125	5
Wednesday	110	4
Thursdays	100	5.5
Friday	80	4.50
Saturday	65	5.00
	600	30.00

Expenses for the week are as follows :

Driver's salary	200	p.m.
Cleaner's salary	100	p.m
Petrol, Oil etc.	0.30	Ps per Mile
Repairs & Maintenance	300	p.m.
Depreciation	4,800	per annum
Other Expenses	200	p.m.

(There are four weeks in a month)

(K.U.D., October 1983)

Solution :

Statement of Operating Cost of Lorry for a Week

	Total Cost	Cost per ton Mile
(I) *Fixed Expenses* :		
(1) Driver's Salary per Quarter Rs. 200 × 1/4	50	
(2) Cleaner's salaries p.m. 100 × 1/4	25	
	75	
Depreciation Rs. 4,800 × 1/12 = 400 × 1/4	100	
Other Expenses p.m. Rs. 200 × ¼	50	
Total Fixed Cost	225	0.0745
(II) *Maintenance* : Repairs & Maintenance 300 × ¼	75	0.0248
(III) *Operating Expenses* : Petrol, Oil etc. 0.30 Ps per Mile for 600 = 180	180	0.0596
Total Cost	480	0.1589

$$\text{Cost per ton mile} = \frac{\text{Total Cost}}{\text{Ton mile}} = \frac{480}{3020} = 0.1589 \text{ Or Re. } 0.16 \text{ per ton Mile.}$$

Working Note

Days	Tons	Tonne Miles
Monday	120 × 6	720
Tuesday	125 × 5	625
Wednesday	110 × 4	440
Thursday	100 × 5.5	550
Friday	80 × 4.5	360
Saturday	65 × 5	325
		3,020 Ton Miles

Problem No. 39

The Iron & Steel works which generates its own Electricity for the purpose of using the same for running the factory gives the following information :

(a) *Fuel* :

(1) Coal consumed during the month is 1000 Quintals @ Rs. 12 per Quintal.

(2) Oil 15 Quitals at Rs. 1,000 per Quintal.

(3) Water 2,00,000 Litres @ Re. 1 per 1000 Litre.

(4) Cost of steam boilers Rs. 50,000 which has the scrap value Rs. 2,000. The Life of the boiler is 10 years.

(b) *Salaries & Wages for Boilers House :*

(1) 20 Men @ Rs. 150 p.m. each.

(2) 50 women @ Rs. 60 p.m. each.

(3) Share of administrative charges Rs. 1,050 per month.

(4) Generating plant cost Rs. 1,50,000 Depreciating is @ 10 p.a.

(c) *Salaries & Wages of Generating Plant :*

(1) 10 Skilled workers @ Rs. 300 p.m. each.

(2) 15 Unskilled workers @ Rs. 100 p.m. each.

(3) Number of units generated 2,00,000 Units.

(4) 1/10 of units generated were used by the Generating Department.

Calculate cost per unit of Electricity generated.

(K.U.D., April 1983)

Statement of Operating Cost of Generating Electricity

(a) *Fuel :*		
(1) Coal consumed (1,000 × 12)	12,000	
(2) Oil (150 × 1,000)	15,000	
(3) Water $\frac{2,00,000}{1,000} \times 1$	200	
(4) Depreciation cost of steam boiler $\frac{50,000 - 2,000}{10 \text{ Years}} = 4,800 \times 1/12$	400	27,600
(b) *Salaries & Wages for boiler House :*		
Men 20 × 150	3,000	
Women 50 × 60	3,000	6,000
Administration Charges		1,650
Depreciation cost Rs. 1,50,000 @ 10% p.a. 15,000 × 1/12		1,250

(c) *Salaries & Wages of generating plant :*

Skilled 100 × 300		3,000	
Unskilled 15 × 100		1,500	4,500
	Total Cost		40,400
Units generated	2,00,000		
Less : 10% used	20,000		
Net units	1,80,000 Units		

$$\text{Total Cost} \quad \frac{40{,}400}{1{,}80{,}000} = 0.224$$

Cost per unit = Re. 0.224

Problem No. 40

Mr. Mohan Singh has started transport business with a fleet of 10 taxies. The various expenses incurred by him are given below :

(1)	Cost of each Taxi	75,000
(2)	Salary of office staff	1,500 p.m.
(3)	Salary of garage staff	2,000 p.m.
(4)	Rent of garage	1,000 p.m.
(5)	Drivers salary (per taxi)	400 p.m.
(6)	Road taxes and Repair (per taxi)	2,160 p.a.
(7)	Insurance premium	4% of cost p.a.

(8) The life of taxi is 3,00,000 Kms. at the end of which it is estimated a Rs. 15,000. A Taxi runs on an average 4000 Kms. p.m. of which 20% runs.

(9) Petrol consumption is 9 Kms. per litre at Rs. 6.30 per litre.

(10) Oil and other sundry expenses amounted to Rs. per 100 Kms.

Calculate the effective cost of running a Taxi per Km. If the hire charges rate is Rs. 1,80 per Km. find out the Profit Mr. Mohan Singh may expect to make in the first year of operation.

(I.C.W.A. Inter, 1983)

Solution :

Statement of Operation Cost

	Total Cost per Month Rs.	Cost per Km. Rs. Ps.
(I) *Standing Charges :*		
(1) Salary of office staff 1,500 × 1/10	150	
(2) Salary of Garage staff 2,000 × 1/10	200	
(3) Garage Rent 1,000 × 1/10	100	
(4) Drivers salary (per taxi)	400	
(5) Road taxes and Repairs (per taxi) 2,160 × 1/10	180	
(6) Insurance (4% p.a.) (75,000 × 4% = 3,000 × 1/12)	250	
(7) Depreciation $\frac{\text{Cost} - \text{Scrap}}{\text{Life}} \times$ Km. per month		
$\frac{75{,}000 - 15{,}000}{3{,}00{,}000} \times 4{,}000 = 800$	800	
Total Standing Charges	2,080	
Standing charges per Km. $= \frac{2{,}080}{3{,}200} = 0.65$		0.65
(II) *Operating Expenses :*		
Petrol cost per litre Rs. 6.30		
Per litre Km. run Rs. 9		
Cost of petrol per Km. $= \frac{6.30}{9} = 0.70$		
Oil and sundry Exp. Rs. 10 per 100 Kms.		
For per Km. $= \frac{10}{100} = 0.10$		0.10
Operating cost per Km.		1.45

Monthly running Km. = 4,000
Less : 20% vacant 800
Effective 3,200

Profit earned per Taxi per Month =

Hire charges per Km.	1.80
Operating cost per Km.	1.45
Profit per Km.	Re. 0.35

Problem No. 41

Praveen Transport company has been given a route 20 Kms long for running buses.

The company has fleet of 10 Buses.

Cost of each bus Rs. 50,000. Life of each Bus 5 years without any scrap value.

From the following estimated expenditures and other details calculate the bus fare to be charged for each passenger :

(1)	Insurance charges 3% per annum	
(2)	Annual tax for each bus	1,000
(3)	Total Garage charges	1,000 p.m.
(4)	Annual repair for each bus	1,000
(5)	Driver's salary for each bus	150 p.m.
(6)	Conductor's salary for each bus	100
(7)	Commission to be shared by drivers and conductors equally 10% of the taking.	
(8)	Cost of stationery	500 p.m.
(9)	Manager's salary	2,000 p.m.
(10)	Accountant's salary	1,500 p.m.
(11)	Petrol and Oil Rs. 25 per 100 Kms.	

Per day each bus will make 3 round trips carrying on an average 40 passengers on each trip. The bus will run on an average 25 days in a month.

(K.U.D., October 1982)

Solution :

Calculations :

Miles run per month – Passenger

No. of bus × Distance × days in a month × No. of trips × No. of passenger
= 1 × 20 × 25 × 3 = 1,500 Miles × 40 = 60,000 passenger Mile.

Solution :

Statement of Operating Cost of Bus Passengers

(I) *Fixed Expenses :*	
(1) Insurance 3% on cost 50,000 × 3% = 1,500 (1,500 × 1/12)	125
(2) Annual tax Rs. 1,000 × 1/12	83
(3) Total Garage Rent 1,000 × 1/10	100
(4) Driver's Salary per month	150
(5) Conductor's salary per month	100

(6) Stationery 500 × 1/10	50
(7) Manager's salary 2,000 × 1/10	200
(8) Accountant Salary 1,500 × 1/10	150
Total	958

(II) *Maintenance :*

Annual repairs — 1,000 × 1/12	83

(III) *Operating Expenses :*

Petrol, Oil etc. Rs. 25 per 100 Kms.

$1 \times 20 \times 3 \times 25 = 1{,}500$ Kms. $= \dfrac{1{,}500}{100} \times 25$	375
Depreciation $= \dfrac{50{,}000}{5} = 10{,}000 \times 1/12$	834
Total cost	2,250

Total cost = 2,250

Total passenger Km 60,000 Kms

Cost per passenger $= \dfrac{2{,}250}{60{,}000} = 0.0375$ Ps.

Calculation of Commission :

10% on taking 0.0375

Total commission = 0.0375 × 10% × 1,500 × 3,000 = Rs. 16,875

Shared Equally by :

Drivers = 16,875 × ½ =	8,437.50
Conductors = 16,875 × ½ =	8,437.50
	16,875.00

Problem No. 42

Bharath Transport Company owns 4 buses each with 40 passengers seats. The firm has the Licence to provide transport between two towns which have 50 Kms. distance.

Each bus makes one trip per day on 30 days in a month on an average 75% of seats are filled.

Estimated Expenses of summary for a month :

(1) Wages of Drivers and Conductors etc.	12,000
(2) Office Salary	5,000
(3) Diesel (Fuel)	20,000
(4) Depreciation	13,000
(5) Repairs and Maintenance	5,000

(6)	Insurance tax and rent of garage	8,000
(7)	Interest and other charges	10,000
(8)	Estimated resale value of tyres etc.	1,000

Calculate cost per passenger Km.

(K.U.D., April 1982)

Solution :

Statement of Operating Cost of Buses Passenger Km.

(I) *Fixed Expenses :*		
(1) Wages of Drivers & Conductors	12,000	
(2) Office Salary	5,000	
(3) Insurance tax and Garage Rent	8,000	
(4) Interest and other charges	10,000	
(5) Depreciation	13,000	
Total	48,000	4.000
(II) *Maintenance :*		
Repairs and Maintenance	5,000	0.416
(III) *Operating Expenses :*		
Diesel Oil etc. (Fuel)	20,000	1.667
Total Cost	73,000	6.083

Total Kms run = 12,000 Kms

$$\text{Cost per Km} = \frac{73{,}000}{12{,}000} = 6.083$$

$$\text{Total Passenger Kms} = 12{,}000 \times 40 \times 75\%$$
$$= 3{,}60{,}000$$

$$\text{Cost per Passenger Km} = \frac{73{,}000}{3{,}60{,}000}$$
$$= 0.2027$$
$$= 0.20 \text{ Ps.}$$

Calculation :

Passenger Km per month = No. of Bus × Distance × No. of trip × No. of day × per cent

= 4 × 50 × 2 × 30 × (40 × 75%)

= 12,000 × 30

= 3,60,000 Passenger Kms.

Problem No. 43

M/s Prakash & Co. own a fleet of taxies and the following information is available from the record :

No. of Taxies = 10 (Ten)	
Cost of each Taxi	20,000
Salary of manager	600 p.m.
Salary of Accountant	500 p.m.
Salary of cleaner	200 p.m.
Salary of mechanic	400 p.m.
Garage Rent	600 p.m.
Annual taxes (per taxi)	600
Annual repairs (per taxi)	1,200
Drivers salary	220 p.m. each
Insurance premium 6% on cost of taxi.	

Total Life of taxi is about 2,00,000 Kms and it runs in a particular month 3,000 Kms. Petrol consumption in one litre for 10 Kms @ Rs. 4.80 per litre. Oil and other sundries are Rs. 5 per 100 Kms.

(K.U.D., October 1980)

Solution :

Statement of Cost Operaing Cost of Taxi

	Total Cost Rs.	Cost per Km.
(I) *Fixed Expenses*		
(1) Salary — Manager 600 × 1/10	60	
(2) Salary — Accountant 500 × 1/10	50	
(3) Salary — Cleaner 200 × 1/10	20	
(4) Salary — Mechanic 400 × 1/10	40	
(5) Garage Rent 600 × 1/10	60	
(6) Insurance premium 6% on cost 20,000 (1,200 × 1/12) =	100	
(7) Driver's salary	220	
(8) Annual Taxies 1,200 × 1/12	100	
Total Fixed Cost	560	
(II) *Maintenance*		
Repairs Annual 600 × 1/12	50	
$\frac{610}{3,000} = 0.20$	610	0.20

		Total Cost Rs.	Cost per Km.
(III) *Operating Charges*			
Depreciation $= \frac{\text{Cost}}{\text{Life}} = \frac{20,000}{2,00,000} \times 3,000$		300	0.10
Petrol 1 Litre 10 Kms. $= \frac{4.80}{10}$			0.48
Oil and other sundries Rs. 5 per 100 Kms. $= \frac{5}{100}$			0.05
Cost per Km.			0.83 Ps

Problem No. 44

SMC is a public school having five buses each plying in different directions for transportation of its students. In view of the large number of students availing of the bus service the buses work two shifts daily both in the morning and in the afternoon. The buses are garaged in the school. The workshed of the students has been so arranged that in the morning the first trip picks up senior students the second trip plying an hour later picks up the Junior students. Similarly in the afternoon the first trip drops the Junior students and an hour later the second trip takes the senior students home.

The distance travelled by each bus one way is 8 Kms. The school works for 25 days in a month and remain closed for vacation in May and June and December. But fee however is payable by students for all the 12 months in a year.

The details of the Expenses for the year are as under :

(1)	Drivers Salary	450 p.m.
(2)	Cleaners Salary (Salary payable for all 12 months and one cleaner employed for all the five buses)	350 p.m.
(3)	Licence fee taxes etc. (per bus p.a.)	860
(4)	Insurance (per bus p.a.)	1,000
(5)	Repairs and maintenance (per bus p.a.)	3,500
(6)	Purchase price of the bus	1,50,000
(7)	Life 12 years.	
(8)	Scrap value	30,000
(9)	Diesel, Oil cost Rs. 2 per litre.	
(10)	Each bus have an average mileage of 4 Kms. per litre of diesel.	
(11)	Seating capacity of each bus 50 students.	

The seating capacity is fully occupied during the whole year.

The students picked up and dropped within a range of up to 4 Kms. of distance from the school and charged half the fare and 50% of the students travelling in each trip are in this category. Ignore interest since the charges are to be based on average cost. You are required to :

(a) Prepare a Statement showing the expenses of operating a single bus and a fleet of five buses for a year.

(b) Work out the average cost per student per month in respect of :

(1) Students coming from a distance up to 4 Kms. from the school.

(2) Students coming from a distance of above 4 Kms. from the school.

(C.A. Inter, 1981)

Solution :

Working Note

(I) Calculations of passenger Kms.

Passenger Kms. = No. of bus × distance × trips × Capacity × No. of days in a month

= 5 × 8 × 8 × 50 × 25 = Passenger Kms. 4,00,000

per month passenger Kms. × 9 month in a year

4,00,000 × 9 = 36,00,000 for 5 (Five) Buses

Passenger Kms. per Bus = $\frac{36,00,000}{5}$ = 7,20,000

(II) Calculations of Kms run for 5 Buses.

Kms. = 5 × 8 × 8 × 25 = 8,000 Kms. per month

For one bus = $\frac{8,000}{5}$ = 1,600 Kms. per month per bus

For 9 months per bus = 9 × 1,600 = 14,400 Kms. run.

(III) Calculations of No. of students per bus — and Five buses.

Bus capacity 50 Students.

No. of bus 5

No. of Students 50.

Half fare for 50% students 50% of 5 = 25 Students

Full fare for remaining students 50% of 50 25 Students

Full fare students 25 are converted into half fare students 25 × 2 = 50 Students

i.e., twice the half fare students

Now the total No. of half fare students 25

Full fare students converted in to half fare 50

75

In single trip — Total No. of half fare students.

In two trips No. of half fare students will 75 × 2 = 150 students Half fare.

Statement of Operating Cost of 5 Buses & One Bus

	Total Cost for One Bus	Total Cost for Five Buses
(I) *Standing Charges*		
(1) Drivers salary Rs. 450 × 12 = 5,400 × 5 = 27,000	5,400	27,000
(2) Cleaners Salary 350 × 12 = 4,200 for 5 buses = $\frac{4,200}{5}$	840	4,200
(3) Licence fee, taxes etc.	860	4,300
(4) Insurance	1,000	5,000
(5) Depreciation = $\frac{\text{Cost} - \text{Scrap}}{\text{Life}} = \frac{1,50,000 - 30,000}{12} = \frac{1,20,000}{12}$	10,000	50,000
Total Standing Charges	18,100	90,500
(II) *Repairs & Maintenance*	3,500	17,500
(III) *Operation Expenses*		
Diesel cost of Diesel per Litre Rs. 2 Mileage 4 Kms. per Litre i.e., cost of diesel per Km. = 0.50 Ps for total Kms. 5 × 8 × 8 × 25 = 8,000 Kms p.m. Per month 8,000 Kms for 9 months 8,000 × 9 = 72,000 Kms run		
	28,800	1,44,000

Cost of diesel per Km 0.50 Ps for 72,000 Kms

0.50 × 72,000 = Rs. 36,000 for 5 Buses.

Cost per month = $\frac{28,000}{12} = 2,400 : \frac{1,44,000}{12} = 12,000$

For one bus = $\frac{36,000}{5} = 7,200$

Total Cost = 2,400 : 12,000

Calculation of fares for half the students per month

$$\text{per bus} = \frac{\text{Total operating cost per month}}{\text{No. of students}}$$

$$= \frac{2{,}400}{150} = \text{Rs. 16 per student for half fare.}$$

Cost per student for Full fare twice the half fare = 2 × 16 = Rs. 32

Answer : (a) Bus fare per month per student at full rate = Rs. 32

(b) Bus fare per month per student at 50% fare = Rs. 16

5

Job Costing, Batch Costing and Contract Costing or Contract Account

(A) JOB COSTING

It is one of the methods of costing. This method of costing is applied in a small engineering firm's operating two or more machines to manufacture the products, specially spare-parts of certain machine and automobile units. The small engineering units who undertake the work of manufacture of spare-parts of specific design, provided by the other manufacturing company. In such cases the accepting firm for manufacture as per specification in required numbers will have to offer quotation for manufacture of one unit cost.

The cost calculated will be on the basis of :

(1) Material cost — per unit.

(2) Wages based on number of hour required.

(3) Machine hours required for completion of work.

(4) And other overhead expenses.

(5) Add to the above the desired percentage of profit.

(6) The total of the above is the total cost for quotation of Job work.

And therefore such nature of work undertaken is known as job costing. If the number of the products to be manufactured is more it is identified as batch and the cost of such Batch is ascertained in a similar manner. In the same way in construction work i.e., Building, Roads and Ship Building etc., are considered under the title of Job costing since, the design, size of the Building differ from one another, each contract work are accounted by the contract or in the form contract Account for each Job separately to ascertain the Profit or Loss in contract business.

In a contract business the contractor maintains the Account called contract Account for the period.

The terms used in contract Business :

(a) Contractor is a person, a firm or a company which undertakes the Job of construction of buildings, Bridges, Roads, Ship Buildings etc., for certain agreed contract price.

(b) Contractee is a person, a firm or a company which invites to do the

Job as per specification design provided by a person, a firm, a company for a price known as contract Price.

(c) *Work-in-Progress*

If the Job undertaken is not completed within the accounting period of contractor the incomplete work is termed as work-in-progress. The terms of contract normally provide the payment of cash to the contractor by the contractee on the basis of certificates issued by an architect appointed by the contractee. The work done certified becomes the qualifying basis for payment normally 80% or 90% of work certified. Similarly the construction work continues to be carried on till the accounting period. The quantum of value of work done but not certified is included in work-in-progress as work done but not certified.

Calculation of Profit in Incomplete Contract Works

(1) For the contract work just started and work done and certified is less than ¼, no profit is taken to the credit of Profit & Loss A/c. All the amount notional profit is transferred to Reserve Account.

(2) If the work done is less than the ½ of the contract price 1/3 of Notional Profit be taken to the credit of Profit & Loss A/c and the balance to Reserve Account.

(3) If work done is more than ½ and less than 3/4, 2/3 of the Notional Profit is to be taken to the credit of Profit & Loss A/c and the Balance to Reserve Account.

(4) If work done is more than 3/4 or nearing completion within two or three months of the accounting period, the profit for that period is calculated considering the additional expenses upto the completion of work. This profit is estimated profit :

$$\text{Estimated Profit} \times \frac{\text{Work certified}}{\text{Contract Price}}$$

Note : In case of 2 and 3 above $\text{Notional Profit} \times \frac{2}{3} \times \frac{\text{Cash received}}{\text{Work certified}}$

= Profit taken to the credit of Profit and Loss Account.

ON JOB COSTING

Problem No. 1

The following records are taken from Vijaya Engineering Works Ltd. whicl has three Production Departments X, Y and Z :

	Total	X	Y	Z
(a) Material	30,000	5,000	10,000	15,000
(b) Direct Wages	11,750	3,500	4,000	4,750
(c) Variable factory overheads	7,500	2,500	2,000	3,000

	Total	X	Y	Z
(d) Fixed factory overheads	7,500	—	—	—
(e) Administrative overheads	5,000	—	—	—
(f) Machine hours (in hours)	10000	3000	2000	5000

Factory overheads are absorbed on the basis of Machine hours and Administrative overheads are absorbed as a percentage of work cost.

The Company has received an order for a job which passes through two departments only i.e. X and Y.

The following particulars are available in respect of the job :

Material	Rs. 750	1,250
Wages	Rs. 350	400
Machine hours	300 hrs.	200 hrs.

Prepare Job Order Cost Sheet and ascertain the selling price, if 25% profit on S.P. (Selling Price) is added.

(K.U.D., October 1995)

Solution :

Job Order Cost Sheet

Material Department	X 750	
	Y 1,250	2,000
Direct Wages Department	X 350	
	Y 400	750
Prime Cost		2,750
Factory overhead (on the basis of Machine hrs.)		
Variable : X $\frac{2,500}{3000} \times 300$	= 250	
Y $\frac{2,000}{2000} \times 200$	= 200	450
Fixed Overhead $\frac{7,500}{10000} \times 500$	=	375
Works Cost		3,575

Administrative Overhead :

As percentage on work cost

Work Cost :

30,000
11,750
7,500
7,500
56,750

$$= \frac{\text{Overhead}}{\text{Works Cost}} \times 100$$

$$56,750 = \frac{5000}{56,750} \times 100 = 8.81\%$$

= Works Cost	= 3,575 × 8.81	315
Total Cost		3,890

Total Cost			3,890
Profit 25% on Selling Price			
Selling Price =	100	Now : 25/75 × 3,890 =	1,297
Profit	25	Selling Price	5,187
Cost	75		
Selling Price	5,187		
Profit 25%	(–) 1,297		
Cost Price	3,890		

Problem No. 2

The following information relates to Job No. 112.

Materials 6,900

Wages :

Department Casting 120 Hours @ Rs. 3 per hour.

Department Machining 40 Hours @ Rs. 4 per hour.

Department Finishing 80 Hours @ Rs. 2 per hour.

Fixed overheads were Rs. 10,000 for 5,000 working hours.

Variable Overheads :

Department Casting — Rs. 4,000 for 2000 Hours.

Department Machine — Rs. 6,000 for 1500 Hours.

Department Finishing — Rs. 2,000 for 500 Hours.

What would be the price to be quoted if profit expected is 20% on Selling Price.

(Gulbarga University, April 1994)

Solution :

Statement of Job Cost Sheet No. 112

Materials			6,900
Wages :			
Department Casting =	120 × 3	360	
Department Machine =	40 × 4	160	
Department Finishing	80 × 2	160	680
	Prime Cost		7,580
Overheads : Fixed :	$\frac{10,000}{5000}$ = Rs. 2 per hour		
Department Casting	: 120 × 2	240	
Department Machining	: 40 × 2	80	
Department Finishing	: 80 × 2	160	480

Variable :

Department Casting :	$\frac{4,000}{2,000}$ = Rs. 2 × 120	240	
Department Machine :	$\frac{6,000}{1500}$ = Rs. 4 × 40	160	
Department Finishing :	$\frac{2,000}{500}$ = Rs. 4 × 80	320	720
	Cost of production		8,780
Add : Profit 20% on Selling Price or 25% on cost			2,195
	Sales Price		10,975

Problem No. 3

From the following information prepare an Estimate of Job No. 250 :

Direct raw materials used	2,000
Direct Wages	4,000

Factory Expenses 60% on Wages.

Office Expenses 20% on Factory cost.

The Tender should include a Profit of 20% on Selling Price.

(Kuvempu University, April 1994)

Solution :

Estimated Cost of Job No. 250

Direct Materials used	2,000
Direct Wages	4,000
Prime Cost	6,000
Factory Overhead 60% on wages (4,000 × 60% = 2,400)	2,400
Works Cost	8,400
Office Overhead 20% on Works Cost (8,400 × 20%)	1,680
Cost of Production	10,080
Profit 20% on Selling Price OR : 25% on Cost = 10,080 × 25% = 2,520	2,520
Sales Price	12,600

Tender Price = Rs. 12,600

Problem No. 4

A Factory is engaged in making a non-standard product to customers specifications processed all production through 3 Departments.

(I) The figures for the month December 1988 was as under :

Particulars	Departments A Rs.	Departments B Rs.	Departments C Rs.
(1) Direct Materials	75,000	64,000	47,000
(2) Direct Wages	60,000	50,000	40,000
(3) Overheads	75,000	60,000	65,000
(4) Labour hours worked (Hours)	2000	3000	1000
(5) Machine Hours worked (Hours)	1200	1200	2600

(II) Following particulars relate to Job-'X' :

Particulars	A	B	C
(1) Direct Materials	1,000	2,000	3,000
(2) Direct Wages	500	600	700
(3) Direct Labour hours (Hours)	20	15	10
(4) Machine hours (Hours)	101	10	20

(III) Overhead recovery rates adopted :

Department A — Percentage on wages.

Department B — Labour Hours Rate.

Department C — Machine Hours Rate.

Find the Cost of Job-X.

(K.U.D., October 1989)

Solution :

Calculations :

Particulars	Departments A	Departments B	Departments C
(1) *Overhead Recovery Rates :*		$\frac{60,000}{50,000} \times 100$ $= 120\%$	
(a) Percentage on wages: $\frac{\text{Overheads}}{\text{Direct Wages}} \times 100 =$	$\frac{75,000}{60,000} \times 100$ $= 125\%$	$\frac{75,000}{60,000} \times 100$ $= 125\%$	$\frac{65,000}{40,000} \times 100$ $= 162\%$

Particulars		Departments A	B	C
(b) Labour Hour Rate :				
$\frac{\text{Overheads}}{\text{Labour Hours}}$		$\frac{75,000}{2,000}$	$\frac{60,000}{3,000}$	$\frac{65,000}{1,000}$
	Rs.	= 37.50	= 20.00	= 65.00
(c) Machine Hours Rate :				
$\frac{\text{Overheads}}{\text{Machine Hour}}$		$\frac{75,000}{1,200}$	$\frac{60,000}{1,200}$	$\frac{65,000}{2,600}$
	Rs.	= 62.50	= 50.00	= 25.00

Calculations : Overhead Recovery Rates :

(i) Percentage on wages (Department — A)

$$\frac{\text{Overhead}}{\text{Wages}} \times 100$$

$$= \frac{75,000}{60,000} \times 100$$

= 125%

(ii) Labour Hour Rate (Department — B)

$$\frac{\text{Overheads}}{\text{Labour Hours}} = \frac{60,000}{3,000}$$

= Rs. 20 per hour rate.

(iii) Machine Hour Rate (Department — C)

$$\frac{\text{Overheads}}{\text{Machine Hours}}$$

$$= \frac{65,000}{2600}$$

= Rs. 25 per hour.

Statement of Cost of Job-'X'

Materials :			
Department : A		1,000	
B		2,000	
C		3,000	6,000
Wages : Department :	A	500	
	B	600	
	C	700	1,800
		Prime Cost	7,800

	Prime Cost		7,800
Factory Overheads :			
Department-A			
125% of Wages = $500 \times \frac{125}{100}$ =		625	
Labour Hours Rate :			
Department-B = Rs. 20 per hour			
= 15 hours × 20 =		300	
Machine Hours Rate :			
Department-C : Rs. 25 per hour			
20 hours × 25 =		500	1,425
	Cost of Production		9,225

Problem No. 5

The following Expenses were incurred for a Job during the year 1987 :

Direct Materials	3,000
Direct Wages	4,000
Chargeable Expenses	1,000
Factory Overhead	2,000
Selling & Distribution Overhead	2,000
Administrative Overhead	3,000
	15,000

Selling Price for the above Job was Rs. 18,000.

You are required to prepare a statement showing the profit earned for the year 1987 from the Job and an Estimated Price of a Job which is to be executed in the year 1988.

Materials	5,000
Wages	7,000
Chargeable Expenses	2,000

Required for the Job :

The various overheads should be recovered on the following basis while calculating the estimated Price :

(a) Factory overhead as a percentage of Direct wages.

(b) Administration and Selling & Distribution overhead as a percentage of factory cost.

(Bangalore University, 1988)

Solution :

Statement of Job Cost Sheet 1987

Direct Materials		3,000
Direct Wages		4,000
Chargeable Expenses		1,000
	Prime Cost	8,000
Factory Overhead		2,000
	Works Cost	10,000
Administrative Overhead		3,000
	Cost of Production	13,000
Selling & Distribution Overhead		2,000
	Cost of Sales	15,000
	Sales Price	18,000
	Profit	3,000

Quotation Price Statement of Estimated Cost for 1988

Materials		5,000
Wages		7,000
Chargeable		2,000
	Prime Cost	14,000
Factory overhead 50% on Direct wages (50% on 7,000)		3,500
	Works Cost	17,500
Administrative overhead (30% on works cost) (17,500 × 30% = 5,250)		5,250
	Cost of Production	22,750
Selling & Distribution overhead 20% on works cost (17,500 × 20%)		3,500
	Cost of Sales	26,250
Profit 20% on 26,250 = 5,250		5,250
	Sales Price	31,500

Working Note

(1) Factory overhead as a percentage on Direct Wages =

$$= \frac{\text{Overhead}}{\text{Direct Wages}} \times 100 = \frac{2{,}000}{4{,}000} \times 100 = 50\% \text{ of Wages}$$

(2) Administrative overhead as a percentage on Factory cost

$$= \frac{\text{Overhead}}{\text{Works Cost}} \times 100 = \frac{3{,}000}{10{,}000} \times 100 = 30\% \text{ on Works Cost}$$

(3) Selling & Distribution as above

$$= \frac{\text{Overhead}}{\text{Works Cost}} \times 100 = \frac{2{,}000}{10{,}000} \times 100 = 20\%$$

Problem No. 6

The following Direct Expenses were incurred on Job No. 55 of Gala T.V. Company :

(1) Materials Rs. 15,030

(2) Wages paid : Departments : A — 40 Hours Rs. 8 per hour.
B — 50 Hours Rs. 9 per hour.
C — 60 Hours Rs. 5 per hour.

(3) Works overhead of these three Departments were estimated as under :
Department A — Rs. 9,000 for 6000 working hours.
Department B — Rs. 10,000 for 5000 working hours.
Department C — Rs. 12,000 for 3000 working hours.

(4) Office expenses were Rs. 75,000 when total wages paid in all the three departments came to Rs. 2,50,000.

It is the practice followed in Gala T.V. Company to recover office overhead as a percentage of direct wages.

You are required to calculate the cost of Job No. 55 and its Price to be quoted which would yield 20% Profit on Selling Price.

(K.U.D., April 1986)

Solution :

Statement of Job Cost Sheet Job No. 55

	Rs.	Rs.
Direct Materials		15,030
Direct Wages : Departments : A — 40 Hours × 8	320	
B — 50 Hours × 9	450	
C — 60 Hours × 5	300	1,070
Prime Cost		16,100
Works Overhead :		
Department : A $\frac{9{,}000}{6{,}000}$ = 1.50 × 40	60	
B $\frac{10{,}000}{5{,}000}$ = 2.00 × 50	100	
C $\frac{12{,}000}{3{,}000}$ = 4 × 60	240	400
Works Cost		16,500

Works Cost	16,821
Office Overhead as a Percentage on Direct Wages	
$\frac{75,000}{2,50,000} \times 100 = 30\%$ of 1,070 =	321
Total Cost	16,821
Add :	
Profit 20% on Selling Price	
OR 25% on Cost = 25% on 16,821 =	4,205
Sales Price =	21,026

Problem No. 7

A work order for 500 units of commodity has to pass through four different machines of which the Machine hour rates are :

Machine No. I	1.25
Machine No. II	3.00
Machine No. III	4.00
Machine No. IV	2.50

The following expenses have been incurred on the work order :

Materials	Rs. 20,000	
Wages	Rs. 1,500	
Machine No. I	Worked for	200 Hours
Machine No. II	Worked for	300 Hours
Machine No. III	Worked for	240 Hours
Machine No. IV	Worked for	100 Hours

After the work order has been executed materials worth of Rs. 1,000 were returned to stores office overhead are to be estimated @ 60% of the works cost.

10% of the production is going to be discarded being unsatisfactory for which ½ the amount can be realised from the sale in Junk market.

Find out the rate of selling price per unit if 20% Profit on selling price desired.

It is presumed that net resulted output is 500 units i.e., the quantum of work order after discarded units have been adjusted for.

(K.U.D., October 1985)

Solution :

Statement of Cost and Selling Price for 500 Units

Direct Material		20,000		
Less : Returned		1,000		19,000
Wages				1,500
	Prime Cost			20,500
Works Overhead :				
Machine No. I	= 200 Hrs × 1.25		250	
Machine No. II	= 300 Hrs × 3.00		900	
Machine No. III	= 240 Hrs × 4.00		960	
Machine No. IV	= 100 Hrs × 2.50		250	2,360
	Works Cost			22,860
Office Overhead :				
60% of works cost 22,860 × 60%				13,716
	Total Cost of Production			36,576
Less : 10% of discarded units (50 units)		3,657.60		
Sold for ½ the amount		1,828.80		1,828.80
	Net Total Cost of Production			34,747.20
Profit 20% on sales price				
OR : 25% on cost 34,747.20 × 25%				8,686.80
	Total units produced 500 Units after discarded units adjusted			43,434.00

Cost per Unit $= \frac{\text{Total Amount}}{\text{Total Units}}$

$= \frac{43,434}{500}$

= Rs. 86.868

= or Rs. 87.00

Problem No. 8

The information given below has been taken from the costing records of an Engineering works in receipts of Job No. 303.

Materials 4,010

Wages :

Departments : A — 60 Hours @ Rs. 3 per hour
B — 40 Hours @ Rs. 2 per hour
C — 20 Hours @ Rs. 5 per hour

Overhead Expenses for these three departments were estimated as follows :

Variable overhead :

Departments : A — Rs. 5,000 for 5000 Labours hours.
B — Rs. 3,000 for 1500 Labours hours.
C — Rs. 2,000 for 500 Labours hours.

Fixed overhead estimated at Rs. 20,000 for 10,000 Normal working hours.

You are required to calculate the cost of Job No. 303 and calculate the Price to give profit of 25 per cent on Selling Price.

(K.U.D., October 1983)

Solution :

Job Costing Sheet — Job No. 303

Direct Materials			4,010
Wages :			
Department :	A — 60 Hours × 3	180	
	B — 40 Hours × 2	80	
	C — 20 Hours × 5	100	360
	Prime Cost		4,370
Works overhead : (Variable)			
Department :	A — 60 hours × $\frac{5,000}{5,000}$ =	60	
	B — 40 hours × $\frac{3,000}{1,500}$ =	80	
	C — 20 hours × $\frac{2,000}{500}$ =	80	220
			4,590
Fixed Overhead =			
(60 + 40 + 20 = 120 Hours) = $\frac{20,000}{10,000}$ × 120			240
	Total Cost		4,830
Add : 25% Profit on Selling Price Or 1/3 on cost			1,610
	Selling Price		6,440

Problem No. 9

A factory is engaged in making standard product which pass through three Departments. The cost figures of the factory for the month of November 1979 are furnished below :

	Total	Departments A	B	C
Direct Materials	37,200	15,000	12,800	9,400
Labours Cost	30,000	12,000	10,000	8,000
Total Overhead Expenses	15,000	6,000	5,000	4,000
Total	82,200	33,000	27,800	21,400

Prepare a simple cost sheet for products X and Y on the basis of data furnished below :

		Departments A	B	C
Product-X :	Material	200	400	600
	Labour	100	120	140
Product-Y :	Materials	100	180	280
	Labour	140	120	160

(Mysore, April 1981)

Solution :

Working Note

(1) Percentage of overheads to Direct Wages :

$$\frac{\text{Overheads}}{\text{Direct Wages}} \times 100$$

Departments : A $= \frac{6{,}000}{12{,}000} \times 100 = 50\%$

B $= \frac{5{,}000}{10{,}000} \times 100 = 50\%$

C $= \frac{4{,}000}{8{,}000} \times 100 = 50\%$

Job Cost Sheet for Products X & Y

Particulars	Product X		Product Y	
Materials : Department A	200		100	
Department B	400		180	
Department C	600		280	
		1,200		560

Particulars	Product X		Product Y	
Labour Cost : Department A	100		140	
Department B	120		120	
Department C	140		160	
		360		420
Prime Cost		1,560		980
Overhead Expenses 50% on Direct Wages :				
Department A	50		70	
Department B	60		60	
Department C	70		80	
(50% on 360 = 180) (50% on 420 = 210)		180		210
Works Cost		1,740		1,190

Problem No. 10

A factory uses Job Costing the following cost data is obtained from its books for the year ended 31st December 1974 :

Direct Materials	90,000
Direct Wages	75,000
Profit	60,900
Selling & Distribution Expenses	52,500
Administrative Overhead	42,000
Factory Overhead	45,000

(a) Prepare a Job cost sheet indicating :

Prime Cost, Works Cost, Cost of Production, Cost of Sales and the Sales Value.

(b) In 1975 factory receives an order for a number of Jobs. It is estimated that the Direct Material required will be Rs. 1,20,000 and the Direct labour will cost of Rs. 75,000. What should be the Price for these Jobs. If the Factory intends to earn the same rate of Profit on sales assuming that :

(i) The Factory overheads as a percentage of direct wages.

(ii) Administration and Selling and Distribution overhead as a percentage of works cost based on cost rate previously in the previous years.

(C.A. Inter)

Solution :

Statement of Job Cost Sheet for the Year 1974

Direct Materials		90,000
Direct Wages		75,000
	Prime Cost	1,65,000
Factory Overheads		45,000
	Works Cost	2,10,000
Administration Overheads		42,000
	Cost of Production	2,52,000
Selling and Distribution Overheads		52,500
	Cost of Sales	3,04,500
Profit		60,900
	Sales Value	3,65,400

Working Note

(a) Factory overhead as percentage of Direct Wages

$$= \frac{\text{Factory Overhead}}{\text{Direct Wages}} \times 100 = \frac{45,000}{75,000} \times 100 = 60\%$$

(b) Administration Overhead as a percentage on works cost

$$= \frac{\text{Administration Overhead}}{\text{Works Cost}} \times 100 = \frac{42,000}{2,10,000} \times 100 = 20\%$$

(c) Selling and Distribution Overhead as percentage on Works Cost

$$= \frac{\text{Selling and Distribution Overhead}}{\text{Works Cost}} \times 100 = \frac{52,500}{2,10,000} \times 100 = 25\%$$

(d) Percentage of Profit on sales

$$= \frac{\text{Profit}}{\text{Sales}} \times 100 = \frac{60,900}{3,65,400} \times 100 = 16.67\%$$

Or Percentage of profit on cost

$$= \frac{\text{Profit}}{\text{Cost}} \times 100 = \frac{60,900}{3,04,500} \times 100 = 20\%$$

Statement of Job Cost Sheet for Quotation

Materials	1,20,000
Wages	75,000
Prime Cost	1,95,000
Factory Overhead (60% on Direct Wages) $75{,}000 \times 60\% = 45{,}000$	45,000
Works Cost	2,40,000
Administration Overhead : 20% on Works cost = 2,40,000 × 20% = 48,000	48,000
Cost of Production	2,88,000
Selling & Distribution Overhead 25% on Works cost = 2,40,000 × 25% = 60,000	60,000
Cost of Sales	3,48,000
Profit 20% on Cost of Sales $3{,}48{,}000 \times 20\% = 69{,}600$	69,600
Sales Price of Rs.	4,17,600

Problem No. 11

A small Engineering firm working on a particular Job work, give you the following particulars :

Materials			108
Direct Wages			90
20 Hours at the Rate of Rs. 4.50 per hour			
Department	X	10 Hours.	
	Y	6 Hours.	
	Z	4 Hours.	
	Prime Cost		198
Add : 50% on cost			99
	Cost of Sales		297

Analysis of the previous year's Profit and Loss A/c shows the following :

Profit and Loss A/c

To Material		1,57,500	By Sales	4,11,750
To Direct Wages				
Dept. X	22,500			
Dept. Y	27,000			
Dept. Z	18,000	67,500		
To Manufacturing Expenses				
Dept. X	22,500			
Dept. Y	13,500			
Dept. Z	13,500	49,500		
Selling & Distribution		54,900		
Profit		82,350		
		4,11,750		4,11,750

You are required to prepare :

(a) Job cost sheet using previous year's figures.

(b) *Add* to the selling Price 20%.

(c) Show what would be the selling price.

Solution :

Job Cost Sheet for Previous Year

Materials			1,57,500
Direct Wages			67,500
	Prime Cost		2,25,000
Factory Overheads :			
Departments : X		22,500	
Y		13,500	
Z		13,500	49,500
	Works Cost		2,74,500
Selling & Distribution Overhead			54,900
	Cost of Sales		3,29,400
Add : Profit 25% on cost			82,350
	Selling Price		4,11,750

Note (1) : Absorption of Factory overhead on the basis of Direct Wages

$$= \frac{\text{Factory Overhead}}{\text{Direct Wages}}$$

Rate per hour in case of wages is Rs. 4.50 per hour and also Factory overheads.

Direct Wages

$$\text{Department X} = \frac{22{,}500}{4.50} = 5000 \text{ Hours.}$$

$$\text{Department Y} = \frac{27{,}000}{4.50} = 6000 \text{ Hours.}$$

$$\text{Department Z} = \frac{18{,}000}{4.50} = 4000 \text{ Hours.}$$

Factory Overhead

$$\text{Department X} = \frac{22{,}500}{4.50} = 5000 \text{ Hours } \frac{5000}{5000} \times 4.50 = 4.50 \text{ Rate per Hour.}$$

Department Y = $\frac{13,500}{4.50}$ = 3000 Hours $\frac{3000}{6000}$ × 4.50 = 2.250 Rate per Hour.

Department Z = $\frac{13,500}{4.50}$ = 3000 Hours $\frac{3000}{4000}$ × 4.50 = 3.375 Rate per Hour.

Factory overhead absorption :

Rate per hour : Department X = 4.50

Y = 2.25

Z = 3.375

Note (2) : Selling & Distribution Expenses on the basis works cost

$$= \frac{\text{Selling \& Distribution Overhead}}{\text{Works Cost}} \times 100 = \frac{54,900}{2,74,500} \times 100$$

$$= 20\%.$$

Job Cost Sheet Revised

		Rs.	Rs.
Materials			108
Direct Wages 20 Hours × 4.50			
Department : X = 10 × 4.50		45.00	
Y = 6 × 4.50		27.00	
Z = 4 × 4.50		18.00	90
	Prime Cost		198
Factory Overheads :			
Department X = 10 × 4.50		45.00	
Department Y = 6 × 2.25		13.50	
Department Z = 4 × 3.375		13.50	72
	Works Cost		270
Selling & Distribution Expenses 20% on works cost 270 × 20%			54
	Cost of Sales		324
Profit 20% on Sales Price Or 25% on Cost Price (324 × 25%)			81
	Selling Price		405

Problem No. 12

A shop floor supervisor of a small factory presented the following costs for Job No. 412 :

	Cost per Unit
Materials	175.00
Direct Wages 18 Hours @ Rs. 6.25 =	112.50
(Department A — 8 Hours, Department B — 6 Hours, Department C — 4 Hours)	
Charged expenses (Special stores)	12.50
	300.00
Add : 33-1/3% for Expenses	100.00
Total Cost	400.00

Analysis of Profit & Loss Account for 1990 shows the following :

To Materials used			3,75,000	By Sales loss Returns	6,25,000
To Direct Wages :					
Department :	A	25,000			
	B	30,000			
	C	20,000	75,000		
To Special stores items			10,000		
To Overheads :					
Department :	A	12,500			
	B	22,500			
	C	5,000	40,000		
To Gross Profit			1,25,000		
			6,25,000		6,25,000
To Selling Expenses			50,000	By Gross Profit	1,25,000
To Net Profit			75,000		
			1,25,000		1,25,000

It is also noted that the average hourly rate for 3 Departments A, B and C are similar.

You are required to :

(a) Draw up a Job Cost Sheet.

(b) Calculate and enter revised cost using 1990 actual figures as basis.

(c) Add 20 per cent to total cost to determine Selling Price.

[ICWA (Modified)]

Solution :

Job Cost Sheet Job No. 412

Particulars		Rs.	Cost per Unit
(1) Materials			175.00
(2) Direct Wages : Department —	A = 8 × 6.25	50.00	
	B = 6 × 6.25	37.50	
	C = 4 × 6.25	25.00	112.50
(3) Chargeable Expenses (Special stores items)			12.50
	Prime Cost		300.00
(4) Overheads : Department :	A = 8 × 3.12	25.00	
	B = 6 × 4.68	28.12	
	C = 4 × 1.56	6.25	59.37
	Cost of Production		359.37
Selling Expenses — 10 per cent Total Cost			
Cost of sales 59.37 of 10%			5.93
	Total Cost		365.30
Add : Profit 20% on Total Cost			
365.30 of 20%			73.06
(of Rs. 448)	Sales Price per unit		448.38

Note : Overheads rates have been competed on the basis of previous year's figures : i.e., $\frac{\text{Overhead}}{\text{No. of Hours}}$

No. of working hours have been ascertained by dividing direct wages in each Department by labour hour rate :

Overhead Rate Per Hour

$$\text{Department A} = \frac{25{,}000}{6.25} = 4000 \text{ Hours} = \frac{12{,}500}{4000} = \text{Rs. } 3.125$$

$$\text{Department B} = \frac{30{,}000}{6.25} = 4800 \text{ Hours} = \frac{22{,}500}{4800} = \text{Rs. } 4.6875$$

$$\text{Department C} = \frac{20{,}000}{6.25} = 3200 \text{ Hours} = \frac{5{,}000}{3200} = \text{Rs. } 1.562$$

Selling Expenses = Percentage of selling expenses on Total Cost

$$= \frac{50{,}000}{5{,}00{,}000} \times 100 = 10\% \text{ on Total Cost}$$

Problem No. 13

A work order for 500 units of a part of Machine has to pass through different Machines of which hour rate are :

Machine No. 1	Rs. 6.25
Machine No. 2	Rs. 12.50
Machine No. 3	Rs. 15.00
Machine No. 4	Rs. 11.25

The following Expenses have been incurred :

Materials	Rs. 40,000
Wages	Rs. 25,000

Machine No. 1 has been engaged for 200 Hours

Machine No. 2 has been engaged for 160 Hours

Machine No. 3 has been engaged for 240 Hours

Machine No. 4 has been engaged for 140 Hours.

After the work order has been completed materials worth Rs. 2,000 are found to be surplus and returned to stores office overhead used to be 60% of work cost but on account of all round rise in the cost of administration there has been a rise of 75% in office overhead expenditure.

It was also found that 10 per cent of the Production will have to be scrapped as not being up to specification and the sales proceeds of the scrapped output will be only 10 per cent of the cost of sales.

If the manufacturer wants to make a profit 25% on the total cost of the work order find out the selling price of a unit of commodity ready for sales.

Solution :

Statement of Job Cost Sheet for 500 Units

Materials		40,000	
Less : Return to stores		2,000	38,000
Direct Wages			25,000
	Prime Cost		63,000
Works overheads :			
Machine No. 1 — 200 × 6.25	=	1,250	
Machine No. 2 — 160 × 12.50	=	2,000	
Machine No. 3 — 240 × 15.00	=	3,600	
Machine No. 4 — 140 × 11.25	=	1,575	8,425
	Works Cost		71,425
Office Overhead :			
75 per cent of works cost 75 per cent of 71,425			53,569
	Cost of production		1,24,994

Cost of production		1,24,994
Less : Scrap 10 per cent of production of Rs. 1,24,994		
Scrap sold cost of 10 per cent 12,499	1,249.9	–1,250
Cost of Production		1,23,744
Add : Profit 25% on Cost of production		
1,23,744 × 25%		30,936
Sales Price		1,54,680

$$\text{Sales price per unit} = \frac{1,54,680}{500} = \text{Rs. } 309.36$$

Note : It is assumed that the not resulted output is 500 units the No. of units ordered. The Scrapped units are adjusted by good units.

Problem No. 14

M/s AB Co. Ltd. a small engineering firm has followed the system of absorption of overheads based on direct labour hour earlier.

It was decided to change the system of absorption of overheads regarding the stores keeping and material handling, Machining and assembling from 1st April 1990.

The estimated of costs and absorption rates are as follows :

Prior to 1st April 1990 :

Overheads absorption rates are :

Production overheads @ Rs. 2.25 per direct labour hour.

Selling keeping and Material handling 15% on Material cost.

Machine Rs. 3.75 per hour.

Assembling Rs. 1.50 per hour.

Selling & Distribution overhead 25% on works cost.

Direct Costs of Job No. 302 are under :

Direct Material cost — Rs. 450

Direct Wages :

Machining 250 Hours @ Rs. 2.75

Assembling 125 Hours @ 2.25

The contract Price for the Job 3,360 and it requires 200 Hours to complete.

Prepare the Job cost Sheet for Job No. 302 :

(a) As would appear prior to 1st April 1990

(b) As would appear after 1st April 1990.

Solution :

Job Cost Sheet Job No. 302 Prior to 1st April 1990

			Rs.
Direct Material Cost			450.00
Direct Wages :			
Machining — 250 × 2.75 =		675.00	
Assembling — 125 × 2.25 =		281.25	956.25
	Prime Cost		1,306.25
Factory Overhead : on Direct Labour Hour (250 + 125) 375 × 2.25 =			843.75
	Works Cost		2,150.00
Selling and Distribution overhead 25 per cent on works cost (25% on 2,150)			537.50
	Cost of Sales		2,687.50
Sales Price			3,360.00
	Profit		672.50

Per cent of Profit on sales $\frac{672}{3,360}$ = 20% on cost $\frac{672}{2,687.5}$ = 25%

Job Cost Sheet Job No. 302 After 1st April 1990

			Rs.
Direct Materials			450.00
Stores Keeping and Materials handling 15% on Materials (450 × 15% = 67.50)			67.50
Machining :	Direct Wages = 250 × 2.75 =	675.00	
	Overhead = 200 × 3.75 =	750.00	
Assembling :	Direct Wages = 125 × 2.25 =	281.25	
	Overhead = 125 × 1.50 =	187.50	1,893.75
Production Cost or Works cost			2,411.25
Selling & Distribution Overhead 25% on works cost (2,411.50 × 25%)			602.75
	Cost of Sales or Total Cost		3,014.00
	Sales Price		3,360.00
	Profit		346.00

(B) CONTRACT ACCOUNTS

Problem No. 1

Happy Homes Ltd., have undertaken a construction work for a contract price of Rs. 2,50,000 construction work commenced on 1-1-1997.

The details given below relate to this contract for the year ended 31 December 1997.

	Rs.
Materials	85,349
Direct Expenses	3,167
Machinery sent to Site	15,000
Materials on Site on 31-12-97	1,883
Work not certified	4,500
Wages paid	74,375
Overhead	4,126
Materials returned (to Stores)	549
Cash received	1,75,500
Works certified	1,95,000
Wages payable	2,690

Company's policy regarding depreciation on Fixed Assets is 20% p.a., expecting severe conditions, the contractors have decided to transfer 1/3 contract profit in cash received proportion to Profit and Loss Account.

Prepare Contract Account and show the item appearing in Balance Sheet.

[K.U.D., April 1998(N)]

Solution :

Contract A/c for the year ended 31-12-1997

		Rs.			Rs.
To Materials		85,349	By Work-in-Progress A/c		
To Direct Expenses		3,167	Work certified		1,95,000
To Machinery sent to Site		15,000	Work not certified		4,500
To Wages paid	74,375		By Materials on site		
Add Payable	2,690	77,065	on 31-12-97		1,883
To Overheads		4,126	By Materials Returned		549
To Notional Profit	29,225		By Machinery	15,000	
Profit to be taken to the credit of Profit and Loss 1/3 on cash bases in 29,225 × 1/3 $\frac{1,75,500}{1,95,000}$			*Less* Depreciation @ 20%	3,000	12,000
To Profit & Loss (8,767.5)		8,768			
To Reserve A/c		20,457			
		2,13,932			2,13,932

Balance Sheet as at 31-12-1997

Liabilities		Assets	
Profit & Loss A/c	8,768	Work-in-Progress	
Outstanding Wages	2,690	Work certified	1,95,000
		Work not certified	4,500
			1,99,500
		Less Reserve	20,457
			1,79,043
		Less Cash received	1,75,500
			3,543
		Materials Returned	549
		Materials on Site	1,883
		Machinery	12,000

Problem No. 2

Better Builders Ltd. commenced construction of a Complex on 1-1-1996 for a contract price of Rs. 5,00,000. The Trial Balance relating to their business as on 31-12-1996 is as under :

Trial Balance as on 31-12-1996

Particulars	Dr. Rs.	Cr. Rs.
Share Capital	—	50,000
Cash received from contractee		
@ 75% of work certified	—	2,25,000
Charged to Contract		
Materials	78,000	
Plant	25,000	
Wages	91,800	
Supervisory Salaries	77,000	
Establishment charges	3,200	
	2,75,000	2,75,000

Additional information :

(a) The company was engaged in only one contract during the year.

(b) Wages for a week and salaries for a month are outstanding.

(c) Plant costing Rs. 5,000 and Materials worth Rs. 6,000 were returned to stores on 31-12-1996.

(d) Material worth Rs. 20,000 were at site
Work not certified was Rs. 45,000.

(e) The Company charges 10% depreciation on its assets.

Prepare Contract Account and show the work-in-progress in the Balance Sheet.

[K.U.D., April 1998(O)]

Solution :

Contract A/c for the year ended 31-12-1996

Particulars		Rs.	Particulars		Rs.
To Materials		78,000	By Work-in-Progress A/c		
To Plant		25,000	Work certified $(2{,}25{,}000 \times \frac{100}{75})$		3,00,000
To Wages - paid for 53 weeks	91,800				
Outstanding for one week	1,800	93,600	Work not certified		45,000
					3,45,000
To Supervisor Salary for 11 months	77,000		By Material Returned to Store		6,000
Outstanding			By Plant Returned to Stores Cost	5,000	
one month	7,000	84,000	*Less* Depreciation 10%	500	4,500
To Establishment Charges		3,200	To Material at Site		20,000
To Total Profit	1,05,200		To Plant at Site		
Profit to be taken			Cost	20,000	
to Profit & Loss A/c			*Less* Returned	5,000	
1,05,200 × 2/3 × 75%			Plant at Site	15,000	
To Profit & Loss A/c		52,600	*Less* Depreciation	1,500	13,500
To Reserve A/C		52,600			
		3,89,000			3,89,000

Note : (1) Wages Paid for 51 weeks 91,800

Outstanding for 1 week = $\frac{91{,}800}{51}$ = 1,800 1,800 93,600

(2) Salary for 11 months paid Rs. 77,000

Outstanding for 1 month = $\frac{77{,}000}{11}$ = 7,000 84,000

Balance Sheet as at 31-12-1996

Liabilities	Rs.	Assets	Rs.
Share Capital	50,000	Work-in-Progress	3,45,000
Profit	52,600	*Less* Reserve	52,600
Outstanding wages for			2,92,400
one week	1,800	*Less* Cash Received	22,500
Salary	7,000	Work-in-Progress	67,400
		Materials Returned to Store	6,000
		Materials at Site	20,000
		Plant Returned to Store	4,500
		Plant at Site	13,500
	1,11,400		1,11,400

Problem No. 3

Marikamba Builders Ltd., have taken a contract in 1996. The contract price was Rs. 6,25,000.

They started work on 1st January 1996.

The following are the details for the year ending 31-12-1996 :

	Rs.
Materials purchased	2,50,000
Wages paid	70,000
Direct Expenditures paid	12,500
Sub-contract Cost	6,250
Plant purchased	2,00,000
Materials returned to stores	25,000
Materials lost by fire sold (Costing Rs. 12,500)	10,000
Plant sold on 1-7-96 (Costing Rs. 25,000)	27,500
Materials at site 31-12-96	37,500
Work certified	5,00,000
Cost of work uncertified	50,000
Rate of Depreciation	10% p.a.
Retention money	10%
Wages accrued	5,000

Prepare Contract Account.

[K.U.D., October 1997(N)]

Solution :

Contract A/c for the year 31-12-1996

Particulars	Amount	Particulars		Amount
To Materials purchased	2,50,000	By Work-in-Progress		
To Wages Paid	70,000	Work certified -	5,00,000	
Add Wages accrued	5,000	Work uncertified -	50,000	5,50,000
To Direct Expenditures	12,500	By Materials Lost by Fire sold		10,000
To Sub-contract cost	6,250	Costing (Rs.12,500 – 10,000)		2,500
To Plant purchased	2,00,000	By Profit & Loss		2,500
To Profit on sales of Plant	3,750	(*Loss* on sales)		
To Notional Profit 2,40,000		By Plant sold on 1-7-96		27,500
Profit and Loss A/c		Cost	25,000	
3/4 × 90/100 × 2,40,000	1,62,000	*Less* Depreciation 10%		
To Reserve A/c	78,000	for six months	1,250	
			23,750	
		Material at Site		37,500
		Plant	2,00,000	
		Less Sales	25,000	
			1,75,000	
		Less Depreciation	17,500	1,57,500
	7,87,500			7,87,500

Note : Profit taken to Profit and Loss A/c on cash Basis 90% work completed more than 3/4 of the contract price.

Problem No. 4

Cosy Home Construction Co. undertook a contract for construction of a Building.

Following are the particulars for the year ended 31-12-1996 :

	Rs.
Work certified by Architect	5,85,000
Plant installed at site	45,000
Material sent to site	2,55,900
Wages paid at site	2,33,125
Direct Expenditures	9,495
Outstanding wages on 31-12-96	8,070
Cost of work uncertified	13,500
Establishment charges	12,360
Materials Returned to Stores	2,400
Materials at site	5,550
Depreciation on Plant upto 31-12-96	12,000
Contract Price	7,50,000
Cash received	5,26,500

Prepare a Contract Account for the year 1996, showing the amount of profit that may be taken to the credit of Profit and Loss Account for the year 1996.

[K.U.D., October 1997(O)]

Solution :

Contract A/c for the year ending 31-12-1996

Particulars		Amount	Particulars		Amount
To Material send to site		2,55,900	By Work-in-progress		
To Wages paid -	2,33,125		Work certified -	5,85,000	
Add Outstanding -	8,070	2,41,195	*Add* Work uncertified -	13,500	5,98,500
To Direct Expenditures		9,494	By Malterials returned to stores		2,400
To Establishment Charges		12,360	By Materials at site		5,550
To Plant installed at site		45,000	By Plant-Cost	45,000	
Nolinal Profit - 75,500			*Less* Depreciation	12,000	33,000
Profit and Loss A/c					
$\frac{3}{4} \times \frac{5,26,500}{5,85,000} \times 75,500$	50,962.50	50,962.50			
To Reserve A/c	24,537.50	24,537.50			
		6,39,450			6,39,450

Profit taken to the credit of Profit and Loss A/c on cash basis $\frac{5,26,500}{5,85,000} = 90\%$

more than 3/4 of the contract completed in 3/4 is taken.

Problem No. 5

Write a Contract Account from the following particulars of Shetty & Company :

Direct Materials	10,200
Wages	16,800
Special Plant	8,000
Stores issued	2,880
Loose tools	1,500
Administrative Expenses	2,555
Cost of Tractor (Fuel, Wages of Drivers etc.)	3,420
Contract Price	40,000

The contract was completed in 20 weeks. The special plant was returned subject to depreciation of 20 per cent per annum on original cost. The value of loose tools and stores returned were Rs. 1,000 and Rs. 400 respectively. The written down value of the tractor used for contract was Rs. 19,500 and the Depreciation on this value was to be charged to this contract @ 20% p.a.

(K.U.D., April 1996)

Solution :

Contract Account

Particulars	Amount	Particulars		Amount
To Direct Materials	10,200	By Contractee A/c		40,000
To Wages	16,800	By Returned to stores		
To Special Plant	8,000	Special Plant	8,000	
To Stores issued	2,880	*Less* : 20% Depr.		
To Loose tools	1,500	(20% × 8000 = 1,600	615	7,385
		$1,600 \times \frac{20}{52}$		
To Administrative Expenses	2,555	By Loose tools		1,000
To Cost of Tractor (Fuel & Wages of Drivers etc.)	3,420	By Stores		400
To Depreciation on Tractor (19,500 × 20% = 3,900 p.a. for 20 weeks)	1,500			
	46,855			48,785
Profit transferred to Profit & Loss A/c	1,930			—
	48,785			48,785

Problem No. 6

The following Trial Balance of Besaveshwar Construction Company engaged in the execution of contract No. 101 for the year ending 31-12-94 :

	Dr	Cr
Share Capital	—	40,000
Creditors	—	4,000
Land & Building	17,000	—
Cash at Bank	4,500	—
Contract Account :		
Material	37,500	
Plant	10,000	
Wages	52,500	
Expenses	2,500	
Cash received for Contractee (80% of work certified)	—	80,000
	1,24,000	1,24,000

Plant costing Rs. 1,500 and material costing Rs. 1,200 were destroyed by fire. On 31-12-94 plant costing Rs. 2,000 was returned to stores. Materials at site at close were Rs. 1,500. Work done but not certified was Rs. 1,000. Charges depreciation on plant at 10% per annum. Prepare Contract Account for the year ended 31-12-94 and Balance Sheet as on that date.

(K.U.D., October 1995)

Solution :

Contract Account for the year ended 31-12-94

Particulars	Amount	Particulars		Amount
To Materials	37,500	By *Work-in-Progress*		
To Plant	10,000	Work certified		
To Wages	52,500	80,000 × 100/80		1,00,000
To Expenses	2,500	Work not certified		1,000
Total	1,02,500	Total		1,01,000
To Notional Profit	10,350	By *Loss by fire*		
		Plant	1,500	
		Material	1,200	2,700
		Plant returned to stores :		
		Cost	2,000	
		Less : Depr. 10%	200	1,800
		Materials at Site		1,500
		Plant	10,000	
		Cost (Loss by fire)	1,500	
			8,500	

Particulars	Amount	Particulars		Amount
		Less : Return to stores	2,000	
			6,500	
		Less : Depr. @ 10% 650		5,850
	1,12,850			1,12,850
To Profit & Loss A/c (10,350 × 2/3 × 80/100)	5,520	By Notional Profit		10,350
To Reserve A/c (Transfer)	4,830			
	10,350			10,350

Balance Sheet as at 31-12-1994

Liabilities		Rs.	Assets		Rs.
Share Capital		40,000	Land & Building		17,000
Creditors		4,000	Cash at Bank		4,500
Profit & Loss A/c	5,520		Work-in-Progress	1,01,000	
Less : Loss by fire	2,700	2,820	*Less* : Reserve	4,830	
				96,170	
			Less : Contractee A/c	80,000	16,170
			Material at Site		1,500
			Plant rate to site		1,800
			Plant at site		5,850
		46,820			46,820

Problem No. 7

The following information is given with reference to contract undertaken by Maya Engineering Co. Ltd. :

Contract Price — Rs. 10,00,000

Contractee pays 90% of the value of work done and certified.

Following are the expenses incurred on the contract :

Materials issued		2,00,000
Materials returned to the stores at cost		10,000
Materials sold (at cost)		10,000
Wages paid	1,90,000	
Wages Payable	10,000	2,00,000
Cost of plant issued (to be depreciated at 15% p.a.)		2,00,000
Administrative Expenses		40,000
Cash received from the Contractee		6,30,000

75% of the work on contract was completed as on 31-12-93. Prepare Contract Account appropriating reasonable profits.

(K.U.D., April 1995)

Solution :

Contract A/c

Particulars	Amount	Particulars	Amount
To Materials Issued	2,00,000	By Materials Returned	10,000
To Wages paid 1,90,000		By Materials sold	10,000
To Wages payable 10,000	2,00,000	By Work certified	
To Plant Cost	2,00,000	630000 × 100/90	7,00,000
To Administrative Exp.	40,000	By Work done but not certified	50,000
To Notional Profit	3,00,000	By Plant cost 2,00,000	
		Less : Depr. @ 5% 30,000	1,70,000
Total	9,40,000	Total	9,40,000
To Profit & Loss A/c 3,00,000 × 2/3 × 90/100	1,80,000	By Notional Profit	3,00,000
To Reserve	1,20,000		
Total	3,00,000	Total	3,00,000

Total Contract Price	10,00,000
Work done 75%	7,50,000
Work certified	7,00,000
Work uncertified	50,000

Problem No. 8

The following figures relate to Contract No. 303 which commenced from 1-1-1993 :

	Rs.
Materials issued from stores	1,60,000
Material purchased for the contract	30,000
Plant installed at site	1,00,000
Wages paid	1,80,000
Direct expenses paid	25,000
Establishment Expenses	6,000
Direct Expenses outstanding on 31-12-93	3,000
Wages outstanding on 31-12-93	4,000

Of the plant and materials charged to the contract, plant which costs Rs. 10,000 and materials costing Rs. 4,000 were lost. Some part of the materials costing Rs. 5,000 were sold at a Profit of Rs. 1,000. On 31-12-93 plant which costs

Rs. 4,000 was returned to stores and plant which costs Rs. 6,000 was transferred to some other contract.

The work certified was Rs. 4,80,000 and 80% of the same is received in cash. The cost of work done but uncertified was Rs. 3,000. Charge depreciation on plant at 10 per cent p.a. You are required to prepare the contract account for the year ended 31-12-93, by transferring to the Profit and Loss Acount, the portion of profit, if any which you consider reasonable.

(K.U.D., October 1994)

Solution :

Contract A/c for the year ended 31-12-93

Particulars		Amount	Particulars		Amount
To Materials issued		1,60,000	By Work-in-progress		
To Materials Purchase		30,000	Work certified	4,80,000	
To Wages paid	1,80,000		Work uncertified	3,000	4,83,000
Add : Outstanding	4,000	1,84,000	By Materials loss		4,000
To Direct Exp.	25,000		By Plant lost		
Add : Outstanding	3,000	28,000	Cost	10,000	
To Establishment Exp.		6,000	By *Less* : Depr. 10%	1,000	9,000
To Plant		1,00,000	By Materials sold		
			Cost	5,000	
To Notional Profit		75,000	*Add* : Profit	1,000	6,000
			By Plant returned to stores cost	4,000	
			Less : Depr. 10%	400	3,600
			To Plant transferred to other contract		
			Cost	6,000	
			Less : Depr. 10%	600	5,400
			To Plant at site Cost	80,000	
			Less : Depr. 10%	8,000	72,000
		5,83,000			5,83,000
To Profit & Loss A/c		40,000	By Notional Profit		75,000
75,000 × 2/3 × 80%					
To Reserve A/c		35,000			
		75,000			75,000

Problem No. 9

Hindustan Construction Co. Ltd. have taken a contract in 1992. The value of the contract is Rs. 6,00,000. They began the work on Ist January 1992. The following are the details for the year ending 31st December 1992 :

Materilas issued	1,68,000
Wages paid	1,70,000
Direct Expenses	4,000
General O.H. apportioned	16,000
Plan issued	30,000

Following are the outstanding expenses as on 31st December 1992 :

Wages — Rs. 1,400; Direct Expenses — Rs. 600. During the year materials of Rs. 500 were returned to the stores and materials worth Rs. 1,500 were at site on 31-12-1992. Rs. 3,00,000 were received from the contractee, being equal to 80% of the work certified. Cost of work done but not certified was Rs. 7,000. Plant is to be depreciated at 20% p.a.

Prepare the Contract Account and Contractee Account for the year ending 31st December 1992 and show the amount of profit to be taken to Profit and Loss Account.

(K.U.D., April 1994)

Solution :

Contract A/c

Particulars		Amount	Particular		Amount
To Materials issued		1,68,000	By Work-in-progress A/c $30{,}000 \times \frac{100}{80}$		3,75,000
To Wages paid	1,70,000		By Work uncertified		7,000
Add : Outstanding	1,400	1,71,400	By Materials returned to stores		500
To Direct Expenses	4,000		By Material on site		1,500
Add : Outstanding	600	4,600	By Plant cost	30,000	
General Expenses		16,000	*Less*: Deprec. 20%	6,000	24,000
Plant — issued		30,000			
Notional Profit		18,000			
		4,08,000			4,08,000
To Profit and Loss a/c 18000 × 2/3 × 4/5		9,600	By Notional Profit		18,000
Reserve A/c		8,400			
Total		18,000	Total		18,000

Contractee A/c

Particulars	Amount	Particulars	Amount
To Balance c/d	3,00,000	By Cash Amount	3,00,000
Total	3,00,000	Total	3,00,000

Problem No. 10

The following information relates to a contract for Rs. 3,75,000. The contractee pays 90% of the value of work certified and the balance on the completion of contract :

	1975	1976	1977
	Rs.	Rs.	Rs.
Material	45,000	55,000	31,500
Wages	42,500	57,500	42,500
Direct Expenses	1,750	6,250	2,250
Indirect Expenses	750	1,000	—
Work certified	87,500	2,82,500	3,75,000
Work uncertified	—	5,000	—
Plant	5,000	—	—

The value of plant at the end of 1975, 1976 and 1977 was Rs. 4,000, Rs. 2,500 and Rs. 1,000 respectively.

Prepare contract account for three years.

(K.U.D., October 1993)

Solution :

Contract A/c for the year 1975

Particulars	Amount	Particulars	Amount
To Materials	45,000	By Work-in-progress A/c (Work certified)	87,500
To Wages	42,500		
To Direct Expenses	1,750	By Plant	4,000
To Plant	5,000	By Profit & Loss A/c (Loss transferred)	3,500
	95,000		95,000

Contract A/c for the year 1976

Particulars	Amount	Particulars	Amount
To Work-in-progress	87,500	By Work-in-progress (work certified)	2,82,500
To Plant	4,000		
To Materials	55,000	" Work uncertified	5,000
To Wages	57,500	" Plant	2,500
To Direct Expenses	6,250		
To Indirect Expenses	1,000		
To Profit (Notional)	78,750		
	2,90,000		2,90,000
To Profit & Loss A/c	47,250	By Notional Profit	78,750
To Reserve	31,500		
	78,750		78,750

Contract A/c for the year 1977

Particulars	Amount	Particulars	Amount
To Work-in-progress (Work certified)	2,82,500	By Contractee A/c	3,75,000
		By Plant	1,000
To Work uncertified	5,000		
	2,87,500		
Less : Reserve	31,500		
	2,56,000		
To Plant	2,500		
To Materials	31,500		
To Wages	42,500		
To Direct Expenses	2,250		
To Profit & Loss A/c	41,250		
Total	3,76,000	Total	3,76,000

Balance Sheet as at 1975

Liabilities	Assets		Amount
	Work-in-progress A/c		
	Work certified		87,500
	Plant		4,000
			91,500
	Less : Cash received		
	90% of 87,500		78,750
			12,750
	Profit & Loss A/c (Loss)		3,500

Balance Sheet as at 31-12-1976

Liabilities	Amount	Assets		Amount
Profit & Loss A/c	47,250	Work-in-progress A/c		
		Work certified	2,82,500	
		Work uncertified	5,000	
			2,87,500	
		Less : Reserve	31,500	
			2,56,000	
		Less : Cash received		
		90% of 2,82,500	2,54,250	1,750
		Plant		2,500

Problem No. 11

Anoop Construction Sirsi undertook a contract for Rs. 4,00,000 on 1st January 1991. From the following particulars, prepare contract account for the year ending 31-12-91 and show how much profit should be appropriated on the basis of estimated total profit.

Materials	90,000
Plant issued	30,000
Wages	1,20,000
Working expenses	2,000
Administrative expenses	5,000
Materials costing Rs. 5,000 were sold for	4,500
Work certified	3,60,000
Plant at site on 31-12-91	15,000
Cost of work not yet certified	10,000

It was estimated that :

(a) The contract would be completed in a further period of 3 months when the plant will have a residual value of Rs. 5,000.

(b) The additional wages required to complete the contract would come to Rs. 20,000.

(c) The additional working expenses would be Rs. 3,000 and administrative expenses would be Rs. 2,000.

(d) The material required would cost Rs. 13,000.

(K.U.D., April 1993)

Solution :

Contract Account for the year ended 31-12-91

Particulars	Amount	Particulars		Amount
To Materials	90,000	By Materials sold	4,500	
To Plant Issued	30,000	(Loss sales)		
To Wages	1,20,00	By Profit & Loss A/c		
To Work Expenses	2,000	transfer	500	5,000
To Administration Expenses	5,000	By Plant at site		15,000
To Notional Profit	1,43,000	By *Work-in-progress*		
		Work certified	3,60,000	
		Work uncertified	10,000	3,70,000
	3,90,000			3,90,000
To Profit & Loss A/c	1,12,500	By Notional Profit		1,43,000
To Balance to Reserve	30,500			
	1,43,000			1,43,000

Working Note

(Statement of Estimated Cost)

Expenses incurred up to this day 31-12-91

Particulars		Amount	Particulars	Amount
I. Expenses incurred		2,47,000	II. Statement of Estimated Profit.	
Less : Cost Material			Contract Price	4,00,000
sold	4,500			
Less : Loss on sale	500		*Less* : Estimated total cost	2,75,000
Plant at site	15,000	20,000		
Cost of completed			Estimated Profit	1,25,000
Contract up to 31-12-91		2,27,000		

Particulars	Amount	Particulars	Amount
Contract up to 31-12-91	2,27,000		
Add : Estimated Additional expenses :		III. Profit to be taken to the Profit & Loss A/c	
Material 13,000		Estimated Profit × $\frac{\text{Work certified}}{\text{Contract Price}}$	
Wages 20,000			
Work Expenses 3,000		$1,25,000 \times \frac{3,60,000}{4,00,000}$ =	1,12,500
Admin. Expenses 2,000		Estimated Profit :	
Plant at site 15,000		Taken Profit & Loss A/c	1,12,500
53,000		Balance Reserve	30,500
Less : Plant			1,43,000
residual value 5,000	48,000		
Estimated Total Cost of Contract	2,75,000		

Problem No. 12

Anand Construction Company undertook a Contract for construction of Building.

Following are the particulars for the year ended 31-12-1988 :

Work certified by Architect	1,43,000
Cost of work uncertified	3,400
Plant installed at site	11,300
Depreciation on Plant up to 31-12-88	3,100
Materials sent at site	65,300
Wages paid at site	54,800
Establishment charges	3,250
Wages accrued on 31-12-1988	1,800
Direct Expenditures	2,400
Materials lost at site	800
Material on hand at site	1,400
Direct expenditure accrued	200
Materials returned to stores	400
Contract Price	2,00,000
Cash received from the contractee	1,30,000

Prepare Contract Account.

(K.U.D., October 1992)

Solution :

Contract A/c

Particulars	Amount	Particulars	Amount
To Material sent to site	65,300	By Work-in-progress A/c	
To Wages paid 54,800		Work certified 1,43,000	
Add : Accrued 1,800	56,600	Work uncertified 3,400	1,46,400
To Establishment charge	3,250	By Profit & Loss A/c	
To Direct Expenses 2,400		Materials Lost at site	800
Add : Accrued 200	2,600	By Material on hand at site	1,400
To Depreciation on Plant	3,100	By Material return to store	400
To Notional Profit	18,150	Total	1,49,000
Total	1,49,000	By Notional Profit	18,150
To Profit & Loss A/c	11,000		
$18{,}150 \times \frac{2}{3} \times \frac{1{,}30{,}000}{1{,}43{,}000}$			
To Reserve Account	7,150		
Total	18,150	Total	18,150

Problem No. 13

The following particulars relate to two contract for the construction of Houses during 1990 :

Particulars	House-A Rs.	House-B Rs.
Work-in-progress on 1-1-1990	14,800	Nil
Materials purchased	23,000	16,600
Wages	20,000	14,000
Electric fitting	1,400	300
Road Making charges	8,000	Nil
Contract Price (Including Road making)	60,000	40,000
Cash received up to 31-12-1990	60,000	24,000
Purchases of cash received to work certified	100%	$66\frac{2}{3}\%$
Materials on hand on 31-12-1990	400	540
Work uncertified	Nil	2,500
Plant	12,000	6,000
Period for which plant is used	10 Months	8 Months

The total administrative charges incurred during 1990 amounted to Rs. 12,240 which are charged to the contract in the ratio of wages depreciation is calculated at the rate of 10% p.a. Prepare two Contract Account for the year 1990.

(K.U.D., April 1992)

Solution :

Contract Account for the year ended 31-12-90

Particulars	House-A	House-B	Particulars	House-A	House-B
To Work-in-progress	14,800	—	By Contract A/c (Cash received 100%)	60,000	—
To Materials purchased	23,000	16,600	By Work-in-progress Work certified		
To Wages	20,000	14,000	$24{,}000 \times \frac{100}{200} \times 3$	—	36,000
To Electricity fitting	1,400	300	Uncertified	—	2,500
To Road making charges	8,000	—	Material in Hand 31-12-90	400	540
To Plant	12,000	6,000	By Plant A 12,000 *Less* : Depr. 10% = 12,000 for 10 months 1,000	11,000	
To Administrative charges $12{,}240 \times \frac{10}{17} = 7{,}200$ $12{,}240 \times \frac{7}{17} = 5{,}040$	7,200	5,040	B 6,000 $(6{,}000 \times 10\% \times \frac{8}{12})$ 400		5,600
To Profit = 2,700 (Notional-B)	—		By Profit & Loss A/c (Loss) Rs. 15,000	15,000	—
Transfer to Profit and Loss A/c $2{,}700 \times \frac{2}{3} \times \frac{24{,}000}{36{,}000} =$		1,200			
Reserve A/c		1,500			
Total	86,400	44,640	Total	86,400	44,640

Problem No. 14

The following information relates to contract No. 1234. You are required to prepare the Contract Account and Contractee's Account assuming that the amount due from contractee was received :

Direct Materials — Rs. 20,250; Direct Wages — Rs. 15,500;

Stores issued — Rs. 10,500; Loose tools — Rs. 2,400. Tractor expenses —

Running materials — Rs. 2,300 and Wages of Drivers — Rs. 3,000; Other direct charges — Rs. 2,650.

The contract price was Rs. 90,000 and the contract took 13 weeks in its completion. The values of loose tools and stores returned at end of the period were Rs. 200 and Rs. 3,000 respectively. The plant was also returned at a value of Rs. 16,000 after charging depreciation at 20%. The value of tractor was Rs. 20,000 and the depreciation was to be charged to the contract at 15% per annum. The administration expenses to be provided is Rs. 5,815.

(K.U.D., October 1991)

Solution :

Contract A/c (No. 1234)

Particulars	Amount	Particulars	Amount
To Direct Material	20,250	By Stores returned	3,000
To Direct Wages	15,500	By Loose tools	200
To Stores issued	10,500	By Plant returned	16,000
To Plant Cost	20,000	By Contractee A/c	90,000
To Loose tools	2,400		
To Tractor Expenses Running material 2,300 Wages of Driver 3,000	5,300		
To Depreciation on Tractor 15% of 20,000 for 13 weeks $20,000 \times 15\% \times \frac{13}{52} = 750$	750		
To Other Direct Charges	2,650		
To Administrative Exp.	5,815		
To Net Profit	26,035		
Total	1,09,200	Total	1,09,200

Contractee A/c

Particulars	Amount	Particulars	Amount
To Contract Account	90,000	By Bank	90,000
Total	90,000	Total	90,000

Ascertainment of Cost of Plant Purchased :

Plant (returned after Depreciation 20%) = Rs. 16,000

Plant costing of Rs. 16,000 being 80% off

$\therefore$ Original Cost = $16,000 \times \frac{100}{80}$ = Rs. 20,000

Problem No. 15

The Engineering Contractors Ltd. having an authorised capital of Rs. 1,00,000 divided in to 500 6 per cent preference share of Rs. 100 each and 5000 Equity shares of Rs. 10 each. Commenced operation on Ist January 1989 and during the year were engaged on one contract of which contract price of Rs. 4,00,000. The Trial Balance extracted from their books on 31-12-1989 stood as follows :

(1) Share Capital 6% 400 preference shares fully paid		40,000
500 Equity shares of Rs. 8 paid up		40,000
(2) Sundry Creditors		8,000
(3) Land & Building	34,000	
(4) Cash at Bank	9,000	
(5) Contract A/c :		
Materials	75,000	
Plant	20,000	
Wages	1,05,000	
Expenses	5,000	
(6) Cash received (80% of work certified)		1,60,000
	2,48,000	2,48,000

Of the plant and materials charged to contract plant costing of Rs. 3,000 and Materials costing Rs. 2,400 were destroyed by an accident. On 31-12-1989 plant costing Rs. 4,000 was returned to the stores. The value of materials on site was Rs. 3,000. Uncertified work was valued Rs. 2,000. Depreciation plant @ Rs. 20% p.a.

Prepare Contract Account for the year 1989 and a Balance Sheet as on that date.

[K.U.D., April 1991, Mysore, October 1986,
M'lore (Modified)]

Solution :

Contract Account for the year 1989

Particulars	Amount	Particulars		Amount
To Materials	75,000	By Work-in-progress A/c		
To Wages	1,05,000	Work certified		
To Expenses	5,000	$(1,60,000 \times \frac{100}{80})$		2,00,000
To Plant	20,000	By Work uncertified		2,000
Total	2,05,000			2,02,000
		By Loss by accident		
		Plant	3,000	
		Material	2,400	5,400

Particulars		Amount	Particulars		Amount
Total		2,05,000	By Plant returned to stores	4,000	
Notional Profit	19,000		*Less* : Depr. 20%	800	3,200
Profit to be taken to Profit & Loss A/c			By Material on site		3,000
			By Plant at site Cost	20,000	
$19{,}000 \times \frac{2}{3} \times \frac{80}{100} =$		10,133	*Less* : Loss in accident	3,000	
				17,000	
Balance transfer to Reserve A/c		8,867	*Less* : Return to stores	4,000	
				13,000	
			Less : Depr. @ 20%	2,600	10,400
		2,24,000			2,24,000

Balance Sheet as at 31-12-1989

Particulars		Amount	Particulars		Amount
Share Capital Authorised			Land & Building		34,000
6% 500 Pref. shares of Rs. 100 each		50,000	Cash at Bank		9,000
5000 Equity shares of Rs. 10 each		50,000	Plant return to stores		3,200
		1,00,000	Plant at site		10,400
Paidup Capital					
6% 400 Pref. shares of Rs. 100 each fully paid		40,000	Material on site		3,000
			Work-in-Progress :		
5000 Equity shares of Rs. 10 Rs. 8 paid up		40,000	Work certified	2,00,000	
			Work uncertified	2,000	
				2,02,000	
Reserve & Surplus					
Profit & Loss Account			*Less* : Reserve	8,867	
Profit	10,133			1,93,133	
Less : Loss on accident	5,400	4,733	*Less* : Cash received	1,60,000	33,133
Sundry Creditors		8,000			
		92,733			92,733

Problem No. 16

In a book of contractor the following information is found on July 31, 1985 :

Materials issued to site	6,000
Plant issued to site	10,000
Direct Labour	4,600
Indirect Labour	635
Overhead Expenses	1,950
Wages accrued	1,500
Value of work certified for payment	12,000
Cost of work uncertified	4,000
Stock of materials	1,050
Depreciation on plant @ 10% p.a.	
Cash received from the contractee	9,600

Show the Contract Account taking 2/3 for the profits on contract in progress. Also show the relevant entries in the Balance Sheet.

(M'lore, October 1990)

Solution :

Contract Account for the year ended 31-7-1985

Particulars		Amount	Particulars		Amount
To Materials issued		6,000	By *Work-in-progress*		
To Direct Labour	4,600		Work certified		12,000
Add : Wages accrued	1,500	6,100	Work uncertified		4,000
					16,000
To Indirect Labour		635			
To Overhead Exp.		1,950	Materials in hand		1,050
To Plant		10,000	Plant cost	10,000	
			Less : Depr. at 10%	1,000	9,000
To Notional Profit		1,365			
		26,050			26,050
To Profit Loss A/c			By Notional Profit		1,365
$(1{,}365 \times 2/3 \times \frac{9{,}600}{12{,}000})$		728			
To Reserve		637			
		1,365			1,365

Balance Sheet as at 31-7-1985

Liabilities	Amount	Assets		Amount
Profit & Loss A/c	728	Material on hand		1,050
		Plant Less Depr.		9,000
		Work-in-progress :	16,000	
		Less : Reserve	637	
			15,363	
		Less : Cash received	9,600	5,763

Problem No. 17

Archana & Co. during 1989 undertook one contract for a price of Rs. 25,00,000 on 1-7-1989. The plant and materials charged to the contract plant which cost of 25,000 and materials Rs. 20,000 were lost by theft on 31-12-1989 plant which originally cost of Rs. 25,000 was returned to stores. The cost of work done but not certified was Rs. 10,000 and materials costing Rs. 25,000 were at site charge depreciation @ 10% p.a. on plant.

Write Contract Account, Profit & Loss A/c and the Balance Sheet from the following Trial Balance as on 31-12-1989.

Trial Balance as on 31-12-1989

	Dr. Rs.	Cr. Rs.
(1) Share Capital	—	6,00,000
(2) Creditors	—	50,000
(3) Contractee A/c (80% of work certified)	—	10,00,000
(4) Land & Building	2,15,000	
(5) Bank	1,25,000	
(6) Contract A/c :		
(a) Material	4,50,000	
(b) Plant (at cost)	1,25,000	
(c) Wages	7,00,000	
(d) Expenses	35,000	
	16,50,000	16,50,000

(Bangalore, October 1990)

Solution :

Contract A/c

Particulars		Amount	Particulars		Amount
To Materials		4,50,000	By Loss by theft		
To Wages		7,00,000	Plant cost	25,000	
			Material	20,000	45,000
To Expenses		35,000	By Plant returned to stores		
To Plant (at Cost)		1,25,000	Cost	25,000	
To Notional Profit		1,20,000			
		14,30,000	*Less* : Depr. @ 10% for		
			6 months	1,250	23,750
To Notional Profit	1,20,000		Plant cost	1,25,000	
Transferred to			*Less* : Loss by theft	25,000	
Profit Loss A/c	64,000			1,00,000	
(1,20,000 × 2/3 × 4/5)			*Less* : Returned to store		
			at site	25,000	
Reserve	56,000			75,000	
	1,20,000		*Less* : Depr.	3,750	71,250
			Material at site		25,000
			Work-in-progress :		
			Work certified	12,50,000	
			$(10,00,000 \times \frac{100}{80})$		
			Work done but not certified	10,000	12,65,000
		14,30,000			14,30,000

Balance Sheet as at 31-12-1989

Liabilities		Amount	Assets		Amount
Share Capital		6,00,000	Plant returned to stores		23,750
Reserve & Surplus			Plant at site		71,250
Profit & Loss A/c	64,000		Material at site		25,000
Less : Abnormal			*Work-in-progress :*		
Loss by theft	45,000	19,000		12,65,000	
Creditors		50,000			
			Less : Reserve	56,000	
				12,09,000	
			Less : Cash received	10,00,000	2,09,000
			Land & Building		2,15,000
			Bank Account		1,25,000
		6,69,000			6,69,000

Problem No. 18

Alcon Contractors Ltd. have undertaken a contract for the construction of a building at a price of Rs. 40,000 on 1st April, 1989. The following informations were obtained from the records of the Company as on 3st December, 1989 :

Materials sent to site	4,150
Labour	10,172
Overheads	1,262

A plant costing Rs. 3,000 has been on the site for 73 days. Its working life is estimated at 5 years and its final scrap value Rs. 400. A supervisor who is paid Rs. 1,200 annually has spent exactly half of his time on this contract. All other expenses amounted to Rs. 2,526 and materials at site on that date cost Rs. 500. The contract price is Rs. 40,000. Two thirds of the contract was completed, architects certificate has been issued for Rs. 20,000 and Rs. 16,000 has been received in cash.

Prepare contract account as on 31st December, 1989 and take a reasonable amount of Profit to the credit of Profit and Loss Account of the Company.

(K.U.D., October 1990)

Solution :

Working Note

Ascertainment of work done but not certified (Work uncertified)

Expenses incurred for 2/3 of the Contract :

Material	4,150	
Labour	10,172	
Overhead	1,262	
Plant	3,000	
Supervisor Salary	450	
Other Expenses	2,526	
Total Expenses		21,560
Less : Credit Items		
Material on site	500	
Plant cost 3,000		
Less : Depr. 104	2,896	3,396
Net Expenses incurred for 2/3 work done		18,164

Now work certified ½ of the contract

For 2/3 work done work certified ½ for expenses incurred 18,164

3/2 × ½ × 18,164 = 4,541 = — 13,623 (–) 13,623

Work Uncertified Rs. 4,541

Contract Account for the year ended 31-12-89

Particulars	Amount	Particulars		Amount
To Materials sent to site	4,150	By Work-in-progress :		
To Labour	10,172	Work certified		20,000
To Overheads	1,262	Work uncertified		4,541
To Plant (for 73 days)	3,000	By Materials on site		500
To Supervisor salary		By Plant on site Cost	3,000	
$(\frac{1}{2} \times 12,000 = 600 \times \frac{9}{12})$	450	*Less* : Depr.	104	2,896
To Other Expenses	2,526			
To Notional Profit	6,377			
Total	27,937	Total		27,937
To Profit & Loss A/c		By Notional Profit		6,377
$\frac{2}{3} \times \frac{16,000}{20,000} \times 6,377$	3,401			
To Reserve A/c (Balance transferred)	2,976			
Total	6,377	Total		6,377

Calculation of Depreciation $= \frac{\text{Cost} - \text{Scrap}}{\text{Life}} \times \frac{73}{365}$

$$= \frac{3000 - 400}{5} \times \frac{73}{365}$$

$$= \frac{2,600}{5} \times \frac{1}{5}$$

$$= \text{Rs. } 104.$$

Problem No. 19

The following particulars relate to a contract for Rs. 4,00,000 :

Particulars	1986 Rs.	1987 Rs.	1988 Rs.
(i) Materials	4,50,000	7,00,000	6,00,000
(ii) Wages	4,30,000	6,00,000	5,00,000
(iii) Carriage	20,000	60,000	50,000
(iv) General Expenses	20,000	50,000	16,000
(v) Work certified	9,00,000	30,00,000	40,00,000
(vi) Work uncertified	10,000	50,000	—

Plant costing Rs. 1,00,000 was bought in the beginning 1986 and depreciation was charged at 25% p.a. on original cost system.

The Contractee was to pay 80% of work certified by the Architect every year and settle the account years and show working notes.

(K.U.D., April 1990)

Solution :

Contract Account for the year ended 1986

Particulars	Amount	Particulars		Amount
To Materials	4,50,000	By *Work-in-Progress*		
To Wages	4,30,000	By Work certified		9,00,000
To Carriage	20,000	By Work uncertified		10,000
To General Expenses	20,000	By Plant cost	1,00,000	
To Plant Cost	1,00,000	*Less* : 25%	25,000	75,000
		By Profit & Loss A/c		35,000
	10,20,000			10,20,000

Contract Account for the year ended 1987

Particulars	Amount	Particulars		Amount
To *Work-in-Progress A/c*		By *Work-in-Progress*		
Work certified	9,00,000	Work certified		30,00,000
Work uncertified	10,000	Work uncertified		50,000
To Plant	75,000	By Plant	75,000	30,50,000
To Materials	7,00,000	*Less* : 25% on		
To Wages	6,00,000	cost Depr.	25,000	50,000
To Carriage	60,000			
To General Expenses	50,000			
To Notional Profit	7,05,000			
	31,00,000			31,00,000
To Profit & Loss A/c	3,76,000	By Notional Profit		7,05,000
7,05,000 × 2/3 × 80/100				
To Reserve A/c (Transfer)	3,29,000			
	7,05,000			7,05,000

Contract Account for the year ended 1988

Particulars	Amount	Particulars		Amount
To *Work-in-Progress A/c*		By Contractee A/c		40,00,000
Work certified	30,00,000	By Plant	50,000	
Work uncertified	50,000	*Less* : Depr.	25,000	25,000
	30,50,000			
Less : Reserve	3,29,000			
	27,21,000			
To Plant	50,000			
To Materials	6,00,000			
To Wages	5,00,000			
To Carriage	50,000			
To General Expenses	16,000			
To Profit & Loss A/c (Net Profit Transfer)	88,000			
	40,25,000			40,25,000

Items in Balance Sheet

	Assets	Amount
	1986	
	Work-in-Progress	
	Work certified	9,00,000
	Work uncertified	10,000
		9,10,000
	Less : Cash received	7,20,000
		1,90,000
	Plant	75,000
	1987	
	Work-in-Progress	30,00,000
	Work uncertified	50,000
		30,50,000
	Less : Reserve	3,29,000
		27,21,000
	Less : Cash Reserve	24,00,000
		3,21,000
	Plant.	50,000

Contractee A/c

Particulars	Amount	Particulars	Amount
1987			
To Balance c/d	7,20,000	By Cash Account 80% of 9,00,000	7,20,000
1988			
To Balance c/d	24,00,000	By Balance b/d	7,20,000
		By Cash A/c 80% of 21,00,000 (30,00,000 – 9,00,000)	16,80,000
	24,00,000		24,00,000
1988			
To Contract A/c	40,00,000	By Balance b/d	24,00,000
		By Cash Balance	16,00,000
	40,00,000		40,00,000

Problem No. 20

Karnatak Construction Co. undertook a contract for construction of Building. Following are the particulars for the year ended 31st December 1988 :

(1)	Work certified by the Architect	1,43,000
(2)	Cost of work uncertified	3,400
(3)	Plant Installed at site	11,300
(4)	Depreciation of plant upto 31-12-88	3,100
(5)	Material sent to site	65,300
(6)	Wages paid at site	54,800
(7)	Establishment charges	3,250
(8)	Wages accrued on 31-12-88	1,800
(9)	Direct Expenditure	2,400
(10)	Materials lost at site	800
(11)	Materials in hand at site	1,400
(12)	Materials returned to stores	400
(13)	Direct Expenditure accrued on 31-12-88	200
(14)	Contract Price	2,00,000
(15)	Cash received from contractee	1,30,000

Prepare a Contract Account for the year ended 31-12-1988 showing the Profit to be taken to the credit of Profit & Loss Account and who show the items appearing in Balance Sheet.

(K.U.D., April 1989)

Solution :

Contract A/c for the year ended 31-12-1988

Particulars		Amount	Particulars	Amount
To Materials sent to site		65,300	By *Work-in-Progress A/c*	
To Wages Paid	54,800		Work certified	1,43,000
Add : Wages accrued	1,800	56,600	Work uncertified	3,400
				1,46,400
To Establishment charges		3,250	By Material Lost at Site (Profit & Loss A/c)	800
To Direct Expenses	2,400			
Add : Exp. accrued	200	2,600	By Materials on hand at site	1,400
To Depreciation on Plant		3,100	By Materials returned to stores	400
To Notional Profit		18,150		
		1,49,000		1,49,000
To Profit & Loss A/c		11,000	By Notional Profit	18,150
$18,150 \times \frac{2}{3} \times \frac{1,30,000}{1,43,000}$				
To Reserve A/c (Transfer)		7,150		
		18,150		18,150

Balance Sheet as at 31-12-1988

Particulars		Amount	Particulars		Amount
Profit and Loss A/c			*Work-in-Progress A/c*		
Profit	11,000		Work certified		1,43,000
Less : Material Loss	800		Work uncertified		3,400
	10,200				1,46,400
Less : Depreciation	3,200	7,100	*Less* : Reserve		7,150
					1,39,250
			Less : Cash received		1,30,000
					9,250
			Material on hand at site		1,400
			Materials return to store		400
			Plant cost :	11,300	
			Less : Depreciation	3,100	8,200

Problem No. 21

The following information relates to a Building contract for Rs. 10,00,000 and for which 80 per cent of the value of work-in-progress as certified by Architect is being paid by the contractee.

Particulars	1976	1977	1978
(1) Material Issued	1,20,000	1,45,000	84,000
(2) Direct Wages	1,10,000	1,55,000	1,10,000
(3) Direct Expenses	5,000	17,000	6,000
(4) Indirect Expenses	2,000	2,600	500
(5) Work certified	2,35,000	7,50,000	10,00,000
(6) Work uncertified	2,800	8,000	—
(7) Materials on site	2,000	5,000	8,000
(8) Value of plant issued	14,000	—	—
The value of plant at the end	1976	1977	1978
of was respectively	11,200	7,000	3,000

Prepare Contract Account for three years.

(K.U.D., April 1988)

Solution :

Items in Balance Sheet

Liabilities	Assets		Amount
	1976		
	Work-in-Progress		
	Work certified	2,35,000	
	Work uncertified	2,800	
		2,37,800	
	Less : Reserve	—	
		2,37,800	
	Less : Cash received	1,88,000	49,800
	Material at site		2,000
	Plant at site		11,200
	1977		
	Work-in-Progress		
	Work certified	7,50,000	
	Work uncertified	8,000	
		7,58,000	
	Less : Reserve	93,053	
		6,64,947	
	Less : Cash reserve	6,00,000	64,947
	Material at site		5,000
	Plant at site		7,000

Contract Account for the year ended 1976

Particulars	Amount	Particulars		Amount
1976				
To Material issued	1,20,000	By *Work-in-Progress A/c*		
To Direct Wages	1,10,000	By Work certified		2,35,000
To Direct Expenses	5,000	By Work uncertified		2,800
To Indirect Expenses	2,000	By Material on site		2,000
To Plant issued	14,000	By Plant	14,000	
		Less : Depr.	2,800	11,200
	2,51,000			2,51,000

Contract A/c

Particulars	Amount	Particulars		Amount
1977				
To *Work-in-Progress A/c*		By *Work-in-Progress A/c*		
To Work certified	2,35,000	By Work certified		7,50,000
To Work uncertified	2,800	By Work uncertified		8,000
To Material	1,45,000	By Material at site		5,000
To Direct Wages	1,55,00	By Plant	11,200	
To Direct Expenses	2,600	*Less* Depreciation	4,200	7,000
To Material at site	2,000			
To Plant at site	11,200			
To Notional Profit	1,99,400			
	7,70,000			7,70,000
To Profit & Loss A/c	1,06,347	By National Profit		1,99,400
199400 × 2/3 × 80/100				
To Reserve	93,053			
	1,99,400			1,99,400

Contract A/c

Particulars	Amount	Particulars	Amount
1978			
To Work-in-Progress A/c	7,58,000	By Contractee A/c	10,00,000
Less : Reserve	93,053	By Material at site	8,000
	6,64,947	By Plant at site	3,000
To Material at site	2,000		
To Plant at Site	11,200		
To Materials issued	84,000		
To Direct Wages	1,10,000		
To Direct Expenses	6,000		
To Indirect Expenses	500		
To Profit & Loss A/c (Profit Transferred)	1,32,353		
	10,11,000		10,11,000

Problem No. 22

The following is the Trial Balance of Novin Construction Co. Ltd. engaged in the execution of Contract No. 189 for the year ended 31-12-1986 :

Particulars	Dr. Rs.	Cr. Rs.
(1) Contractee Account		3,60,000
(2) Creditors		70,000
(3) Capital		5,50,000
(4) Building	1,78,000	—
(5) Bank Balance	1,05,000	—
(6) Materials bought (Purchased during the year)	2,20,000	—
(7) Wages paid during the year	1,80,000	—
(8) Expenses paid during the year	47,000	—
(9) Plant as on 1-1-1986	2,50,000	—
	9,80,000	9,80,000

The work on contract was commenced on 1st January 1986.

Additional Information :

(1) Material costing Rs. 1,98,000 were sent to site but there of Rs. 10,500 were destroyed in accident and the Insurance Company agreed to settle claims for Rs. 7,500 only.

(2) Materials costing Rs. 8,500 were at site on 31-12-1986.

(3) Plant costing Rs. 50,000 was used on the contract all through the year.

(4) Plant costing Rs. 2,00,000 was used only for six months from 1st January to 30th June and was returned to stores.

(5) The contract was for Rs. 6,00,000 and the contractee pays 75% of Work certified. Work certified was 80% of the total contract Price. Work uncertified was estimated at Rs. 15,000 on 31-12-1986.

(6) Expenses were charged to contract @ 25% of wages.

(7) Plant is to be depreciated @ 10% p.a.

Prepare Contract Account for the year ended 31-12-1986 and show also the following items in the Balance Sheet — Material Plant, Work-in-Progress and Profit & Loss A/c.

(K.U.D., April 1987)

Solution :

Contract Account for the year ended 31-12-86

Particulars		Amount	Particulars		Amount
To Materials sent to store		1,98,000	By Material Destroyed in accident		10,500
To Wages paid		1,80,000	By Insurance Co.	7,500	
To Expenses	47,000		Profit & Loss A/c	3,000	
Charges @ 25%	45,000	45,000	By Material at site		8,500
of wages (1,80,000)	2,000				
Unabsorbed wages transferred to P & L A/c.			By Plant costing	50,000	
			Less : Depr. 10% at site	5,000	45,000
To Plant Cost from 1-1-86 to 31-12-86	50,000		By Plant returned to store	2,00,000	
			Less : Depr. (6 Months)	10,000	1,90,000
Plant cost (1-1-86 to 30-6-86)	2,00,000	2,50,000	By *Work-in-Progress A/c*		
Notional Profit		76,000	Work certified (Contract Price × 80/100)		4,95,000
			6,00,000 × 80/100 =	4,80,000	
Profit & Loss A/c (2/3 × 3/4 × 76.000)	38,000		Work Uncertified	15,000	
Reserve A/c	38,000				
	76,000				
		7,49,000			7,49,000

Balance Sheet as at 31-12-1986

Liabilities	Rs.	Rs.	Assets	Rs.	Rs.
Capital		5,50,000	*Work-in-Progress*		
			Work certified	4,80,000	
Profit & Loss A/c	38,000		Work uncertified	15,000	
				4,95,000	
Less : Depr. of Plant return to store	10,000		*Less* : Reserves	38,000	
				4,57,000	
	28,000		*Less* : Contractee A/c	3,60,000	97,000
Less : Loss in accident	3,000		Materials at site		8,500
	25,000		Material in store	2,20,000	
			Less : Issued	1,98,000	22,000
Less : Wages unabsorbed	2,000	23,000	Plant at site		45,000
			Plant in store	1,90,000	
Sundry Creditors		70,000	*Less* : Depr. (6 Months)	10,000	1,80,000
			Building		1,78,000
			Bank Balance		1,05,000
			Insurance Co.		7,500
		6,43,000			6,43,000

Problem No. 23

Following is the summary of the entries in a Contract Ledger as on 31st December 1981 :

(1) Material Purchased directly	35,000
(2) Materials Issued from stores	7,000
(3) Wages paid	18,000
(4) Direct Expenses	7,000
(5) Administrative Expenses	8,000
(6) Plant	34,200
(7) Scrap sold	1,820

Further information is as follows :

(a) Wages accrued due on 31-12-1981 Rs. 900 and Direct expenses accrued due Rs. 1,200.

(b) The cost of work uncertified included :

Materials	2,600
Wages	1,000
Expenses	1,500

(c) Rs. 2,000 worth of pland and Rs. 3,000 worth of materials were destroyed by fire.

(d) Depreciation on plant till 31-12-1981 was Rs. 10,000.

(e) Materials at site on 31-12-1981 — Rs. 10,000.

(f) Cash received from contractee — Rs. 60,000 being 80 per cent of work certified.

(g) Contract Price of Rs. 1,00,000.

Prepare Contract A/c and show how the Work-in-progress Account as would appear in Balance Sheet.

(K.U.D., October 1986)
(Kolhapur University,
M. Com. 1988, Gulbarga, 1985)

Solution :

Contract Account for the year ended 31-12-81

Particulars		Amount	Particulars		Amount
To Material Purchased	35,000		By Scrap sold		1,820
Add : Issued	7,000	42,000	By Profit & Loss A/c		
To Wages paid	18,000		Plant destroyed by fire	2,000	
Add : Accrued	900	18,900	Materials destroyed by fire	3,000	5,000
To Direct Exp.	7,000		By Plant	34,200	
Add : Accrued	1,200	8,200	*Less* : Destroyed	2,000	
To Administration Exp.		8,000		32,200	
To Plant		34,200	*Less* : Depr.	10,000	22,200
To Notional Profit		7,820	*Work-in-Progress*		
			Work certified 80% of cash received 60,000 × 100/80 =	75,000	
			Uncertified Materials 2,600 Wages 1,000 Expenses 1,500	5,100	80,100
			Materials at site		10,000
		1,19,120			1,19,120
To Profit & Loss A/c 7820 × 2/3 × 80/100 =		4,170	By Notional Profit		7,820
To Reserve		3,650			
		7,820			7,820

Balance Sheet as at 31-12-1981

Liabilities	Rs.	Rs.	Assets	Rs.	Rs.
Profit & Loss A/c			*Work-in-Progress A/c*		
Profit	4,170		Work certified	75,000	
Add : Scrap sold	1,820		Work uncertified	5,100	
	5,990			80,100	
Less : Loss	5,000		*Less* : Reserve	3,650	
	990			76,450	
Less : Depreciation	10,000		*Less* : Cash received	60,000	16,450
Net Loss to be shown Assets side	(–) 9,010		Plant		22,200
			Materials at Site		10,000

Problem No. 24

From the following data relating is a contract extracted from the books of the company as on 31-3-1986. Prepare a Contract Account.

(1) Materials Issued for work	90,000
(2) Wages paid on site	50,00
(3) Plant issued to site	75,000
(4) Salary of supervisory staff	5,500
(5) Work certified for payment	1,76,000
(6) Work not certified	9,000
(7) Amount received on certifed	1,58,400

Additional Information :

(a) The wages of workers for a week and salary of supervisory staff for a month were outstanding at the end of the period.

(b) The Contract commenced on 1st October 1985.

(c) Depreciation on plant is required @ 10% p.a.

(d) Materials at site on 31-3-1986 — Rs. 4,200.

(e) Full contract rice agreed Rs. 2,50,000.

Note : Profit to be transferred to Profit and Loss A/c. 2/3 of the Notional Profit to the extent of realised cash.

(K.U.D., October 1987)

Solution :

Contract Account for the year ended 31st March 1986

Particulars			Amount	Particulars		Amount
To Materials Issued			90,000	By *Work-in-Progress A/c*		
To Wages Paid	50,000			Work certified		1,76,000
Add : Outstanding for one week				Work not certified		9,000
$\frac{50,000}{25}$ =	2,000		52,000			1,85,000
				By Material at Site		4,200
To Salary of supervising staff paid	5,500					
Add : Outstanding for 1 month						
$\frac{5,500}{5}$ =	1,100		6,600			

Particulars	Amount	Particulars	Amount
To Depreciation on plant @ 10% p.a. $75{,}000 \times \frac{10}{100} = 7{,}500 \times \frac{6}{12} = 3{,}750$			
To Notional Profit	36,850		
	1,89,200		1,89,200
To Profit & Loss A/c $36{,}850 \times \frac{2}{3} \times \frac{1{,}58{,}400}{1{,}76{,}000}$	22,110	By Notional Profit	36,850
To Reserve to Transfer	14,740		
	36,850		36,850

Note : Contract work start from 1-10-1985 to 31-3-1986 = Only 6 months.

Problem No. 25

. A Building contractor furnishes the following records about the contract which was started on 1-4-1985. Expenses incurred on the contract up to 31-12-1985 were :

Material Purchased	21,500
Labour charged	50,110
Forman's Salary	6,310
Administrative Expenses	12,610
Machinery Purchases	15,000

A supervisor was paid monthly Rs. 1,000, he spent half of his time on this contract.

Material on Site on 31-12-1985 — Rs. 2,480.

The Machinery purchased was used only for 73 days on this contract the estimated life of the machinery in five years with Scrap value of Rs. 1,000.

Contract Price was fixed at Rs. 2,00,000 on 31-12-1985.

2/3 of the contract was completed. However work certified was worth of Rs. 1,00,000 and 80% of the same was paid in cash on account.

Prepare Contract Account and give the necessary working notes.

(K.U.D., M'lore, 1986, Gulbarga, 1988)

Solution :

Contract A/c for the year ended 31-12-1985

Particulars	Amount	Particulars		Amount
To Materials	21,500	By Work-in-progress A/c		
To Wages	50,110	By Work certified		1,00,000
To Forman's Salary	6,310	By Work uncertified (see Working Note)		23,277
To Administrative Exp.	12,610	By Materials on site		2,480
To Machinery Purchased	15,000	By Machinery Cost	15,000	
To Supervisor's Salary 1,000 × 9 = 9,000 (1/2 × 9,000)	4,500	*Less* : Depr.	560	14,440
To Notional Profit	30,167			
	1,40,197			1,40,197
To Profit & Loss A/c (2/3 × 80/100 × 30,167)	16,089	By Notional Profit		30,167
To Reserve	14,078			
	30,167			30,167

Working Note

Ascertainment of Work done but not certified

Expenses incurred for 2/3 of contract			
Material		21,500	
Labour charges		50,110	
Forman's Salary		6,310	
Administrative Expenses		12,610	
Machinery Purchased		15,000	
Supervisor Salary		4,500	
		1,10,030	
Less : Material on site	2,480		
Machinery Cost Less Depr. (15,000-560)	14,440	(–)16,920	
		93,110	93,110

$$\text{Depreciation} = \frac{\text{Cost} - \text{Scrap}}{\text{Life}} \times \text{No. of days}$$

$$= \frac{15{,}000 - 1{,}000}{5} \times \frac{73}{365}$$

$$= 560$$

Less : Expenses incurred for 2/3 work	69,833
Ascertainment of Work certified Expenses :	
$3/2 \times 1/2 \times 93{,}110 = 69{,}832.50$	
Work uncertified of Rs.	23,277

Problem No. 26

Doddamane Ltd. obtained a contract for the construction of a Building. Construction work started in July 1982. The Contract price was Rs. 9,00,000 on 30th June 1983 the end of the Account year the cash received on Account Rs. 3,60,000 being 80% of the work certified.

Other Information :

(1)	Material issued on Contract	1,80,000
(2)	Material on hand at site on 30-6-1983	75,000
(3)	Wage	2,46,000
(4)	Plant purchased specially for contract and Depreciation charged @ 10% p.a.	30,000
(5)	Direct Expenses	12,900
(6)	Work finished but not certified (cost)	15,000
(7)	Overhead allocated to contract	7,600

You are required to prepare the Contract Account and Statement showing the Profit on Contract upto 30th June 1983, stating what proposition of Profit should take to the credit of Profit and Loss A/c and show what are the items that would appear in the Balance Sheet.

(K.U.D., October 1985)

Contract Account for the year ended 30th June 1983

Particulars	Amount	Particulars		Amount
To Materials issued	1,80,000	By Materials in hand at site		7,500
To Wages	2,46,600	By Plant cost	30,000	
To Plant	30,000	*Less* : Depr. 10%	3,000	27,000
To Direct Expenses	12,900	By *Work-in-progress*		
To Overhead	7,600	Work certified		
To Notional Profit	22,400	Cash received		
		$3,60,000 \times \frac{100}{80} =$		4,50,000
		Work uncertified		15,000
Total	4,99,500	Total		4,99,500
To Profit & Loss A/c 22,400 × 2/3 × 4/5 = 11,947	11,947	By Notional Profit		22,400
To Reserve	10,453			
	22,400			22,400

Note : Profit taken to the Credit of Profit & Loss Account :

(1) Work completed 1/2 of the Total contract Price.

(2) 2/3 of Profit to be taken on cost basis i.e., 80% cash received on work certified

$$22,400 \times 2/3 \times \frac{80}{100} = 11,946.66 \text{ (Rs. 11,947)}$$

Balance Sheet

Liabilities	Rs.	Assets	Rs.
Profit & Loss A/c	11,947	*Work-in-Progress*	
		Work certified	4,50,000
		Work uncertified	15,000
			4,65,000
		Less : Reserve	10,453
			4,54,547
		Less : Cash received	3,60,000
			94,547
		Material in hand at site	7,500
		Plant cost *Less* Depr. (30,000 – 3,000)	27,000

Problem No. 27

Three Contracts commenced on 1st January, and 1st July 1983 and 1st October 1983 respectively. They are undertaken by Sunderam contractors and their accounts on 31st December 1983. Showed the following position :

Particulars	Contract-I	Contract-II	Contract-III
Contract Price	4,00,000	2,70,000	3,00,000
Expenditures :			
Materials	72,000	58,000	20,000
Wages paid	1,10,000	1,12,000	14,000
Plant Charges	4,000	2,800	1,000
Plant Installed	20,000	16,000	12,000
Materials on hand	4,000	4,000	2,000
Wages accrued	4,000	4,000	1,800
Work certified	2,00,000	1,60,000	36,000
Cash received in respect thereon	1,50,000	1,20,000	27,000
Work finished but not certified	6,000	8,000	2,100

The Plant was installed on the date of commencement of each of contract. Depreciation thereon is to be taken @ 10% p.a. Prepare Contract A/cs and show what are the items which would appear on the work-in-progress A/c as on 31st December 1983.

(K.U.D., April 1985)

Solution :

Contract Account for the year ended 31-12-1983

Particulars	Contract I	Contract II	Particulars	Contract I	Contract II
Materials	72,000	58,000	By Materials in hand	4,000	4,000
To Wages paid	1,10,000	1,12,400	By Work certified	2,00,000	2,00,000
To General Espenses	4,000	2,800	By Plant Cost (Less Depr.)		
To Wages accrued	4,000	4,000	(20,000 - 2,000)	18,000	—
To Plant Installed	20,000	16,000	By Plant Cost (Less Depr. 10% for 6 months.		
To Notional Profit	18,000	—	16,000 – 800)		15,200
			By Profit & Loss A/c	—	6,000
	2,28,000	1,93,200		2,28,000	1,93,200
To Profit & Loss A/c			By Notional Profit	18,000	
$18,000 \times 2/3 \times \frac{1,50,000}{2,00,000}$	9,000				
To Reserve	9,000				
	18,000			18,000	

Contract No. III A/c (1st October to 31-12-1983)

Particulars		Rs.	Particulars		Rs.
To Materials		20,000	By Materials in hand		2,000
To Wages paid		14,000	By Plant cost	12,000	
Add : Accrued		1,800	*Less* : Depr. @ 10%		
To General charges		1,000	for 3 months	300	11,700
To Plant installed for			By *Work-in-progress*		
1st October 83		12,000	Work certified	36,000	
Profit transfer to Reserve		3,000	Work uncertified	2,100	38,100
		51,800			51,800

Note : Since work completed is less than 1/4 of the Total contract the entire Profit is transferred to Reserve A/c.

Balance Sheet for the year ended as at 31-12-1983

Liabilities		Rs.	Assets		Rs.
Profit and Loss A/c			*Contract No. 1*		
Contract-I	9,000		Materials in hand		4,000
Less : Contract-II			Plant		18,000
(Loss)	3,000	6,000	*Work-in-progress*		
			Work certified	2,00,000	
			Work uncertified	6,000	
				2,06,000	
			Less : Reserve	9,000	
				1,97,000	
			Less : Cash in hand	1,50,000	47,000
			Contract No. II		
			Material in hand		4,000
			Plant		15,200
			Work-in-progress		
			Work certified	1,60,000	
			Work uncertified	8,000	
				1,68,000	
			Less : Cash received	1,20,000	48,000
			Loss		3,000
			Contract No. III		
			Material in hand		2,000
			Plant		11,700
			Work-in-progress		
			Work certified	36,000	
			Work uncertified	2,100	
				38,100	
			Less : Reserve	3,000	
				35,100	
			Less : Cash received	27,000	8,100

Problem No. 28

The following Trial Balance was extracted on 31-12-1979 from the books of Swastik Co. Ltd. Contractor :

Trial Balance as on 31-12-1979

	Dr. Rs.	Cr. Rs.
(1) Share Capital (shares of Rs. 10 each)	—	3,51,800
(2) Profit & Loss A/c on 1st Jan. 1979	—	25,000
(3) Provision for depreciation on machinery	—	63,000
(4) Cash received on Account (from Contractee)	—	12,80,000
(5) Contractor	—	81,200
(6) Land & Building (at cost)	74,000	—
(7) Machinery (at cost)	52,000	—
(8) Bank	45,000	—
(9) Contract A/c No. 7 :		
Materials	6,00,000	—
Direct Labour	8,30,000	—
Expenses	40,000	—
Machinery sent to site (cost)	1,60,000	—
	18,01,000	18,01,000

Contract No. 7 was began on 1st January 1979. The contract price is Rs. 24,00,000 and the custom has so far paid Rs. 12,80,000 being 80% of work certified. The cost of work done since certification is estimated at Rs. 16,000. On December 31st, 1979 after the above trial balance was extracted, machinery costing Rs. 32,000 was returned to stores to and materials were valued at Rs. 27,000, provision to be made for Direct labour due Rs. 6,000 and depreciation of all machinery @ 12½% on cost p.a. You are required to prepare

(1) The Contract Account.

(2) The Statement of profit if any to be properly credited to Profit and Loss Account for 1979.

(3) The Balance Sheet of Swastik Co. Ltd. as on 31-12-1979.

(Gulbarga, April 1985)

Solution :

Contract Account for the year 1979

Particulars		Amount	Particulars		Amount
To Materials		6,00,000	By Work-in-progress		
To Direct Labour	8,30,000		Work certified		16,00,000
Add : Due	6,000		$(1,20,000 \times \frac{100}{80})$		
		8,36,000	By Work done but not certified		16,000
To Expenses		40,000			16,16,000
To Machinery		1,60,000			
To Notional Profit		1,47,000	By Machinery Returned		
			Cost	32,000	
			Less: Dep @ 12½%	4,000	28,000
			By Machinery on site		
			Cost	1,60,000	
			Less: Returned	32,000	
				1,28,000	
			Less: Depr.	16,000	11,200
			Material on site		27,000
		17,83,000			17,83,000
To Profit & Loss A/c			By Notional Profit		1,47,000
$(1,47,000 \times 2/3 \times \frac{80}{100})$		78,400			
Reserve Account		68,600			
		1,47,000			1,47,000

Balance Sheet as at 31-12-1979

Liabilities		Rs.	Assets		Rs.
Share Capital			Land & Building (at cost)		74,000
Shares of Rs. 10 each		3,51,800	Machinery at cost	52,000	
Profit and Loss A/c			*Less* : Depr.	6,500	45,500
Balance 1-1-79	25,000		Machinery at site		1,12,000
Add : Profit for the year	78,400		Machinery return to stores		28,000
	1,03,400		Materials at site		27,000
Less : Provision for Depr. Machinery @ 12½ % of 52,000	6,500	96,900	Bank Balance		45,000
			Work-in-progress	16,16,000	
			Less : Reserve	68,600	
				15,47,400	
Provision for Depr. on Machinery		63,000	*Less* : Contractee A/c	12,80,000	2,67,400
Provision for Labour		6,000			
Creditors		81,200			
		5,98,900			5,98,900

Problem No. 29

The following information relates to a Contract for Rs. 7,50,000 (the Contractee pays 90% of the value of work done and certified by the Architect and rest on completion of the Contract) :

Particulars	1979 Rs.	1980 Rs.	1981 Rs.
Materials	90,000	1,10,000	63,000
Wages	85,000	1,15,000	85,000
Indirect Expenses	1,500	2,000	—
Direct Expenses	3,500	12,500	4,500
Work certified	1,75,000	5,65,000	7,50,000
Work uncertified	—	10,000	—
Plant	10,000	—	—

The value of the plant at the end of 1979, 1980 & 1981 was Rs. 8,000, Rs. 5,000, and Rs. 2,000 respectively. Prepare the Contract Account for three years.

(K.U.D., October 1984)

Solution :

Contract Account for the year 1979

Particulars	Amount	Particulars	Amount
To Material	90,000	By *Work-in-Progress*	
To Wages	85,000	By Work certified	1,75,000
To Direct Expenses	3,500	By Plant	8,000
To Indirect Expenses	1,500	By Profit & Loss A/c (Loss)	7,000
To Plant	10,000		
Total	1,90,000	Total	1,90,000

Contract Account for the year ended 1980

Particulars	Amount	Particulars	Amount
To *Work-in-progress A/c*		By *Work-in-Progress*	
Work certified	1,75,000	Work certified	5,65,000
To Materials	1,10,000	Work uncertified	10,000
To Wages	1,15,000	By Plant	5,000
To Direct Expenses	12,500		
To Indirect Expenses	2,000		
To Plant	8,000		
To Profit & Loss A/c	1,57,500		
Total	5,80,000	Total	5,80,000
To Profit & Loss A/c		By Notional Profit	1,57,500
1,57,500 × 2/3 × 90/100	94,500		
To Reserve	63,000		
Total	1,57,500	Total	1,57,500

Contract Account for the year ended 1981

Particulars	Amount	Particulars	Amount
To *Work-in-Progress*			
Work certified	—	By Contractee A/c	7,50,000
Work uncertified	5,75,000	By Plant	2,000
Less : Reserve	63,000		
	5,12,000		
To Materials	63,000		
To Wages	85,000		
To Direct Expenses	4,500		
To Plant	5,000		
To Net Profit (Transfer to P & L A/c)	82,500		
Total	7,52,000	Total	7,52,000

Problem No. 30

M/s Bahubali Builders of Dharmastal undertook a contract on 1-1-1981 at an agreed contract price of Rs. 10,00,000. On 31-12-1981, 75 per cent of the contract was completed. The following figures relate to this contract for 1981 :

Materials (Direct Purchases)	2,00,000
Materials (Issued from stores)	1,00,000
Plant Issued	80,000
Wages paid	2,80,000
Working Expenses	12,000
Administration Expenses	20,000
On 31-12-1981	
Materials at site	60,000
Wages unpaid	20,000
Plant at site	40,000
Cost of work not yet approved	32,000

During the year material costing Rs. 20,000 were sold for Rs. 21,000 only. 70% of the contract has been certified for payment of which 80% of each received.

It is expected that the contract would be finished by March 1982 incurring additional expenditure as under :

(1)	Materials (besides materials at site)	42,000
(2)	Wages	1,30,000

(3) Work Administrative Expenses 18,000

(4) The plant will have a resident value of Rs. 10,000 on the completion of the contract.

Prepare Contract Account as on 31-12-1981 taking Profit on Estimated basis.

(K.U.D., October 1982)

Solution :

Contract Account for the year 1981

Particulars		Amount	Particulars		Amount
To Material			By Material at site		60,000
To Direct Purchases	2,00,000		By Plant at site		40,000
To Issued from stores	1,00,000		By Material cost Rs. 20,000 sold for Rs. 21,000		21,000
		3,00,000	By *Work-in-progress*		
To Wages paid	2,80,000		Work certified 70%	7,00,000	
Add : Wages payable	20,000		Work not yet certified	32,000	7,32,000
		3,00,000			
To Work Expenses		12,000			
To Administration Exp.		20,000			
To Profit on Material Cost		1,000			
To Plant Issued		80,000			
To Notional Profit		1,40,000			
Total		8,53,000	Total		8,53,000
To Profit & Loss A/c $(1,28,000 \times \frac{7,00,000}{10,00,000})$ (See Note)		89,600	By Notional Profit		1,40,000
To Reserve		50,400			
		1,40,000			1,40,000

Estimated Profit on completion of contract on March 1982

Total Expenses upto 31-12-1981 :

Material (2,00,000 + 1,00,000)	3,00,000
Wages (2,80,000 + 20,000)	3,00,000
Work Expenses	12,000
Administration Expenses	20,000
Plant	80,000
Total Cost	7,12,000

Less : Closing Stock :		
Material at site	60,000	
Plant	40,000	
Cost of material sold	20,000	1,20,000
	Total cost up to 31-12-81	5,92,000
Add : Additional Expenses :		
Material	60,000	
Additions	42,000	
Wages	1,30,000	
Working Expenses	18,000	
Plant 40,000		
Less :		
Reserve 10,000	30,000	2,80,000
	Total	8,72,000
Total Contract Price		10,00,000
Less Estimated Total Expenses		8,72,000
	Estimated Profit	1,28,000

On Completion of Contract.

Note :

Profit to be taken to the credit of Profit and Loss Account on the basis of estimated profit. Estimated profit (as above) Rs. 1,28,000 since the estimated profit is calculated on completion of the contract work.

Profit taken being in proportion to the work certified to contract Price.

$$= \text{Estimated Profit} \times \frac{\text{Work Certified}}{\text{Contract Price}}$$

$$= 1,28,000 \times \frac{7,00,000}{10,00,000} = \text{Rs. } 89,600$$

Profit taken to the credit of Profit and Loss A/c Rs. 89,600.

Profit to be taken to the credit of Profit & Loss Account out of the Profit earned for the year 1981 Rs. 89,600.

Profit earned on contract being Notional Profit	1,40,000
Less : Profit & Loss A/c	89,600
(On basis of Estimated Profit on completion of contract Balance amount transferred to Reserve A/c on 31-12-1981.)	50,400

Problem No. 31

Following was the expenditure incurred on a Contract for Rs. 5,00,000 commenced on 1-7-1979 :

Materials	1,00,000
Wages	1,35,000
Plant used	18,000
Overhead	75,000

Cash received from the Contractee upto 31st December 1979 amounted to Rs. 2,00,000 being 4/5 of the work certified.

Value of materials on hand at the close of the year Rs. 9,500 and Depreciate plant @ 20% p.a.

Prepare the Contract A/c for the six months ending 31st December 1979. Transferring the reasonable Profit to the Profit & Loss A/c.

(K.U.D., October 1980)

Solution :

Contract A/c

Particulars	Amount	Particulars		Amount
To Materials	1,00,000	By *Work-in-Progress A/c*		
To Wages	1,35,000	By Work certifed		
To Overhead Expenses	75,000	(Cash received 2,00,000)		
To Plant used	18,000	being 4/5 of work certified		
		2,00,000 × 5/4		2,50,000
		By Materials in hand		9,500
		By Plant	18,000	
		Less : Depr. 20% p.a		
		for 6 months	1,800	16,200
		By Profit & Loss		52,300
		(Loss transfer)		
	3,28,000			3,28,000

There is Loss on contract. Therefore transferring reasonable Profit does not arise.

6

Process Costing : Joint Product – By-Product Process Profit – Equivalent Process

Problem No. 1

In manufacturing the Main product, a company processes the incidental waste into two by-products A and B. From the following data relating to the products, you are required to prepare a statement showing apportionment of Joint Cost among Main product and By-products.

Total cost upto the point of separation was Rs. 3,10,400

		Main Product	By-Products	
		Rs.	A Rs.	B Rs.
(1)	Sales	8,00,00	64,000	96,000
(2)	Cost after separation	80,000	12,800	14,400
(3)	Estimated net Profit as a percentage of sales value	—	20%	20%
(4)	Estimated selling expenses as percentage of sales value	20%	10%	15%

[K.U.D., April 1998(N)]

Solution :

Statement Showing Estimated Costs of By-Products up to Separation Point

	By-Products	
	A Rs.	B Rs.
Sales value	64,000	96,000
Less Estimated Profit on Sales 20% : 20%	–12,800	–19,200
Estimated Total Cost	51,200	76,800
Less Selling Expenses % on Sales 10% & 15%	5,120	11,520
Works Cost	46,080	65,280
Less Actual Cost after separation	12,800	14,400
Estimated Cost up to the point of separation	33,280	50,880

Share in Joint Cost

	Total	Main Product	By-Products A	By-Products B
	Rs.	Rs.	Rs.	Rs.
Total Joint Cost share in Joint Cost	3,10,400	2,26,240	33,280	50,880

Problem No. 2

A by-product Beta is obtained in Processing Product Alpha. These products are further processed and the Cost details are as under :

Particulars	Joint Cost	Further Processing Costs Alpha	Further Processing Costs Beta
	Rs.	Rs.	Rs.
Materials	15,000	9,000	750
Wages	10,500	7,500	3,000
Other Expenses	3,750	2,250	900

Ascertain the cost per Kg. of Alpha and Beta with the help of the following additional information :

Output of Alpha - 400 Kg; Beta - 100 Kg.

Sales Price of Beta - Rs. 200 per Kg.

Yielding 30% Profit on sales

[K.U.D., April 1998(O)]

Solution :

Statement Showing the Apportionment of Joint Cost of By-Product Beta

		Rs.
Sales price of Beta - Rs. 200 per Kg. Output - 100 Kg.		20,000
Less Estimated Profit 30% on sales 30% on 20,000		6,000
Total Cost		14,000
Less Cost after separation or Further Individual Process Cost		
Material	750	
Wages	3,000	
Other Expenses	900	4,650
Share in Joint Cost		9,350

Total Cost of By-Product Beta = Rs. 14,000

Output 100 Kg.

Cost per Kg. = $\frac{14,000}{100}$ = Rs. 140

Statement Showing the Cost of Main Product Alpha

	Rs.	Rs.
Joint Costs		
Materials	15,000	
Wages	10,500	
Other Expenses	3,750	29,250
Less Share in Joint Cost of By-Product Beta (as in above Statement)		9,350
Share in Joint Cost of Main Product Alpha		19,900
Add Costs after separation or Further Individual Process Costs		
Materials	9,000	
Wages	7,500	
Other Expenses	2,250	18,750
Total Cost of Main Product Alpha		38,650

Total Cost of Main Product Alpha Rs. 38,650

Total Output - Alpha 400 Kg.

$$\text{Cost per Kg.} = \frac{38,650}{400} = 96.625$$

Cost per Kg. Rs. 96.625

Main Product Alpha A/c

	Rs.		Rs.
To Joint Cost		By Share in Joint Cost of By-Product (Transfer)	9,350
Material	15,000		
Wages	10,500		
Other Expenses	3,750		
Add			
To Further Process Costs		By Cost of Product of Main Product Alpha	38,650
Material	9,000		
Wages	7,500		
Other Expenses	2,250		
	48,000		48,000

By-Product Beta A/c

	Rs.		Rs.
To Share in Joint Cost	9,350	By Sales 100 × 200	20,000
To Further Process Costs	4,650		
To Profit 30% on 20,000	6,000		
	20,000		20,000

$$\frac{\text{Total Cost}}{\text{Output}} = \frac{38,650}{400 \text{ Kg}} = \text{Rs. } 140$$

$$\frac{\text{Total Cost}}{\text{Output}} = \frac{14,000}{100} = \text{Rs. } 140$$

Problem No. 3

In a factory three Joint Products M, N and O are produced. For the Month of January 1997 the following data were available :

	Products :	M	N	O
Selling Price per Kg.	Rs.	4	8	25
Post Separation Cost	Rs.	8,000	4,000	12,000
Output	Kgs	2,000	800	1,200

Pre-separation Cost amounted to Rs. 16,000. The Joint products are manufactured in one common process after which they are separated and may under go further individual processing. The Pre-separation point costs are apportioned to the Joint products according to weight. You are required to prepare a statement showing the estimated Profit or Loss for each Product and in total.

[K.U.D., October 1997(N)]

Solution :

Statement Showing Estimated Profit or Loss

		Products : M	N	O	
(1) Selling Price per Kg. (a)	Rs.	4	8	25	
(a) Output in Kg. (b)	Rs.	2,000	800	1,200	Total
Total Sales price – (A × B) Rs.		8,000	6,400	30,000	44,400
Less Post-separation Cost		– 8,000	– 4,000	12,000	24,000
		—	2,400	18,000	20,400
Less apportionment of Joint Cost on the loss of weight =		– 8,000	– 3,200	– 4800	– 16000
2,000 800 1,200 = 5/10 × 16,000					
20 8 12 = 2/10		– 8,000	– 800	+ 13200	+ 4,400
5 2 3 = 3/10					
		Loss	Loss	Profit	Profit

Total Sales Price —	44,400	Estimated Profit or Loss	
Less Separate Cost —	240,00	Estimated Profit — Product O - 13200	
	20,400	*Less* Estimated Loss M — 8,000	
Less Joint Cost	16,000	N — 800	
Total Estimated Profit	4,400	8,800	Rs. 4,400 Profit

Problem No. 4

A product passes through three processes A, B and C. The Normal wastage of each Process is as follows :

Process-A — 10%, Process-B — 20% and Process-C — 25% on input

Wastage of Process A — was sold at Rs. 2 per unit

Process B — at Rs. 4 per unit and

Process C — at Rs. 5 per unit

Expenses	Total	Processes		
		A	B	C
	Rs.	Rs.	Rs.	Rs.
Sundry Materials	5,625	2,600	2,000	1,025
Direct wages	7,330	2,250	3,680	1,400
Production Overhead	7,330	—	—	—
Actual Output	—	450 units	340 units	270 units

500 units were introduced @ Cost of Rs. 4 per unit in Process A

Production overheads are absorbed as a percentage of Direct wages

There is no stock or work-in-progress.

Show Three Process Accounts.

[K.U.D., April 1997(N)]

Solution :

Working Note

Calculations of Abnormal Loss or Abnormal Gain

Process-A A/c	Units	Total Cost
Units Introduced	500	9,100
Less Normal Loss 10%	50	100
Normal Output & Cost	450	9,000
Actual Output	450	
No Loss — No Gain		

Process — B A/c	Units	Total Cost
Input	450	18,360
Less Normal Loss 20%	90	360
Normal Output & Normal Cost	360	18,000
Actual Output	340	
Less than actual Abnormal Loss	20	

Cost of Abnormal

$$\text{Loss} = \frac{\text{Total cost}}{\text{Normal Output}} = \frac{18,000}{360}$$

Abnormal Loss Unit 20 × 50 = Rs. 1,000 Rs. 50 per unit

Process-C A/c	Units	Amount
Input	340	20,825
Less Normal Loss 25%	85	425
Normal output & Normal Cost	255	20,400
Actual output	270	
More than Actual output	15	

Abnormal Gain — 15 units

Cost of Abnormal Gain = $\frac{\text{Total cost}}{\text{Unit}} = \frac{20,400}{255}$

Abnormal Gain Rs. 80 per unit

Units 15 × 80 = Rs. 1,200 Abnormal Gain

Process-A A/c

Particulars	Units	Rate	Amount Rs.	Particulars	Units	Rate	Amount Rs.
To Units Introduced	500	4	2,000	By Normal Loss	50	2	100
To Sundry Materials			2,600	10% of 500			
To Direct Wages			2,250	Sold out Rs. 2			
To Production Overhead			2,250	By Process-B A/c	450	20	9,000
	500		9,100		500		9,100

Process-B A/c

Particulars	Units	Rate	Amount Rs.	Particulars	Units	Rate	Amount Rs.
To Process A/c Input	450	20	9,000	By Normal Loss	90	4	360
				450 × 20% =			
To Sundry Materials			2,000	Sold at Rs. 4			
To Direct Wages			3,680	By Abnormal Loss	20	50	1,000
To Production Overhead			3,680	By Process-C A/c	340	50	17,000
				Rs. 50 per unit			
	450		18,360		450		18,360

Process-C A/c

Particulars	Units	Rate	Amount	Particulars	Units	Rate	Amount
To Process-B A/c	340	50	17,000	By Normal Loss	85	5	425
To Sundry Materials			1,025	25% of 340			
To Direct Wages			1,400	Sold at Rs. 5			
To Production Overhead			1,400	By Finished Stocks	270	80	21,600
To Abnormal Gain	15	80	1,200	Transfer A/c			
	355		22,025		355		22,025

Abrormal Loss A/c

Particulars	Units	Rate	Amount	Particulars	Units	Rate	Amount
To Process-B A/C	20	50	1,000	By Banks Value of Scrap sold	20	4	80
				By Costing Profit/Loss Balance Transferred			920
	20		1,000		20		1,000

Abnormal Gain A/c

Particulars	Units	Rate	Amount Rs.	Particulars	Units	Rate	Amount Rs.
To Reduction in Scrap Process	15	5	75	By Process-C A/c	15	80	1,200
To Costing Profit & Loss A/c Balance Transferred			1,125				
			1,200				1,200

Problem No. 5

A product of a company passes through three different processes. Prepare process accounts from the following information :

	Particulars	Total	Process I	Process II	Process III
1.	Sundry Materials	8,482	2,000	3,020	3,462
2.	Wages	12,000	3,000	4,000	5,000
3.	Direct Expenses	726	500	226	—
4.	Products overhead	6,000	—	—	—

1000 Units @ Rs. 5 per unit were issued to Process-I production overhead is recovered 50 per cent of wages. The following additional information was obtained :

Process	Output	Normal Loss	Value of Scrap
I	920 Units	10%	Rs. 3 per unit
II	870 Units	5%	Rs. 5 per unit
III	800 Units	10%	Rs. 6 per unit

There was no opening or closing stock of any type.

(K.U.D., April 1996)

Solution :

Statement showing Abnormal Loss or Gain

Particulars	Process-I Units	Process-I Total	Process-II Units	Process-II Total	Process-III Units	Process-III Total
Units Issued	1000	12,000	920	21,206	870	31,842
Less : Normal Loss 10%	100	300	—	—	87	230
Normal Loss 5%	—	—	46	230	—	—
Normal output of Normal Cost	900	11,700	874	20,976	783	31,320
Actual output	920		870		800	

Particulars	Process I Units	Process I Total	Process-II Units	Process-II Total	Process-III Units	Process-III Total
More than Normal output (Abnormal Gain)	20		—		17	
Less than Normal output (Abnormal Loss)	—		4		—	

$$\text{Cost of Abnormal Gain} = \frac{\text{Normal cost of Normal output}}{\text{Normal output}} \times \text{Units of Abnormal Gain}$$

$$\text{Process-I} = \frac{11{,}700}{900} \times 20 = \text{Rs. } 260$$

$$\text{Process-III} = \frac{31{,}320}{783} \times 17 = \text{Rs. } 680$$

$$\text{Cost of Abnormal Loss} = \frac{\text{Normal cost of Normal output}}{\text{Normal output}} \times \text{Units of Abnormal Loss}$$

$$\text{Process-II} = \frac{20{,}976}{874} \times 4$$

$$= \text{Rs. } 96.$$

Process-I A/c

Particulars	Units	Amount	Particulars	Units	Amount
To Units Issued @ Rs. 5 per unit	1000	5,000	By Normal Loss 10% of 1000	100	
To Sundry Materials		2,000	By Scrap sold		
To Wages		3,000	Rs. 3 per unit		300
To Direct Expenses		500	By Process-II transferred	920	11,960
To Production overhead 50% of wages 50% × 3000		1,500	(@ Rs. 12 per unit)		
To Abnormal Gain @ Rs. 13 per unit	20	260			
	1020	12,260		1020	12,260

Process-II A/c

Particulars	Units	Amount	Particulars	Units	Amount
To Process-I A/c	920	11,960	By Normal Loss 5% of 920	46	
To Sundry Materials		3,020	By Scrap sold @ Rs. 5 per unit		230
To Wages		4,000			
To Direct Expenses		226	By Abnormal Loss @ Rs. 24 per unit	4	96
To Production overhead 50% of wages (4,000 × 50%)		2,000	By Process-III A/c	870	20,880
	920	21,206		920	21,206

Process-III A/c

Particulars	Units	Amount	Particulars	Units	Amount
To Process-II A/c	870	20,880	By Normal Loss 10% of 870	87	522
To Sundry Materials		3,462	Scrap sold @ Rs. 6 per unit		
To Wages		5,000	By Finished stock transfer @ Rs. 40 per unit	800	32,000
To Production overhead 50% of wages (5,000 × 50%)		2,500			
To Abnormal Gain @ Rs. 40 per unit	17	680			
	887	32,522		887	32,522

Problem No. 6

A product of a company passes through two separate processes. Prepare process Cost Account from the following details :

	Process-I	Process-II
Materials	60,000	6,000
Wages	20,000	24,000
Indirect Expenses	14,000	17,200
Input	40000 Units	35000 Units
Normal Loss	10%	4%
Scrap Value	Re. 1 per unit	Rs. 2 per unit

There was no opening or closing stock of any type. The final output from Process-II was 34,000 units.

(K.U.D., October 1995)

Solution :

Process-I A/c

Particulars	Units	Amount	Particulars	Units	Amount
Material	40000	60,000	By Normal Loss 10% of 40,000	4000	4,000
Wages		20,000	Scrap Sold @ (Re. 1 per unit)		
Indirect Expenses		14,000	By Abnormal Loss	1000	2,220
			By Process-II A/c (Transfer)	35000	77,780
	40000	84,000		40000	84,000

Process-II A/c

Particulars	Units	Amount	Particulars	Units	Amount
To Process-I A/c	35000	77,780	By Normal Loss (4% of 35,000)	1400	2,800
To Materials		6,000	Scrap sold Rs. 2 per unit		
To Wages		24,000			
To Indirect Expenses		17,200	By Finished stock (Rs. 3.63 × 34000)	34000	1,23,636
To Abnormal Gain (Rs. 3.64 × 400)	400	1,456			
	35400	1,26,436		35400	1,26,436

Note : Calculations of Abnormal Loss/Gain

Process-I	Units	Amount
Input	40000	84,000
Less : Normal Loss 10% of 40,000	4000	4,000
Normal output	36,000	80,000
Actual output	35000	
Less than the Normal output so there is Abnormal Loss	1000	

$$\text{Cost of Abnormal Loss} = \frac{\text{Total Cost of Normal output}}{\text{Units of Normal output}} \times \text{Units of Abnormal Loss}$$

$$= \frac{80,000}{36,000} = 2.22$$

$$= 1000 \times 2.22$$

$$= \text{Rs. } 2,220$$

Process-II	Units	Amount
Input	35000	1,24,980
Less : Normal Loss 4% of 35,000 Scrap sold	1400	2,800
Normal output	33600	1,22,180
Actual output	34000	
More than normal output so, there is abnormal gain	400	

$$\text{Cost of Abnormal Gain} = \frac{\text{Cost Normal output}}{\text{Units of Normal output}} \times \text{Units of abnormal gain}$$

$$= \frac{1{,}22{,}180}{33{,}600} = 3.64$$

$$= 400 \times 3.64$$

$$= \text{Rs. } 1{,}456.$$

Problem No. 7

A product passes through two processes "M" and "N" and then to finished stock. Prepare process accounts and calculate abnormal loss or gain from the following figures :

	Process-M Rs.	Process-N Rs.
Materials — 10,000 units at Rs. 5 per unit	50,000	—
Sundry materials	10,000	8,000
Wages	20,000	42,000
Overheads	8,400	11,180
Normal Loss (per cent of Input)	2%	4%
Scrap value per unit	Re. 1.00	Rs. 2.00
Actual output	9500 Units	9200 Units

There was no opening or closing stock

(K.U.D., April 1995)

Solution :

Process-'M' A/c

Particulars	Units	Amount	Particulars	Units	Amount
To Materials (@ Rs. 5 per unit)	10000	50,000	By Normal Loss	200	
To Sundry Materials		10,000	By Scrap sold (Rs. 1 × 200)		200
To Wages		20,000	By Abnormal Loss (300 × 9)	300	2,700
To Overheads		8,400	By Process N A/c transferred (9500 × 9)	9500	85,500
	10000	88,400		10000	88,400

Working Note

	Units	Rs.
Process-M		
Input	10000	88,400
Less : Normal Loss 2% of 10000	200	
Scrap sold		200
Normal output	9800	88,200
Actual output	9500	
Less than Normal output		
∴ Abnormal Loss	300	

$$\frac{\text{Total cost Normal output}}{\text{Normal output}} = \frac{\text{Rs. } 88{,}200}{9800}$$

Cost per unit = Rs. 9

$$\text{Cost of Abnormal Loss } \frac{88{,}200}{9800} \times 300$$

= Rs. 2,700

(Cost per unit = 9 × 300 = Rs. 2,700)

Process-N A/c

Particulars	Units	Amount	Particulars	Units	Amount
To Process-M A/c @ Rs. 9 per unit (From M)	9500	85,500	By Normal Loss (4% of 9,500)	380	
To Sundry Materials		8,000	By Scrap sold (380 × 2)		720
To Wages		42,000	By Finished stock (9200 @ Rs. 16 p. unit)	9200	1,47,200
To Overhead		11,180			
To Abnormal Gain (@ Rs. 16 p. unit)	80	1,280			
	9580	1,47,960		9580	1,47,960

Process-N :

Input	9500	1,46,680
Less : Normal Loss 4% of 9500	380	760
Normal output	9120	1,45,920
Actual output	9200	
Abnormal Gain	80	

$$\frac{\text{Cost of Normal Output}}{\text{Normal output}} = \text{Cost per unit}$$

$$\frac{1{,}45{,}920}{9120} = \text{Cost per unit} = \text{Rs. } 16$$

$$\text{Cost of abnormal Gain} = \frac{1{,}45{,}920}{9120} \times 80$$

$$= \text{Rs. } 1{,}280$$

Problem No. 8

Daneshwari Ltd. make and sell their chemicals manufactured by three consecutive processes.

The products of these processes are dealt with as under :

	Process-I	Process-II	Process-III
Transferred to next process	66-2/3	60%	—
Transferred to warehouse for sale	33-1/3	40%	100%

In each process 4 per cent of the weight put in is lost and 6 per cent is scrapped, which realise Rs. 4 per ton, Rs. 6 per ton and Rs. 8 per ton from Process-I, Process-II and Process-III respectively. The following information relates to March 1994 :

	Process-I	Process-II	Process-III
Raw materials used	1000 tons	200 tons	268 tons
Rate per ton	Rs. 12	Rs. 20	Rs. 15
Wages and other expenses	Rs. 4,440	Rs. 3,488	Rs. 4,416

Prepare process accounts, showing cost per ton of each process.

(K.U.D., October 1994)

Solution :

Process-I A/c

Particulars	Qty. (Ton)	Amount	Particulars	Qty. (Ton)	Amount
To Raw Materials @ Rs. 12 per ton	1000	12,000	By Weight Loss of 4% of 1000	40	—
To Wages and other Expenses		4,440	By Scrap 6% of 1000 @ Rs. 4 per ton	60	240
			By Process-II A/c 66-2/3% transfer @ Rs. 18 per ton	600	10,800
			By Warehouse 33½ %	300	5,400
	1000	16,440		1000	16,440

Working Note

	Qty.	Total Cost
Input	1000	16,440
Less : Weight loss 4% of 1000	40	
	960	
Less : Scrap 6% of 1000 @ Rs. 4 per ton	60	240
	900	16,200

Cost per ton = $\frac{16,200}{900}$ = Rs. 18 per ton

Transferred :

66-2/3 of 900 = 600

33-1/3 of 900 = 300

Process-II A/c

Particulars	Qty. (Ton)	Amount	Particulars	Qty. (Ton)	Amount
To Process-I Account transferred from @ Rs. 18 per ton	600	10,800	By Weight loss 4% of 800	32	
To Raw material @ Rs. 20 per ton	200	4,000	By Scrap 6% of 800 @ Rs. 6 per ton	48	288
To Wages & other Exp.		3,488	By Process-III A/c 60% of 720 @ Rs. 25 per ton	432	10,800
			By Warehouse 40% of 720 @ Rs. 25 each	288	7,200
	800	18,288		800	18,288

Working Note

	Qty.	Rs.	
Input	800	18,288	Cost per ton = $\frac{18,000}{7200}$
Less : Weight Loss 4% of 800	32		= Rs. 25 per ton
	768		Process-III A/c
Less : Scrap 6% of 800			60% of 720 = 432
	48	288	40% of 720 = 288
	720	18,000	

Process-III A/c

Particulars	Qty.	Amount	Particulars	Qty.	Amount
To Process-II A/c @ Rs. 25 per ton	432	10,800	By weight loss 4% of 700	28	
To Raw Material @ Rs. 15 per ton	268	4,020	By Scrap 6% of 700 @ Rs. 8 per ton	42	336
To Wages and other expenses		4,416	By Finished stock @ Rs. 30 per on	630	18,900
	700	19,236		700	19,236

Working Note

	Qty.	Rs.
Input	700	19,236
Less : Weight loss 4% of 700	28	
	672	
Less : Scrap 6% of 700	42	336
	630	18,900

Cost per ton $= \frac{18,900}{630}$

= Rs. 30 per ton.

Problem No. 9

Following is the information in respect of a product that passes through two processes namely Process-I and Process-II :

	Process I Rs.	Process II Rs.
20,000 units of material introduced @ Rs. 10 per unit	2,00,000	—
Sundry materials	—	60,000
Labour	50,000	70,000
Overheads	36,000	36,500
Normal Loss (per cent of input)	5%	4%
Scrap value per unit (Re.)	1	Nil
Output (In units)	18,500	18,200

18,000 units were sold @ Rs. 30 per unit, the selling expenses amounted to Rs. 2 per unit.

Prepare Process Accounts and a statement showing the profit or loss (after adjustment of abnormal loss and abnormal gain, if any) assuming that there were no opening stocks of any type in any process.

(K.U.D., April 1994)

Solution :

Process-I A/c

Particulars	Units	Amount	Particulars	Units	Amount
To Materials	20000	2,00,000	By Normal Loss 5% of 20000	1000	
To Labour		50,000	By Scrap @ Re. 1		1,000
To Overheads		36,000	By Abnormal loss @ 15 per unit	500	7,500
			By Process-II A/c transfer	18500	2,77,500
	20000	2,86,000		20000	2,86,000

Working Note

	Units	Amount
Units issued	20000	2,86,000
Less : Normal Loss 5% of 20000	1000	1,000
Normal output	19000	2,85,000
Actual output	18500	
Less than Normal output abnormal Loss	500	

Cost of Abnormal Loss :

$= \frac{2,85,000}{19000} = 15\ (15 \times 500 = 7,500)$

Rs. 7,500 Abnormal Loss

Process-II A/c

Particulars	Units	Amount	Particulars	Units	Amount
To Process-I A/c transferred from @ Rs. 15 per unit	18500	2,77,500	By Normal Loss 4% of 18500	740	
			By Scrap sold		
To Sundry Material		60,000	By Finished stock A/c @ cost Rs. 25 each	18200	4,55,000
To Labour		70,000			
To Overheads		36,500			
To Abnormal Gain	440	11,000			
	18940	4,55,000		18940	4,55,000

Working Note

	Units	Amount	
Units issued	18500	4,44,000	
Less : Normal Loss 4% of 18500	740		
	17760	4,44,000	Cost of Abnormal gain = $\frac{4,44,000}{17760}$
Actual output more than normal output	18200		= Rs. 25 per unit
Abnormal gain	440		for 440 × 25 = 1,11,000

Abnormal Loss A/c

Particulars	Amount	Particulars	Amount
To Process-I A/c	7,500	By Value of Scrap	500
		By Costing (Profit and Loss) Loss A/c	7,000
	7,500		7,500

Abnormal Gain A/c

Particulars	Amount	Particulars	Amount
To Reduction in Scrap	—	By Process-II A/c	11,000
To Profit Costing (Profit and Loss A/c) Profit	11,000		
	11,000		11,000

Statement of Profit on Sales A/c

Cost of Production of units sold (18000 × 25)	4,50,000
Add : Selling Expenses @ Rs. 2 per unit (18000 × 2)	36,000
Cost of Sales	4,86,000
Sales 18000 × 30 =	5,40,000
Profit on Sales	54,000
Profit as per cost =	54,000
Abnormal Gain – Abnormal Loss (11,000 – 7,500) = Net Gain	3,500
(Process-II – Process-I) Net Profit :	57,500

Problem No. 10

A Product passes through two processes A and B and then to finished stock. Prepare process account and calculate loss or gain from the following figures :

	Process-A	Process-B
Materials 5000 units @ Rs. 4 per unit	20,000	—
Sundry Materials	7,000	9,000
Wages	5,000	10,000
Overheads	2,100	3,080
Normal Loss (per cent of input)	3%	5%
Scrap value (per unit)	Re. 1	Rs. 4
Actual output	4800 units	4600 units.

There was no opening or closing stock.

(K.U.D., October 1993)

Solution :

Working Table

Particulars	Process-A Input	Process-A Amount	Process-B Input	Process-B Amount
Inputs	5000	34,100	4800	55,680
Less : Normal Loss 3%	150	—	240	—
Scrap sold	—	150	—	960
	4850	33,950	4560	54,720
Actual output	4800		4600	
Abnormal Loss	50		—	
Abnormal Gain	—		40	
Cost of Abnormal Loss = $\frac{33,950}{4850}$ = 7 × 50 = Rs. 350			—	—
Cost of Abnormal Gain = $\frac{54,720}{4560}$ = Rs. 12 —		—	40 × 12 = Rs. 480	

Process-A A/c

Particulars	Units	Amount	Particulars	Units	Amount
To Material @ Rs. 4 per unit	5000	20,000	By Normal Loss 3% of 5000	150	
To Sundry Materials		7,000	By Scrap sold @ Re. 1 per unit		150
To Wages		5,000	By Abnormal Loss	50	350
To Overheads		2,100	By Process-B A/c (transfer)	4800	33,600
Total	5000	34,100	Total	5000	34,100

Process-B A/c

Particulars	Units	Amount	Particulars	Units	Amount
To Process-A A/c	4800	33,600	By Normal Loss 5% of 4800	240	
To Sundry Material		9,000	By Scrap value @ Rs. 4 Per unit		960
To Wages		10,000			
To Overheads		3,080	By Finished stock (4600 × 12)	4600	55,200
To Abnormal Gain	40	480			
Total	4840	56,160	Total	4840	56,160

Problem No. 11

A Product passes through three processes. The following information relates to January 1990 :

	Process-I Rs.	Process-II Rs.	Process-III Rs.
Sundry Materials	2,600	1,980	2,962
Wages	2,600	3,000	4,000

Production overhead of Rs. 9,000 is recovered at 100% on Direct Wages. 1000 units of material at Rs. 3 per unit were introduced in to Process-I. The following additional data are obtained :

Process	Output	Normal Loss	Scrap value per unit
Process-I	950 Units	5%	Rs. 2
Process-II	840 Units	10%	Rs. 4
Process-III	750 Units	15%	Rs. 5

There was no stock of materials or work-in-progress at the beginning or end of the period.

Prepare Cost Accounts.

(K.U.D., April 1993)

Solution :

Working Chart

Particulars	Process-I		Process-II		Process-III	
	Units	Cost	Units	Cost	Units	Cost
Input	1000	9,600	950	17,480	840	27,762
Less : Normal Loss (Scrap sold)	50	100	95	380	126	630
Cost of Normal output	950	9,500	855	17,100	714	27,132
Actual output	950	9,500	840		750	
Abnormal Loss	—	—	15	—	—	—
Abnormal Gain	—	—	—	—	36	—

Cost of Abnormal Loss = $\frac{17,100}{855} \times 15$ = Rs. 300

Cost of Abnormal Gain = $\frac{27,132}{714}$ = Rs. 38

38 × 36 = 1,368 Abnormal gain.

Process-I A/c

Particulars	Units	Amount	Particulars	Units	Amount
To Material Cost of units introduce	1000	3,000	By Normal Loss 5% of 1000	50	100
To Sundry Materials		2,600	By Scrap sold		
To Wages		2,000	By Process-II A/c	950	9,500
To Production overhead 100% of Direct wage		2,000			
	1000	9,600		1000	9,600

Process-II A/c

Particulars	Units	Amount	Particulars	Units	Amount
To Process-I A/c	950	9,500	By Normal Loss 10% of 950	95	380
To Sundry Material		1,980	Scrap sold @ Rs. 4		
To Wages		3,000	By Abnormal Loss	15	300
To Production overhead		3,000	$\frac{17,100}{8550}$ = Rs. 20		
100% of Direct Wages			By Process-III A/c transfer	840	16,800
	950	17,480		950	17,480

Process-III A/c

Particulars	Units	Amount	Particulars	Units	Amount
To Process-II A/c (transfer)	840	16,800	By Normal Loss 15% of 840	126	630
To Sundry Material		2,962	Scrap sold @ Rs. 5%		
To Production overhead 100% of Direct wage		4,000	By Finished stock @ Rs. 38 per unit	750	28,500
To Wages		4,000			
To Abnormal gain 36 Units @ Rs. 38 per unit (36 × 38)	36	1,368			
Total	876	29,130		876	29,130

Problem No. 12

A Product of a company passes through two separate processes. From the following information prepare process Accounts. Units of Materials introduced into Process-A — 10000 Units — Rs. 80,000.

Other Particulars :

	Process-A	Process-B
Sundry Material	8,000	12,000
Wages	40,000	64,000
Overheads	8,400	9,500
Normal Loss	3%	5%
Scrap Value per unit	2	4
Actual Production in Units	9500	9100

(K.U.D., October 1992)

Solution :

Working Table

Particulars	Process-A		Process-B	
Inputs	10000	1,36,400	9500	2,18,500
Less : Normal Loss	300		475	
Scrap Value				
Process-A = 300 × 2		600		
Process-B = 475 × 4				1,900
	9700	1,35,800	9025	2,16,600
Actual Output	9500		9100	
Abnormal Loss	200		—	
Abnormal Gain	—		75	

$$\text{Abnormal Loss} = \frac{\text{Cost of Normal output}}{\text{Units of Normal loss}} \times \text{Units of Abnormal Loss}$$

$$= \frac{1,35,800}{9700} = 14 \times 200 = 2,800$$

$$\text{Abnormal Gain} = \frac{2,16,600}{9025} \times 24 \times 75$$

$$= \text{Rs. } 1,800$$

Process-A A/c

Particulars	Units	Amount	Particulars	Units	Amount
To Material introduce	10000	80,000	By Normal Loss 3% of 10000	300	600
To Sundry Materials		8,000	Scrap sold @ Rs. 2 per unit		
To Wages		40,000	By Abnormal Loss	200	2,800
To Overheads		8,400	By Process-B A/c transferred	9500	1,33,000
Total	10000	1,36,400	Total	10000	1,36,400

Process-B A/c

Particulars	Units	Amount	Particulars	Units	Amount
To Process-A A/c	9500	1,33,000	By Normal Loss 5% of 9500	475	
To Sundry Material		12,000	By Scrap sold @ Rs. 4 per unit		1,900
To Wages		64,000	By Finished stock Account	9100	2,18,400
To Overheads		9,500			
To Abnormal Gain	75	1,800			
Total	9575	2,20,300	Total	9575	2,20,300

Problem No. 13

A product of a company passes through 3 separate processes. From the following information prepare Process Accounts.

Units of Materials introduced in to Process-A — 20000 Units — Rs. 8,000

Particulars	Process A	Process B	Process C
Sundry Materials	Rs. 6,000	2,000	2,000
Direct Labour	Rs. 4,000	3,000	3,000
Overheads	Rs. 4,000	2,000	1,000
Normal Loss	2%	5%	10%
Scrap value per 100 units	Rs. 5	20	10
Output (Units)	Rs. 19,600	18,400	16,700

(K.U.D., April 1992)

Solution :

Working Table

Particulars	Process-A Unit	Process-A Cost	Process-B Unit	Process-B Cost	Process-C Unit	Process-C Cost
Input	20000	22000	19600	28980	18400	34444
Less Normal Loss	400	20	980	196	1840	184
A - 2% of input						
B - 5% of input						
C - 10% of input						
Normal cost of Normal output	19600	21,980	18620	28,784	16,560	34,260
Actual output	19600		18400		16700	
	Nil		220 Less		140 more	

No Loss/Gain

Process-B Actual output is less than normal output

∴ Abnormal Loss of 220 units

Cost of Abnormal Loss = $\frac{\text{Total cost}}{\text{Normal Unit}} \times$ Units Abnormal Loss

$\frac{28,784}{18,620} \times 220$ = Rs. 340 Loss

Loss

Process-C Gains Actual output Abnormal Gain

Abnormal Gain

$= \frac{34,260}{16,560} \times 140$

= 289.6

= 290 Approx.

Process-A A/c

Particulars	Units	Amount	Particulars	Units	Amount
To Materials introduce	20000	8,000	By Normal Loss 2% of 20000	400	
To Sundry Materials		6,000	By Scrap sold Rs. 5 for 100 Units		20
To Direct Labour		4,000	By Transferred to Process-B	19600	21,980
To Overheads		4,000			
	20000	22,000		20000	22,000

Process-B A/c

Particulars	Units	Amount	Particulars	Units	Amount
To Process A A/c transfer	19600	21,980	By Normal Loss 5% on 19,600	980	
To Sundry Material		2,000	By Scrap sold Rs. 20 for 100 units		196
To Direct Labour		3,000	By Abnormal Loss	220	340
To Overheads		2,000	By Process-C transfer	18400	28,444
	19600	28,980		19,600	28,980

Process-C A/c

Particulars	Units	Amount	Particulars	Units	Amount
To Process-B A/c	18400	28,444	By Normal Loss 10% of 18400	1840	184
To Sundry Materials		2,000	Scrap sold 10 for 100 Units		
To Direct Wages		3,000	By Finished stock A/c	16700	34,550
To Overhead		1,000			
To Abnormal Gain	140	290			
Total	18540	34,734	Total	18540	34,734

Problem No. 14

A by-product A is produced in the course of manufacture of Product is further processed for sale. The following is the information for the month of March 1991 :

Elements	Joint Expense	Separate Expense A	Separate Expense B
	Rs.	Rs.	Rs.
Materials	20,000	12,000	1,000
Labour	14,000	10,000	4,000
Overheads	5,000	3,000	1,200

The quantities produced during the month were : A — 100 units and B — 50 units.

The selling price of B is Rs. 240 per unit on which the profit earned is estimated at 30%.

Prepare an account to show the cost price of A per unit.

(K.U.D., October 1991)

Solution :

Selling price of "B" per unit	240.00
Less : Estimated Profit 30% (240 × 30%)	72.00
Total Cost	168.00
Total Cost of 50 Units = 168 × 50 = Rs. 8,400	8,400.00

	Total Cost		8,400.00
Less : Separate Expenses on "B"			
Material		1,000	
Labour		4,000	
Overhead		1,200	6,200.00
	Share in Joint Cost		2,200.00

A Products Production A/c

Particulars	Amount	Particulars	Amount
To Materials (20,000 + 12,000)	32,000	By "B" Production A/c	2,200
		" Cost of "A" Product	61,800
To Wages Labour (14,000 + 10,000)	24,000		
To Overhead (5,000 + 3,000)	8,000		
Total	64,000	Total	64,000

Cost per unit of 'A' Product

$$= \frac{\text{Total Cost}}{\text{No. of units}}$$

$$= \frac{61{,}800}{100}$$

= 618 per unit.

Problem No. 15

A product of a company passes through three processes to completion are known as A, B and C. From the past experience it is ascertained that wastage is incurred in each process as under : Process-A 2%, Process-B — 5% and Process-C — 10%. In each case percentage of wastage computed on the number of units entering into the process concerned.

The wastage of each process is possessing scrap value. Process-A and B is sold at Rs. 5 per 100 Units and that of C is sold at Rs. 20 per 100 Units. The output of each process passes immediately to the next process and the finished units are passed from Process-C into finished stock Account.

The following information is obtained :

Particulars	Process		
	A	B	C
Materials consumed	6,000	4,000	2,000
Direct Labour	8,000	6,000	3,000
Manufacturing Expenses	1,000	1,000	1,500

20,000 Units are issued to Process-A at a cost of Rs. 10,000. The output of each process is :

Process-A	19,500 Units
Process-B	18,800 Units
Process-C	16,000 Units

Prepare Process Accounts and the calculation should be made to the nearest rupee.

(K.U.D., April 1991)

Solution :

Working Notes

Process 'A' Account		Units	Amount
Input		20,000	25,000
Less : Normal Loss 2% of 20,000		400	20
Normal cost of Normal output		19,600	24,980
Actual Output	19,500	19,500	
Abnormal Loss		100	

$$\text{Cost of Abnormal Loss} = \frac{\text{Normal Cost}}{\text{Normal Output}} \times \text{Units of Abnormal Loss}$$

$$= \frac{24{,}980}{19{,}600} \times 100 = 127$$

$$= \text{Cost per Unit} = 1.27$$

Process 'B' Account		
Input	19,500	35,853
Less : Normal Loss	975	49
Normal cost of Normal output	18,525	35,804
Actual output	18,800	
More than Normal output	275	

It is Abnormal Gain :

$$\text{Cost of Abnormal Gain} = \frac{\text{Normal Cost}}{\text{Normal Output}} \times \text{Units of Abnormal Gain}$$

$$= \frac{35{,}804}{18{,}525} \times 275 = 532$$

Cost per Unit = Rs. 1.93

Process 'C' Account		
Input	18,800	42,836
Less: Normal Loss 10% of 18800	1,880	376
Normal cost of Normal output	16,920	42,460
Actual output	16,000	
Abnormal Loss	920	

$$\text{Cost of Abnormal Loss} = \frac{\text{Normal Cost}}{\text{Normal Output}} \times \text{Units of Abnormal Loss}$$

$$= \frac{42{,}460}{16{,}920} \times 920 = 2309$$

Cost per unit = Rs. 2.51.

Process 'A' A/c

Particulars	Units	Amount	Particulars	Units	Amount
To Units	20000	10,000	By Normal Loss	400	
To Materials consumed		6,000	By 2% of 20,000		
To Direct Labour		8,000	By Scrap sold Rs. 5 per 100 Units		20
To Manufacturing Exp.		1,000	By Abnormal Loss	100	127
			By Process 'B' A/c Transfer	19500	24,853
	20000	25,000		20000	25,000

Process 'B' A/c

Particulars	Units	Amount	Particulars	Units	Amount
To Process 'A' A/c	19500	24,853	By Normal Loss 5% of 19500	975	
To Materials		4,000	By Scrap sold @ Rs. 5 per 100 units		49
To Manufacture Exp.		1,000	By Process 'C' A/c	18800	36,336
To Abnormal Gain	275	532			
	19775	36,385		19775	36,385

Process 'C' A/c

Particulars	Units	Amount	Particulars	Units	Amount
To Process 'B' A/c	18800	36,336	By Normal Loss (10% of 18800)	1880	
To Materials		2,000	By Scrap sold @ Rs. 20 per 100 units		376
To Direct Labour		3,000	By Abnormal Loss	920	2,309
To Manufacture Exp.		1,500	By Finished goods	16000	40,151
	18800	42,836		18800	42,836

Abnormal Loss A/c

Particulars	Amount	Particulars	Amount
To Process 'A' A/c	127	By Sale of Scrap 100 @ Rs. 5	5
To Process 'C' A/c	2,309	By Sale of Scrap @ Rs. 20 per 100 units	184
		By Costing Profit & Loss A/c	2,247
	2,436		2,436

Abnormal Gain A/c

To Reduction in sale of Scrap $\left(\frac{275}{100} \times 5\right)$	13.75	By Process 'B' A/c	532
To Costing Profit & Loss A/c	518.25		
	532.00		532

Problem No. 16

A product passes through two distinct Processes 'A' and 'B'. Prepare process cost account from the following details :

	Particulars	Process A Rs.	Process B Rs.
(i)	Materials	60,000	43,250
(ii)	Labour	35,000	24,000
(iii)	Overheads	12,000	17,100
(iv)	Inputs (in units)	40000	35000
(v)	Normal Loss	10%	4%
(vi)	Scrap Value (per unit)	Rs. 2	3

There was no opening or closing stock of any type. The final output from Process 'B' was 34,000 units. Prepare process account and show the calculation for abnormal gain and abnormal loss resulting in the processes.

(K.U.D., October 1990)

Solution :

Working Table

Particulars	Process-A Units	Process-A Cost	Process-B Units	Process-B Cost
Inputs	40000	1,07,000	35000	1,80,600
Less : Normal Loss				
Process-A 10%	4000	8,000		
Process-B 4%			1400	4,200
Cost of Units of normal output	36000	99,000	33600	1,76,400
Actual output	35000		34000	
Abnormal Loss	1000		—	
Abnormal Gain	—		400	

$$\text{Cost of Abnormal Loss} = \frac{\text{Cost of Normal output}}{\text{Units of Normal output}} \times \text{Units of Abnormal loss}$$

$$\text{(Process-A)} = \frac{99{,}000}{36{,}000} \times 1000 = 2750$$

Cost per Unit = Rs. 2.75.

$$\text{Cost of Abnormal Gain} = \frac{\text{Cost of Normal output}}{\text{Normal output}} \times \text{Units of Abnormal gain}$$

$$= \frac{1{,}80{,}600}{33600} \times 400 = 2150$$

Cost per Unit = Rs. 5.375

Process-A A/c

Particulars	Units	Amount	Particulars	Units	Amount
To Units Input	40000		By Normai Loss 10% of 40000	4000	
To Materials		60,000	By Scrap sold @ Rs. 2 per unit		8,000
To Labour		35,000	By Abnormal Loss	1000	2,750
To Overheads		12,000	By Process-B A/c	35000	96,250
	40000	1,07,000		40000	1,07,000

Process-B A/c

Particulars	Units	Amount	Particulars	Units	Amount
To Process-A A/c	35000	96,250	By Normal Loss 4% of 35000	1400	
To Materials		43,250	By Scrap sold Rs. 3		4,200
To Labour		24,000	By Finished Stock	34000	1,78,550
To Overheads		17,100			
To Abnormal Gain	400	2,150			
	35400	1,82,750		35400	1,82,750

Problem No. 17

Product 'A' passes through three abstract processes for completion. The following information relates for the month of December 1989 :

Particulars	Total	Process A	Process B	Process C
Materials	6,455	2,600	1,915	1,940
Direct Wages	7,330	2,250	3,680	1,400
Production Overhead	10,995	—	—	—

500 Units @ Rs. 4 per unit were introduced into process 'A'. Production overhead to be distributed @ 150% on Direct Wages. The actual output and Normal loss of the respective.

Process are as a follows :

Process	Output in units	Normal Loss on inputs	Sale of Scrap per unit
A	450	10%	2.00
B	340	20%	4.00
C	270	25%	5.00

There was no opening and closing work-in-progress at any stage in any process.

You are require to prepare :

(1) Process Accounts.

(2) Abnormal Gain and Abnormal Loss A/c.

(K.U.D., April 1990)

Solution :

Working Chart

Particulars	Process 'B' Units	Process 'B' Rs.	Process 'C' Units	Process 'C' Rs.
Input	450	20,880	240	25,160
Less : Normal Loss 20% of 450	90	360	—	—
Normal Loss 25% of 340	—	—	85	425
Scrap sold : 90 × 4				
	360	20,880	255	24,735
Actual Output	340		270	
Abnormal Loss	20		—	
Abnormal Gain	—		15	

Cost of Abnormal Loss $= \frac{20,880}{360} = 58$ Cost of Abnormal Gain $= \frac{24,735}{255} = 97$

58 × 20 = Rs. 1,160 Abnormal Gain 97 × 15 = Rs. 1,455

Process 'A' A/c

Particulars	Units	Amount	Particulars	Units	Amount
To Units introduced @ cost 4 per unit	500	2,000	By Normal Loss 10% of 500 units sold @ Rs. 2 per unit	50	100
To Materials		2,600	By Process 'B' A/c transfer	450	10,125
To Direct Wages		2,250			
To Prduction overhead 150% on 2,250		3,375			
	500	10,225		500	10,225

Process 'B' A/c

Particulars	Units	Amount	Particulars	Units	Amount
To Process 'A' A/c	450	10,125	By Normal Loss 20% on 450 Scrap sold Rs. 4	90	360
To Materials		1,915			
To Direct Wages		3,680	By Abnormal Loss @ Rs. 58	20	1,160
To Production output 150% of 3,680		5,520	By Process 'C' A/c 58 × 340	340	19,720
	450	21,240		450	21,240

Process 'C' A/c

Particulars	Units	Amount	Particulars	Units	Amount
To Process 'B' A/c	340	19,720	By Normal Loss 25% on 340 Scrap sold @ 5	85	425
To Materials		1,940			
To Direct Wages		1,400	By Finished Stock transfer cost Rs. 97	270	26,190
To Production overhead 150% of 1,400		2,100			
To Abnormal Gain @ Rs. 97	15	1,455			
	355	26,615		355	26,645

Abnormal Loss A/c

Particulars	Units	Amount	Particulars	Units	Amount
To Process 'B' A/c	20	1,160	By Scrap Value		80
			By Costing Profit & Loss A/c		1,080
		1,160			1,160

Abnormal Gain A/c

Particulars	Units	Amount	Particulars	Units	Amount
To Process 'C' A/c Reduction in scrap (15 × 5)		75	By Process 'C' A/c	15	1,455
To Costing Profit & Loss A/c		1,380			
		1,455			1,455

Problem No. 18

A product passes through two distant Processes A & B and then to Finished stock.

The normal wastage of each process is as follows :

Process-A 3% on the units entering the process.

Process-B 5% on the units entering the process.

Wastage of process 'A' was sold at Re. 0.50 per unit and that the process 'B' was @ Re. 1 per unit.

10,000 units were issued to Process-A @ a cost of Rs. 2 per unit. The other Expenses are as following :

	Process-A	Process-B
Sundry Material	2,000	3,000
Wages	10,000	16,000
Manufacturing Expenses	2,100	2,375
The actual output were	9500 Units	9100 Units

Prepare Process Account assuming that there was no opening and closing stock.

(K.U.D., October 1989)

Process 'A' A/c

Particulars	Qty.	Amount	Particulars	Qty.	Amount
To Units Issued Input @ Rs. 2 per unit	10000	20,000	By Normal Wastage @ 3% on 10000	300	150
To Sundry Material		2,000	By Abnormal Loss Cost = 34100 – 150 $= \frac{33,950}{9700} \times 200$	200	700
To Wages		10,000			
To Manufacturing Exp.		2,100	By Process 'B' A/c transfer	9500	33,250
Total	10000	34,100	Total	10000	34,100

Process 'B' A/c

Particulars	Qty.	Amount	Particulars	Qty.	Amount
To Process 'A' A/c	9500	33,250	By Normal Wastage	475	475
To Sundry Materials		3,000	5% on 9500 sold		
To Wages		16,000	@ Re.1 per unit		
To Manufacturing Exp.		2,375	By Finished stock	9100	54,600
To Abnormal Gain	75	450	Rs. 6 per unit		
Cost = 54,625 – 475 = 54,150; $= \frac{54,150}{9,025} = 6$; = 6 × 75 = 450					
Total	9575	55,075	Total	9575	55,075

Problem No. 19

A Factory is engaged in the production of chemical 'X' and in the course of its manufacture a by-product 'Y' is produced which after a separate process has a commerical value. For the month of January 1989, the following are the summarised costing data :

	Joint Expenses	Separate Expenses	
		Main Product	By-Product
	Rs.	X	Y
Materials	19,200	7,360	780
Labour	11,700	7,680	2,642
Overhead	3,450	1,500	544

The output for the month was 142 tons of 'X' and 49 tons of 'Y' and the Selling price of 'Y' averaged Rs. 280 per ton. Assuming that the profit on 'Y' is estimated at 50% of the Selling price.

Prepare Cost Account of 'X'.

(K.U.D., April 1989)

Solution :

Statement of Cost of By-product 'Y'

Selling Price Rs. 280 per ton (280 × 49)		13,720
Less : Estimated profit (50% on 13,720)		6,860
Estimated total cost		6,860
Less : Separate Expenses of 'Y'		
Material	780	
Labour	2,642	
Overhead	544	3,966
Estimated cost up to the Point of separate		
Or : Share in Joint cost		2,894

Statement of Cost of Main Product 'X'

Output 142 tons		
Joint cost : Material	19,200	
Labour	11,700	
Overhead	3,450	34,350
Less : Cost of by-product 'Y' share in Joint cost		2,894
Cost of main product 'X' share in Joint cost		31,456
Add : Separate Expenses : Material	7,360	
Labour	7,680	
Overhead	1,500	15,540
Total Cost of Production 'X'		47,996

$$\text{Cost per unit} = \frac{47,996}{142} = \text{Rs. } 338.$$

Main Product 'X' A/c

Particulars		Amount	Particulars	Amount
To *Joint Cost*			By 'Y' by-product A/c share in Joint cost	2,894
Material	19,200			
Labour	11,700		By Cost of production	47,996
Overhead	3,450	34,350	(Output — 142 units)	
To Separate Expenses of X			By Cost per unit = $\frac{47,996}{142}$ = Rs. 338	
Material	7,360			
Labour	7,680			
Overhead	1,500	16,540		
		50,890		50,890

By-Product 'Y' A/c

Particulars		Amount	Particulars	Amount
To 'X' Main Product		2,894	By Sales (49 × 280)	13,720
To *Separate Expenses*				
Material	780			
Labour	2,642			
Overhead	544	3,966		
To Profit Estimate 50% on sales		6,860		
Total		13,720	Total	13,720

Problem No. 20

Modern Process Limited manufactured its products by three consecutive process. The products of these processes are dealt with as under :

Particulars	A	B	C
Transferred next process	66-2/3%	60%	—
Transferred to warehouse for sale	33-1/3%	40%	100%

In each process 4% of weight put into lost and 6% is scrapped which from Process-A realise Rs. 3 per ton, from Process-B and Process-C @ Rs. 5 and Rs. 6 per ton respectively.

The following information relate to July 1987 :

Particulars	Process A	Process B	Process C
Raw Material used (in ton)	1400	160	1260
Rate per Ton (in Rs.)	10	16	7
Wages and other Exp. (in Rs.)	5,152	3,140	2,895

Prepare Process Account showing cost per ton of each process.

(K.U.D., October 1988)

Solution :

Process 'A' A/c

Particulars	Qty.	Amount	Particulars	Qty.	Amount
To Raw Materials	1400	14,000	By Normal Loss weight 4% of 1400	56	
To Wages and other Expenses		5,152	By Scrap sold @ Rs. 3 (6% of 1400)	84	252
			By Process 'B' A/c 66-2/3 % of 1260	840	12,600
			By Warehouse for	420	6,300
Total		19,152	Total		19,152

Cost per ton = 19,152
Less : Scrap 251
18,900

$$= \frac{18,900}{1260} = \text{Rs. } 15 \text{ per ton.}$$

Process 'B' A/c

Particulars	Qty.	Amount	Particulars	Qty.	Amount
To Process 'A' A/c	840	12,600	By Normal Loss weight loss 4% on 1000	40	
To Raw material @ Rs. 16	160	2,560			
To Wages and other Expenses		3,140	By Scrap sold @ Rs. 5 6% on 1000	60	300
			By Process 'C' A/c 60% of 900	540	10,800
			By Warehouse for sale 40% of 900 @ Rs. 20	360	7,200
Total		18,300	Total		18,300

Cost per ton 18,300
Less : Scrap 300
18,000

$$= \frac{18,000}{900} = 20 \text{ (Rs. 20 per ton)}$$

Process 'C' A/c

Particulars	Qty.	Amount	Particulars	Qty.	Amount
To Process 'C' A/c	540	10,800	By Normal Loss Weight loss 4% on 1800	72	
To Material	1260	8,820			
To Wages & Other Exp.		2,895	By Scrap sold @ Rs. 6 6% on 1800	108	648
			By Finished stock	1620	21,867
Total		22,515	Total		22,515

Cost per unit = 22,515

Less : Scrap 648

21,867

$= \frac{21,867}{1,620}$

= 13.498 or Rs. 13.50

Problem No. 21

Excell Ltd. produces a patent materials used in Building in the Manufacture of which three processes are involved. The material is produced in three consecutive grades namely, Soft, Medium and Hard. Figure relating to production for the first six months of 1986 are as follows :

Particulars	A	B	C
Raw material used (ton)	1000	—	—
Cost per ton (Rs.)	200	—	—
Manufacturing wages and Expenses (Rs.)	72,500	40,800	10,710
Weight Lost	5%	10%	20%
Scrap (sold @ Rs. 50 per ton)	50 tons	30 tons	51 tons

Two-thirds of process A and one-half of Process B are passed to the next process and the balance are sent to warehouse for sale.

You are required to prepare account for each process showing the cost per ton.

(K.U.D., October 1987)

Solution :

Process 'A' A/c

Particulars	Qty.	Amount	Particulars	Qty.	Amount
To Material used	1000	2,00,000	By Normal Loss 5% on 1000	50	
To Manufacturing Wages & Exp.		72,500	By Scrap sold @ Rs. 50 (50 tons)	50	2,500
			By Process 'B' A/c 2/3 × 900	600	1,80,000
			By Warehouse A/c balancing figure	300	90,000
Total	1000	2,72,500	Total	1000	2,72,500

Cost per ton	= 2,72,500
Less : Scrap sold	2,500
	2,70,000

$$= \frac{2,70,000}{900} = 300 \text{ per ton.}$$

Process 'B' A/c

Particulars	Qty.	Amount	Particulars	Qty.	Amount
To Process 'A' A/c	600	1,80,000	By Normal Loss 10% on 600	60	
To Manufacturing Wages & Other Exp.		40,800	By Scrap sold @ Rs. 50 per ton	80	1,500
			By Process 'C' A/c ½ of 510 @ Rs. 430	255	1,09,650
			By Warehouse transfer	255	1,09,650
Total	600	2,20,800	Total	600	2,20,800

Process 'C' A/c

Particulars	Qty.	Amount	Particulars	Qty.	Amount
To Process 'B' A/c	255	1,09,650	By Normal Loss 20% on 255	51	
			By Scrap sold @ Rs. 50	51	2,550
			By Finished stock transferred	153	1,17,810
Total	255	1,20,360	Total	255	1,20,360

Cost per ton	= 1,20,360
Less : Scrap sold	2,550
Net	1,17,810

$$= \frac{1,17,810}{153} = \text{Rs. } 770 \text{ per ton.}$$

Problem No. 22

The Antibiotics Drugs Manufacturing concern produces medicine 'M' and in the course of manufacture a by-product 'N' is produced which after a separate process has a commercial value.

Following is the information for the month of January 1986 :

Particulars	Joint Exp.	Separate Expenses Main Product M	Separate Expenses By-product N
	Rs.	Rs.	Rs.
Materials	25,000	5,000	7,000
Labour	10,000	6,250	6,250
Expenses	6,250	3,500	2,500

The output for the month was 150 units of 'M' and 50 units of 'N'. The selling price of product 'N' is Rs. 500 per unit. Profit on 'N' product is 33-1/3% on cost.

Prepare an account to show cost price of 'M' product per unit.

(K.U.D., April 1987)

Solution :

Statement of Cost of Product 'N' (Units — 50)

Sales price @ Rs. 50 per unit (500 × 50)	25,000	
Less : Profit 33-1/3% on cost 25% on sale 25,000	6,250	
Estimated Total Cost		18,750
Less : Cost after separation :		
Material	7,000	
Labour	6,250	
Expenses	2,500	15,750
Estimated cost up to the point of separation OR : Share in the Joint cost		3,000

Statement of Cost of Product 'M' (Main Product)

Joint Cost : Material		25,000	
Labour		10,000	
Expenses		6,250	41,250
Less : Cost of product (Share in Joint cost)			3,000
			38,250
Add : Separate Expenses :	Material	5,000	
	Labour	6,250	
	Expenses	3,500	14,750
	Total Cost of product		53,000

Alternatively :

Product 'M' (Main Product)

Particulars	Qty.	Amount	Particulars	Qty.	Amount
To Joint Cost :			By Product 'N' transfer		3,000
Material	25,000		By Cost of production		
Labour	10,000		Balancing figure		53,000
Expenses	6,250	41,250			
To Separate Expenses :					
Material	5,000				
Labour	6,250				
Expenses	3,500	14,750			
Total		56,000	Total		56,000

Product 'N' (By-product)

Particulars		Amount	Particulars		Amount
To Share in Joint Cost transfer from main product 'M'		3,000	By Sales (500 × 50 Units)		25,000
To Separate Expenses :					
Material	7,000				
Labour	6,250				
Expenses	2,500	15,750			
Add : Profit 25% on sales (25,000 × 25%)		6,250			
Total		25,000	Total		25,000

Problem No. 23

Product 'A' yields by-products B & C. Joint expenses of manufacture are :

Material	19,000
Labour	10,000
Overheads	700
	29,700

Subsequent Expenses are as follows :

Particulars	Main Product A	By-Products B	By-Products C
Materials	8,000	4,000	2,000
Labour	4,000	3,000	1,000
Overhead	600	500	500
Total	12,600	7,500	3,500
Selling Price	51,000	21,000	10,000
Estimated Profit on sales	40%	30%	20%

Prepare a statement showing the apportionment of Joint Expenses of manufacture over different products and also show the cost of production of A, B and C.

(K.U.D., October 1986)

Solution :

Apportionment of Joint Expenses

Particulars		Main Product A	By-Products B	By-Products C	Total
Selling Price		51,000	21,000	10,000	82,000
Less : Estimated Profit		40%	30%	20%	
		20,400	6,300	2,000	28,700
Total Cost		30,600	14,700	8,000	53,300
Less : Subsequent Expenses		12,600	7,500	3,500	23,600
Share in Joint Cost		18,000	7,200	4,500	29,700
Joint Expenses :	Material		19,000		
	Labour		10,000		
	Overhead		700		
			29,700		

Main Product-'A' A/c

Particulars	Qty.	Amount	Particulars	Qty.	Amount
To Material Joint	19,000		By Transfer share in Joint		
Separate	8,000	27,000	Expenses 'B' Product A/c		7,200
To Labour Joint	10,000		By 'C' Product Account		4,500
Separate	4,000	14,000	By Sales		51,000
To Overhead Joint	700				
Separate	600	1,300			
To Profit		20,400			
Total		62,700	Total		62,700

By-Product-'B' A/c

Particulars	Amount	Particulars	Amount
To Main 'A' Product transfer	7,200	By Sales	21,000
To *Separate Expenses*			
Material	4,000		
Labour	3,000		
Overhead	500		
To Profit	6,300		
Total	21,000	Total	21,000

By-Product-'C' A/c

Particulars	Amount	Particulars	Amount
To Main Product 'A' A/c	4,500	By Sales	10,000
To *Separate Expenses*			
Material	2,000		
Labour	1,000		
Overhead	500		
Profit	2,000		
Total	10,000	Total	10,000

Problem No. 24

Trilok Industries produces a forged product 'Sun-beam' after it passes three distinct processes. The following information has been obtained from the Cost Accounts for the month ending 31-12-1985 :

	Total	Process I	Process II	Process III
	Rs.	Rs.	Rs.	Rs.
Direct Material	7,542	2,600	1,980	2,962
Labour	9,000	2,000	3,000	4,000
Production Overhead	9,000	—	—	—

Production overhead recovered 100% of direct wages.

1000 units @ Rs. 3 per unit were interduced in process-I.

There was no Opening and Closing stock.

The output of each process passes direct to the next process and final to finished stock.

The following additional data are provided :

	Process I	Process II	Process III
Output in units	950	840	750
Percentage of Normal Loss to input	5%	10%	15%
Value of Scrap per unit	Rs. 2	Rs. 4	Rs. 5

Prepare Process and Cost Account.

(K.U.D., April 1986)

Working Note

Note : Process-I A/c there was no abnormal Loss or Gain.

Ascertainment of Abnormal Gain and Abnormal Loss.

Working Table

Particulars		Process-II Qty.	Process-II Amount	Process-III Qty.	Process-III Amount
Inputs		950	17,480	840	27,762
Less : Normal Loss :	10% of 950	95	380		
	15% of 840			126	630
Normal Cost of Normal Output		855	17,100	714	27,132
Actual Output		840		750	
Abnormal Loss		15		—	
Abnormal Gain		—		36	

$$\text{Cost of Abnormal Loss} = \frac{\text{Normal Cost}}{\text{Normal Output}} \times \text{Units of Abnormal Loss}$$

$$= \frac{17{,}100}{855} \times 15 = 300 \quad \text{Cost per Unit Rs. 20}$$

$$\text{Cost of Abnormal Gain} = \frac{\text{Normal Cost}}{\text{Normal Output}} \times \text{Units of Abnormal Gain}$$

$$= \frac{27{,}132}{714} \times 36 = 1{,}368$$

Cost per unit = Rs. 38.

Process-I A/c

Particulars	Qty.	Amount	Particulars	Qty.	Amount
To Units issued	1000	3,000	By Normal Loss 5% of 1000	50	
To Direct Material		2,600	By Scrap sold @		100
To Labour		2,000	Rs. 2 per unit		
To Product overhead 100% of Direct wages		2,000	By Process-I A/c	950	9,500
Total	1000	9,600	Total	1000	9,600

Process-II A/c

Particulars	Qty.	Amount	Particulars	Qty.	Amount
To Process-I A/c @ Rs. 10 per unit	950	9,500	By Normal Loss 10% of 950	95	
To Direct Material		1,980	By Scrap sold		380
To Labour		3,000	@ Rs. 4 per unit		
To Production overhead 100% of labour		3,000	By Abnormal Loss @ Rs. 20 per unit	15	300
			By Process-III A/c	840	16,800
Total	950	17,480	Total	950	17,480

Process-III A/c

Particulars	Qty.	Amount	Particulars	Qty.	Amount
To Process-II A/c @ Rs. 20 per unit	840	16,800	By Normal Loss 15% of 840	126	
To Direct Material		2,962	By Scrap sold @ Rs. 5 each		630
To Labour		4,000	By Finished stock	750	28,500
To Production overhead 100% of Labour		4,000			
To Abnormal Gain @ Rs. 38 p. unit	36	1,368			
Total	876	29,130	Total	876	29,130

Abnormal Loss A/c

Particulars	Amount	Particulars	Amount
To Process-II A/c 15 units @ Rs. 20 each	300	By Scrap Sold 15 units @ 4	60
		By Costing Profit & Loss A/c	240
	300		300

Abnormal Gain A/c

Particulars	Amount	Particulars	Amount
To Reduction in sale in scrap 36 units @ 5 each	180	By Process-III A/c	1,368
To Costing P & L A/c	1,188		
Total	1,368	Total	1,368

Problem No. 25

Product 'A' is obtained after passes through three distinct processes. The following cost information is available for the month :

Particulars	Total	Process		
		I	II	III
Materials	5,625	2,600	2,000	1,025
Labour Direct wages	7,330	2,250	3,680	1,400
Production Overhead	7,330	—	—	—

500 units @ Rs. 4 per unit were introduced in Process-I. Production overhead to be distributed as 100% on Direct Wages. The actual output and Normal Loss of the respective process are :

Particulars	Process		
	I	II	III
Output in units (in Rs.)	450	340	270
Normal Loss on Input	10%	20%	25%
Value of Scrap per unit (in Rs.)	2	4	5

There was no stock or work-in-progress in any of the Process A/c. Show

(a) Process Account.

(b) Normal Loss Account.

(c) Abnormal Loss and Abnormal Gain Account.

(K.U.D., April 1985)

Solution :

Working Table

Particulars	Process-II		Process-III	
	Qty.	Amount	Qty.	Amount
Inputs	450	18,360	340	20,825
Less : Normal Loss	20%		25%	
Cost of Normal output	90	360	85	425
	360	18,000	255	20,400
Actual Output	340		270	
Normal (Abnormal Loss)	20			
Abnormal Gain			15	

$$\text{Abnormal Loss : Cost} = \frac{\text{Cost of Normal output}}{\text{Normal output}} \times \text{Units Abnormal Loss}$$

$$= \frac{18{,}000}{360} \times 20 = \text{Rs. } 1{,}000. \text{ Cost per unit Rs. } 50.$$

$$\text{Abnormal Gain} = \frac{\text{Cost of Normal output}}{\text{Normal output}} \times \text{Units Abnormal Gain}$$

$$= \frac{20{,}400}{255} \times 15 = 1{,}200. \text{ Cost per unit Rs. 80.}$$

Process-I A/c

Particulars	Qty.	Amount	Particulars	Qty.	Amount
To Units introduced @ Rs. 4 per unit	500	2,000	By Normal Loss 10% of 500	50	
To Materials		2,600	By Scrap sold @ Rs. 2 p. unit		100
To Direct wages		2,250	By Process-II A/c transfer	450	9,000
To Production overhead 100% of 2,250		2,250			
Total	500	9,100	Total	500	9,100

Process-II A/c

Particulars	Qty.	Amount	Particulars	Qty.	Amount
To Process-I A/c	450	9,000	By Normal Loss 20% of 450	90	
To Materials		2,000			
To Direct Wages		3,680	By Scrap sold @ Rs. 4 each		360
To Production overhead 100% of 3680		3,680			
			By Abnormal Loss 50 × 20	20	1,000
			By Process-III A/c transfer	340	17,000
Total	450	18,360	Total	450	18,360

Process-III A/c

Particulars	Qty.	Amount	Particulars	Qty.	Amount
To Process-II A/c	340	17,000	By Normal Loss 25% of 340	85	
To Material		1,025			
To Direct Wages		1,400	By Scrap sold at Rs. 5		425
To Production overhead 100% of 1400		1,400	By Finished stock @ Rs. 80 p. unit	270	21,600
To Abnormal Gain @ Rs. 80 p. unit	15	1,200			
Total	355	22,025	Total	355	22,025

Normal Loss A/c

Particulars	Qty.	Amount	Particulars	Qty.	Amount
To Process-I A/c @ Rs. 2 per unit	50	100	By Abnormal Gain A/c Process-III	15	75
To Process-II A/c @ Rs. 4	90	360	By Costing Profit & Loss A/c transfer	210	815
To Process-III A/c @ Rs. 5 per unit	85	425			
	225	885		225	885

Abnormal Loss A/c

Particulars	Units	Amount	Particulars	Units	Amount
To Process-II A/c	20×50	1,000	By Sales of Scrap	20×4	80
			By Costing Profit & Loss A/c Transfer		920
	20	1,000		20	1,000

Abnormal Gain A/c

Particulars			Particulars		
To Reduction in Scrap	15×5	75	By Process-III A/c	15×80	1,200
To Costing Profit & Loss A/c Transfer		1,125			
	15	1,200		15	1,200

Problem No. 26

The product passes through three processes A, B and C. 10,000 units were issued to process A at cost of Rs. 100 per unit. The expenses were as follows :

Particulars	Process A	Process B	Process C
Materials	10,000	15,000	5,000
Labour	50,000	80,000	65,000
Direct Expenses	10,450	15,895	20,070
Actual output in units	9500	9100	8100
Normal Loss	3%	5%	8%
Scrap sold @ per unit (in Rs.)	2.50	5.00	8.50

Prepare Process Account; there was no opening or closing stock in any process; give the working notes.

(K.U.D., October 1985,
M'lore, April 1988)

Solution :

Working Note

Particulars	Process-A Qty.	Process-A Amount	Process-B Qty.	Process-B Amount	Process-C Qty.	Process-C Amount
Inputs	10000	10,70,450	9500	10,96,539	9100	11,93,346
Less : Normal Loss	300		475		728	
Scrap sold		750		2,375		6,188
	9700	10,69,700	9025	10,94,164	8372	11,87,158
Actual Output	9500		9100		8100	
Abnormal Loss	200		—		272	
Abnormal Gain	—		75		—	

Abnormal Gain or Loss $= \dfrac{\text{Normal Cost}}{\text{Normal Output}} \times$ Units of Abnormal Gain or Loss

Process-A $= \dfrac{10{,}69{,}700}{9700} \times 200 = 22{,}056$ Cost per unit = Rs. 110.27 Abnormal Loss

Process-C $= \dfrac{11{,}87{,}158}{8372} \times 272 = 38{,}570$ Cost per unit = Rs. 141.80 Abnormal Loss

Process-B $= \dfrac{\text{Normal Cost}}{\text{Normal Output}} \times$ Units of Abnormal Gain

$= \dfrac{10{,}94{,}164}{9025} \times 75 = 9{,}092$ Cost per unit = Rs. 11.237 Abnormal Loss

Process 'A' A/c

Particulars	Qty.	Amount	Particulars	Qty.	Amount
To Units Issued	10000	10,00,000	By Normal Loss 3% of 10000	300	
To Materials		10,000	By Scrap sold @ 2.50 per unit		750
To Labour		50,000			
To Direct Expenses		10,450	By Abnormal Loss	200	22,056
			By Process-B A/c transferred	9500	10,47,644
	10000	10,70,450		10000	10,70,450

Process 'B' A/c

Particulars	Qty.	Amount	Particulars	Qty.	Amount
To Process 'A' A/c @ Rs. 110.27	9500	10,47,644	By Normal Loss 5% of 9500	475	
To Material		15,000	By Scrap sold @ Rs. 5 each		2,375
To Labour		18,000	By Process 'C' A/c transferred @ Rs. 121.23	9100	11,03,256
To Direct Expenses		15,895			
To Abnormal Gain	75	9,092			
	9575	11,05,631		9575	11,05,631

Process 'C' A/c

Particulars	Qty.	Amount	Particulars	Qty.	Amount
To Process 'B" A/c	9100	11,03,256	By Normal Loss 8% of 9100	728	
To Material		5,000	By Scrap sold @ Rs. 8.50		6,188
To Labour		65,000	By Abnormal Loss @ Rs. 141.8	272	38,570
To Direct Expenses		20,090	By Finished Stock	8100	11,48,588
	9100	11,93,346		9,100	11,93,346

Abnormal Loss A/c

Particulars	Qty.	Amount	Particulars	Qty.	Amount
To Process 'A' A/c @ Rs. 110.28	200	22,056	By Scrap sold @ Rs. 2.50	200	500
To Process 'C' A/c	272	38,570	By Scrap sold @ Rs. 8.50	272	2,312
			By Costing Profit & Loss A/c		57,814
	472	60,626		472	60,626

Abnormal Gain A/c

Particulars	Qty.	Amount	Particulars	Qty.	Amount
To Reduction in sale of scrap @ Rs. 5 each 75		375	By Process 'B' A/c @ Rs. 121.23 each	75	9,092
To Costing Profit & Loss A/c		8,717			
		9,092			9,092

Problem No. 27

A Product of a company passes through three separate processes for completion. From the following information prepare Process A/c: Units introduced in to process 'A' 20000 @ Rs. 8,000.

Particulars	Process A	Process B	Process C
Normal Loss	2%	5%	10%
Scrap sold per 100 units (in Rs.)	5.	20	10
Materials consumed (in Rs.)	6,000	2,000	2,000
Direct Labour (in Rs.)	4,000	3,000	3,000
Manufacturing Expenses (in Rs.)	4,000	2,000	1,000
Output (in units)	19600	18400	16700

(K.U.D., October 1980)

Solution :

Working Table

Particulars	Process-A		Process-B		Process-C	
	Units	Amount	Units	Amount	Units	Amount
Units introduced	20000	22,000	19600	28,980	18400	34,444
Less : Normal Loss	2%		5%		10%	
	400		980		1840	
Scrap sold		20		196		184
Normal Cost of Normal output	19600	21,980	18620	28,784	16560	34,260
Actual output	19600		18400		16700	
Abnormal Loss	—		220		—	
Abnormal Gain	—		—		140	

$$\text{Cost of Abnormal Loss} = \frac{\text{Cost of Normal output}}{\text{Units of Normal}} \times \text{Units of Abnormal Loss}$$

$$= \frac{28{,}784}{18620} \times 220 = \text{Rs. } 340$$

$$\text{Cost of Abnormal Gain} = \frac{\text{Cost of Normal output}}{\text{Units of Normal}} \times \text{Abnormal Gain}$$

$$= \frac{34{,}260}{16560} \times 140 = \text{Rs. } 289.63$$

Process 'A' A/c

Particulars	Units	Amount	Particulars	Units	Amount
To Units introduced	20000	8,000	By Normal Loss @ 2% 20000	400	
To Material consumed		6,000	By Scrap sold @ Rs. 5 per 100		20
To Direct Labour		4,000	By Process 'B' A/c transfer	19600	21,980
To Manufacturing Exp.		4,000			
Total	20000	22,000	Total	20000	22,000

Process 'B' A/c

Particulars	Units	Amount	Particulars	Units	Amount
To Process 'A' A/c	19600	21,980	By Normal Loss @ 5% on 19600	980	
To Materials		2,000	By Scrap sold @ Rs. 20 per 100		196
To Direct Labour		3,000	By Abnormal Loss	220	340
To Manufacturing Exp.		2,000	By Process 'C'	18400	28,444
Total	19600	28,980	Total	19600	28,980

Process 'C' A/c

Particulars	Units	Amount	Particulars	Units	Amount
To Process 'B' A/c	18400	28,444	By Normal Loss 10% of 18400	1840	184
To Materials		2,000	By Finished Stock	16700	34,550
To Direct Labour		3,000			
To Manufacturing Exp.		1,000			
To Abnormal Gain @ 2.068	140	290			
Total	18540	34,734	Total	18540	34,734

Problem No. 28

Calculate the Estimated cost of production of by-products 'X' and 'Y' at the point of separation from the main product.

	By-Product 'X'	By-Product 'Y'
Selling price per unit	Rs. 12	24
Cost per unit after separation from main product	3	5
Units produced	500	200

Selling expenses amounted to 25% of the total works cost including both pre-separation and post-separation works cost.

Selling prices are arrived at by adding 20% of total cost i.e., sum of works cost and selling cost.

(C.A. Final)

Solution :

Statement of Cost showing Share in Joint Cost

X — Produce - 500 Units Y — Produce - 200 Units.	By-Product 'X' per unit Rs.	By-Product 'X' Total Cost Rs.	By-Product 'Y' per unit Rs.	By-Product 'Y' Total Cost Rs.
Selling Price (500 units & 200 units)	500×12	6,000	200×24	4,800
Less : Profit 20% on Cost or 1/6 of selling price	2	1,000	4	800
Total Cost	10	5,000	20	4,000
Less : Selling Expenses 25% on works cost or 20% on Total Cost	2	1,000	4	800
Works Cost	8	4,000	20	3,200
Less : Cost after separation	3	1,500	5	1,000
Share in Joint Cost	5	2,500	15	2,200

Problem No. Extra-1/29

A certain Chemical was put into process and yields 75% of materials introduced as main product, 20% as a by-product and 5% loss in process. The percentage of material consumed by main product and by-product is 80 : 20. Time taken to produce one unit of by-product is half of the time taken of Main Product. Overheads have been allocated 200% of wages of each product.

Cost Data :

Raw Material	25,000	5000 Units.
Labour	21,250	
Overhead	42,500	
Total	88,750	

Solution :

Note : (1) Total No. of units produced.

5000 × 75% = 3,750 Units Main Product.

5000 × 20% = 1,000 Units By-Product.

5000 × 5% = 2,500 Wastage process Loss.

(2) Time taken to produce (One) 1 unit of by-product.

(a) is half the time taken by main product
= 3,750 × 2 = 7,500

Main Product 7,500 : By-Product 1000

Ratio 75 : 10

15 : 2 Wages

(b) Material consumed ratio = 80 : 20 = 4 : 1

(c) Overhead are @ 200% of wages.

Statement of Apportionment Cost

	Ratio	Total	Main Product Total	Main Product Cost per unit	By-Product Total	By-Product Cost per unit
Units Produced			3750		1000	
Material	80 : 20	25,000	20,000	5.33	5,000	5.00
Wages	15 : 2	21,200	18,750	5.00	2,500	2.50
Overhead	200% of Wages	42,500	37,500	10.00	5,000	5.00
Total Cost		88,750	76,250	20.33	12,500	12.50

Problem No. Extra-2/30 (Where Balance of Cost is more than the Joint Cost)

A factory producing article 'P' also produce a by-product 'Q' which is further processed into finished product. Joint cost and subsequent cost are as follows :

Particulars	Joint Cost	Subsequent Cost P	Subsequent Cost Q
Materials	22,500	13,500	6,750
Labour	13,500	6,300	4,500
Overheads	9,000	2,700	2,250
	45,000	22,500	13,500
Selling Price	—	72,000	36,000
Estimated Profit on selling price	—	25%	20%

[C.A. (Inter) Modified]

Solution :

Statement showing Apportionment of Joint Cost

	Main Product 'P'	By-Product 'Q'	Total Rs.
Selling Price	72,000	36,000	1,08,000
Less : Estimated Profit on Selling Price (P-25%, Q-20%)	18,000	7,200	25,200
	54,000	28,800	82,800
Less : Subsequent Cost	22,500	13,500	36,000
Total Cost	31,500	15,300	46,800
Less : Joint Cost	—	—	45,000
Difference being Selling & Distribution Expenses			1,800
Total Cost as above	31,500	15,300	46,800
Less : Selling & Distribution Expenses ratio : 2 : 1	1,200	600	1,800
Share in Joint Cost	30,300	14,700	45,000

'P' Main Product A/c

Particulars	Amount	Particulars	Amount
To Material (22,500 + 13,500)	36,000	By Sales	72,000
To Labour (13,500 + 6,300)	19,800	By Q A/c (Transfer) Balancing figure Share in Joint cost of 'Q'	14,700
To Overhead (9,000 + 2,700)	11,700		
To Selling & Distribute Expenses	1,200		
Total Cost	68,700		
Add : Profit	18,000		
Total	86,700	Total	86,700

By-Product A/c

Particulars	Amount	Particulars	Amount
To Transferred from 'P' A/c	14,700	By Sales	36,000
To Material	6,750		
To Labour	4,500		
To Overhead	2,250		
To Selling & Distribute Expenses	600		
Total Cost	28,800		
Add : Profit	7,200		
Total	36,000	Total	36,000

Cost of Production of Main Product 'P'

Particulars	Amount	Particulars	Amount
To Share in Joint Cost	30,300	By Sales	72,000
To *Add* : Subsequent cost :			
Material	13,500		
Labour	6,300		
Overhead	2,700		
Total Cost	52,800		
Add : Selling & Distribute			
Expenses	1,200		
Cost of Sales	54,000		
Add : Profit	7,800		
Total	72,000	Total	72,000

Problem No. Extra 3/31

A Co. Ltd. manufactures product X Main, which yield two By-products 'Y' and 'Z'. Following are the details.

Amount spent upto the point of separation (i.e., Joint cost) Rs. 6,18,000 subsequent Expenses were :

Particulars	Products		
	X	Y	Z
Materials	25,000	6,000	5,000
Labour	22,500	9,000	5,500
Overhead	12,500	8,100	8,400
	60,000	23,100	18,900

Gross sales value of products X, Y and Z was Rs. 5,00,000, Rs. 3,00,000 and Rs. 1,50,000 respectively. It was estimated that the net profit as a percentage on sales of Y and Z products would be 25% and 20% respectively. Ascertain profit earned on product X.

Solution :

To ascertain profit on X main product it is necessary to find out Share in Joint Cost.

Ascertainment of Share in Joint Cost of Y and Z (By-product)

Particulars			By-Products Y	By-Products Z
Gross sale value			3,00,000	1,50,000
Less : Estimated profit	Y : 25%		75,000	
	Z : 20%			30,000
Cost of Sales			2,25,000	1,20,000
Less : Subsequent Expenses			23,100	18,900
			2,01,900	1,02,100
Share in Joint cost of Y and Z				
Total Joint Cost				6,18,000
Less : Share in Joint Cost of :	Y	2,01,900		
	Z	1,01,100		3,03,000
Share in Joint Cost of 'X' Main product				3,15,000
Add : Separate Expenses				60,000
Total Cost				3,75,000
Gross Sales				5,00,000
Profit				1,25,000

Percentage of Profit on sales value of 'X' Main Product

$$= \frac{\text{Profit}}{\text{Sales}} \times 100 = \frac{1,25,000}{5,00,000} \times 100 = 25\% \text{ on sales}$$

Alternatively :

'X' Main Product A/c

Particulars	Amount	Particulars	Amount
To Joint Cost	6,18,000	By Sales	5,00,000
To Separate Expenses of 'X' Main		By Share in Joint Cost :	
		Y	2,01,900
Material	25,000	Z	1,01,100
Labour	22,500	(as per above statement)	
Overhead	12,500		
To Profit	1,25,000		
	8,03,000		8,03,000

$$\text{Percentage of Profit of 'X' Main product} = \frac{\text{Profit}}{\text{Sales}} \times 100$$

$$= \frac{1,25,000}{5,00,000} \times 100 = 25\%$$

'Y' By-product A/c

Particulars	Amount	Particulars	Amount
To 'X' Account Share in Joint Cost	2,01,900	By Sales	3,00,000
To Subsequent Expenses		$= \frac{\text{Profit}}{\text{Sales}} \times 100$	
Material	6,000		
Labour	9,000	$= \frac{75{,}000}{3{,}00{,}000} \times 100$	
Overhead	8,100	= 25%	
To Profit	75,000		
	3,00,000		3,00,000

'Z' By-product A/c

Particulars	Amount	Particulars	Amount
To 'X' Main product Share in Joint Cost	1,01,100	By Sales	1,50,000
To Subsequent Expenses :		$= \frac{\text{Profit}}{\text{Sales}} \times 100$	
Material	5,000		
Labour	5,500	$= \frac{30{,}000}{1{,}50{,}000} \times 100$	
Overhead	8,400		
To Profit	30,000	= 20%	
Total	1,50,000	Total	1,50,000

Problem No. Extra-4/32

In a manufacturing company a product passes through three processes. The following informations were provided for January 1990 :

Particulars	Processes I	Processes II	Processes III
Direct Materials	7,800	5,940	8,856
Direct Wages	6,000	9,000	12,000
Product in overhead 100% of Direct Wages			
Output in units	950	840	750
Normal Loss	5%	10%	15%
Value of Scrap sold @ Rs. per unit	6	12	15

Additional information :

1000 units @ Rs. 9 per unit were introduced into Process-I.

There was no Opening or Closing stock.

Prepare :

(a) Process Accounts.

(b) Abnormal Gain and Abnormal Loss Account.

Solution :

Working Table

Particulars	Process-I		Process-II		Process-III	
	Unit	Amount	Unit	Amount	Unit	Amount
Input	1000	28,800	950	52,440	840	83,286
	5%		10%		15%	
Less : Normal Loss	50		95		126	
Scrap Sold		300		1,140		1,890
Normal Cost of Normal output	950	28,500	855	51,300	714	81,396
Actual output	950		840		750	
Abnormal Loss	—		15		—	
Abnormal Gain	—		—		36	

$$\text{Abnormal Loss Cost} = \frac{\text{Normal Cost}}{\text{Normal Output}} \times \text{Units of Abnormal Loss}$$

$$= \frac{51{,}300}{855} \times 15 = \text{Rs. } 900$$

$$\text{Abnormal Gain Cost} = \frac{\text{Normal Cost}}{\text{Normal Output}} \times \text{Units of Abnormal Gain}$$

$$= \frac{81{,}396}{714} \times 36 = \text{Rs. } 4{,}104.$$

Solution :

Process-I A/c

Particulars	Qty.	Amount	Particulars	Qty.	Amount
To Units introduced @ Rs. 9 each	1000	9,000	By Normal Loss 5% of 1000	50	
To Direct Materials		7,800	By Scrap sold @ Rs. 6 each		300
To Direct Wages		6,000	By Process-II A/c transferred @ Rs. 30 each	950	28,500
To Production overhead 100% of Direct wages		6,000			
Total	1000	28,800	Total	1000	28,800

Process-II A/c

Particulars	Qty.	Amount	Particulars	Qty.	Amount
To Process-I A/c	950	28,500	By Normal Loss 10% of 750	95	
To Direct Material		5,940	By Scrap sold @ Rs. 12 each		1,140
To Direct Wages		9,000	By Abnormal Loss @ Rs. 60 each	15	900
To Production overhead 100% of Wages		9,000	By Process-III A/c @ Rs. 60 each	840	50,400
	950	52,440		950	52,440

Process-III A/c

Particulars	Qty.	Amount	Particulars	Qty.	Amount
To Process-III A/c	840	50,400	By Normal Loss 15% of 480	126	
To Direct Material		8,886	By Scrap sold @ Rs. 15 each		1,890
To Direct Wages		12,000	By Finished stock	750	85,500
To Production overhead		12,000			
To Abnormal gain	36	4,104			
	876	87,390		876	87,390

Abnormal Loss A/c

Particulars	Qty.	Amount	Particulars	Qty.	Amount
To Process-II A/c	15	900	By Scrap sold @ Rs. 12 each	15	180
			By Costing Profit & Loss Account		720
	15	900		15	900

Abnormal Gain A/c

Particulars	Qty.	Amount	Particulars	Qty.	Amount
To Reduction in Scrap value @ Rs. 15 each	36	540	By Process-III A/c @ Rs. 114	36	4,104
To Costing Profit & Loss A/c		3,564			
	36	4,104		36	4,104

Problem No. Extra 5/33

The Joint cost it is to be treated as selling expenses and apportioned on the basis of sales (i.e. in the ratio of sales).

A manufacturing company produces an article 'X' and also a by-product 'Y' which is further processed into finished product. Following are the particulars of Joint costs and subsequent cost.

Particulars	Total Cost	Subsequent Cost	
	Rs.	X	Y
Materials	2,25,000	1,35,000	67,500
Labour	1,35,000	63,000	45,000
Overheads	90,000	27,000	22,500
	4,50,000	2,25,000	1,35,000
Selling Price		7,20,000	3,60,000
Estimated Profit on Selling Price		25%	20%

Assuming that the Selling & Distribution Expenses are in proportion to sales price. Show how you would apportion the Joint cost of manufacture and prepare a Statement of Cost of Production of products X and Y.

Solution :

Particulars	Main Product X	By-product Y	Total Cost
Selling Price	7,20,000	3,60,000	10,80,000
Less : Estimated Profit X — 25%	1,80,000	72,000	
Y — 20%			2,52,000
Total Cost	5,40,000	2,88,000	8,28,000
Less : Subsequent cost	2,25,000	1,35,000	3,60,000
Cost upto the point of separate	3,15,000	1,53,000	4,68,000
Less : Total Joint Cost			4,50,000
Difference amount is treated as Selling & Distribution Expenses			18,000
Apportion on sales 2 : 1	3,15,000	1,53,000	4,68,000
Less : Selling & Distribution cost (2 : 1)	12,000	6,000	18,000
Share in Joint Cost	3,03,000	1,47,000	4,50,000

Statement of Cost of Production

Particulars	Main Product	By-product	Total
(1) Share in Joint cost	3,03,000	1,47,000	4,50,000
(2) Subsequent Costs :			
Material	1,35,000	67,500	2,02,500
Labour	63,000	45,000	1,08,000
Overhead	27,000	22,500	49,500
Cost of Production	5,28,000	2,82,000	8,10,000
(3) Selling & Distribution Expenses	12,000	6,000	18,000
Cost of Sales	5,40,000	2,88,000	8,28,000
Selling Price	7,20,000	3,60,000	10,80,000
Estimated Profit	1,80,000	72,000	2,52,000
Percentage of Profit on sales	25%	20%	

In form of Accounts :

Main Products 'X' A/c

Particulars		Amount	Particulars	Amount
To Share in Joint cost		3,03,000	By Sales	7,20,000
To *Add : Subsequent Exp.*				
Material	1,35,000			
Labour	63,000			
Overhead	27,000	2,25,000		
Cost of Production		5,28,000		
Add : Selling & Distribution Exp.		12,000		
Total Cost		5,40,000		
Profit to Profit & Loss A/c		1,80,000		
		7,20,000		7,20,000

By-Product 'Y' A/c

Particulars		Amount	Particulars	Amount
To Share in Joint cost		1,47,000	By Sales	3,60,000
Add : Subsequent Exp.				
Material	67,500			
Labour	45,000			
Overhead	22,500	1,35,000		
Cost of Production		2,82,000		
Add : Selling & Distribution		6,000		
Total Cost of sales		2,88,000		
Profit to Profit & Loss A/c		72,000		
		3,60,000		3,60,000

Problem No. Extra 6/34

A factory is engaged in the production of chemical 'X' and in the course of manufacture a By-product 'Y' is produced which after a separate process has a commercial value.

Following are the particulars for the month of October 1990 :

Particulars	Joint Expenses	Separate Expenses 'X'	Separate Expenses 'Y'
Materials	4,50,000	90,000	1,26,000
Labour	1,80,000	1,12,500	1,12,500
Overhead	1,12,500	63,000	45,000
Total	7,42,500	2,65,500	2,83,500

The output for the month was 625 units of 'X' and 225 units of 'Y'. The selling price of 'Y' is Rs. 2,520 per unit.

The profit on 'Y' product is 33-1/3 on Cost.

Prepare an Account to show the cost price of 'X' product.

Solution :

Statement of Cost Estimate of Product 'Y'

	Rs.	Rs.
Selling Price per unit Rs. 2,520 (225 Units)		5,67,000
Less : Estimated Profit 1/3% on cost OR 25% on Selling Price 25% on 5,67,000		1,41,750
Estimated Cost Total		4,25,250
Less : Cost after separation :		
Material	1,26,000	
Labour	1,12,500	
Overhead	45,000	2,83,500
Share in Joint cost of 'Y' product upto the point of separation		1,41,750

Statement of Cost of Product 'X'

	Rs.	Rs.
Joint cost	4,50,000	
Materials	1,80,000	
Overhead	1,12,500	7,42,500
Less : Share in Joint cost of 'Y' By-product		1,41,750
Share in Joint cost of product 'X'		6,00,750
Add : Separate Expenses :		
Materials	90,000	
Labour	1,12,500	
Overhead	63,000	
		2,65,500
Total Cost of production of product 'X' Main		8,66,250

$$\frac{\text{Total Cost}}{\text{Total Units}} = \frac{8,66,250}{625} = \text{Rs. } 1,386 \text{ cost per unit.}$$

Main Product 'X' A/c

Particulars		Amount	Particulars	Amount
To Joint Cost :			By Share 'Y' product	1,41,750
Material		4,50,000	By Cost of product of 'X' product (Balancing figure)	8,66,250
Labour		1,80,000		
Overhead		1,12,500		
		7,42,500		
To Separate Exp.				
Material	90,000			
Labour	1,12,500			
Overhead	63,000			
		2,65,500		
Total		10,08,000	Total	10,08,000

Problem No. Extra-7/35

(Problem on where Balance of Cost is more than Joint Cost)

In a manufacturing concern a certain product 'X' yields by-products 'Y' and 'Z'.

The Joint Expenses of manufacture are :

Material	3,83,500
Labour	4,05,000
Overhead	3,37,500
	11,25,000

Subsequent expenses are as follows :

Particulars	Main Product	By-Products	
	X	Y	Z
Materials	1,12,500	54,000	63,000
Labour	85,500	72,000	90,000
Overhead	67,500	40,500	47,250
Total Cost	2,65,500	1,66,500	2,00,250
Selling Price	13,50,000	9,00,000	6,75,000
Estimated Profit on Selling Price	40%	30%	25%

Show how would you apportion the Joint Expenses of manufacture.

Solution :

Particulars	Main Product X	By-Products Y	By-Products Z	Total Cost
Selling Price	13,50,000	9,00,000	6,75,000	29,25,000
Less : Estimated Profit X — 20 %, Y — 30%, Z — 25%	5,40,000	2,70,000	1,68,750	9,78,750
Total Cost	8,10,000	6,30,000	5,06,250	19,46,250
Less : Subsequent Expenses	2,65,500	1,66,500	2,00,250	6,32,250
	5,44,500	4,63,500	3,06,000	13,14,000
Less : Joint Cost				11,25,000
Difference amount is treated as Selling & Distribute Exp.				1,89,000
Total Cost as above	5,44,500	4,63,500	3,06,000	13,14,000
Less : Selling & Distributed Exp. (in the ratio 6:4:3)	87,228	58,155	43,615	1,89,000
Share in Joint Cost	4,57,272	4,05,345	2,62,385	11,25,000

Main Product 'X' A/c

Particulars		Amount	Particulars	Amount
To Share in Joint Cost		4,57,270	By Sales	13,50,000
Add : Separate Exp.				
Material	1,12,500			
Labour	85,500			
Overhead	67,500	2,65,500		
To Selling & Distribution Expenses (Balancing figure)		87,230		
To Estimated Profit 40% on 13,40,000		5,40,000		
		13,50,000		13,50,000

By-Product 'Y' A/c

Particulars		Amount	Particulars	Amount
To Share in Joint cost		4,05,345	By Sales	9,00,000
To Separate Expenses :				
Material	54,000			
Labour	72,000			
Overhead	40,500	1,66,500		
To Selling & Distribution Exp. (Balancing figure)		58,155		
To Estimated Profit 30% of 9,00,000		2,70,000		
		9,00,000		9,00,000

By-Product 'Z' A/c

To Share in Joint cost		2,62,385	By Sales	6,75,000
To Separate Exp. :				
Material	63,000			
Labour	90,000			
Overhead	47,250	2,00,250		
To Selling & Distribution Exp. (Balancing figure)		43,615		
To Estimated Profit 25% on 6,75,000		1,68,750		
Total		6,75,000	Total	6,75,000

Problem No. Extra-8/36

'X' Co. Ltd. manufactures product 'A' which yields two by-products 'B' and 'C' during the month of May 1990 the amount spent upto point of separation Rs. 9,27,000. The subsequent expenses are as follows :

Particulars	Main Product	By-Products	
	A	B	C
Materials	13,500	9,000	6,750
Labour	18,000	13,500	9,000
Overhead	13,500	12,150	12,600
Total	45,000	34,650	28,350
Gross sales value of product	6,75,000	4,50,000	2,25,000
Estimated Profit as a percentage to sales in case 'B' and 'C'		25%	20%

Ascertain Profit earned on Product 'A' main.

Solution :

Statement showing share of B and C By-Product in Joint cost

Particulars		By-Products B	By-Products C
Sales value		4,50,000	2,25,000
Less : Estimated Profit (B — 25%, C — 20%)		1,12,500	45,000
Total Cost		3,37,500	1,80,000
Less : Subsequent Expenses		34,650	28,350
Share in Joint cost of By-Product B and C		3,02,850	1,51,650
Total Share in Joint cost of			
B	3,02,850		
C	1,51,650		
Total B & C	4,54,500		
Total Joint cost of 'A' main and 'B' and 'C' by-products			
Total	9,27,000		
Less : Share in Joint cost B and C	4,54,500		
Share in X Joint Cost of 'A' main product	4,72,500		

Statement of Cost and Profit of 'A' Main Product

Share in Joint cost before separation	4,72,500
Add : Subsequent cost	45,000
Cost of production total cost	5,17,500
Sales	6,75,000
Main Product 'A' Profit	1,57,500
Percentage profit on sales — 23.33%	
Percentage Profit on Cost — 30.43%	

Problem No. Extra 9/37 (Joint Product & By-product)

Where balance of cost is more than Joint cost

In a manufacturing concern a certain Product 'A' yields by-products 'B' and 'C'.

Material	12,750
Labour	13,500
Overhead	11,250
	37,500

Subsequent expenses are as follows :

	Main	By-Products	
	A	B	C
Material	3,750	1,800	2,100
Labour	2,850	2,400	3,000
Overhead	2,250	1,350	1,575
	8,850	5,550	6,675

Selling prices of the products are : A — Rs. 45,000, B — Rs. 30,000
C — Rs. 22,500

Estimated Profit : A — 40%, B — 30% and C — 25%

Show how you would apportion the Joint Expenses of manufacture.

Solution :

Apportionment of Joint Expenses

Particulars	Total Cost Rs.	Main Product A	By-Products B Rs.	By-Products C Rs.
Selling Price	97,500	45,000	30,000	22,500
Less : Estimated Profit (A — 40%, B — 30% & C — 25%)	32,675	18,000	9,000	5,625
Cost of Product	64,875	27,000	21,000	16,875
Less : Subsequent cost	21,075	8,850	5,550	6,675
	43,800	18,150	15,450	10,200
Less : Joint cost	37,500			
More than Joint Selling Exp.	(–) 6,300			
To be apportioned in the sales ratio 450 : 300 : 225 6 : 4 : 3	(–) 6,300	2,908	1,938	1,454
	37,500	15,242	13,512	8,746

Problem No. 38 (Problem on Equivalent Production)

X Co. Ltd. a manufacturing company provides the following particulars :

Materials	20,000
Labour	8,000
Overhead	12,000
Input (in units)	400

Completed output 90% of Inputs

Abnormal Loss 6% of Input.

Normal Loss 4% of Input.

Prepare Process Account.

Solution :

Process A/c

Particulars	Qty.	Amount	Particulars	Qty.	Amount
To Material @ Rs. 52.08	400	20,000	By Normal Loss 4% of 400	16	
To Labour Rs. 20.83		8,000	By Abnormal Loss 6% of 400 Rs. 104.16	24	2,500
To Overhead Rs. 31.25		12,000	By Finished Goods Rs. 104.16	360	37,500
	400	40,000		400	40,000

Working Note

(a) Calculation of cost of Material Labour and overhead per unit :

Input units	400
Less : Normal Loss 4% 400	16
Normal output	384

(b) Calculation of cost of Abnormal Loss

Input	400	40,000
Less : Normal Loss	16	—
	384	40,000

(a) Cost of Material 20,000

Normal output 384

Cost per unit = $\frac{20,000}{384} = 52.08$

(b) Labour $\frac{8,000}{384} = 20.83$

(c) Overhead $\frac{12,000}{384} = 31.25$

Normal Cost × Normal output = Cost of Abnormal Loss

$$= \frac{\text{Normal Cost}}{\text{Normal output}} \times \text{Abnormal Units.}$$

$$= \frac{40,000}{384} = 104.16 \text{ Cost per unit.}$$

104.16 × 24 units = Rs. 2,500 Abnormal Loss.

Problem No. 1/39

In the present problem the wastage, Abnormal Loss accrued in the process of production and before completion. In such a situation the cost of Material Labour and overhead incurred on units of Abnormal Loss is to be ascertained assuming that :

Material	100%
Labour	50%
Overhead	50%

The position in such situation is as follows :

	%	Units	Wages and Overhead			
Completed units	100	360	100%	360	100%	360
Abnormal Loss in Process	100	24	50%	12	50%	12
Equivalent units		384		372		372

Equivalent Production Cost per unit :

Material $\frac{20,000}{384}$ 52.08 per unit

Wages $\frac{8,000}{372}$ 21.50 per unit

Overhead $\frac{12,000}{372}$ 32.26 per unit

Equivalent Production			Process Account	Revised	
To Material	400	20,000	By Normal 4% of 400	16	
To Wages		8,000	By Abnormal Loss	24	1,895
To Overhead		12,000	By Finished stock	360	38,105
	400	40,000		400	40,000

Cost of Abnormal Loss units	24	
Material Cost Rs. 52.08 × 24		1,250
Wages 50% of 24 units @ 21.50 = 12 × 21.50		258
Overhead 50% of 24 Units 32.26 = 12 × 32.26		287
Total Cost of Abnormal Loss		1,895

Total Cost	40,000
Less : Cost of Abnormal Loss	1,895
Cost of Finished stock	38,105

Cost per unit = $\frac{38,105}{360}$ = Rs. 105.84

Problem No. 2/39

'X' Co. Ltd. produces a certain product. The following particulars are provided :

Input 6000 units and output was 5000 units and closing stock work-in-progress 1000 units.

Degree of incomplete units of 1000 is as follows :

Material 80% completed cost of Rs. 26,100.

Overhead 60% completed cost Rs. 15,400.

Wages 75% completed cost of Rs. 14,375.

Find out :

(a) Equivalent production.

(b) Cost per unit of Equivalent production.

(c) Process Account assuming there was no Loss in Process.

Solution :

Statement of Equivalent Production

Input 6000 Units	Unit	Material		Wages		Overhead	
		%	Units	%	Units	%	Units
Output							
Finished unit closing stock	5000	100	5000	100	5000	100	5000
(Work-in-progress)							
Incomplete units	1000	80%	800	75%	750	60%	600
Units of Equivalent production			5800		5750		5600

Statement of Cost per Unit Equivalent Production

	Total Cost	Equivalent production	Cost per unit
Material	26,100	5,800	4.50
Wages	14,375	5,750	2.50
Overheads	15,400	5,600	2.75
	55,875		9.75

Statement of Equivalent Cost of Production

	Per unit	Total Cost
Finished stock 5000 units @ Rs. 9.75 each		48,750
Closing stock :		
Work-in-progress 1000 units completed		
Material 80% = 800 × 4.50	3,600	
Wages 75% = 750 × 2.50	1,875	
Overhead 60% = 600 × 2.75	1,650	7,125
Total Cost		55,875

Process A/c

Particulars	Units	Rate	Amount	Particulars	Units	Rate	Amount
To Material	5800	4.5	26,100	By Finished stock	5000	9.75	48,750
To Wages	5750	2.5	14,375	By Closing stock	1000		7,125
To Overhead	5600	2.75	15,400	(Work-in-progress as above)			
			55,875				55,875

Calculation of cost per unit :

Input 6000 units, output 5000 units, Incomplete 1000 units.

% of work completed 80% in 5000 $= 800 + 5000 = 5800 = \frac{26,100}{5800} = 4.50$

Wages 75% of 1000 $= 750 + 5000 = 5750 = \frac{14,375}{5750} = 2.50$

Overhead 60% of 1000 $= 5000 + 600 = 5600 = \frac{15,400}{5600} = 2.75$

Problem No. 40

A Co. Ltd. manufactured certain products. Following are the particulars produced :

No. of units introduced in process	20000 Units
No. of units completed and transferred to next process	15000 Units
No. of units in process at the end work-in-progress	4000 Units

State of completion :

Materials	90%
Labour	80%
Overhead	75%

Normal Loss at the end of process	1000 units
Value of Scrap per unit	Rs. 5
Cost of Raw materials	Rs. 51,500
Direct Wages	Rs. 59,150
Overheads	Rs. 36,000

Calculate : (a) Equivalent production

(b) Cost per unit of Equivalent production

(c) Process Account.

Solution :

Statement of Equivalent Production Units

Particulars	Units	Material		Labour		Overhead	
		%	Units	%	Units	%	Units
Completed units transferred to next process	15000	100	15000	100	15000	100	15000
Closing stock incomplete and stage of completion	4000	90	3600	80	3200	75	3000
			18600		18200		18000

Statement of Cost per Unit of Equivalent Product

		Total Cost	Equivalent production	Cost per Unit
Cost of Raw material	51,500			
Less : Normal Loss 1000 Scrap sold @ Rs. 5 per unit	5,000	46,500	18,600	2.50
(2) Labour		59,150	18,200	3.25
(3) Overhead		36,000	18,000	2.00
				7.75

Process A/c

Particulars	Units	Amount	Particulars	Units	Amount
Input	20000		By Finished stock @ Rs. 7.75 each	15000	1,16,250
To Materials		51,500	By Closing stock Work-in-progress	4000	25,400
Less : Normal Loss Scrap sold @ Rs. 5 each	1000	5,000			
		46,500			
To Labour (18200 × 3.25)		59,150			
To Overhead (18000 × 2)	2	36,000			
	19000	1,41,650		19000	1,41,650

Cost of Finished Stock :

Material	15000	2.50	37,500
Labour	15000	3.25	48,750
Overhead	15000	2.00	30,000
			1,16,250

Closing Stock : *Work-in-Progress :*

Material	90% of 4000 = 3600 × 2.50	9,000
Labour	80% of 4000 = 3200 × 3.25	10,400
Overhead	75% of 4000 = 3000 × 2.00	6,000
	Closing Stock	25,400
Cost of Finished Stock		1,16,250
Add : Closing Stock		25,400
		1,41,650
Add : Normal Loss 1000 units deducted from material Scrap sold @ Rs. 5 each (1000 × 5)		5,000
		1,46,650

Problem No. 41

X Y Co. Ltd. manufacturing certain products. The following particulars are provided for the month of December 1994 :

Units introduced to Process A/c 10000 units. Normal process Loss was estimated @ 5% of input. The finished product 7000 units are transferred to next process.

The incomplete to product at the end of the month. The incompleted products work-in-progress reached the stage of production as under :

Material	100%
Labour	75%
Overhead	60%

The cost of Direct Material introduced to process	23,750
Direct Labour	17,850
Overheads	15,015

Normal Loss scrap realise @ Re. 1 per unit.

Stage of completion of these units were 100% of material, labour and overhead.

Prepare a Statement showing :

(a) Equivalent production units.

(b) Equivalent product cost per unit.

(c) Process Account.

Solution :

Working Note

	Units	Amount
(a) Units introduced	10000	43,250
Less : Normal Loss 5% of 10000 = 500 Units		
Scrap sold @ Re. 1 per unit (500 × 1)	500	500
	9500	42,750
(b) Completed units 100%	7000	
	2500	
(c) Incompleted units (work-in-progress)	2300	
(d) Balance of units being Abnormal Loss	200	

(a) Statement of Equivalent Production in Units

Input	Particulars	Units	Material %	Material Units	Labour %	Labour Units	Overhead %	Overhead Units
Introduced	Normal Loss	500	100	7000	100	7000	100	7000
in to process	Completed Units	7000	100	2300	75	1725	60	1380
10000 Units	Incompleted Units (Work-in-progress)	2300						
	Abnormal Loss	200	100	200	100	200	100	200
	Equivalent Production	10000		9500		8925		8580

(b) State of Cost Equivalent production per unit

Particulars	Units	Cost	Total Cost	Equivalent product	Cost per Unit
(I) Cost of Units Introduced	10000	45,250			
Less : Normal Loss Scrap sold @ Re. 1 per unit	500	500			
	9500	42,750	42,750	9500	4.50
(II) Material			23,750	9500	2.50
Labour			17,850	8925	2.00
Overhead			15,015	8580	1.75
Total			99,365		10.75

Statement showing the Cost of Finished Stock, Abnormal Loss and Incompleted units work-in-progress

Particulars	Element of cost	Equivalent production	Cost per Unit	Cost	Total Cost
(a) Finished stock Or completed units	Material Labour Overhead	7000	10.75	75,250	75,250
(b) Abnormal Loss	Material Labour Overhead	200	10.75	2,150	2,150
(c) Incompleted units Or (Work-in-progress)	Material-I	2300	4.50	10,350	
	Material-II	2300	2.50	5,750	
				16,100	
	Labour	1725	2.00	3,450	
	Overhead	1380	1.75	2,415	21,965
	Total Cost				99,365

Process A/c

Particulars	Units	Amount	Particulars	Units	Amount
To Cost Material of units introduced	10000	43,250	By Finished stock @ Rs. 10.75 each	7000	75,250
To *Less* : Normal Loss Scrap sold @ Rs. 1 each	500	500	By Abnormal Loss @ Rs. 10.75 each	200	2,150
	9500	42,750	By Incompleted units (Work-in-progress)	2300	21,965
To Material		23,750			
To Labour		17,850			
To Overhead		15,015			
	9500	99,365		9500	99,365

Problem No. 42

A B Co. Ltd. manufactures a product in one process, process costing is followed and work-in-progress stock at the end of each month are valued on FIFO Method.

At the beginning of the month of October 1990, the inventory of work-in-progress showed 2000 units 75% complete value of as follows :

Material		42,000
Labour		45,000
Overhead		12,750
	Total	99,750

During the month of October 1990 they have spent on production :

On Material		3,90,000
Labour		4,50,625
Overhead		1,87,500
	Total	10,28,125

The finished units of output taken in stock in the month were 12500 units. At the end of the month work-in-progress inventory was 2500 units completed stores is :

Material	80%
Labour	75%
Overhead	60%

You are required to show the following :

(a) Statement of production unit

(b) Statement of Equivalent production unit

(c) Process cost sheet

(d) Process cost Account.

[ICWA, Final (Modified)]

Solution :

Computation of New Units of input :

Computated units of output	12500
Add : Closing stock work-in-progress at end	2500
Total units	15000
Less : Opening stock work-in-process in the beginning	2000
New units Input	13000

Statement showing Equivalent Production in Units

Particulars	No. of Units	Equivalent product in units					
		Material		Labour		Overhead	
		%	Units	%	Units	%	Units
Completed units	12500	100	12500	100	12500	100	12500
Add : Work-in-process Closing stock incomplete stage	2500	80%	2000	75%	1875	60%	1500
Total Units	15000		14500		14375		14000
Less : Work-in-process Opening stock incomplete stage	2000	75%	1500	75%	1500	75%	1500
	13000		13000		12875		12500

Statement of Cost per Unit of Equivalent Units

	Total Cost	Equivalent Units	Cost per Unit
Material	3,90,000	13,000	30.00
Labour	4,50,625	12,875	35.00
Overhead	1,87,500	12,500	15.00
Total	10,28,125		80.00

Process Cost Sheet for the month of June

Statement of Cost of Equivalents Units of Process Cost per Unit

	Total Process Cost	Equivalent units in process	Cost per Unit Rs.
Opening stock : 2000 Units. Work-in-process Completed stage of 75%			
Material 2000 × 75%	42,000	1500	28.00
Labour 2000 × 75%	45,000	1500	30.00
Overhead 2000 × 75%	12,750	1500	8.50
(A) Total	99,750		66.50
Put in Process cost :			
Material	3,90,000	13000	30.00
Labour	4,50,625	12875	35.00
Overhead	1,87,500	12500	15.00
(B) Total	10,28,125		80.00
Total of A	99,750		66.50
Total of B	10,28,125		80.00
Total	11,27,875		

Analysis of Cost Sheet (FIFO Method)

Cost of completed and Incompleted units	Equivalent Units	Cost per unit	Total Cost Rs.
(A) Work-in-process opening stock 1-10-90			
Completed stage 2000 × 75%	1500	66.50	99,750
for completing remain 25% of 2000			
Material 25% of 2000	500	30.00	15,000
Labour 25% of 2000	500	35.00	17,500
Overhead	500	15.00	7,500
	2000		1,39,750
(B) Put it process and completed (12500 - 2000)	10500	80.00	8,40,000
(C) Work-in-process closing stock at the end of the month completed stage of 2500 units of : Material 80%	2000	30.00	60,000
Labour 75%	1875	35.00	65,625
Overhead 60%	1500	15.00	22,500
			1,48,125
Total of A, B & C			
A			1,39,750
B			8,40,000
C			1,48,125
			11,27,875

Process Cost A/c

Particulars	Units	Amount	Particulars	Units	Amount
To Opening stock work-in-process in the beginning 75% @ Rs. 66.5 each	2000	99,750	By Compeleted units Finished stock (2500 + 10500)	12500	1,39,750 8,40,000
To Material	13000	3,90,000	By Closing stock Work-in-process	2500	1,48,125
To Labour		4,50,625			
To Overhead		1,87,500			
Total		11,27,875	Total		11,27,875

Problem No. 43 (Inter Process Profit)

A B Co. Ltd. manufactures certain product which passes through the process namely Process-I, II and III. The output of each process is charged to the next process at a profit of 20% on transfer price. The output of Process-III is charged to Finished stock on similar basis (i.e., 20% Profit on transfer price).

	Process I	Process II	Process III
	Rs.	Rs.	Rs.
Material consumed	18,000	27,000	9,000
Wages paid	27,000	18,000	36,000
Stock on 31st March 1990	9,000	18,000	27,000

The stocks in each process were valued at prime cost to the process. There was no stock in hand on 1st April 1989. Overheads are ignored of the goods passed into finished stock. Rs. 18,000 remained in hand on 31st March 1990 and the Balance of Finished stock were sold at Rs.1,62,000.

Write the Process Account and also calculate reserve for unrealised Profit for each process.

Solution :

Process-I A/c

Particulars	Total Cost	Cost	Profit	Particulars	Total Cost	Cost	Profit
To Material	18,000	18,000		By Process II (transfer)	45,000	36,000	9,000
Wages	27,000	27,000					
	45,000	45,000					
Less : Closing stock	9,000	9,000					
Prime Cost	36,000	36,000					
Add : 25% on cost	9,000						
	45,000	36,000	9,000				
			9,000		45,000	36,000	9,000
To Stock Bal. B/d	9,000	9,000					

Process-II A/c

Particulars	Total Cost	Cost	Profit	Particulars	Total Cost	Cost	Profit
To Process-I A/c (transferred)	45,000	36,000	9,000	By Process-III (transferred)	90,000	64,800	25,200
To Materials	27,000	27,000					
To Wages	18,000	18,000					
	90,000	81,000	9,000				
Less : Closing stock	18,000	16,200	1,800				
Prime Cost	72,000	64,800	7,200				
Add : Profit 25% on cost	18,000	—	18,000				
	90,000	64,800	25,200		90,000	64,800	25,200
To Stock Bal. B/d	18,000	16,200	25,200				

Process-III A/c

Particulars	Total Cost	Cost	Profit	Particulars	Total Cost	Cost	Profit
To Process-III A/c (transferred)	90,000	64,800	25,200	By Finished stock A/c	1,35,000	87,840	47,160
To Material	9,000	9,000					
To Wages	36,000	36,000					
	1,35,000	1,09,800	25,200				
Less : Closing Stock	27,000	21,960	5,040				
Prime Cost	1,08,000	87,840	20,160				
Add : Profit 25% on Cost	27,000		27,000				
	1,35,000	87,840	47,160		1,35,000	87,840	47,160
To Stock B/d	27,000		5,040				

Finished Stock A/c

Particulars	Total Cost	Cost	Profit	Particulars	Total Cost	Cost	Profit
To Process-III A/c transfer	1,35,000	87,840	47,160	By Sales	1,62,000	76,128	85,872
To *Less* : Closing stock	18,000	11,712	6,288				
	1,17,000	76,128	40,872				
To *Add* : Profit	45,000	—	45,000				
	1,62,000	76,128	85,872		1,62,200	76,128	85,852
To Stock B/d	18,000	11,712	6,288				

Working Note 1

Calculations of Profit on closing stock = Cost of stock = $\frac{\text{Cost}}{\text{Total Cost}} \times \text{Stock}$

(I) Process-I $= 45{,}000 \times 9{,}000 = 9{,}000$ 9,000

No Profit is included in the process cost of stock

(II) Process-II $= \frac{81{,}000}{90{,}000} \times 18{,}000 = 16{,}200$

$18{,}200 - 16{,}200 = 1{,}800$ 1,800

(III) Process-III $= \frac{1{,}09{,}800}{1{,}35{,}000} \times 27{,}000 = 21{,}960$

$27{,}000 - 21{,}960 = 5{,}040$ 5,040

(IV) Finished stock :

(a) $\frac{87,840}{1,35,000} \times 18,000 = 117.12$

Closing stock – Cost = 18,000 – 11,712 = 6,288	6,288
(b) Sales – Total cost = 1,62,000 – 1,17,000 = 45,000	45,000

Working Note 2

Actual Profit Realised :

	Process Profit	Unrealised Profit Closing Stock	Actual Profit
Process-I	9,000	—	9,000
Process-II	18,000	1,800	16,200
Process-III	27,000	5,040	21,960
Finished stock	45,000	6,288	38,712
Total	99,000	13,128	85,872

Valuation of Closing stock for Balance Sheet.

	Cost of closing stock
Process-I	9,000
Process-II	16,200
Process-III	21,960
Finished stock	11,712
Total of Rs.	58,872

Verification

Individual Costs of Process :

	Material + Wages	Cost
Process-I	18,000 + 27,000	45,000
Process-II	27,000 + 18,000	45,000
Process-III	9,000 + 36,000	45,000
	Total of Rs.	1,35,000

Total Cost of Process - I, II & III	1,35,000
Less : Cost of Sales of Finished stock	76,128
Closing stock of Rs.	58,872

Problem No. 44 (Inter Process Profit)

The manufacturing company produces certain product which passes through three Processes namely X, Y & Z and transferred to Finished stock. The following particulars are provided :

Particulars	Process X	Process Y	Process Z
Direct Materials	50,000	12,500	10,000
Direct Wages	37,500	25,000	50,000
Closing stock	12,500	16,250	23,750

Sales of finished stock amounted to Rs. 2,75,000. Finished stock valued @ Rs. 12,500.

The output of each process is transferred to next process at a profit of 20% on transfer amount the transfer from process 'Z' to Finished stock is to be treated similarly.

Prepare the Process Account and the Finished Stock Account.

(Panjab University)

Solution :

Process 'X' A/c

Particulars	Total Cost	Cost Rs.	Profit Rs.	Particulars	Total Cost	Cost Rs.	Profit Rs.
To Material	50,000	50,000		By Process 'Y'	93,750	75,000	18,750
To Wages	37,500	37,500					
	87,500	87,500					
Less : Closing stock	12,500	12,500					
Prime Cost	75,000	75,000					
Add : Profit 25% on cost	18,750		18,750				
	93,750	75,000	18,750		93,750	75,000	18,750
To Stock b/d	12,500	12,500	—				

Process 'Y' A/c

Particulars	Total Cost	Cost Rs.	Profit Rs.	Particulars	Total Cost	Cost Rs.	Profit Rs.
To Process 'X'	93,750	75,000	18,750	By Process 'Z' transferred	1,43,750	98,572	45,178
To Material	12,500	12,500					
To Wages	25,000	25,000					
	1,31,250	1,12,500	18,750				
Less : Closing stock	16,250	13,928	2,322				
Prime Cost	1,15,000	98,572	16,428				
Add : Profit 25% on cost	28,750		28,750				
	1,43,750	98,572	45,178		1,43,750	98,572	45,178
To Stock b/d	16,250	13,928	2,322				

Process 'Z' A/c

Particulars	Total Cost	Cost Rs.	Profit Rs.	Particulars	Total Cost	Cost Rs.	Profit Rs.
To Process 'Y'	1,43,750	98,572	45,178	By Finished stock A/c transferred	2,25,000	1,40,088	84,912
To Material	10,000	10,000					
To Wages	50,000	50,000					
	2,03,750	1,58,572	45,178				
Less : Closing stock	23,750	18,484	5,266				
Prime Cost	1,80,000	1,40,088	39,912				
Add : Profit 25% on cost	45,000	—	45,000				
	2,25,000	1,40,088	84,912		2,25,000	1,40,088	84,912
Closing stock b/d	23,750	18,484	5,266				

Finished Stock A/c

Particulars	Total Cost	Cost Rs.	Profit Rs.	Particulars	Total Cost	Cost Rs.	Profit Rs.
To Process 'Z'	2,25,000	1,40,088	84,912	By Sales	2,75,000	1,32,305	1,42,695
Less : Closing Stock	12,500	7,783	4,717				
	2,12,500	1,32,305	80,195				
Add : Profit 20% on cost	62,500	—	62,500				
	2,75,000	1,32,305	1,42,695		2,75,000	1,32,305	1,42,695

Working Note 1

(a) Calculations of Profit included in closing stock

$$\text{Cost of Stock} = \frac{\text{Cost}}{\text{Total Cost}} \times \text{Closing Stock}$$

(1) Process 'X' $= \frac{87,500}{87,500} \times 12,500 = 12,500$ — 12,500

No profit is included in closing stock.

Cost of closing stock

(2) Process 'Y' $= \frac{1,12,500}{1,31,250} \times 16,250 = 13,298$

Total Cost – Cost = Profit

16,250 – 13,298 = 2,322 — 2,322

(3) Process 'Z' $= \frac{1,58,572}{2,03,750} \times 23,750 = 18,484$

= 23,750 – 18,484 = 5,266 — 5,266

(4) Finished Stock $= \frac{1,40,088}{2,25,000} \times 12,500 = 7,783$

= 12,500 – 7,783 = 4,717 — 4,717

(b) Sales – Total Cost = Profit

= 2,75,000 – 2,12,500 = Profit Rs. 62,500

Working Note 2

Actual Profit Realised

	Process Profit Rs.	Unrealised Profit in Closing stock Rs.	Actual Profit Rs.
Process - 'X'	18,750	—	18,750
Process - 'Y'	28,750	2,322	26,428
Process - 'Z'	45,000	5,266	39,734
Finished Stock	62,500	4,717	57,783
Total	1,55,000	12,305	1,42,695

Process Profit	1,55,000
Less : Unrealised Profit included in closing stock	12,305
Actual Profit Realised of Rs.	1,42,695

Verification of Profit :

Sales Price – Finished stock

= 2,75,000 – 1,32,350

= 1,42,695

Verification

Individual cost of Process	Material	+	Wages		Cost of Stock
Process 'X' =	50,000	+	37,500	87,500	12,500
Process 'Y' =	12,500	+	25,000	37,500	13,928
Process 'Z' =	10,000	+	50,000	60,000	18,484
Total Cost				1,85,000	44,912
Less : Cost of sales of Finished stock				1,32,305	+7,783
				52,695	52,695

Closing stock in Process Accounts = Rs. 52,695

Problem No. 45

A manufacturing company produces certain article which passes through three processes namely A, B & C. The output of Process A charged to Process B at a Profit 25 per cent on cost and the out of process B is charged to Process C on similar basis. The completed product is transferred to Finished stock at a price which gives Process C a Profit of 25 per cent on cost.

From the following particulars prepare :

(a) Process Cost Account and Finished Stock in each process have been valued at prime cost.

Particulars	Process A	Process B	Process C
Material consumed	35,000	52,500	17,500
Wages	52,500	35,000	70,000
Closing Stock	17,500	35,000	52,500

Sales of Finished stock of Rs. 3,15,000.

Closing stock of Finished Products of Rs. 35,000.

(b) Show also the actual realised profit to be taken to the credit of Profit & Loss Account.

Solution :

Process 'A' A/c

Particulars	Total Cost	Cost Rs.	Profit Rs.	Particulars	Total Cost	Cost Rs.	Profit Rs.
To Material	35,000	35,000		By Process 'B' transferred	87,500	70,000	17,500
To Wages	52,500	52,500					
	87,500	87,500					
Less : Closing stock	17,500	17,500					
Prime Cost	70,000	70,000					
Add : Profit 25% on cost	17,500		17,500				
	87,500	70,000	17,500		87,500	70,000	17,500
Stock B/d	87,500	70,000	17,500				

Process 'B' A/c

Particulars	Total Cost	Cost Rs.	Profit Rs.	Particulars	Total Cost	Cost Rs.	Profit Rs.
To Process 'A' transferred from	87,500	70,000	17,500	By Process 'C' transferred	75,000	1,26,000	49,000
To Material	52,500	52,500					
To Wages	35,000	35,000					
	1,75,000	1,57,500	17,500				
Less : Closing stock	35,000	31,500	3,500				
Prime Cost	1,40,000	1,26,000	14,000				
Add : Profit 25% on cost	35,000		35,000				
	1,75,000	1,26,000	49,000		1,75,000	1,26,000	49,000
Stock B/d	35,000	31,500	3,500				

Process 'C' A/c

Particulars	Total Cost	Cost Rs.	Profit Rs.	Particulars	Total Cost	Cost Rs.	Profit Rs.
To Process'B'	75,000	1,26,000	49,000	By Finished Stock A/c	2,62,500	1,70,000	91,700
To Material	17,500	17,500					
To Wages	70,000	70,000					
	2,62,500	2,13,500	49,000				
Less : Closing stock	52,500	42,700	9,800				
Prime Cost	2,10,000	1,70,800	39,200				
Add : Profit 25% on cost	52,500		52,500				
	2,62,500	1,70,800	91,700		2,62,500	1,70,000	91,700
Closing Stock	52,500	42,700	9,800				

Finished Stock A/c

Particulars	Total Cost	Cost Rs.	Profit Rs.	Particulars	Total Cost	Cost Rs.	Profit Rs.
To Process'C' Account	2,62,500	1,70,800	91,700	By Sales	3,15,000	1,48,027	1,66,973
To *Less* : Closing stock	35,000	22,773	12,227				
	2,27,500	1,48,027	79,473				
Add : Profit 25% on Cost	87,500		87,500				
	3,15,000	1,48,027	1,66,973		3,15,000	1,48,027	1,66,973
Stock	55,000	22,773	12,227				

Working Note 1

Calculation of Profit included in closing stock = $\frac{\text{Cost}}{\text{Total Cost}}$ × Closing stock

(1) Process 'A' = $\frac{70,000}{70,000} \times 17,500$ — 17,500

No Profit is included in closing stock.

(2) Process 'B' = $\frac{1,57,500}{1,75,000} \times 35,000 = 31,500$

Profit = Closing stock – Cost = Profit

35,000 – 31,500 = 3,500 — 3,500

(3) Process 'C' = $\frac{2,13,500}{2,62,500} \times 52,500 = 42,700$

= 52,500 – 42,700 = 9,800 — 9,800

(a) Finished stock = $\frac{1,70,800}{2,62,500} \times 35,000 = 22,773$

= 35,000 – 22,773 = 12,227 — 12,227

(b) Sales – Total Cost = 3,15,000 – 2,27,500 = Profit Rs. 87,500.

Working Note 2

Statement of Actual Profit Realised

Particulars	Process	Unrealised Profit	Actual Profit
Process 'A' A/c	17,500	—	17,500
Process 'B' A/c	35,000	3,500	31,500
Process 'C' A/c	52,500	9,800	42,700
Finished stock	87,500	12,227	75,273
Total	1,92,500	25,527	1,66,973

Process Profit	1,92,500	Verification :
		= Sales – Cost of sales of Finished goods
Less :		
Unrealised profit	25,527	= 3,15,000 – 1,48,027
Actual Profit	1,66,973	= 1,66,973

Working Note 3

Valuation of closing stock for Balance sheet

	Cost of closing stock
Process-A	17,500
Process-B	31,500
Process-C	42,700
Finished stock	22,773
	1,14,473

Verification

Process	Material + Wages		
Process-A	35,000 + 52,500 =		87,500
Process-B	52,500 + 35,000 =		87,500
Process-C	17,500 + 70,000 =		87,500
	Total Cost		2,62,500
Less : Sales of Finished stock			1,48,027
Cost of Closing stock of		Rs.	1,14,473

Problem No. 46

A manufacturing company produces certain product which passes through three processes namely X, Y & Z and then is transferred to Finished stock account. The output of process 'X' is transferred to process Y at a Profit of 25 per cent on transfer price and the output of process. Y and Z is transferred at profit of 20 per cent transfer price.

The following information was provided for the month :

Particulars	Process X	Process Y	Process Z
Opening stock	12,500	15,000	10,000
Direct Materials	25,000	26,250	37,500
Direct Wages	18,750	18,750	20,000
Works overhead	17,500	7,500	50,000
Closing stock	6,250	7,500	5,000
Inter process Profit for opening stock	—	2,500	2,500

Finished stock – Opening Balance	37,500
Closing Balance	18,750
Inter Process Profit opening stock	13,750

Stocks in the process are valued at Prime cost. The Finished stock has been valued at the price at which it was received from the process 'Z'.

Sales of Finished stock Rs. 4,37,500.

You are required to prepare :

(a) Process Account and

(b) Finished stock Account showing the Profit element at each stage.

(c) Actual realised Profit.

Process 'X' A/c

Particulars	Total Cost	Cost Rs.	Profit Rs.	Particulars	Total Cost	Cost Rs.	Profit Rs.
To Opening stock	12,500	12,500		By Process 'Y' A/c	90,000	67,500	22,500
To Material	25,000	25,000					
	37,500	37,500					
To Wages	18,750	18,750					
	56,250	56,250					
Less : Closing stock	6,250	6,250					
Prime Cost	50,000	50,000					
To Overhead	17,500	17,500					
	67,500	67,500					
To Gross Profit 1/3 on cost	22,500		22,500				
	90,000	67,500	22,500		90,000	67,500	22,500
Stock b/d	6,250	6,250	—				

Process 'Y' A/c

Particulars	Total Cost	Cost Rs.	Profit Rs.	Particulars	Total Cost	Cost Rs.	Profit Rs.
To Opening stock	15,000	12,500	2,500	By Process 'Z' A/c	1,87,500	1,26,250	61,250
To Process 'Y' A/c	90,000	67,500	22,500				
To Material	26,250	26,250					
To Wages	18,750	18,750					
	1,50,000	1,25,000	25,000				
Less : Closing stock	7,500	6,250	1,250				
Prime Cost	1,42,500	1,18,750	23,750				
To Overhead	7,500	7,500					
	1,50,000	1,26,250	23,750				
To Gross Profit 25% on cost	37,500	—	37,500				
	1,87,500	1,26,250	61,250		1,87,500	1,26,250	61,250
To Stock B/d	7,500	6,250	1,250				

Process 'Z' A/c

Particulars	Total Cost	Cost Rs.	Profit Rs.	Particulars	Total Cost	Cost Rs.	Profit Rs.
To Opening stock	10,000	7,500	2,500	By Finished Stock transfer	3,75,000	2,37,500	1,37,500
To Process Z's A/c	1,87,500	1,26,250	61,250				
To Material	37,500	37,500	—				
To Wages	20,000	20,000	—				
	2,55,000	1,91,250	63,750				
Less : Closing stock	5,000	3,750	1,250				
Prime Cost	2,50,000	1,87,500	62,500				
To Overhead	50,000	50,000	—				
	3,00,000	2,37,500	62,500				
To Gross Profit 25% on Cost	75,000		75,000				
	3,75,000	2,37,500	1,37,500		3,75,000	2,37,500	1,37,500
To Stock B/d	5,000	3,750	1,250				

Finished Stock A/c

Particulars	Total Cost	Cost Rs.	Profit Rs.	Particulars	Total Cost	Cost Rs.	Profit Rs.
To Opening stock	37,500	23,750	13,750	By Sales	4,37,500	2,49,375	1,88,125
To Process 'Z'	3,75,000	2,37,500	1,37,500				
	4,12,500	2,61,250	1,51,250				
Less : Closing stock	18,750	11,875	6,875				
Prime Cost	3,93,750	2,49,375	1,44,375				
To Gross Profit	43,750		43,750				
	4,37,500	2,49,375	1,88,125		4,37,500	2,49,375	1,88,125
Stock B/d	18,750	11,875	6,875				

Profit = Sales – Cost of sales of finished goods

= 4,37,500 – 2,49,375

= Rs. 1,88,125

Working Note 1

(a) Calculation of Profit on closing stock = Closing stock = $\frac{\text{Cost}}{\text{Total Cost}} \times \text{Stock}$

Process 'X' $= \frac{56{,}250}{56{,}250} \times 6{,}250 = 6{,}250$ cost of closing stock

No profit is included in process closing stock

Process 'Y' $= \frac{1{,}25{,}000}{2{,}55{,}000} \times 7{,}500 = 6{,}250$

Profit = Closing stock – Cost = Profit.

= 7,500 – 6,250 = Rs. 1,250

Process 'Z' $= \frac{1{,}91{,}250}{2{,}55{,}000} \times 5{,}000 = 3{,}750$

Profit = 5,000 – 3,750 = Rs. 1,250

Finished stock $= \frac{2{,}16{,}250}{4{,}12{,}500} \times 18{,}750 = 11{,}875$

Profit = 18,750 – 11,875 = Rs. 6,875

(b) Sales – Total = Finished stock

= 4,37,500 – 3,93,750 = Rs. 43,750

Working Note 2

Statement of Actual Profit Realised

Process A/cs	Process profit	Unrealised Profit in Stock: Opening stock	Unrealised Profit in Stock: Closing stock	Actual Profit
Process-X	22,500 +	—	–	22,500
Process-Y	37,500 +	2,500	–1,250	38,750
Process-Z	75,000 +	2,500	–1,250	76,250
Finished stock	43,750 +	13,750	–6,875	50,625
Total	1,78,750 +	18,750	–9,375	1,88,125

Process Profit	1,78,750
Add : Unrealised Profit in opening stock	18,750
Unrealised Profit	1,97,500
Less : Closing stock	9,375
Actual Profit realised	Rs. 1,88,125

Working Note 3

Valuation of Closing Stock for Balance Sheet

Element of Cost	Processes X	Processes Y	Processes Z	Finished stock
Opening stock	12,500	12,500	7,500	23,750
Material	25,000	26,250	37,500	
Wages	18,750	18,750	20,000	
Overhead	17,500	7,500	50,000	
Total	73,750	65,000	1,15,000	23,750

Process-X	6,250
Process-Y	6,250
Process-Z	3,750
Finished stock	11,875
Total	28,125

Verification

Closing Stock for Balance Sheet

Elements of Cost	Processes X	Processes Y	Processes Z	Finished stock
Opening Stock	12,500	12,500	7,500	23,750
Materials	25,000	26,250	37,500	
Wages	18,750	18,750	20,000	
Overhead	17,500	7,500	50,000	
Total	73,750	65,000	1,15,000	23,750

Total Cost of :			
X	73,750	Total Cost	2,77,500
Y	65,000	*Less* Cost of Sales of Finished Stock	2,49,375
Z	1,15,000	Cost of Closing Stock	Rs. 28,125
Finished stock	23,750		
	2,77,500		

Problem No. 47

X Co. Ltd. a manufacturing company process a certain product which passes through two processes namely X and Y and passed on to a finished stock Account. The output of process X is transferred to process Y at a price which gives process X a profit of 25% thereon and the output of process Y is transferred to Finished stock account at a price which given process 'Y' a profit of 20% on transferred amount.

The following information is provided in respect of October, 1990 :

Particulars	Process X Rs.	Process Y Rs.
Stock on 1st October 1990	14,400	9,000
Materials consumed	28,800	12,150
Wages paid	56,250	38,250
Overhead	11,250	7,650
Stock on 31st October 1990	9,450	4,050

Process stock consists of products which have passed through process completely and are valued at prime cost to the process concerned.

Finished Goods were in stock on 1st October 1990 to the value of Rs. 45,900 and on 31st October 1990 to the value of Rs. 27,900. Both opening and closing stock were valued at a price at which they were transferred from process 'Y'.

The sales value amounted to Rs. 3,07,800 and included all the stock in the beginning of the month.

The reserve on 1st October 1990 for unrealised profit included in the stock valuation were process Y Rs. 1,575 and Finished stock Rs. 15,435.

Prepare : (a) The Process Account and Finished Stock Account.

(b) Show Statement of Actual Profit.

Process 'X' A/c

Particulars	Total Cost	Cost Rs.	Profit Rs.	Particulars	Total Cost	Cost Rs.	Profit Rs.
To Opening stock	14,400	14,400		By Process 'Y' transferred	1,35,000	1,01,250	33,750
To Material	28,800	28,800					
To Wages	56,250	56,250					
	99,450	99,450					
Less : Closing stock	9,450	9,450					
	90,000	90,000					
Add : Overhead	11,250	11,250					
Total Cost	1,01,250	1,01,250					
Add : Profit 25% Or 1/3 on cost	33,750	—	33,750				
	1,35,000	1,01,250	33,750		1,35,000	1,01,250	33,750
Stock b/d	9,450	9,450	—				

Process 'Y' A/c

Particulars	Total Cost	Cost Rs.	Profit Rs.	Particulars	Total Cost	Cost Rs.	Profit Rs.
To Opening Stock	9,000	7,425	1,575	By Finished Stock A/c	2,47,500	1,63,411	84,089
To Process Y	1,35,000	1,01,250	33,750				
To Material	12,150	12,150					
To Wages	38,250	38,250					
	1,94,400	1,59,075	35,325				
Less : Closing stock	4,050	3,314	736				
	1,90,350	1,55,761	34,589				
To Overhead	7,650	7,650					
	1,98,000	1,63,411					
Add : Profit 25%	49,500	—	49,500				
	2,47,500	1,63,411	84,089		2,47,500	1,63,411	84,089
Stock b/d	4,050						

Finished Stock A/c

To Opening Stock	45,900	30,465	15,435	By Sales	3,07,800	1,75,440	1,32,360
To Process Y	2,47,500	1,63,411	84,089				
	2,93,400	1,93,876	99,524				
Less : Closing stock	27,900	18,436	9,464				
	2,65,500	1,75,440	90,060				
Add : Profit	42,300	—	42,300				
	3,07,800	1,75,440	1,32,360		3,07,800	1,75,440	1,32,360

Working Note 1

Calculation of profit included in stock :

$$\text{Cost of closing stock} = \frac{\text{Cost}}{\text{Total Cost}} \times \text{Closing stock}$$

(1) Process X $= \frac{99{,}450}{99{,}450} \times 9{,}450 = 9{,}450$ cost of closing stock

No Profit included in closing stock.

(2) Process Y $= \frac{1{,}59{,}075}{1{,}94{,}400} \times 4{,}050 = 3{,}314$ Cost of closing stock

Profit $= 4{,}040 - 3{,}314 = 736$

(3) Finished stock $= \frac{1{,}93{,}876}{2{,}93{,}400} \times 27{,}900 = 18{,}436$ cost of closing stock

Profit = Closing stock – Cost

$= 27{,}900 - 18{,}436 = 9{,}464$

(b) Sales – Cost of sales = Profit

$3{,}07{,}800 - 1{,}75{,}440 = 1{,}32{,}360$

(c) Finished stock – Profit = Sales – Total Cost

$= 3{,}07{,}800 - 2{,}65{,}500 = 42{,}300$

Working Note 2

Statement of Actual Profit

	Process Profit Rs.	Unrealised Profit Opening stock	Closing stock	Actual Profit Rs.
Process X	33,750	—	—	33,750
Process Y	49,500	+ 1,575	–736	50,339
Finished stock	42,300	+15,435	–9,464	48,271
	1,25,550	+17,010	–10,200	1,32,360

Process Profit	1,25,550
Add : Profit in Opening stock	17,010
	1,42,560
Less : Profit in closing stock	10,200
Actual Profit	1,32,360

Working Note 3

Valuation of Closing Stock for Balance Sheet

Process 'X' Account	9,450
Process 'Y' Account	3,314
Finished Stock Account	18,436
Closing stock of	Rs. 31,200

Verification :

	Process X	Process Y
Material	28,800	12,150
Wages	56,250	38,250
Overhead	11,250	7,650
Total Cost	96,300	58,050
Opening Stock	14,400	7,425
	1,10,700	65,475

Total : Process X	1,10,700
Process Y	65,475
Finished Stock	1,76,175
Add : Opening Stock	30,465
Total Cost	2,06,640
Total Cost	2,06,640
Less : Cost of sales of finished stock	1,75,440
Closing Stock	31,200

7

Reconciliation Statement

RECONCILIATION STATEMENT OF COST PROFIT AND FINANCIAL PROFIT

Where Cost and Financial Accounts are maintained independent of each other, it is necessary to reconcile the accounts, as the profits shown by cost accounts and the financial accounts differ. It is therefore, necessary to findout the reasons for the difference between Cost Accounts Profits and Financial Accounts Profit.

Reasons for Disagreement in Profit

Cost Profit and Financial Profit

(I) *Items shown only in Financial Accounts* : There are number of items which are included only in Financial Accounts but do not find place in Cost Accounts.

They are : items of expenditure or Appropriation of Profit-Reduce Financial Profit, items of Incomes increase the Profits.

(a) *Purely Financial Charges :*

(1) Loss on sale of Fixed Assets & Investments.

(2) Discount on debenture.

(3) Interest on Bank Loan.

(4) Expenses of share Transfer office etc.

Effect-Reduce Financial Profit.

(b) *Items of Appropriation of Profits :*

(1) Income tax.

(2) Dividend paid.

(3) Transfer to Reserves and sinking fund.

(4) Amount written off, Goodwill, Preliminary Expenses.

(5) Donations and Charities.

Effect-Reduce Financial Profits.

(II) *Purely Financial Incomes :*

(1) Rent Receivable.

(2) Profit on sale of fixed Assets.

(3) Transfer fees Received.

(4) Interest received on Bank Deposits.

(5) Dividend received — Effect Increase in Financial Profit.

(III) *Items shown in Cost Accounts Only :* There are items included in Cost Accounts only but not in Financial Accounts.

Eg: Interest may be calculated on capital employed in production to show nominal cost though in fact no interest has been paid.

Similarly : Nominal Rent for Premises is charged.

(IV) *Over absorption or Under absorption of Overheads :* Overhead absorption in Cost Accounts is on the basis of estimates as a percentage on direct material or direct labour, wages etc. It may be more or less than the actual amount incurred.

If the overhead is not fully absorbed i.e. the amount in Cost Accounts is less than the actual Amount, the shortfall is called Under absorption of overhead.

On the other hand, if overhead expenses in Cost Accounts are more than the actual, it is called Over absorption of overhead. Under absorption or Over absorption of overheads, lead to difference in two accounts.

(V) *Difference in basis in Valuation of Stock and Depreciation :* Valuation of stock in Financial Account — Cost price or Market value, whereas in Cost Accounts — Basis Methods of Pricing Materials i.e. F.I.F.O. L.I.F.O. Average methods, etc.

Depreciation-Methods of depreciation followed :

PROCEDURE OF RECONCIALATION

Reconciliation Statement

		Rs.	Rs.
(I) Profit as per Cost Accounts			—
Add : (1)	Over recovery of overheads (or over absorption of overheads) in Cost Accounts	—	
(2)	Items of expenses included in cost Account but not in Financial Accounts	—	
	e.g. (i) Interest on Capital	—	
	(ii) Rent on owned premises	—	
(3)	Items of Incomes credited in Financial Accounts only	—	
(i)	Interest Received	—	
(ii)	Dividend Received	—	
(iii)	Profit on sale of Fixed stock	—	
(4)	Higher value of opening stock in Cost Accounts	—	
(5)	Lower value of closing stock in Cost Accounts		(+)

	Rs.	Rs.
Less : (1) Under recovery of overheads in Cost Accounts. (or under absorption of overheads)	—	
(2) Items of incomes included in cost but not in Financial Accounts	—	
(3) Items of Expenses & Losses debited in Financial Accounts but not included in Cost Account	—	
(4) Lower value of opening stock in cost	—	
(5) Higher value of closing stock in cost		(–)
Profit as per Financial Accounts		—

Reconciliation Statement

	Rs.	Rs.
(II) Profit as per Financial Account		
Note : Reverse the above items i.e., items deducted above be added and items added be deducted		
Profit as per Cost Account		

Reconciliation Statement

	Rs.	Rs.
(III) Net Loss as per Financial Account		
Add : (1) Under recovery of overheads in Cost A/c	–	
(2) Items debited in Financial Account only	–	
(3) Lower value of opening stock in Cost A/c	–	
(4) Over value of closing stock in Cost A/c		(+)
Less : (1) Over recovery of overheads in Cost A/c	–	
(2) Items of income credited in Financial A/c	–	
(3) Higher value of opening stock in cost	–	
(4) Lower value of closing stock in cost		(–)

Reconciliation Statement

	Rs.	Rs.
(IV) Net Loss as per Cost Account		
(*Note* : Reverse the above)		
(1) Items deducted above be added and Items added be deducted.		
Ans. : Net Loss per Financial Account		

Problem No. 1

The Financial details of a company for a certain period are given below :

Trading and Profit & Loss A/c

Particulars	Rs.	Particulars	Rs.
To Opening Stock	6,00,000	By Sales	34,65,000
Purchases	30,92,000	By Closing Stock	7,50,000
Direct Wages	2,30,000		
Factory Overhead	2,10,000		
Gross Profit	4,83,000		
	42,15,000		42,15,000
To Salaries and Administrative Exp.	95,000	By Gross Profit	4,83,000
Selling Expenses	2,25,000	By Sundry Incomes	5,000
Net Profit	1,68,000		
	4,88,000		4,88,000

Costing Records reveal —

(a) Profit for the year Rs. 2,40,000

(b) Closing Stock at Rs. 7,80,000

(c) Recovery of Factory overhead — Rs. 1,89,800

(d) Recovery of Administrative overhead @ 3% on selling price

(e) Direct wages — Rs. 2,46,000 absorbed in cost

(f) Selling expenses @ 5% on Sales price

(g) Miscellaneous Income not considered.

Reconcile the Cost and Financial Profits.

[K.U.D., April 1998(O)]

Solution :

Working Note

	In Financial A/c	In Cost A/c	In Cost Over/Under recovery	
(1) Direct Wages	2,30,000	2,46,000	Excess	16,000
(2) Factory Overhead	2,10,000	1,89,800	Less	20,200
(3) Administrative Overhead 3% on Selling Price 34,65,000	95,000	1,03,950	Excess	8,950
" Selling Expenses 5% on selling price 34,65,000	2,25,000	1,73,250	Less	51,750
" Sundry Income	5,000	—	Less	5,000
" Closing stock	7,50,000	7,80,000	Higher value	30,000

Reconciliation Statement

		Rs.	Rs.
Profit as per Cost records			2,40,000
Add I. (a) Over recovery of overheads in cost —			
(1) Administrative Overhead in cost			
3% on Selling Price 34,65,000	1,03,950		
Charged in Financial A/c	95,000		
Over recovery in cost		8,950	
(2) Direct Wages in cost	2,46,000		
in Financial A/c	2,30,000	16,000	
(b) Items Credited in Financial A/c on			
Sundry Income		5,000	
(c) Higher value of opening stock in cost			
(d) Lower value of closing stock in cost		—	29,950
			2,69,950
II. Under recovery of overheads in cost			
(a) Factory Overheads			
in Cost	1,89,800		
in Financial A/c	2,10,000	20,200	
Selling Expenses in Cost	1,73,250		
in Financial A/c	2,25,000	51,750	
(b) Items debated in Financial A/c only		—	
(c) Lower value of opening stock in cost		—	
(d) Higher value of closing stock in cost		30,000	–1,01,950
Net Profit as per Financial A/c			1,68,000

Problem No. 2

From the following figures prepare a Reconciliation Statement :

	Rs.
Net Loss as per Cost Records	95,670
Net Loss as per Financial Records	1,00,140
Factory on Cost under recovered in Cost books	8,550
Administrative overhead recovered in excess	6,375
Depreciation charged in Financial books	5,490
Depreciation in Cost books	5,925
Interest received recorded in Financial books	675
Income Tax provided in Financial books	900

Banks interest received not included in Cost books	345
Stores Adjustment (credited in Financial books)	630
Depreciation of stocks charged in Financial books	1,290
Dividend appropriated in Financial books	1,800
Loss due to theft provided in Financial books only	390

[K.U.D., October 1997(N)]

Solution :

Reconciliation Statement

				Rs.
	Net Loss as per cost books			95,670
Add (i)	Items – under recovery of overheads in cost :			
	(a) Factory on cost under recovered in cost		8,550	
(ii)	Items debited in Financial books only :			
	(a) Income-tax provided in Financial books		900	
	(b) Depreciation of stocks charged in Financial books		1,290	
	(c) Dividend apportioned in Financial books		1,800	
	(d) Loss due to theft provided in Financial books		390	
(iii)	Lower value of opening stock		—	
(iv)	Higher value of closing stock		—	+12,930
				1,08,600
Less (1)	Items of over recovery of overhead in Cost :			
	(i) Administrative overhead over recovered in Cost		6,375	
	(ii) Depreciation recovered in Cost	5,925		
	Charged in Financial books	5,490	435	
	Excess in Cost			
(II)	Items credited in Financial books only :			
	(i) Interest received recorded in Financial books		675	
	(ii) Bank interest received credited on F.B. only		345	
	(iii) Stores Adjustment credited in F.B. only		630	8,460
	Net Loss as per Financial books			1,00,140

Problem No. 3

Prepare a Reconciliation Statement from the following information :

	Rs.
Net Profit as per Cost Account	1,29,690
Income Tax provided in Financial A/c only	30,000
Directors fees shown in Financial A/c only	12,000
Works overhead charged in Financial A/c	42,000
Works overhead charged in Cost Accounts	51,000
Depreciation charged in Financial Accounts	8,400
Depreciation recovered in Cost Accounts	9,000
Administrative overhead over recovered	1,275
Interest on Investments not included in Cost Accounts	6,000
Provision for Doubtful Debts	25,000

[K.U.D., October 1997(O)]

Solution :

Reconciliation Statement

			Rs.	Rs.
	Net Profit as per Cost Accounts			1,29,690
Add (a)	Over recovery of overheads in cost :			
(1)	Works overhead – recovered in cost	51,000		
	Charged in Financial A/c	42,000	9,000	
	Over recovery in Cost			
(2)	Depreciation charged in Cost	9,000		
	Depreciation charged in Financial A/c			
	Over recovery	8,400	600	
(3)	Administrative Overhead over recovered in cost		1,275	
(b)	Items credited in Financial books only		6,000	
	Interest on Investment not included in cost			
(c)	Higher value of opening stock in cost		—	
(d)	Lower value of closing stock in cost		—	+16,875
				1,46,565
Less (i)	Under recovery of overheads in cost		—	
(ii)	Items debited in Financial A/c only :			
	(a) Income Tax provided in Financial books		30,000	
	(b) Directors fees shown only in Financial A/c		12,000	
	(c) Provision for Doubtful Debts		6,000	
(iii)	Lower value of opening stock in cost		—	
(iv)	Higher value of closing stock in cost		—	–48,000
	Net Profit as per Financial Accounts			98,565

Problem No. 4

From the following information of Sahadri Paper Products calculate Profits in Financial Accounts and Profits in Cost Accounts. Reconcile the Profits between Cost and Financial Accounts.

	Rs.
Sales	80,000
Purchase of Materials	32,000
Closing Stocks of Materials	2,000
Direct wages	4,000
Indirect wages	2,000
Indirect Factory Expenses	8,000
Selling Commission	400
Interest on Bank Loan	500
Profit on Sale of Machinery	700
Advertisement and Sales Promotion	8,000
Distribution Expenses	4,000
Office Salary	1,000
Printing and Stationery	200

In Cost Account :

(1) Manufacturing overhead was recovered at 300% on Direct wages
(2) Selling overhead was recovered @ 10% on sales
(3) Distribution overhead recovered @ 4% on sales
(4) Administrative overhead was recovered @ 2% on sales.

[K.U.D., April 1997(N)]

Solution :

Manufacturing A/c (Financial A/c)

To Purchases of Materials	32,000	By Sales	80,000
To Direct Wages	4,000	By Closing Stock of Materials	2,000
To Indirect Wages	2,000		
To Indirect Factory Exp.	8,000		
To Gross Profit Transfer	36,000		
To Profit & Loss	82,000		82,000

Profit & Loss A/c

To Office Salary	1,000	By Gross Profit	36,000
To Printing & Stationery	200	By Profit on sale & Machinery	700
To Selling Commission	400		
To Interest on Bank Loan	500		
To Advertisement & Sales Production	8,000		
To Destribution Exp.	4,000		
To Net Profit	22,600		
	36,700		36,700

In Cost Books

Statement of Cost

			Rs.
Materials :			
Purchases	32,000		
Less Closing Stock	2,000	Materials Consumed	30,000
Direct Wages			4,000
		Prime Cost	34,000
Factory overhead :			
300% on Direct Wages 300% × 4,000			12,000
		Factory Cost	46,000
Office overhead or Administrative overhead			
2% on sales 2% on 80,000			1,600
		Total Cost	47,600
Selling of Distribution overhead :			
Selling overhead 10% on sales 10% on		80,000 – 8,000	
Distribution overhead 4% on sales = 4% × 80,000		3,200	11,200
		Cost of Sales	58,800
Sales			80,000
		Profit	Rs. 21,200

Reconciliation Statement

			Rs.
Net Profit as per Cost Accounts			21,200
Add (i) Over recovery of overheads in cost :			
Factory overhead in cost	12,000		
in Financial A/cs	10,000	2,000	
Office overhead – in cost	1,600		
in Financial A/c	1,000	600	
(ii) Items credited in Financial Books only			
Profit on Sale of Machinery		700	3,300
			24,500
Less (i) Under recovery of overheads in cost			
Selling & Distribution overhead in cost	11,200		
in Financial A/c	12,400	1,200	
(ii) Items debited in Financial A/c only		200	
Printing & Stationery Interest on Bank Loan		500	1,900
Net Profit as per Financial A/c			22,600

Problem No. 5

The Financial Profit and Loss Account of a company for the year ended 30-4-1994 was as follows :

Profit and Loss A/c for the year ended 30-4-94

Particulars	Amount	Particulars	Amount
To Materials	50,000	By Sales	1,24,000
To Carriage	1,000		
To Direct Wages	34,000		
To Works Expenses	12,000		
To Administrative Expenses	4,500		
To Selling & Distribution Expenses	6,500		
To Debenture Interest	1,000		
To Net Profit	15,000		
	1,24,000		1,24,000

The Net Profit as per Cost Accounts for the same period is Rs. 16,270. A scrutiny of two sets of books revealed the following facts :

(a) The amount charged in Cost Account in respect of overheads are as follows :

Works Expenses — 11,500

Administrative Expenses — Rs. 4,590

Selling & Distribution Expenses — Rs. 6,640

(b) No monitor is made in cost account about debenture interest.

You are required to reconcile the profit shown by the two accounts.

(K.U.D., April 1996)

Solution :

Reconciliation Statement

	Rs.	Rs.	Rs.
Net Profit as per Cost Account			16,270
Add : (1) Overabsorption of overheads in cost :			
Administrative Expenses in cost	4,590		
In Financial Account	4,500	90	
Selling & Distribution Expenses in cost	6,640		
In Financial Account	6,500	140	230
			16,500

	Rs.	Rs.	Rs.
			16,500
(2) Items credited in Financial Account			—
(3) Over valuation of opening stock in cost			—
(4) Under valuation of closing stock in cost			—
Less : (1) Under absorption overheads in cost :			
Works Expenses in cost	11,500		
In Financial Account	12,000	500	
(2) Items debited in Financial Account only		1,000	
(3) Under valuation opening stock in cost		—	
(4) Over valuation of closing stock in cost		—	–1,500
Net Profit as per Financial Account			15,000

Problem No. 6

The Net Profit of company appeared at Rs. 1,28,754 as per Financial Records for the year ended 31-12-93. A scrutiny of Financial and Cost records revealed the following facts :

(a)	Works overheads under recovered in Cost Accounts	3,120
(b)	Administrative overheads over recovered in Cost Accounts	1,700
(c)	Depreciation charged in Financial Accounts	11,200
(d)	Depreciation recovered in Cost Accounts	12,500
(e)	Interest on Investments not included in cost books	8,000
(f)	Obsolescence loss charged in Financial Accounts	5,700
(g)	Income tax provided in Financial Accounts	40,300
(h)	Bank interest and transfer fees credited in Financial Accounts	750
(i)	Stores adjustment credited in Financial Accounts	474
(j)	Loss due to depreciation in stock values charged in Financial Accounts	6,750

Prepare a Reconciliation Statement and find out profit or loss as per Cost Accounts.

(K.U.D., October 1995)

Solution :

Reconciliation Statement

		Rs.	Rs.
Net Profit as per Financial Accounts			1,28,754
Add : (1) Under recovery of overhead in cost :			
Works overhead under recovered in cost		3,120	
(2) Items debited in Financial Accounts only :			
Obsolescence Loss charged in Financial A/c		5,700	
Income Tax provided in Financial A/c		40,300	
Loss due to depreciation in stock values charged in Financial Accounts		6,750	
(3) Lower value of opening stock in cost		—	
(4) Higher value of closing stock in cost		—	55,870
			1,84,624
Less : (1) Over recovery of overheads in cost			
Administrative overheads over recovered		1,700	
Depreciation charged in Financial A/c	11,200		
Depreciation charged in Cost A/c	12,500	1,300	
(2) Items credited in Financial Account only :			
(a) Interest on Investment not included in cost (i.e. credited in Financial A/c)		8,000	
(b) Bank Interest and transfer fees credited in Financial Accounts		750	
(c) Stores Adjustment credited in Financial Account only		474	
(3) Higher value of opening stock in cost		—	
(4) Lower value of closing stock in cost		—	(–) 12,224
Net Profit as per Cost Accounts			1,72,400

Problem No. 7

From the following figures prepare a Reconciliation Statement :

Net Loss as per Cost Account	10,000
Net Profit as per Financial Accounts	15,000
Works overheads under recovered in Cost Account	3,000
Administrative overhead over recovered in Cost Accounts	6,000
Depreciation charged in Financial Accounts	10,000

Depreciation recovered in Cost Account	14,000
Interest received on Securities	25,000
Obsolescence loss charged in Financial Account	5,000
Income tax provided in Financial Accounts	10,000
Bank interest credited	10,000
Stores adjustment credited in Financial A/c only	2,000
Value of opening stock in Cost Accounts	52,000
Value of opening stock in Financial A/c	54,000
Value of closing stock in Cost A/c	50,000
Value of closing stock in Financial A/c	47,000
Interest charged in Cost A/c but not in Financial Accounts	6,000
Preliminary expenses written off	1,000
Provision for Doubtful debts	4,000

(K.U.D., April 1995)

Solution :

Reconciliation Statement

		Rs.	Rs.
Net Profit as a Financial Accounts			15,000
(I) *Add* : (a) Under recovery of overheads in cost works overhead under recovery		3,000	
(b) Items Debited in Financial Account only :			
(i) Obsolescence loss charged in Financial A/c		5,000	
(ii) Income tax provided in Financial A/c		10,000	
(iii) Preliminary Expenses written off		1,000	
(iv) Provision for Doubtful Debts		4,000	
(c) Lower value of opening stok in cost :			
In Cost Account	52,000		
In Financial A/c	54,000	2,000	
(d) Higher value of closing stock in cost :			
In Cost Account	50,000		
In Financial A/c	47,000	3,000	28,000
			43,000
(II) *Loss* : (a) Over recovery of overheads in Cost A/c :			
(i) Administrative overheads over recovered		6,000	
(ii) Depreciation :			
In Financial Account	10,000		
In Cost Account	14,000	4,000	

	Rs.	Rs.
(iii) Interest charged in Cost A/c	6,000	
(b) Items credited in Financial A/c only :		
(i) Interest received on securities	25,000	
(ii) Bank interest credited	10,000	
(iii) Stores Adjustment credited	2,000	
(c) Higher value of opening stock in cost	—	
(d) Lower value of closing stock in cost	—	–53,000
Net Loss as per Cost Accounts		–10,000

Or

Reconciliation Statement

	Rs.	Rs.
Net Loss as per Cost Accounts		–10,000
I. *Add* : Over recovery of overheads in Cost A/c :		
(i) Administrative overhead over recovery	6,000	
(ii) Depreciation charged recovered :		
In Financial A/c 10,000		
In Cost A/c 14,000	4,000	
(iii) Interest charged in Cost A/c only	6,000	
(b) Items credited in Financial Account only :		
(i) Interest received on security	25,000	
(ii) Bank interest credited	10,000	
(iii) Stores Adjustment credited	2,000	
(c) Higher value of opening stock in cost	—	
(d) Lower value of closing stock in cost	—	+53,000
		+43,000
II. *Less* : (a) Under recovery of overheads in cost		
(i) Works overhead under recovered	3,000	
(b) Items Debited in Financial A/c only :		
(i) Obsolescence loss charged	5,000	
(ii) Income Tax proved	10,000	
(iii) Preliminary Expenses written off	1,000	
(iv) Provision for Doubtful Debts	4,000	
	23,000	
(c) Lower value of opening stock :		
In Cost 52,000		
In Financial 54,000	2,000	
(d) Higher value of closing stock :		
In Cost Account 50,000		
In Financial A/c 47,000	3,000	–28,000
Net. Profit as per Financial Account		+15,000

Problem No. 8

The Trading and Profit Loss Account of Prasad Ltd. was as follows :

Trading and Profit and Loss Account for the year ending 31-03-1994

Particulars		Amount	Particulars	Amount
To Purchase	25,210		By Sales	75,000
			50000 units @ Rs. 1.50 each	
Closing Stock	4,080	21,130	By Discount Received	260
To Direct wages		10,500	By Profit on sale of old plant	2,340
To Work Expenses		12,130		
To Administrative Expenses		5,340		
To Selling Expenses		7,100		
To Depreciation		1,100		
To Preliminary Expenses (written off)		1,000		
To Net Profit		19,300		
		77,600		77,600

The following information is available from the costing records :

(a) Cost Account valued closing stock at Rs. 4,280.

(b) The works expenses in Cost Accounts were taken at 100% of Direct Wages.

(c) Selling expenses and Administrative expenses were charged in Cost Accounts at 10% of sale and 10 Ps per unit respectively.

(d) Depreciation in Cost Accounts was Rs. 800.

Prepare the Profit Reconciliation Statement to show profit as per Cost Accounts.

(K.U.D., October 1994)

Solution :

Profit Reconciliation Statement

Particulars	Rs.	Rs.	Rs.
Net Profit as per Financial Accounts			19,300
(I) *Add* : (1) Under recovery of overheads in cost			
(a) Work expenses in Cost A/c :			
100% Direct wages	10,500		
In Financial Account	12,130	1,630	
(b) Administrative Expenses			
In Cost Account (50000 × .10)	5,000		
In Financial A/c	5,340	340	
(c) Depreciation charged in Cost A/c	800		
In Financial Accounts	1,100	300	

Particulars	Rs.	Rs.	Rs.
(II) Items debited in Financial A/c only :			
Preliminary Expenses		1,000	
(III) Lower value of opening stock in cost			
(IV) Higher value of closing stock in Cost			
In Cost Account	4,280		
In Financial Account	4,080	200	+3,470
			22,770
Less : (1) Over recovery of overheads in Cost :			
Sales Expenses in Cost	7,500		
In Financial Account	7,100	400	
(2) Items credited in Financial A/c only			
Discount received		260	
Profit on sale of Assets		2,340	
(3) Higher value of opening stock in cost			
(4) Lower value of closing stock in cost		—	– 3,000
Profit as per Cost Accounts			19,770

Problem No. 9

Following information is derived from the records of a company for the year ended 31st March 1991. You are required to prepare :

(i) A statement showing the Profit as per Cost Account; and

(ii) A statement of reconciliation.

Following is taken from the financial records :

Profit and Loss Account for the year ended 31-3-91

Particulars	Amount	Particulars	Amount
To Opening stock of finished goods (400 units)	16,000	By Sales (10,200 units)	7,14,000
Materials	2,50,000	Closing stock of finished goods (200 units)	9,000
Wages	1,60,000		
Factory overhead	94,000		
Administrative overhead	1,05,000		
Selling expenses	50,000		
Bad debts	10,000		
Preliminary Expenses	4,000		
Net Profits	34,000		
	7,23,000		7,23,000

Following are found out in costing books :

Materials – Rs. 25 per unit.

Labour cost – Rs. 16 per unit.

The factory overheads are absorbed at 60 per cent of labour cost and administration overheads are at 20 per cent of factory cost. Selling expenses are charged at Rs. 6 per unit sold. In Cost Accounts, the opening stock is valued at Rs. 45 per unit and the closing stock at Rs. 60 per unit. There is opening or closing stock of materials or work-in-progress except that of finished goods.

(K.U.D., April 1994)

Solution :

Working Notes

Units Produced = Sales – 10,200 units

Add : Closing stock 200 units

10,400

Less : Opening stock 400

10,000 Units produce during the year.

Statement of Cost and Profit

Material @ Rs. 25 × 10000	2,50,000
Wages – @ Rs. 16 × 10000 =	1,60,000
Prime Cost	4,10,000
Factory overhead 60 per cent of wages = 1,60,000 × 60%	96,000
Works Cost	5,06,000
Administrative overhead 20% of Factory cost	
5,06,000 × 20% =	1,01,200
Cost of production	6,07,200
Opening stock of finished goods (400 × 45)	18,000
	6,25,200
Less : Closing stock of finished goods (200 × 60)	12,000
	6,13,200
Add : Selling expenses (10200 × 6)	61,200
Cost of Sales	6,74,400
Selling Price 10200	7,14,000
Profit	39,600

Reconciliation Statement

Particulars	Rs.	Rs.	Rs.
Net Profit as per Cost Accounts			39,600
(I) *Add* : Over recovery of overheads :			
Factory overhead – In Cost	96,000		
In Finance	94,000	2,000	
Selling Expenses – In Cost	61,200		
In Finance	50,000	11,200	
(2) Items credited in Finance A/c only	—		
(3) Higher value of opening stock :			
in Cost	18,000		
in Finance	16,000	2,000	
(4) Lower value of closing stock in cost		—	15,200
			54,800
(II) *Less* : Under recovery of overhead in cost :			
(1) Administrative overhead in cost	1,01,200		
in Finance A/c	1,05,000	3,800	
(2) Items debited in Financial A/c only :			
Bad Debts	10,000		
Preliminary Expenses	4,000	14,000	
(3) Lower value of opening stock in cost			
(4) Higher value of closing stock in cost	12,000		
in Financial A/c	9,000	3,000	20,800
Net Profit as per Financial Account			Rs. 34,000

Problem No. 10

From the information given below, prepare Reconciliation Statement :

Loss as per financial records	50,000
Works overheads under recovered in Cost A/c	8,000
Depreciation overcharged in Cost A/c	2,000
Depreciation in stock value written off in Financial books	3,500
Stores adjustment credited in Financial books	100
Interest on investment	7,500
Income Tax	30,000
Goodwill Written off	5,000
Administrative overheads overcharged in cost books	3,000

(K.U.D., October 1993)

Solution :

Reconciliation Statement

Particulars	Rs.	Rs.
Net Loss as per Financial Records		– 50,000
Add : (1) Works overhead under recover in cost	8,000	
(2) Items debited in Financial A/c only :		
(a) Depreciation in stock value written off in Financial Books	3,500	
(b) Income Tax paid	30,000	
(c) Goodwill written off	5,000	+ 46,500
		– 3,500
(3) Lower value of opening stock in cost	—	
(4) Higher value of closing stock in cost	—	
Less : (1) Over recovery of overhead in cost :		
(a) Administrative overheads over charged	3,000	
(b) Depreciation over charged in cost	2,000	
(2) Items credited in Financial A/c :		
(a) Interest in investment	7,500	
(b) Stores Adjustment credited in Financial Book	100	
(3) Higher value of opening stock in cost	—	
(4) Lower value of closing stock in cost	—	– 12,600
Net Loss as per Cost Accounts		–16,100

Problem No. 11

Profits as disclosed by Cost Accounts was Rs. 17,240 for the year 1989. From the following information prepare Reconciliation Statement and find out profit or loss as per Financial books :

Works overheads under recovered in costing	312
Office overheads recovered in excess in cost	170
Depreciation in Financial records	1,120
Depreciation in cost records	1,250
Interest received Investments	800
Obsolescence loss charged in Financial records	570
Income tax provided in Financial books	4,030
Bank interest credited in Financial books	75
Stores adjustment credited in Financial books	47
Depreciation of stock charged in Financial books	675

(K.U.D., April 1993)

Solution :

Reconciliation Statement

Particulars		Rs.	Rs.
Profit as per Cost Accounts			17,240
(I) *Add* : Over recovery of overhead in cost :			
(a) (i) Office overhead recovered in Excess in cost		170	
(ii) Depreciation Financial A/c	1,120		
Depreciation in Cost A/c	1,250	130	
(b) Items credited in Financial Account only :			
(i) Interest on investment		800	
(ii) Bank Interest credited in Financial book		75	
(iii) Stores Adjustment credited in Financial book		47	
(c) Higher value of opening stock in cost		—	
(d) Lower value of closing stock in cost		—	+1,222
			+18,462
(II) *Less* : Under recovery of overheads in cost :			
(a) Works overhead under recovered in cost : Items debited in Financial A/c only		312	
(b) (i) Obsolescence loss charged in Financial A/c		570	
(ii) Income Tax provided in Financial A/c		4,030	
(iii) Depreciation of stock charged in Financial A/c		675	
(c) Lower value of opening stock in cost		—	
(d) Higher value of closing stock in cost		—	−5,587
Profit as per Financial Account.			12,875

Problem No. 12

The following relates to 31-12-1985 :

Sales for the year	1,60,000
Raw materials	48,000
Wages	36,000

Works overhead and administrative overheads charged in cost accounts stand 3 : 1 ratio sales price included 30 per cent Profit.

Actual expenses were :

Manufacturing	26,000
Office Expenses	11,000

Find out profit as per Cost and Finance account and reconcile the statement.

(Gulbarga, April 1993 & K.U.D., 1986)

Solution :

Working Note

Ascertainment of cost of production :

Sales (as given)	1,60,000
Less : Profit 30 per cent included	48,000
Cost of production of Rs.	1,12,000

Cost of production = Prime cost + Factory overhead + Office overhead.

1,12,000 = (48,000 + 36,000) + Factory overhead + Office overhead

= 84,000 + Factory overhead + Office overhead

1,12,000 - 84,000 = 28,000 = Factory overhead + Office overhead

= 28,000 = 3 : 1

= Apportioned 28,000 × 3/4 : 28,000 × ¼

21,000 7,000

Now Prime cost	84,000	
Factory O/H	21,000	
Office O/H	7,000	
	1,12,000	Cost of production.

Statement of Cost Sheet

Raw material		48,000
Wages		36,000
	Prime Cost	84,000
Factory overhead		21,000
	Works Cost	1,05,000
Office overhead		7,000
	Cost of production	1,12,000
Sales		1,60,000
	Profit	48,000
Being 30 per cent on sales of Rs. 1,60,000		
Profit 30 per cent of 1,60,000 = 48,000		
Net Profit as per cost		48,000
Net Profit as per Financial Account		39,000

Trading and Profit and Loss Account

Particulars	Amount	Particulars	Amount
To Raw material	48,000	By Sales	1,60,000
To Wages	36,000		
To Factory Expenses	26,000		
To Gross Profit	50,000		
	1,60,000		1,60,000
To Office Expenses	11,000	By Gross Profit	50,000
To Net Profit	39,000		
	50,000		50,000

Reconciliation Statement

Particulars	Rs.	Rs.	Rs.
Net Profit as per Cost Account			48,000
Add : (1) Over recovery of overhead in cost		—	
(2) Items credited in Financil Account		—	
(3) Higher value of opening stock in cost		—	
(4) Lower value of closing stock in cost		—	—
Less : Under recovery of overhead in cost :			
(a) Factory overhead in cost	21,000		
In Financial Account	– 26,000	– 5,000	
(b) Office overhead in cost	7,000		
In Financial Account	– 11,000	– 4,000	–9,000
Net Profit as per Financial Account			39,000

Problem No. 13

Profits as disclosed by a company's Cost Accounts for the year ended 31-12-1990 was Rs. 2,00,000. A scrutiny of the figures from both Cost and Financial Accounts revealed the following :

(a) Income Tax provided in Financial Account	60,000
(b) Share transfer fee credited in Financial Account	4,000
(c) Company provided for doubtful debts	20,000
(d) Overhead costs as per Cost Account estimated	34,000
Whereas in Financial Account charged	28,000
(e) Directors fees shown in the Financial Accounts	8,000
(f) Depreciation charged in Financial Accounts	7,000
(g) Value of closing stock in Cost Accounts	18,750
(h) Value of closing stock in Financial Accounts	20,750

(i) Interest on Investments not included in Cost A/c 4,000
(j) Goodwill written off in Financial Accounts 9,000
(k) Stores Adjustment Credited in Financial Accounts 1,000

Prepare Reconciliation Statement.

(K.U.D., October 1992)

Solution :

Reconciliation Statement for the year 1990

Particulars		Rs.	Rs.
Net Profit as per Cost Account			2,00,000
Add : (1) Over Recovery of overheads in Cost A/c			
Overhead in Cost Account		34,000	
Overhead in Financial Account		28,000	
		6,000	
(2) Items credited in Financial Account :			
Share transfer fee credited in Financial A/c		4,000	
Interest on Investment not included in Cost A/c		4,000	
Stores Adjustment credited in Financial A/c		1,000	
(3) Higher value of opening stock in Cost A/c		—	
(4) Lower value of closing stock in Cost A/c :			
Closing stock in Cost A/c	18,750		
Closing stock in Financial A/c	20,750	2,000	+17,000
			2,17,000
Less : (1) Under recover of overheads			—
(2) Items debited in Financial A/c only :			
Income Tax provided		60,000	
Provision for doubtful debts		20,000	
Directors fees		8,000	
Depreciation		7,000	
Goodwill		9,000	–1,04,000
Profit as per Financial Account			1,13,000

Problem No. 14

Prepare a Reconciliation Statement from the following data :

(1) Net Profit as per cost 2,00,000
(2) Income tax provided in Financial Account 60,000
(3) Share transfer fee credited in Financial Account 4,000
(4) Provision for doubtful debts 20,000
(5) Overheads as per Cost Account 34,000

(6)	Overheads as per Financial Account	28,000
(7)	Depreciation charged in Financial A/c	7,000
(8)	Directors fees shown in Financial A/c	8,000
(9)	Value of closing stock in Financial A/c	20,750
(10)	Value of closing stock in Cost Account	18,750
(11)	Goodwill written off in Financial Account	9,000
(12)	Stores adjustment (credited in Financial A/c)	1,000
(13)	Interest on Investment not included in cost	4,000

(K.U.D., April 1992)

Solution :

Reconciliation Statement

Particulars	Rs.	Rs.	Rs.
Net Profit as per Cost Account			2,00,000
Add : (1) Over recovery of overheads in cost :			
Overheads in cost	34,000		
In Financial A/c	28,000	6,000	
(2) Items credited in Financial A/c only :			
(a) Share transfer fee credited		4,000	
(b) Stores adjustment (creditors)		1,000	
(c) Interest on Investment		4,000	
(3) Higher value of opening stock in cost		—	
(4) Lower value of closing stock in cost :			
Closing stock in cost	18,750		
In Financial Account	20,750	2,000	+ 17,000
			2,17,000
Less : (1) Under recovery of overheads in cost			
(2) Items debited in Financial A/c only :			
(a) Income tax provided		60,000	
(b) Provision for doubtful debts		20,000	
(c) Direct Fees		8,000	
(d) Depreciation		7,000	
(e) Goodwill written off		9,000	
(3) Lower value of opening stock in cost		—	
(4) Higher value of closing stock in cost		—	– 1,04,000
Net Profit as per Financial Account			1,13,000

Problem No. 15

In a factory two types of Radios are manufactured viz., "Popular" and "Delux" models. There is no opening or closing stock.

Expenses	'Popular'	Delux
Labour	46,800	62,920
Materials	81,900	1,08,680

Works overheads is charged @ 80% on labour.

Office overheads taken @ 15 per cent on works cost.

Popular Radios sold during the year were 234 @ Rs. 1,000 each and Delux radios sold 286 @ Rs. 1,100 each. Ascertain Total Profit as per cost Books from the above particulars. If the actual works expenses are Rs. 87,000 and Office expenses Rs. 58,000 find out the actual Profit made.

(K.U.D., October 1991)

Solution :

Statement of Cost and Profit

Particulars	Popular 234	Delux 286
Materials	81,900	1,08,680
Labour	46,800	62,920
Prime Cost	1,28,700	1,71,600
Works overhead 80 per cent of wages	37,440	50,336
Works Cost	1,66,140	2,21,936
Office overhead 15 per cent on works cost	24,921	33,290.40
Total Cost	1,91,061	2,55,226.40
Sales Price		
Popular = 234 × 1,000 =	2,34,000	
Delux = 286 × 1,100 =		3,14,600
Profit as per Cost	42,939	59,374

Profit and Loss Account

Particulars		Amount	Particulars		Amount
To Materials		1,90,580	By Sales		5,48,600
Popular	81,900		Popular -	2,34,000	
Delux	1,08,680		Delux -	3,14,600	
To Labour		1,09,720			
Popular	46,800				
Delux	62,920				
To Overhead Works		87,000			
To Office Overhead		58,000			
To Net Profit		1,03,300			
Total		5,48,600	Total		5,48,600

Reconciliation Statement

Profit as Cost Account	1,02,313
Add : Works overhead over recovered	776
	1,03,089
Add : Office overhead over recovered	211
Profit as Financial Account	1,03,300

Problem No. 16

The Profits as per Cost Account is Rs. 1,65,300. The following details are ascertained on comparison of Cost and Financial A/c :

Particulars	Cost A/c	Financial A/c
(a) Opening stock :		
Materials	32,600	33,000
Works-in-progress :	20,000	21,000
(b) Closing stock		
Materials	36,000	34,400
Work-in-progress	16,000	15,200

(c) Interest remitted but ignored in Cost Account Rs. 800.

(d) Interest charged but not considered in Financial A/c Rs. 600

(e) Preliminary Expenses charged in :

Financial Accounts Rs. 1,21,200

but overhead recovered in Cost A/c. Rs. 1,26,000

Find out Profit as per Financial A/c by drawing up Reconciliation Statement.

(K.U.D., April 1991)

Solution :

Reconciliation Statement

Particulars	Rs.	Rs.	Rs.
Profit as per Cost Account			1,65,300
Add : Over recovery of overhead in Cost Accounts :			
(1) Overhead Expenses recovered :			
in Cost	1,26,000		
in Finance	1,21,200	4,800	
Interest charged in Cost A/c only but not considered in Financial A/c		6,000	10,800
			1,76,100

Particulars	Rs.	Rs.	Rs.
			1,76,000
(2) Items credited in Financial A/c		—	
(3) Higher value of opening stock in Cost		—	
(4) Lower value of closing stock in Cost A/c		—	
Less : Under recovery of overheads in cost :			
(1) Items debited in Financial Account only		800	
(2) Interest remitted but ignored in cost preliminary expenses written off		13,000	
(3) Lower value of opening cost :			
Material : 32,600 33,000	400		
20,000 21,000	1,000	1,400	
(4) Higher value of closing stock :			
Material	1,600		
Work-in-progress	800	2,400	–17,600
Profit as per Financial Account			1,58,500

Problem No. 17

Find out Profits as per costing records and financial accounts from the following information and reconcile the results :

Particulars	Product-A	Product-B
(1) Number of Units produced and sold	600	400
(2) Total Direct Material	Rs. 3,600	Rs. 2,800
(3) Total Direct Wages	Rs. 3,000	Rs. 2,400
(4) Selling Price per Unit	25	30

Works on cost is charged at 80 per cent of direct wages and office on cost at 25 per cent of works cost. Actual works expenses amounted to Rs. 4,500 and office expenses to Rs. 3,900. There was no opening or closing stock.

(K.U.D., October 1990)

Solution :

Statement of Cost and Profit

Particulars	Product A	Product B	Total
No. of units produced	600	400	
Direct Materials	3,600	2,800	6,400
Direct Wages	3,000	2,400	5,400
Prime Cost	6,600	5,200	11,800
Works on cost 80% of wages	2,400	1,920	4,320
Works Cost	9,000	7,120	16,120
Office on Cost 25% on Works Cost	2,250	1,780	4,030
Total Cost	11,250	8,900	20,150
Sales (600 × 25) (400 × 30)	15,000	12,000	27,000
Net Profit	3,750	3,100	6,850

Financial Account Manufacturing and Profit and Loss A/c

Particulars		Amount	Particulars	Amount
To Material - A	3,600		By Sales	
To Material - B	2,800	6,400	A - 600 × 25 =	15,000
To Wages - A	3,000		B - 400 × 30 =	12,000
To Wages - B	2,400	5,400		
To Factory Expenses		4,500		
		16,300		
To Gross Profit		10,700		
Total		27,000	Total	27,000
To Office Expenses		3,900	By Gross Profit	10,700
To Net Profit		6,800		
Total		10,700	Total	10,700

Profit as per Cost Accounts Rs. 6,850

Profit as per Financial Account Rs. 6,800

Reconciliation Statement

Particulars	Rs.	Rs.	Rs.
Profit as per Cost Accounts			6,850
Add Over recovery of overhead in cost			
office expenses - in cost	4,030		
in Financial Account	3,900	130	+ 130
			6,980
Less Under recovery of overhead in Cost A/c			
Factory overhead - in Cost	4,320		
in Financial Account	4,500	180	– 180
Net Profit as per Financial A/c			6,800

Problem No. 18

In a factory two models of T.V. sets are manufactured namely A and B. From the following particulars ascertain profits as per Cost Account and Financial Account. Prepare Reconciliation Statement.

	Models A	Models B
	Rs.	Rs.
Material	7,37,100	9,78,120
Labour	4,21,200	5,66,280
Output and sales (in Nos.)	234	286
Sales price per T.V. Set	10,000	11,000

In Cost Account works overhead is charged @ 80% of Labour and Office overhead @ 15% of works cost.

Actual Factory Expenses are Rs. 8,70,000 and Office Expenses are Rs. 5,80,000.

(B'lore, October 1990)

Solution :

Trading and Profit & Loss A/c

Particulars		Amount	Particulars	Amount
To Material			By Sales	
A -	7,37,100		Model A = 234 × 10,000	23,40,000
B -	9,78,120	17,15,220	Model B = 286 × 11,000	31,46,000
To Labour				
A -	4,21,200			
B -	5,66,280	9,87,480		
To Factory Exp.		8,70,000		
To Gross Profit		19,13,300		
		54,86,000		54,86,000
To Office Expenses		5,80,000	By Gross Profit	19,13,300
To Net Profit		13,33,300		
		19,13,300		19,13,300

Statement and Profit

	Model A	Model B	Total Rs.
Materials	7,37,100	9,78,120	17,15,220
Labour	4,21,200	5,66,280	9,87,480
Prime Cost	11,58,300	15,44,400	27,02,700
Factory Overhead 80% of Labour	3,36,960	4,53,024	7,89,984
Works Cost	14,95,260	19,97,424	34,92,684
Office Overhead 15% on Works Cost	2,24,289	2,99,614	5,23,903
Total Cost or Cost of production	17,19,549	22,97,038	40,16,587

	Model A	Model B	Total Rs.
Sales : Model A = 234 × 10,000	23,40,000		
B = 286 × 11,000		31,46,000	54,86,000
Profit	6,20,451	8,48,962	14,69,413

Total Net Profit as per cost Rs. 14,69,413

Reconciliation Statement

Particulars	Rs.	Rs.	Rs.
Net Profit as per Cost Account			14,69,413
Add : (1) Over recovery of overhead		—	
(2) Items credited in Financial Account only		—	
(3) Higher value of opening stock in cost		—	
(4) Lower value of closing stock in cost		—	—
Less : Under recovery of overhead in cost :			
Factory overhead in cost	7,89,984		
In Financial Account	8,70,000	80,016	
Office overhead in cost	5,23,903		
In Financial Account	5,80,000	56,097	–1,36,113
Net Profit as per Financial Account			13,33,300

Problem No. 19

Prepare a Reconciliation Statement from the following data :

(1)	Net Loss as per Cost Account	3,44,800
(2)	Net Loss as per Financial Account	4,32,090
(3)	Works overhead under recovered in Cost A/c	6,240
(4)	Depreciation overcharged in Cost A/c	2,600
(5)	Administration overhead recovered in Excess	3,400
(6)	Interest on Investment	17,500
(7)	Goodwill written off in Financial A/c	11,400
(8)	Income Tax paid	80,600
(9)	Stores Adjustment (Credited in Financial A/c)	950
(10)	Depreciation of stock charged Financial A/c	13,500

(K.U.D., April 1990)

Solution :

Reconciliation Statement

Particulars	Rs.	Rs.
Net Loss as per Cost Account		–3,44,800
Add : (1) Under recovery of overheads in Cost A/c :		
Works overhead under recovered	6,240	
(2) Items debited in Financial A/c only :		
(a) Goodwill written off in Financial A/c	11,400	

Particulars	Rs.	Rs.
(b) Income tax paid debited Financial A/c	80,600	
(c) Depreciation on stock charged Financial A/c	13,500	–1,11,740
		–4,56,540
Less : Over recovery of overhead in Cost :		
(a) Depreciation over charged in cost	2,600	
(b) Administration overhead recovered in excess in cost	3,400	
(2) Items credited in Financial Account :		
(a) Interest on Investments	17,500	
(b) Stores Adjustment	950	+ 24,450
Net Loss as per Financial Account		– 4,32,090

Problem No. 20

The Net Profit of Bharati Engineering Co. appeared to Rs. 1,78,980 in the Financial Account for the year ended 31-12-1988. The cost Books however showed a Net Profit Rs. 1,48,755. Following errors were found in the accounts :

(1)	Works overhead under recovered in cost	1,700
(2)	Administrative overheads recovered in excess in cost	31,200
(3)	Depreciation recovered in cost	14,000
(4)	Depreciation charged in Financial Account	11,500
(5)	Interest on investments not included in cost	8,000
(6)	Loss on sales of Assets debited in Financial Account	4,700
(7)	Income tax provided in Financial Account	4,100
(8)	Stores adjustment (credited in Financial Account)	450
(9)	Loss on stock value (charged in Financial Account)	725
(10)	Debenture interest charged in Financial Account	700

You are required to prepare a Reconciliation Statement.

(M'lore, April 1990)

Solution :

Reconciliation Statement for the year 1988

Particulars		Rs.	Rs.
Net Profit as per Cost Account			1,48,755
Add : (1) Over recovery of overheads in cost :			
(a) Administrative overhead recovered in excess		31,200	
(b) Depreciation recovered in cost	14,000		
In Financial Account	11,500	2,500	
(2) Items credited in Financial Account only :			
(a) Interest on investment		8,000	
(b) Stores Adjustment (credit in Financial A/c)		450	

Particulars	Rs.	Rs.
(3) Higher value of opening stock in cost	—	
(4) Lower value of closing stock in cost	—	+42,150
		1,90,905
Less : (1) Under recovery of overheads in cost :		
Works overhead under recovered	1,700	
(2) Items debited in Financial A/c only :		
(a) Loss on sale of Assets	4,700	
(b) Income tax provided in Financial A/c	4,100	
(c) Loss on stock value	725	
(d) Debenture Interest debited	700	
(3) Lower value of opening stock in cost	—	
(4) Higher value of closing stock	—	−11,925
Net Profit as per Financial Account		1,78,980

Problem No. 21

The following is the Profit and Loss Account of a manufacturing company for the year 1979 :

Trading and Profit and Loss A/c for the year 1979

Particulars	Amount	Particulars		Amount
To Materials	48,000	By Sales		96,000
To Wages	36,000	By Closing stock		
To Works Expenses	24,000	Finished goods		18,000
To Gross Profit	12,000	*Work-in-progress*		
		Materials	3,000	
		Labour	1,800	
		Works Expenses	1,200	6,000
	1,20,000			1,20,000
To Administrative Exp.	6,000	By Gross Profit		12,000
To Net Profit	6,000			
	12,000			12,000

During the year 6000 units were manufactured and 4800 units were sold. The costing records show that works expenses have been worked out at Rs. 3 per unit and administrative expenses @ Rs. 1.50 per unit. The cost books show the profit of Rs. 11,040.

Prepare necessary accounts and show the reconciliation of profits.

(M'lore, April 1989 and Mysore, April 1982)

Solution :

Statement of Cost and Profit

	Units	Rs.
Output Units	6000	
Materials		48,000
Wages		36,000
Prime Cost		84,000
Factory Expenses Rs. 3 per unit (6000 × 3)		18,000
Works Cost		1,02,000
Office Expenses Rs. 1.50 per unit 1.50 × 6000 (No. of units production 6000 Units)		9,000
Cost of production		1,11,000
Less : Closing stock of work-in-progress (Material + Labour + Work Exp. (3,000 + 1,800 + 1,200)		6,000
	6,000	1,05,000

Cost of production of 6000 Units — Rs. 1,05,000

$$\text{Cost per unit} = \frac{1,05,000}{6000} = \text{Rs.}17.50 \text{ per unit}$$

	Units	Rs.
Less : Closing stock of Finished goods 1200 × 17.5	1200	21,000
	4,800	84,000
Selling Expenses Re. 0.20 Ps per unit (4800 × .20)		960
Cost of Finished unit (4800 Units sold)	4800	84,960
Sales value Rs. 20 per unit (4800 × 20)		96,000
Net Profit as per cost		11,040

Reconcilation Statement

Particulars	Rs.	Rs.	Rs.
Net Profit as per Financial A/c			6,000
Add : (1) Under recovery of overhead in cost			
Works Expenses factory expenses :			
In Cost	18,000		
In Financial Account	24,000	6,000	
(2) Items debited in Financial Account		—	
(3) Lower value of opening stock in cost			
(4) Higher value of closing stock in cost :			
Closing stock in cost (Finished goods)	21,000		
In Financial Account	18,000	3,000	+ 9,000
			15,000

Particulars	Rs.	Rs.	Rs.
			15,000
Less : Over recovery of overheads in cost :			
(a) Office Expenses in cost	9,000		
In Financial Account	6,000	3,000	
(b) Selling Expenses recovered in cost only		960	
(2) Items credited in Financial Account only		—	
(3) Higher value of opening stock in cost		—	
(4) Lower value of closing stock in cost		—	– 3,960
Net Profit as per Cost Account			11,040

Problem No. 22

From the following information prepare :

(1) Profit and Loss Account

(2) Cost sheet – calculating :

Factory overhead @ 25 per cent on Prime cost and

Office Overhead @ 75 per cent of Factory overhead

(3) A profit reconciliation statement :

Stock on 1-1-1987	
Raw Material	4,000
Finished Stock	8,000
Stock on 31-12-1987	
Raw Material	6,000
Finished stock	2,000
Purchases of Raw materials	24,000
Wages	10,000
Sales	65,000
Factory overhead	7,750
Office Expenses	6,100

Selling price in fixed cost plus 25 per cent.

[Mysore, October 1988 (Modified), Gulbarga, 1988, April 1991]

Solution :

Statement of Cost and Profit

Raw materials : Opening stock	4,000	
Add : Purchases	24,000	
	28,000	
Less : Closing stock	6,000	
Raw material consumed		22,000
Wages		10,000
Prime Cost		32,000
Factory Overhead 25% on Prime cost of Rs. 32,000		8,000
Works Cost		40,000
Office Overhead 75% of factory overhead (75% of 8,000)		6,000
Cost of production		46,000
Add : Opening stock of finished goods		8,000
		54,000
Less : Closing stock Finished goods		2,000
Cost of production		52,000
Add : Profit 25% on cost (25% on 52,000)		13,000
Sales Price		65,000

Trading and Profit & Loss Account

Particulars	Amount	Particulars	Amount
To *Opening Stock*		By Sales	65,000
Raw material	4,000	By *Closing Stock*	
Finished Goods	8,000	Raw material	6,000
To Purchases	24,000	Finished goods	2,000
To Wages	10,000		
To Factory Expenses	7,750		
To Gross Profit	19,250		
	73,000		73,000
To Office Expenses	6,100	By Gross Profit	19,250
To Net Profit	13,150		
	19,250		19,250

Net Profit as per cost = Rs. 13,000

Net Profit as per Financial A/c 13,150

Reconciliation Statement

Particulars	Rs.	Rs.	Rs.
Net Profit as per Cost Account			13,000
Add : Over recovery of overheads in cost :			
Factory overhead in cost	8,000		
In Financial Account	7,750	250	+ 250
			13,250
Less : Under recovery of overhead in cost :			
Office overhead recovered in cost	6,000		
In Financial Account	6,100		– 100
Net Profit as per Financial Account			13,150

Problem No. 23

The profit disclosed by Financial Account was Rs. 8,900 for the year 1986 of Prasad Ltd.

From the following information prepare Profit Reconciliation Statement and find out Profit or Loss as per costing Books :

(1) Cver recovery of administrative overheads in Cost A/c Rs. 1,000
(2) Loss due to obsolescence charged in Financial A/c only Rs. 3,000
(3) Depreciation charged in Cost Accounts of Rs. 1,200
(4) Depreciation charged in Financial A/c was Rs. 850
(5) Interest on Investment received credited in Financial A/c Rs. 750
(6) Loss due to depletion in stock charged in Financial A/c. Rs. 600
(7) Works overhead under recovered in Cost A/c of Rs. 1,250
(8) Value of closing stock in Cost A/c of Rs. 19,000
(9) Value of closing stock in Financial A/c of Rs. 17,250.

(K.U.D., October 1987)

Solution :

Reconciliation Statement

Particulars	Rs.	Rs.	Rs.
Net Profit as per Financial Account			8,900
Add : (1) Under recovery of overhead in cost :			
Works cost		1,250	
(2) Items of expenses debited in Financial A/c :			
(a) Loss due to obsolescence charged in Financial A/c		3,000	
(b) Loss due to depletion in stock charged		600	

Particulars	Rs.	Rs.	Rs.
(3) Lower value of opening stock in cost		—	
(4) Higher value of closing stock in cost	19,000		
In Financial A/c	17,250	1,750	6,600
			15,500
Less : (1) Over recovery of overhead in cost :			
Administrative Overhead		1,000	
(2) Depreciation in Cost Account	1,200		
Financial Account	850	350	
(3) Items credited in Financial A/c :			
Interest recover		750	– 2,100
Profit as per Cost Account			13,400

Problem No. 24

Prakash Industries Ltd. Financial Account prepared the following Profit and Loss Account for the year 31-12-1986 :

Trading and Profit and Loss A/c for the year ended 31-12-1986

Particulars	Amount	Particulars	Amount
To Opening stock	2,47,179	By Sales	3,46,500
To Purchases	80,200	By Closing Stock	75,121
To Direct Wages	24,867		
To Factory Overhead	20,826		
To Gross Profit	48,329		
	4,21,621		4,21,621
To Administrative Exp.	9,845	By Gross Profit	48,329
To Selling Expenses	22,176	By Sundry Income	316
To Net Profit	16,624		
Total	48,645	Total	48,645

The Profit as per company Cost Account was Rs. 24,797.

The following additional information is available from costing records :

(a) Closing stock was Rs. 78,197.

(b) Factory overhead absorption was Rs. 19,714.

(c) Administration over absorption was @ 3% of the selling Price.

(d) Selling overhead was @ 5% on sales.

(e) No credit for sundry Income was given.

Prepare Reconciliation Statement.

(K.U.D., April 1987)

Solution :

Particulars	Financial A/c	Cost A/c	+ or – in Cost
(1) Closing Stock	75,121	78,197	3,076 Over charged
(2) Factory Overhead	20,826	19,714	1,112 Under charged
(3) Administration Expenses	9,845	10,395	550 Over charged
(4) Selling Overhead	22,176	17,325	4,851 Under charged
(5) Sundry Income	316	—	Income credited in Financial A/c.

Reconciliation Statement

Particulars	Rs.	Rs.	Rs.
Profit as per Cost Account			24,797
Add : Over absorption of overhead in cost :			
Administration Exp. in Cost	10,395		
Administration Exp. in Financial A/c	9,845	550	
(2) Items credit in Financial A/c Sundry Income		316	
(3) Over valuation of opening stock in Cost		—	
(4) Under valuation of closing stock in Cost		—	+ 866
			25,663
Less : Under absorption of overheads in cost :			
(a) Factory overhead in Cost	19,714		
Factory overhead in Financial A/c	20,826	1,112	
(b) Selling Exp. in Cost	17,325		
Selling Exp. in Financial A/c	22,176	4,851	
(2) Items debited in Financial A/c only		—	
(3) Under valuation opening stock in cost		—	
(4) Over valuation of closing stock in cost :			
In Cost A/c	78,197		
In Financial A/c	75,121	3,076	–9,039
Profit as per Financial Account			16,624

Problem No. 25

During the year a company's Profits have been estimated from the costing system to be Rs. 23,063 whereas the Financial Accounts prepared by the Auditors disclose a Profit of Rs. 16,624.

From the following information you are required to prepare a Reconciliation Statement showing reason for difference :

Profit and Loss A/c for the year ended 31-3-1980

Particulars		Amount	Particulars	Amount
To Opening stock	2,47,179		By Sales	3,46,500
Add : Purchases	82,154			
	3,29,333			
Less : Closing stock	75,121	2,54,212		
To Direct Wages		23,133		
To Factory overhead		20,826		
To Gross Profit c/d		48,329		
		3,46,500		3,46,500
To Administrative Exp.		9,845	By Gross Profit	48,329
To Selling Expenses		22,176	By Sundry Income	316
To Net Profit		16,624		
		48,645		48,645

The costing Records show :

(a) A stock Ledger closing stock Rs. 78,197.

(b) A Direct wages absorption A/c of Rs. 24,867.

(c) A Factory overhead absorption A/c of Rs. 19,714.

(d) Administration Expenses calculated @ 3% of Selling Price.

(e) Selling Expenses are 5% on sales.

(f) No mention of sundry Income.

(K.U.D., April 1987)

Solution :

Reconciliation Statement

Particulars	Rs.	Rs.	Rs.
Profit as per Cost Accounts			23,063
Add : (1) Over absorption of overhead in Cost A/c :			
(a) Direct wages Cost Account	24,867		
Direct wages in Financial Account	23,133	1,734	
(b) Administrative Expenses : in Cost A/c	10,395		
In Financial A/c	9,845	550	
(2) Items of income credited in Financial A/c only		316	
(3) Higher valuation of opening stock in cost		—	
(4) Lower valuation of closing stock in cost		—	+2,600
			25,663

Particulars	Rs.	Rs.	Rs.
			25,663
Less : (1) Under absorption of overhead in Cost A/c (Under recovery of overhead in Cost A/c) :			
(a) Factory overhead in Cost A/c	19,714		
Factory overhead in Financial A/c	20,826		
		1,112	
(b) Items Selling overhead :			
In Cost A/c	17,325		
In Financial Account	23,176		
		4,851	
(2) Items of Expenses and Less Debited in Financial Account only		—	
(3) Lower value of opening stock in Cost A/c		—	
(4) Higher value of closing stock in Cost A/c :			
In Cost Account	78,197		
In Financial Account	75,121	3,076	– 9,039
Profit as per Financial Account			16,624

Problem No. 26

The Net Profit of a company for the year ended 31-12-1980 as shown by the Cost Account was Rs. 6,89,600. A scrutiny of the figures from the Financial Books and the Cost Accounts revealed the following facts :

(1) Interest on Investment	32,000
(2) Loss due to Depreciation in stock value (Charged in Financial Account only)	27,000
(3) Works overhead under recovered in Cost A/c only	12,480
(4) Bank Interest and Dividend received	4,900
(5) Obsolescence loss charged in Financial A/c only	22,800
(6) Depreciation charged in Financial A/c only	44,800
(7) Depreciation recovered in Cost A/c	50,000
(8) Income Tax paid	1,61,200
(9) Administrative overheads over recovered in Cost A/c	6,800

Prepare Reconciliation Statement showing the profit as per Financial Account.

(K.U.D., October 1986)

Solution :

Reconciliation Statement

Particulars		Rs.	Rs.
Profit as per Cost Account			6,89,600
Add : (I) Over recovery of overhead :			
(a) Depreciation in Cost A/c	50,000		
Depreciation in Financial A/c	44,800	5,200	
(b) Over recovery of Administrative overhead		6,800	
(c) *Items Credited in Financial A/c only :*			
(1) Interest in Investment		32,000	
(2) Bank Interest and Divided credited		4,900	
(d) Higher value of opening stock in cost		—	
(e) Lower value of closing stock in cost		—	+48,900
			+7,38,500
Less : (II) (a) Under recovery of overhead in cost :			
Works overhead under recovery in cost		12,480	
(b) Items debited in Financial Account only :			
(1) Loss due to Depreciation in Stock value		27,000	
(2) Obsolescence loss charged in Financial A/c		22,800	
(3) Income tax paid debited in Financial A/c		1,61,200	
(c) Lower value of opening stock in cost		—	
(d) Higher value of closing stock in cost		—	−2,23,480
Profit as per Financial Account			5,15,020

Problem No. 27

The following figures relate to 31st December 1985 :

Particulars	Rs.
Sales for the year	1,60,000
Raw Materials	48,000
Wages	36,000

Works overhead and administrative overhead charged in Cost Account stand in 3 : 1 ratio sales price include 30 per cent Profit.

Actual expenses incurred were :

Manufacturing	26,000
Office	11,200

Find out the Profit as per Cost Accounts and Financial A/c. Reconcile the same.

(K.U.D., April 1986 & Gulbarga, 1993)

Solution :

Trading & Profit and Loss A/c for the year ended 31-12-1985

Particulars	Amount	Particulars	Amount
To Raw materials	48,000	By Sales	1,60,000
To Wages	36,000		
To Manufacturing Expenses	26,000		
To Gross Profit	50,000		
	1,60,000		1,60,000
To Office Expenses	11,200	By Gross Profit	50,000
To Net Profit	38,800		
	50,000		50,000

Statement of Cost and Profit

Raw Material		48,000
Wages		36,000
	Prime Cost	84,000
Works Overhead		21,000
	Works Cost	1,05,000
Administrative Overhead		7,000
	Total Cost	1,12,000
Profit 30% of sales 1,60,000		48,000
		1,60,000

Note : Ascertainment of works overhead and Administrative overhead :

Sales	1,60,000	
Less : Profit 30%	48,000	
Total Cost		1,12,000
Less : Prime Cost		84,000
Cost of Works overhead and Administrative		28,000

Works Overhead (3:1) $28{,}000 \times \frac{3}{4} = 21{,}000$

Administrative Overhead $28{,}000 \times \frac{1}{4} = 7{,}000$

Reconciliation Statement

Particulars		Rs.	Rs.
Net Profit as per Cost A/c		—	48,000
Add : (1) Over recovery of overhead in cost		—	
(2) Items credited in Financial A/c		—	
(3) Higher value of opening stock in cost		—	
(4) Lower value of closing stock in cost		—	—
			48,000
Less : (1) Under recovery of overhead in cost :			
(a) Manufacturing Expenses :			
In Financial Account	26,000		
In Cost Account	21,000	5,000	
(b) Administrative Expenses :			
In Financial Account	11,200		
In Cost Account	7,000	4,200	–9,200
Net Profit as per Financial Account			38,800

Problem No. 28

During a particular year the auditor certified the Financial Accounts showing a Profit of Rs. 1,68,000 whereas the same as per Cost accounting Rs. 2,40,000.

From the following information you are required to prepare a Reconciliation Statement :

Particulars	Amount	Particulars	Amount
To Opening stock	8,20,000	By Sales	34,65,000
To Purchases	24,72,000	By Closing Stock	7,50,000
To Direct Wages	2,30,000		
To Factory overheads	2,10,000		
To Gross Profit	4,83,000		
Total	42,15,000	Total	42,15,000
To Administrative Exp.	95,000	By Gross Profit B/d	4,83,000
To Selling Expenses	2,25,000	By Sundry Income	5,000
To Net Profit	1,68,000		
Total	4,88,000	Total	4,88,000

The Costing Records show :

(a) The Book value of closing stock Rs. 7,80,000

(b) Factory overheads has been absorbed Rs. 1,89,800

(c) Sundry Incomes not considered.

(d) Administrative Expenses are recovered @ 3% on selling price.

(e) Total Absorption of Direct wages — Rs. 2,46,000.

(f) Selling Price includes 5 per cent for selling Expenses

(K.U.D., October 1985)

Reconciliation Statement

Particulars	Rs.	Rs.	Rs.
Net Profit as per Cost Account			2,40,000
Add : (I) (a) Over recovery of overheads in cost :			
In Cost A/c	2,46,000		
In Financial A/c	2,30,000	16,000	
(b) Administrative Expenses			
@ 3% on 34,65,000 : In Cost A/c	1,03,950		
In Financial A/c	95,000	8,950	
(II) Incomes credited in Financial A/c only :			
Sundry Income		5,000	
(III) Higher value of opening stock in cost		—	
(IV) Lower value of closing stock in cost		—	29,950
			2,69,950
Less : (I) Under recovery overheads in cost :			
(a) Selling Expenses in Cost			
@ 5% on 34,65,000	1,73,250		
In Financial A/c	2,25,000	51,750	
(b) Factory overhead in cost	1,89,800		
In Financial Account only	2,10,000	20,200	
(II) Items debited in Financial A/c only		—	
(III) Lower value opening stock in cost		—	
(IV) Higher value in closing stock :			
In Cost A/c	7,80,000		
In Financial A/c	7,50,000	30,000	1,01,950
Net Profit as per Financial Account			1,68,000

Problem No. 29

Find out profits as per costing records and as per Financial Accounts from the following information and reconcile the results by preparing Reconciliation Statement :

Particulars	Products	
	Ball	Bat
Number of units produce and sold	900	600
	Rs.	Rs.
Total Direct Materials	5,400	4,200
Total Direct Wages	4,500	3,600
Selling Price per unit	37.50	45

Works on cost is charged @ 80 per cent of Direct Wages and Office on cost @ 25% of works cost.

Actual Works Expenses amounted to Rs. 6,750 and Office Expenses Rs. 5,850. There was no opening and closing stock.

(K.U.D., April 1985)

Solution :

Statement of Cost and Profit

Particulars	Ball	Bat	Total
No. of units produced	900	600	
Direct Material	5,400	4,200	9,600
Direct Wages	4,500	3,600	8,100
Prime Cost	9,900	7,800	17,700
Works on cost 80% of Direct Wages :			
Ball : 80% of 4,500	3,600		
Bat : 80% of 3,600		2,880	6,480
Works Cost	13,500	10,680	24,180
Office Overhead 25% on Works cost :			
Ball : 25% on 13,500 = 3,375	3,375		
Bat : 25% on 10,680 = 2,670		2,670	6,045
Total cost or Cost of production	16,875	13,350	30,225
Sales Ball : 37.50 × 900	33,750		
Bat : 45 × 600		27,000	60,750
Profit	16,875	13,650	30,525

Trading and Profit and Loss Account

Particulars		Amount	Particulars	Amount
To Direct Material			By Sales	
Ball	5,400		Ball 37.50 × 900	33,750
Bat	4,200	9,600	Bat 45 × 600	27,000
To Direct Wages				
Ball	4,500			
Bat	3,600	8,100		
To Works Exp.		6,750		
To Gross Profit		36,300		
		60,750		60,750
To Office Expenses		5,850	By Gross Profit	36,300
To Net Profit		30,450		
		36,300		36,300

Reconciliation Statement

Particulars	Rs.	Rs.	Rs.
Net Profit as per Cost Account			30,525
Add : (1) Over recovery of overheads in cost :			
Office Overhead recovery in cost	6,045		
In Financial Account	5,850	195	
(2) Items credited in Financial Account only		—	
(3) Over valuation of opening stock in cost		—	
(4) Lower valuation of closing stock in cost		—	+ 195
			30,720
Less : (1) Under recovery of overhead in cost :			
Works Expenses recovered in cost	6,480		
In Financial Account	6,750	270	
(2) Items debited in Financial Account only		—	
(3) Low valuation of opening stock in cost		—	
(4) Higher valuation of closing stock in cost		—	– 270
Net Profit as per Financial Account			30,450

Problem No. 30

Profit disclosed by the company's cost Books amounted for the year ended 31-12-82 was Rs. 1,00,000. Whereas the Net Profit as disclosed by the Financial Accounts was Rs. 59,500.

Following information is available :

(a) Provision for Income Tax was Rs. 30,000

(b) Shares transfer fees received during the year Rs. 2,000

(c) Director fees show in Financial Account Rs. 4,000

(d) Provision for doubtful debts Rs. 10,000

(e) Overhead as per Cost accounts of Rs. 17,000
Overhead as per Financial Account — Rs. 14,000

(f) Work was commenced during the year.

On a New factory an expenditure of Rs. 60,000 was made depreciation at Rs. 5% per annum was provided for the Financial Account for 6 months.

From the above information prepare a Statement of Reconciliation.

(K.U.D., October 1984)

Solution :

Reconciliation Statement

Particulars	Rs.	Rs.	Rs.
Profit as per Cost Account			1,00,000
Add : (1) Over recovery of overhead in cost :			
Overhead in Cost	17,000		
Overhead in Financial A/c	14,000	3,000	
(2) Items credited in Financial A/c shares transfer fees.		2,000	
(3) Higher value of opening stock in cost		—	
(4) Lower value of closing stock in cost		—	+5,000
			1,05,000
Less : (1) Under recovery of overheads in cost		—	
(2) Items of Expenses debited in Financial A/c :			
(a) Income tax provision		30,000	
(b) Directors fees		4,000	
(c) Provision for Doubtful Debts		10,000	
(d) Depreciation on 60,000 at 5% $60{,}000 \times \frac{5}{100} = 3{,}000 \times ½$		1,500	
(3) Lower value of opening stock in Cost A/c		—	
(4) Higher value of closing stock in Cost A/c		—	−45,500
Profit as per Financial Account			59,500

Problem No. 31

The Net Profit of Shakti Automobile Manufacturing Co. Ltd., operated at Rs. 64,500 as per financial accounts for the year ended 31-12-1982. The cost Books however, showed a Net Profit of Rs. 86,460 for the same period. A careful scrutiny of the figures from both the sets of accounts revealed the following facts :

(1)	Income tax provided in Financial Account	20,000
(2)	Bank interest credited in Financial Account	250
(3)	Works overhead under recovered in cost	1,550
(4)	Depreciation charged in Financial books	5,600
(5)	Depreciation recovered in cost	6,000
(6)	Administrative overhead over recovered in cost	850
(7)	Loss due to obsolescence charged in Financial Accounts	2,800
(8)	Interest on investments not included in cost	4,000
(9)	Stores adjustments credited in Financial Accounts	240
(10)	Loss due to depreciation in stock value charged in Financial Accounts	3,350

(K.U.D., April 1984 & Gulbarga, April 1991)

Solution :

Reconciliation Statement

Particulars	Rs.	Rs.	Rs.
Net Profit as per Financial Account			64,500
Add : (1) Under recovery of overhead in cost :			
Works overhead under recovery in cost		1,550	
(2) Items debited in Financial Account only :			
(a) Income tax provided		20,000	
(b) Loss due to obsolescence charged		2,800	
(c) Loss due to depreciation in stock value	3,350		
(3) Lower value of opening stock in cost		—	
(4) Higher value of closing stock in cost		—	+27,700
			92,200
Less : (1) Over recovery of overhead in cost :			
(a) Administrative overhead over recovered in cost		850	
(b) Depreciation recovered in cost	6,000		
Depreciation charged in Financial A/c	5,600	400	
(2) Items credited in Financial A/c only :			
(a) Bank interest		250	
(b) Interest on Investment		4,000	
(c) Stores Adjustment (credited in Financial)		240	
(3) Higher value of opening stock in cost		—	
(4) Lower value of closing stock in cost		—	– 5,740
Net Profit as per Cost Account			86,460

Problem No. 32

From the details given below ascertain the profit as per Financial Accounts :

	Cost A/c	Financial A/c
(1) Opening Stock	28,000	30,000
(2) Closing Stock	32,000	30,000
(3) Interest charged but not yet paid	—	10,000
(4) Preliminary Expenses written off	—	500
(5) Goodwill written off	—	1,500
(6) Dividend received	—	1,000
(7) Works overhead recovered	75,500	80,000
(8) Profit	98,350	?

(Mysore, October 1984)

Solution :

Reconciliation Statement

Particulars	Rs.	Rs.	Rs.
Net Profit as per Cost Account			98,350
Add : (1) Over recovery of overheads in cost		—	
(2) Items credited in Financial Account only :			
Dividend received		1,000	
(3) Higher value of opening stock in cost		—	
(4) Lower value of closing stock in cost		—	+1,000
			99,350
Less : (1) Under recovery of overheads in cost :			
Works overhead recovered in cost	75,500		
Recovered in Financial Account	80,000	4,500	
(2) Item debited in Financial Account only :			
(a) Interest charged		10,000	
(b) Preliminary Expenses written off		500	
(c) Goodwill written off		1,500	
(3) Lower value of opening stock cost :			
(a) Opening stock in cost	28,000		
In Financial Account	30,000	2,000	
(4) Higher value of closing stock in cost :			
Closing stock in cost	32,000		
In Financial Account	30,000	2,000	−20,500
Net Profit as per Financial Account			78,850

Problem No. 33

M/s Ajanta Traders have furnished the following information. Financial Books for the year ended 30th June 1983 :

Trading and Profit and Loss Account for the year ended 30-6-1983

Particulars	Amount	Particulars	Amount
To Opening Stock (500 units @ Rs. 35)	17,500	By Sales (10250 Units)	7,17,500
		By Closing stock (250 units @ Rs. 50 each)	12,500
To Materials consumed	2,60,000		
To Wages	1,50,000		
To Gross Profit	3,02,500		
	7,30,000		7,30,000
To Factory Overhead	94,700	By Gross Profit	3,02,500
To Office Overhead	1,06,000	By Interest	250
To Selling Expenses	55,000	By Rent	10,000
To Bad Debts	4,000		
To Goodwill written off	5,000		
To Net Profit	48,050		
	3,12,750		3,12,750

The cost sheet shows the following :

(a) Cost of materials @ Rs. 26 per unit on unit produced. Labour cost Rs. 15 per unit on units produced.

(b) Factory overheads are absorbed @ 60% of labour cost.

(c) Office overheads are absorbed @ 20% on works cost.

(d) Selling expenses are charged @ Rs. 6 per unit.

(e) Opening stock of finished goods valued at Rs. 45 per unit.

(f) You are required to prepare :

(i) A Statement of Cost and Profit as per Cost Account for the year ended 30-6-1983 and

(ii) A Statement showing Reconciliation of Profits in Cost and Financial Account.

(Mysore, April 1984)

Solution :

Working Note

Calculation of Units Produced :	
Sales in units	10250
Add : Closing stock	250
	10500
Less : Opening Stock	500
Units produced during the year	10000

Statement of Cost and Profit for the year ended 30-6-83

Particulars		Rs.	Rs.
(1) Materials consumed	(10000 Units @ Rs. 26 each)	2,60,000	
(2) Wages	(10000 Units @ Rs. 15 each)	1,50,000	
	Prime Cost		4,10,000
(3) Factory Overhead @ 60% of Labour cost	(1,50,000 × 60%)		90,000
	Works Cost		5,00,000
(4) Office Overhead 20% on works cost (5,00,000 × 20%)			1,00,000
	Total cost or cost of production		6,00,000

$$\text{Cost per unit} = \frac{6,00,000}{10,000} = \text{Rs. 60 per unit}$$

Add : Opening stock of Finished goods (500 × 45)	22,500
	6,22,500
Less : Closing stock of Finished goods (250 × 60)	15,000
Cost of goods sold	6,07,500
Selling Exp. (10250 units @ Rs. 6 per unit)	61,500
Cost of goods sold	6,69,000
Sales Price (Sales price per unit of Rs. 70)	7,17,500
Net Profit as per Cost A/c	48,500

Opening Stock	500
Add : Units Produced	10000
	10500
Less : Closing stock	250
Units Sold	10250

Reconciliation Statement

Particulars	Rs.	Rs.	Rs.
Net Profit as per Cost Account			48,500
Add :			
(1) Over recovery of overhead in cost :			
Selling Expenses in cost	61,500		
In Financial Account	55,000	6,500	
(2) Items credited in Financial Account only :			
Interest		250	
Rent		10,000	
(3) Higher value of opening stock in cost :			
Opening stock in cost	22,500		
In Financial Account	17,500	5,000	
(4) Lower value of closing stock in cost :		—	+21,750
			70,250
Less :			
(1) Under recovery of overhead in cost :			
(a) Factory overhead in cost	90,000		
In Financial Account	94,700	4,700	
(b) Office overhead recovered :			
In cost	1,00,000		
In Financial Account	1,06,000	6,000	
(2) Items debited in Financial Account only :			
Bad Debts		4,000	
Goodwill written off		5,000	
(3) Lower value of opening stock in cost		—	
(4) Higher value of closing stock in cost :			
Closing stock in cost	15,000		
In Financial Account	12,500	2,500	– 22,200
Net Profit as per Financial Account			48,050

Problem No. 34

In a factory works overheads are absorbed 60 per cent of the labour and office over expenses @ 20% of works cost. The total expenditure is as follows :

Materials	2,00,000
Labour	1,50,000
Factory Expenses	98,000
Office Expenses	85,000

10 per cent of output is in stock at the end and the total sales value of Rs. 5,10,000.

Prepare a statement of showing the profits as per Cost Accounts and Financial Accounts and Reconcile the profits of both.

(K.U.D., April 1983)

Trading and Profit and Loss Account

Particulars	Amount	Particulars	Amount
To Materials	2,00,000	By Sales	5,10,000
To Labour	1,50,000	By Closing Stock (10% of production cost 48,000 × 10%)	44,800
To Factory Expenses	98,000		
	4,48,000		
To Gross Profit	1,06,800		
	5,54,800		5,54,800
To Office Expenses	85,000	By Gross Profit	1,06,800
To Net Profit	21,800		
	1,06,800		1,06,800

Statement of Cost and Profit

Material	2,00,000
Labour	1,50,000
Prime Cost	3,50,000
Factory overhead 60% of Labour cost (1,50,000 × 60%)	90,000
Works Cost	4,40,000
Office Expenses 20% of works cost (4,40,000 × 20%)	88,000
Cost of production	5,28,000
Less : Closing stock of Finished goods 10% of 5,28,000	52,800
Cost of goods sold	4,75,200
Sales Value	5,10,000
Profit	34,800

Reconciliation Statement

Particulars	Rs.	Rs.	Rs.
Net Profit as per Cost Account			34,800
Add : (1) Over recovery of overheads in cost :			
Office Expenses recovered in cost	88,000		
In Finanical Account	85,000	3,000	
(2) Items credited in Financial Account only		—	
(3) Higher value of opening stock in cost		—	
(4) Lower value of closing stock in cost		—	+3,000
			37,800
Less : (1) Under recovery of overhead in cost :			
Factory overhead in cost	90,000		
In Financial Account	98,000	8,000	
(2) Items debited in Financial Account only		—	
(3) Lower value of opening stock in cost		—	
(4) Higher value of closing stock in cost :			
Closing stock in cost	52,800		
In Financial Account	44,800	8,000	– 16,000
Net Profit as per Financial Account			21,800

Problem No. 35

In a Factory workers overhead are absorbed 60% of Labour and Office Expenses @ 20% on works cost.

The total expenditures are as follows :

Material	9,00,000
Labour	6,75,000
Factory Expenses	4,41,000
Office Expenses	3,82,500
Total	23,98,500

10 per cent of the output is in stock at the end and the total sales valued at Rs. 22,95,000. Prepare a Statement showing the profit as per Financial Account and Cost Account and prepare Reconciliation Statement of the two Profits.

[K.U.D., April 1983 (Modified)]

Solution :

Profit and Loss A/c

Particulars	Amount	Particulars	Amount
To Materials	9,00,000	By Sales	22,95,000
To Labour	6,75,000	By Closing stock	2,01,600
To Factory Expenses	4,41,000	10% of output	
To Office Expenses	3,82,500	(9,00,000 + 6,75,000 +	
To Net Profit	98,100	4,41,000 = 20,16,000)	
		10% of 20,16,000	
Total	24,96,600	Total	24,96,600

Statement of Cost and Profit

Materials	9,00,000	
Labour	6,75,000	
Prime Cost		15,75,000
Works on Cost 60% of 6,75,000 =		4,05,000
Works Cost		19,80,000
Office Overheads : 20% of 19,80,000		3,96,000
Cost of Production		23,76,000
Less : Closing stock of Finished goods 10% of 23,76,000		2,37,600
Cost of Goods sold		21,38,400
Sales Price		22,95,000
Net Profit		1,56,600

Reconciliation Statement

Particulars	Rs.	Rs.	Rs.
Net Profit as per Cost Account			1,56,600
Add : (1) Over recovery of overhead in cost :			
Office overhead in Cost	3,96,000		
In Financial A/c	3,82,500	13,500	
(2) Items credited in Financial A/c only		—	
(3) Higher value of opening stock in cost		—	
(4) Lower value of closing stock in cost		—	+ 13,500
			1,70,100

Particulars	Rs.	Rs.	Rs.
			1,70,100
Less : (1) Under recovery of overheads in cost :			
In Financial Factory overheads	4,41,000		
In Cost Factory overheads	4,05,000	36,000	
(2) Items debited in Financial A/c only		—	
(3) Lower value of opening stock in cost			
(4) Higher value of closing stock in cost :			
Closing stock in cost	2,37,600		
Closing stock in Financial	2,01,600	36,000	– 72,000
Net Profit as per Financial Account			98,100

Problem No. 36

The Net Profit of the Manufacturing Co. Ltd. appeared at Rs. 64,377 as per Financial records for the year ended 31-12-1974. The cost books showed a net profit of Rs. 86,200 for same period. A scrutiny of the figures from both the sets of accounts revealed the following facts :

		Rs.
(1)	Works overhead under recovered in cost	1,560
(2)	Administrative overheads over recovered in cost	850
(3)	Depreciation charged in Financial Accounts	5,600
(4)	Depreciation recovered in cost	6,250
(5)	Interest on Investment not included in cost	4,000
(6)	Loss due to obsolescence charged in Financial A/c	2,850
(7)	Income provided in Financial Account	20,150
(8)	Bank interest and transfer fees in Financial A/c	375
(9)	Stores adjustment (credited in Financial A/c)	237
(10)	Loss due to depreciation in stock values (Charged in Financial Account)	3,375

(K.U.D., October 1982)

Solution :

Reconciliation Statement

Particulars		Rs.	Rs.
Net Profit as per Financial Account			64,377
Add : (1) Under recovery of overheads in cost :			
Works overhead under recovered in cost		1,560	
(2) Items debited in Financial Account only :			
(a) Loss due to obsolescence charged		2,850	
(b) Income Tax provided		20,150	
(c) Loss due to depreciation in stock		3,375	
(3) Lower value of opening stock in cost		—	
(4) Higher value of closing stock in cost		—	+27,935
			92,312
Less : (1) Over recovery of overhead in cost :			
(a) Administrative overhead		850	
(b) Depreciation recovered in cost	6,250		
Depreciation charged in Financial	5,600	650	
(2) Items credited in Financial Account only :			
(a) Interest on investment		4,000	
(b) Bank interest & Transfer fees		375	
(c) Stores adjustment credited in Financial A/c			237
(3) Higher value of opening stock in cost		—	
(4) Lower value of closing stock in cost		—	− 6,112
Net Profit as per Cost Account			86,200

Problem No. 37

Prepare profits reconciliation statement between Cost and Financial A/cs.

(1) Net Profit as per Cost Account	1,72,400
(2) Works overheads under recovered in cost	3,120
(3) Depreciation over charged in cost	1,300
(4) Over recovery of office overhead in cost	1,700
(5) Depreciation on stock charged in Financial books	6,750
(6) Profit on sale of Land included in Financial books	475
(7) Goodwill written off in Financial books	5,700
(8) Interest on investment credited in Financial books	8,750
(9) Income Tax paid debited in Financial books	40,300

(K.U.D., April 1982)

Solution :

Reconciliation Statement

Particulars	Rs.	Rs.
Net Profit as per Cost Account		1,72,400
Add : (1) Over recovery of overheads in cost :		
(a) Depreciation over charged in cost	1,300	
(b) Over recovery of office overhead in cost	1,700	
(2) Items credited in Financial A/c only :		
(a) Profit on sale of Land	475	
(b) Interest on investment	8,750	
(3) Higher value of opening stock in cost	—	
(4) Lower value of closing stock in cost	—	+ 12,225
		1,84,625
Less : (1) Under recovery of overhead in cost :		
Works overhead under recovered in cost	3,120	
(2) Items debited in Financial A/c only :		
(a) Depreciation on stock value charged in Financial books	6,750	
(b) Goodwill written off	5,700	
(c) Income tax paid	40,300	
(3) Lower value of opening stock in cost	—	
(4) Higher value of closing stock in cost	—	− 55,870
Net Profit as per Financial Account		1,28,755

Problem No. 38

The financial Profit and Loss Account of a manufacturing company for the year ended 31st March 1980 is given below :

Trading and Profit and Loss A/c for the year ended 31-3-1980

Particulars		Amount	Particulars		Amount
To Opening stock :			By Sales		4,60,000
Raw materials	25,000		By Closing stock		
Works-in-progress	12,500		Raw material	30,000	
Finished stock	40,000	77,500	Works-in-progress	20,700	
To Purchases		1,20,000	Finished stock	15,000	65,700
To Wages		30,000			
To Electric power (Factory)		65,000			

Particulars	Amount	Particulars	Amount
To Factory overhead	45,000		
To Gross profit	1,88,200		
	5,25,700		5,25,700
To Administrative Exp.	20,500	By Gross Profit	1,88,200
To Selling Expenses	46,500	By Miscellaneous Revenue	26,800
To Bad debts	15,600		
To Net Profit	1,32,400		
	2,15,000		2,15,000

To cost account of the company showed the costing records as the following :

(a) Works overheads are recovered @ 75 per cent of Prime cost.

(b) Office on costs absorbed @ 20% on works cost.

(c) Selling and distribution overheads @ 8% on sales.

You are required to prepare Cost statement and show Cost profit and also reconcile the Cost profit with Financial profit.

[C.A. Final (Modified)]

Solution :

Statement of Cost and Profit for the year ended 31-3-1980

(1) Raw materials :		
Opening stock	25,000	
Add : Purchases	1,20,000	
	1,45,000	
Less : Closing stock	30,000	
Raw materials consumed		1,15,000
(2) Wages		30,000
Prime Cost		1,45,000
(3) Factory overhead Work-in-progress (75% of prime cost — 75% × 1,45,000)		1,08,750
Works Cost		2,53,750
Add : Opening stock		12,500
		2,66,250
Less : Closing stock		20,700
Total Works Cost		2,45,550
(4) Office overhead Finished stock (20% on works cost : 20% of 2,45,550)		49,110
Cost of Production		2,94,660

	2,94,669
Add : Opening stock	40,000
	3,34,660
Less : Closing stock	15,000
Total cost of finished goods	3,19,660
(5) Selling and Distribution overhead (8% on sales value : 8% × 4,60,000)	36,800
Total cost of sales	3,56,460
Sales value	4,60,000
Net Profit as per Cost Account	1,03,540

Reconciliation Statement

Particulars	Rs.	Rs.	Rs.
Net Profit as per Cost Account			1,03,540
Add : (1) Over recovery of overhead in cost :			
Office overhead in cost	49,110		
In Financial Account	20,500	28,610	
(2) Items credited in Financial A/c only			
Miscellaneous Revenue		26,800	
(3) Higher value of opening stock in cost		—	
(4) Lower value of closing stock in cost		—	55,410
			1,58,950
Less : (1) Under recovery of overheads in cost :			
(a) Factory overhead in cost	1,08,750		
In Financial Account (Power + Factory overhead 65,000 + 45,000)	1,10,000	1250	
(b) Selling and Distribution overhead :			
In Cost Account	36,800		
In Financial Account	46,500	9,700	
(2) Items debited in Financial A/c only		15,600	
(3) Lower value of opening stock in cost		—	
(4) Higher value of closing stock in cost		—	– 26,550
Net Profit as per Financial A/c			1,32,400

Problem No. 39

The following figures were available in receipt of Amat Engineering Co. for year ended 31-3-1989 :

	Particulars	Financial A/c	Cost A/c
(1)	*Opening Stock :*		
	Raw materials	18,000	15,000
	Work-in-progress	21,000	19,500
	Finished stock	15,000	13,500
(2)	*Closing Stock :*		
	Raw Materials	12,000	12,900
	Work-in-progress	9,000	11,100
	Finished stock	17,700	18,600
(3)	Purchases	1,20,000	
(4)	Direct Wages	60,000	
(5)	Indirect Wages	9,000	
(6)	Factory Expenses	51,000	65,000 Absorbed
(7)	Selling Expenses	12,000	14,500 Absorbed
(8)	Administrative Expenses	15,400	12,800 Absorbed
(9)	Reserve for Doubtful debts	5,000	
(10)	Interest and dividend received	4,500	
(11)	Transfer to Reserve	11,000	
(12)	Dividends	25,000	
(13)	Sales	3,60,000	
(14)	Last year Profit	24,000	

Compute Profit in Financial Account as well as in Cost Accounts and prepare Reconciliation Statement.

Solution :

Statement of Cost and Profit

Particulars	Rs.	Rs.
Raw Materials :		
Opening stock	15,000	
Add : Purchases	1,20,000	
	1,35,000	
Less : Closing stock	12,900	
Material consumed		1,22,100
Direct Wages		60,000
Prime Cost		1,82,100
Factory Overhead		65,000
Works Cost		2,47,100
Add : *Work-in-Progress*		
Opening stock		19,500
		2,66,600
Less : Closing stock		11,100
Net Works Cost		2,55,500
Add : Administrative overhead		12,800
Total Cost		2,68,300
Add : Finished opening stock		13,500
		2,81,800
Less : Closing Stock		18,600
Total cost of Finished goods sold		2,63,200
Add : Selling Overhead		14,500
Cost of Sales		2,77,700
Sales Price		3,60,000
Profit as per Cost Account		82,300

Trading A/c for the year ended 31-3-1989

Particulars	Amount	Particulars	Amount
To Opening stock	54,000	By Sales	3,60,000
To Purchases	1,20,000	By Closing Stock	38,700
To Direct wages	60,000		
To Indirect wages	9,000		
To Factory Expenses	51,000		
To Gross Profit	1,04,700		
Total	3,98,700	Total	3,98,700

Profit & Loss A/c for the year ended 31-3-1989

Particulars	Amount	Particulars	Amount
To Administrative Expenses	15,400	By Gross Profit	1,04,700
To Selling Expenses	12,000	By Interest and Dividend received	4,500
To R.D.D.	5,000	By Profit Last year Balance	24,000
To Transfer to Reserve	11,000		
To Dividend	25,000		
To Net Profit	64,800		
Total	1,33,200	Total	1,33,200

Working Notes

	Cost	Financial	Difference	
(1) Opening Stock	48,000	54,000	(–) 6,000	Less
(2) Closing stock	42,600	38,700	+ 3,900	More
Overheads :				
(1) Factory Expenses	65,000	60,000	+ 5,000	More
(2) Administrative Exp.	12,800	15,400	– 2,600	Less
(3) Selling Expenses	14,500	12,000	+ 2,500	More

Reconciliation Statement

Particulars	Rs.	Rs.
Profit as per Financial Account		64,800
Add : Under recovery of overhead		
(a) Administrative Expenses	2,600	
(b) Items debited in Financial Account :		
(a) R.D.D.	5,000	
(b) Transfer to Reserve	11,000	
(c) Dividend	25,000	
(3) Lower value of opening stock	6,000	
(4) Higher value of closing stock	3,900	+ 53,500
		1,18,300
Less : Over recovery of overheads :		
(1) Factory Expenses	5,000	
(2) Selling Expenses	2,500	
(3) Items credited in Financial A/c	4,500	
Financial A/c	24,000	–36,000
Profit as per Cost Account		82,300

Problem No. 40

The following is the summary of the Trading and Profit and Loss Account of X Co. Ltd. for the year ending 31-12-1984 :

Trading and Profit & Loss Account

Particulars	Amount	Particulars		Amount
To Materials consumed	27,40,000	By Sales (120000 Units)		60,00,000
To Wages	15,10,000	By Finished Stock (4000 units)		1,60,000
To Factory Expenses	8,30,000	By Work-in-progress :		
To Administration Exp.	3,82,400	Materials	64,000	
To Selling Distribution Expenses	4,50,000	Wages	36,000	
		Factory Exp.	20,000	1,20,000
To Preliminary Expenses (Written off)	40,000	By Dividend Received		18,000
To Goodwill written off	20,000			
To Net Profit	3,25,600			
Total	62,98,000	Total		62,98,000

The company manufactures standard units in the Cost Account :

(1) Factory Expenses have been allocated to the production @ 20% on Prime Cost.

(2) Administration Expenses @ Rs. 3 per unit on units produced.

(3) Selling and Distribution Expenses @ Rs. 4 per unit on units sold.

You are required to prepare Statement of Cost and Profit in the Cost Books of the Company and reconcile the Profit disclosed by the Financial A/c.

Solution :

Statement of Cost and Profit

Units Sold	1,20,000	
Finished Stock	4,000	
	1,24,000	Units Produced.

	Rs.	Rs.
Materials	27,40,000	
Wages	15,10,000	
Prime Cost		42,50,000
Factory Overheads (20% on Prime cost 42,50,000)		8,50,000
		51,00,000
Less : Works-in-progress closing stock (64,000 + 36,000 + 20,000)		1,20,000
Works Cost		49,80,000

	Rs.
	49,80,000
Administrative Overheads Rs. 3 per unit on units produced (124000 × 3)	3,72,000
Cost of Production	53,52,000
Less : Finished stock 4000 units $= \left(\frac{4000}{124000} \times 53,52,000\right) =$	1,72,645
Cost of Goods sold (Units sold = 120000)	51,79,355
Selling and distribution Expenses Rs. 4 per unit On units sold (120000 × 4)	4,80,000
	56,59,355
Sales 120000 units	60,00,000
Profit as per Cost Account	3,40,645

Reconciliation Statement

Particulars	Rs.	Rs.	Rs.
Profit as per Cost Account			3,40,645
Add : (1) Over recovery of overheads in cost :			
Factory Overhead in cost	8,50,000		
In Financial A/c	8,30,000	20,000	
Selling and Distribution in Cost	4,80,000		
In Financial A/c	4,50,000	30,000	
(2) Items credited in Financial A/c only :			
Dividend received		18,000	+ 68,000
			4,08,645
Less : (1) Under recovery of overheads in cost :			
Administrative Expenses : in cost	3,72,000		
In Financial A/c	3,82,000	10,400	
(2) Items debited in Financial A/c only :			
Preliminary Expenses	40,000		
Goodwill written off	20,000		
(3) Higher value of closing stock in cost :			
Cost Account	1,72,645		
Financial A/c	1,60,000	12,645	− 83,045
Net Profit as per Financial Account			3,25,600

Problem No. 41

Following is the summary of Trading and Profit and Loss A/c for the year ended 31-12-1990 :

Trading Account for the year ended 31-12-90

Particulars		Amount	Particulars	Amount
To Stock on 1-1-90		7,500	By Sales (315000 Units @ Rs. 1.5 each)	4,72,500
To Purchases	2,05,000			
Less : Returns	2,500	2,02,500		
To Factory Expenses		15,750	By Stock on 31-12-90	12,750
To Wages		63,750		
To Depreciation on Plant		18,300		
To Gross Profit		1,77,450		
Total		4,85,250	Total	4,85,250

Profit and Loss A/c for the year ended 31-12-90

Particulars	Amount	Particulars	Amount
To Office Expenses	32,685	By Gross Profit	1,77,450
To Selling and Distribution Expenses	51,330	By Profit sale of Land	3,750
To Reserve for bad debts	2,000	By Interest on Investment	1,875
To Loss on sale of Investments	1,500		
To Interest on Bank Overdraft	705		
To Goodwill written off	4,000		
To Net Profit	90,855		
Total	1,83,075	Total	1,83,075

Note : Stock valuation is done as under :

	Opening	Closing stock
Material	4,050	6,300
Labour	2,250	3,600
Overheads	1,200	2,250
	7,500	12,750

In Cost Account : (a) Recovery rate applied were :

Factory on Cost @ 5% of sales. Selling and Distribution on cost @ 12% of sales.

(b) Stock is valued at Prime cost only.

(c) Non cost items should strictly be excluded.

Ascertain Profit shown by Cost A/c by preparing Reconciliation Statement.

Solution :

Calculations : Stock in cost valued at Prime Cost only.

	Opening stock	Closing stock
Materials	4,050	6,900
Labour	2,250	3,600
	6,300	10,500

Differences	Cost A/c	Financial A/c	+ or – in Cost A/c
(1) Stock valued : Opening	6,300	7,500	– 1,200 (Loss)
(2) Closing	10,500	12,750	– 2,250 (Loss)
Overheads Recovery :			
(3) Factory Overhead (5% on 4,72,500)	23,625	15,750	+ 7,875 (More)
(4) Office Overhead	28,000	32,685	– 4,685 (Loss)
(5) Selling & Distribution (12% on 4,72,500)	56,700	51,330	+ 5,370 (More)

Reconciliation Statement

Particulars	Rs.	Rs.	Rs.
Profit as per Financial Account			90,855
Add : (1) Under recovery of overhead in cost :			
Office overhead		4,685	
(2) Items debited in Financial A/c only :			
(a) R.D.D.	2,000		
(b) Interest on Bank Overdraft	705		
(c) Loss on sale of Investment	1,500		
(d) Goodwill — written off	4,000	8,205	
(3) Lower value of opening stock in cost		1,200	
(4) Higher value of closing stock in cost		—	+ 14,090
			1,04,945
Less : (1) Over recovery of overhead in cost :			
(a) Factory Overhead		7,875	
(b) Selling & Distribution Overhead		5,370	
(2) Items credited in Financial A/c only :			
(a) Profit on sale of land		3,750	
(b) Interest on Investment		1,875	
(3) Higher of opening stock in cost		—	
(4) Lower value of closing stock in cost		2,250	– 21,120
Profit as per Cost A/c			83,825

Note : Depreciation on Plant is a cost item. Therefore it is considered and charged in cost.

Problem No. 42

The Net Profit of A Co. Ltd. showed Rs. 90,978 as per Financial records for the year ended 1990.

The Cost books however showed a Net Profit of Rs. 1,29,300 for the same period.

A scrutiny of the figures from the both the sets of Books of Accounts revealed the following facts :

(1)	Works overhead under recovered in Cost	2,340
(2)	Administrative overhead over recovered in cost	1,275
(3)	(a) Depreciation charged in Financial A/c	8,400
	(b) Depreciation recovered in Cost A/c	9,375
(4)	Interest on Investment not included in cost	6,000
(5)	Loss due to obsolescence charged in Financial A/c	4,275
(6)	Income Tax provided in Financial A/c	30,225
(7)	Bank Interest and Transfer fees in Financial Account credited	562
(8)	Stores Adjustment (credited) in Financial A/c	356
(9)	Value of opening stock : in Cost Account	37,200
	in Financial Account	39,450
(10)	Value of closing stock : in Cost Account	37,500
	In Financial A/c	34,500
(11)	Interest charged in Cost Account only	3,000
(12)	Goodwill written off	7,500
(13)	Loss on sale of furniture	900

Prepare a statement showing Reconciliation between the fiures of Net Profit as per Cost Accounts and the Financial Account.

Solution :

Reconciliation Statement

Particulars	Rs.	Rs.	Rs.
Net Profit as per Cost Account			1,29,300
Add : (1) Over recovery of overheads in Cost A/c			
(a) Administrastive overhead over recovered in Cost Account		1,275	
(b) Depreciation : In Financial A/c	8,400		
In Cost A/c	9,375		
Over recovered in Cost		975	
(2) Items credited in Financial A/c only :			
(a) Interest on Investment not included		6,000	

Particulars	Rs.	Rs.	Rs.
(b) Bank Interest and transfer fees credited in Financial Account		562	
(c) Stores Adjustment credited in Financial A/c		356	
(3) Items debited in Cost A/c only :			
Interest charged in Cost A/c only		3,000	
(4) Higher value of opening stock in cost		—	
(5) Higher value of closing stock in cost		—	+ 12,168
			1,41,468
Less : (1) Under recovery of overheads in cost :			
Works overhead under recovered in cost		2,340	
(2) Items of expenses debited in Financial A/c :			
(a) Income Tax provided in Financial A/c		30,225	
(b) Loss due to obsolescence		4,275	
(c) Goodwill written off		7,500	
(d) Loss on sale of Furniture		900	
(3) Lower value of opening stock in cost :			
Value of opening stock in cost	37,200		
Value of opening stock in Financial	39,450	2,250	
(4) Higher value of closing stock in cost	37,500		
Higher value of closing stock in Financial	34,500	3,000	– 50,490
Net Profit as per Financial Account			90,978

Problem No. 43

From the following particulars of Ashok Engineering Works Ltd. compute profit in Financial Account as well as Cost Accounts and reconcile profits between Cost and Financial Accounts showing reasons for variation in two Profit figures :

Sales	3,00,000
Purchases of raw materials	4,50,000
Closing stock raw materials	7,500
Direct wages	15,000
Indirect wages	7,500
Indirect Expenses	30,000
Bad Debts	1,500
Interest on Bank Loan	750
Profit on sale of assets	15,000

Selling Expenses	30,000
Distribution Expenses	15,000

In Cost Account :

(a) Manufacturing overhead recovered @ 300% of Direct Wages.

(b) Selling overhead at Rs. 22,500.

(c) Distribution overhead @ Rs. 10,500.

Solution :

Profit and Loss Account

Particulars	Amount	Particulars	Amount
To Purchases raw material	45,000	By Sales	3,00,000
To Direct Wages	15,000	By Closing stock raw materials	7,500
To Indirect Wages	7,500	By Profit on sale of Assets	15,000
To Indirect Expenses	30,000		
To Selling Expenses	30,000		
To Distribution Expenses	15,000		
To Bad Debts	1,500		
To Interest on Bank Loan	750		
To Net Profit	1,77,750		
	3,22,500		3,22,500

Note: Profit as per Financial Account of Rs. 1,77,750.

Statement of Cost and Profit

Raw Materials :		
Purchases	45,000	
Less : Closing Stock	7,500	37,500
Direct Wages		15,000
Prime Cost		52,500
Factory Overhead 300% of Direct Wages		
$(15,000 \times \frac{300}{100} = 45,000)$		45,000
Works Cost		97,500
Selling Overhead		22,500
Distribution Overhead		10,500
Total Cost of Sales		1,30,500
Sales Price		3,00,000
Profit as per Cost Account		1,69,500

Reconciliation Statement

Particulars	Rs.	Rs.	Rs.
Net Profit as per Cost Accounts			1,69,500
Add : (1) Over absorption of overhead in cost :			
Factory overhead in Cost	45,000		
Factory overhead in Financial A/c	37,500	7,500	
Indirect Wages 7,500			
Indirect Exp. 30,000			
(2) Items of Incomes credited in Financial A/c only		15,000	
(3) Higher value of opening stock in Cost A/c		—	
(4) Lower value of closing stock in Cost A/c		—	+ 22,500
			1,92,000
Less : (1) Under absorption of overhead in cost :			
Selling Expenses in cost	22,500		
Distribution Expenses	10,500		
	33,000		
In Financial A/c Selling Exp. 30,000			
Distribution 15,000	45,000	12,000	
(2) Items debited in Financial A/c only :			
Bad Debts	1,500		
Interest on Bank Loan	750	2,250	
(3) Lower value of opening stock in cost		—	
(4) Higher value of closing stock in cost		—	14,250
Net Profit as per Financial Account			Rs. 1,77,750

Problem No. 44

From the following figures prepare a Reconciliation Statement :

	Rs.
Net Loss as per Financial Accounts	2,08,045
Net Loss as per Cost Account	1,72,400
Works overhead under recovered in costing	3,120
Administrative overhead recovered in Excess	1,700
Depreciation charged in Financial Account	11,200
Depreciation recovered on costing	12,500
Interest received not included in costing	8,000
Obsolescence loss charged in Financial Account	5,700
Income tax provided in Financial Books	40,300

Bank Interest credited in Financial Books		750
Stores Adjustment (credit Financial Books)		475
Value of opening stock :	in Cost Account	52,600
	in Financial Account	54,000
Value of closing stock :	in Cost Account	52,000
	in Financial Account	49,600
Interest charged in Cost Account but not in Financial Accounts		6,000
Preliminary expenses written off in Financial A/c		800
Provisions for Doubtful Debt in Financial A/c		150

Solution :

Reconciliation Statement

Particulars		Rs.	Rs.
Net Loss as per Cost Account			−1,72,400
Add : Under recovery of overheads in Cost Account :			
(1) Works overhead under recovered in cost		3,120	
(2) Items of expenses debited in Financial A/c :			
(a) Obsolescence loss charged in Financial A/c		5,700	
(b) Income tax provided in Financial A/c		40,300	
(c) Preliminary Expenses written off in Financial Account		800	
(d) Provision for Doubtful debts in Financial A/c		150	
(3) Lower value in opening stock : in Cost	52,600		
In Financial Account	54,000	1,400	
(4) Higher value in closing stock : in Cost	52,000		
In Financial Account	49,600	2,400	+53,870
			−2,26,270
Less : (1) Over recovery of overheads in cost :			
(a) Administrative overheads recovered in Excess in cost		1,700	
(b) Depreciation recovered in excess in cost :			
In Cost Account	12,500		
In Financial Account	11,200	1,300	
(2) Items of Income credited in Financial Account :			
(a) Interest received in Financial A/c		750	
(b) Interest received not included in cost		8,000	
(c) Interest charged in cost not in Financial A/c		6,000	
(d) Stores adjustment credited in Financial A/c		475	−18,225
Net Loss as per Financial Account only			−2,08,045

8

Marginal Costing

Marginal Costing is a technique of costing. It is not a method of costing. The technique of marginal costing is used to provide a basis for interpretation of cost figures for management decision than to arrive at the cost of product.

Definition I.C.W.A., London :

(1) Marginal costing is "the ascertainment of Marginal cost and of effect on Profit of changes in the volume or type of output by differentiating between Fixed cost and Variable costs".

(2) Marginal cost is defined as "The amount at any given volume of output by which aggregate costs are changed if the volume of output is increased or decreased by one unit."

The Marginal cost is the additional cost of producing one additional unit.

Illustration :

		Cost per 1000 units Rs.	Cost Extra 300 units Rs.	Total Cost of 1300 units Rs.
Raw Materials		6,000	1,800	7,800
Direct Labour		3,000	900	3,900
Variable Cost		1,500	450	1,950
Marginal Cost		10,500	3,150	13,650
Fixed Costs		4,550	—	4,550
Total		15,050	3,150	18,200
Cost per Unit	=	$\frac{15,050}{1000}$	$\frac{3,150}{300}$	$\frac{18,200}{1300}$
	=	15.05	10.50	14.00

The Marginal cost differentiate between Fixed costs and Variable costs. All variable costs vary in proportion to the volume of output whereas fixed costs remain the same as before the increase in the volume of output. Fixed costs are the period cost.

Marginal cost is the total of Prime cost + Variable overheads :

Material	—
Labour	—
Variable overhead	—
Marginal cost	—

Equations :

(1) Sales = Variable cost + Fixed costs ± Profit/Loss

Or Sales – Variable cost = Fixed costs ± Profit/Loss

(2) Contribution = Fixed cost ± Profit/Loss

Contribution – Fixed costs = ± Profit/Loss

(3) Sales = Variable costs + Contribution

Or Sales – Variable costs = Contribution.

(4) Break-Even Point = It is the point where total sales are equal to total costs. It is a volume of sales at which there is neither profit nor loss. The contribution is just sufficient to cover the fixed cost.

Calculation of B.E.P. Formula :

(1) $\text{B.E.P. (in Units)} = \dfrac{\text{Fixed cost}}{\text{Contribution}}$

$= \dfrac{\text{Fixed cost}}{\text{Sales Prime} - \text{Variable cost (Per Unit)}}$

(2) $\text{B.E.P. (in Sales value)} = \dfrac{\text{Fixed cost} \times \text{Sales}}{\text{Sales} - \text{Variable costs}}$

(3) $\text{Sales to earn a given profit} = \dfrac{(\text{Fixed cost} + \text{Profit}) \times \text{Sales}}{\text{Sales} - \text{Variable cost}}$

Profit Volume Ratio

Formula : (1) $\text{P/V Ratio} = \dfrac{\text{Contribution}}{\text{Sales}} = \dfrac{C}{S}$

Contribution = Sales – Variable cost

= Fixed cost ± Profit/Loss

(2) P/V Ratio $= \dfrac{\text{Sales} - \text{Variable cost}}{\text{Sales}}$

$= \dfrac{\text{Fixed cost} + \text{Profit}/\ -\text{Loss}}{\text{Sales}}$

(3) P/V Ratio $= \dfrac{\text{Changes in Profit}}{\text{Changes in Sales}}$

$= \dfrac{\text{Changes in contribution}}{\text{Changes in Sales}}$

Use of P/V Ratio :

(1) B.E.P. Sales $= \dfrac{\text{Fixed Cost}}{\text{P/V Ratio}}$

(2) Contribution = Sales × P/V Ratio

(3) Fixed Cost = Sales at B.E.P. × P/V Ratio

(4) Sales to earn a given amount of Profit :

$= \dfrac{\text{Fixed cost} + \text{Profit}}{\text{P/V Ratio}}$

Margin of Safety (M/S)

Margin of safety is the range of sales over B.E.P. sales above the B.E.P. sales indicate the profitability of the organisation. At B.E.P. sales fixed costs are covered the additional sales above B.E.P. sales would bring additional contribution and therefore additional profits.

Calculation of Margin of Safety Formula :

M/S $= \dfrac{\text{Profit}}{\text{P/V Ratio}}$

M/S = Sales (Actual) – Sales at B.E.P.

Problem No. 1

A Manufacturer, manufactures and sells 3000 Units. The cost structure is as under :

	Rs.
Material	6 per Unit
Wages	4 per Unit
Variable overhead	2 per Unit
Fixed Expenses	6,000
Selling Price	18 per Unit

He wants to sell another 3000 units in the foreign market at Rs. 14 per unit. Additional distribution cost for export will be at Re. 1 per unit.

Should he try to sell in foreign market.

Suggest the minimum which may be quoted in the foreign market.

[K.U.D., April 1998(N)]

Solution :

In Local Market

Sales 3000 units @ Rs. 18 per unit

Cost per unit . Total

Foreign Market

Selling price Rs. 14

3000 units

Cost per unit	Rs.	Total	Rs.	3000 units	Rs.
Sales. price	18 p. unit	3000 × 18 =	54,000	3000 × 14 =	42,000
Less Material 6		*Less* 18,000		Sales Price	
Wages 4		M. · 12,000		Total Variable	
Variable		Overhead 6,000		Cost remain	
Overhead 2		Total Variable		Same 36,000	
Total Variable Cost	12	Cost	36,000	+ Additional	
Contribution per unit	6	Contribution	18,000	Distribution	
		Less Fixed Cost	6,000	Cost Re. 1	
		Profit Rs.	12,000	per unit 3,000	
				Total Cost	39,000
				Contribution	3,000

Note : In the Local market 3000 units sold at Rs. 18 per unit and earned Rs. 12,000 Net Profit.

Though he wants to sell in foreign market @ Rs. 14 per unit in earning additional cost of Re. 1 per unit. There is a contribution per unit earned i.e. Contribution Rs. 3,000 is additional earning is Profit. Total Profit Rs. 12,000 + 3,000 = Rs. 15,000/Minimum Price Rs. 13 equal to Marginal Cost.

Problem No. 2

Lucky Buckets sold 14000 buckets and 18000 buckets at Rs. 50 per bucket in two consecutive years. The company incurred a loss of Rs. 10,000 in the First year and earned a profit of Rs. 10,000 in second year.

Find out :

(a) The amount of Fixed Cost

(b) Break-even quantity (point)

(c) Sales required to earn a Profit of Rs. 35,000.

[K.U.D., April 1998 (O)]

Solution :

	I Year		II Year	
Sales of bucket Nos.	14000		18000	
Sales in Value Rs. 50 per bucket	7,00,000		9,00,000	
Profit/Loss	10,000	Loss	10,000	Profit
	Sales		Profit	Loss
Changes in Sales & Profits/Loss				
II Year	9,00,000		+ 10,000	Profit
I Year	7,00,000		– 10,000	Loss
Changes in Sales & Profit	2,00,000		20,000	

$$\text{P/V Ratio} = \frac{\text{Changes in Profits}}{\text{Changes in Sales}}$$

$$= \frac{20000}{2,00,000} = 10\% \text{ or } 1/10$$

Contribution for I Year = Sales × P/V Ratio

= 7,00,000 × 1/10

Contribution = 70,000

Contribution = Fixed Cost + Profit/ – Loss

Fixed Cost = Contribution – Profit/ + Loss

= 70,000 + 10,000

(a) Fixed Cost = 80,000

$$\text{Or BEP Sales} = \frac{\text{Fixed Cost}}{\text{P/V Ratio}}$$

$$= \frac{80,000}{1/10} = 80,000 \times \frac{10}{1} = \text{Rs. } 8,00,000$$

(b) BEP Sales = Rs. 8,00,000

(c) Sales required to earn a Profit of Rs.

$$= \frac{\text{Fixed Cost + Profit}}{\text{P/V Ratio}}$$

$$= \frac{80{,}000 + 35{,}000}{1/10}$$

$$= 1{,}15{,}000 \times 10$$

Sales in value = 11,50,000

Sales in No. of buckets $= \frac{11{,}50{,}000}{50}$

= 23000 buckets to be sold

Alternatively :

II Year P/V Ratio $= \frac{1}{10}$ or 10% remains the same

Contribution = Sales × P/V Ratio

= 9,00,000 × 1/10

Contribution = 90,000

Now Fixed Costs = Contribution – Profit

= 90,000 – 10,000

Fixed Cost = Rs. 80,000

Now BEP Sales $= \frac{\text{Fixed Cost}}{\text{P/V Ratio}}$

$$= \frac{80{,}000}{1/10}$$

= 80,000 × 10 = 8,00,000

BEP Sales in value = 8,00,000

BEP Sales in Units $= \frac{8{,}00{,}000}{\text{50 per Unit}}$

= 16000 Units buckets

Sales required to earn Profit of Rs. 35,000

$$= \frac{\text{Fixed Cost + Profit}}{\text{P/V Ratio}}$$

$$= \frac{80{,}000 + 35{,}000}{1/10}$$

Sales required to earn Units $= \frac{11{,}50{,}000}{50}$

Profit of Rs. 35,000 : 1,15,000 × 10/1 = 23000 Units

= Rs. 11,50,000

Problem No. 3

Find P/V ratio and sales to earn Profit of Rs. 1,000.

Fixed Cost — Rs. 4,000

Break-even Sales — Rs. 20,000

Selling Price per Unit — Rs. 20.

[K.U.D., October 1997(N)]

Solution :

$$\text{P/V Ratio} = \frac{\text{Contribution}}{\text{Sales}} \text{ or } \frac{\text{Fixed Cost + Profit}}{\text{Sales}}$$

$$\text{BEP Sales} = \text{Fixed Cost} \div \text{P/V Ratio}$$

$$\therefore \text{P/V ratio} = \frac{\text{Fixed Cost}}{\text{BEP Sales}}$$

Now factors given =

Fixed Cost = Rs. 4,000

BEP Sales = Rs. 20,000

(1) $$\text{Now P/V ratio} = \frac{\text{Fixed Cost}}{\text{BEP Sales}} = \frac{4{,}000}{20{,}000} = \frac{1}{5} \text{ ratio or } 20\%$$

P/V ratio = 1/5 ratio or 20%

(2) Sales to earn a Profit of Rs. 1,000

$$\text{Desired Sales} = \frac{\text{Fixed cost + Profit}}{\text{P/V ratio}}$$

$$= \frac{4{,}000 + 1{,}000}{1/5}$$

$$= \frac{5{,}000}{1/5} = 5{,}000 \times \frac{5}{1} = 25{,}000$$

Sales to earn a Profit of Rs. 1,000 = is Rs. 25,000

Ans. (1) P/V Ratio - 1/5 or 20%

(2) Sales required to ear Profit of Rs. 1,000 is Rs. 25,000

Problem No. 4

The following information relates to the Product of a Company :

Selling Price per unit	Rs. 30
Variable Manufacturing cost per unit	Rs. 17
Variable selling cost per unit	Rs. 3
Fixed Factory overhead	Rs. 1,50,000
Fixed selling cost	Rs. 30,000

Calculate :

(a) BEP in amount and in unit

(b) Sales to earn a Profit of Rs. 60,000 is value and in units.

(c) Profit or Loss of sales are @ 15000 units

[K.U.D., October 1997(O)]

Solution :

		Rs.
Selling Price per unit		30
Less Variable Cost :		
Variable Manufacturing Cost	17	
Variable Selling Cost	3	
Total Variable Cost	20	20
Contribution per Unit		10
Fixed Cost :		
Factory Overhead		1,50,000
Selling Overhead		30,000
Total Fixed Cost		1,80,000

$$\text{P/V ratio} = \frac{\text{Contribution}}{\text{Sales}} \text{ or } \frac{\text{Fixed Cost + Profit}}{\text{Sales}}$$

$$= \frac{10}{30} = \frac{1}{3} \text{ or } 33\%$$

$$\text{BEP Sales} = \frac{\text{Fixed Cost}}{\text{P/V Ratio}} = \frac{1{,}80{,}000}{1/3} = 1{,}80.000 \times \frac{3}{1} = 5{,}40{,}000$$

BEP Sales in amount Rs. 5,40,000

$$\text{In units} \quad \frac{5{,}40{,}000}{30} = 18000 \text{ units}$$

Verification :

Selling Price per unit Rs. 30 × 18000 =	5,40,000
BEP Sales	5,40,000
Less Variable Cost 20 × 18000	3,60,000
Contribution	1,80,000
(Contribution per unit 10 × 18000 = 1,80,000)	
Less Fixed Cost = Total	1,80,000
Profit	Nil

BEP Sales in Amount Rs. 5,40,000 } No Profit
in units 18000 } No Loss

(2) Sales to earn a Profit Rs. 6,000 in value and in units

$$\text{Desired Sales} = \frac{\text{Fixed Cost + Profit}}{\text{P/V Ratio}}$$

$$= \frac{1,80,000 + 60,000}{1/3}$$

$$= 2,40,000 \times \frac{3}{1} = 7,20,000 \text{ Sales in value}$$

$$\text{Sales - in value} = \text{Rs. } 7,20,000$$

$$\text{in units} = \frac{7,20,000}{30} = 24000 \text{ units}$$

Verification :

= Sales	7,20,000
Less Variable cost Rs. 20 per unit for 24,000	
20 × 24,000 =	4,80,000
Contribution	2,40,000
Less Fixed Cost	1,80,000
Profit	60,000

(3) Profit or Loss if sales are at 15000 units

BEP sales in units are 18000

Therefore there is a Loss at sales in 15000 units

Sales - Rs. 30 per unit for 15000 × 30 =	4,50,000
Less Valuable Cost - Rs. 20 per unit for 15000 × 20 =	3,00,000
Contribution	1,50,000
Less Fixed Cost	1,80,000
Loss on Sales of 15000 units	Rs. 30,000

Problem No. 5

Denta Ltd., provides the following details relating to the manufacture of Delta Tooth Brush :

	Rs.
Selling Price per piece	15.00
Direct materials cost per piece	4.50
Direct Wages per piece	3.00
Fixed overheads	11,250.00
Variable overheads per piece	30.00

Find out BEP and P/V ratio if trade commission allowed is 5%

What will be the Profits if sales price are 10% and 15% above the BEP calculate above?

[K.U.D., April 1997(N)]

Solution :

	Rs. per piece	Rs.
Present Position		
Selling Price per unit		15.00
Less Variable Costs		
Direct Material Cost	4.50	
Direct Wages	3.00	
Variable overhead	3.00	
Total Variable Cost	10.50	10.50
Contribution per unit		4.50

$$\text{BEP} = \frac{\text{Fixed Cost}}{\text{Contribution per unit}} = \frac{11,250}{4.50} = 2500 \text{ units} \times \text{Sales per unit}$$

$$= 2500 \times 15 = \text{Rs. } 37,500$$

BEP Sales (in amount) = Rs. 37,500 Ans.

$$\text{P/V ratio} = \frac{\text{Contribution per unit}}{\text{Sales per unit}}$$

$$= \frac{4.50}{15} = 30\% \text{ Ans.}$$

$$\text{BEP Sales} = \frac{\text{Fixed Cost}}{\text{P/V Ratio}}$$

$$= 11,250 \times \frac{100}{30} = \text{Rs. } 37,500 \text{ Ans.}$$

Verification :

BEP Sales @ Rs. 15 per unit × 2500 units	Rs. 37,500
Less Variable Cost Rs. 10.50 × 2500	26,250
Contribution	11,250
Less Fixed Cost	11,250
Profit	Nil

BEP Sales — No Profit - No Loss

If trade Commission is considered @ 5%

Selling Price per unit		Rs. 15.00
Trade Commission @ 5% of 15 =		0.75
		14.25
Direct material cost	4.50	
Direct wages	3.00	
Variable overhead	3.00	
Total Variable Cost =	10.50	10.50
Contribution per unit		3.75

$$\text{BEP} = \frac{\text{Fixed Cost}}{\text{Contribution per unit}} = \frac{11{,}250}{3.75} = 3000 \text{ units Ans}$$

BEP sales in units = 3000

BEP sales in value = 3000 × 14.25 = 42,750 Ans.

$$\text{P/V ratio} = \frac{\text{Contribution per unit}}{\text{Sales per unit}}$$

$$= \frac{3.75}{14.25} 26.3157 = 26.32$$

OR

$$\text{P/V ratio} = \frac{\text{Fixed Cost}}{\text{BEP Sales}} = \frac{11{,}250}{42{,}750} = 26.3157 = 26.32$$

Verification :

BEP sales 3000 × 14.25 =	42,750
Less Variable Cost 10.50 × 3000 =	31,500
Contribution	11,250
Less Fixed Cost	11,250
	Nil

BEP Sales – Covers Just Fixed Cost only

There is No Profit or No Loss

Sales Price before allowing Trade Commission is Rs. 15
BEP sales – @ Rs. 15 × 2500 units = – Rs. 37,500
Profit if sales Price are 10% and 15% above BEP sales

above	I 10%	II 15%
BEP Sales Rs. 37,500	41,250	43,125
Less Variable Cost 2500 × 10.50	26,250	26,250
Contribution	15,000	16,875
Less Fixed Cost	11,250	11,250
Profit	Rs. 3,750	Rs. 5,625 Ans.

Problem No. 6

Find out P/V ratio and Fixed Cost from the following information :
Selling Price per unit — Rs. 10

Year	Sales (in units)	Total Cost (Rs.)
1994	15000	1,30,000
1995	17000	1,45,000

[K.U.D., April 1997(N)]

Solution :

(1) P/V Ratio $= \dfrac{\text{Contribution}}{\text{Sales}}$

(2) P/V Ratio $= \dfrac{\text{Sales} - \text{Variable Cost}}{\text{Sales}}$

$= \dfrac{\text{Fixed Cost} + \text{Profit}}{\text{Sales}}$

Contribution = Fixed Cost + Profit

(3) P/V Ratio $= \dfrac{\text{Changes in Profits}}{\text{Changes in Sales}}$

Sales – Total Cost = Profits
Total Cost = Variable Cost + Fixed Cost
Fixed Cost = Total Cost – Variable Cost

Now P/V Ratio $= \dfrac{\text{Changes in Profits}}{\text{Changes in Sales}}$

Profits = Sales – Total Cost
For Period 1994 : Profit = 1,50,000 – 1,30,000
= 20,000
For Period 1995 : Profit = 1,70,000 – 1,45,000
Profit = 25,000

1994 Sales – 1,50,000 Profit – 20,000

1995 Sales – 1,70,000 Profit – 25,000

Changes in Sales 20,000 in Profit = 5,000

$$\text{Now P/V Ratio} = \frac{\text{Changes in Profits}}{\text{Changes in Sales}}$$

$$= \frac{5{,}000}{20{,}000} = \frac{1}{4} \text{ or } 25\%$$

$$\text{P/V Ratio} = \frac{1}{4} \text{ or } 25\%$$

Ascertainment of Fixed Cost :

Contribution = Sales × P/V Ratio

For 1994 = 1,50,000 × 1/4

Contribution = 37,500

Fixed Cost = Contribution – Profit

= 37,500 – 20,000

Fixed Cost = 17,500

For 1995

Contribution = Sales × P/V Ratio

= 1,70,000 × 1/4

Contribution = 42,500

Fixed Cost = Contribution – Profit

= 42,500 – 25,000

Fixed Cost = 17,500

Fixed Cost for 1994 – Rs. 17,500

1995 Rs. 17,500

Fixed Cost for 1994 and 1995 remains the same

Alternatively

$$\text{Variable Cost} = \frac{\text{Changes in Total Cost}}{\text{Changes in Sales}}$$

1994 Sales – 1,50,000 Total Cost = 1,30,000

1995 Sales 1,70,000 Total Cost = 1,45,000

Changes in Sales – 20,000 in Total Cost = 15,000

$$\text{Variable Cost} = \frac{\text{Changes in Total Cost}}{\text{Changes in Sales}}$$

$$\text{Variable Cost} = \frac{15{,}000}{20{,}000} = \frac{3}{4} \text{ or 75\% Variable Cost}$$

Variable Cost = 75% of sales

For 1994 Variable Cost = 75% or 1,50,000

Variable Cost = 1,12,500

For 1995 Variable Cost = 75% of 1,70,000

Variable Cost = 1,27,500

For 1994 Contribution = Sales – Variable Cost

= 1,50,000 – 1,12,500

= 37,500

For 1995 Contribution = 1,70,000 – 1,27,500

Contribuition = 42,500

1994 P/V Ratio = $\frac{\text{Contribution}}{\text{Sales}}$

= $\frac{37{,}500}{1{,}50{,}000} = \frac{1}{4}$ or 25%

1995 P/V Ratio = $\frac{42{,}500}{1{,}70{,}000} = \frac{1}{4}$ or 25%

Calculation of Fixed Cost = Total Cost – Variable Cost

For 1994 = 1,30,000 – 1,12,500

Fixed Cost = Rs. 17,500

For 1995 Fixed Cost = 1,45,000 – 1,27,500

Fixed Cost = Rs. 17,500

Extra Answer :

Now BEP Sales = $\frac{\text{Fixed Cost}}{\text{P/V Ratio}}$

1994 = Fixed Cost × P/V Ratio

= 17,500 × 4/1

BEP Sales = Rs. 70,000

Sales required to earn Profit of Rs. 40,000

Required sales = $\frac{\text{Fixed Cost + Desired Profit}}{\text{P/V ratio}}$

= $\frac{17{,}500 + 40{,}000}{1/4} = 57{,}500 \times \frac{1}{4} = 2{,}30{,}000$

S	2,30,000
VC	1,72,500
25%	
Contr.	57,500
FC	17,500 Profit Rs. 40,000
	40,000

Problem No. 7

X Co. Ltd. has the profit volume ratio (P/V) 30% and its Margin of safety is 40%. Find out the net profit and the Break-Even point if Sales are at Rs. 2,00,000.

(C.A. Modified)

Solution :

Sales = Rs. 2,00,000
P/V Ratio = 30%
M/s = 40%

Formula : (1) P/V Ratio $= \frac{\text{Contribution}}{\text{Sales}}$

(2) Contribution = Sales × P/V ratio

(3) B.E.P. $= \frac{\text{Fixed Cost}}{\text{P/V Ratio}}$

Contribution at B.E.P. sales is equal to Fixed cost

Contribution at B.E.P. = Sales at B.E.P. × P/V Ratio

Fixed cost at B.E.P. = Sales at B.E.P. × P/V Ratio

(4) Margin of Safety $= \frac{\text{Profit}}{\text{P/V Ratio}}$

Margin of Safety = Sales – B.E.P. Sales

Profit = % of M/S × % P/V Ratio

Net Profit = Contribution – Fixed cost

Now

(1) Margin of Safety = Sales – B.E.P. Sales

B.E.P. Sales = Sales – M/S%
= 2,00,000 – 40% of 2,00,000
= 2,00,000 – 80,000
= 1,20,000

At B.E.P. Sales contribution = Fixed cost since B.E.P. sales just covers only fixed cost so contribution arrived at B.E.P. Sales is equal to fixed cost.

Now contribution = Sales at B.E.P. × P/V ratio
= 1,20,000 × 30%

Contribution = 36,000

Therefore Fixed cost = Contribution = 36,000

Fixed cost = 36,000

Now net profit at sales of Rs. 2,00,000

Profit = Contribution – Fixed cost

Contribution at sales of Rs. 2,00,000

Contribution = Sales × P/V Ratio
= 2,00,000 × 30%
= 60,000

Now Profit = Contribution – Fixed cost

= 60,000 – 36,000

Profit = Rs. 24,000

Alternatively :

Sales	2,00,000
Less : 40% M/S	80,000
B.E.P. Sale	1,20,000

Net Profit = M/S % × P/V Ratio %

= 40% × 30%

= 40/100 × 30/100

= 0.40 × 0. 30

= 0. 12%

Profit = 0.12% of Rs. 2,00,000 Sales

= 0.12% × 2,00,000

Profit = Rs. 24,000

Problem No. 8

The sales turnover and the profits during the periods were as follows :

Year	Sales	Profit
1993	Rs. 1,50,000	Rs. 20,000
1994	Rs. 1,70,000	Rs. 25,000

Calculate :

(a) P/V Ratio (b) B.E.P. sales (c) Sales to earn a profit of Rs. 40,000 (d) Profit when sales are Rs. 2,50,000.

(K.U.D., April 1996)

Solution :

(a) P/V Ratio = $\frac{\text{Changes in Profit}}{\text{Changes in Sales}}$

1994	Sales	1,70,000	Profit	25,000
1993	Sales	1,50,000	Profit	20,000
Changes		20,000		5,000

Now P/V Ratio = $\frac{\text{Changes in Profits}}{\text{Changes in Sales}} = \frac{5,000}{20,000} = \frac{1}{4}$ Or 25%

(b) B.E.P. Sales = $\frac{\text{Fixed cost}}{\text{P/V Ratio}}$

Now ascertain contribution = Sales × P/V Ratio

= 1,50,000 × ¼ = 37,500

Fixed cost = Contribution – Profit

= 37,500 – 20,000

= 17,500

Now B.E.P. = $\frac{\text{Fixed cost}}{\text{P/V Ratio}}$

$$= \frac{17,500}{1/4}$$

$$= 17,500 \times 4/1$$

$$= \text{Rs. } 70,000$$

(c) Sales to earn a Profit of Rs. 40,000

$$= \frac{\text{Fixed Cost + Profit}}{\text{P/V Ratio}}$$

$$= \frac{17,500 + 40,000}{1/4}$$

$$= 57,500 \times 4/1$$

$$= \text{Rs. } 2,30,000$$

Sales to earn a profit of Rs. 40,000 is Rs. 2,30,000

(d) Profit when sales are @ Rs. 2,50,000

Now contribution when sales are @ Rs. 2,50,000

Contribution = Sales × P/V Ratio

= 2,50,000 × ¼

= 62,500

Profit = Contribution – Fixed cost

= 62,500 – 17,500

= 45,000

Profit is Rs. 45,000 when sales are @ Rs. 2,50,000.

Problem No. 9

Akashwani Tape-recorder Company sold 5,000 tape-recorder last year at a price of Rs. 1,000 each.

The cost structure is as follows :

Material	200
Wages	100
Variable overheads	50
Marginal cost	350
Fixed overheads	400
Total cost	750
Profit	250
Selling Price	1,000

Due to heavy competition, the price will have to be reduced to Rs. 850 in the coming year. Assuming no changes in costs, calculate the number of tape-recorders that should be sold at the new price to get the same total profit as earned last year.

(K.U.D., October 1995)

Solution :

$$\text{Expected Sales} = \frac{\text{Fixed Cost + Profit}}{\text{P/V Ratio}}$$

$$\text{P/V Ratio} = \frac{\text{Sales – Variable Cost}}{\text{Sales}}$$

$$\text{Or : P/V Ratio} = \frac{\text{Contribution}}{\text{Sales}}$$

Marginal Cost (Variable Cost) = 350

Fixed Cost = 400

Sales Price = 1,000

Profit = 250

Now let us know the Total Profit for the last year for sales of 5000 units.

Profit per unit = 250 × 5000 = 12,50,000

Fixed Cost per unit = 450 × 5000 = 20,00,000

Existing Sales Price – Rs. 1,000

Future-Reduced sales Price	850
Variable cost (Marginal cost)	350
Contribution	500

$$\text{Now P/V Ratio} = \frac{\text{Contribution}}{\text{Sales}} = \frac{500}{850} = \frac{10}{17}$$

Sales required to earn desired Profit of Rs. 12,50,000

$$\text{Sales (in Amount)} = \frac{\text{Fixed Cost + Profit}}{\text{P/V Ratio}}$$

$$= \frac{20,00,000 + 12,50,000}{10/17}$$

$$= 32,50,000 \times \frac{17}{10} = 55,25,000$$

$$\text{Sales in units} = \frac{55,25,000}{850} = 6500 \text{ Units.}$$

No. of Tape Recorder to be sold = 6500 Units

At reduced-price to earn same Profit = 12,50,000

Verification :

Future Sales Price Per unit Rs. 850 × 6500 =	55,25,000
Variable Cost (Marginal Cost) 350 × 6500 =	22,75,000
Contribution	32,50,000
Less : Fixed Cost	20,00,000
Profit	12,50,000

Problem No. 10

The following information relates to Poornima Ltd. :

Sales	2,00,000
Variable cost	1,20,000
Fixed cost	60,000

Find out the P/V ratio and Break-even point. Calculate the New P/V ratio and Break-even point by considering the following changes :

(a) 20% increase in sale price accompanied by an increase of fixed cost by Rs. 20,000.

(b) 20% increase in sale price accompanied by 10% decrease in variable cost and 10% increase in fixed cost.

(K.U.D., April 1995)

Solution :

Sales Price 10,000 units	2,00,000
Less : Variable cost	1,20,000
Contributation	80,000
Less : Refixed cost	60,000
Profit	20,000

$$\text{P/V Ratio} = \frac{\text{Contribution}}{\text{Sales}}$$

$$= \frac{80{,}000}{2{,}00{,}000}$$

$$= 2/5 \text{ or } 40\%$$

$$\text{B.E.P. Sales} = \frac{\text{Fixed Cost}}{\text{P/V Ratio}}$$

$$= \frac{60{,}000}{2/5}$$

$$= 60{,}000 \times \frac{5}{2}$$

$$= 1{,}50{,}000$$

In units $= \dfrac{1,50,000}{20}$

$= 7500$ Units.

Verification : B.E.P.

Sales 7500 × 20 =	1,50,000
Less : Variable cost 7500 × 12	90,000
Contribution	60,000
Less : Fixed Cost	60,000
Profit	Nil

(a) 20% increase in Sales Price and Rs. 20,000 increase in fixed cost.

Sales Price (10000 Units)	2,00,000	
Add : Increase 20%	40,000	2,40,000
Less : Variable cost		1,20,000
Contribution		1,20,000
Less : Fixed cost	60,000	
Add : Increase	+20,000	80,000
Profit		40,000

New P/V ratio $= \dfrac{\text{Contribution}}{\text{Sales}}$

$= \dfrac{1,20,000}{2,40,000} = 1/2$ or 50%

B.E.P. sales $= \dfrac{\text{Fixed Cost}}{\text{P/V Ratio}}$

$= \dfrac{80,000}{1/2} = 80,000 \times 2/1 = 1,60,000$

Sales in units $= \dfrac{1,60,000}{24} = 6667$ units.

Verification of B.E.P. sales	=	
Sales 6667 × 24	=	1,60,000
Less : Variable cost (6667 × 12)	=	80,000
Contribution		80,000
Less : Fixed Cost		80,000
Profit		Nil

(b) 20% increase in sale Price, 10% decrease in Variable cost and 10% increase in Fixed cost.

Now sale Price 10000 =	2,00,000	
Add : Increase 20%	+40,000	2,40,000
Less : Variable cost	1,20,000	
Add : Decrease 10%	– 12,000	1,08,000
Contribution		1,32,000
Less : Fixed cost	60,000	
Add : Increase 10%	+6,000	66,000
Profit		66,000

New P/V ratio $= \dfrac{\text{Contribution}}{\text{Sales}}$

$= \dfrac{1,32,000}{2,40,000} = 11/20$

B.E.P. Sales $= \dfrac{\text{Fixed Cost}}{\text{P/V Ratio}}$

$= \dfrac{66,000}{11/20} = 66,000 \times 20/11$

$= 1,20,000$

Sales in Units $= \dfrac{1,20,000}{24} = 5000$ Units.

Verification of B.E.P. Sales :

Sales 5000 × 24	=	1,20,000
Less : Variable cost		54,000
Contribution		66,000
Fixed Cost		66,000
Profit		Nil

Problem No. 11

The following figures are obtained form the accounts of "Goldstar Ltd"

Year	Sales (in units)	Profit/Loss Rs.
1992	4000	5,000 Loss
1993	6000	5,000 Profit

The selling price per unit can be assumed to be Rs. 20.

Calculate :

(a) P/V ratio

(b) Fixed cost

(c) Break-even sales

(d) Profit at sales of Rs. 2,00,000

(e) Sales earn a profit of Rs. 30,000.

(K.U.D., October 1994)

Solution :

(a) P/V ratio $= \dfrac{\text{Changes in Profit}}{\text{Changes in Sales}}$

(i) Changes in profit = –5,000 – +5,000 = 10,000 Profit

(ii) Changes in sales = 1993 = 6000 units × Rs. 20 = 1,20,000

1992 = 4000 units × Rs. 20 = 80,000

40,000

Now P/V ratio $= \dfrac{10{,}000}{40{,}000} = 1/4$ or 25%

Ascertainment of Fixed Cost :

Now contribution = Sales × P/V ratio

Contribution for 1992 = 80000 × 1/4

= 20,000

Now Fixed Cost = Contribution – Profit / + Loss

= 20000 + 5000 Loss

Fixed Cost = Rs. 25,000

(c) Break-even Point $= \dfrac{\text{Fixed Cost}}{\text{P/V Ratio}}$

$= \dfrac{25{,}000}{1/4}$

= 25000 × 4 = 1,00,000

B.E.P. Sales in value = 1,00,000

B.E.P. Sales in units $= \dfrac{1{,}00{,}000}{20}$

= 5000 Units.

(d) Profit at sales of Rs. 2,00,000

Ascertain contribution when sales are Rs. 2,00,000

Contribution = Sales × P/V ratio

= 2,00,000 × 1/4

= Rs. 50,000

Profit = Contribution – Fixed Cost

= 50,000 – 25,000

= Rs. 25,000

(e) Sales to earn a Profit of Rs. 30,000

$$\text{Sales} = \frac{\text{Fixed Cost + Profit}}{\text{P/V Ratio}}$$

$$= \frac{25{,}000 + 30{,}000}{1/4}$$

$$= 55{,}000 \times 4/1$$

$$\text{Sales} = \text{Rs. } 2{,}20{,}000$$

Problem No. 12

Following details pertain to a company :

		Period-I	Period-II
Number of units sold	:	10000	30000
Selling Price per unit (Rs.)	:	50	50
Profit or Loss made (Rs.)	:	1,00,000 (Loss)	1,00,000 (Profit)

Calculate :

(1) The amount of fixed cost;

(2) The number of units to break-even; and

(3) The number of units to be sold earn a profit of Rs. 4,00,000.

(K.U.D., April 1994)

Solution :

$$\text{P/V ratio} = \frac{\text{Changes in Profits}}{\text{Changes in Sales}}$$

Changes in profit = Period-I – Period-II

= $-1{,}00{,}000 - +1{,}00{,}000$

Profit = $+2{,}00{,}000$

Changes in sales = Period-II 30000 × 50 = 15,00,000

Period-I 10000 × 50 = 5,00,000

Rs. 10,00,000

$$\text{P/V ratio} = \frac{2{,}00{,}000}{10{,}00{,}000} = 2/10 = 1/5 \text{ or } 20\%$$

$$\text{Now} = \frac{\text{Fixed Cost}}{\text{Contribution}} = \text{Sales} \times \text{P/V ratio}$$

Period-I = 500000 × 1/5

Contribution = Rs. 1,00,000

Fixed Cost = Contribution – Profit or + Loss

= 1,00,000 + 1,00,000 Loss = 2,00,000

Contribution = Sales × P/V ratio (Period-II)

= 15,00,000 × 1/5 =

= Rs. 3,00,000

Fixed Cost = Contribution – Profit (Period-II)

= 3,00,00 – 1,00,000

= 2,00,000

Now B.E.P. in sales volume = $\frac{\text{Fixed Cost}}{\text{P/V Ratio}} = \frac{2,00,000}{1/5}$

= 2,00,000 × 5/1

= Rs. 10,00,000

B.E.P. in units = $\frac{10,00,000}{50}$

= 20000 units.

Sales to earn Profit of Rs. 4,00,000 = $\frac{\text{Fixed Cost + Profit}}{\text{P/V Ratio}}$

= $\frac{2,00,000 + 4,00,000}{1/5}$

= 6,00,000 × 5

= 30,00,000

= $\frac{30,00,000}{50}$

= 60000 Units.

Problem No. 13

(a) Give the meaning of fixed costs, variable cost and semi variable costs.

(b) Calculate from the following particulars :

(1) P/V Ratio (2) B.E.P. (3) Net Profit from the sales of Rs. 3,00,000 (4) Sales to earn a profit of Rs. 70,000.

Sales		2,00,000
Variable costs		1,50,000
	Gross Profit	50,000
Fixed Overheads		15,000
	Net Profit	35,000

(Gulbarga, April 1994 & K.U.D., April 1988)

Solution :

(1) P/V Ratio $= \dfrac{\text{Contribution}}{\text{Sales}}$

Contribution = Sales – Variable cost

= 2,00,000 – 1,50,000

= 50,000

Now P/V Ratio $= \dfrac{\text{Contribution}}{\text{Sales}}$

$= \dfrac{50,000}{2,00,000} = 1/4 \text{ or } 25\%$

(2) B.E.P. Sales $= \dfrac{\text{Fixed Cost}}{\text{P/V Ratio}}$

$= \dfrac{15,000}{1/4}$

$= 15,000 \times 4/1 = 60,000$

B.E.P. (Sales) = Rs. 60,000

(3) Net Profit when sales are Rs. 3,00,000. Now ascertain contribution and P/V Ratio.

P/V Ratio $= \dfrac{\text{Contribution}}{\text{Sales}}$

Contribution = Sales × P/V Ratio

= 3,00,000 × 1/4

= 75,000

Now Profit when sales are Rs. 3,00,000

Contribution = Fixed Cost + Profit

Profit = Contribution – Fixed Cost

= 75,000 – 15,000

= 60,000

(4) Desired sales to earn a profit of Rs. 70,000

Desired Sales $= \dfrac{\text{Fixed Cost + Profit}}{\text{P/V Ratio}}$

$= \dfrac{15,000 + 70,000}{1/4}$

$= \dfrac{85,000}{1/4}$

$= 85{,}000 \times 4/1$

$= 3{,}40{,}000$

Sales required to earn a profit of Rs. 70,000 = Rs. 3,40,000.

Problem No. 14

The P/V ratio of Anand Ltd. is 40% and margin of safety is 30%. Calculate :

(i) B.E.P.

(ii) Profit if sales are Rs. 2,40,000

(iii) Fixed Cost.

(K.U.D., October 1993)

Solution :

Given : P/V ratio = 40% and Margin Safety = 30%

$$\text{P/V ratio} = \frac{\text{Contribution}}{\text{Sales}}$$

$$\text{Sales} = \frac{\text{Contribution}}{\text{P/V Ratio}}$$

Contribution = Sales × P/V ratio

= 2,40,000 × 40/100 on sales

= 96,000

Margin of Safety = Sales – B.E.P. sales

Now B.E.P. Sales = Sales – Margin of Safety

= 2,40,000 – 30% of 2,40,000

= 2,40,000 – 72,000

= 1,68,000.

Sales at B.E.P. contribution = Fixed Cost

Fixed Cost = Contribution at B.E.P.

= 40% of 1,68,000

= 67,200

Now Net Profit = Contribution – Fixed Cost

= 40% of sales – 67,200

= 40% of 2,40,000 – 67,200

= 96,000 – 67,200

Profit at sales of 2,40,000 = Rs. 28,800

Verification :

$$\text{Margin of Safety} = \frac{\text{Fixed Cost}}{\text{P/V Ratio}}$$

$$= \frac{28,800}{40\% \ (2/5)}$$

$$= 28,800 \times \frac{5}{2}$$

$$= 72,000$$

$$\text{Now Margin of Safety} = 30\% \text{ of sales}$$

$$= 30\% \text{ of } 2,40,000$$

$$= 72,000$$

$$\text{Sales} = \frac{\text{Fixed Cost + Profit}}{\text{P/V Ratio}}$$

$$= \frac{67,200 + 28,800}{40\% \ (2/5)}$$

$$= 96,000 \times \frac{5}{2}$$

$$= \text{Rs. } 2,40,000$$

Problem No. 15

Alphas Ltd. manufactures and sells four types of products under four Brand names as A, B, C & D respectively.

The sales Mix in value comprises of 33-1/3%, 41-2/3%, 16-2/3% and 8-1/3% of A, B, C and D respectively.

The total Budgeted Sales (100%) are Rs. 60,000 per month.

Variable costs are :

Product	A	60% of the selling price.
	B	68% of the selling price.
	C	80% of the selling price
	D	40% of the selling price.

Fixed costs are Rs. 14,700 per month.

Calculate :

B.E.P. for the products on the overhead basis and also find out the net profit on Budgeted sales.

(K.U.D., April 1993)

Solution :

	Products A	B	C	D	Total
Sales Mix (in %)	33-1/3	41-2/3	16-2/3	8-1/3	100
Sales in Amount	20,000	25,000	10,000	5,000	60,000
Less : Variable cost 60%, 68%, 80% & 40%	12,000	17,000	8,000	2,000	39,000
Contribution	8,000	8,000	2,000	3,000	21,000
Less : Fixed cost					14,700
Total Profit					6,300

$$\text{P/V Ratio} = \frac{\text{Contribution}}{\text{Sales}} \quad \frac{8,000}{20,000} \quad \frac{8,000}{25,000} \quad \frac{2,000}{10,000} \quad \frac{3,000}{5,000}$$

40% 32% 20% 60%

$$\text{B.E.P. Sales} = \frac{\text{Fixed}}{\text{P/V Ratio}} = \frac{14,700}{7/20} = 14,700 \times \frac{20}{7} = 42,000$$

B.E.P. Sales = Rs. 42,000

$$\text{P/V Ratio} = \frac{21,000}{60,000} = \frac{7}{20}$$

Problem No. 16

Prakash Enterprises have a plant which can produce two types of articles – X and Y. The following information is available on per unit basis :

Materials :	Product X	Product Y
X – 2 Kgs. at Rs. 6 per Kg.	Rs. 12	—
Y – 3 Kgs. at Rs. 6 per Kg.	Rs. 4	Rs. 18
Wages :		

Variable overheads – 100% of direct labour.

Fixed Cost : Rs. 1,20,000.

Selling Price : X – Rs. 30 per unit.
Y – Rs. 40 per unit.

Calculate :

(i) P/V ratio of each product.
(ii) State which product is preferable, if material is in shortage.
(iii) State which of the following sales mixes will you recommend and why :

	X	Y
Sales Mix I	14,000	6,000
Sales Mix II	10,000	10,000
Sales Mix III	8,000	12,000

(K.U.D., April 1993)

Solution : (Marginal Costing)

Key Factor Material in Shortage Sales Mix

Particulars		Product X	Product Y
Materials : X – 2 Kg. @ Rs. 6 per Kg.		12	—
Y – 3 Kg. @ Rs. 6 per Kg.		–	18
Wages		4	4
Variable overhead 100% of Direct Wages		4	4
	Marginal Cost	20	26
Selling Price		30	40
	Contribution	10	14
(1) P/V ratio = $\frac{\text{Contribution}}{\text{Sales}}$		$\frac{10}{30}$	$\frac{14}{40}$
=		$\frac{1}{3}$	$\frac{7}{20}$

(2) When Material is in shortage :

Ascertain contribution per unit of Material.

$$X - \text{Contribution per unit} = \frac{10}{2} = 5.$$

$$Y - \text{Contribution per unit} = \frac{14}{3} = 4.66.$$

The contribution per unit of material in case of product X is more than that of product Y. The available material should be used first to product X and after meeting the requirement of X, Y should be produced.

		Sales Mix		
		I	II	III
Sales Mix :	X	14,000	10,000	8,000
	Y	6,000	10,000	12,000
Contribution :				
X – 10 × 14,000		1,40,000	1,00,000	80,000
Y – 14 × 6,000		84,000	1,40,000	1,68,000
Total Contribution		2,24,000	2,40,000	2,48,000
Less : Fixed Cost		1,20,000	1,20,000	1,20,000
Profit		1,04,000	1,20,000	1,28,000

Sales Mix-III is the best combination as it gives maximum contribution and the profit.

Problem No. 17

From the information given below calculate :

(a) P/V ratio and (b) Sales required to earn a Profit of Rs. 400.

Sales 200 units at Rs. 10 per unit.

Fixed overheads – Rs. 400. Variable Cost of Rs. 6 per unit.

(K.U.D., October 1992)

Solution :

(a) P/V Ratio $= \dfrac{\text{Sales} - \text{Variable Cost}}{\text{Sales}}$

$= \dfrac{10-6}{10} = \dfrac{4}{10} = \dfrac{2}{5}$

$= \dfrac{2}{5}$ or 40%.

(b) Sales required to earn a profit of Rs. 400

Sales $= \dfrac{\text{Fixed Cost + Profit}}{\text{P/V Ratio}}$

$= \dfrac{400+400}{2/5} = 800 \times \dfrac{5}{2} = \text{Rs. } 2{,}000.$

Present Position :

Sales 200 units Rs. 10 per unit 200 × 10	2,000
Less : Variable Cost = Rs. 6 per unit 200 × 6	1,200
Contribution :	800
Less : Fixed Cost	400
Profit	400

(a) P/V ratio $= \dfrac{\text{Sales} - \text{Variable Cost}}{\text{Sales}}$

$= \dfrac{2{,}000 - 1{,}200}{2{,}000} = \dfrac{800}{2{,}000}$

$= \dfrac{2}{5}$

(b) Sales required to earn a profit of Rs. 400

Sales $= \dfrac{\text{Fixed Cost + Profit}}{\text{P/V Ratio}}$

$= \dfrac{400+400}{2/5} = 800 \times \dfrac{5}{2} = \text{Rs. } 2{,}000.$

Problem No. 18

The following information relates to the product of a company :

Selling price per unit – Rs. 10.

Variable Manufacturing cost per unit – Rs. 3.

Fixed Cost are :	Manufacturing	Rs. 1,75,000
	Administrative	Rs. 15,000
	Selling	Rs. 10,000

The company pays to its agents a commission of 30% on sales.

Calculate :

(a) B.E.P. in units and amount.

(b) P/V ratio.

(c) Sales to earn a Profit of Rs. 30,000.

(d) If the company is earning a Profit of Rs. 30,000 margin of safety available to it.

(K.U.D., April 1992)

Solution :

	Selling Price Rs.		10
Less :	Variable cost Rs.	3	
	Sales Commission (30% of 10)	3	6
	Contribution		4

Fixed Cost :

Manufacturing Expenses	1,75,000
Administrative Expenses	15,000
Selling Expenses	10,000
Total Fixed Cost	2,00,000

(1) Margin Safety = Sales – B.E.P.

$$\text{B.E.P. (In Units)} = \frac{\text{Fixed Cost}}{\text{Contribution per unit}}$$

$$= \frac{2,00,000}{4} = 50000 \text{ Units.}$$

B.E.P. (In Rs.) = 50000 × 10 = Rs. 5,00,000.

$$\text{(2) P/V ratio} = \frac{\text{Fixed Cost + Profit}}{\text{Sales}}$$

$$\text{Or} = \frac{\text{Sales – Variable Cost}}{\text{Sales}}$$

$$= \frac{10-6}{10} = \frac{4}{10} = \frac{2}{5}$$

Sales to earn of Profit of Rs. 30,000 $= \dfrac{\text{Fixed Cost + Profit}}{\text{P/V Ratio}}$

Or $= \dfrac{\text{Sales – Variable Cost}}{\text{P/V Ratio}}$

$= \dfrac{2,00,000 + 30,000}{2/5}$

$= \dfrac{2,30,000}{2/5}$

$= 2,30,000 \times \dfrac{5}{2}$

= Rs. 5,75,000

Margin of Safety = Sales actual – B.E.P.

= 5,75,000 – 5,00,000

= Rs. 75,000.

Problem No. 19

A company produces and sells 4 types of products under 4 brand names A, B, C and D respectively. The sales mixture of each product is as follows :

A – 33-1/3%; B – 41-2/3%, C – 16-2/3%; D – 8-1/3%

Total budgeted sales representing 100% capacity is Rs. 90,000 per year.

Variable costs are :

A – 20% of selling price

B – 40% of selling price

C – 50% of selling price

D – 70% of selling price

Fixed costs are Rs. 28,125 per year.

Calculate :

1. BEP for the products in total as per sales volume.
2. Profit on budgeted sales.

(K.U.D., October 1991)

Solution :

	Variable Costs				Total
	A	B	C	D	
% of Sales mix	33-1/3	41-2/3	16-2/3	8-1/3	100%
∴ Sales	30,000	37,500	15,000	7,500	90,000
∴ Variable Cost	6,000	15,000	7,500	5,200	33,750

Sales :

$$A = 90{,}000 \times \frac{100}{3} \times \frac{1}{100} = \text{Rs. } 30{,}000$$

$$B = 90{,}000 \times \frac{125}{3} \times \frac{1}{100} = \text{Rs. } 37{,}500$$

$$C = 90{,}000 \times \frac{50}{3} \times \frac{1}{100} = \text{Rs. } 15{,}000$$

$$D = 90{,}000 \times \frac{25}{3} \times \frac{1}{100} = \text{Rs. } 7{,}500$$

Variable Cost :

$$A = \frac{20}{100} \times 30{,}000 = \text{Rs. } 6{,}000$$

$$B = \frac{40}{100} \times 37{,}500 = \text{Rs. } 15{,}000$$

$$C = \frac{50}{100} \times 15{,}000 = \text{Rs. } 7{,}500$$

$$D = \frac{70}{100} \times 7{,}500 = \text{Rs. } 5{,}250$$

(1) B.E.P

$$= \frac{\text{Fixed Cost} \times \text{Sales}}{\text{Sales} - \text{Variable Cost}}$$

$$= \frac{28{,}125 \times 90{,}000}{90{,}000 - 33{,}750}$$

$$= \text{Rs. } 45{,}000$$

(2) Profit

$$= \text{Sales} - \text{Variable cost} - \text{Fixed cost}$$

$$= 90{,}000 - 33{,}750 - 28{,}125$$

$$= \text{Rs. } 28{,}125.$$

Problem No. 20

The following information relates Shivayogi Ltd. :

Sales	10000 Units @ Rs. 20 per unit.
Variable cost	Rs. 10 per unit.
Fixed cost	Rs. 80,000.

Find out : (1) Break-even point in units and in amount and profit earned.

(2) Sales to earn a profit of Rs. 60,000.

(3) P/V Ratio.

(K.U.D., April 1991 and October 1985)

Solution :

(1) Break-even point (B.E.P.) $= \dfrac{\text{Fixed Cost}}{\text{Sales Price} - \text{Variable (per unit)}}$

$= \dfrac{80,000}{20 - 10}$

$= \dfrac{80,000}{10}$

= 8,000 Units.

B.E.P. (in value) = Units × Sales per unit

= 8,000 × 20

= 1,60,000 (in Rs.)

Profit earned = S – V = F + P

= (10000 × 20) – (10000 × 10)

= 2,00,000 – 1,00,000 – 80,000 = 20,000

Profit = Rs. 20,000

(2) Sales to earn a profit of Rs. 60,000

$= \dfrac{(\text{Fixed Cost} + \text{Profit}) \times \text{Sales}}{\text{Sales} - \text{Variable cost}}$

$= \dfrac{(80,000 + 60,000)\ 2,00,000}{2,00,000 - 1,00,000}$

$= \dfrac{1,40,000 \times 2,00,000}{1,00,000}$

= 2,80,000

Sales (in units) $= \dfrac{2,80,000}{20}$

= 14000 Units.

Alternative Answer by use of P/V Ratio :

(1) P/V Ratio $= \dfrac{\text{Contribution}}{\text{Sales}}$

(b) Contribution = Sales – Variable cost

= 20 – 10

= 10

Now P/V Ratio $= \dfrac{\text{Contribution}}{\text{Sales}}$

$= \dfrac{10}{20} = \dfrac{1}{2}$ or 50%

Now B.E.P. $= \frac{\text{Fixed Cost}}{\text{P/V Ratio}}$

$= \frac{80,000}{½}$

$= 80,000 \times 2/1$

$= 1,60,000$

B.E.P. (in units) $= \frac{1,60,000}{20}$

$= 8000$ Units.

(2) Sales to earn a profit of Rs. 60,000

$= \frac{\text{Fixed Cost + Profit}}{\text{P/V Ratio}}$

$= \frac{80,000 + 60,000}{½}$

$= 1,40,000 \times 2/1$

$= 2,80,000$

Sales to earn profit of Rs. 60,000 = 2,80,000

(in units) $= \frac{2,80,000}{20}$

$= 14000$ Units.

Verification :

		Rs.
(1) B.E.P. Sales (in units)	= Units × Rate	
	= 8000 × 20 =	1,60,000
Less : Variable cost	= 8000 × 10	80,000
	Contribution	80,000
Less : Fixed Cost		80,000
	Profit/Loss	Nil
(2) Sales to earn a profit of Rs. 60,000		
Sales 14000 × 20		2,80,000
Less : Variable cost 14000 × 10		1,40,000
	Contribution	1,40,000
Less : Fixed cost		80,000
	Profit	60,000

Problem No. 21

The following figures for profit and sales are obtained from the account of 'A' Co. Ltd. :

Year	Sales Rs.	Profit Rs.
1988	40,000	4,000
1989	60,000	8,000

Calculate:

(a) P/V ratio (b) Fixed Cost

(c) Break Even Sales (d) Profit at sales of Rs. 95,000

(e) Sales to earn a Profit of Rs. 9,000.

(K.U.D., October 1990)

Solution :

(a) P/V Ratio $= \dfrac{\text{Contribution}}{\text{Sales}}$

Or $= \dfrac{\text{Changes in contribution in two periods}}{\text{Changes is sales in two periods}}$

$= \dfrac{\text{Changes in Profit in two periods}}{\text{Changes in Sales in two periods}}$

$= \dfrac{8{,}000 - 4{,}000}{60{,}000 - 40{,}000} = \dfrac{4{,}000}{20{,}000}$

$=$ 1/5 or 20%

(b) Fixed Cost = Contribution – Profit

Now calculate contribution for the year 1988.

When sales are Rs. 40,000 and P/V ratio – $\dfrac{1}{5}$

Contribution = Sales × P/V ratio

= 40,000 × 20%

= 8,000

Now Fixed Cost = Contribution – Profit

= 8,000 – 4,000

= Rs. 4,000.

(c) Break-even Point B.E.P. $= \dfrac{\text{Fixed Cost}}{\text{P/V Ratio}}$

$= \dfrac{4{,}000}{1/5}$

$= 4{,}000 \times 5$

$=$ Rs. 20,000

(d) Profit when sales are @ Rs. 95,000 :

Profit = Contribution – Fixed Cost

Now calculate contribution for sales Rs. 95,000

Contribution $=$ Sales × P/V ratio

$= 95{,}000 \times \dfrac{1}{5}$

$=$ Rs. 19,000.

Now Profit $=$ Contribution – Fixed Cost

$= 19{,}000 - 4{,}000$

$=$ Rs. 15,000

(e) Sales to earn a Profit of Rs. 9,000 :

$= \dfrac{\text{Fixed Cost + Profit}}{\text{P/V Ratio}}$

$= \dfrac{4{,}000 + 9{,}000}{1/5}$

$= 13{,}000 \times 5$

$=$ Rs. 65,000.

(f) Variable Cost in two periods :

1988 Variable Cost $=$ Sales – (Fixed Cost + Profit)

$= 40{,}000 - (4{,}000 + 4{,}000)$

$= 40{,}000 - 8{,}000$

$=$ Rs. 32,000

1989 Variable Cost $= 60{,}000 - (4{,}000 + 8{,}000)$

$= 60{,}000 - 12{,}000$

$=$ Rs. 48,000.

Problem No. 22

The cost figures for 1985 are given below :

Variable cost	5
Fixed cost	2,00,000
Sales	5,00,000

In view of intense competition to maintain the sales it is proposed to reduce the selling Price from present Rs. 10 per unit to Rs. 9 per unit in 1986. Find out the number of units to be sold to maintain the profit at the same level in 1985. Tabulate the result of 1985 and 1986 including :

(1) The number of units to be produced.

(2) The selling price realised.

(3) Required sales.

(4) The Profit earned.

(K.U.D., April 1990)

Solution :

(1) Present profit *i.e.*, for 1985

	Rs.
Sales Price of Rs. 10 per unit = 50000 × 10	5,00,000
Less : Variable cost Rs. 5 per unit (5 × 50000)	2,50,000
Contribution	2,50,000
Less : Fixed Cost	2,00,000
Present Profit (for 1985)	50,000

(2) Future Sales and Profit for 1986

When sales Price (1985)		10
Reduced to Rs. (1986)		9
Future sales price	Rs.	9 per unit
Variable cost		5
Contribution		4

$$\text{Future P/V Ratio} = \frac{\text{Contribution}}{\text{Sales}}$$

$$\text{P/V Ratio} = \frac{4}{9}$$

$$\text{Now B.E.P.} = \frac{\text{Fixed Cost}}{\text{P/V Ratio}}$$

$$= \frac{2,00,000}{4/9}$$

$$= 2,00,000 \times \frac{4}{9} = 4,50,000$$

$$\text{B.E.P. (in units)} = \frac{4,50,000}{9}$$

$$= 50000 \text{ Units.}$$

Verification :

Sales 50000 × 9	=	4,50,000
Less : Variable cost 50000 × 5		2,50,000
	Contribution	2,00,000
Less : Fixed Cost		2,00,000
	Profit/Loss	Nil

(2) Sales to earn present profit of Rs. 50,000

$$= \frac{\text{Fixed Cost + Profit}}{\text{P/V Ratio}}$$

$$= \frac{2,00,000 + 50,000}{4/9}$$

$$= 2,50,000 \times \frac{9}{4}$$

= Rs. 5,62,500

Sales required to earn a profit of Rs. 50,000 = 5,62,500 (in Rs.)

Verification :

Sales required to earn profit of Rs. 50,000 of 1985 and in 1986

Sales in units × Rate = 62500 × 9	=	5,62,500
Less : Variable cost 62500 × 5		3,12,500
	Contribution	2,50,000
Less : Fixed Cost		2,00,000
	Profit	50,000

In 1986 :

Sales Price per unit Rs. 9	5,62,500
Profit	50,000

No. of units to be produced 62500 Units.

Problem No. 23

The Anup Radio Co. manufacture and sold 10000 Radios last year at a price of Rs. 500 each. The cost structure per Radio is as follows :

Material	100
Labour	50
Variable overhead	25
Marginal Cost	175
Fixed Cost	200
Total cost	375
Profit	125
Selling Price	500

Due to heavy competition price has to be reduced to Rs. 425 for coming year.

Assuming no change in cost state the number Radios that would have to be sold at the new price to ensure the same amount of profit as that of last year.

(K.U.D., October 1989)

Solution :

Profit of Rs. 125 per Radio when selling price was Rs. 500.

Total profit = 125 × 10000 = 12,50,000

Present Sales Price	500	Fixed Cost	20,00,000
Future Sales Price	425		

Variable cost remains the same in both cases. Variable cost Rs. 175.

Now Sales to earn a profit of Rs. 12,50,000 (@ future selling Price Rs. 425)

$$= \frac{\text{Fixed Cost + Profit}}{\text{Selling Price – Variable Cost (per unit)}}$$

$$= \frac{20,00,000 + 12,50,000}{425 - 175} = \frac{32,50,000}{250} = 13000 \text{ Units to be sold.}$$

Problem No. 24

Videocon Appliances Ltd. manufactured and sold 1000 washing machines. Last year at a price of Rs. 5,000 each. Cost structure per machine is as follows :

Direct Material		1,000
Direct Wages		500
Variable Overhead		250
	Marginal Cost	1,750
Fixed Overhead		2,000
	Total cost	3,750
Profit		1,250
Selling Price		5,000

Due to heavy competition Price has to be reduced to Rs. 4,250 for the coming year. Assuming no change in cost state the number of machines that would have to be sold at the new Price to ensure the same amount of total profits as the last year.

(K.U.D., April 1989)

Solution :

Profit for 1000 Machines – Rs. 1,250 × 1000	=	12,50,000
Fixed Cost (1000 × 2,000)	=	20,00,000
Contribution @ Reduced Price Rs. 4,250	=	Sales – Variable cost
Present 5,000 & Future – 4,250	=	4,250 – 1,750
Contribution	=	Rs. 2,500 per month.

Sales required to earn profit of Rs. 12,50,000
The Price is @ 4,250

$$\text{Formula} = \frac{\text{Fixed Cost + Profit}}{\text{P/V Ratio}}$$

$$\text{P/V Ratio} = \frac{\text{Contribution per unit}}{\text{Selling Price per unit}}$$

$$= \frac{2{,}500}{4{,}250}$$

$$= \frac{10}{17}$$

Now Sales @ Rs. 4,250 required to earn profit of Rs. 12,50,000

$$\text{B.E.P. (in value)} = \frac{\text{Fixed Cost + Profit}}{\text{P/V Ratio}}$$

$$= \frac{20{,}00{,}000 + 12{,}50{,}000}{10/17}$$

$$= 32{,}50{,}000 \times \frac{17}{10}$$

$$= 55{,}25{,}000$$

$$\text{B.E.P. (in units)} = \frac{55{,}25{,}000}{4{,}250}$$

= 1300 Machines to be sold.

Verification :

$$\text{Sales in Units} = \frac{\text{Fixed Cost + Profit}}{\text{Contribution per unit}}$$

$$\text{Contribution} = 4{,}250 - 1{,}750$$

$$= 2{,}500$$

$$\text{Sales in Units} = \frac{20{,}00{,}000 + 12{,}50{,}000}{2{,}500}$$

$$= \frac{32{,}50{,}000}{2{,}500}$$

= 1300 Units.

Problem No. 25

The price and cost structure of a product in a company are as follows :

Selling Price per unit Rs. 30

Variable cost per unit Rs. 9

Fixed costs are :

(1) Manufacturing Rs. 2,25,000 per annum.

(2) Administration Rs. 36,000 per annum.

(3) What should be value of sales to earn a Profit of Rs. 60,000.

(4) In the above situation the company wants to reduce its price to Rs. 27 per unit from the present Rate of Rs. 30.

(5) What should be the value of sales to maintain this level of profit.

(K.U.D., October 1988)

Solution :

Sales price per unit	Rs.	30
Variable cost per unit	Rs.	9
Total Fixed cost :		
(a) Manufacturing	Rs.	2,25,000
(b) Administrative	Rs.	36,000
Total Fixed cost	Rs.	2,61,000

(1) P/V Ratio $= \dfrac{\text{Contribution}}{\text{Sales}}$

Contribution (per unit) = Sales – Variable cost

= 30 – 9

= 21 per unit

Now P/V Ratio $= \dfrac{\text{Contribution}}{\text{Sales}}$

$= \dfrac{21}{30}$

$= \dfrac{7}{10}$

(2) Desired sales to earn a profit of Rs. 60,000

Desired Sales $= \dfrac{\text{Fixed Cost + Profit}}{\text{P/V Ratio}}$

$= \dfrac{2{,}61{,}000 + 60{,}000}{7/10}$

$= 3{,}21{,}000 \times 10/7$

$= 4{,}58{,}571.42$

In Units $= \dfrac{4{,}58{,}571.42}{30}$

$= 15285.714$ Or 15286 Units.

Verification :

Sales Units × Rate =	15286 × 30	=	4,58,580
Variable cost	15286 × 9	=	1,37,574
	Contribution		3,21,000
Contribution (rouded up)			3,21,000
Less : Fixed Cost			2,61,000
	Profit		60,000

(3) When the sales price reduced to Rs. 27 from Rs. 30 what should be sales to earn the same previous profit of Rs. 60.

Present sales price Rs. 30 per unit

Reduced to Rs. 27 per unit

Future sales price	27
Variable cost	9
Contribution	18 per unit

Now P/V Ratio = Contribution

P/V Ratio $= \dfrac{18}{27}$

$= \dfrac{2}{3}$ Or 67%

Now sales to earn a profit of Rs. 60,000

$= \dfrac{\text{Fixed Cost + Profit}}{\text{P/V Ratio}}$

$= \dfrac{2{,}61{,}000 + 60{,}000}{2/3}$

$= 3{,}21{,}000 \times \dfrac{3}{2} = 4{,}81{,}500$

Sales to earn a profit of Rs. 60,000 = Rs. 4,81,500

Sales in units $= \dfrac{4{,}81{,}500}{27} = 17833.33$ Or 17834 Units.

Verification :

Sales unit 17833.33 × 27 =		4,81,500
Less : Variable cost 17833.33 × 9 =		1,60,500
	Contribution	3,12,000
Less : Fixed Cost		2,61,000
	Profit	Rs. 60,000

Problem No. 26

Electronic Equipment Ltd. manufactures calculators. The following particulars are provided :

Materials Cost (per unit)	80.00
Conversion (variable) cost	60.00
Dealers Commission	20.00
Selling Price	200.00 per unit
Fixed cost	Rs. 5,00,000
Present sales	18000 Units
Capacity utilisation	60%

There is acute competition, increased efforts are needed to sell the produce. Suggestions have been made for increasing sales.

(a) By reducing sales Price by 5%.

(b) By increasing Dealers commission over the existing rate would of the two suggestions would you recommend earn present profit.

(K.U.D., October 1987)

Solution :

Calculation of Present Profit

Present Variable cost (cost per unit) :

Materials	80
Conversion cost	60
Dealers commission	20
Variable cost	120

Now *Contribution per unit*

Selling Price (per unit)	200
Less : Variable cost	160
Contribution (per unit)	40
Total contribution = 18000 × 40 =	7,20,000
Less : Fixed cost	5,00,000
Present Profit	2,20,000

Suggested courses – Profit desired of Rs. 2,20,000

(a) If sales Price reduced by 5%

Present sales Price	200
Less : Reduced by 5% of 200	10
Future Selling Price	190

The present dealers commission is Rs. 20 when sales price was Rs. 200. The dealers commission is 10% on selling Price.

The dealers commission @ Rs. 190 selling Price :

10% of 190 =		19
New *Contribution* :		
Selling Price (per Unit)		190
Less : Variable cost :		
Materials	80	
Conversion cost	60	
Dealers Commission	19	159
New Contribution		31

Sales (in units) required to earn profit of Rs. 2,20,000 :

$$= \frac{\text{Fixed Cost + Profit}}{\text{Contribution (per unit)}}$$

$$= \frac{5,00,000 + 2,20,000}{31}$$

$$= 23226 \text{ Units}$$

Or if Dealers commission Rs. 20 per unit remains unchanged :

Contribution	=	Sales	190
		Less : Variable cost	160
		Contribution	30

Now Sales (in units) to earn a profit of Rs. 2,20,000 :

$$= \frac{\text{Fixed Cost + Profit}}{\text{Contribution per unit}}$$

$$= \frac{5,00,000 + 2,20,000}{30}$$

$$= \frac{7,20,000}{30}$$

$$= 24000 \text{ Units.}$$

(b) If dealers commission is increased by 20%

Dealers Commission	=	Rs. 20.00
Add : Increase 20% of Rs. 20	=	Rs. 4.00
		24.00

Sales	200
Less : Variable Cost (80 + 60 + 24)	164
Contribution	36

$$\text{Sales in Units} = \frac{\text{Contribution}}{\text{Contribution (per unit)}}$$

$$\begin{aligned}\text{Contribution} &= \text{Fixed Cost + Profit}\\ &= 5{,}00{,}000 + 2{,}20{,}000\\ &= 7{,}20{,}000\end{aligned}$$

$$\begin{aligned}\text{Sales (in Units)} &= \frac{\text{Contribution}}{\text{Contribution (per unit)}}\\ &= \frac{7{,}20{,}000}{36}\\ &= \text{20000 Units.}\end{aligned}$$

Problem No. 27

A company is producing 500000 units @ a variable cost of Rs. 20 :
The fixed costs are Rs. 20,00,000
The selling price is Rs. 30 per unit.
What is B.E.P. in terms of sales in unit?
The company is thinking of reducing the selling price by Rs. 5 per unit in view of the severe competition. What will be the effect on B.E.P.?

(K.U.D., April 1987)

Solution :

$$\begin{aligned}\text{B.E.P. Sales in units} &= \frac{\text{Fixed Cost}}{\text{Contribution per unit}}\\ &= \frac{\text{Fixed cost}}{\text{Selling price} - \text{Variable cost (per unit)}}\end{aligned}$$

Now : Selling price per unit = 30
Variable cost per unit = 20
Fixed Cost = Rs. 20,00,000

$$\begin{aligned}\text{B.E.P. Sales (in units)} &= \frac{\text{Fixed Cost}}{\text{Selling price} - \text{Variable cost (per unit)}}\\ &= \frac{20{,}00{,}000}{30-20} = \frac{20{,}00{,}000}{10}\\ &= \text{200000 Units.}\end{aligned}$$

$$\begin{aligned}\text{B.E.P. Sales in value} &= 200000 \times 30\\ &= \text{Rs. } 60{,}00{,}000\end{aligned}$$

When selling price is reduced by Rs. 5

Future selling Price = 30 – 5 = Rs. 25 per unit

$$\text{B.E.P. sales} = \frac{20{,}00{,}000}{25-20} = \frac{20{,}00{,}000}{5}$$

= 400000 Units.

Verification :

			Rs.
Sales Price	= 25 × 400000	=	1,00,00,000
Variable cost	= 20 × 400000	=	80,00,000
	Contribution		20,00,000
Fixed Cost			20,00,000
	No Profit/No Loss		– Nil –

Problem No. 28

A manufacturing company sells its products under the Brand names of X, Y & Z. The sales Mix value of each product is given below :

X – 20%, Y 50% and Z – 30%.

The total budgeted sales representing (100% capacity) is estimated at Rs. 6,00,000 per year.

Variable Costs are :

Product X – 30% of Selling Price

Product Y – 60% of Selling Price

Product Z – 40% of Selling Price.

Fixed costs for the year is Rs. 1,24,800.

Your are required to :

(1) Find out Profit on budgeted sales.

(2) Ascertain B.E.P. for the products in total as per sales value.

(K.U.D., October 1986)

Solution :

Statement showing Profit & B.E.P.

	Products			Total
	X	Y	Z	
Sales Mix	20%	50%	30%	100%
Sales Value	1,20,000	3,00,000	1,80,000	6,00,000
Less : Variable cost (30%, 60% & 40%)	36,000	1,80,000	72,000	2,88,000
Contribution	84,000	1,20,000	1,08,000	3,12,000
Less : Fixed Cost	—	—	—	1,24,800
Profit				Rs. 1,87,200

		Products			Total
		X	Y	Z	
P/V Ratio =	$\frac{\text{Contribution}}{\text{Sales}}$	$\frac{84,000}{1,20,000}$	$\frac{1,20,000}{3,00,000}$	$\frac{1,08,000}{1,80,000}$	$\frac{3,12,000}{6,00,000}$
		7/10 Or 70%	2/5 Or 40%	3/5 Or 60%	13/25 Or 52%

$$\text{B.E.P. (in value)} = \frac{\text{Fixed Cost}}{\text{Contribution}}$$

$$= \frac{1,24,800}{3,12,000} \times 40\% \text{ of total sales of Rs. } 6,00,000$$

= Rs. 2,40,000 B.E.P. Sales in value.

Alternatively

(I) *Sales Value of the Products :*

X – 20% of Rs. 6,00,000 = 1,20,000

Y – 50% of Rs. 6,00,000 = 3,00,000

Z – 30% of Rs. 6,00,000 = 1,80,000

(II) *Variable Cost of the Products :*

X – 30% of Selling Price of 1,20,000	=	36,000	
Y – 60% of Selling Price of 3,00,000	=	1,80,000	
Z – 40% of Selling Price of 1,80,000	=	72,000	2,88,000

(III) Contribution = Sales – Variable cost

= 6,00,000 – 2,88,000

= Rs. 3,12,000

$$\text{B.E.P. (Sales)} = \frac{\text{Sales} \times \text{Fixed Cost}}{\text{Contribution}}$$

$$= \frac{6,00,000 \times 1,24,800}{3,12,000}$$

= Rs. 2,40,000

Profit on Budgted Sales :

Profit = Contribution – Fixed Cost

= 3,12,000 – 1,24,800

= Rs. 1,87,200.

Problem No. 29

From the particulars given below calculate :

(1) B.E.P.

(2) P/V Ratio

(3) Profit on budgeted sales

(4) Profit on 100% capacity (Assuming no changes to Rs. 80,000).

The particulars are :

(a) Budgeted sales during 1984-85 amounted to Rs. 80,000 (80% capacity)

(b) Direct material costs — 40% of sales.

(c) Direct labour costs — 20% of sales.

(d) Variable factory overheads — 10% of sales.

(e) Variable administrative overheads — 5% of sales.

(f) Fixed cost — Rs. 10,000.

(K.U.D., April 1986)

Solution :

If sales price is	100	100%
Variable costs :		
Material cost	40% of sales	
Labour cost	20% of sales	
Factory overhead	10% of sales	
Administrative overhead	5% of sales	
Total variable costs		75%
Contribution		25%

(1) P/V Ratio $= \frac{\text{Contribution}}{\text{Sales}}$

$= \frac{25\%}{100\%}$

$= \frac{1}{4}$ Or 25%

(2) B.E.P. Sales $= \frac{\text{Fixed Cost}}{\text{P/V Ratio}}$

$= \frac{10{,}000}{1/4}$

$= 10{,}000 \times 4/1$

= Rs. 40,000

(3) Profit on budgeted sales of Rs. 80,000 :

Sales	80,000
Less : Variable cost (75% or 80,000)	60,000
Contribution	20,000
Less : Fixed cost	10,000
On budgeted sales profit	Rs. 10,000

(4) Profit on 100% Capacity :

For 80% capacity	80,000
For 100% capacity	1,00,000
Less : Variable cost (75% of sales)	75,000
Contribution	25,000
Less : Fixed cost	10,000
On 100% Capacity sales Profit	Rs. 15,000

Problem No. 30

Star Ltd. furnishes you the following data relating to the year 1983 :

	First Half of the year Rs.	Second Half of the year Rs.
Sales	45,000	50,000
Total cost	40,000	43,000

Assuming there is no change in prices and variable cost.

The Fixed costs are incurred equally in the two half year periods.

Calculate :

(1) P/V Ratio

(2) Fixed Cost

(3) Break-Even Point (B.E.P.) Sales

(4) Percentage of Margin of Safety.

(K.U.D., October 1985)

Solution :

First calculate profit in two periods :

	First half	Second half
Sales	45,000	50,000
Less : Total Cost	40,000	43,000
Profit	5,000	7,000

Now ascertain changes in sales and profit in two periods :

	Sales	Profit
Second half	50,000	7,000
First half	45,000	5,000
Changes in Sales & Profit	5,000	2,000

(a) Calculation of P/V Ratio :

$$\text{P/V Ratio} = \frac{\text{Changes in Profits}}{\text{Changes in Sales}}$$

$$= \frac{2{,}000}{5{,}000} = \frac{2}{5} \text{ Or } 40\%$$

(b) Calculation of Fixed Cost :

Now ascertain contribution for First half when sales are Rs. 45,000 :

Contribution = Sales × P/V Ratio

= 45,000 × 2/5

= Rs. 18,000

Fixed cost = Contribution – Profit

= 18,000 – 5,000

= Rs. 13,000

(c) Now B.E.P. Sales

$$= \frac{\text{Fixed Cost}}{\text{P/V Ratio}}$$

$$= \frac{13{,}000}{2/5}$$

$$= 13{,}000 \times \frac{5}{2}$$

= Rs. 32,500

(d) Margin of Safety (First half period) = Sales – B.E.P. Sales

= 45,000 – 32,500

= Rs. 12,500

Or : M/S

$$= \frac{\text{Profit}}{\text{P/V Ratio}}$$

$$= \frac{5{,}000}{2/5}$$

$$= 5{,}000 \times \frac{5}{2}$$

= Rs. 12,500

Margin of Safety (Second half period) = Sales – B.E.P. Sales

= 50,000 – 32,500

= Rs. 17,500

OR : M/S = $\frac{\text{Profit}}{\text{P/V Ratio}}$

= $\frac{7,000}{2/5}$

= $7,000 \times \frac{5}{2}$

= Rs. 17,500.

Problem No. 31

From the following data which product would you recommend to be manufactured in a factory time being Key factor.

Particulars	Per unit Product-A	Per unit Product-B
Direct Materials	24	14
Direct Labour (Re. 1.00 per hour)	2	3
Variable cost (Re. 2 per hour)	4	6
Selling Price	100	100
Standard time to produce	2 Hours	3 Hours

(K.U.D., April 1985)

Solution :

			Product A	Product B
Selling Price			100	100
Less : Variable cost	A	B		
Material	24	14		
Labour (Re. 1 per Hour)	2	3		
Variable Overhead (Rs. 2 per hour)	4	6		
	30	23	30	23
	Contribution		70	77

P/V Ratio = $\frac{\text{Contribution}}{\text{Sales}} = \frac{70}{100} = \frac{7}{10}$ Or 70% 77%

When Time is Key factor Contribution per hour = 70/2 = Rs. 35

77/3 = Rs. 25.67

Recommendation : If time is Key factor contribution per Labour Hour is high in Product A than that of Product B.

During the labour shortage product A is to be produced. During Normal period P/V Ratio in product B is higher and therefore product B is more profitable.

Problem No. 32

From the below given information, determine the Net Profit if sales are 10% and 15% above the Break-Even Point :

Selling Price	Rs. 10.00
Trade Discount	5%
Direct Material cost per unit	3%
Direct labour cost per unit	2%
Fixed overhead	Rs. 10,000

Variable overhead 100% of Direct Wages.

(K.U.D., October 1984)

Solution :

Selling Price		10.00
Less : *Variable cost* :		
(1) Trade discount 5% of Rs. 10 =	0.50	
(2) Material cost per unit	3.00	
(3) Labour cost	2.00	
(4) Variable overhead (100% of direct Labour)	2.00	7.50
Contribution		2.50

$$\text{B.E.P. (sales in units)} = \frac{\text{Fixed Cost}}{\text{Contribution per unit}}$$

$$= \frac{10{,}000}{2.50} = 4000 \text{ Units.}$$

B.E.P. (sales in value) = 4000 × 10 = Rs. 40,000

	Rs.	Units
B.E.P. Present sales	40,000	4000
If 10% increase above B.E.P. *Add* : 10% of 4000 =		400
		4400
Contribution for 4400 × 2.50 =	11,000	
Less : Fixed Cost	10,000	
Profit	1,000	

If 15% increase above B.E.P. sales of 4000 Units.

Present Sales		4000 Units	
Increase 15%		600	
	Total Sales	4600 Units	Rs.
Contribution 4600 × 2.50 =			11,500
Less : Fixed Cost			10,000
	Profit		1,500

Problem No. 33

The cost and the price structure of a product of a company are as follows :

Selling Price per unit	Rs. 10
Variable manufacturing cost	Rs. 3
Fixed costs :	
Manufacturing	Rs. 75,000 per year.
Selling	Rs. 13,000 per year.
Administration	Rs. 12,000 per year.

The company has to pay to its agents a commission of 20% on sales. Compute :

(a) B.E.P. in the above situation

(b) P/V Ratio

(c) If the company want to have a profit of Rs. 20,000 what would be the level of sales.

(K.U.D., October 1983)

Solution :

(1) P/V Ratio = $\frac{\text{Contribution}}{\text{Sales}}$

Now Sales		10
Less : Variable Cost (manufacturing)	3	
Less : Commission on sales (20% of 10)	2	5
Contribution		5

(2) P/V Ratio $= \frac{\text{Contribution}}{\text{Sales}}$

$= \frac{5}{10} = ½$ or 50%.

(3) Sales to earn a Profit of Rs. 20,000

$$= \frac{\text{Fixed Cost + Profit}}{\text{P/V Ratio}} = \frac{1{,}00{,}000 + 20{,}000}{½}$$

Sales $= 1{,}20{,}000 \times 2 =$ Rs. 2,40,000

Verification :

Sales		2,40,000
Less : Contribution ½ of sales		1,20,000
		1,20,000
Less : Fixed Cost		1,00,000
	Profit	Rs. 20,000

Problem No. 34

Alphas Ltd. manufactures and sells four types of products under four Brands named as A, B, C & D respectively.

The sales mix in value comprises of :

A – 33-1/3%, B – 41-2/3%, C – 16-2/3% and D – 8-1/3%.

The total budgeted sales (100%) are Rs. 60,000 per month.

Variable costs are :

Product A – 60% of the selling Price.

Product B – 68% of the selling Price.

Product C – 80% of the selling Price

Product D – 40% of the selling Price.

Fixed costs are Rs. 14,700.

(a) Calculate B.E.P. for the production on the overall basis and also find out the Net Profit on the Budgeted sales.

(K.U.D., April 1983)

(b) It has been proposed to change the sales Mix as follows : The total sales per month remaining Rs. 60,000

Product A - 25%

B - 40%

C - 30%

D - 5%

Assuming that the proposal is implemented, calculate the Break-Even Point and state the main factor which contribute to the shift in B.E.P. in the New position.

(I.C.W.A. Final)

Solution-I :

Calculation of B.E.P. and the Net Profit

Particulars	Product A	Product B	Product C	Product D	Total
(a) Sales Mix (in %)	33-1/3	41-2/3	16-2/3	8-1/3	100
(b) Sales Values	20,000	25,000	10,000	5,000	60,000
(c) *Less* : Variable (cost 60%, 68%, 80% & 40%)	12,000	17,000	8,000	2,000	39,000
Contribution	8,000	8,000	2,000	3,000	21,000
Less : Fixed Cost	—	—	—	—	14,700
	Profit				6,300

P/V Ratio :

$= \frac{\text{Contribution}}{\text{Sales}}$	$\frac{8,000}{20,000}$	$\frac{8,000}{20,000}$	$\frac{2,000}{10,000}$	$\frac{3,000}{5,000}$
=	2/5	8/25	1/5	3/5
B.E.P. = $\frac{\text{Fixed Cost}}{\text{Contribution}}$	40%	32%	20%	60%

$$= \frac{14,700}{21,000} \times 100 = 70\% \text{ of the total sales } i.e., 60,000 \times 70\%$$

$$= \text{Rs. } 42,000$$

Solution-II :

Proposed Changes in Sales Mix Calculation of B.E.P. & Profit

Particulars	Product A	Product B	Product C	Product D	Total
Sales Mix (in %)	25%	40%	30%	5%	100%
Sales value	15,000	24,000	18,000	3,000	60,000
Less : Variable cost (60%, 68%, 80% & 40%)	9,000	16,320	14,400	1,200	40,920
Contribution	6,000	7,680	3,600	1,800	19,080
Fixed Cost					14,700
	Profit				4,380
P/V ratio		40%	32%	20%	60%

$$\text{B.E.P.} = \frac{\text{Fixed Cost}}{\text{Contribution}} = \frac{14,700}{19,080} = 77\% \text{ of the Total Sales.}$$

B.E.P. Sales in value = 77% of 60,000 = Rs. 46,200

The B.E.P. has shifted to the right $\frac{\text{curtailing}}{\text{(reducing)}}$ the margin of safety by Rs. 4,200 (46,200 – 42,000).

The proposed sales Mix has an adverse effect in as much as product D and A which were contributing the highest P/V Ratio have been made to go down and product 'C' which was contributing the lowest (*i.e.*, 20%) has gone up considerably in production. As a result of it, the total profit — has gone down — (reduced) from Rs. 6,300 to Rs. 4,380 = Rs. 1,920 Net Loss.

KEY FACTOR OR LIMITING FACTOR

Key factor is one which limits production and profits of business. It may be scarcity of any factor of production such as material, labour, capital, plant capacity etc.

It is a scarce factor :

Where a concern has two or more production and a factor of production is in scarce the problem of utilising such a factor in best possible manner arises.

In such cases a decision has to be taken regarding choice of production increase or reduce or stop completely. Usually when there is no limiting factor the choice of product will be on the basis of higher P/V Ratio.

But when there are scarce or limiting factor, selection of product will be on the basis of contribution per unit of limiting factor of production.

Therefore scarce resource should be utilised where contribution per unit of limited resources is maximum.

Problem No. 35

Key Factor Material/Choice of Profitable Mix.

M/s Pande Enterprises has a plant which can produce two types of articles namely A & B. They supply you the following information (per unit bases) :

Materials	Product A	Product B
	Rs.	Rs.
A – 2 Kgs. @ Rs. 3	6.00	
B – 3 Kgs. @ Rs. 3		9.00
Wages	2.00	2.00
Variable overhead	2.00	2.00
Selling Price	15.00	20.00

Fixed Costs – Rs. 80,000 per annum

You are required to :

(a) Find out P/V Ratio of each product.

(b) State which product will you prefer if raw material is in short?

(c) State which of the following sales Mix will you recommend and why?

Sales Mix – I	A – 12,000	B – 8,000
Sales Mix – II	A – 10,000	B – 10,000
Sales Mix – III	A – 9,000	B – 11,000

(K.U.D., October 1982)

Solution :

Marginal cost of products & contribution per unit.

	A	B	Product A Rs.	Product B Rs.
Sales Price			15.00	20.00
Less : Marginal Cost				
Material	6	9		
Wages	2	2		
Variable Overhead	2	2	10.00	13.00
Contribution			5.00	7.00

(I) P/V Ratio = $\frac{\text{Contribution}}{\text{Sales}}$ A: $\frac{5}{15}$ = 1/3   B: $\frac{7}{20}$ = 7/20

(II) Material is in scarce (shortage)

	Product A	Product B
Contribution per Unit	5	7
Material used	2 Kgs	3 Kgs
Ratio : $\frac{\text{Contribution}}{\text{Material in Kg}}$ =	$\frac{5}{2}$	$\frac{7}{3}$
	2.50	2.33

Since contribution per unit of material in product A is more that of product B. Therefore the available material should be used to produce product A and after meeting the demand, it should be used to produce product B.

(III) Contribution and Profit from each of the Sales Mix.

		Sales Mix I	Sales Mix II	Sales Mix III
	A	12,000	10,000	9,000
	B	8,000	10,000	11,000
Contribution : on Sales Mix				
	A-5	60,000	50,000	45,000
	B-7	56,000	70,000	77,000
Total contribution		1,16,000	1,20,000	1,22,000
Less : Fixed Cost		80,000	80,000	80,000
Profit		36,000	40,000	42,000

Suggested Sales Mix-III is the best combination as it gives maximum contribution and the profit and therefore it is recommended Sales Mix-III.

Problem No. 36

Due to labour strike labour being limiting factor you are required to find out the profitability of producing one of the two products. Following are the particulars :

	Product X	Product Y
Direct Material	125	125
Direct Wages @ Rs. 2.50 per hour	50	25
Veriable Overhead 100% of Direct Wages	50	25
Fixed Overhead Rs. 50,000 Sales	250	200

Solution :

Statement of Cost	Product X	Product Y
Direct Material	125	125
Direct Wages Rs. 2.50 per hour	50	25
Prime Cost	175	150
Variable Overhead 100% Direct Wages	50	25
Total of Variable cost Or Marginal cost	225	175
Sales	250	200
Contribution	25	25

Contribution in both the cases is the same and labour is key factor.
Product-X, 20 Hours, Product-Y, 10 Hours

$$\text{Profitability} = \frac{\text{Contribution}}{\text{Key Factor Labour}}$$

$$\text{Product-X} = \frac{25}{20} = \text{Rs. } 1.25 \qquad \text{Product-Y} = \frac{25}{10} = \text{Rs. } 2.50$$

Therefore product-Y yields Rs. 2.50 per hour whereas product-X yields Rs. 1.25 and therefore during strike period product-Y is more profitable.

Problem No. 37

Standard Co. Ltd. gives you the following information :

Period	Sales	Profit
I	1,50,000	4,000
II	1,90,000	11,500

Calculate :

(a) P/V Ratio

(b) Profit when sales are Rs. 1,20,000

(c) Sales required to earn a profit of Rs. 20,000

(d) Break-Even Point (B.E.P.).

(K.U.D., April 1982)

Solution :

B.E.P. (in sales) $= \dfrac{\text{Fixed Cost}}{\text{P/V Ratio}}$

(a) P/V Ratio $= \dfrac{\text{Changes in profit}}{\text{Changes in sales}}$

Changes in	Sales	Profit
Period-II	1,90,000	11,500
Period-I	1,50,000	4,000
	40,000	7,500

Now P/V Ratio $= \dfrac{\text{Changes in profit}}{\text{Changes in sales}}$

$= \dfrac{7,500}{40,000}$

$= \dfrac{3}{16}$ Or 18.75%

Now contribution for period-I when sales of Rs. 1,50,000 :

Contribution = Sales × P/V Ratio

= 1,50,000 × 3/16

= Rs. 28,125

Now Fixed Cost = Contribution − Profit

= 28,125 - 4,000

= Rs. 24,125

(b) Profit when sales are Rs. 1,20,000 :

Contribution = Sales × P/V Ratio

= 1,20,000 × 3/16

= Rs. 22,500

Profit Or Loss = Contribution − Fixed Cost

= 22,500 – 24,125

Loss = Rs. – 1,625.

(c) Sales required to earn a profit of Rs. 20,000 :

$$\text{Sales} = \frac{\text{Contribution}}{\text{P/V Ratio}}$$

$$\text{Or} = \frac{\text{Fixed Cost + Profit}}{\text{P/V Ratio}}$$

$$= \frac{24{,}125 + 20{,}000}{3/16}$$

$$= 44{,}125 \times \frac{16}{3}$$

$$= 2{,}35{,}333.32$$

$$= \text{Rs. } 2{,}35{,}333$$

$$\text{(d) B.E.P. (in Sales)} = \frac{\text{Fixed Cost}}{\text{P/V Ratio}}$$

$$= \frac{24{,}125}{\frac{3}{16}}$$

$$= 24{,}125 \times \frac{16}{3}$$

$$= \text{Rs. } 1{,}28{,}667.$$

Problem No. 38

The operating results of a company for the last two years are as follows :

Year	Sales Rs.	Profit Rs.
1979	2,00,000	20,000
1980	3,00,000	40,000

(1) What would be the profit when sales are Rs. 1,80,000.

(2) What sales yield a profit of Rs. 50,000.

(3) Calculate Break-Even Point – Sales and Fixed cost.

(K.U.D., April 1981)

Solution :

$$\text{(1) B.E.P. Sales} = \frac{\text{Fixed Cost}}{\text{P/V Ratio}}$$

$$\text{P/V Ratio} = \frac{\text{Contribution}}{\text{Sales}}$$

$$\text{OR} = \frac{\text{Changes in profits in two periods}}{\text{Changes in sales in two periods.}}$$

Changes in	Sales	Profit
1980	3,00,000	40,000
1979	2,00,000	20,000
	1,00,000	20,000

Now P/V Ratio $= \dfrac{\text{Changes in Profit}}{\text{Changes in Sales}}$

$= \dfrac{20,000}{1,00,000}$

$= \dfrac{1}{5}$ or 20%

Contribution during 1979 when sales are Rs. 2,00,000 :

Contribution = Sales × P/V Ratio

$= 2,00,000 \times \dfrac{1}{5}$

= Rs. 40,000

Fixed Cost = Contribution – Profit

= 40,000 – 20,000

= Rs. 20,000

Now B.E.P. Sales $= \dfrac{\text{Fixed Cost}}{\text{P/V Ratio}}$

$= \dfrac{20,000}{1/5}$

$= 20,000 \times \dfrac{5}{1}$

= Rs. 1,00,000.

(2) Profit when sales are Rs. 1,80,000 :

Contribution = Sales × P/V Ratio

$= 1,80,000 \times \dfrac{1}{5}$

= 1,80,000 × 1/5

= Rs. 36,000

Profit = Contribution – Fixed Cost

= 36,000 – 20,000

= Rs. 16,000.

Sales required when profit are Rs. 50,000 calculate contribution :

Contribution = Fixed Cost + Profit

= 20,000 + 50,000

= 70,000

Now sales to earn a profit of Rs. 50,000

$$\text{Sales} = \frac{\text{Contribution}}{\text{P/V Ratio}}$$

$$= \frac{70{,}000}{1/5}$$

$$= 70{,}000 \times \frac{5}{1}$$

Sales = Rs. 3,50,000.

Problem No. 39

Mr. Basavaraj carries on Trading Business and earns a Gross Profit of 25% (before charging commission) on cost. He has appointed a sole selling agent to whom a commission at 10% on Selling price has been given. There are no other variable costs. Fixed expenses are Rs. 600 per month. Calculate the number of units he has to sell in a year to earn a profit of Rs. 6,000 if the selling price is fixed at Rs. 25% per unit.

(K.U.D., October 1980)

Solution :

	Rs.
Selling Price per unit	25
Less : Profit 25% on cost or 20% on sales	
$\frac{25}{125} \times 25 = 5$ or 20% on 25 = 5	5
Total Cost	20
Direct variable cost	
Add : 10% commission on selling Price	
$25 \times \frac{10}{100}$	2.50
Total Variable cost	22.50
Fixed Expenses Rs. 600 per month	
(for one year 600 × 12)	7,200

No. of units to earn a profit of Rs. 6,000 per year

$$\text{Sales} = \frac{\text{Fixed Cost + Profit}}{\text{Selling Price – Variable cost (per unit)}}$$

$$= \frac{7{,}200 + 6{,}000}{25 - 22.5}$$

$$= \frac{13{,}200}{2.50} = 5280 \text{ Units.}$$

Sales in values = 5280 × 25 = Rs. 1,32,000

Verification :

Sales 5280 × 25	1,32,000
Less : Variable cost (5280 × 22.50)	1,18,800
Contribution	13,200
Less : Fixed cost	7,200
Profit	Rs. 6,000

Problem No. 40

PROFIT PLANNING

$$\text{Expected Sales} = \frac{\text{Fixed Cost + Profit}}{\text{P/V Ratio}}$$

$$\text{P/V Ratio} = \frac{\text{Sales – Variable Cost}}{\text{Sales}}$$

$$\text{Or} = \frac{\text{Contribution}}{\text{Sales}}$$

Solid Radios Co. sold 10000 Radios last year at a price of Rs. 500 each. The cost structure is as follows :

	Rs.
Material	100
Labour	50
Variable overhead	25
Marginal Cost	175
Fixed Overhead	200
Total Cost	375
Profit	125
Sales Price	500

Due to heavy competition the price will have to be reduced to Rs. 425 in the coming year. Assuming no changes in the cost calculate the number of Radios that should be produced at the price to get the same total Profit.

(K.U.D., October 1979)

Solution :

Profit for 10000 Radios at Sales Price Rs. 500 each

Profit = 12,50,000
(10,000 × 125)

New Sales Price (10000 × 425) Per Unit = 425.00

Now change in cost

∴ Contribution = Sales – Variable cost

= 425 – 175

Contribution = 250 per Radio.

$$\text{Now P/V Ratio} = \frac{\text{Contribution}}{\text{Sales}}$$

$$= \frac{250}{425}$$

$$= \frac{10}{17}$$

Sales required to earn profit of Rs. 12,50,000

$$= \frac{\text{Fixed Cost + Profit}}{\text{P/V Ratio}}$$

Fixed Cost Rs. 200 per Radio for 10000 units

(200 × 10000) = 20,00,000

$$= \frac{\text{Fixed Cost + Profit}}{\text{P/V Ratio}}$$

$$= \frac{20{,}00{,}000 + 12{,}50{,}000}{10/17}$$

$$= 32{,}50{,}000 \times \frac{17}{10}$$

Sales (in Amount) = 55,25,000

$$\text{Sales in Units} = \frac{\text{Total Sales amount}}{\text{Cost per unit}}$$

$$= \frac{55{,}25{,}000}{425}$$

Sales (in Units) = 13000 Radios.

Problem No. 41

The sales of 'X' Co. Ltd. :

	Sales	Profit
First half of 1976	2,70,000	7,200
Second half of 1976	3,42,000	20,700

Assuming no change in the Fixed cost, calculate :

(a) P/V Ratio.

(b) The profit when sales are Rs. 2,16,000.

(c) The amount and Sales required to earn a profit of Rs. 36,000.

(d) B.E.P. Sales.

(K.U.D., April 1978)

Solution :

(1) P/V Ratio $= \frac{\text{Contribution}}{\text{Sales}}$

Or $= \frac{\text{Changes in Profit in two periods}}{\text{Changes in sales in two periods}}$

Changes	Sales	Profits
1976 Second half	3,40,000	20,700
1976 First half	2,70,000	7,200
	70,000	13,500

Now P/V Ratio $= \frac{\text{Changes in Profits}}{\text{Changes in Sales}}$

$= \frac{13,500}{70,000}$

$= \frac{3}{16}$ Or 18.75%

Contribution during the 1976 First half when sales are Rs. 2,70,000.

Contribution = Sales × P/V Ratio

= 2,70,000 × 3/16

= Rs. 50,625

Now Fixed Cost = Contribution – Profit

= 50,625 – 7,200

= Rs. 43,425

(2) Profit when sales are Rs. 2,16,000

Now contribution = Sales × P/V Ratio

= 2,16,000 × 3/16

= Rs. 40,500

Profit Or Loss = Contribution – Fixed Cost

= 40,500 – 43,425

Loss = Rs. – 2,925

Loss of Rs. 2,925 when sales are Rs. 2,16,000.

(3) Sales to earn a Profit of Rs. 36,000

$$\text{Sales} = \frac{\text{Fixed Cost + Profit}}{\text{P/V Ratio}}$$

$$= \frac{43{,}425 + 36{,}000}{3/16}$$

$$= 79{,}425 \times \frac{16}{3}$$

Sales = Rs. 4,23,600.

Sales to earn a Profit of Rs. 36,000 sales to be made of Rs. 4,23,600.

$$\text{(4) B.E.P.} = \frac{\text{Fixed Cost}}{\text{P/V Ratio}}$$

$$= \frac{43{,}425}{3/16}$$

$$= 43{,}425 \times \frac{16}{3}$$

B.E.P. Sales = Rs. 2,31,600.

Problem No. 42

(a) Write short notes on any of the following.
(1) Contribution (2) Angle of incidence
(3) Break-Even Point (4) Key factor.

(b) From the following particulars calculate :
(1) Break-Even Point (B.E.P.).
(2) P/V Ratio.
(3) Margin of Safety.

Particulars :

(i)	Selling price per unit	Rs. 100
(ii)	No. of Units sold	10,000
(iii)	Variable cost per unit	Rs. 60
(iv)	Fixed Cost	Rs. 3,00,000

(K.U.D.)

Solution : Part-B (only)

	Rs.
Sales in value Rs. 100 × 10000 units	10,00,000
Less Variable Cost Rs. 60 × 10000	6,00,000
Contribution	Rs. 4,00,000
Less Fixed Cost	3,00,000
Profit	Rs. 1,00,000

(1) B.E.P. Sales $= \frac{\text{Fixed Cost}}{\text{P/V Ratio}}$

P/V Ratio $= \frac{\text{Contribution}}{\text{Sales}}$

or $= \frac{\text{Fixed Cost + Profit}}{\text{Sales}}$

Now P/V Ratio $= \frac{\text{Fixed Cost + Profit}}{\text{Sales}}$

$= \frac{3,00,000 + 1,00,000}{10,00,000}$

$= \frac{4,00,000}{10,00,000} = \frac{2}{5}$ or 40%

(2) ∴ P/V Ratio $= \frac{2}{5}$

Now B.E.P. Sales (in value) $= \frac{\text{Fixed Cost}}{\text{P/V Ratio}}$

$= \frac{3,00,000}{2/5}$

$= 3,00,000 \times \frac{5}{2}$

B.E.P. Sales = Rs. 7,50,000

in units $= \frac{7,50,000}{\text{Rs. } 100}$ = 7500 units.

Verification :

	Rs.
Sales at B.E.P. = 7500 × 100	7,50,000
Less Veriable Cost = 7500 × 60	4,50,000
Contribution	Rs. 3,00,000
Less Fixed Cost	Rs. 3,00,000
Profit	Nil

(3) Margin of Safety (M/S) $= \frac{\text{Profit}}{\text{P/V Ratio}}$

$= \frac{1,00,000}{2/5}$

$= 1,00,000 \times \frac{5}{2}$

M/S = Rs. 2,50,000

or M/S = Sales − B.E.P. Sales

= 10,00,000 − 7,50,000

= Rs. 2,50,000.

Problem No. 43

From the following information calculate :

(1) B.E.P. Sales

(2) P/V Ratio

(3) Sales to earn a profit of Rs. 1,50,000

(4) Margin of Safety.

Selling Price per unit of Rs. 25

Variable cost per unit of Rs. 10

Fixed overheads of Rs. 1,05,000.

[C.A. Final (Modified)]

Solution :

(1) P/V Ratio $= \dfrac{\text{Contribution}}{\text{Sales}}$

Contribution = Sales – Variable cost

= 25 – 10

= Rs. 15 per Unit.

P/V Ratio $= \dfrac{\text{Contribution}}{\text{Sales}}$

$= \dfrac{15}{25} = \dfrac{3}{5}$ or 60%

(2) B.E.P. sales (in value) $= \dfrac{\text{Fixed Cost}}{\text{P/V Ratio}}$

$= \dfrac{1,05,000}{3/5}$

Sales in value $= 1,05,000 \times \dfrac{5}{3}$

= Rs. 1,75,000

Sales in units $= \dfrac{\text{Sales in value}}{\text{Cost per unit}}$

$= \dfrac{1,75,000}{25}$

= 7000 Units

Verification :

		Rs.
Sales – 7000 Units × 25	=	1,75,000
Less : Variable cost 7000 × 10	=	70,000
Contribution		1,05,000
Fixed cost		1,05,000
Profit – Nil at B.E.P. Sales		– Nil –

(3) Sales to earn a Profit of Rs. 1,50,000 :

Sales $= \dfrac{\text{Fixed Cost + Profit}}{\text{P/V Ratio}}$

$$= \frac{1,05,000 + 1,50,000}{3/5}$$

$$= 2,55,000 \times \frac{5}{3}$$

Sales in value $= 4,25,000$

Sales in units $= \frac{4,25,000}{25}$

$= 17000$ Units.

Verification :

Sales	17000 × 25 =	4,25,000
Less : Variable cost 17000 × 10 =		1,70,000
Contribution		2,55,000
Less : Fixed Cost		1,05,000
Profit		1,50,000

Margin of Safety = Actual Sales – Sales at B.E.P.

= 4,25,000 – 1,75,000

= Rs. 2,50,000

Margin Safety (in units) = 17000 – 7000

= 10000 Units.

Problem No. 44

Following are the particulars of a manufacturing company :
Sales Price Rs. 30 per unit
Variable cost Rs. 21 per unit
Fixed cost for the year Rs. 11,88,000
Calculate :

(a) Break-Even Point in sales volume and units.
(b) Number of units be sold to earn a profit of Rs. 90,000 p.a. (Sales to earn a profit of Rs. 90,000)
(c) How many units must be sold to earn a net profit of 10% on sales.

(I.C.W.A. Final)

Solution :

Sales Price per unit = 30
Less : Variable cost = 21
Contribution per unit = 9

$$\text{P/V Ratio} = \frac{\text{Contribution}}{\text{Sales}}$$

$$= \frac{9}{30}$$

$$= \frac{3}{10} \text{ Or } 30\%.$$

$$\text{(a) B.E.P. (Sales in value)} = \frac{\text{Fixed Cost}}{\text{P/V Ratio}}$$

$$= \frac{11,88,000}{3/10}$$

$$= 11,88,000 \times \frac{10}{3}$$

B.E.P. (Sales in value) = Rs. 39,60,000

$$\text{B.E.P. (in units)} = \frac{\text{Total Sales Value}}{\text{Cost per unit}}$$

$$= \frac{39,60,000}{30}$$

= 132000 Units.

Verification :

B.E.P. Sales (132000 × 30)	=	39,60,000
Less : Variable cost (132000 × 21)	=	27,72,000
Contribution	=	11,88,000
Less : Fixed cost	=	11,88,000
B.E.P. Sales in value No profit No loss		– Nil –

(b) No. of units to be sold to earn a Profit of Rs. 90,000 p.a. Now sales to earn a profit of Rs. 90,000.

$$\text{Sales (in Value)} = \frac{\text{Fixed Cost + Profit}}{\text{P/V Ratio}}$$

$$= \frac{11,88,000 + 90,000}{3/10}$$

$$= 12,78,000 \times \frac{10}{3}$$

$$= \frac{1,27,80,000}{3}$$

Sales in Value = 42,60,000

$$\text{Sales in Units} = \frac{42,60,000}{30}$$ Sales Price per unit.

= 142000 Units.

Verification :

	Rs.
Sales Value	
142000 units × Rs. 30 per unit	42,60,000
Less Variable Cost	
142000 units — Rs. 21 per unit	29,82,000
Contribution	12,78,000
Less Fixed Cost	11,88,000
Profit	90,000

(c) No. of units to be sold to earn 10% of profit on sales.

Sales Price Rs. 30

Profit 10% on sales = 30 × 10% = Rs. 3

Variable Cost Rs. 21

Now Sales – Variable Cost = Fixed Cost + Profit

Fixed Cost = Sales – Variable – Profit

= 30 – 21 – 3

Fixed Cost per unit = 6

$\therefore$ Sales in No. of Units = $\frac{\text{Total Fixed Cost}}{\text{Fixed per Unit}}$ = No. of units

Sales in No. of Units = $\frac{11,88,000}{6}$

= 198000 Units to be sold to earn 10% profit on sales.

Verification :

Sales (198000 × 30)	=	59,40,000
Less : Variable cost (198000 × 21)	=	41,58,000
Contribution	=	17,82,000
Less : Fixed Cost	=	11,88,000
Profit	=	5,94,000

Profit of Rs. 5,94,000 is 10% on sales of Rs. 59,40,000.

Problem No. 45

Any change in fixed cost, variable cost and selling price has the effect of shifting the Break-Even Point although the impact of each change on the Break-Even Point, and the profit is different. The following figures assuming 10% increase individually in each of the elements of cost and also show how the profit figure is effected if all the elements increase collectively each by 10%.

	Rs.
Sales (45000 Units)	1,80,000
Per Unit = $\frac{1,80,000}{45000}$ = Rs. 4	
Variable cost	60,000
Fixed cost	75,000

(I.C.W.A. Final)

Solution :

Present Position :

Sales (45000 × 4) (per unit Rs. 4)		1,80,000
Less : Variable cost		60,000
	Contribution	1,20,000
Less : Fixed cost		75,000
	Profit	Rs. 45,000

(a) P/V Ratio $= \frac{\text{Sales} - \text{Variable Cost}}{\text{Sales}}$ or $= \frac{\text{Contribution}}{\text{Sales}}$

$= \frac{1,80,000 - 60,000}{1,80,000} \quad \frac{1,20,000}{1,80,000}$

$= \frac{1,20,000}{1,80,000}$

P/V Ratio $= \frac{2}{3}$

B.E.P. Sales (in value) $= \frac{\text{Fixed Cost}}{\text{P/V Ratio}}$

$= \frac{75,000}{2/3}$

$= 75,000 \times \frac{3}{2}$

$=$ Rs. 1,12,500

B.E.P. (in units) $= \frac{\text{Total Sales}}{\text{Sales per Unit}}$

$$= \frac{1,12,500}{4}$$

$= 28125$ Units.

Effect on Break-Even Point (B.E.P.) in each of the following factor :

(a) Increase in the Fixed cost by 10%, P/V Ratio remains unchanged 2/3

Present Fixed Cost	75,000
Add : Increase by 10%	7,500
Future Fixed Cost	82,500

Break-Even Point :
(Sales in value) $= \dfrac{\text{Fixed Cost}}{\text{P/V Ratio}}$

$$= \frac{82,500}{2/3}$$

$$= 82,500 \times \frac{3}{2}$$

= Rs. 1,23,750

B.E.P. (in units) $= \dfrac{1,23,750}{4}$

= 30937.5

= Or 30938 Units.

(b) Increase in variable cost 10%

	Rs.
Present Variable cost	60,000
Add : Increase by 10%	6,000
Future Variable cost	66,000

Future P/V Ratio $= \dfrac{\text{Sales} - \text{Variable Cost}}{\text{Sales}}$

$$= \frac{1,80,000 - 66,000}{1,80,000}$$

$$= \frac{1,14,000}{1,80,000}$$

$= \dfrac{19}{30}$ Or 63.33%.

B.E.P. (in Value) $= \dfrac{\text{Fixed Cost}}{\text{P/V Ratio}}$

$$= \frac{75,000}{19/30}$$

$$= 75{,}000 \times \frac{30}{19}$$

B.E.P. Sales in value $= 1{,}18{,}421.5$ Or Rs. 1,18,422

B.E.P. (in units) $= \frac{1{,}18{,}422}{4}$

$= 29605.5$ Or 29606 Units.

(c) Increase in selling price by 10%

	Rs.
Present sales	1,80,000
Add : Increase by 10%	18,000
Future Sales Price	1,98,000

P/V Ratio $= \frac{\text{Sales} - \text{Variable Cost}}{\text{Sales}}$

$$= \frac{1{,}98{,}000 - 60{,}000}{1{,}98{,}000}$$

$$= \frac{1{,}38{,}000}{1{,}98{,}000}$$

$$= \frac{23}{33}$$

= Or 69.69% Or 69.7%

B.E.P. (Sales in value) $= \frac{\text{Fixed Cost}}{\text{P/V Ratio}}$

$$= \frac{75{,}000}{69.7/100}$$

$$= 75{,}000 \times \frac{100}{69.7}$$

= Rs. 1,07,604.

B.E.P. (in Units) $= \frac{\text{Total Sales Value}}{\text{Sales Value per unit}}$

$$= \frac{1{,}07{,}604}{4}$$

= 26901 Units.

Problem No. 46

Ashok Co. Ltd. has provided the budget estimates for the year 1993-94.

Sales in units	22500
Sales Price	3,37,500
Variable cost per unit	Rs. 9
Fixed Cost	Rs. 51,000

You are required to find out :

I. (a) P/V Ratio (b) B.E.P. Sales (c) Margin of Safety (d) Sales required to earn Profit of Rs. 84,000.

II. Calculate also the revised :

(a) P/V Ratio (b) B.E.P. (Sales) (c) Margin of Safety in each of the following cases :

(i) Decrease of 10% in selling price.
(ii) Increase of 10% in variable cost
(iii) Increase in volume of sales by 3000 Units.
(iv) Increase in the Fixed cost by Rs. 9,000.

(C.A. Inter)

Solution :

I. (a) P/V Ratio $= \dfrac{\text{Contribution}}{\text{Sales}}$

Contribution = Selling price (per unit) – Variable per unit

Selling Price (per unit) $= \dfrac{\text{Total Sales Value}}{\text{Sales Value per unit}}$

$= \dfrac{3{,}37{,}500}{22500}$

= Rs. 15 per unit.

Now contribution = Sales – Variable cost

= 15 – 9 = Rs. 6

P/V Ratio $= \dfrac{\text{Contribution}}{\text{Sales}}$

$= \dfrac{6}{15} = \dfrac{2}{5}$ Or 40%

(b) B.E.P. Sales $= \dfrac{\text{Fixed Cost}}{\text{P/V Ratio}}$

$= \dfrac{51{,}000}{2/5}$

$= 51{,}000 \times \dfrac{5}{2}$

= Rs. 1,27,500

$$\text{B.E.P. (in units)} = \frac{1,27,500}{15}$$

= 8500 Units.

(c) Margin of Safety = Actual Sales – B.E.P. Sales

= 3,37,500 – 1,27,500

= 2,10,000

Verification :

		Rs.
B.E.P. – 8500 × 15	=	1,27,500
Less : Variable cost (8500 × 9)	=	76,500
Contribution		51,000
Fixed cost		51,000
Profit		– Nil –

(d) *Profit at Budgeted Sales :*

Sales (22500 × 15)	=	3,37,500
Less : Variable cost (22500 × 9)	=	2,02,500
Contribution		1,35,000
Less : Fixed Cost		51,000
Profit		Rs. 84,000

II. (i) *Decrease of 10% in Selling Price :*

Present Selling Price of Rs. 15 per unit	=	15.00
Less : Decrease 10% of 15	=	1.50
Future Selling Price		13.50
Less : Variable cost	=	9.00
Contribution		4.50 per unit

$$\text{(a) P/V Ratio} = \frac{\text{Contribution}}{\text{Sales}}$$

$$= \frac{4.50}{13.50} = \frac{9/2}{27/2} = \frac{9}{2} \times \frac{2}{27}$$

$$= \frac{9}{27} = \frac{1}{3}$$

$$\text{(b) B.E.P. Sales} = \frac{\text{Fixed Cost}}{\text{P/V Ratio}}$$

$$= \frac{51,000}{1/3}$$

$= 51{,}000 \times 3$

$= 1{,}53{,}000$

B.E.P. (in Units) $= \dfrac{1{,}53{,}000}{13.50}$

$= 11333$ Units.

Verification :

Sales 11333 × 13.50	=	1,53,000
Less : Variable cost (11333 × 4.50)	=	1,02,000
Contribution		51,000
Fixed Cost		51,000
Profit		–Nil–

(c) *Margin of Safety* : = Actual Sales – B.E.P. Sales.

Present Sales 22500 × 13.5	=	3,03,750
B.E.P. Sales	=	1,53,000
Margin of Safety	=	1,50,750

Or Margin of Safety = Actual Sales – B.E.P. Sales.

$= 3{,}03{,}750 - 1{,}53{,}000$

= Rs. 1,50,750

(d) Sales required to earn present profit of Rs. 84,000

$= \dfrac{\text{Fixed Cost + Profit}}{\text{P/V Ratio}}$

$= \dfrac{51{,}000 - 84{,}000}{1/3}$

$= 1{,}35{,}000 \times \dfrac{3}{1}$

= Rs. 4,05,000

Sales to earn Profit of Rs. 84,000 = 4,05,000

Sales in units $= \dfrac{4{,}05{,}000}{13.50}$

$= 30000$ Units.

Verification :

Sales 30000 × 13.50	=	4,05,000
Less : Variable cost 30000 × 9	=	2,70,000
Contribution		1,35,000
Less : Fixed Cost		51,000
Profit		Rs. 84,000

(ii) Increase of 10% in Variable cost		Rs.
Present Variable cost	=	9.00
Add : Increase 10% of Rs. 9	=	0.90
Future Variable cost	=	9.90
Sales Present	=	15.00
Less : Variable cost	=	9.90
Contribution	=	5.10

(a) P/V Ratio $= \frac{\text{Contribution}}{\text{Sales}}$

$= \frac{5.10}{15}$

$= 34\%$

(b) B.E.P. Sales $= \frac{\text{Fixed Cost}}{\text{P/V Ratio}}$

$= \frac{51,000}{34/100}$

$= 51,000 \times \frac{100}{34}$

= Rs. 1,50,000

B.E.P. (in units) $= \frac{1,50,000}{15}$

= 10000 Units.

Verification :

Sales 10000 × 15	=	1,50,000
Less : Variable cost (10,000 × 9.90)	=	99,000
Contribution		51,000
Less : Fixed Cost		51,000
Profit		– Nil –

(c) Margin of Safety (Present) = Actual Sales – B.E.P. Sales

= 3,37,500 – 1,50,000

= Rs. 1,87,500

(d) Sales required to earn Present Profit of Rs. 84,000.

$$= \frac{\text{Fixed Cost + Profit}}{\text{P/V Ratio}}$$

$$= \frac{51{,}000 - 84{,}000}{34/100}$$

$$= 1{,}35{,}000 \times \frac{100}{34} = \text{Rs. } 3{,}97{,}058.82$$

$$\text{Sales (in units)} = \frac{3{,}97{,}058.82}{15}$$

$$= 26470.88 \text{ Or } 26471 \text{ Units.}$$

Verification :

Sales Units 26471 × 15 =	3,97,065	
Less : Variable cost (26471 × 9.9)	2,62,063	
Contribution	1,35,002	
Less : Fixed Cost	51,000	
Present Profit	84,002	Or Rs. 84,000

Margin of Safety (future) = Actual Sales – B.E.P. Sales

= 3,97,065 – 1,50,000

= Rs. 2,47,065

(iii) Increase in the volume of sales :

Present sales in units	22500
Add : Increase in units	3000
Total future sales in units	25500

Sales per unit Rs. 15 remain the same.

Variable cost per unit Rs. 9 remains the same.

Fixed cost Rs. 51,000 remains the same.

(a) P/V Ratio $= \frac{\text{Contribution}}{\text{Sales}}$ Remains the same

$$= \frac{6}{15} = 2/4 \text{ Or } 40\%$$

(b) B.E.P. Sales $= \frac{\text{Fixed Cost}}{\text{P/V Ratio}}$

$$= \frac{51{,}000}{2/5}$$

$$= 51{,}000 \times \frac{5}{2}$$

B.E.P. Sales = Rs. 1,27,500 remains the same before increase in units.

B.E.P. (in units) $= \frac{1{,}27{,}500}{15} =$ 8500 Units.

(c) M/S = Actual Sales – B.E.P. Sales

here Sales $= 25500 \times 15 = 3{,}82{,}500$

$= 3{,}82{,}500 - 1{,}27{,}500$

= Rs. 2,55,000

Future Profits at (22500 + 3000) 25500 Units.

Sales 25500 Units @ Rs. 15 per unit	3,82,500
Less : Variable cost 25500 × 9	2,29,500
Contribution	1,53,000
Less : Fixed cost	51,000
Profit	Rs. 1,02,000

(d) Sales to earn a profit of Rs. 84,000

$$\text{Sales} = \frac{\text{Fixed Cost + Profit}}{\text{P/V Ratio}}$$

$$= \frac{51{,}000 + 84{,}000}{2/5}$$

$$= 1{,}35{,}000 \times \frac{5}{2}$$

Sale in value = Rs. 3,37,500

$$= \frac{3{,}37{,}500}{15}$$

= 22500 Units.

(iv) Increase in the Fixed Cost by Rs. 9,000. Present sales Price Rs. 15 per unit. No. of units 22500. Variable cost Rs. 9 per unit.

Fixed cost = 51,000 + 9,000 = 60,000 Future.

(a) P/V Ratio $= \frac{\text{Contribution}}{\text{Sales}}$

$= \frac{6}{15}$ Or $\frac{2}{15}$ Or 40% remain the same.

(b) B.E.P. Sales $= \dfrac{\text{Fixed Cost}}{\text{P/V Ratio}}$

$= \dfrac{60,000}{2/5}$

$= 60,000 \times \dfrac{5}{2}$

B.E.P. (Sales in value) = Rs. 1,50,000

B.E.P. (in units) $= \dfrac{1,50,000}{15}$

= 10,000 Units.

(c) Margin of Safety = Actual Sales – B.E.P. Sales

= 3,37,500 – 1,50,000

= Rs. 1,87,500.

Profit when fixed cost increase by Rs. 9,000

Sales (22500 × 15)	=	3,37,500
Less : Variable cost (22500 × 9)	=	2,02,500
Contribution		1,35,000
Less : Fixed cost		60,000
Profit		Rs. 75,000

Sales to earn profit of Rs. 84,000 (Present)

$= \dfrac{\text{Fixed Cost + Profit}}{\text{P/V Ratio}}$

$= \dfrac{60,000 - 84,000}{2/5}$

$= 1,44,000 \times \dfrac{5}{2}$

= Rs. 3,60,000

Sales (in value) = 3,60,000

Sales (in units) $= \dfrac{3,60,000}{15}$

= 24000 Units.

Verification :

Sales (24000 × 15)	=	3,60,000
Less : Variable cost (24000 × 9)		2,16,000
Contribution		1,44,000
Less : Fixed cost		60,000
Profit		Rs. 84,000

Problem No. 47

X Co. sold in successive years :

	I Year	II Year
Units sold	105000	135000
Selling Price (per unit)	100	100
Profit Or Loss	1,50,000 (Loss)	1,50,000 (Profit)

Calculate :

(a) Amount of Fixed cost (b) P/V Ratio

(c) Break-Even Point (in units)

(d) No. of units to be sold to earn a Profit of Rs. 5,00,000.

[I.C.W.A. Inter (Modified)]

Solution :

(1) B.E.P. Sales $= \dfrac{\text{Fixed Cost}}{\text{P/V Ratio}}$

(2) P/V Ratio $= \dfrac{\text{Contribution}}{\text{Sales}}$

OR $= \dfrac{\text{Changes in Profit}}{\text{Changes in Sales}}$

Now changes in sales and Profit :

II Year 135000 × 100	1,35,00,000	1,50,000
I Year 105000 × 100	1,05,00,000	1,50,000 Loss
	30,00,000	3,00,000

Now P/V Ratio $= \dfrac{\text{Changes in Profit}}{\text{Changes in Sales}}$

$= \dfrac{3,00,000}{30,00,000}$

$= \dfrac{1}{10}$ Or 10%

Ascertain contribution of I year :

Contribution = Sales × P/V Ratio

= 1,05,00,000 × 1/10

= 10,50,000

(a) Now Fixed Cost = Contribution – Profit + Loss

= 10,50,000 + 1,50,000

= 12,00,000

(b) B.E.P. Sales $= \frac{\text{Fixed Cost}}{\text{P/V Ratio}}$

$= 12,00,000 \times \frac{10}{1}$

= 1,20,00,000

(c) B.E.P. (in units) $= \frac{1,20,00,000}{100}$

= 120000 Units.

(d) Sales required to earn profit of Rs. 5,00,000

$= \frac{\text{Fixed Cost + Profit}}{\text{P/V Ratio}}$

$= \frac{12,00,000 + 5,00,000}{1/10}$

$= 17,00,000 \times \frac{10}{1}$

Sales in value = 1,70,00,000

Sales in units $= \frac{1,70,00,000}{100}$

= 170000 Units.

Margin of Safety = Actual Sales – Sales B.E.P.

I Year (87.5% of B.E.P.) = 1,05,00,000 – 1,20,00,000 (12.5% Negative)

= Rs. 15,00,000

II Year M/S = 1,35,00,000 – 1,20,00,000 (112.5% Positive)

= Rs. 15,00,000.

Problem No. 48

From the following particulars calculate (a) B.E.P. (b) P/V Ratio and Sales required to earn a profit of Rs. 1,20,000 :

Direct Material per unit	4.50
Direct Labour per unit	3.00
Variable Overhead 100% of Direct Labour	
Fixed Cost	2,40,000 per year
Selling Price	15 per unit
Trade Discount	5% on sales

[C.A. Inter (Modified)]

Solution :

		Rs.
Sales Price		15.00
Less : Trade Discount 5% on Rs. 15		00.75
Net Selling Price		14.25
Ascertain contribution		
Material cost per unit	4.50	
Labour cost	3.00	
Variable cost 100% of Labour	3.00	10.50
Contribution per unit		3.75

$$\text{Now P/V Ratio} = \frac{\text{Contribution}}{\text{Sales}}$$

$$= \frac{3.75}{15}$$

$$= 25\% \text{ Or } \frac{1}{4}$$

$$\text{B.E.P. Sales in Value} = \frac{\text{Fixed Cost}}{\text{P/V Ratio}}$$

$$= \frac{2,40,000}{1/4}$$

$$= 2,40,000 \times \frac{4}{1}$$

$$= \text{Rs. } 9,60,000$$

$$\text{B.E.P. Sales in units} = \frac{9,60,000}{15}$$

$$= 64000 \text{ Units.}$$

Problem No. 49

Sales Price	Rs.	30 per unit
Variable manufacturing cost	Rs.	16 per unit
Variable selling cost	Rs.	5 per unit
Fixed factory overhead	Rs.	8,10,000 per year
Fixed selling cost	Rs.	3,78,000 per year

You are required to find out :

(1) P/V Ratio.

(2) Break-Even Point (B.E.P.) in amount of sales.

(3) No. of units to be sold to earn a profit of Rs. 90,000 per year.

(4) Profit if sales at Rs. 60,00,000.

[I.C.W.A. Final (Modified)]

Solution :

(1) P/V Ratio $= \frac{\text{Contribution}}{\text{Sales}}$

Now Contribution = Sales – Variable Cost

= 30 – 21

= Rs. 9

P/V Ratio $= \frac{\text{Contribution}}{\text{Sales}}$

$= \frac{9}{30}$ Or $\frac{3}{10}$ Or 30%.

(2) B.E.P. $= \frac{\text{Fixed Cost}}{\text{P/V Ratio}}$

$= \frac{8,10,000 + 3,78,000}{3/10}$

$= 11,88,000 \times \frac{10}{3}$

= Rs. 39,60,000

B.E.P. (in units) $= \frac{39,60,000}{30}$

= 132000 Units.

Sales required to earn a Profit of Rs. 90,000

$$= \frac{\text{Fixed Cost + Profit}}{\text{Contribution}}$$

$$= \frac{11{,}88{,}000 + 90{,}000}{9} = 142000 \text{ Units.}$$

Sales in Value = 1,42,000 × 30 = Rs. 42,60,000.

Verification :

(1) Sales required to earn Profit of Rs. 90,000 in units 142000

Sales Price 142000 × 30	=	42,60,000
Less : Variable cost		
142000 × 21	=	29,82,000
Contribution		12,78,000
Less : Fixed cost		11,88,000
Profit		90,000

(2) Profit when sales are at Rs. 60,00,000 sales per unit of Rs. 30

$$\text{No. of units sold} = \frac{60{,}00{,}000}{30} = 200000 \text{ Units.}$$

Sales (units 200000 × 30)	=	60,00,000
Less : Variable cost		
200000 × 21	=	42,00,000
		18,00,000
Less : Fixed cost	=	11,88,000
Profit	=	6,12,000

Verification :

Sales required to earn profit of Rs. 6,12,000

$$= \frac{\text{Fixed Cost + Profit}}{\text{P/V Ratio}}$$

$$= \frac{11{,}88{,}000 + 6{,}12{,}000}{3/10}$$

$$= 18{,}00{,}000 \times \frac{10}{3}$$

Sales = Rs. 60,00,000

required to earn a Profit of Rs. 6,12,000.

Problem No. 50

Fixed cost Rs. 1,50,000 and the P/V Ratio 25%.

Find out (a) Sales to earn a profit of Rs. 1,25,000.

(b) B.E.P.

(c) B.E.P. when P/V Ratio is shifted to 40%.

Solution :

Sales to earn a profit of Rs. 1,25,000

When P/V ratio is 25% and

Fixed costs are Rs. 1,50,000

(a) Sales to earn a profit of Rs. 1,25,000

$$= \frac{\text{Fixed Cost + Profit}}{\text{P/V Ratio}}$$

$$= \frac{1,50,000 + 1,25,000}{25\%}$$

$$= 2,75,000 \times \frac{100}{25}$$

= Rs. 11,00,000 Sales to earn a Profit of Rs. 1,25,000.

(b) Break-Even Point =

Sales at B.E.P. $= \frac{\text{Fixed Cost}}{\text{P/V Ratio}}$

$$= \frac{1,50,000}{25\%}$$

$$= 1,50,000 \times \frac{100}{25}$$

= Rs. 6,00,000

(c) B.E.P. Sales when P/V Ratio is shifted to 40%

B.E.P. Sales $= \frac{\text{Fixed Cost}}{\text{P/V Ratio}}$

$$= \frac{1,50,000}{40\%}$$

$$= 1,50,000 \times \frac{100}{40}$$

= Rs. 3,75,000.

Problem No. 51

Fixed cost — Rs. 2,00,000

Variable cost — 60% of sales

Calculate :

(a) Break-Even Point (B.E.P.).

(b) New B.E.P. if Fixed increase by Rs. 50,000.

(c) If variable costs increase by 15% on sales.

(d) Sales price increase by 20%.

(e) Variable cost decrease by 10%.

Solution :

(a) B.E.P. Sales $= \dfrac{\text{Fixed Cost}}{\text{P/V Ratio}}$

Now P/V Ratio $= \dfrac{\text{Contribution}}{\text{Sales}}$

Now Contribution = Sales – Variable Cost

If sales are at 100 Variable Cost 60

Now Contribution = 100 – 60 = 40%

P/V Ratio $= \dfrac{\text{Contribution}}{\text{Sales}}$

= 40%

B.E.P. Sales $= \dfrac{\text{Fixed Cost}}{\text{P/V Ratio}}$

$= 2{,}00{,}000 \times \dfrac{100}{40}$

B.E.P. Sales = Rs. 5,00,000

(b) New B.E.P. if Fixed cost increase by Rs. 50,000

i.e., 2,00,000 + 50,000 = 2,50,000

New B.E.P. Sales $= \dfrac{\text{Fixed Cost}}{\text{P/V Ratio}}$

$= 2{,}50{,}000 \times \dfrac{100}{40}$

New B.E.P. in Sales = Rs. 6,25,000

(c) B.E.P. Sales if variable cost increase by 15% on Sales :

Present Variable Cost	60% on Sales
Add : increase by Variable cost	15%
New Variable Cost	75% on Sales

If sales are at 100 – Variable cost 75% and the contribution is 25%

$$= 100 - 75$$

$$\text{Contribution} = 25\%$$

$$\text{Now P/V Ratio} = \frac{\text{Contribution}}{\text{Sales}} = \frac{25}{100} \times 100 = 25\%$$

$$\text{P/V Ratio} = 25\% \text{ or } 1/4$$

$$\text{Now B.E.P. Sales} = \frac{\text{Fixed Cost}}{\text{P/V Ratio}}$$

$$= \frac{2{,}00{,}000}{1/4}$$

$$= 2{,}00{,}000 \times 4 = 8{,}00{,}000$$

$$\text{B.E.P. at Sales} = \text{Rs. } 8{,}00{,}000.$$

(d) B.E.P. Sales when sales price increased by 20%.

Note : Increase or decrease in sales price variable cost does not affect variable cost remains.

Sales at Present	=	100 – Variable cost Rs. 60
Increase by 20%	=	20
Future Sales Price		120 – Variable cost Rs. 60

$$\text{B.E.P. Sales} = \frac{\text{Fixed Cost} \times \text{Sales}}{\text{Sales} - \text{Variable Cost}}$$

$$= \frac{2{,}00{,}000 \times 120}{120 - 60}$$

$$= \frac{2{,}40{,}00{,}000}{60}$$

$$\text{B.E.P. Sales} = \text{Rs. } 4{,}00{,}000.$$

Alternatively

(d) When sales increase by 20% Sales

Sales Present	=	100 Variable Cost of Rs. 60
Increase by 20%	=	20
Future Sales		120 Variable Cost of Rs. 60
Contribution	=	Sales – Variable cost
	=	120 – 60
	=	Rs. 60

$$\text{P/V Ratio} = \frac{\text{Contribution}}{\text{Sales}}$$

$$= \frac{60}{120} \times 100$$

$$= 50\%$$

$$= \frac{1}{2}$$

$$\text{B.E.P. Sales} = \frac{\text{Fixed Cost}}{\text{P/V Ratio}}$$

$$= \frac{2{,}00{,}000}{1/2}$$

$$= 2{,}00{,}000 \times 2 = 4{,}00{,}000$$

B.E.P. Sales = Rs. 4,00,000.

(e) B.E.P. Sales when variable cost decrease by 10% :

Present Variable cost 60% on sales

Less : Decrease by 10%

Future Variable cost 50% on Sales.

Now contribution = Sales – Variable Cost

Contribution = 100 – 50 = 50%

$$\text{Now P/V Ratio} = \frac{\text{Contribution}}{\text{Sales}}$$

$$= \frac{50}{100} = \frac{1}{2}$$

$$\text{P/V Ratio} = 50\% \text{ or } \frac{1}{2}$$

$$\text{B.E.P. Sales} = \frac{\text{Fixed Cost}}{\text{P/V Ratio}}$$

$$= \frac{2{,}00{,}000}{1/2} = 2{,}00{,}000 \times 2 = 4{,}00{,}000$$

B.E.P. Sales = Rs. 4,00,000

Problem No. 52

The following particulars provided by a manufacturing company which produces two different types of products :

Particulars	Product M	Product N
Units of Material consumed	10 Units	15 Units
Cost of Material per unit	Rs. 50	Rs. 75
Direct Wages cost (Per hour Rs. 10)	Rs. 100	Rs. 75
Direct Expenses	Rs. 25	Rs. 30
Machine Hour used	15 Hours	10 Hours
Overhead Expenses :		
Variable	Rs. 75	Rs. 100
Fixed	Rs. 25	Rs. 50
Sales price per unit	Rs. 300	Rs. 350

You are required to show which of the two products are profitable in the following Key factor :

(a) Sales potential in units/Value is limited.

(b) Raw material is in short supply.

(c) Product-capacity (in terms of Machine hour limiting factor).

(d) Labour is limiting factor.

Solution :

Statement of Cost Contribution

Particulars		Product M	Product N
		Rs.	Rs.
Cost per unit :			
Material		50	75
Direct Wages per hour Rs. 10	M – 5 Hours	100	
	N – 7.5 Hours		75
Direct Expenses		25	30
	Prime Cost	175	180
Overhead Expenses :			
Variable		75	100
	Total Variable Cost Or Marginal Cost	250	280
Sales Price		300	350
	Contribution :	50	70

Particulars	Product M	Product N
	Rs.	Rs.
P/V Ratio = $\frac{\text{Contribution}}{\text{Sales}}$	$\frac{50}{300}$	$\frac{70}{350}$
	$= \frac{1}{6}$	$= \frac{1}{5}$
	= 16.67	20%
Contribution per Kg of Material Material = M – 10, N – 15	$\frac{50}{10}$	$\frac{70}{15}$
	= Rs. 5	= Rs. 4.67
(3) Contribution per Machine hours M – 15, N – 10	$\frac{50}{15}$	$\frac{70}{10}$
	= Rs. 3.33	= Rs. 7
(4) Labour Hours : M – 5 Hours, N – 7.4 Hours	$\frac{50}{5}$	$\frac{70}{7.5}$
	= Rs. 10	= Rs. 9.33

If the limiting factor (Key factor) is :

(a) Sales profitability is higher with N Product.

(b) Material profitability of M Product is higher.

(c) Machine Hours : Production capacity profitability is higher with 'N' Product.

(d) Labour shortage (or strike Profitability) is higher with Product 'M'.

Problem No. 53

P/V Ratio is 40% and the Marginal cost of the product is Rs. 75 what will be the Selling Price ?

[Fixing Selling Price (Decision-making)]

Solution :

$$\text{P/V Ratio} = \frac{\text{Contribution}}{\text{Sales}} = \frac{40}{100}$$

$$\text{Sales} - \text{Contribution} = \left(\frac{\text{Variable cost}}{\text{Marginal cost}}\right)$$

$$100 - 40 = 60 \text{ Marginal cost}$$

If Marginal Or Variable cost is 60 : 75 : 100 Selling price

$$\frac{75}{60} \times 100 = \text{Rs. } 125$$

Selling price of product is Rs. 125 when its Marginal cost is Rs. 75 and the contribution would be 40% of 125 = Rs. 50

$$\text{Now P/V Ratio} = \frac{\text{Contribution}}{\text{Sales}}$$

$$= \frac{50}{125}$$

$$= 40\%.$$

Problem No. 54

From the following particulars find out Break-Even Point (B.E.P.) :

Selling Price (per unit)	Rs. 60
Variable cost	Rs. 40
Fixed Expenses	Rs. 2,00,000

What will be the selling price per unit if the B.E.P. is brought down to 8000 units. Further show also :

(1) P/V Ratio

(2) Sales to earn a Profit of 2,50,000.

Solution :

Selling Price per unit	60
Less : Variable cost per unit	40
Contribution	20

$$\text{B.E.P. Sales} = \frac{\text{Fixed Cost}}{\text{Contribution per unit}}$$

$$= \frac{2,00,000}{20} = 10000 \text{ Units.}$$

$$\text{P/V Ratio} = \frac{\text{Contribution}}{\text{Sales}}$$

$$= \frac{20}{60} = \frac{1}{3}$$

$$\text{B.E.P. Sales (in Value)} = \frac{\text{Fixed Cost}}{\text{P/V Ratio}}$$

$$= 2,00,000 \times \frac{3}{1}$$

$$= \text{Rs. } 6,00,000$$

Break-Even Point is proposed to be brought down to 8000 units. The fixed cost of Rs. 2,00,000 are to be recovered from 8000 units to have no Profit no Loss.

$$\therefore \text{ Fixed Expenses per unit} = \frac{2,00,000}{8000} = \text{Rs. } 25$$

Now Sales Price of Variable Cost		40
+ Fixed Expenses		25
Sales Price	Rs.	65

Verification :

Selling Price per unit	Rs.	65
Less : Variable cost	Rs.	40
Contribution		25

$$\text{B.E.P. Sales (in units)} = \frac{\text{Fixed Cost}}{\text{Contribution}}$$

$$= \frac{2,00,000}{25}$$

$$= 8000 \text{ Units.}$$

$$\text{P/V Ratio} = \frac{\text{Contribution}}{\text{Sales}}$$

$$= \frac{25}{65} = \frac{5}{13}$$

$$= 2,00,000 \times \frac{13}{5}$$

$$= \text{Rs. } 5,20,000$$

$$\text{B.E.P. (in units)} = \frac{5,20,000}{65}$$

$$= 8000 \text{ Units.}$$

Now Sales 8000 × 65	=	5,20,000
Less : Variable cost (8000 × 40)		3,20,000
Contribution		2,00,000
Less : Fixed Cost		2,00,000
		–Nil–

Sales to earn a profit of Rs. 2,50,000 when sales price of Rs. 60

$$= \frac{\text{Fixed cost + Profit}}{\text{Sales} - \text{Variable}} \times \text{Sales}$$

$$= \frac{2,00,000 + 2,50,000}{6,00,000 - 4,00,000} \times 6,00,000$$

$$= \frac{4,50,000}{2,00,000} \times 6,00,000$$

$$= \text{Rs. } 13,50,000$$

Verification :

Sales @ Rs. 60 per unit	13,50,000
Less : Variable cost (40 × 22,500)	9,00,000
Contribution	4,50,000
Less : Fixed cost	2,00,000
Profit	Rs. 2,50,000

Alternatively :

Sales required to earn a Profit of Rs. 2,50,000

$$= \frac{\text{Fixed Cost + Profit}}{\text{P/V Ratio}}$$

$$= \frac{2,00,000 + 2,50,000}{1/3}$$

$$= 4,50,000 \times \frac{3}{1}$$

Sales = Rs. 13,50,000

Problem No. 55

Standard Product Ltd. manufactured sold a single product. The following are the details of cost structure :

	Rs.
Material	24
Conversion cost	16
Dealer's Margin	6
Selling Price	60
Fixed Expenses	7,50,000
Present sales	135000 Units.
Capacity untilisation	60%

There is acute competition, extra efforts are necessary to sell. Suggestions have been made for increasing sales :

(a) By reducing sales price by 5%.

(b) By increasing dealer's margin by 25% over the existing rates.

Which of these two suggestions would you recommend if the company desires to maintain the present profit ? Give reasons.

Solution :

Present Marginal Cost Per Unit

		Rs.
Material		24
Conversion cost		16
Dealers Margin		6
Total Variable cost		46
Contribution per unit :		
Selling Price	60	
Less : Variable cost	46	
Contribution	14 per unit	
Total Contribution =		Rs.
(14 × 135000)		18,90,000
Less : Fixed Cost		7,50,000
Present Profit		11,40,000

Verification :

Present Sales (135000 × 60)		81,00,000
Less : Variable cost (135000 × 46)	62,10,000	
Fixed Cost	7,50,000	69,60,000
Present Profit		11,40,000

In the both suggested courses for increasing sales the fixed costs remain unaffected.

Therefore the present profit can be maintained by maintaining the total contribution at the present level of Rs. 18,90,000.

Suggestion (a) : By reducing sales Price by 5%

Present Sales Price	60
Less : Reducing Price by 5% of Rs. 60	3
Suggested Selling Price	57

Present dealers margin of Rs. 6 and it is 10% of Selling Price.

The dealers commission of 10% of Rs. 57 = 5.70

New Selling Price		57
Less : Variable cost :		
Material	24	
Conversion cost	16	
Dealers Margin	5.7	45.70
New Contribution		11.30

Sales (in units) required to maintain present level of Profit of Rs. 11,40,000

$$\frac{\text{Total Contribution}}{\text{Contribution per unit}}$$

$$\frac{18,90,000}{11.30} = 1,67,256.63 \quad \text{Or } 167257 \text{ Units}$$

Verification :

Sales 167257 × 57		95,33,649
Less : Variable cost		
(167257 × 45.70)	76,43,649	
Fixed cost	7,50,000	83,93,649
Profit		11,40,000

OR

Sales 167257 × 57 =	95,33,649	
Less Variable Cost		
167257 × 45.70 =	76,43,645	
Contribution	18,90,004	
Less Fixed Cost	7,50,000	
Profit	Rs. 11,40,004	(fraction 4 rounded up)
Profit =	Rs. 11,40,000	

Suggestion (b) : By increasing dealer's commission by 25%

Present dealer's commission 10%

Add : Increase by 25% i.e., $10 \times \frac{25}{100} = 2.50$

Suggested dealer's commission 12.50% of Sales Price = 7.50

(60 × 12.5% = 7.50)

Selling Price per unit		60.00
Less : Material	24	
Conversion cost	16	
Dealer's Margin	7.5	47.50
Contribution		12.50

Sales required to earn profit of Rs. 11,40,000

$$= \frac{\text{Total Contribution}}{\text{Contribution per unit}}$$

$$= \frac{18,90,000}{12.50}$$

Sales in Units = 151200 Units × Rs. 60 per unit

Sales in value = Rs. 90,72,000

Verification :

Sales 151200 × 60	=	90,72,000
Less : Variable cost (151200 × 47.50)		71,82,000
		18,90,000
Contribution		18,90,000
Less : Fixed Cost		7,50,000
Profit		11,40,000

Problem No. 56

X Co. Ltd. manufactures and sells 2000 Units per month at Rs. 40 each.

Fixed Costs are Rs. 6000 per month.

Variable costs are Rs. 24 per unit.

There is a proposal to reduce Selling Price by 10%.

Calculate : (a) Present and future P/V Ratio.

(b) B.E.P. Sales at present and future.

(c) How many units to be sold to maintain present Profit?

Solution :

(a) Present Sales and Profit

Selling Price per unit	40
Less : Variable cost per unit	24
Contribution per unit	16
Present sales 2000 × 40	80,000
Less : Variable cost 2000 × 24	48,000
Contribution 2000 × 16	32,000
Less : Fixed cost	6,000
Present Profit	26,000

$$\text{Present P/V Ratio} = \frac{\text{Contribution}}{\text{Sales}}$$

$$= \frac{32{,}000}{80{,}000} = \frac{2}{5}$$

$$\text{B.E.P. Sales} = \frac{\text{Fixed Cost}}{\text{P/V Ratio}}$$

$$= \frac{6{,}000}{2/5}$$

$$\text{B.E.P. Sales} = 15{,}000 \text{ in units } \frac{15{,}000}{40} = 375 \text{ Units.}$$

Verification :

Sales 375 × 40 =	15,000
Less : Variable cost (375 × 24)	9,000
Contribution	6,000
Less : Fixed cost	6,000
Profit	Nil

(b) Future Selling Price :

Present Selling Price	40
Less : Reducing 10%	4
Future Selling Price	36
Future Selling Price	36
Less : Variable cost	24
Contribution	12

$$\text{Future P/V Ratio} = \frac{\text{Contribution}}{\text{Sales}}$$

$$= \frac{12}{36} = \frac{1}{3}$$

$$\text{P/V Ratio} = \frac{1}{3}$$

Sales to earn present Profit of Rs. 26,000

$$\text{Sales in Units} = \frac{\text{Fixed Cost + Profit}}{\text{Selling Price − Variable cost (per Unit)}}$$

$$= \frac{6{,}000 + 26{,}000}{36 - 24}$$

$$= \frac{32{,}000}{12} = 2666.66 \text{ Or } 2667 \text{ Units.}$$

Verification :

Sales 2667 × 36 =	96,012	
Less : Variable cost (2667 × 24)	64,008	
Contribution	32,004	
Less : Fixed cost	6,000	
Profit	26,004	Or 26,000

$$\text{B.E.P. Sales} = \frac{\text{Fixed Cost}}{\text{P/V Ratio}} = \frac{6{,}000}{1/3}$$

$$= 6{,}000 \times \frac{3}{1}$$

$$= \text{Rs. } 18{,}000$$

$$\text{B.E.P. in units } \frac{18{,}000}{36} = 500 \text{ Units.}$$

Verification :

Sales 500 × 36 =	18,000
Less : Variable cost (500 × 24)	12,000
Contribution	6,000
Less : Fixed cost	6,000
Profit	Nil

Problem No. 57

X Co. Ltd. manufacture products and sells and earned gross profit (before charging commission) of 25% on cost.

The company appointed a sole selling agent to whom a commission of 10% on Selling Price has been given. There are no other variable cost. Fixed costs are Rs. 1,200 per month.

Selling price per unit is Rs. 50.

Calculate :

The number of units he must sell every year so that he may earn a net profit of Rs. 12,000 per year.

Solution :

Selling price per unit	50
Less : Profit 25% on cost or 20% on sales	
(on cost $\frac{25}{125}$ × 100) 20% on 50 or $\frac{25}{125}$ = 1/5	10
Direct Variable cost	40
Add : Commission 10% on Selling Price	5
Total Variable cost Or Marginal cost	45
Fixed Expenses Rs. 1,200 per month (1,200 × 12)	14,400 per year

Sales to earn profit of Rs. 12,000 per year.

$$= \frac{\text{Fixed Cost + Profit}}{\text{Selling Price − Marginal cost (per Unit)}}$$

$$= \frac{14{,}400 + 12{,}000}{50 - 45} = \frac{26{,}400}{5}$$

= 5280 Units.

Sales in Amount = 5280 × 50 = Rs. 2,64,000

OR

$$\text{P/V Ratio} = \frac{\text{Contribution}}{\text{Sales}}$$

$$= \frac{5}{50} = \frac{1}{10}$$

P/V Ratio = 1/10

Sales to earn profit of Rs. 12,000

$$= \frac{\text{Fixed Cost + Profit}}{\text{P/V Ratio}}$$

$$= \frac{14{,}400 + 12{,}000}{1/10}$$

= 26,400 × 10

= Rs. 2,64,000

$$\text{in Units} = \frac{2{,}64{,}000}{50}$$

= 5280 Units.

Verification :

Sales 5280 × 50		= 2,64,000
Less : Variable cost		
5280 × 45	= 2,37,600	
Fixed Cost	14,400	2,52,000
	Profit	Rs. 12,000

Problem No. 58

The following are the data of manufacturing Co. The variable cost 60% on sales price. The Break-Even Point (B.E.P.) accrues at 80%. Find out a capacity sales when Fixed costs are Rs. 4,00,000. Determine Profit at 90% and 100% capacity.

Solution :

Let the Sales to be Rs. 100

Now Sales	100
Less : Variable cost	60
Contribution per unit	40

$$\text{Sales at B.E.P.} = \frac{\text{Fixed Cost}}{\text{P/V Ratio}}$$

$$\text{P/V Ratio} = \frac{\text{Contribution}}{\text{Sales}}$$

$$= \frac{40}{100} = \frac{2}{5}$$

$$\text{Sales at B.E.P.} = \frac{\text{Fixed Cost}}{\text{P/V Ratio}}$$

$$= 4{,}00{,}000 \times \frac{5}{2}$$

$$= 10{,}00{,}000$$

B.E.P. Sales (in Rs.) Rs. 10,00,000

Particulars	B.E.P. 80% Capacity	90% Capacity	100% Capacity
Sales Price	10,00,000	11,25,000	12,50,000
Less : Variable cost 60% of sales	6,00,000	6,75,000	7,50,000
Contribution	4,00,000	4,50,000	5,00,000
Less : Fixed cost	4,00,000	4,00,000	4,00,000
Profit	Nil	50,000	1,00,000

Problem No. 59

Following are the particulars of a manufacturing company :

Selling Price per unit	40
Variable cost per unit	12
Fixed Cost	3,50,000

Calculate :

(a) P/V Ratio

(b) Break-Even Point (B.E.P.)

(c) Sales to earn a Profit of Rs. 72,000

(d) Margin of Safety (M/S).

Solution :

Selling Price per unit	40
Less : Variable cost per unit	12
Contribution	28

(1) P/V Ratio $= \dfrac{\text{Contribution}}{\text{Sales}}$

$= \dfrac{28}{40} = \dfrac{7}{10}$

P/V Ratio $= \dfrac{7}{10}$

(2) B.E.P. Sales $= \dfrac{\text{Fixed Cost}}{\text{P/V Ratio}}$

$= 3{,}50{,}000 \times \dfrac{10}{7}$

= Rs. 5,00,000

B.E.P. Sales (in Units) $= \dfrac{5{,}00{,}000}{40}$

= 12500 Units.

Verification :

	Rs.
Sales of B.E.P. (12500 × 40)	5,00,000
Less : Variable cost (12500 × 12)	1,50,000
Contribution	3,50,000
Less : Fixed cost	3,50,000
Profit	Nil

Sales to earn Profit of Rs. 72,000

$$\text{Sales} = \frac{\text{Contribution}}{\text{P/V Ratio}}$$

$$\text{Contribution} = \text{Fixed Cost} + \text{Profit} = 3,50,000 + 72,000$$

$$= 4,22,000$$

$$= \frac{4,22,000}{7/10}$$

$$= 4,22,000 \times \frac{10}{7}$$

$$= \text{Rs. } 6,02,857$$

Now Sales (in amount) = Rs. 6,02,857

$$\text{In Units} = \frac{6,02,857}{40}$$

$$= 15071 \text{ Units.}$$

Verification :

Sales (15071 × 40)	=	6,02,857.14
Less : Variable cost (15071 × 12)	=	1,80,857.13
Contribution		4,22,000.01
Less : Fixed Cost		3,50,000
Profit		72,000

Margin of Safety = Sales (Actual) – Sales at B.E.P.

= 6,02,857 – 5,00,000

= Rs. 1,02,857

Alternative :

$$\text{M/S} = \frac{\text{Profit}}{\text{P/V Ratio}}$$

$$= 72,000 \times \frac{10}{7}$$

$$= \text{Rs. } 1,02,857$$

$$\text{(in Units)} = \frac{1,02,857}{4}$$

$$= 2571 \text{ Units}$$

Problem No. 60

(a) What is Profit/Volume Ratio

(b) The following are the sales and profit for the period 1992 :

	Sales	Profit
First half	3,60,000	9,600
Second half	4,56,000	27,600

Assuming no change in the Fixed costs.

Calculate : (1) P/V Ratio

(2) B.E.P.

(3) The amount of Profit when Sales are Rs. 2,88,000

(4) The amount of sales required to earn a profit of Rs. 48,000.

Solution-I :

Profit/Volume Ratio Or P/V Ratio.

It is the ratio contribution to sales

$$\text{P/V Ratio} = \frac{\text{Contribution}}{\text{Sales}}$$

$$\text{Contribution} = \text{Sales} - \text{Variable cost}$$

$$= \text{Fixed Cost} + \text{Profit}$$

$$\text{Now P/V Ratio} = \frac{\text{Sales} - \text{Variable cost}}{\text{Sales}}$$

$$\text{Or} = \frac{\text{Fixed Cost} + \text{Profit}}{\text{Sales}}$$

$$\text{P/V Ratio} = \frac{\text{Changes in Profit}}{\text{Changes in Sales}}$$

$$= \frac{\text{Changes in Contribution}}{\text{Changes in Sales}}$$

Importance of P/V Ratio

It is used to ascertain profitability of products or operations and decision making. Higher the ratio reflects higher profitability and lower the ratio lower the profitability. The Management should always make efforts to raise P/V Ratio by increasing gap between selling price and variable cost. It is done (a) By increasing sales price (b) Reducing variable cost (c) Changing over more profitable products. P/V Ratio is the Key to decision making.

Use of P/V Ratio :

$$\text{(1) B.E.P.} = \frac{\text{Fixed Cost}}{\text{P/V Ratio}}$$

(2) Sales to earn a given amount of Profit

$$= \frac{\text{Fixed Cost + Profit}}{\text{P/V Ratio}}$$

(3) Contribution = Sales × P/V Ratio

(4) Fixed Cost = Sales at B.E.P. × P/V Ratio.

Solution-II :

(1) P/V Ratio $= \frac{\text{Contribution}}{\text{Sales}}$

(2) P/V Ratio $= \frac{\text{Changes in Profit in two periods}}{\text{Changes in Sales in two periods}}$

Now P/V Ratio $= \frac{27{,}600 - 9{,}600}{4{,}56{,}000 - 3{,}60{,}000}$

$$= \frac{18{,}000}{96{,}000}$$

$$= \frac{3}{16} \text{ or } 18.75\%$$

(3) B.E.P. $= \frac{\text{Fixed Cost}}{\text{P/V Ratio}}$

Now calculate Fixed Cost :

First ascertain contribution. Contribution during first half will be

P/V Ratio $= \frac{\text{Contribution}}{\text{Sales}}$

Contribution = Sales × P/V Ratio

$$= 3{,}60{,}000 \times \frac{3}{16}$$

$$= 22{,}500 \times 3$$

= Rs. 67,500

Contribution during first half = Rs.	67,500
Less : Profit	9,600
Fixed Cost	57,900

Now B.E.P. $= \frac{\text{Fixed Cost}}{\text{P/V Ratio}}$

$$= \frac{57{,}900}{3/16}$$

$$= 57{,}900 \times \frac{16}{3}$$

B.E.P. Sales = Rs. 3,08,800

(4) Profit when sales are Rs. 2,88,000

Contribution when sales are Rs. 2,88,000

Contribution = Sales × P/V Ratio

$$= 2{,}88{,}000 \times \frac{3}{16} = \text{Rs. } 54{,}000$$

Contribution	=	54,000
Less : Fixed Cost		57,900
Loss		–3,900

(5) Sales required to earn a profit of Rs. 48,000

$$= \frac{\text{Fixed Cost + Profit}}{\text{P/V Ratio}}$$

$$= \frac{57{,}900 + 48{,}000}{3/16}$$

$$= 1{,}05{,}900 \times \frac{16}{3}$$

= Rs. 5,64,800

(6) B.E.P. Sales as above Rs. 3,08,800

Contribution = Sales × P/V Ratio

$$= 3{,}08{,}800 \times \frac{3}{16} = 57{,}900$$

Contribution at B.E.P. Sales	=	Rs. 57,900
Fixed Cost	=	57,900
Profit		Nil

At B.E.P. sales contribution is equal to fixed cost i.e., contribution is just sufficient to cover Fixed Cost. Therefore sales at B.E.P. is the position of No profit No Loss.

Problem No. 61

A B Co. Ltd. manufacture and sell the products during 1990 and the Selling price and the cost structure of the product remain the same during the periods as shown below :

Calculate :

(a) Profit / Volume Ratio (P/V Ratio)

(b) Break-Even Point (B.E.P.) for sale

(c) Profit when sales are Rs. 1,20,000

(d) Sales required to earn profit of Rs. 30,000

(e) Margin of Safety in Period-II (M/S in Period-II)

Periods	Sales Rs.	Profit Rs.
I	1,50,000	14,000
II	1,80,000	20,000

Solution :

(a) P/V Ratio $= \dfrac{\text{Changes in Profit}}{\text{Changes in Sales}}$

Change in Sales and Profit

Periods-II	1,80,000	20,000
Periods-I	1,50,000	14,000
Changes in Sales and Profit	30,000	6,000

Now P/V Ratio $= \dfrac{\text{Changes in Profit}}{\text{Changes in Sales}}$

$= \dfrac{6,000}{30,000}$

$= \dfrac{1}{5}$ Or 20%

(b) B.E.P. Sales $= \dfrac{\text{Fixed Cost}}{\text{P/V Ratio}}$

It is necessary to ascertain Fixed costs and contribution in period-I when sales are at Rs. 1,50,000 and the P/V Ratio is 1/5.

Contribution = Sales × P/V Ratio

= 1,50,000 × 1/5

= Rs. 30,000

Fixed Cost = Contribution – Profit

= 30,000 – 14,000

= Rs. 16,000

Here contribution and fixed costs are for period-I.

Now B.E.P. (Sales) $\dfrac{\text{Fixed Cost}}{\text{P/V Ratio}}$

$= 16,000 \times \dfrac{5}{1}$

= Rs. 80,000

(c) Profit when Sales are Rs. 1,20,000

Sales	1,20,000	
Contribution @ 1/5 of Sales		
	1,20,000 × 1/5	24,000
Less : Fixed cost		16,000
	Profit	8,000

(d) Sales required to earn a profit of Rs. 30,000

Contribution = Fixed Cost + Profit

= 16,000 + 30,000

= 46,000

Sales required to earn contribution of Rs. 46,000

$$= \frac{\text{Contribution}}{\text{P/V Ratio}} = \frac{46{,}000}{1/5}$$

$$= 46{,}000 \times 5 = \text{Rs. } 2{,}30{,}000 \text{ Sales}$$

Or $$= \frac{\text{Fixed cost + Profit}}{\text{P/V Ratio}}$$

$$= 46{,}000 \times 5 = \text{Rs. } 2{,}30{,}000$$

(e) Margin of Safety during period-II = Sales – Sales at B.E.P.

= 1,80,000 – 80,000

= 1,00,000

M/S $$= \frac{\text{Profit}}{\text{P/V Ratio}} = 20{,}000 \times \frac{5}{1}$$

= Rs. 1,00,000.

Problem No. 62

The Sales of X Co. Ltd. during the two periods were as follows :

Period	Sales Rs.	Profit Rs.
1990	1,80,000	30,000
1991	2,40,000	45,000

You are required to calculate :

(1) P/V Ratio

(2) B.E.P. Sales

(3) The sales required to earn a profit of Rs. 60,000

(4) Variable costs of the two period

(5) Margin of Safety at a Profit of Rs. 75,000

(6) Profit when Sales are Rs. 3,50,000.

Solution :

(1) P/V Ratio $= \dfrac{\text{Contribution}}{\text{Sales}}$

$= \dfrac{\text{Changes in Profit}}{\text{Changes in Sales}}$

Changes Sales and Profit =	Sales	Profit
1991	2,40,000	45,000
1990	1,80,000	30,000
	60,000	15,000

Now P/V Ratio $= \dfrac{15{,}000}{60{,}000} = \dfrac{1}{4}$ Or 25%

(2) B.E.P. Sales $= \dfrac{\text{Fixed Cost}}{\text{P/V Ratio}}$

It is necessary to ascertain Fixed costs contribution in Period 1990 when sales are @ Rs. 1,80,000 and the P/V Ratio is $\dfrac{1}{4}$

Now contribution = Sales × P/V Ratio

= 1,80,000 × 1/4

Contribution = Rs. 45,000

Fixed Cost = Contribution – Profit

= 45,000 – 30,000

Fixed Cost = Rs. 15,000

Now B.E.P. Sales $= \dfrac{\text{Fixed Cost}}{\text{P/V Ratio}}$

$= 15{,}000 \times \dfrac{1}{4} = 15{,}000 \times 4/1$

= Rs. 60,000

(3) Sales required to earn a Profit of Rs. 60,000

$= \dfrac{\text{Fixed Cost + Profit}}{\text{P/V Ratio}}$

$= \dfrac{15{,}000 + 60{,}000}{1/4}$

= 75,000 × 4

= Rs. 3,00,000

(4) Profit when sales are Rs. 3,50,000

Now contribution = Sales × P/V Ratio

= 3,50,000 × 1/4

= Rs. 87,500

Profit = Contribution – Fixed Cost

= 87,500 – 15,000

= Rs. 72,500

(5) Variable cost = Sales – Fixed Cost – Profit

Period 1990 = 1,80,000 – 15,000 – 30,000

= 1,80,000 – 45,000

= Rs. 1,35,000

Period 1991 = 2,40,000 – 15,000 – 45,000

= 2,40,000 – 60,000

Variable cost = Rs. 1,80,000

(6) Margin of Safety = $\frac{\text{Profit}}{\text{P/V Ratio}}$

When Profit of Rs. 75,000 = 75,000 × 4/1

= Rs. 3,00,000.

Problem No. 63

The Statement of cost of a children computer is as follows :

Material	2,000	
Labour	600	
Variable overhead	1,400	
Fixed overheads	600	4,600
Profit		400
Sales Price		5,000

The number of computer sets manufactured and sold is 8000. Find out :

(a) Break-Even Point

(b) How many computers must be produced and sold if the price is reduced by Rs. 200 to be the same profit as above.

Solution :

(a) *Marginal cost* :

	Per Unit
Material	2,000
Labour	600
Variable Overhead	1,400
Marginal cost Or Variable costs	4,000

(b) Fixed cost per unit Rs. 600 remain the same though there is changes in the output :

Fixed Cost $= 600 \times 8000 = 48{,}00{,}000$

$$\text{B.E.P. in Units} = \frac{\text{Fixed Cost}}{\text{Selling Price} - \text{Variable cost (per Unit)}}$$

$$= \frac{48{,}00{,}000}{5000 - 4000}$$

$$= \frac{48{,}00{,}000}{1000}$$

$= 4800$ Units.

Present Profit for 8000 units $= 400 \times 8000 = 32{,}00{,}000$

Present Selling Price =	5,000
Less : Reduce in Sales Price =	200
Proposed Selling Price =	4,800

Ascertain number of units to be produced and sold to earn the present profit of Rs. 32,00,000. Now sales to earn a profit of Rs. 32,00,000.

$$= \frac{\text{Fixed Cost + Profit}}{\text{Selling Price} - \text{Variable cost (per Unit)}}$$

$$= \frac{48{,}00{,}000 + 32{,}00{,}000}{4{,}800 - 4000}$$

$$= \frac{80{,}00{,}000}{800} = 10000 \text{ Units.}$$

$$\text{OR :} = \frac{\text{Fixed Cost + Profit}}{\text{Contribution per unit}}$$

Contribution = Sales – Variable cost

$= 4{,}800 - 4{,}000$

$= 800$

$$= \frac{80{,}00{,}000}{800} = 10000 \text{ Units.}$$

(c) Sales to earn a Profit of Rs. 32,00,000

Sales Price (Reduced) Rs. 4,800 for 10000 Units.

$4{,}800 \times 10000$ = Rs. 4,80,00,000

Original Sales 8000 × 500	= 40,00,000
Present Profit (8000 × 400)	32,00,000
Future Profit (10000 × 320)	32,00,000

$$\text{Fixed Cost per Unit} = \frac{48,00,000}{10000} = \text{Rs. } 480$$

Cost structure per unit =

Material	2,000
Labour	600
Variable overhead	1,400
Fixed overhead	480
Total Cost	4,480
+ Profit	320
Sales Price	Rs. 4,800

Problem No. 64

Surya Electricals Ltd. manufactures Electrical Switches is working at 40% capacity producing 25000 Units per year. The cost structure for each unit is as follows :

Material	55
Labour	25
Overheads	25 (40% variable)

Each unit is sold for Rs. 120

The selling price falls by 3% when production is at 50% capacity by 5% if worked at 90%.

The fall in selling price is accompanied by similar fall in material price.

You are required to find out :

(a) Profit at 50% capacity and at 90% capacity.

(b) Break-even point at both levels.

Solution :

For 40% capacity 25000 For 100% capacity $\frac{100}{40} \times 25000 = 62,500$		@ 40% Capacity 40% of 25,000 = 10,000		@ 50% Capacity 60% of 62,500 = 31,250		@ 90% Capacity 90% 62,500 = 56,250	
		Cost per Unit	Total Cost	Cost per Unit	Total Cost	Cost per Unit	Total Cost
(A) Sales Price	120.00	120	30,00,000	116.40	36,37,500	114	64,12,500
@ 50% reduced by 3%	3.60						
	116.40						
	120						
@ 90% reduced by 5%	6						
	114						
(B) Material	55.00	55.00	13,75,000	53.35	16,67,187.5	52,25	29,39,062.5
@ 50% reduced by 3%	1.65						
	53.35						
	55.00						
@ 90% reduced by 5%	2.75						
	52.25						
Labour Overhead	25	25	6,25,000	25	7,18,250	25	14,06,250
40% Variable (40% of 25)	10	10	2,50,000	10.00	3,12,500	10	5,62,500
Total Variable cost Or Marginal Cost		90	22,50,000	88.35	27,60,937.5	87.25	49,07,812.25
Contribution (A – B)		30	7,50,000	28.05	8,76,562.5	26.75	15,04,687.5
Less : Fixed Cost (60% of 25)	15	15	3,75,000	15	4,68,750	15	8,43,750
Profit		15	3,75,000	13.05	4,07,812.5	11.75	6,60,937.5
B.E.P. Sales = $\frac{\text{Fixed Cost}}{\text{Contribution}} \times$ Sales			15,00,000		19,45,186.9		35,95,973.9

Problem No. 65

X Co. Ltd. manufactures as sells its products capacity sales Rs. 8,00,000 @ Sales price Rs. 2 per unit. Variable cost is Re. 0.70 price per unit.

Fixed cost Rs. 2,00,000 per year.

Find out the profit made during year at above sales price. Further the management is interested to know the Profit or Loss @ 50% and 80% capacity at sales price Rs. 2.50 and at Rs. 1.60.

Solution :

@ 100% capacity sales 400000 units × Rs. 2 per unit	8,00,000
Less : Variable cost 400000 × 0.70	2,80,000
Contribution	5,20,000
Less : Fixed cost	2,00,000
Profit	Rs. 3,20,000

$$\text{B.E.P. Sales} = \frac{\text{Fixed Cost}}{\text{Contribution per unit}}$$

$$= \frac{2,00,000}{2.00 - .70}$$

$$= \frac{2,00,000}{1.30}$$

$$= 153846 .15 \text{ units}$$

B.E.P. Sales in amount	=	153486.15 × 2
Sales Price	=	3,07,692.3
Less : Variable cost	=	1,07,692.3
Contribution		2,00,000.0
Less : Fixed cost		2,00,000
Profit		– Nil –

100% Capacity sales – Rs. 8,00,000 Statement of Profit/Loss Rs. 2 per unit No. of unit 400000

	Sales Price at Rs. 2.50 per unit			Sales Price at Rs. 1.60 per unit		
Units sold	@ 50%	@80% Cap	@ 100%	@ 50%	@ 80%	@ 100%
Units sold	200000	320000	400000	200000	320000	400000
Sales Price	5,00,000	8,00,000	10,00,000	3,20,000	5,12,000	6,40,000
Less : Variable Cost @ Rs. .70 (per unit)	1,40,000	2,24,000	2,80,000	1,40,000	2,24,000	2,80,000
Contribution	3,60,000	5,76,000	7,20,000	1,80,000	2,88,000	3,60,000
Less : Fixed Cost	2,00,000	2,00,000	2,00,000	2,00,000	2,00,000	2,00,000
Profit/Loss	1,60,000	3,76,000	5,20,000	– 20,000 (Loss)	88,000 (Profit)	1,60,000 (Profit)

Problem No. 66

A manufacturing company operating @ 60% capacity. The sales proceeds of the product realise Rs. 6,00,000. The fixed cost of operation Rs. 1,20,000 and the variable cost Rs. 4,00,000.

Find out the percentage of capacity at which manufacturing operation should work so that profit of Rs. 1,60,000 is realised.

Also show (a) P/V Ratio (b) B.E.P.

Solution :

	Rs.
Sales Price	6,00,000
Variable cost	4,00,000
Contribution	2,00,000
Less : Fixed Cost	1,20,000
Profit	80,000

Sales required to earn a profit of Rs. 1,60,000

$$\text{Sales in value} = \frac{\text{Fixed Cost + Profit}}{\text{Sales – Variable cost}} \times \text{Sales}$$

$$= \frac{1{,}20{,}000 + 1{,}60{,}000}{6{,}00{,}000 - 4{,}00{,}000} \times 6{,}00{,}000$$

$$= 2{,}80{,}000 \times 3 = \text{Rs. } 8{,}40{,}000$$

At 60% capacity sales value is Rs. 6,00,000 for sales value of Rs. 8,40,000

$$= \frac{60\% \times 8{,}40{,}000}{6{,}00{,}000} = 84\%$$

Operating capacity = 84% at sales value Rs. 8,40,000

$$\text{(a) P/V Ratio} = \frac{\text{Contribution}}{\text{Sales}} = \frac{2{,}00{,}000}{6{,}00{,}000} = \frac{1}{3}$$

$$\text{(b) B.E.P. Sales} = \frac{\text{Fixed Cost}}{\text{P/V Ratio}} = 1{,}20{,}000 \times \frac{3}{1}$$

$$= \text{Rs. } 3{,}60{,}000.$$

Problem No. 67

From the following data find out :

(a) P/V Ratio (b) B.E.P. Sales (c) Sales required to earn a Profit of Rs. 2,40,000 (d) Profit when sales are Rs. 7,50,000.

Selling Price per unit		60
Variable cost per unit :		
Material	15	
Labour	10	
Variable overhead	10	
100% of Direct wages		35
Fixed Cost		96,000

Solution :

		Rs.
Selling price per unit		60
Less : Variable cost per unit :		
Material	15	
Labour	10	
Variable overhead	10	
100% of Direct wages		35
Contribution		25

(a) P/V Ratio $= \dfrac{\text{Contribution per unit}}{\text{Sales per unit}}$

$= \dfrac{25}{60} = \dfrac{5}{12}$

(b) B.E.P. Sales $= \dfrac{\text{Fixed Cost}}{\text{P/V Ratio}}$

$= 96{,}000 \times \dfrac{12}{5}$

B.E.P. Sales (in value) 2,30,400 in value

B.E.P. (in units) $= \dfrac{2{,}30{,}4000}{60}$

$=$ 3840 Units

(c) Sales to earn a profit of Rs. 2,40,000

$= \dfrac{\text{Fixed cost + Profit}}{\text{P/V Ratio}}$

$= \dfrac{96{,}000 + 2{,}40{,}000}{5/12}$

$= 3{,}36{,}000 \times \dfrac{12}{5}$

$=$ Rs. 8,06,400

Sales 8,06,400 in value to earn Profit of Rs. 2,40,000.

In units $= \frac{8,06,400}{60}$

$= 13440$ Units.

Verification of the above sales figure :

Sales 13440 × 60	=	8,06,400
Less : Variable cost		
13440 × 35	=	4,70,400
Contribution		3,36,000
Less : Fixed Cost		96,000
Profit as above		Rs. 2,40,000

(d) Profit when sales are Rs. 7,50,000

Ascertain contribution when sales are Rs. 7,50,000

Now contribution = Sales × P/V Ratio

$= 7,50,000 \times \frac{5}{12}$

Contribution = Rs. 3,12,500

Profit = Contribution – Fixed Cost

= 3,12,500 – 96,000

= Rs. 2,16,500

Verification :

Sales Price (12500 × 60)	=	7,50,000
Less : Variable cost (12,500 × 35)	=	4,37,500
Contribution		3,12,500
Less : Fixed Cost		96,000
Profit		Rs. 2,16,500

Problem No. 68

Fixed cost for the year — Rs. 3,60,000

Variable cost per unit — Rs. 18

Budgeted sales for the period — Rs. 12,00,000

Selling price per unit — Rs. 30

Calculate : (1) B.E.P. sales in value and in units.

(2) Sales required to earn a Profit of Rs. 1,25,000

(3) Selling price per unit to bring up break-even point to 45000 Units.

Solution :

(1) B.E.P. Sales $= \dfrac{\text{Fixed Cost}}{\text{P/V Ratio}}$

P/V Ratio $= \dfrac{\text{Contribution}}{\text{Sales}}$

Contribution = Sales – Variable Cost

= 30 – 18 = 12

Now P/V Ratio $= \dfrac{\text{Contribution}}{\text{Sales}}$

$= \dfrac{12}{30} = \dfrac{2}{5}$ Or 40%

B.E.P. Sales (in Value) $= \dfrac{\text{Fixed Cost}}{\text{P/V Ratio}}$

$= \dfrac{3{,}60{,}000}{2/5} = 3{,}60{,}000 \times \dfrac{5}{2}$

= Rs. 9,00,000

B.E.P. Sales (in units) $= \dfrac{9{,}00{,}000}{30}$

= 30000 Units.

(2) Selling Price per unit to bring up B.E.P. to 45000 Units.

B.E.P. Sales (in Units 45000) = Variable cost + Fixed cost only

$= 45{,}000 \times 18 + 3{,}60{,}000$

$= 8{,}10{,}000 + 3{,}60{,}000$

Sales Price = 11,70,000

Per Unit $= \dfrac{11{,}70{,}000}{45{,}000}$

= Rs. 26 per unit.

(3) Sales required to earn a profit of Rs. 1,25,000.

Sales $= \dfrac{\text{Fixed Cost + Profit}}{\text{P/V Ratio}}$

$= \dfrac{3{,}60{,}000 + 1{,}25{,}000}{2/5}$

$= 4{,}85{,}000 \times \dfrac{5}{2}$ = Rs. 12,12,500

Sales in Value = Rs. 12,12,500

$$\text{Sales in units} = \frac{12,12,500}{30} \quad \frac{\text{Sales in Value}}{\text{Cost per unit}}$$

= Rs. 40,416.66 Or Rs. 40,417

Verification :

		Rs.
Variable cost Rs. 18 per unit		
40,417 × 18	=	7,27,506
Fixed Cost	=	3,60,000
Profit	=	1,25,000
Total Sales Price		12,12,000

Problem No. 69

The sales turnover and the profit during two years were as follows :

Year	Sales	Profit
1978	1,50,000	20,000
1979	1,70,000	25,000

You are required to calculate :

(1) P/V Ratio

(2) B.E.P.

(3) Sales required to earn a profit of Rs. 40,000

(4) Profit when sales are Rs. 2,50,000

(5) Margin of Safety at a profit of Rs. 50,000

(6) Variable costs of two periods.

(Extra)

Solution :

$$\text{(1) P/V Ratio} = \frac{\text{Changes in profit of two periods}}{\text{Changes in sales of two periods}}$$

Changes in Sales and Profit	Sales	Profit
Period-II 1979	1,70,000	25,000
Period-I 1978	1,50,000	20,000
	20,000	5,000

$$\text{(1) P/V Ratio} = \frac{\text{Changes in profit}}{\text{Changes in sales}}$$

$$= \frac{5,000}{20,000}$$

= ¼ Or 25%

(2) B.E.P. $= \dfrac{\text{Fixed Cost}}{\text{P/V Ratio}}$

Now ascertain Fixed Cost

Contribution in period-I — 1978 when sales are at Rs. 1,50,000 and the P/V Ratio is ¼

Contribution = Sales × P/V Ratio

= 1,50,000 × ¼

= Rs. 37,500

Contribution = Fixed Cost + Profit

Now Fixed Cost = Contribution -- Profit

= 37,500 – 20,000

Fixed Cost = Rs. 17,500

Here contribution and Fixed costs are for period-I — 1978

37,500 – 17,500

= Rs. 20,000

Now B.E.P. Sales $= \dfrac{\text{Fixed Cost}}{\text{P/V Ratio}}$

$= \dfrac{17{,}500}{1/4}$

= 17,500 × 4/1

B.E.P. Sales = Rs. 70,000

(3) Sales required to earn a profit of Rs. 40,000

$= \dfrac{\text{Fixed cost + Profit}}{\text{P/V Ratio}}$

$= \dfrac{17{,}500 + 40{,}000}{1/4}$

= 57,500 × 4/1

= Rs. 2,30,000

(4) Profit when sales are Rs. 2,50,000

Now ascertain new contribution when sales are 2,50,000

P/V Ratio $= \dfrac{\text{Contribution}}{\text{Sales}}$

Now contribution = Sales × P/V Ratio

= 2,50,000 × ¼

= Rs. 62,500

Now Profit when sales are Rs. 2,50,000

Profit = Contribution − Fixed Cost

= 62,500 − 17,500

= Rs. 45,000

(5) Margin of Safety at Profit of Rs. 50,000

$$M/S = \frac{\text{Profit}}{\text{P/V Ratio}}$$

$$= \frac{50,000}{1/4}$$

= 50,000 × 4/1

= 2,00,000

M/S = Rs. 2,00,000

(6) Variable cost = Sales − Contribution

Or Sales − (Fixed Cost + Profit)

Period-I (1978) = 1,50,000 − 17,500 − 20,000

= Rs. 1,12,500

Period-II (1979) = 1,70,00 − 17,500 − 25,000

= Rs. 1,27,500

Variable cost in 1978 − Rs. 1,12,500

1979 − Rs. 1,27,500.